How to Use Maps in This

Here are some basic map concepts and simple tips to help you get the most from the maps in this textbook.

- There are many different types of maps intended to illustrate different types of information. A few of the kinds most frequently used in history books are political, demographic, topographic, and military maps.

  - **Political maps** traditionally show territorial boundaries (such as state and country borders).
  - **Demographic maps** use shading or cross-hatching to show trends relating to population density and distribution.
  - **Topographic maps** illustrate both natural and man-made surface features, such as mountain ranges, rivers, and dams.
  - **Military maps** zoom in on a specific battlefield or show a broad theater of war, and illustrate troop movements over a period of time.

  Many maps, such as the one in this foldout, combine multiple features into one document, illustrating more than one kind of information.

- Always look at the scale, which allows you to determine the distance, in miles or kilometers, between locations on the map.

- Examine the legend carefully (it's usually contained in a boxed inset). It explains the colors, shading, and symbols used on the map.

- If the map is accompanied by a caption, read it thoroughly. Captions usually provide clues to what the author thinks is important about the geography, and offer additional interesting details that may not be covered in the surrounding text.

- Note the mountains, rivers, oceans and other topographic features and consider how these features would affect human activities such as agriculture, trade, communication, travel, and warfare during the period being discussed.

- Refer often to the maps as you read surrounding text, and go back to study them after you have finished reading. Maps can enhance your understanding of events and places discussed.

World History

COMPACT FOURTH EDITION

VOLUME I

BEFORE 1600: THE DEVELOPMENT
OF EARLY CIVILIZATION

Jiu-Hwa L. Upshur
EASTERN MICHIGAN UNIVERSITY

Janice J. Terry
EASTERN MICHIGAN UNIVERSITY

James P. Holoka
EASTERN MICHIGAN UNIVERSITY

Richard D. Goff
EASTERN MICHIGAN UNIVERSITY

George H. Cassar
EASTERN MICHIGAN UNIVERSITY

THOMSON
™
WADSWORTH

Australia • Canada • Mexico • Singapore • Spain
United Kingdom • United States

THOMSON

WADSWORTH

Executive Editor: Clark Baxter
Assistant Editor: Paul Massicotte
Editorial Assistant: Richard Yoder
Technology Project Manager: Melinda Newfarmer
Marketing Manager: Lori Grebe-Cook
Marketing Assistant: Mary Ho
Advertising Project Manager: Stacey Purviance
Project Manager, Editorial Production: Matt Ballantyne
Art Director: Maria Epes
Print/Media Buyer: Rebecca Cross

Permissions Editor: Chelsea Junget
Production Service: Lachina Publishing Services
Photo Researcher: Connie Hathaway, Penmarin Books
Illustrator: Graphic World, Inc.
Cover Designer: Janet Bollow Design
Cover Images: Art Today, Corel Corporation,
    Instructional Resources Corporation
Cover Printer: Coral Graphic Services
Compositor: Lachina Publishing Services
Printer: Courier–Westford

For more information about our products,
contact us at:
Thomson Learning Academic Resource Center
1-800-423-0563

For permission to use material from this text
or product, submit a request online at
http://www.thomsonrights.com.
Any additional questions about permissions
can be submitted by email to
thomsonrights@thomson.com.

Library of Congress Control Number: 200408492

ISBN-13: 978-0-495-12924-0
ISBN-10: 0-495-12924-0

Thomson Wadsworth
10 Davis Drive
Belmont, CA 94002-3098
USA

Asia
Thomson Learning
5 Shenton Way #01-01
UIC Building
Singapore 068808

Australia/New Zealand
Thomson Learning
102 Dodds Street
Southbank, Victoria 3006
Australia

Canada
Nelson
1120 Birchmount Road
Toronto, Ontario M1K 5G4
Canada

Europe/Middle East/Africa
Thomson Learning
High Holborn House
50/51 Bedford Row
London WC1R 4LR
United Kingdom

#422949302

About the Authors

JIU-HWA L. UPSHUR received her B.A. at the University of Sydney in Australia and Ph.D. in history at the University of Michigan. She is the author of two catalogs on Chinese art and many articles on Chinese history and has lived and traveled extensively in China, Taiwan, and other parts of Asia. She is co-author of *The Twentieth Century: A Brief Global History* (6th edition, 2001) and co-editor of *Lives and Times: Readings in World History* (1994). She served on the world history committee of the College Board between 1993 and 1999. She is currently a member of the review board of Teaching World History for the Twentieth Century, funded by the National Endowment for the Humanities and the National Advisory Committee for Social Studies of the Educational Testing Service.

JANICE J. TERRY is a graduate of the School of Oriental and African Studies, University of London. She is author of *The Wafd, 1919–1952: Cornerstone of Egyptian Political Power, Mistaken Identity: Arab Stereotypes in Popular Writing,* and numerous articles on contemporary events in western Asia. Dr. Terry has lived and traveled extensively throughout western Asia and Africa. She is co-author of *The Twentieth Century: A Brief Global History* (6th edition, 2001). In 1990, she received an award for excellence in teaching from the state of Michigan.

JAMES P. HOLOKA received his B.A. from the University of Rochester, his M.A. from SUNY, Binghamton, and his Ph.D. from the University of Michigan, where he was a Rackham Prize Fellow. He has taught Greek and Latin, classical humanities, and ancient history since 1974; he received a teaching excellence award in 1980 and a scholarly recognition award in 1991. He is a published translator and the author of three textbooks and over eighty scholarly articles and reviews in such journals as *American Historical Review; Classical World; Greek, Roman, and Byzantine Studies;* and *Transactions of the American Philological Association.*

RICHARD D. GOFF received his B.A. and Ph.D. from Duke University and his M.A. from Cornell University. He has taught courses in Western civilization and specializes in teaching twentieth-century world history. He is the author of *Confederate Supply* and encyclopedia articles on southern U.S. history and culture. In 1983 he received a distinguished faculty service award. He is co-author of *The Twentieth Century: A Brief Global History* (6th edition, 2001), and lead author of R. Goff et al., *A Survey of Western Civilization* (2nd edition, 1997).

GEORGE H. CASSAR received his B.A and M.A. from the University of New Brunswick and his Ph.D. from McGill University. He is currently Professor of History at Eastern Michigan University, where he has taught European and military history since 1968. His output is extensive and includes half a dozen books on various aspects of the First World War as well as co-authorship of *A Survey of Western Civilization* (2nd edition, 1997). In 1985 he received the prestigious Faculty Award for Research and Publication from Eastern Michigan University. He is currently working on a book about Kitchener and British strategy during the Great War.

Brief Contents

Contents

Maps

Preface

Modern communications and transportation have linked the world's continents closer together and made them more integrated politically, economically, and culturally than ever before. Our technological society is predicated on a world economy and depends on a precarious ecological balance that makes events in the forests of Brazil or the deserts of Africa and Asia vitally important to people all around the globe.

Many institutions of higher learning have come to realize that students need insights into the historical backgrounds of other cultures in order to respond effectively to the currents that make us all citizens of a global village. As a result, many are now emphasizing world history as an essential part of the basic undergraduate curriculum, rather than traditional courses in Western civilization.

The five of us have aimed to produce a truly global and well-balanced world history text, since we have expertise in different regions, periods, and topics of history: the classics and Greco-Roman history, modern Europe, military history, the Western Hemisphere, the Islamic world, the United States, and South and East Asia. We are conversant in more than a half-dozen ancient and modern languages. Each has more than thirty years' experience teaching college survey courses of Western and world history and advanced courses in special subjects. All have extensive experience in writing successful textbooks and editing primary source materials in world history and Western civilization. The result is a smooth integration of diverse materials.

Our first edition, widely adopted across the United States and Canada, was a success. Our second and third editions were even more successful. Thus encouraged, we have now updated the current edition.

While other world history textbooks have stressed specific themes, human civilizations, in our view, have produced too rich a tapestry of experience to limit our examination of them to any single theme. Our consistent goal has been not only to show students the diversity and distinctive qualities of the various civilizations, but to trace their social, cultural, and economic influences and interactions. Furthermore, we point out the many dimensions of the lives of individual men and women across cultures, religions, social classes, and times.

Several distinctive features of our book bear enumeration.

First, we have divided world history into seventeen chapters, each highlighting a major trend (emergence of civilization, early empires, invasion and disruption, and so on) during a distinct chronological era. The subsections of each chapter are devoted to the areas of the world affected by this trend. This effective organization has been continued from previous editions, with revisions based on the latest discoveries and advances in scholarship. Chapter 17 has been carefully reworked and updated to incorporate recent events up to 2004.

Second, we have placed twelve comparative essays at strategic points in the book. These lay the groundwork for the historical concepts examined in detail in subsequent chapter sections. For example, the essay "The Defining Characteristics of Great Empires," which discusses the dynamics of large states, precedes Chapter 4, which covers the roughly contemporary Hellenistic, Roman, Mauryan, and Han Empires. For this edition, we have added quotations from original sources at the opening of each essay to demonstrate the pertinence of such material and to heighten the essays' interest and relevance.

Third, we have included many charts and maps; each chapter features helpful maps to accentuate the geographical contexts of historical events. In each chapter the "Summary and Comparisons" section is accompanied by a timeline of important events that occurred during the period covered by that chapter, an important learning aid for students.

Fourth, we have added new boxes to each chapter; most of these consist of quotations from primary sources. Students, reviewers, and professors have praised this engaging and useful enhancement of the text.

Fifth, expanding on a successful feature, we have added more short essays entitled "Lives and Times Across Cultures." These informative, often unusual, and entertaining pieces present facts and details of life not found in traditional textbooks.

Sixth, the chapter summaries, titled "Summary and Comparisons," stress the comparative aspect of historical study. Since each chapter contains much information about diverse regions of the world, this emphasis on comparison ensures a better integration of the various materials of a given chapter and a clearer overall view of world events.

Seventh, at the end of each chapter we have compiled an updated list of sources to guide interested students to well-written monographs, fiction, dramas, films, and television programs that provide historical perspective.

Eighth, the publisher has put together an invaluable package of ancillary materials. These include aids for instructors:

- **Instructor's Manual and Testbank.** Includes a multimedia guide, chapter outlines, recommended readings, paper topics, identification questions, multiple-choice questions, short-essay questions, and new to this edition, Internet resources. One comprehensive volume.
- **ExamView for Windows and Macintosh.** Create, deliver, and customize tests and study guides (both print and online) in minutes with this easy-to-use assessment and tutorial system. ExamView offers both a Quick Test Wizard and an Online Test Wizard that guide you step by step through the process of creating tests, while its unique "WYSIWYG" capability allows you to see the test you are creating on the screen exactly as it will print or display online. You can build tests of up to 250 questions

using up to 12 question types. Using ExamView's complete word-processing capabilities, you can enter an unlimited number of new questions or edit existing questions.

- *Map Acetates and Commentary for World History.* Contains maps from the text and from other sources as well as commentary on each map. The commentary, by James Harrison of Siena College, includes not only the text caption but also additional points of interest about the map, such as what it shows and its relevance to the study of world history. Possible discussion questions for student involvement are included.
- **Wadsworth Video Library: History.** Recommended Films for the Humanities & Sciences videos are available free upon adoption, subject to terms of the Wadsworth video policy.
- **CNN Today Video: *World History, Volumes I and II.*** Launch lectures with riveting footage from CNN, the world's leading twenty-four-hour global news television network. CNN Today: *World History, Volumes I and II*, allows you to integrate the news-gathering and programming power of CNN into the classroom to show students the relevance of course topics to their everyday lives. Organized by topics covered in a typical course, these videos are divided into short segments—perfect for introducing key concepts. A Wadsworth/Thomson exclusive.
- **Sights and Sounds of History Videodisk/Video.** Short, focused video clips, photos, artwork, animations, music, and dramatic readings are used to bring life to historical topics and events that are most difficult for students to appreciate from a textbook alone. For example, students will experience the grandeur of Versailles and the defeat felt by a German soldier at Stalingrad. The video segments (average length, four minutes) are available on VHS and make excellent lecture launchers.

The following ancillaries are also available for students:

- *Study Guide for World History, Volumes I and II.* The study guide contains identifications, true-or-false questions, essay study questions for further reading, and map exercises.
- *Migrations in History CD-ROM.* An interactive multimedia curriculum on CD-ROM by Patrick Manning and the World History Center. Includes over 400 primary source documents; analytical questions to help the student develop his/her own interpretations of history; timelines; and additional suggested resources, including books, films, and websites.
- *Journey of Civilization CD-ROM.* This CD-ROM takes the student on eighteen interactive journeys through history. Enhanced with QuickTime movies, animations, sound clips, maps, and more, the journeys allow students to engage in history as active participants rather than as readers of past events.
- *Magellan World History Atlas.*
- *Lives and Times: A World History Reader.* Assembled by two of the text authors, James Holoka and Jiu-Hwa Upshur, the reader includes 150 short and lively selections, most of them biographical.

■ **Web page.** Both instructors and students will enjoy our web page. Visit Historic Times, the Wadsworth History Resource Center at http://history.wadsworth.com. From this full-service site, instructors and students can access many selections, such as a career center, lessons on surfing the web, and links to great history-related websites.

In sum, we have striven to make this book not only accurate and informative but also exciting for students and other readers. Our textbook combines key characteristics to work effectively in various learning situations. It offers a clear narrative focusing on major histor-ical forces and concepts, uncluttered by minute detail. This edition gives greater attention to social, economic, cultural, and gender history in order to provide a more balanced and comprehensive account of human experience.

We have nevertheless kept our book relatively short—short enough to be suitable for courses at most colleges, so that instructors may assign supplementary readings without overwhelming their students.

To provide a true world perspective, we have adopted several special conventions. First, because the text will be used mostly in North American colleges, we have based our gen-eral chronology on the traditional Christian/Western calendar; however, we have desig-nated year dates as B.C.E. (Before the Common Era) instead of B.C. (Before Christ) and C.E. (Common Era) instead of A.D. (Anno Domini). Next, wherever possible we have eliminated Eurocentric geographical terms such as *Far East, Levant, New World,* and the like. Finally, we have generally transliterated (rather than Latinized or Anglicized) names and terms from their original language; thus, *Qur'an* instead of *Koran, Tanakh* instead of *Old Testa-ment,* and (post–1949) *Mao Zedong* instead of *Mao Tse-tung* and *Beijing* instead of *Peking* (see also "Romanizing Chinese Words" at the end of this volume). However, we have made exceptions of such familiar Westernized spellings as *Confucius, Averroës, Christopher Columbus,* and *Aztec.*

An enterprise of this magnitude and complexity succeeds only through the dedicated efforts of many people. Wadsworth Publishing secured the services of reviewers whose insights and information materially strengthened this and the previous three editions. The list follows this preface.

We wish to thank our colleagues at Eastern Michigan University—in particular, Ronald Delph and Joseph Engwenyu for their assistance at several stages in the writ-ing—and Gersham Nelson, head of the History Department, for his constant support and encouragement. Nancy Snyder and her assistants were stalwart helpers in handling innumer-able practical and technological chores. Raymond Craib at Yale University supplied informa-tion and text on women's history and Mexican history. From the outset of this project, Sally Marks, in Providence, Rhode Island, has been exceptionally helpful in suggesting improve-ments. We also wish to thank Margot Duley of Eastern Michigan University and Richard Edwards of the University of Michigan for making available to us photographs of historical interest from their personal collections. We are grateful to John Nystuen of the University of

Michigan for photographing some of the artifacts illustrated in this edition. The authors' spouses furnished copious practical and moral support and showed a high tolerance for hectic writing and production schedules. Thanks also go to Pat Manning at the World History Center at Northeastern University and his graduate assistants, Stacy Tweedy, Tiffany Olson, and Bin Yang. A final word of thanks goes to Clark Baxter, Sharon Adams Poore, Nancy Crochiere, and other members of the Wadsworth Publishing team for their patient attention to all manner of details. Their collective skills have once again transformed our project into a most attractive textbook.

THE AUTHORS

Reviewers

INTRODUCTION

Paleolithic and Neolithic Cultures around the World

●

• Human Development in the Old Stone Age •

• The Neolithic Food-Producing Revolution in West Asia •

• Neolithic Times in Europe •

• Neolithic Times in Africa •

• Neolithic Times in Asia •

• Neolithic Times in the Western Hemisphere •

What are we? To the biologist we are . . . Homo sapiens sapiens. . . . But what is particularly interesting about our species? For a start, we walk upright on our hind legs at all times, which is an extremely unusual way of getting around for a mammal. There are also several unusual features about our head, not least of which is the very large brain it contains. . . . Unlike the apes, we are not covered by a coat of thick hair. . . . Very probably this has something to do with [the fact that] the skin is richly covered with millions of microscopic sweat glands. . . . Our forelimbs, being freed from helping us to get about, possess a very high degree of manipulative skill. . . . No other animal manipulates the world in the extensive and arbitrary way that humans do. . . . Unlike any other animal, we have a spoken language which is characterized by a huge vocabulary and a complex grammatical structure. . . .

All [these] . . . are characteristics of a very intelligent creature, but humans are more than just intelligent. Our sense of justice, our need for aesthetic pleasure, our imaginative flights and our penetrating self-awareness, all combine to create an indefinable spirit which I believe is the "soul."

*Richard E. Leakey, The Making of Mankind (New York: Dutton, 1981), pp. 18, 20.

This passage by anthropologist Richard Leakey states the dual nature of human beings—physical and spiritual. Students of history are particularly concerned to identify how these various distinguishing traits have found expression in the accomplishments of mankind. Such historical study records advances in production of food, in technology, in the building of social groups and their habitations, and in general in the more efficient control of the environment. It also seeks to define what it is to be human. This means that historians also study the ways human beings have viewed the world around them, that is, how people have understood its working through science, answered unfathomable questions through religion, and expressed their thoughts in art, literature, and philosophy.

Through such investigation, students of history have ascertained that, to begin with, humans survived precariously through hunting and gathering. Eventually, after hundreds of thousands of years, humans living in several continents created first the agricultural and then the urban revolutions noted in the passage above, thus bringing about civilized life in both the Eastern and Western Hemispheres. This section of *World History* surveys these initial advances of humankind. It first discusses what modern researchers have reconstructed about the emergence of the human species and about life in the hunter-gatherer era around the world. It then takes up the dramatic material changes brought by the invention of agriculture.

Human Development in the Old Stone Age

The story of humanity's achievement began with the Paleolithic or Old Stone Age sometime around 2,000,000 B.C.E., probably in East Africa, as the famous finds in the Olduvai Gorge show. (The labeling of Ages as "Stone," "Bronze," and "Iron" refers to the materials used in the making of tools at a given stage in history.) After 1,000,000 B.C.E., hominids of the *Homo erectus* type moved out of East Africa into West Asia, Europe, East Asia, and Indonesia. This whole vast stretch of time cannot be described with great confidence or detail because there are no written records to illumine it. Instead, we have had to rely on the conclusions and conjectures which modern scientists have drawn from materials obtained from archaeological excavations.

In response to changes in the natural environment, Old Stone Age people made physical and cultural adaptations fundamental for subsequent human development. Crucial physiological refinements included the ability to stand and walk easily in an upright position, changes in the position and size of teeth (especially the canines) in response to changing diet, the evolution and increasing dexterity of an opposable thumb, and changes in the size and configuration of the skull.

Particularly dramatic was the doubling of their brain size. This gave men and women mental superiority over other species, demonstrated in creating artifacts, particularly tools. They could both expand and perfect their cultural equipment and transmit knowledge of how to use that equipment through language, the most flexible and finely calibrated tool of all.

A series of four major ice ages, marked by the movement of ice sheets hundreds of feet thick over vast areas of the earth, stimulated human development. The glaciations changed land formations, sea levels, and plant and animal life and habitats. People had to be innovative and able to modify their patterns of living to survive. Many animals, solely dependent on physical equipment for their survival, were often unable to adjust to changing environmental conditions and became extinct.

By 100,000 B.C.E., modern humans (*Homo sapiens sapiens*) had evolved in Africa. By 40,000 B.C.E. they had occupied the areas originally settled by *Homo erectus*, and afterwards spread into northern Eurasia and into Australia. The South Pacific was settled much later, between 1100 B.C.E. and 1300 C.E.

Modern *Homo sapiens* also migrated through Siberia, across to Alaska, and then east and south throughout North America. Most scholars think that, as in Australia, the greater number of movements occurred during the last ice ages, when glaciers locked up some of the world's water, thus lowering sea levels and exposing land bridges.

As elsewhere in the world at this time, these *Homo sapiens* migrants were still hunters and gatherers, fire-users with chipped stone tools, whose relics in the Western Hemisphere date from about 40,000 B.C.E. By 20,000 B.C.E. humans had arrived in Middle America (the southern two-thirds of Mexico and parts of current Central America south to Panama). It appears that they soon spread thereafter throughout South America, although isolated archaeological finds hinting at settlements even as early as 30,000 B.C.E. may require a revision of our chronology.

The Arctic zone of North America, though it was on the migration route from Asia, was in fact the last part of the continent to be settled. The earliest Paleolithic culture of the Eskimos dates to about 7000 B.C.E. in the region of the Bering Strait. Succeeding cultures known as Pre-Dorset and Dorset combined influences from East Asia and from regions to the south in North America. They were characterized by hunting of caribou, rabbits, and birds, with a gradual shift to fishing and the hunting of polar bears and marine creatures such as walrus and seals. By the first millennium B.C.E., these Eskimo cultures were prevalent in the Arctic from Alaska in the west through northern Canada to Greenland in the east.

By the late Paleolithic era, human beings around the world had (1) manufactured a range of stone or bone implements (knives, scrapers, borers) and weapons (blades, bows

The Ascent of Mankind

Fossil skulls have been found in Southern Africa . . . which establish the characteristic structure of the head when it began to be man-like. . . . A historic skull, found [in 1924] . . . at a place called Taung, by . . . Raymond Dart . . . is [that of] a baby, five to six years old. . . . Dart called this creature Australopithecus [Southern Ape]. . . . For me the little Australopithecus baby has a personal history. In 1950, . . . I was asked to do a piece of mathematics. Could I combine a measure of the size of the Taung child's teeth with their shape, so as to discriminate them from the teeth of apes? I had never held a fossil skull in my hands, and I was by no means an expert on teeth. But it worked pretty well; and it transmitted to me a sense of excitement which I remember at this instant. I, at over forty, having spent a lifetime in doing abstract mathematics about the shape of things, suddenly saw my knowledge reach back two million years and shine a searchlight into the history of man. . . . I do not know how the Taung baby began life, but to me it still remains the primordial infant from which the whole adventure of man began. *

Thus Jacob Bronowski described the excitement he felt as he looked at a bit of evidence of ancient human life on our planet. The title of his book, *The Ascent of Man*, is an allusion to Charles Darwin's famous book *The Descent of Man*, published a century earlier, which advanced evidence for the hypothesis that human beings had evolved from more primitive life forms. Darwin's claim released a torrent of controversy by its challenge to the traditional belief in the biblical story of Creation, but it also stimulated the sciences of physical anthropology and archaeology. Researchers have made stunning discoveries about the ancestry of our species through excavations at sites such as the Olduvai Gorge in East Africa and Hsihoutu in Shansi province in China. Their work has yielded insights into the earliest achievements that brought humanity from primitive origins to the creation of civilized life, from crude stone implements to spacecraft, from the rudiments of spoken language to the art of poetry, from nomadic hunting and gathering to the complex socioeconomic and political structures of city life.

**Jacob Bronowski, The Ascent of Man (Boston: Little Brown, 1973), pp. 28–30.*

and arrows, spears and spear throwers), (2) controlled fire for cooking and for giving heat and light, (3) developed spoken language in addition to the nonverbal gestures used by all primates, (4) formulated an artistic tradition, seen for example in the famous cave paintings at Lascaux in France and Altamira in Spain, (5) created ritual practices connected chiefly with fertility and with burial of the dead, and (6) organized themselves into social groups for more efficient collection and sharing of food.

Also by late Paleolithic times, human beings had probably acquired the superficial physical traits conventionally known as racial. Differences in skin, hair, and eye color, in size and shape of the nostrils, and perhaps in stature and cranial shape likely resulted from adaptation to environmental conditions in various parts of the world.

The Neolithic Food-Producing Revolution in West Asia

Because Paleolithic humans lived by hunting animals and by gathering wild fruits, nuts, and grains, they needed a relatively large space to support even a single family. This severely restricted the size of human communities and made settled life in one area impossible, since the group had to follow its food supply and move in conjunction with animal migrations and vegetation cycles. Only when people shifted from the random collection of food to its regular cultivation did they overcome such limitations. In the Neolithic or New Stone Age, humans assured themselves of a regular food supply by developing agricultural techniques and domesticating food-producing animals. Stable food supplies in turn produced a rapid increase in population and the founding of permanent settlements, which later became the basis for the more complex social structures and more dynamic technologies of urban civilization. These characteristics of the Neolithic revolution varied from region to region and emerged much earlier in some parts of the world than in others. Indeed, to speak of a "revolution" is somewhat misleading, since the transformation in most areas was very gradual. Still, in terms of the vast time frame of human evolution, the change was comparatively quick. In 10,000 B.C.E., 100 percent of the world's population of ca. 10 million were hunters and gatherers; by 1500 C.E., only 1 percent of the world's roughly 350 million people were hunters and gatherers; today, less than 0.001 percent of the world's population—for example, Eskimos, African !Kung San people, and the aborigines of Australia—still live in pre-Neolithic conditions.

With the retreat of the last ice age, beginning around 10,000 B.C.E., climatic conditions in that part of West Asia called the Fertile Crescent became well suited to raising grain and domesticating animals. The valleys and foothills of this region were home to the wild ancestors of domesticable plants (barley, wheat, millet, and so on) and animals (goats, donkeys, and the like). During a transitional period, the Mesolithic or Middle Stone Age (10,000 to 7000 B.C.E..), at places like Mount Carmel in Palestine, humans made tentative efforts to move from hunting-gathering subsistence methods to the systematic harvesting of grain.

By 7000 B.C.E. the residents of West Asia had developed the true farming villages that typify the Neolithic era. These centers consisted of at most a few thousand inhabitants

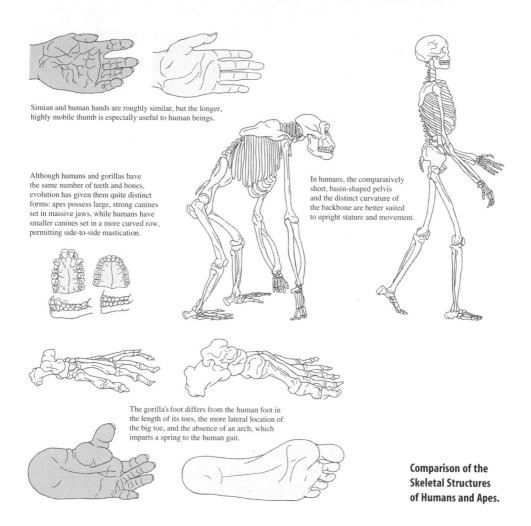

Simian and human hands are roughly similar, but the longer, highly mobile thumb is especially useful to human beings.

Although humans and gorillas have the same number of teeth and bones, evolution has given them quite distinct forms: apes possess large, strong canines set in massive jaws, while humans have smaller canines set in a more curved row, permitting side-to-side mastication.

In humans, the comparatively short, basin-shaped pelvis and the distinct curvature of the backbone are better suited to upright stature and movement.

The gorilla's foot differs from the human foot in the length of its toes, the more lateral location of the big toe, and the absence of an arch, which imparts a spring to the human gait.

Comparison of the Skeletal Structures of Humans and Apes.

engaged in the cultivation of wheat, barley, peas, beans, and lentils and in the raising of goats, sheep, pigs, and cattle. These early farmers continued to supplement their diet with wild fruits, nuts, and grains. They lived in caves or pit houses or huts made of mud, reeds, logs, or stones, grouped in small open communities or in larger fortified towns like Jericho, in the Jordan Valley near the Dead Sea, or Çatal Hüyük in the Anatolian Peninsula (modern Turkey). The point of such communities was to concentrate labor both for agricultural work—plowing, sowing, harvesting, and the like—and for the protection of the farmland on which the community's survival now depended.

Early farmers also devised techniques for making porridge, bread, and beer, and developed ovens for cooking and, later, for firing pottery. (Pottery in particular is a joy for archaeologists because it is almost imperishable and once a culture starts to make pottery, it leaves behind a trail of broken shards, often distinctively decorated and therefore datable.) They wove baskets and textiles from wool and flax, and began to work metals like gold, silver, and copper. Finally, they discovered the wheel and made wagons and pottery wheels, and they invented the plow, which superseded digging sticks and hoes. Food surpluses freed some members of the community, generally males, to become at least part-time specialists: smiths, potters, weavers, artists, and perhaps priests.

Gender roles in Neolithic communities were affected by the production of food surpluses. Plow agriculture required the physical strength of males, rather than of females, whose energies were taken up by pregnancy and the nursing and rearing of children. Animal husbandry, too, was likely a male occupation. The males' control of surpluses of livestock, meat, pelts, and grain gave them an economic advantage that translated into the leisure to develop and engage in the specializations mentioned above. In short, males managed production, while to women fell the lifetime-consuming and labor-intensive tasks of reproduction.

Once the agricultural revolution had occurred in the Fertile Crescent, it quickly spread to other regions in Asia, North Africa, and Europe. By contrast, farming emerged independently in North and South America (see Map I.1). In all these areas, the revolution in food production enabled humans to take the next major step toward civilization, from village to city. Before turning to that major change, we will consider Neolithic culture elsewhere in the world.

Neolithic Times in Europe

The earliest agricultural villages in Europe appeared about 6500 B.C.E. in Greece, probably as a result of colonization by Anatolians across the Aegean. The farmers lived in square mudbrick buildings, sometimes with one larger building as a meeting place. Their economy centered on the raising of sheep and the cultivation of wheat and legumes. By 4000 B.C.E., Neolithic settlements had spread throughout Europe along two major routes: the Vardar-Danube-Rhine corridor, and the coastal areas of the Mediterranean Sea. Wooden longhouses were . . . more common than mud brick huts outside the Balkans. Initially, the pattern of farming settlements was dictated by the location of fertile soil that had resulted from the weathering of loess (layers of wind-blown dust that had formed like silt along the rims of glaciers in earlier times). Eventually, however, as incoming farmers carved land from the European forests, the hunters who had lived there since the early postglacial period (ca. 10,000 B.C.E.) left their former mode of life to swell the ranks of the agriculturalists.

The earliest progress toward civilization on the European continent took place along the Mediterranean coasts, especially in the Balkan and Italian peninsulas. Northern and western Europe was another matter; this area made few contributions (mainly in the form of natural resources) to the general advance of civilization before 500 B.C.E. It was largely unreceptive to external cultural influences (metalworking was an exception). Literacy, for example, came very late, imposed by conquerors. However, one ancient European art form does remain noteworthy: the megalithic (literally "large stone") construc-

Map I.1 The Origins of Agricultural Crops and of Domestic Animals. This map shows the areas where particular plant and animal species were first cultivated of domesticated. Some species (for example, the pig) seem to have developed independently in different areas. In most cases, however, contact between neighboring cultures facilitated the rapid spread of plant and animal cultivation around the globe.

tions scattered from Scandinavia in the north to Corsica, Sardinia, and Malta in the south. Some of these are older than the great pyramids of Giza in Egypt, though they are by comparison very crude both in form and arrangement. Many of them are tombs; others are laid out in symmetrical patterns selected for religious or astronomical reasons. The most famous of these megaliths is Stonehenge in southern England. Here, in late Neolithic and early Bronze Age times (c. 2800–1800 B.C.E.), the prehistoric builders collected about 136 massive stones, some as large as thirty feet long and weighing fifty tons. The megaliths, transported over some eighteen miles, were assembled in a hundred-foot-diameter circle with an inner horseshoe consisting of five massive post and lintel gateways. The structure as a whole is aligned to the movements of sun, moon, and stars at specific points in the year, thus constituting a kind of gigantic observatory. All this argues a remarkably precise awareness of astronomical movements, unassisted by the mathematical theorems later developed by Babylonians and Egyptians. Stonehenge also bespeaks both an elaborate cooperation of labor activity and a careful organization of religious and social observances.

Neolithic Times in Africa

The Neolithic Revolution spread to the Nile Valley between 5000 and 4000 B.C.E. Wheat and barley, and goats, sheep, and pigs were introduced very likely from the Fertile Crescent, especially Palestine and Mesopotamia. Irrigation by control of the Nile flood started at this time. Such developments laid the agricultural foundations for the first historical dynasties of ancient Egypt, beginning about 3000 B.C.E., discussed later in this chapter. Elsewhere, African peoples in the Saharan region, which did not become uninhabitably arid till after 3000 B.C.E., adopted the domestication of animals and, more slowly, the practice of agriculture from the neighboring Nile Valley. With the desiccation of the Sahara, these peoples carried their Neolithic skills with them in migrations to central and western Africa, though hunting-gathering cultures persisted in many areas. The barrier that the Sahara desert imposed by 2500 B.C.E. prevented the spread of the urban civilization that flowered with such magnificence in Old Kingdom Egypt. It was not until the first millennium B.C.E. that settled agricultural life and the practice of metallurgy became more widespread in sub-Saharan Africa. In all cases, however, the scarcity of water has meant that African peoples engaged in long-term agriculture have lived within the limits of a precariously balanced ecological system.

A very few African peoples remained at the hunter-gatherer stage till quite recently. Thus anthropologists could observe directly the cultural implications of changeover to an agricultural mode of life, for example, among the !Kung San people (formerly called "bushmen") of southern Africa (the ! symbolizes an explosive sound or "click" common to the language). Here the transition to settled farming meant a shift from the mentality of sharing to that of saving. Among hunter-gatherers, survival of the group depends on the sharing of food collected into a common supply by all members, and all who contribute in any way to the general store of food are valued equally, regardless of sex. Among farmers, by contrast, a desire to conserve for oneself what one has produced is predominant. There is also an intensified possessiveness of and willingness even to fight for land that one has labored long and hard to make productive. Socially, hunter-gatherer !Kung exhibited little differentiation in status or rigidity in the definition of sex roles. Among agriculturalist !Kung, however, women are confined to work in the fields, while men tend to animals. Because there is often a surplus of animals and not of crops, the men gain power by controlling cattle as a medium of exchange for other goods or for money; thus the work of the women is undervalued. The division of gender roles begins even in childhood: in hunter-gatherer societies, children play together in the same manner. By contrast, the children of !Kung farmers split by sex: girls' play is modeled on the behavior of women, boys' on that of men.

Neolithic Times in Asia

The Neolithic age in India dates from about 5000 B.C.E. It was centered in modern-day Baluchistan and Sind in northwest India, then well watered and wooded, today almost a waterless desert. Several distinct cultures evolved, distinguished from each other by different types of painted pottery and burial practices. Pottery figurines made by these Neolithic peoples show that they practiced fertility rites (Mother Goddess, phallic symbols) and that the bull was important to them. The Neolithic Age came to an end around 2500 B.C.E. with the beginning of the Indus civilization. This also is the subject for the next chapter.

The Neolithic Age began in China about 6000 B.C.E. with three separate Neolithic cultures. The first was in North China, called the Yangshao culture, whose people lived in semisubterranean round and rectangular houses and cultivated millet. Another was located in the Hwai (a river in east-central China) and lower Yangtze valleys, where rice was grown. A third, which extended along the South China coast and possibly included coastal Southeast Asia and Taiwan, cultivated edible tubers (taro and yam) and fruit. Each culture had its distinct and characteristic pottery ware. In time each outgrew its immediate surroundings and interactions resulted. Around 3000 B.C.E., silkworms were domesticated and weaving of silk cloth began. At about the same time, technology for working neghrite jade, an extremely hard stone, was developed. The Chinese have been making jade tools, ornaments, and ritual items ever since.

Around 2500 B.C.E., an advanced late Neolithic culture, the Lungshan, developed in northeastern China. Its people made a thin, high-fired, almost porcelain-quality pottery on the wheel, began to work metals, had specialized crafts, and began to live in small urban settlements. Differentiated graves indicate the development of a ranked society. According to traditional accounts, great rulers of this period created the first dynasty, called the Hsia. To date, we have no documentary evidence of the Hsia dynasty. Undoubtedly, however, the Lungshan culture provided a basis for later development of the first documented dynasty, the Shang, which began around 1700 B.C.E. The Shang dynasty and its immediate successors will be examined in Chapter 2.

Although the earliest Japanese written records date from about 500 C.E., archaeology and Chinese records enable us to reconstruct information for earlier periods. The archaeological record shows that the first Japanese culture, called the Jomon (rope pattern), appeared during the third millennium B.C.E. It is named after pots made and decorated by coiling clay. These people did not practice agriculture, but were hunters and gatherers. To judge from the huge shell mounds they left behind, shellfish was important to their diet.

About the third century B.C.E., in western Japan, there emerged a Neolithic culture that made pottery on wheels, knew both bronze and iron, and used irrigation to grow rice. It is called the Yayoi culture after one of its sites. Strong Chinese influence is suggested in the introduction of irrigation and in the Han bronze mirrors, weapons, and coins found at Yayoi sites. Technology transfer is evident in the local imitation of metal prototypes introduced from China.

The earliest Chinese historic records containing definite information on Japan were compiled in the third century B.C.E. They provide interesting information about the political and social organization of the island people whom the Chinese called Wa. According to the records, the Wa were divided into many tribes, ruled over by hereditary kings and queens. The most powerful tribe, called the Yamatai (possibly a rendition of

Yamato, the old capital district of the later Japanese imperial line), was ruled by a queen who was also a high priestess. The Chinese also commented on the marked social differences between members of society.

Neolithic Times in the Western Hemisphere

In the Western Hemisphere, undisputed evidence of Mesolithic farming exists in the semiarid Mexican highlands, but the climate, at least in the areas where the first civilizations rose, is less favorable to preserving the evidence archaeologists need than are the deserts of Mesopotamia or Egypt. Nevertheless, the early Middle Americans had domesticated gourds by 6500 B.C.E., and they selectively bred maize (commonly called "corn") into a cultivated staple between 7000 and 3500 B.C.E. In comparison, the first cereals were grown in the area of present-day Europe about 3000 B.C.E.

Maize would be the agricultural basis for the development of later civilization in Middle America, filling the role that rice did in Asia and cereals did in the Middle East. Weighed against those staples, maize produces more nourishment with less effort than rice or wheat and can grow in drier conditions. The Middle American peoples recognized their debt to the crop: maize gods figure in every Middle American culture as equals, at least, of rain and other environmental deities.

From 3500 to 2500 B.C.E., roughly contemporaneously with the civilization of Sumer and the founding of Egypt's dynasties, permanent Neolithic settlements appeared in Middle America. The oldest pottery found dates to about 2500 B.C.E. By 1500 B.C.E., full-time agriculturists had appeared in the central highlands and the Gulf Coast regions of Middle America. The earliest known civilization in the Western Hemisphere, the Olmec, appeared here south of Vera Cruz; it will be taken up in Chapter 1.

Turning to South America, in Peru some farming of both gourds and cotton took place before 2500 B.C.E. In this early phase, many cultural centers existed in different river valleys, but intervening highlands limited contact between them. We know from the archaeological record that sedentary cultures evolved between 2500 and 1800 B.C.E. in most of the river valleys, with the people there, as well as some of the highland groups, building temples and altars. On the seacoast, the basis of the economy was not agriculture, although farming was done in the fertile soil that seasonal flooding left on the rivers' banks. The main source of food was the sea, which provided not only fish, shellfish, and birds but also seaweed. By the end of this period, some highlanders grew maize, the cultivation of which had spread from Middle America, although most still depended largely on hunting and gathering. Unlike the Middle Americans, the Peruvians domesticated animals, and they had the dog, guinea pigs, and fowl for food; and the American cousins of the camel family—the llama, alpaca, guanaco, and vicuña—for carrying burdens and also for wool. Along the central coast, pottery appeared about 1800 B.C.E. and may represent a diffusion of the technology from Colombia, where it was being made by about 3100 B.C.E. Cultivation of the potato, whose later export to Europe profoundly affected the Old World, was general in suitable climates. During the period when pottery was just beginning, some of the Peruvian coastal cities also began to raise

CHRONOLOGY

2,500,000 B.C.E.	Earliest evidence of stone tools
2,000,000	Earliest examples of the genus *Homo*
1,000,000	Premodern humans spread out of Africa
100,000	Appearance of *Homo sapiens sapiens* in East Africa
40,000	*Homo sapiens* in the Western Hemisphere
15,000	Cave paintings at Altamira and Lascaux
10,000	Retreat of the last ice age Transition from Paleolithic to Mesolithic era Beginnings of agriculture
7000	The Neolithic Revolution in West Asia Cultivation of maize in Mesoamerica
6500	Earliest agricultural villages in Europe
6000	Neolithic period begins in China
5000	Agriculture in the Nile Valley Neolithic settlements in Mesoamerica
3000	Neolithic period in India Cultivation of silkworms Megalithic construction begins at Stonehenge Desiccation of the Sahara
2500	Neolithic settlements begin in Peru

peanuts and manioc. Because those plants originated east of the Andes, their presence on the Peruvian coast argues long-range trade.

Selected Sources

Items indicated with an asterisk (*) are available in paperback.

Annaud, Jean-Jacques, director. *Quest for Fire*. 1982. This film depicts a variety of Stone Age discoveries, including fire starting and spoken language.

Barber, Elizabeth W. *Women's Work: The First 20,000 Years: Women, Cloth, and Society in Early Times*. 1994. An informative book that draws on archaeological and other evidence for the development of weaving and many other aspects of women's lives; covers the era from later Paleolithic through classical Greece.

*Bronowski, Jacob. *The Ascent of Man*. 1973. Chapters 1 and 2 of this best-seller, based on the BBC television series, offer a lively account of Stone Age developments.

*Chang Kwang-chih. *The Archaeology of Ancient China*. 3d ed. 1977. The most authoritative book on the subject. Many illustrations, maps, and charts make it interesting and informative.

*Ehrenberg, Margaret. *Women in Prehistory.* 1989. An interesting study of deductions that can be made about the important role of women in Stone Age cultures.

Fagan, Brian M. *The Journey from Eden: The Peopling of Our World.* 1990. A useful treatment of human evolution and migration patterns in Paleolithic times.

Fiedel, Stuart J. *Prehistory of the Americas.* 1988. A recent and splendid attempt to integrate the new knowledge about pre-Colombian America that has appeared in many fields.

Gimbutas, Marija A. *The Civilization of the Goddess: The World of Old Europe.* 1991. A good examination of the question of prehistoric religions and the place of mother goddesses in early human culture.

*Hawkes, Jacquetta. *The Atlas of Early Man: The Rise of Man across the Globe from 35,000 B.C. to A.D. 500.* 1976; rev. ed. 1993. An extremely well-written book, enhanced by more than 1,000 superb illustrations and maps.

*Leakey, Richard E., and Roger Lewin. *Origins Reconsidered: In Search of What Makes Us Human.* 1992. A readable and well-illustrated update of the popular first edition of Leakey's discussion of human origins.

Lloyd, Seton. *The Archaeology of Mesopotamia: From the Old Stone Age to the Persian Conquest.* Rev. ed. 1984. An excellent survey of the origins and early course of civilization in Mesopotamia.

Mohen, J. P. *The World of Megaliths.* 1990. A current discussion of the megalithic monuments and their builders in the Neolithic era.

Piggott, S. *Prehistoric India.* 1950. Still the classic work on this subject.

Wilson, Peter J. *The Domestication of the Human Species.* 1988. Particularly strong on prehistoric social evolution, land settlement patterns, and dwellings.

Additional resources, exercises, and Internet links related to this chapter are available at the Book Companion Web site: http://history.wadsworth.com/upshurcompact4/

COMPARATIVE ESSAY 1
The Defining Characteristics of Civilization

Appetite for food and sex is nature.
Kao Tzu, fourth-century B.C.E. philosopher.

The range of variations is infinitely wider in food than in sex. . . . People who have the same culture share the same food habits, that is, they share the same assemblage of food variables. People of different cultures share different assemblages of food variables. We might say that different cultures have different food choices.
K. C. Chang, *Food in Chinese Culture: Anthropological and Historical Perspectives* (New Haven: Yale University Press, 1977), p. 3.

The first cities appeared in the Fertile Crescent and Egypt about 3000 B.C.E. as a result of the Agricultural Revolution, which began in those regions after about 10,000 B.C.E. This momentous achievement enabled humans to acquire food with much greater efficiency and regularity and in greater quantities than had been possible during the earlier hunting-gathering stage. Thus larger groups of people could live from the produce of less land. As food production increased, so did population and consequently population density. More efficient food production led to a surplus that allowed some people to engage in specialized occupations. Trade developed as a result. These advances changed the human condition so significantly that they are collectively termed the Agricultural Revolution.

Some historians speculate that agriculture spread from the Fertile Crescent and Egypt to other parts of the globe. This thesis is difficult to prove, however, and it is possible that agriculture was independently invented in several areas of the world and under different geographic conditions. For example, most early centers of the Agricultural Revolution in Asia and North Africa were located in the temperate zones, and most early civilizations began in large river valleys: the Tigris-Euphrates in Mesopotamia, the Nile in Egypt, the Indus in India, and the Huang Ho in China. However, the Amerindians of Mesoamerica and South America developed advanced civilizations in tropical jungles, in hot arid highlands and coasts, and in cool plateaus and uplands, but not along major river valleys. These cultures differed in their food assemblages (for example, cereal grains in West Asia, rice in East Asia, maize in Mesoamerica), and in the evolution of city-based societies. Thus no set rules regarding the preconditions for civilization are universally applicable.

Many people use the word *civilized* to mean "urbane" or "sophisticated." The term is often applied to one's own group; other groups are deemed to be less civilized or uncivilized "barbarians." For example, the Greeks considered the Persians "barbarians" because they did not speak Greek and embrace Greek cultural values; in the same way, the Persians called the Arabs barbarians, and the Chinese referred to most of their neighbors by the same epithet. In North America, the Inuit and Sioux spoke of themselves as "human beings" or "the people," as if those outside their group were somehow less than human. The origin myths of many peoples support such claims.

Professionals who deal with the past use the word *civilized* in a neutral, descriptive way. Increasingly, historians tend to define civilization in terms of urbanization. Whatever the particular circumstances of their origin, early civilizations manifested similar urban characteristics: new and specialized vocations, advances in the arts and technology, and complex political and cultural institutions. Physically, a city is functionally distinct from the surrounding countryside, often with defensive walls demarcating the entire city or at least its religious and administrative center. It also includes palaces, temples, private residences, and markets. Socially, most early cities included people of distinct social classes and occupational groups, ranging from the ruling elite and religious leaders to artisans, merchants, and slaves.

The city-centered government also ruled surrounding territories, often by military force. It also organized labor for public works. Depending on the resources at their disposal, governments devoted great technological and artistic skills to building canals and dikes, roads, palaces, rulers' tombs, and monuments.

Another approach to defining civilization is to link it with writing. In the opinion of some, no matter how urbanized and how technologically, culturally, and artistically advanced a culture is, it must also have a system of writing to be termed civilized. Applying this criterion to Amerindian cultures, the Maya and the Aztecs were civilized but the Olmec and Inka were not.

Another issue related to the concept of civilization is the meaning of the term *prehistoric*. Most of us use the term to mean "primitive," as in the sense of Neolithic "cave dwellers." Some professionals, however, use *prehistoric* in a special technical sense to denote a culture that had no writing or whose writing has not been deciphered. According to this point of view, an era is designated *historic* if written materials provide us with a deeper understanding of its culture than can be gained from archaeological artifacts alone. Thus, although the people of the Indus civilization used writing, their civilization is prehistoric, because the few surviving samples of their writing remain undeciphered.

This essay has defined civilization and its preconditions largely in material terms. In closing our discussion, we must also remember that every civilization represents a triumph of the human spirit. In the words of Arnold J. Toynbee, a renowned historian of world civilizations:

> How are we to describe . . . any . . . of the ten or twenty civilizations which we can count up on our fingers? In human terms . . . , each of these civilizations is . . . a distinctive attempt at a single great common human enterprise . . . , an effort to perform an act of creation. (Civilization on Trial [New York: Oxford University Press, 1948], p. 55)

The next two chapters will focus on the distinguishing features and achievements of the world's oldest known civilizations in West Asia and Africa, along the Mediterranean, in Central and South America, and in South and East Asia.

1

Early Civilization in West Asia, Africa, the Aegean, and the Western Hemisphere

•

• Mesopotamian Civilization •

• African Civilization •

• Early Aegean Civilization •

• Ancient Persian Civilization •

• Amerindian Civilization •

• Summary and Comparisons •

On [the shield, Hephaestus] wrought in all their beauty two cities of mortal men. And there were marriages in one, and festivals. They were leading the brides along the city from their maiden chambers under the flaring of torches, and the loud bride song was arising. The young men followed the circles of the dance, and among them the flutes and lyres kept up their clamor as in the meantime the women standing each at the door of her court admired them. The people were assembled in the marketplace, where a quarrel had arisen, and two men were disputing over the blood price for a man who had been killed. One man promised full restitution in a public statement, but the other refused and would accept nothing. Both then made for an arbitrator, to have a decision; and people were speaking up on either side, to help both men. But the heralds kept the people in hand, as meanwhile the elders were in session on benches of polished stone in the sacred circle and held in their hands the staves of the heralds who lift their voices. The two men rushed before these, and took turns speaking their cases, and between them lay on the ground two talents of gold, to be given to that judge who in this case spoke the straightest opinion.

But around the other city were lying two forces of armed men shining in their war gear. For one side counsel was divided whether to storm and sack, or share between both sides the property and all the possessions the lovely citadel held within it. But the city's people were not giving way, and armed for an ambush. Their beloved wives and their little children stood on the rampart to hold it, and with them the men with age upon them, but meanwhile the others went out. . . .

But the other army . . . went after, and soon overtook them. These stood their ground and fought a battle by the banks of the river, and they were making casts at each other with their spears bronze-headed; and Hate was there with Confusion among them, and Death the destructive.

The Iliad of Homer, trans. Richmond Lattimore (Chicago: University of Chicago Press, 1951), pp. 388–389.

In this passage from Homer's epic story of the Trojan War, we read the description of a shield adorned with an elaborate relief sculpture that the smith-god Hephaestus has crafted for the greatest of the Greek heroes, Achilles. The subject matter of the god's art is a tale of two cities, of peace and of war, of the good things and the bad of civilized life. The Shield of Achilles depicts the human potential for both creativity and destruction. This chapter surveys the results of that potential in several of the earliest civilizations around the world.

The study of ancient societies is rewarding for many reasons. There is the allure of origins, of people in remote times and distant places who were first in so many crucial endeavors. The early inhabitants of West Asia, Egypt, the Aegean area, and, in the Western Hemisphere, of Mesoamerica and the Andean region confronted the problems of survival and developed the earliest examples of civilized life. The cities of Mesopotamia, Babylon, and Ur of the Chaldees, the ever-fascinating great pyramids at Giza, the massive sculpted heads at the Olmec city of La Venta, the Lion Gate in the imposing walls at Mycenae, and the spectacular royal palace at Persepolis in Iran—all are the visible signs of energetic people who had marvelous creative talents and ambition to match. Because of their remoteness in time, these civilizations have an air of the exotic and mysterious. We cannot help but be curious about the conditions of life and the personal motivations of the people who fashioned these ancient worlds: in short, what made them tick? To pursue this question is to explore the early, prototypical accomplishments of the human race. Such study is its own reward.

For the student of history, there are additional reasons for studying ancient civilizations. This chapter and the next examine the cultural traits of a number of peoples who built some of the earliest societies based on an urban mode of existence. The preconditions for those societies and their political, social, economic, and cultural common denominators are sketched in the preceding comparative essay. Though the early civilizations examined in this chapter died out in the course of history, they demand attention because of their lasting contributions to subsequent societies: the development of writing, city living, metal working, hydraulic engineering, complex governments, rational codes of law, and quasi-monotheistic religions.

For students living in Western societies, the study of ancient civilizations, as indeed of world history itself, is a good antidote to Eurocentrism (overemphasis on European historical achievements). For West Asia and Africa were the cradles of the very earliest civilizations, and it is increasingly clear that the first European civilization, ancient Greece, owed a large debt to its non-European predecessors. Furthermore, great civilizations were emerging in the rain forests and highlands of Mesoamerica and on the Peruvian coast and the adjacent slopes of the Andes long before the heyday of the classical Greeks.

Mesopotamian Civilization

The fenlands are in bloom, the fields are green,
The uplands are drenched, the dykes are watered;
Ravine and slope carry down the mountain-torrents

That rush into the dykes, watering the fields.
The soil . . . becomes a plantation,
The grass grows in wood and in meadow,
The bountiful womb of the earth is opened,
Giving plenteous food for cattle and abundance for the
        homes of men.
An ox and a horse struck up a friendship.
The rich pasture had sated their bellies,
And glad of heart they lay resting.
The ox opened his mouth to speak, and said to the
        horse, glorious in battle:
"I seem to have been born under a lucky star:
From beginning to end of the year I find food;
I have fodder in abundance and spring water in
        profusion. . . .
Change thy way of life and come away with me!"
[Said the horse:] "Strong brass to cover my body
Have they put upon me, and I wear it as a garment.
Without me, the fiery steed,
Nor king nor prince nor lord nor noble fares upon his
        way . . . .
The horse is like a god, stately of step,
Whilst thou and the calves wear the cap of servitude."*

*Sabatino Moscati, *The Face of the Ancient Orient* (Garden City, NY: Doubleday, 1962), pp. 85–86.

This Assyrian beast fable offers a parable of the contrasting aspects of civilized life. The ox praises the settled and orderly life of peace, an idyllic life in a land made lush and fertile by the efforts of men and women who build dikes, divert water, sow seeds, reap the harvest, and raise the animals. The horse, by contrast, praises war, scorning the slavish life of its bovine friend and glorying in the armor and magnificence of the great warriors, lords, and kings who depend on it for success in battle. The following section examines both peace and war in several ancient Mesopotamian civilizations.

The Sumerian Exemplar of Civilized Life

The constituents of civilization appeared first in Mesopotamia (Greek for "the land between the rivers"), in the Tigris and Euphrates river valleys of West Asia. Climatically, Mesopotamia, a region larger than Texas, was sometimes a hot, arid dust bowl but at other times suffered from unpredictable floods and unhealthful swamps. To surmount these problems, a succession of peoples over the centuries—Sumerians, Babylonians, Assyrians, and Chaldeans—mobilized large, well-organized labor forces that gained control over the water supply by constructing and maintaining a system of canals, dikes, drainage ditches, and reservoirs. Properly irrigated and cultivated, Mesopotamian crops yielded as much as a hundredfold return on seed planted and thus supported a much larger population than regions outside Mesopotamia still practicing Neolithic agriculture.

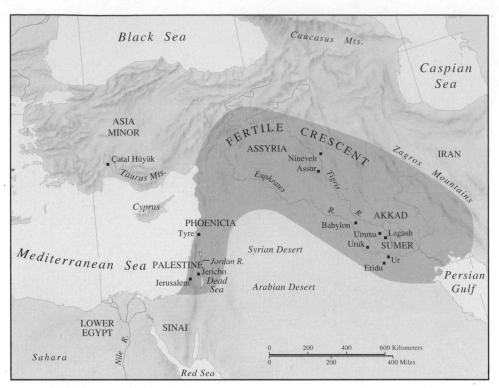

Map 1.1 Ancient Mesopotamia. The two great rivers of Mesopotamia flow out of Anatolia (present-day Turkey): in Mesopotamia the Euphrates runs some 800 miles and the Tigris about 440, from northwest to southeast, before they join as the present-day Shatt al-Arab, whose 100-mile course ends in the Persian Gulf.

Soon after 3500 B.C.E. the Sumerians began to exploit the potential of the lower Tigris-Euphrates Valley. They built several city-states of ten to fifty thousand inhabitants, notably Ur, Uruk, and Lagash, and sustained themselves both by the agricultural produce of the land they controlled and by trade, which provided various imported goods and materials in exchange for surplus crops of cereals and vegetables. On this agricultural base the Sumerians erected in the next 1,500 years a civilization of great sophistication and durability essentially based on a cluster of independent city-states that occasionally made war on each other. Because the Sumerians established enduring patterns for Mesopotamian civilization, they receive the greatest attention here.

The Sumerian city-states showed a striking advance in agriculture, architecture, engineering, and technology over the farming villages of the Neolithic era. The Sumerians parceled out the land in tracts of almost geometrical regularity, and efficiently watered them through an elaborate irrigation system of dams and canals, with smaller channels supplying individual plots. They built a network of roads and waterways and used pack asses, wagons, boats, and barges to carry goods to the urban center.

Sumerian social, economic, and political life was as elaborately organized and controlled as were its natural surroundings. Around 85 percent of the inhabitants of a city

Ram Caught in a Thicket. This mid-third-millennium sculpture is one of the most beautiful objects found in the royal tombs at the Sumerian city of Ur. Standing seventeen inches high and made of gold, silver, lapis lazuli, copper, and other materials, it foreshadows the ram caught in a thicket that Abraham sacrificed in place of his son Isaac (Genesis 22:13).

were little more than human farm machines. Most were slaves or tenant farmers who went out from the city to their plots or to the water control works and, by ceaseless toil, produced the abundant crops that sustained their society. They exchanged part of their produce for the wares of the city's artisans—metal workers, weavers, potters, and others. They also bartered for the foods available from fisherfolk, bakers, and brewers and for the merchandise brought from outside Mesopotamia by a host of traders.

This intense economic activity made Sumerian cities very impressive indeed. Fortifications were common. The city wall at Uruk, for example, nearly six miles in circuit, enclosed about 1,000 acres and contained some 900 defense towers. Within the walls were thousands of humble farmers' hovels and the more elaborate homes of civic and priestly officials and other members of the upper class. Though one could find some broad and straight avenues, the city as a whole gave the impression of a densely packed hive. Most conspicuous were the temples, set apart in walled-off enclosures and often raised on distinctive, stepped artificial mounds called *ziggurats* (the probable inspiration of the biblical tower of Babel).

Much of the peasants' produce went to support the many religious and civic activities controlled by the temples. Increasingly, in the Sumerian period the secular leaders of the state became identical with the religious hierarchy. The *ensi* (city ruler) was considered the agent of the city god and acted on his behalf. He coordinated the various temple communities within the city and assigned work on public buildings and on the water-control

Original pictograph	Pictograph in position of later cuneiform	Early Babylonian	Assyrian	Original or derived meaning
				Bird
				Fish
				Donkey
				Ox
				Sun Day
				Grain
				Orchard
				To plow To till
				Boomerang To throw To throw down
				To stand To go

Evolution of Sumerian Writing. After earlier experimentation with pictographic writing, the Sumerians devised a script called cuneiform (wedge-shaped). Since this system of signs transcribed sounds rather than pictures or ideas, it was adaptable to other languages as well; thus cuneiform writing was used by the Babylonians and Assyrians.

"Fill Your Belly with Good Things"

Gilgamesh, where are you hurrying to? You will never find that life for which you are looking. When the gods created man they allotted him death, but life they retained in their own keeping. As for you, Gilgamesh, fill your belly with good things; day and night, night and day, dance and be merry, feast and rejoice. Let your clothes be fresh, bathe yourself in water, cherish the little child that holds your hand, and make your wife happy in your embrace; for this too is the lot of man.*

The attractive and nubile Siduri, barmaid and vintner to the gods, gives this consoling advice to the hero Gilgamesh during his unsuccessful quest for eternal life. The *Epic of Gilgamesh* was composed in the third millennium B.C.E., some 1,500 years before the earliest European literature (Homer). It was known to the Babylonians, Hittites, Assyrians, and perhaps to the Greeks. A seventh-century B.C.E. copy inscribed in cuneiform on clay tablets was found by excavators at Nineveh in 1853.

*N. K. Sandars, trans., The Epic of Gilgamesh, rev. ed. (Baltimore: Penguin, 1972), p. 102.

installations. He imposed taxes and made legal decisions of various kinds. The city ruler also dictated the foreign policy of the state, including its defense policy and trade relations. The soldiers were under his direct command. Recognized by his subjects as the supreme earthly authority, the *ensi* was given gifts and shown other signs of deference.

Writing is one of the most notable achievements of the Sumerians. Archaeologists have found thousands of clay tablets inscribed in cuneiform ("wedge-shaped"; see the illustration) dating from nearly all periods of Mesopotamian civilization. These tablets mainly record business transactions, inventories of supplies, production and taxation figures, and wage payments. They show, too, that the Mesopotamians employed such mathematical functions as multiplication and division and had devised both a base 12 system of numerical computation and a calendar correlated to the phases of the moon.

Cuneiform records give invaluable insights into the Sumerians' view of the world. Anthropomorphic (having human forms and/or personalities) deities, all-powerful and often fickle, populated their religion. The gods were chiefly personifications of natural forces: Inanna, goddess of fertility; Enlil, storm god of earth, wind, and air; Ereshkigal, queen of the underworld; Dumuzi, cyclically dying god of vegetation. Humans were subject to these and a whole host of lesser but still awe-inspiring divine forces.

akg-images

King Sargon I. Sargon I, ruler of Akkad, founded a dynasty that dominated the cities of Sumer for two centuries. This imposing sculptural head was found at Nineveh and dates to around 2350 B.C.E.

Sumerian religion offered no comforting theology of love and salvation and no clearly defined ethical code by which men and women might order their individual lives. Humans might only hope to ensure the security of their society by the proper observance of rituals, involving the sacrifice of animals, demanded by imperious gods. The following hymn to the god Ninurta gives some sense of the intensity of "fear of the lord" in ancient Sumer:

> Lord Ninurta who vanquishes the houses of the rebellious lands, great lord of Enlil,
>> You, with power you are endowed. . . .
> Lord Ninurta, when your heart was seized by anger,
>> You spat venom like a snake. . . .

> Lord Ninurta, of the house of the contentious and disobedient, you are its adversary,
>   Of their city, you are its enemy. (Trans. S. N. Kramer)

Further, after death one could expect to experience only a shadowy, limbolike existence in the underworld. The outlook here is in striking contrast to the more optimistic expectations of Egyptian religion. Still, there was a time for laughter and dancing as well as for weeping and mourning, as may be seen in such literary remains as the great *Epic of Gilgamesh*.

Political and Cultural Developments of the Babylonians, Assyrians, and Chaldeans

After 2400 B.C.E. the land of Mesopotamia witnessed political upheavals and shifts in centers of power. New peoples rose to prominence by gradual infiltration or by conquest. The rulers of Akkad (2350–2150), known as Sargonids after King Sargon I, subjugated the city-states of Sumer and forced them into a federation under Akkadian direction. However, this early instance of empire building was terminated by the violent incursion of outside groups. A later reassertion of Sumerian control (2150–1950) was cut short by an invasion of the Amorites, who organized the city-states of Sumer and Akkad into an empire centered at Babylon.

This Old Babylonian Empire lasted four centuries. The Babylonians assimilated and refined many of the elements of Sumerian civilization, just as Rome later built on Greek cultural foundations. To cite one example, the law code of Hammurabi (1792–1750 B.C.E.),

---

"I Cut Their Throats Like Lambs"—Memoirs of an Assyrian Warrior-King

With the weapons of [the god] Assur, my lord, and the terrible onset of my attack, I stopped their advance, I succeeded in surrounding them [or turning them back], I decimated the enemy host with arrow and spear. All of their bodies I bored through like a sieve.... Speedily I cut them down and established their defeat. I cut their throats like lambs. I cut off their precious lives [as one cuts] a string. Like the many waters of a storm, I made [the contents of] their gullets and entrails run down upon the wide earth. My prancing steeds, harnessed for my riding, plunged into the streams of their blood as [into] a river. The wheels of my war chariot, which brings low the wicked and the evil, were bespattered with blood and filth. With the bodies of their warriors I filled the plain, like grass. [Their] testicles I cut off, and tore out their privates like the seeds of cucumbers.... Their hands I cut off. The heavy rings of brightest gold [and] silver which [they had] on their wrists I took away. With sharp swords I pierced their belts and seized the girdle daggers of gold and silver which [they carried] on their persons.... The chariots and their horses,

whose riders had been slain at the beginning of the terrible onslaught, and who had been left to themselves, kept running back and forth.... I put an end to their [the riders'] fighting. [The enemy] abandoned their tents and to save their lives they trampled the bodies of their [fallen] soldiers, they fled like young pigeons that are pursued. They were beside themselves ... they held back their urine, but let their dung go in their chariots. In pursuit of them I dispatched my chariots and horses after them. Those among them who had escaped, who had fled for their lives, wherever they [my charioteers] met them, they cut them down with the sword.*

The ruler who records one of his military successes with such relish in the inscription quoted above was Sennacherib (704–681 B.C.E.). This typically brutal Assyrian warrior-king established an imperial capital at Nineveh on the Tigris River, using thousands of slave laborers to construct the royal palaces and monuments of the new city.

*Daniel D. Luckenbill, Ancient Records of Assyria and Babylonia, vol. 2 (Chicago: University of Chicago Press, 1927), pp. 126–128.

Babylon's most famous dynast, set out in an orderly way, in some 280 articles, the body of law as it had evolved over 1,500 years of Mesopotamian history. Designed to replace capricious blood feuds as the basis for justice, Hammurabi's laws dealt in a ponderous, rational manner with a wide variety of actionable offenses. Most of the code was primarily concerned with indebtedness and breach of business contracts (reflecting a commercial orientation among the Mesopotamians), but it also applied to marriage, adultery, and divorce, legitimacy and inheritance, incest, treatment of slaves, personal injury and property damage, and even medical malpractice. Clearly evident in the code is a stratification of society into upper, lower, and slave classes. The penal aspects are dominated by the law of retaliation, "an eye for an eye." As with many early codifications of law, Hammurabi's code imposed harsh penalties—including capital punishment for many crimes—usually according to the status of the aggrieved party. For example, it stipulated, "If a physician performed a major operation on a free man with a bronze lancet and has caused the free man's death, or he opened up the eye-socket of a free man and has destroyed his eye, they shall cut off his hand" (trans. Theophile J. Meek), while the same offense against a slave entailed only replacement of the damaged "property." The general severity of the law code was necessitated in part by the absence of a highly developed ethical doctrine in Mesopotamian religion.

The Babylonians also improved on Sumerian innovations in mathematics and science, especially astronomy. In religion, their deity Marduk presided over a pantheon of Sumerian gods with Babylonian names: for example, Babylonian Ishtar was equivalent to Sumerian Inanna. These deities would survive in various guises down through the periods of Assyrian and Chaldean predominance.

The sudden arrival around 1550 B.C.E. of the Kassites from the neighboring Iranian highlands to the east brought another transition in the sequence of Mesopotamian civilizations. The Kassites in their turn melded with existing Babylonian civilization and remained dominant in Sumer and Akkad for some 400 years.

During the Kassite period, the focus of Mesopotamian development shifted northward. Between about 1300 and 900 B.C.E. the Assyrians rose to prominence in northern Mesopotamia. Although the Kassites for a time prevented consolidation of the entire Tigris-Euphrates Valley, ruthless Assyrian militarism won out after 900 and reached its peak in the careers of a succession of victorious warrior-kings. By the seventh century nearly all of Asia Minor (present-day Turkey), Mesopotamia, Syria, Palestine, and Egypt were at one time or another under Assyrian domination

In 612, however, another Iranian people, the Medes, allied with resurgent Babylon, succeeded in destroying Assyrian power at its center, the capital of Nineveh. The Neo-Babylonian or Chaldean era that followed was a time of conquests of foreign lands, though not on the Assyrian scale. The most famous Neo-Babylonian king, Nebuchadnezzar (reigned 605–562), beautified Babylon with such adornments as the Hanging Gardens (an elaborate terraced garden area) and the magnificently decorated Ishtar Gate; he also sought to revive Babylonian religious devotion.

Religion in the Chaldean period of Mesopotamia was marked by equating the gods with planets: for example, Ishtar (later, Venus), Marduk (later, Jupiter), and so on. The Chaldeans were the best astronomers of the ancient world; they developed a detailed method of time reckoning, employing a seven-day week and a day of twelve 120-minute hours. Astronomy had also a religious or astrological function. Chaldeans believed that charting the positions and movements of the planets and the stars provided a key that would reveal the intentions of the gods, thus enabling mankind to foresee future events.

The long story of Mesopotamian civilization closed in 539 B.C.E., when the Persian ruler Cyrus conquered Babylon and incorporated Mesopotamia into his huge empire.

African Civilization

One generation of men passes to another, and God, who knows characters, has hidden Himself, . . . so worship God upon his way. . . . The soul goes to the place it knows. . . . Beautify your mansion in the West, embellish your place in the necropolis with straightforwardness and just dealing; . . . more acceptable is the character of the straightforward man than the ox of the wrongdoer. Serve God, that He may do the like for you, with offerings for replenishing the altars and with carving; . . . God is aware of whoever serves Him. Provide for men, the cattle of God, for He made heaven and earth at their desire. He suppressed the greed of the waters, he gave the breath of life to their noses, for they are likenesses of Him which issued from His flesh. He shines in the sky for the benefit of their hearts; He has made herbs, cattle, and fish to nourish them. He has killed His enemies and destroyed His own children, because they had planned to make rebellion; He makes daylight for the benefit of their hearts, and He sails around in order to see them, . . . and when they weep, He hears.*

*Leonard H. Lesko, trans., "Egyptian Religion: An Overview," in *The Encyclopedia of Religion*, vol. 5, ed. M. Eliade (New York: Macmillan, 1987), p. 41.

The passage quoted above comes from an ancient Egyptian "coffin text" (so called because it was painted inside a coffin) of about 2040 B.C.E. It provides a concise summary of the theology and philosophy of the religion of Re, the sun god, whose cult was preeminent through most of Egyptian history. Re is a hidden, all-knowing, and just god. His gifts of life and of the good things of the world must be matched by humankind's worship of his godhead and fair treatment of fellow human beings. The pyramids of Giza are the most lasting testimony of the Egyptians' faithfulness to these central beliefs in the power and justice of their gods and of the kings thought to be descended from them. They also bespeak a thriving society of teeming thousands whose labor—skilled and unskilled—was mustered and directed by a highly sophisticated organization. Ancient Egyptian civilization, the earliest to develop on the continent of Africa, has fascinated later ages both because of its great antiquity and because of the marvelous works of art and architecture that have outlived it.

The Land of the Nile and the Emergence of Egyptian Civilization

Because of the topographical uniformity of its location, Egyptian civilization (see Map 1.2) was more homogeneous, both geographically and politically, than was the case in Mesopotamia, with its numerous, densely populated city-states. Compared with Mesopotamia, Egypt had few cities; administrative activity was highly centralized and concentrated in a few major capitals, such as Memphis and Thebes. The mass of people in Egypt lived in thousands of villages more or less evenly distributed in the twelve

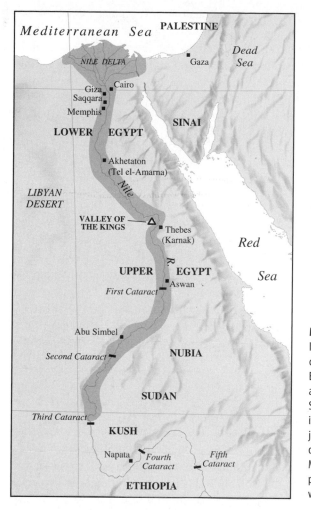

Map 1.2 Ancient Egypt. The Nile—the longest river in the world—literally defines the country of Egypt. Its sources are in the lakes of Ethiopia and Uganda, which give rise to the Blue and White Niles. These two join at Khartoum in Sudan. The river is about one-half mile wide, and its valley is about five miles wide down to a point just west of present-day Cairo, where the river divides to form the great Nile delta on the Mediterranean. Throughout Egyptian history, 95 percent of the population has lived in the Nile valley and delta.

thousand square miles of arable land in the valley and delta of the mighty Nile, where the dependable pulse of the river's yearly cycle of flood and subsidence regulated Egyptian life. The arid land was fertile only where its waters reached or could be made to reach.

Besides bringing water during its annual flood stage, June to October, the Nile brought deposits of some 200 million tons of rich, fertile soil and minerals per year. The diversion of floodwaters and draining of swamplands in the Nile Valley made Egypt the most productive agricultural land of the ancient world. The reliable rhythm of the Nile also affected the people of Egypt in subtler ways: in particular, it fostered a more optimistic outlook on life, a confidence in the natural order of things that is not evident in, for example, Mesopotamia.

Menes, the first king of Egypt's First Dynasty (royal family line), is credited with unifying Upper and Lower Egypt around 3000 B.C.E. The next 2,000 years of Egyptian history are customarily divided into three periods of strong political unity, the Old, Middle, and New Kingdoms, separated by periods of weak central government, social unrest, and foreign invasions.

The preeminent central authority in the Old Kingdom was the pharaoh, a god-king, seen variously as the son or the manifestation of certain deities. He exercised his supreme will through a simple but rigid hierarchy ranging from royal agents and elite nobles to local officials who ruled some forty administrative districts. This political superstructure and the many building projects and other activities it supervised were supported by the tremendous agricultural surplus produced by the mass of peasants. The god-governed state engaged in exploration of and trade with neighboring lands, including Nubia, Ethiopia, the Sinai Peninsula, and Phoenicia. To build monuments or flood-control installations, the pharaohs dictated the enlistment and provisioning of a large, skilled labor force: masons and stonecutters, sculptors, carpenters, and painters, as well as construction managers, surveyors, draftsmen, scribes, and others. These worked chiefly during the inundation phase of the Nile's cycle, when transport by water was easiest and farm workers were free to quarry, haul, and position stone building materials.

The pharaoh wielded such extensive powers because service to him on any state project was a religious as well as a civic duty. Egyptian religion, like that of Sumer, was a thoroughgoing polytheism (belief in many gods), in which most major and minor divinities were associated with the agrarian rhythms of fertility and germination, death and regeneration. The gods were mainly anthropomorphic, but could also have the form of a beast, such as a beetle, bull, or snake, or a half-beast, such as a human torso with the head of a jackal, crocodile, or cow.

Perhaps the most universal Egyptian myths concerned the god Osiris, slain by the evil Set but reborn through the efforts of his sister/wife Isis. Osiris was the father of Horus, who, in most periods of Egyptian history, was embodied in the person of the king. After death, the pharaoh became one with Osiris, the king of the dead who influenced the life cycles governing the natural world. In a continuing cycle, the new pharaoh, his son, was the dutiful Horus, who led the state in the worship of his father Osiris. Thus the security not only of the state but also of the whole universe was directly linked to the well-being of the king, both during and after his life on earth. He had to be accorded all due honors and signs of deference in this life as well as in the next. This accounts for the practice of mummification, which was an attempt to ensure the continued comfort and goodwill of the deceased king in the afterworld. Hence, too, the fantastic expenditure of time and resources on funeral monuments, temples, and tombs, of which the pyramids are the most notable.

Early in their history, the ancient Egyptians evolved and perfected the pyramid, the architectural form that has ever after been the distinguishing mark of their civilization. Of the Great Pyramids built at Giza, the largest is that of Khufu (or Cheops), which dates from about 2600 B.C.E. It was 460 feet high and 755 feet on each side, and was made from some 2.3 million stone blocks averaging 2.5 tons each. The whole was sheathed with limestone casing blocks (stripped in later centuries to supply building stone for new cities like Cairo) that gave the pyramid the appearance of one massive unit. The complex at Giza—the three Great Pyramids and the famous Sphinx—was only one of

LIVES AND TIMES ACROSS CULTURES

Diverse Burial Customs

Death, birth, and marriage are the cardinal events in all societies throughout history. Humans have evolved a wide range of rituals of celebration and mourning. Burial practices vary depending on the climate and topography in which various societies have emerged. In tropical, hot regions where bodies decompose quickly, or in densely populated areas like India, corpses are often cremated and the ashes returned to the land, air, or sea. In hot desert regions like the Middle East, simple burials are held usually within twenty-four hours of death.

As civilizations became more complex, so too did burial practices. Powerful and wealthy rulers and elites were often buried in huge, ornate tombs and adorned with costly jewels and clothing. In Han China, rulers were buried with full regalia and replicas of their armies, horses, and trappings of power. Similarly, in the Western Hemisphere, Chaco and Aztec warriors were buried with their armor, gold jewelry, and armaments.

The burial customs of the ancient Egyptians were among the most complex in human history. The pyramids in Giza and tombs in the Valleys of the Kings and Queens are 3,000-year-old monuments to the Egyptian preoccupation with death and the afterlife. The burial chamber of the pharaoh Tutankhamon, uncovered by Howard Carter in 1922, contained a veritable treasure trove of artifacts. Upon seeing the chamber for the first time, Carter exclaimed that he saw "wonderful things, strange animals, statues and gold, everywhere the glint of gold." One elaborately painted chest took Carter three weeks to unpack. The items found in "King Tut's" tomb—including gold jewelry, alabaster vases, and a jewel-inlaid, golden funerary mask—amaze and delight even present-day viewers.

---

many Old Kingdom burial places in the region of Memphis; some eighty tombs are marked by pyramids.

The Pyramids at Giza are among the best examples of Egyptian architecture, not only in scale but also in the precision of their construction. This is particularly remarkable considering the lack of sophisticated hoisting equipment. It is likely that earthen ramps were used to haul the stones up and into position. Moreover, the tombs and temples, here and elsewhere in Egypt, were adorned with magnificent sculptures (full-figure and relief), paintings, and hieroglyphic inscriptions. The last were perhaps inspired by a knowledge of cuneiform, but they differ from that script by combining pictographs with syllable signs and letter signs. Thus the Egyptians did not develop true alphabetic writing.

Although the pyramids were the eternal homes of royalty, the possibility of life after death was open to others besides the pharaoh, as the evidence of nobles' tombs indicates. Moreover, Egyptian religion had a slight ethical emphasis, a concern for justice that we do not see in Mesopotamia. The gods ruled a cosmos based on the Egyptian notion of moral right. The pharaoh was expected to treat his subjects equitably, and those subjects were required to be fair in their dealings with one another. Those with the means to do so were to assist the less well off, such as widows and orphans.

Career Counseling in Ancient Egypt

The washerman's day is going up, going down. All his limbs are weak, [from] whitening his neighbor's clothes every day, from washing linen.

The maker of pots is smeared with soil, like one whose relations have died. His hands, his feet are all full of clay; he is like one who lives in the bog.

The cobbler mingles with vats. His odor is penetrating. His hands are red with madder [dye], like one who is smeared with blood. He looks behind him for the kite, like one whose flesh is exposed.

The watchman prepares garlands and polishes vase-stands. He spends a night of toil just as one on whom the sun shines.

The merchants travel downstream and upstream. They are as busy as can be, carrying goods from one town to another. . . . But the tax collectors carry off the gold, that most precious of metals.

The ships' crews from every house [of commerce], they receive their loads. They depart from Egypt for Syria, and each man's god is with him. [But] not one of them says: "We shall see Egypt again!"

The carpenter who is in the shipyard carries the timber and stacks it. If he gives today the output of yesterday, woe to his limbs! The shipwright stands behind him to tell him evil things. . . .

The scribe, he alone, records the output of all of them. Take note of it! . . . Set your sight on being a scribe. . . . You will not be like a hired ox.

The preceding passage is from an ancient Egyptian document (the *Papyrus Lansing* in the British Museum) dating to about 1150 B.C.E. It is part of a letter of advice written to a young man about to decide on a profession. The document provides some interesting reflections on the conditions of work in a variety of jobs.

Miriam Lichtheim, comp. Ancient Egyptian Literature: A Book of Readings, vol. 2, The New Kingdom (Berkeley: University of California Press, 1976), pp. 168–173.

Discontinuities and the Rise and Decline of an Imperial Culture

Just as Sumerian archetypes gave an enduring pattern to Mesopotamian civilization, the Old Kingdom originated many aspects of the political, religious, and artistic worldview of the Egyptians. In Mesopotamia, change often came as a result of intrusions from the Iranian uplands to the east and north or from Arabia to the west and south. Egypt, by contrast, was better protected from invasion by vast tracts of uninhabitable desert wasteland. Internal social and political upheavals, however, occasionally led to weakness and disunity.

During the first intermediate period (2150–2050 B.C.E.), the central administration was replaced by a fragmented system of hereditary local leadership. The succeeding Middle Kingdom (2050–1750) had its capital at Thebes, some 400 miles up the Nile from Memphis; Upper and Lower Egypt were reunited. About 1750, however, either a succession of weak kings or stiffer competition from local nobility with royal aspirations apparently once again eroded central authority. Vulnerable because of its domestic disarray, Egypt suffered the "Great Humiliation," a successful invasion, probably from Palestine, by a people whom the Egyptians called the Hyksos. Unlike the Amorites or the Kassites, who were ultimately absorbed by the civilizations they attacked in Mesopotamia, the Hyksos remained an alien force. They maintained themselves in lower Egypt by superior military ability and technology: the horse-drawn chariot and improved weapons. After about 200 years they were ejected by Theban rulers, who were in turn followed by the ambitious and imperialistic kings of the New Kingdom era.

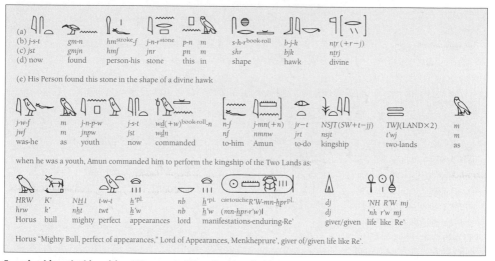

(a)
(b) *j-s-t* | *gm-n* | *hm*stroke-*f* | *j-n-r*stone | *p-n* m | *s-h-r*book-roll | *b-j-k* | *nt̲r* (+*r*−*j*)
(c) *jst* | *gmjn* | *hmf* | *jnr* | *pn* m | *shr* | *bjk* | *nt̲rj*
(d) now | found | person-his | stone | this in | shape | hawk | divine

(e) His Person found this stone in the shape of a divine hawk

j-w-f | *m* | *j-n-p-w* | *j-s-t* | *wd̲*(+*w*)book-roll-*n* | *n-f* | *j-mn*(+*n*) | *jr-t* | *NSJT* (*SW*+*t*−*jj*) | *TWJ*(LAND×2) | *m*
jwf | *m* | *jnpw* | *jst* | *wd̲n* | *nf* | *nmnw* | *jrt* | *nsjt* | *t'wj* | *m*
was-he | as | youth | now | commanded | to-him | Amun | to-do | kingship | two-lands | as

when he was a youth, Amun commanded him to perform the kingship of the Two Lands as:

HRW | *K'* | *NH̲I* | *t-w-t* | *h̲'*pl. | *nb* | *h̲'*pl. | cartouche*R'W-mn-h̲pr*pl. | *dj* | *'NH R'W mj*
hrw | *k'* | *nh̲t* | *twt* | *h̲'w* | *nb* | *h̲'w* | (*mn-h̲pr-r'w*)I | *dj* | *'nh r'w mj*
Horus | bull | mighty | perfect | appearances | lord | manifestations-enduring-Re' | giver/given | life like Re'

Horus "Mighty Bull, perfect of appearances," Lord of Appearances, Menkheprure', giver of/given life like Re'.

Egyptian hieroglyphic writing. This example of Egyptian hieroglyphic writing is from a temple of Thutmose IV (reigned 1406–1398 B.C.E.). Line (a) shows original hieroglyphics, (b) and (c) show two kinds of transcription, (d) gives a word-by-word translation, and (e) gives a smooth English version. Hieroglyphic writing passed out of use around 400 C.E. It remained undeciphered until the discovery of the Rosetta stone (now in the British Museum) by the French during their occupation of Egypt in 1799. The stone bears an inscription from the reign of Ptolemy V (196 B.C.E.) in three versions: hieroglyphic Egyptian, demotic Egyptian, and Greek. Using this as a key, the French scholar Jean François Champollion was able to decipher hieroglyphic writing in 1822.

The Egyptian Empire, as the New Kingdom (1550–1150 B.C.E.) is sometimes labeled, restored much of the prestige lost during the Hyksos occupation. Egyptian control again reached across the Sinai into Palestine and Syria and to the Euphrates. At home, foreign conquest meant peace and prosperity; tribute and valuable materials poured into Egypt. Strong trade contacts were developed, for example, with the land of "Punt," in the region of modern Somalia, and with Arabia; these contacts brought incense, ivory, myrrh, and slaves to Egypt in exchange for jewelry, weapons, and tools. The pride taken in these achievements can be seen in the art and architecture sponsored by the conquering pharaohs of the New Kingdom, who launched massive building programs to honor the gods and to publicize and magnify their own accomplishments. The colossal temple complex of Amon at Karnak near Thebes is an especially noteworthy example, as are the huge, lavishly furnished temples and tombs built in the Valley of the Kings across the Nile from Thebes and at Abu Simbel above Aswan. The tomb of an unimportant king, Tutankhamon (reigned 1352–1344), which escaped grave robbers, gives us a tantalizing glimpse of the wealth of these kings and nobles of imperial Egypt. The discovery of the tomb of Tutankhamon (or "King Tut") by the British archaeologist Howard Carter in 1922 caused a worldwide sensation and a frenzy of interest in ancient Egypt, seen in new styles of architecture and interior decoration, as well as in such popular entertainments as the horror film *The Mummy*. As Carter himself said in recalling the discovery:

A feeling of intrusion had descended heavily upon us with the opening of the doors, heightened, probably, by the almost painful impressiveness of a linen pall, decorated with golden

Temple at Abu Simbel. Pictured is the façade of the great temple at Abu Simbel with its colossal figures of Ramses II (reigned 1290–1224 B.C.E.), more than sixty feet in height. At a cost of $40 million, a UNESCO team of German, Italian, French, and Swedish engineers dismantled and moved the temple to higher ground to prevent its submersion by the rising waters of Lake Nasser after the completion of the Aswan High Dam; the move took four years (1964–1968).

© Roger Wood/Corbis

rosettes, which dropped above the inner shrine. We felt that we were in the presence of the dead King and must do him reverence, and in imagination could see the doors of the successive shrines open one after the other till the innermost disclosed the King himself.

Amenhotep IV (reigned 1369–1353 B.C.E.), unlike most of the militaristic pharaohs who preceded him, was most notable for his innovations in religion. A rebel in his attitudes toward art and theology, he recognized as gods only himself and the solar disk, Aton. He changed his name to Akhenaton ("it pleases Aton") and founded a new capital called Akhetaton ("place of the Glory of Aton") at present-day Tel el-Amarna (see Map 1.2). Compared with the polytheism prevalent in the ancient world, his religion closely approached monotheism. Akhenaton and his queen, Nefertiti, are familiar from artistic depictions. The pharaoh's reform efforts, however, were short-lived. His successor, Tutankhamon, reinstated the previous polytheism with Amon as chief deity, pleasing the numerous priests who derived wealth and prestige at the restored capital of Thebes and elsewhere. Indeed, the ever-rising power of the various priesthoods, which Akhenaton had tried to curb, was a principal symptom of yet another decline of the central authority.

Egypt after 1100 B.C.E. was only intermittently a unified state. Despite sporadic reassertions of independence, Egypt proper never regained the political autonomy and confident imperialism of its glorious past. Ancient Egyptian history became an adjunct of Kushitic, Assyrian, Persian, Macedonian, and Roman history.

The Kushite Kingdom in Upper Egypt and the Sudan

Once an extension of the ancient Egyptian empire, the Kushite kingdom emerged as an independent power by 700 B.C.E. Located around the border of present-day Egypt and

Sudan, with their capital at Napata, the Kushites had long served as intermediaries for the transport of goods traded between the Egyptian kingdom and eastern Africa. In the course of their contacts with, and eventual subjugation by, Egypt, the Kushites assimilated many of the cultural, religious, and social values of ancient Egypt.

As Egypt declined in military strength and cultural dynamism, the Kushite kingdom evolved into a distinctive Sudanic empire. By 750 B.C.E., Kushite kings began attacking the weakened Egyptian forces and, under King Shabako (reigned 707–696 B.C.E.), conquered Egypt. After almost 100 years of rule over Egypt, the Kushite empire was attacked by the stronger military might of the Assyrians. Following the Assyrian conquest of Egypt, the Kushites hastily withdrew to the Sudan. By 591 the Egyptians renewed their attacks on the Kushites, who then moved their capital further south to Meroë. Meroë, approximately 100 miles north of contemporary Khartoum, had substantial deposits of iron ore and wood, good grazing land for cattle, and a navigable harbor; it also had control of the rich gold mines in the Sudan (known in Rome as Nubia).

In Meroë, the Kushites prospered from trade with Egypt and East Africa. Documents and relics indicate that the Kushites also had indirect contacts with China, India, and Arabia. Following the Macedonian conquest of Egypt in 332 B.C.E., they also established close relations with the Greeks. Much of Meroë's prosperity was based on the production of high-grade iron used to manufacture weapons. Meroë was known throughout the Hellenistic world as an iron-producing center, and remnants of slag heaps from smelting factories are still visible around the ancient monuments of the city. As Meroë declined in wealth and power, some Kushites may have migrated to West Africa, where they transmitted their skills in iron production and knowledge of the lost-wax process for bronze casting. At present it is not known whether these skills were transmitted from East Africa or whether West African societies developed the techniques independently.

Once literate in the Egyptian language, the Kushites gradually developed a written language of their own; based on hieroglyphics, the signs have yet to be interpreted. As a result, much of what is known about Kushite society has been transmitted in accounts by foreign travelers, traders, or historians who had contact with the Kushite Empire.

It is known that the Kushites were literate and had an extremely hierarchical society similar to that of ancient Egypt. The ruling families lived lavishly, owned slaves, and were probably revered as divine. Most Kushites earned their livelihoods from herds of cattle, sheep, and goats. The many depictions of royal women in sculptures and reliefs on temples may indicate that the society was matrilineal. Documentary evidence shows that the Kushite kingdom was ruled by a queen in 45 B.C.E. The extensive ruins of temples, palaces, and pyramids around Meroë attest to the wealth, building skills, and complexity of the society. Pottery, sculpture, and other objects show influences of pharaonic, Hellenistic, and sub-Saharan African societies. As in Egypt, Kushite royalty and nobility, along with their personal possessions, were buried in lavish tombs. Some of these tombs have provided archaeologists with a rich source of information about the Kushites; however, many of these tombs and other Kushite monuments have not yet been excavated, and much remains to be learned.

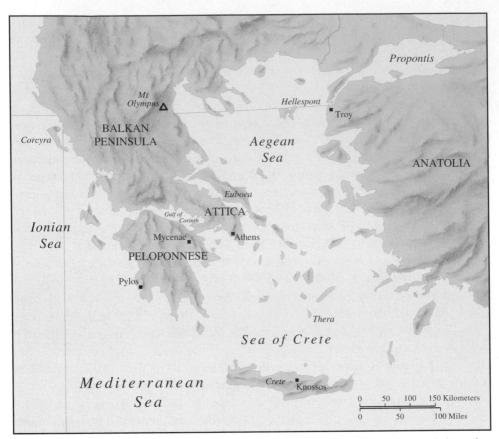

Map 1.3 Greece and the Aegean Basin. Shown in this map are the mainland regions and islands that were the home of Aegean civilization. Some of the more important Bronze Age sites are indicated.

Early Aegean Civilization

At a depth of twenty-five feet from the surface of the [Mycenaean] Acropolis, [Heinrich] Schliemann cried out, "Sophia! Sophia!"

When she joined him . . . she exclaimed, "My God!"

He had found three bodies "smothered"—Schliemann's word—in gold. Each body was draped with five gold diadems; two of the bodies were each adorned with gold laurel leaves. The sepulcher, cut out of rock, also contained "many curious objects," including cow-shaped idols, fragments of colored glass, small knives of obsidian, the fragments of a gold-plated silver vase, a bronze knife. The bones and skulls had been preserved but they had suffered so much from moisture that when he reached out and touched them, they dissolved as if in a dream. . . .

Returning to the surface in a frenzy, he ordered the work gangs to dig up the whole area beneath the other grave markers. Schliemann behaved like a man possessed.*

*Arnold C. Brackman, *The Dream of Troy* (New York: Mason & Lipscomb, 1974), pp. 180–81.

This passage captures the thrill of discovery that makes archaeology so appealing. Of course, when Schliemann was excavating at Mycenae in 1876, the science was in its infancy and many mistakes were made; as one scholar put it, Schliemann excavated as if he were digging for potatoes, and the atmosphere was more that of a treasure hunt than of a scientific investigation. Schliemann has even been accused of "salting" his dig sites with modern forgeries. Today, as a mature field of study, archaeology involves careful examination of sites and painstaking methods of handling, labeling, and recording materials brought to light. There still remains, however, the romantic allure of revealing the lives of men and women who lived thousands of years ago. This was particularly the case for Schliemann, who later claimed to be seeking to verify the Homeric poems, with their glorious and bloodthirsty kings and warriors, magnificent palaces, and heroic quests and warfare. However rudimentary his efforts at Troy and "golden Mycenae," he proved that Homer's world of heroes was not merely a figment of poetic imagination. This section focuses on the earliest civilizations of the Aegean region.

The Flowering of Minoan Civilization

The Aegean world encompassed the southern end of the Balkan Peninsula (see Map 1.3), the west coast of Asia Minor, the islands that dot the Aegean and Ionian Seas, and the large islands of Crete and Cyprus. This region (in land area about the size of Alabama) was not so blessed as Mesopotamia or Egypt with fertile soil or other natural resources. Its physical geography consisted of many mountains, small and scattered coastal plains and river valleys, and the ever-present sea.

LIVES AND TIMES ACROSS CULTURES

Risking Death to Gain the Favor of the Gods

Many early cultures around the world have sought to pay homage to supernatural powers by means of perilous athletic contests. Among the Olmec, for example, such competitions centered on ball games in which the losing participants often lost their lives. Spectators at these events no doubt also felt the presence of supernatural forces. The general intent was probably to placate the gods and to ensure their goodwill toward the community.

Similarly, the Minoan people of Bronze Age Crete appear to have enjoyed life-threatening feats of acrobatic skill. A number of famous wall-paintings and sculptures depict young athletes performing death-defying vaults over charging bulls. Since archaeological evidence from Crete features bulls in contexts of religious sacrifice, it seems likely that the bull-jumping events were designed, like the Mesoamerican athletic competitions, to honor or influence the gods. So, too, in classical Greece and Rome, the athletic games at Olympia, Delphi, and hundreds of other sites, while not generally life-endangering, were held to honor gods such as Zeus and Apollo.

The Roman gladiatorial contests are perhaps the best-known examples of the association of physical competition with the awe-inspiring force of death. Though they became thoroughly secularized, the bloody Roman games likely originated with an earlier, Etruscan practice of a specialized type of human sacrifice, in which pairs of warriors fought to the death as part of the funeral rites in honor of deceased noblemen.

Knossos. An artist's rendering of the great Minoan palace complex discovered by Sir Arthur Evans at Knossos, on Crete. The palace's mazelike complexity may have inspired the myth of the labyrinth, in which the Greek hero Theseus slew the Minotaur.

Such topographical features contributed to the political fragmentation of the Aegean world and the scarcity of arable land; less than 20 percent of the land was fit for cultivation, and even in antiquity the land suffered from deforestation and generally poor soil management. The area was hot and arid in summer, in winter cool and moderately watered by rainfall. The grapevine and the olive tree were best suited to the soil and weather of the region, though wheat and barley were grown on virtually every acre of suitable land. There was sufficient grazing land for sheep and goats, but not usually for cattle and horses. It was and is a beautiful region, one of stunning contrasts, of crystalline skies and "wine-dark" seas, of brilliant, sun-drenched vistas of steep river valleys and mountain peaks.

Human beings had lived in the Aegean area in the Neolithic era (7000–3000 B.C.E.) and, in a few places, even earlier. Around 3000, a change occurred, marked by new types of pottery and the introduction of metallurgy (specifically in bronze, hence the term Bronze Age). This transition from Stone to Bronze Age likely reflects the arrival of a new people. In the next 1,500 years the most rapid cultural advances in the region took place on the large island of Crete, on the southern edge of the Aegean Sea, where the Minoan civilization flourished.

The culture of the Minoans was unknown until modern times, when Sir Arthur Evans excavated Knossos (see Map 1.3), beginning in 1899. He uncovered a vast, multistory palace complex and eventually found that the astonishingly rich and distinctive Minoan civilization had pervaded the whole island, some 150 miles long by 35 miles wide. The palace walls and floors were brightly decorated with fresco paintings showing plants and animals and aquatic and marine life. People were pictured in a wide variety of activities, including ritual sports such as the famous bull-jumping events. The style of this art was vivid and distinctively impressionistic.

Less is known about the people who built and adorned the palaces. The architectural grandeur implies a strongly centralized administration, as does the evidence of two non-alphabetic forms of writing, called Linear A (used to transcribe the language of Crete) and Linear B (used to transcribe Greek). Inscribed clay tablets contain inventories of raw materials and manufactured goods, of agricultural production and stored goods, suggesting that Crete was heavily populated and that the various palace centers controlled surrounding farmsteads, pastures, and villages.

A king called "Minos," perhaps an honorific title, controlled the palace complex, and was assisted by a corps of specially trained bureaucrats and scribes who supervised and recorded the activities of farmers, artisans, and slaves. Priests may have been in charge of religious observances, in which the bull figured prominently; whether the animal was a sacrificial offering or a god image is unclear, but it may have provided the kernel of the myth of the Minotaur, a monster usually depicted as a man with the head of a bull, who was slain by the Athenian hero Theseus. Snake-handling mother goddesses, sacred trees, and caves also figured in Minoan religion. As in Egypt and Mesopotamia, fertility,

Boxing Children. This charming fresco painting comes from the island of Thera (present-day Santorini) and dates to the time of the volcanic eruption around 1625 B.C.E. The fresco is in the typical style of the Minoan civilization of Crete and surrounding islands.

© Gianni Dagli Orti/Corbis

death, and regeneration were major concerns of this religion.

The people of Crete had learned from Egypt how to construct ships that could sail the Mediterranean. Though we have stories of Cretan naval vessels dominating neighboring islands and even mainland sites, the influence of the Minoans appears to have been commercial and cultural rather than imperialistic. Unlike the Mycenaeans later, they neither protected their palaces by fortifications nor included military scenes and weapons in their art.

The Minoan civilization was dealt crippling blows by a devastating earthquake around 1700 B.C.E. and a huge volcanic eruption on the neighboring island of Thera around 1625. The Minoans seem not to have recovered fully from these disasters when, sometime after 1380, their palaces were again destroyed, this time by Indo-European invaders, the Mycenaeans. Minoan traditions, however, continued to live in the culture of the conquerors.

The Advent of the Indo-Europeans

Beginning in the third millennium B.C.E. and continuing into the first millennium C.E., a new linguistic class of people, the Indo-Europeans, radiated out from the steppe region north of the Black Sea into Greece, Anatolia (Asia Minor), Iran, and India. Written

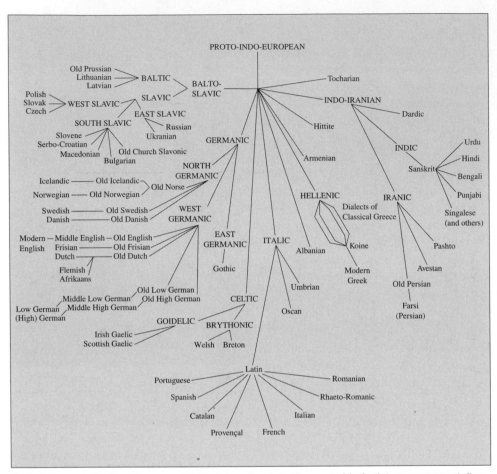

The Indo-European Family of Languages. This chart shows the principal languages of the family in an arrangement indicating genetic relationships and geographic distribution.

records for the earliest periods of Indo-European migration are very scarce and appear only after the migrating peoples settled in their new homes. The languages recorded are distinct (including Greek, Hittite, Persian, and Sanskrit) and reflect a mingling of immigrant and indigenous populations. There are no written specimens whatever of the parent Indo-European language, which antedated the advent of writing. Although there is controversy regarding particular word roots, it is possible to recreate some of its basic vocabulary by arguing backward from later, "descendant" languages. Thus, many dictionaries list reconstructed Indo-European roots (usually preceded by an asterisk [*]) for words in modern languages. For example, *bhrater lies behind Sanskrit bhratar, Greek phrater, Latin frater, German Bruder, French frère, Italian fratello, and English brother, friar, and fraternal.

Since so many modern tongues, including English and most other languages of Europe as well as of Iran and, to a lesser extent, India are Indo-European (see the illustration), linguists and historians have given special attention to the history of its speakers. By recreating the vocabulary of this protolanguage, specialists may reconstruct details of the lives of its speakers and their community. Deductions from vocabulary provide a different perspective on a society than does archaeology. The lack of a general word for sea argues that the original Indo-Europeans were an inland people, unfamiliar with seafaring. Indo-Europeans had words for time and the seasons that reflect life in an agricultural society. Words for plowing, sowing, plucking, and grinding, as well as for furrow, wheat, rye, and so forth point to the cultivation of grains. The vocabulary also attests to the domestication of animals (cows, sheep, pigs, horses) and, in the technical sphere, to weaving, pottery manufacture, metal working (copper and possibly bronze), and the use of carts with solid (not spoked) wheels. That the Indo-Europeans also had a word for apple trees, but not for citrus fruits, indicates a northern rather than Mediterranean locale. Words for fish were rare and there were none for camel, lion, or tiger.

As regards socioeconomic matters, the Indo-Europeans had many terms for familial relations within a strongly patriarchal (father-ruled) society and for the household or tribal groups of households as basic units. There were also words for fortified high places. Kingship or warlordship and priesthood appear to have been complementary aspects of political sovereignty. The principles of gift exchange and mutual obligation binding hosts and guests, familiar from later Greek customs, existed in Indo-European society. The invaders infused various indigenous Neolithic peoples with an active, mobile, patriarchal, and aggressive culture. When they conquered and joined or merged with civilized societies, they often adopted or assimilated many elements of those cultures.

The impact of an early Indo-European culture may be gauged from the accomplishments of the Hittites in the second millennium B.C.E. Although Mesopotamia and Egypt enjoyed for two millennia the best natural resources and strongest political organizations in West Asia, archaeologists have shown that another very significant power was located in Asia Minor. The Hittites came to this region sometime before 2000, as part of the general movement of Indo-European peoples mentioned above. Between 1600 and 1200, the Hittites played a major role in the power politics of West Asia. This was in part due to a technology they monopolized for a time: iron working. The use of iron weapons, together with another innovation, the chariot, gave the Hittites a decided advantage in warfare. Iron was also used in the manufacture of improved farming implements. The Hittites successfully invaded Babylonia and fought a great battle against New Kingdom Egypt at Kadesh in Syria. The Egyptian pharaoh, Ramses II, later decorated many temple walls with carved depictions of his exploits at this battle, though in fact the battle was a draw. The Hittites themselves then fell to a new wave of Indo-European invaders after 1200.

In western Asia Minor, the chief successor state of the Hittites was the kingdom of Lydia, which rose to prominence beginning in the eighth century. The Lydians enjoyed the economic advantages of excellent farmland and rich natural resources. The Greek cities that had sprung up in western Asia Minor became tribute-paying subject states of Lydia. In Greek accounts of his life, the last and most famous of Lydian kings, Croesus, became an archetype of the fabulously wealthy eastern potentate. It is thus fitting that the Lydians' principal gift to posterity should have been the invention of coined money.

The Rise and Fall of Mycenaean Warrior-Kings

The Greeks, another Indo-European people active at the same time as the Hittites, played a more influential role in world history. Around 2000, the first Greek speakers arrived on the tip of the Balkan Peninsula and founded powerful states centering on citadels at Athens, Pylos, Mycenae (from which the culture gets its name), and other sites. These were the heroes that the Greek poets spoke of, people called Achaeans in Homer's epic poems. The uncovering of Troy and Mycenae by Heinrich Schliemann in the 1870s sent shock waves through the scholarly world.

Each Mycenaean site was a heavily fortified center from which a king governed surrounding territory. Administrative organization was quite intricate and, as on Crete, was overseen by a corps of bureaucrats and scribes who classified, counted, and recorded millions of bits of information in Linear B.

This civilization was wealthy and, at least in its art, cosmopolitan. It imported amber from the Baltic Sea coast, ivory from Syria, alabaster from Crete, lapis lazuli from Mesopotamia, and even ostrich eggs from Nubia in Africa. At Mycenae, excavation revealed royal graves exceedingly rich in gifts, including crowns, sword scabbards, pommels of ivory and gold, bronze daggers inlaid with scenes of lion hunts, vases of gold, silver, bronze, and alabaster, numerous articles of jewelry, arrowheads, boars' tusks like those of a helmet in Homer's *Iliad,* axes, tridents, and many other valuables. The workmanship is very fine and points to influence from Asia Minor, Egypt, and especially Crete. Schliemann thought one of the gold masks he found was the death mask of Homer's King Agamemnon, and indeed the stern and angular features do give an impression of majesty and a will to power.

How did Mycenaean royalty acquire such wealth and power? A far-flung network of trade contacts and a firm agricultural base offer part of the answer, but warfare played an

---

The Creation of Homer's Epic Poems

The Homeric poems belong to the period of transition from an oral to a literary technique. . . . Homer . . . was an oral poet living in an age of writing. Oral songs can be collected either by phonograph apparatus, which is obviously out of the question here; or by dictation to a scribe; or by a literate oral poet who has been asked to write down his song for someone else who, for some reason, wants it in writing. The last of these possibilities is highly unlikely, because the oral poet, if he is at all literate, can have only a smattering of writing, if he is to remain an oral poet. Had he enough facility in writing to record 27,000 lines of text [of the Iliad *and the* Odyssey], *his style could not be that of an oral technique, which Homer's demonstrably is. In my own mind*

there remains no doubt that Homer dictated the Iliad *to someone else who wrote it down, because the Homeric poems have all the earmarks of dictated texts of oral epic songs.**

Albert Lord reached these conclusions about the origins of our texts of the Homeric poems on the basis of knowledge gained while he did field research with his teacher and mentor, Milman Parry. This research was conducted among illiterate singer-poets in Yugoslavia during the 1930s. Lord's theory of the oral dictated text has won wide acceptance among students of Homer and other early oral traditions of epic poetry.

*Albert B. Lord, "Homer's Originality: Oral Dictated Texts," Transactions of the American Philological Association, *84 (1953), 131.*

Bronze Age Bureaucrats

Astonishing and significant is the omniscience, the insatiable thirst for intimate detail [of Mycenaean officials]. Sheep may be counted up to a glittering total of twenty-five thousand: but there is still a purpose to be served by recording the fact that one animal was contributed by Komawens and another by Etewano. Restless officialdom notes the presence in Pesero's house of one woman and two children; the employment of two nurses, one girl, and one boy, in a Cretan village; the fattening of an insignificant number of hogs. . . ; the existence somewhere of a single pair of brassbound chariot wheels labelled "useless,"—these things and hundreds

more of the same type were duly recorded in the palaces of Pylos and Knossos.*

The records described in this passage come from thousands of clay tablets inscribed with the nonalphabetic script called Linear B. For a half century after their first discovery by archaeologists in 1900, it was thought that the language of the tablets was not Greek. Then, in 1952, a young British architect named Michael Ventris deciphered Linear B and showed it to be a primitive form of Greek. This amazing discovery forced researchers to rewrite the history of Greek civilization.

*Denys L. Page, History and the Homeric Iliad (Berkeley: University of California Press, 1959), p. 181.

important role too. The weapons buried with the warrior-kings show this, and so do the massive fortification walls later built to protect Mycenaean fortresses. The walls at Mycenae were adorned by the Lion Gate, the first large-scale sculpture in Europe. Indeed, the Mycenaeans engaged in one of the most famous military conflicts in ancient history. Around 1200 B.C.E. they attacked and destroyed Troy, located at the northwest corner of Asia Minor near the Dardanelles. The Trojan War was celebrated in heroic song orally transmitted by epic poets down to the eighth century, when the *Iliad* and the *Odyssey* of Homer were recorded in a written form made possible by the adaptation of the Phoenician alphabet to the transcription of the Greek language (see Chapter 3).

Homer's great poems are the earliest landmarks of European literature. Greek myth told of the abduction of Helen, the most beautiful woman on earth, from her husband Menelaus by the Trojan prince Paris. The Greek expedition to Troy, which in legend lasted ten years, was mounted to recover Helen. In fact, the real goal of the mission was the wealth of Troy, which was a great center of textile manufacturing and likely also extracted toll payments from ships passing through the nearby Dardanelles Straits. Whatever the actual goal and the true scale of the Trojan War of legend, it was for the Greeks the earliest major event in their history.

Around 1200 B.C.E., most Mycenaean centers were devastated by roving warriors during the movement of the "Sea Peoples" in the eastern Mediterranean region. There followed a large-scale influx from the north of Dorians, a culturally backward Greek subgroup. Internal strife may also have hastened the Mycenaean world's demise. By 1050 a whole civilization had disappeared, with its royal ruling elite, administrative apparatus, writing system, monumental art and architecture, transport and trade networks, armed forces, fortifications and citadels, and elaborate burial practices. In the period that followed, the Greek dark age, down to 800, the population of Greater Greece fell by about 80 percent. Many people had died in the times of trouble just before and during the Dorian invasion; others fled to new settlements on the west coast of Asia Minor.

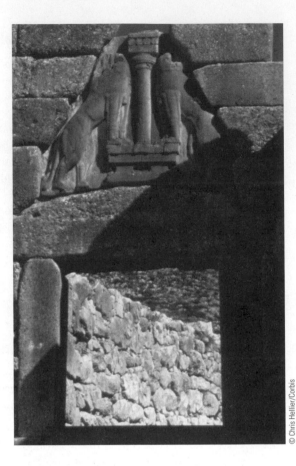

The Lion Gate at Mycenae. The massive structure of the main entrance to the citadel at Mycenae. The lions stand symmetrically in a heraldic pose on either side of a central, Minoan-style column resting on two altars. This earliest piece of monumental sculpture in Europe (c. 1250 B.C.E.) symbolizes the religious and political power of the Mycenaean king.

© Chris Hellier/Corbis

Although Lefkandi on the island of Euboea and a very few other sites remained active in trading with cities in the eastern Mediterranean, commercial contacts with lands outside the Aegean basin virtually ceased, and in most cases loosely organized tribal groups replaced the former strongly centralized governments.

The Dorians completed the ethnic picture of the Greek people and created a great divide in Greek history. For Greece in the dark age witnessed a transition to another, quite distinct civilization, which will be discussed in Chapter 3.

Ancient Persian Civilization

When I entered Babylon as a friend and . . . established the seat of the government in the palace of the ruler under jubilation and rejoicing, Marduk, the great lord, induced the magnanimous inhabitants of Babylon to love me, and I was daily endeavoring to worship him. My numerous troops walked around in Babylon in peace; I did not allow anyone to terrorize any place of the country of Sumer and Akkad. . . . As to the inhabitants . . . , I abolished the yoke which was against their standing. I brought relief to their dilapidated housing, putting an end to their main complaints. Marduk, the great lord, was well pleased with my deeds and sent friendly blessings to myself, Cyrus, the king who worships him, to Cambyses, my son . . . as well as to all my troops, and we all praised his godhead joyously, standing before him in peace.

> *All the kings of the entire world from the Upper to the Lower Sea, those who are seated in throne rooms . . . , as well as all the kings of the West lands living in tents, brought their tributes and kissed my feet in Babylon.**

*James B. Pritchard, ed., The Ancient Near East: An Anthology of Texts and Pictures (Princeton: Princeton University Press, 1958), pp. 207–208.

Leaders of new regimes often sing their own praises while damning their predecessors. In the passage above, Cyrus the Great, founder of the mighty Persian Empire, describes the allegedly happy acceptance of his rule by the conquered people and gods of Babylon. While civil discord during the reign of the last Chaldean king, Nabonidus, had in fact made life miserable for many, we may doubt whether Cyrus's contemporaries fully realized the significance of the changes the "king of kings" had made in the political map of ancient West Asia.

The Rise of the Persian Empire

The Persians lived in a number of tribes dispersed throughout southwestern Iran. They were ethnically related to their overlords, the Medes, a warrior people who temporarily controlled Upper Mesopotamia, Syria, and Iran. During the reign of Cyrus (559–530 B.C.E.), the Indo-European-speaking Persians achieved a spectacularly swift rise to power that radically changed the political map of West Asia. In 550 they not only freed themselves from Median authority but conquered their former masters and annexed their territory. The Lydian king, Croesus, now made the mistake of attacking the Persians; in 547 he lost both his life and his kingdom. The realm of the Chaldeans, which was suffering from political disorder internally, fell to Persian arms in 539.

Cyrus next turned his attention to the northeastern quadrant of his far-flung dominions. In 530 he died in Bactria (modern Turkestan) defending the Persian Empire's frontier on the Jaxartes River against nomadic invaders. Cyrus's son and successor, Cambyses (reigned 530–522), added Egypt to the empire. Faced with a major revolt within his empire and perhaps afflicted with mental illness, Cambyses committed suicide in 522. After a period of bloody civil strife, a rather distant relative of the royal Achaemenid family, Darius I (reigned 522–486), became king.

During his long reign, Darius proved as energetic and effective as his forerunners. He eventually enlarged the empire to the Indus River in the east, the Caucasus Mountains in the north, and Upper Egypt in the south, while in the west he seized a foothold in Europe.

Darius made his most significant contribution in creating one model for the organization and administration of large empires composed of ethnically, religiously, and linguistically diverse groups. Royal inscriptions, for example, were written in three official languages: Persian, Elamitic, and Babylonian. In the ancient world, only the Roman Empire would surpass the Persian in the degree of unity achieved despite cultural differences among subject peoples. Imperial China attained a similar degree of administrative unity, but among a population that was much more culturally and ethnically homogeneous. The empire Darius and his predecessors had fashioned embraced various tributary kingdoms and twenty provinces. Although strategically stationed garrisons ensured military

Map 1.4 Persian Empire. The Persian Empire at its greatest extent was by far the largest of the ancient West Asian imperial domains.

control, the Persians allowed considerable autonomy in local governments and respected religious preferences. The relative leniency of Persian rule as compared with the earlier Assyrian hegemony enabled Darius to recruit willing mercenary forces both for maintaining internal security and for defending borders.

Military and civil officials were drawn primarily from the elite of the Iranian nobility. Darius appointed provincial governors called satraps, who enjoyed considerable individual autonomy, to collect tribute, taxes, soldiers, and military provisions for delivery to the king, whose personal supervisors, called "Eyes and Ears," made regular rounds of the provinces. The revenue generated by this method not only paid administrative expenses but also ensured brimming royal treasuries. Although internal uprisings did occur, especially at times of transition in leadership, the administrative apparatus Darius set in place endured until Alexander's conquest in 330 B.C.E.

To ease the task of governing their huge empire, the Persian monarchs created the most elaborate public works system yet seen in West Asia. Communication (including a postal system) and transport were facilitated by an extensive network of good roads, including the Royal Road from Ephesus on the Aegean to Susa, some 1,600 miles away in Iran. These were to be traveled by armies, ambassadors, distinguished visitors, prisoners of war, caravans, and merchants. Only Han China and the Roman Empire equaled or surpassed the Persian Empire in their elaborate public works systems. Darius also provided for a uniform standard of weights and measures and, borrowing an idea from Lydia, introduced gold and silver coinage.

Master of all this was the supreme autocrat, Darius, the earthly viceroy of Ahura Mazda, the Zoroastrian god of light. To quote one inscription, he was "the great king,

© Gianni Dagli Ort /Corbis

Archers of the Persian Royal Guard. This relief sculpture, done in colored brick, depicts two members of the imperial guard. It adorned the palace of King Darius I at Susa.

The Great King Darius Crushes a Rebellion

I am Darius, the great king, the king of kings, the king of Persia, the king of the provinces, the son of Hystaspes, the grandson of Arsames, the Achaemenian....

Says Darius the king—There are eight of my race who have been kings before me; I am the ninth; nine of us have been kings in succession....

Says Darius the king—Then I went to Babylon against that Nidintabelus, who was called Nabochodrossor. The people of Nidintabelus held the Tigris; there they were posted, and they had boats. There I approached with a detachment in rafts. I brought the enemy into difficulty. I carried the enemy's position. Ahura Mazda brought help to me. By the grace of Ahura Mazda I crossed the Tigris. There I slew many of the troops of Nidintabelus. On the 26th day of the month Atriyata, then it was we so fought.

Says Darius the king—Then I went to Babylon. When I arrived near Babylon, at the city named Zazana, on the Euphrates, there that Nidintabelus, who was called Nabochodrossor, came with his forces against me, to do battle. Then we fought a battle. Ahura Mazda brought help to me. By the grace of Ahura Mazda I slew many of the troops of that Nidintabelus—the enemy was driven into the water—the water destroyed them. On the 2nd day of the month Anamaka, then it was we so fought.

Says Darius the king—Then Nidintabelus with the horsemen that were faithful to him fled to Babylon. Then I went to Babylon. By the grace of Ahura Mazda I both took Babylon, and seized that Nidintabelus. Then I slew that Nidintabelus at Babylon.

Says Darius the king—While I was at Babylon, these are the countries which revolted against me: Persia, Susiana, Media, Assyria, Armenia, Parthia, Margiana, Sattagydia, Sacia....

Says Darius the king—[After his lieutenants had quelled many of the revolts] then I went out from Babylon. I proceeded to Media. When I reached . . . a city . . . named Kudrusia, there that Phraortes, who was called king of Media, came with an army against me, to do battle. Then we fought a battle. Ahura Mazda brought help to me; by the grace of Ahura Mazda, I entirely defeated the army of Phraortes. On the 26th day of the month Adukanish, then it was we thus fought the battle.*

This passage is from an inscription carved around 520 B.C.E. on a cliff face near the site of one of Darius's famous battles. The Persian king records a successful mission to quell a rebellion mounted against him after the death of his predecessor, Cambyses.

*Henry Rawlinson, trans., "The Behistun Inscription of Darius" [1847], in The Greek Historians, *vol. 2, ed. Francis R. B. Godolphin (New York: Random House, 1942), pp. 623–628.*

king of Kings, king of the countries possessing many kinds of people, king of this great earth far and wide." In the Greek world, the earlier Mycenaean kings had been mere local warlords by comparison; the powers of the Persian kings were to be rivaled by a Greek only briefly in the reign of Alexander the Great, who saw himself as their supplanter and successor. Roman emperors provide the closest analogy to the Persian model of absolute monarchy, although the earlier (and wiser) emperors tried to avoid the appearance of such unlimited monopoly of power.

Persian Culture and Religion

Persia's artistic and intellectual accomplishments did not match its military and governmental performance. Little literature was produced, except for the Avesta, the collected sacred scriptures of Zoroastrianism. Science and mathematics did not advance beyond the substantial inheritance from Babylonia and Egypt. In art and architecture, Assyria, Babylonia, Greece, and Egypt often provided the models and sometimes the expertise: Greek stonecutters and sculptors, for example, worked on the mammoth palace complexes at Susa and Persepolis. In at least one respect, the Persian structures were novel, for they were erected to celebrate not the gods but an earthly ruler of a mighty empire, the all-powerful "king of kings."

The Persians did show great originality in religion. The traditional Iranian religion was a typical Indo-European polytheism, whose chief officials were magi (priest-astrologers). In the early sixth century, however, a reformer named Zoroaster (Zarathustra in Persian), removed the magical elements from the religion. According to the new faith, Zoroastrianism, the world was ruled not by a horde of supernatural beings but by one only. Representing goodness, light, and truth, Ahura Mazda was the supreme being,

The Genius of Zoroaster

With a history of some three thousand years, Zoroastrianism is one of the most ancient living religions. It is the most important and best-known religion of ancient, or pre-Islamic, Iran. . . . It was . . . the religion of Iran under the rule of the Iranian-speaking Aryan populations, members of the Aryan or Indo-Iranian group of the more extended Indo-European family. Another name for Zoroastrianism, Mazdaism, is derived from the name of the religion's supreme god, Mazda ("wise"), or Ahura Mazda ("wise lord"). . . . The primary innovation of Zoroastrianism, which sets it apart from the religions of other Indo-European peoples, . . . is its emphasis on monotheism. . . . The concept of Ahura Mazda as the creator of heaven and earth, day and night, and light and darkness, . . . as well as the ethical context in which

Zarathustra conceived his answer to the problem of evil, demonstrates that the prophet was an original thinker, a powerful religious figure who introduced radical changes to the spiritual and cultural world in which he was reared.*

It is important in assessing the achievement of the Persians to avoid the bias of ancient Greek historians like Herodotus. In writing of political and military affairs, they often labeled the Persians "barbarians" and saw their civilization as culturally decadent and, because monarchical, politically despotic. The truth is that Persian religious beliefs at any rate were in crucial ways very much in advance of contemporary Greek polytheism.

*Gherardo Gnoli, "Zoroastrianism," in Religions of Antiquity, ed. R. M. Seltzer (New York: Macmillan, 1989), pp. 128, 131.

but he was opposed by another supernatural power, Ahriman, who represented darkness and evil. The two were locked in a universal struggle, which Ahura Mazda was destined to win. On a future judgment day, all human beings, living and dead, would be consigned to heaven or hell. This notion of last judgment later figured significantly in Christianity and Islam. Zoroastrianism was a strongly ethical religion; it taught that men and women possessed free will and were expected to avoid sin and abide by divine laws. Each person's choices mattered in the struggle. The king of kings himself was a devotee and example to his people. Later, Mithras, Ahura Mazda's lieutenant, played a prominent part in the religious ferment of the Roman Empire. Zoroastrianism, though modified by resurgence of old Iranian ritual and magic and by contact with other religious traditions, survived the fall of the Persian Empire to Macedon and the subsequent period of Hellenistic overlordship. After the Arab conquest, it was handed on from generation to generation during Mongol hegemony and the reign of Muslim rulers in Persia. Today there are small Zoroastrian communities in Iran and more influential ones among the Parsee of India (for example, in Bombay) and Pakistan.

In warfare, politics, religion, and material culture, the Persian Empire equaled or surpassed its West Asian predecessors. It brought lasting stability to a vast region of diverse peoples and cultures. In the ancient world, only the Roman Empire and Han China would match that achievement.

Amerindian Civilization

I [came] face to face with Colossal Head Number 1, buried up to its eyes near the base of the great mound at La Venta. Now, retrieved and revered anew, it stares sightlessly with a certain air that seems to me to verge on smugness, perhaps because it has survived a span of time that began long before the Parthenon rose on the heights above Athens.*

*George E. Stuart, "New Light on the Olmec," *National Geographic* 184 (November 1993): 104.

Standing up to eleven feet tall, these intimidating sculptures portray the rulers of the city-states of the early Olmec culture of Mesoamerica. They are among the most impressive archaeological finds from the early Amerindian civilizations that arose in the Western Hemisphere beginning in 1800 B.C.E., some 1,200 years after humans had established civilizations in Mesopotamia and Egypt. One cultural center, Andean civilization, originated on the Pacific coast of present-day Peru and quickly extended into the Andean highlands from Ecuador to Chile. The other center of civilization arose in Mesoamerica (present-day eastern Mexico, Guatemala, Belize, El Salvador, and western Honduras) about 400 years later.

Archaeologists are currently undertaking extensive projects in both Mesoamerica and the Andes, and their investigations are quickly enlarging our understanding of the antiquity, complexity, and geographic extent of these Amerindian civilizations. In this section of the text we focus on the two earliest Amerindian cultures, Chavin society along the arid coast of Peru and Olmec society in the humid rain forests along the Gulf of Mexico southeast of Vera Cruz.

Map 1.5 Early Peruvian-Andean Civilization.
The Chavin culture (900–300 B.C.E.) was the first stage of a series of increasingly sophisticated Amerindian cultures that first flourished on the coast of present-day Peru and spread up into the high plateaus of the Andes. The Chavin built monumental religious structures and were experts in making fine pottery and exquisite gold jewelry.

The Opening of Andean Civilization: The Chavin Culture

The Andean cultural area, a region of great environmental diversity where the distance from the ocean shore to high mountain valleys averages seventy miles, is best conceived of on a vertical rather than a horizontal scale. Off the coast, a cold current supports a rich marine life that usually provides a major element of the diet of the dwellers on the narrow, arid coastal plain. On occasion, however, the waters run warm, producing the effect called El Niño, destroying marine life and disrupting the interior climates. The narrow coastal plain is cut by some forty rivers that bring the fertile soil down from the adjacent highlands. Amerindian farmers grew maize, vegetables, avocados, potatoes, and peanuts on the soil deposits in these short, narrow valleys. As one moves into the Andean foothills and mountains that rise next to the arid plains, rainfall increases, and the puna, a high plateau of varying elevations interspersed among the Andean mountain ranges, is well watered. The Amerindians living in these uplands grew maize at the lower levels and potatoes farther up and herded llamas and alpacas on the high grasslands. Some Andean villagers attended to all three areas by walking a few miles up or down the slopes. The warm eastern face of the Andes drops down into the Amazon basin; here the inhabitants grew cotton and coca and gathered tropical fruit.

The civilizations in the Andean region existed in relative isolation from those of Mesoamerica. All that exists of Peru's history before the Spanish Conquest is the archaeological record of nonliterate peoples, which can reveal much about the way that people lived, but less about why they did so. By 3000 B.C.E. the Amerindians had established

The University of Pennsylvania Museum (neg. #T4-132)

A Chavin Jaguar. This stone mortar was carved in the shape of a puma, or jaguar. Stone carving was a specialty of the Chavin, and the jaguar was an important figure in Peruvian and Andean culture as well as in Mesoamerica.

permanent agricultural settlements on the coast and shortly thereafter in the Andean highlands, and by 2700 the inhabitants were making pottery. By 1800 B.C.E. Amerindians were building religious centers marked by large stone buildings throughout Ecuador and Peru, both on the coast and in the highlands.

The first known widespread civilization in Peru was the Chavin culture, which flourished from 900 to 200 B.C.E. Archaeologists have uncovered some aspects of this culture, and it is known that the Chavin religion promoted two deities that archaeologists call the Smiling God and the Staff God. The Chavin religion was so powerful that in less than a century its missionaries won converts throughout the vast area of Peru, yet scholars to date have little knowledge of its ideas or rituals. Chavin artwork was as influential as its religion. Its artisans worked in ceramics, textiles, and jade; jaguars were a key motif. In these years, metals were smelted for the first time, almost solely for decoration. Chavin artisans first worked with gold and copper and later with silver, platinum, and tin. They also began to cast bronze, also usually for decoration, not for tools or weapons.

About 350 B.C.E. major changes occurred. Coastal populations began to build major irrigation works, a hint that population growth may have been pressing on natural resources. Many Peruvian cities began to build strong fortifications, and their art began to feature warriors, an indication that cities were warring with each other over control of neighboring farmlands. Urban centers constructed fortifications, undertook prolonged wars, built irrigation systems, and allocated water, suggesting that strong central authority and stratified social systems had developed by this stage. By 200 B.C.E. the Chavin culture had faded away in a welter of urban ministates.

The Advent of Mesoamerican Civilization: The Olmec

Mesoamerica is a geographic area of great variety in altitude and rainfall, and the Amerindian cultures there developed in many different environments. The great mountain spine that runs from Alaska to the tip of South America dominates the physical terrain of Mesoamerica, running close to the Pacific coast. There are, however, extensive lowlands, including the Yucatán Peninsula, along the Gulf of Mexico and the Caribbean Sea. Rainfall varies over different lowland and highland areas.

Map 1.6 Early Mesoamerican Civilization.
The Olmec culture (1200–500 B.C.E.) was the first stage of a series of increasingly sophisticated Amerindian cultures centered in Mesoamerica (present-day eastern Mexico, Guatemala, Belize, and western Honduras) for almost 3,000 years. The Olmec built large earthen temple mounds, imported huge boulders that they carved into likenesses of their rulers, and set up an extensive trading network throughout the area.

Olmec society appeared about 1400 B.C.E. Most archaeological excavations have centered on the area southeast of Vera Cruz, but work at new sites in the highlands south of Mexico City and in southern Guatemala has revealed additional centers of Olmec culture.

As early as 2200 B.C.E., the Olmec were living in agricultural villages, cultivating large maize crops in the lush, steamy environment along the gulf coast, supplementing their diet with abundant seafood and shellfish, game, and dogs. The plentiful food supply supported an increasingly populous and sophisticated village and town life.

The Olmec were traders as well as farmers and fisherfolk. They prospered by selling and trading throughout Mesoamerica. They trafficked in tar, rubber, salt, fine clay for pottery, metal ores for coloring, basalt for monuments, shells, skins, exotic bird feathers, cacao, jade, incense, medicines, textiles, obsidian (volcanic glass), and jadite (a special variety of jade). The Olmec especially prized obsidian and jadeite. In cultures without smelted metals, obsidian is particularly valuable because, properly worked, it can be made into razor-sharp, though somewhat brittle, tools or weapons. Access to obsidian sources in the highlands around present-day Mexico City was an important element in the rise and fall of Mesoamerican civilizations. The Olmec craved jadeite for religious purposes.

Where traders went, cultural influence was not far behind. Artifacts found over a wide area of Mesoamerica indicate that the Olmec traders also spread their culture to less advanced maize-growing villages in the central highlands of Mexico and founded a major city, Copan, in southern Guatemala 400 miles from the Olmec heartland.

The culture of the Olmec dominated Mesoamerican civilization from 1400 to 500 B.C.E. Recent studies now indicate that both writing and the famous Mesoamerican calendar (described in the Maya section in Chapter 7), first known to be employed at Monte Alban in the highlands about 450 B.C.E., may have originated in Olmec civilization.

Like the Chavin before them and the Maya after them, the Olmec lived in a world of ministates. In the Olmec heartland three major centers based on temple complexes—San

The Head of an Olmec Ruler. The most striking artistic expressions of the Olmec culture are the heads carved from basalt boulders, apparently advertising the authority of specific rulers. This particular six-foot representation was carved about 700 B.C.E.

Lorenzo (1400–900 B.C.E.), Tres Zapotes (900–350 B.C.E.), La Venta (900–350 B.C.E.)—arose. San Lorenzo was the first religious center in the Western Hemisphere, and the sacred ball game (described below) may have originated there. As with the Chavin culture, what we know about the Olmec comes from archaeological assessments. At the San Lorenzo stage in Olmec culture, there is no sign of writing.

✳ La Venta, the largest Olmec city, best illustrates aspects of Olmec culture. It was situated on an island whose population numbered about 18,000; another 350,000 people lived in adjacent areas. La Venta was symmetrically laid out on an axis eight degrees west of true north and was dominated by a pyramid of packed earth more than one hundred feet high, probably flattened on top to serve as the center of religious ceremonies. A number of lower mounds were probably the sites of other public buildings or homes for the nobility. In the hot climate, both private homes and public buildings were apparently made with thatched roofs and open walls to catch any cooling drafts. The city was guarded by huge, stern-visaged heads that proclaimed to all outsiders, human and non-human, the temporal and spiritual power of La Venta's rulers.

The Olmec, and the Amerindian cultures that succeeded them in Mesoamerica, constructed their temples and other major buildings without the wheel, metal tools, or draft animals. Olmec farmers, probably working in the dry season as forced labor, hauled burdens such as the ten-ton monumental heads; they used rafts on waterways where possible and sleds and rolling poles on land where necessary. Historians of ecology see the lack of draft animals as the greatest handicap for the Olmec, because these animals not only perform labor but also provide a ready source of high-protein food.

La Venta was a center for artisans, traders, and farmers who lived in a highly stratified society dominated by a class of nobles and absolute rulers. Unlike the Chavin, Olmec artisans did little metalworking, but rather concentrated their efforts on sculpting, whether huge stone heads or tiny jadite jewelry. Overall, the artistic and spiritual power of the Olmec artisans was immense. Most of the numerous Mesoamerican cultures that followed the Olmec—including the Maya and the Aztec—show distinct Olmec influence.

La Venta was above all a religious complex. What precisely the Olmec asked of their gods is not clear, because they had plenty of rain, an unfailing agriculture, and no strong enemies. Perhaps, as in many religions, they sought the continuation of the natural order, praying that their state would not fall to social anarchy or natural catastrophes.

The Olmec and later Mesoamericans depicted most of their gods as part human and part animal, a practice also common in ancient Egyptian and Indian religions. At different times, the eagle, the serpent, the alligator, and the jaguar rose to special distinction. The jaguar, a fearsome predator in nature, was even more terrible and powerful when deified; jadeite was the medium chosen to represent the jaguar god.

Like all humans, the Olmec had death rituals. They evidently believed in an underworld. The seated figures they commonly carved may have been their rulers sitting in the passageway to that underworld. The rulers, in animal-shaman form, could perhaps pass in and out of the underworld as mediators, and determine who went there and under what conditions.

The Olmec developed the "divine" or "sacred" ball game that later spread into almost every Mesoamerican culture, although they did not construct the walled enclosures for it that became typical later. The ball game was an athletic contest in which the object was to put a heavy rubber ball through a tight-fitting ring set vertically in a wall at both ends of the court. The players could not use their hands, but powered the ball by bouncing it off heavy plates on their forearms, chests, and hips. There may have been professional teams that played for money and glory; apparently there was considerable betting. Certainly in later Mesoamerican civilizations and probably in the Olmec, the players often fought for high stakes—their lives. In these instances, the ball game served as a ritual for the perpetuation of the state. A captured ruler and his men, suitably weakened, were forced to play in a hopeless contest against the local ruler and his rested men. The captives eventually lost the game and were sacrificed to the gods. The ball game in later times also played a role in predicting the future and had other religious overtones.

Summary and Comparisons

The story of civilization begins in Mesopotamia, a fertile land claimed from swamp and desert by dint of hard work that became the locus for the development of cities. Around 3500 B.C.E. the Sumerians, who lived in the region, began an urban mode of life with a diversified social structure and labor force. The development of writing both facilitated public and private business transactions and made possible the creation of a rich literary tradition. The Babylonians added further refinements in mathematics, astronomy and the calendar, and law; the Assyrians' achievements were in imperialism and military conquest. Finally, in the Chaldean or Neo-Babylonian phase, Mesopotamian civilization was revitalized under Nebuchadnezzar.

In Egypt, too, regular crop production supported a vibrant and long-lived civilization. In the Old Kingdom, the god-king pharaoh presided over a strongly centralized govern-

CHRONOLOGY

3000 B.C.E.	King Menes unifies Egypt
	Bronze metallurgy in West Asia
	Great Pyramids at Giza
	Olmec agricultural villages in Mesoamerica
2000	Indo-Europeans arrive in Balkan Peninsula
	Hammurabi's Code
	Hyksos domination in Egypt
	Height of Minoan civilization on Crete
	Eruption of Thera
	Akhenaton and Nefertiti rule in Egypt
	Rise of Olmec civilization in Mesoamerica
	Introduction of chariot warfare by the Hittites
	The Trojan War
	Collapse of Mycenaean civilization
1000	Spread of iron metallurgy
	Kushite kingdom in Africa
	Amerindian Chavin culture begins to flourish in Peru
	Greeks adopt Phoenician alphabet
	Homer composes *Iliad* and *Odyssey*
	Zoroaster in Persia
	Nebuchadnezzar builds the Hanging Gardens in Babylon
	Persian royal road network
	Conquests of King Cyrus
500	

ment, and massive labor forces built irrigation systems and the Great Pyramids. Priests supervised the rituals of an elaborate polytheism. Later, New Kingdom pharaohs built an Egyptian Empire that extended into West Asia. They, too, engaged in extensive building programs at Karnak, Abu Simbel, the Valley of the Kings, and elsewhere. The New Kingdom also experimented briefly with a form of monotheism.

In the Aegean region, Crete and the southern Balkan Peninsula saw the flourishing of Minoan-Mycenaean civilization. Mycenaean culture emerged from the mixture of indigenous elements and borrowings from Crete by a Greek-speaking Indo-European people around 2000 B.C.E. The Minoan-Mycenaean culture excelled in painting, sculpture, jewelry, and architecture. The surviving written materials show a degree of literacy in both Crete and Greece. A combination of disruptive forces, including foreign invasion, brought an end to the Mycenaean world.

The Persians, also an Indo-European people, reshaped West Asia when Cyrus fashioned a larger and better-organized empire than any up to Roman times. Racially, linguistically, and religiously diverse populations were governed through a carefully devised network of semiautonomous local officials. The public works infrastructure included an unprecedented imperial road network. Culturally, Zoroastrianism brought an advance in beliefs about the nature of the divine and superseded the older, more traditional Iranian polytheism.

In the Western Hemisphere, civilization appeared in the Mesoamerican rain forests and highlands and also in the coastal and Andean region centered in present-day Peru, again because of a thriving agriculture. Amerindian cultures built cities around religious complexes. There was extensive internal trade within the cultures, but apparently little or none between them. The Chavin culture in Peru, like that of the Mesopotamians, demonstrated advanced engineering skills in constructing an extensive irrigation system.

Amerindian religious practices flourished and spread widely; typical were painstakingly constructed temples and arenas for sacred ball games. Artwork was impressive, including the monumental sculpted heads of the Olmec and the advanced metalwork of the Chavin culture. In these matters the Western Hemisphere civilizations were as advanced as those elsewhere in the world.

The magnitude of the material and intellectual developments of early civilizations described in this chapter is impossible to overestimate. Certainly the differences stand out. Geographically, some cultures, like Egypt and Mesopotamia, developed in great river valleys, others on the edge of the sea or in steaming jungles. Urbanization for some of these cultures, as in Mesopotamia, meant large cities that reorganized a prosperous agricultural society for commerce. For other societies, like Egypt and the Olmec, it meant having a religious center for the most effective communication with the powers of the next world. Some, such as Persia, were conquering civilizations that could sustain military operations in faraway lands; some, like the Chavin, stayed home. Some civilizations, like Mesopotamia, Persia, and the Olmec, added to the sum of human knowledge in mathematics, astronomy, highway engineering, hydraulics, and the calendar; others specialized in body adornments. Though some of these early cultures remained completely illiterate, in others literacy could mean prayers for priests only, commercial and stockyard receipts, or even transcriptions of poetry.

If one were to seek a common denominator, perhaps the most pervasive underlying factor in the human experience was the striving for order. The impulse to exploit the order of nature had earlier led to agriculture. The need to impose order on the relationships of men and women to the environment and to one another now led to civilized communities. The attempt to detect order in the dispositions of the invisible powers also stimulated more complex intellectual speculation. Egyptians; Mesopotamians; Indo-European peoples like the Hittites, Persians, and Greeks; and Amerindians all attempted to grasp and somehow control the workings of their world and have influence on the other world. They did this by developing mathematics and astronomy, some by creating writing systems, and all by applying their religious insights. In all these arenas, later participants in the various civilizations of the world were heavily indebted to their ancient forebears. Chapter 2 will round out the picture of early civilizations by examining those of South and East Asia.

Selected Sources

Items indicated with an asterisk (*) are available in paperback.

Archaeology. This reasonably priced magazine (six issues annually) provides information on recent discoveries and interpretations of archaeological sites around the world. Excellent photographs.

Brosius, Maria. *Women in Ancient Persia (559–331 B.C.).* 1996. An excellent, very current examination of a neglected subject.

Burger, Richard. *Chavin and the Origins of Andean Civilization.* 1992. A good, well-illustrated overview of Chavin culture as it has been revealed by archaeological excavation.

*Burstein, Stanley, ed. and trans. *Ancient African Civilizations: Kush and Axum.* 1997. Based on Greek and Roman sources, the collection describes the cultures and governments of two major African kingdoms.

*Castleden, Rodney. *Minoans: Life in Bronze Age Crete.* 1990. A very attractive presentation of the evidence about Minoan Crete.

*Chadwick, John. *The Mycenaean World.* 1976. A well-written general account with helpful illustrations.

*Crawford, Harriet. *Sumer and the Sumerians.* 1991. A good, concise treatment of the Sumerian people and their achievements.

*Ferry, David, trans. *Gilgamesh: A New Rendering in English Verse.* 1992. A recent, lively translation of the world's first heroic epic.

Ghirshman, Roman. *Persia: From the Origins to Alexander the Great.* Trans. S. Gilbert and J. Emmons. 1964. An excellent, highly readable survey.

*Gurney, O. R. *The Hittites.* Rev. ed. 1990. A good, concise work on the subject.

*Harris, James E., and Kent R. Weeks. *X-Raying the Pharaohs.* 1973. This description of a radiological examination of mummies in the Egyptian Museum in Cairo includes an astounding "Portfolio of Pictures."

Hawkes, Jacquetta. *King of the Two Lands.* 1966. A historical novel set in the time of Akhenaton and Nefertiti, by an eminent British archaeologist.

*Hobson, Christine. *The World of the Pharaohs: A Complete Guide to Ancient Egypt.* 1987; reprinted 1993. A clearly organized treatment with marvelous color illustrations.

*Knapp, A. Bernard. *The History and Culture of Ancient West Asia and Egypt.* 1988. A succinct, current survey.

*Latacz, Joachim. *Homer: His Art and His World.* Trans. James P. Holoka. 1996. This recent study places the great Greek epic poet in his historical and literary contexts. Contains helpful discussions of the *Iliad* and the *Odyssey.*

*Mallory, J. P. *In Search of the Indo-Europeans: Language, Archaeology, and Myth.* 1989. A recent work with many illustrations; includes a judicious assessment of rival theories.

Markman, Roberta H., and Peter T. *The Flayed God: The Mythology of Mesoamerica.* 1992. A combination of original text and contemporary commentary that leads the reader into the mythology of the Mesoamerican cultures.

*Phillipson, David W. *African Archaeology.* 2d ed. 1993. A revised version of the author's broad survey of the archaeology of Africa, beginning with the origins of humankind. Well illustrated.

*Pritchard, James B. *The Ancient Near East: An Anthology of Texts and Pictures.* 1958. A convenient, widely available collection of interesting and important materials.

*Romer, John. *Ancient Lives: Daily Life in the Egypt of the Pharaohs.* 1984. A fascinating study of daily lives of the people—on all social strata—in a village near ancient Thebes.

Soustelle, Jacques. *The Olmecs: The Oldest Civilization in Mexico.* Trans. Helen R. Lane. 1985. The distinguished French anthropologist shows his affection for the Olmec in this work.

Stuart, George E. "New Light on the Olmec." *National Geographic* 184, no. 5 (1993), 88.

Welsby, Derek A. *The Kingdom of Kush: The Napatan and Meroitic Empires.* 1996; reprinted 1998. This up-to-date examination of these very ancient civilizations is enhanced by more than 200 illustrations.

Wilber, Donald N. *Persepolis: The Archaeology of Parsa, Seat of the Persian Kings.* 1969. A well-written and illustrated presentation of the ancient Persian capital.

*Wood, Michael. *In Search of the Trojan War.* 1985. A well-illustrated and clearly written account of the archaeological adventures of the search for ancient Troy; a companion to the six-part BBC television series.

Additional resources, exercises, and Internet links related to this chapter are available at the Book Companion Web site: http://history.wadsworth.com/upshurcompact4/

2

The Early Civilizations of South and East Asia

•

• The Indus Civilization •

• The Aryan Invasion and Early Vedic Age •

• The Late Vedic Age •

• China from the Neolithic Age to the Shang Dynasty •

• The Chou Dynasty •

• Summary and Comparisons •

Hitherto it has commonly been supposed that the pre-Aryan peoples of India were on an altogether lower plane of civilization than their Aryan [Caucasian, Indo-European] conquerors; that to the latter they were much what the Helots were to the Spartans, . . .—a race so servile and degraded, that they were commonly known as Dasas or slaves. . . . Never for a moment was it imagined that five thousand years ago, before ever the Aryans were heard of, the Punjab and Sind, if not other parts of India as well, were enjoying an advanced and singularly uniform civilization of their own, closely akin but in some respects even superior to that of contemporary Mesopotamia and Egypt. . . . They exhibit the Indus people of the fourth and third millennia B.C., in possession of a highly developed culture.*

In [1899], Liu Tieh-yun . . . was visiting the capital [Peking] as a house guest of Wang I-yung. The host of Liu Tieh-yun was attacked by malarial fever. The doctor's prescriptions included an ingredient of decayed tortoise shell purchased at the drug store. On the tortoise shells Liu Tieh-yun saw seal characters, which he picked out and showed to his host; both of them were somewhat astonished at this discovery. Wang, a student of bronze inscriptions, immediately realized that these tortoise shells must be ancient. He went to the drugstore, to inquire about the source of supply of these ingredients. The manager told him that they came from T'ang-yin and Anyang of Honan province. They were sold at a very low price. Liu Tieh-yun went to the drugstore in the city and purchased them all.**

*John Marshall, ed., *Mohenjo-Daro and the Indus Civilization* (Delhi: Indological Book House, 1973), pp. v, vii.
**Li Chi, *Anyang* (Seattle: University of Washington Press, 1997), p. 8.

The author of the first passage quoted above, Sir John Marshall, headed the first systematic excavation of Indus sites in the 1920s. Workers digging foundations for a railway line in the Indus River valley uncovered remains of brick walls and streets that, as archaeologists confirmed, belonged to the earliest civilization on the Indian subcontinent, a discovery as exciting and important as those of Heinrich Schliemann at Troy in Asia Minor and Mycenae in Greece.

In the second passage, from the journal of a specialist in ancient Chinese writing, the writer tells of the accidental discovery of the earliest specimens of writing, incised on tortoise shells and scapula bones of cattle, and the tracing of those items to the last capital of the Shang dynasty at Anyang. Scientific excavations began at Anyang in the late 1920s just when Marshall was working along the Indus River.

These passages illustrate how archaeological work has enormously increased our knowledge of the past and unlocked its secrets throughout the world. This chapter looks at South Asia (the Indian subcontinent) and East Asia, which is dominated by China. South Asia is bounded by the Hindu Kush range in the northwest and the Himalayas in the northeast, the Arabian Sea in the southwest, and the Bay of Bengal in the southeast. It comprises five nations: India, Pakistan, Bangladesh, Nepal, and Sri Lanka. East Asia is situated between the Pacific Ocean to the east, the Gobi Desert to the north, and the Tien Shan and Himalaya mountains on the west. China, Korea, and Japan occupy eastern Asia.

As happened slightly earlier in Mesopotamia and Egypt, civilizations in South and East Asia first emerged in the Indus River valley in India and the Yellow River valley in China, because the rivers made transportation easy and brought silt that renewed the soil's fertility. China was isolated from other ancient civilizations by the nearly impassable Gobi Desert and the high Himalayas and Tien Shan; the Hindu Kush posed a somewhat lesser barrier between India and western Asia. Current archaeological evidence points to independent indigenous developments of higher civilization in these two regions from Neolithic times.

Both regions underwent periodic invasions that brought new settlers. The Aryan invaders who superseded the first Indus civilization infused large numbers of settlers of a different racial makeup and linguistic heritage. In China, by contrast, the earliest historic dynasty was overtaken by people of the same racial and cultural background, so that its early development suffered no discontinuity. As a result, the people of historic northern India spoke Indo-European languages introduced by the Aryans, while southern Indians spoke languages of the indigenous Dravidian group. No such divide affected the Chinese, whose current writing system evolved in form directly from the first extant script.

The Indus Civilization

The most striking feature of the Indus Civilization is its homogeneity. Within the farthest limits of the Indus Empire its uniform products are easily distinguishable from those of the Mesopotamian and Egyptian civilizations. This remarkable uniformity in the form and content of its products should be attributed to the early realization of the advantages of standardization on the part of the Harappans. Wherever they settled down they introduced a uniform system of civic administrations, built towns and cities on identical gridiron plans with neatly laid-out streets and lanes, maintained a high standard of public sanitation, used similar earthen and metalwares, produced the same types of tools and weapons, and organized trade of a uniform pattern. Even the sizes of houses and bricks, tools and ornaments were standardized. . . .

Another remarkable feature of the Indus Civilization is its individuality, which was zealously guarded against any serious inroads by alien cultures. In spite of extensive trade contacts with the Mesopotamians and Egyptians, Harappans did not adopt the western system of writing. The rectangular steatite seals and cubical stone weights of the Indus people differed as much from the duck- and barrel-shaped weights and cylinder seals of the Mesopotamians as did their pictographic script from the cuneiform writing of the latter. *

*S. R. Rao, Lothal and the Indus Civilization (New York: Asia Publishing House, 1973), p. 5.

S. R. Rao is an eminent Indian archaeologist of the Indus civilization and author of the above passage. Since the 1920s, the excavation of dozens of sites along the Indus River and in other parts of northwestern India and Pakistan has led him and other archaeologists to conclude that this highly developed civilization was homogeneous. They also agree that the Indus civilization remained unique in important ways despite extensive trade with Mesopotamia and other regions to the west.

The Land of India

The Indian subcontinent, also called South Asia, is a little less than half the size of the United States. It is bordered on the north by the Hindu Kush and Himalayas, the latter the world's tallest mountain range; with their extensions to the east and west, these separate India from the rest of Asia and make it a distinct subcontinent. Formidable though the mountains are, they did not prevent the movement of settlers, traders, and warriors to and from India. The mountains are also the source of two great river systems. To the west is the Indus, which gave its name to India and which empties into the Arabian Sea. To the east the Ganges joins the Brahmaputra to form the largest delta in the world, as the two mighty rivers empty into the Bay of Bengal. The Thar, or Desert of Rajastan, divides the Indus from the Ganges River. In more recent times the Gangetic Plain, together with that of the Brahmaputra, has been the heartland of India.

South of the great river plains is peninsular India, whose core is the Deccan Plateau, bordered by the Eastern and Western Ghats, or hills, and beyond them, the coastal plains. The Tamil Plain at the southeastern tip of the peninsula is home to a distinct ethnic and cultural group. Geographically the island of Sri Lanka (formerly Ceylon) is a continuation of south India. From north to south the subcontinent spans approximately 2,000 miles.

India has a wide variety of climates, from cold winters in the Himalayan foothills to searing summers in the northern plains, to year-round high temperatures in the south. Climate and natural conditions have changed significantly since the dawn of civilization. From Neolithic times down through the third and second millennia B.C.E. when the first civilization developed along the banks of the Indus and its tributaries, the region was well watered and featured marshes and jungles. Later, more arid climatic conditions in the lower Indus contributed to the decline of the Indus civilization. By the time Alexander the Great and his army reached this area in 326 B.C.E., much of it was already a barren desert, as it remains today.

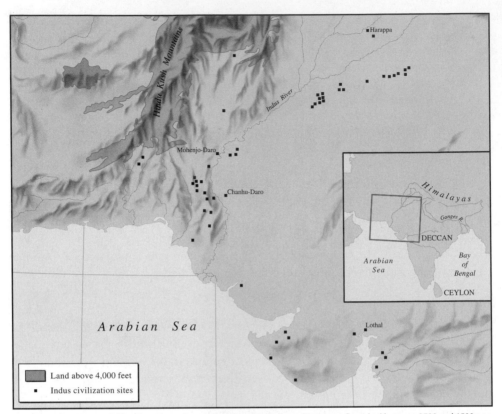

Map 2.1 Indus Valley Civilization. The earliest civilization on the Indian subcontinent flourished between 2500 and 1500 B.C.E. in an 800-mile stretch extending along the banks of the Indus River and its tributaries to the coast of the Arabian Sea. Indus cities were planned and prosperous, and the peoples traded with other parts of India and Mesopotamia.

The most important feature in the Indian climate is the monsoon ("the rain"), which comes pelting down from June until September. These rains bring relief from the suffocating heat, turn the parched land green, and make agriculture possible. To this day, the quality of the harvest depends on the intensity and timing of the monsoon season. Not surprisingly, Indians look on rain-laden dark clouds and thunder and lightning as beneficent signs from heaven. Between October and May hardly a drop of rain falls in most of India, making irrigation indispensable for farming.

The Beginning of the Indus Civilization

By around 3000 B.C.E., Neolithic peoples who lived in the Indus valley evolved the first civilizations in India, just as civilizations were emerging in the Nile and Tigris-Euphrates valleys. Sites and artifacts of the earliest stages of the Indus civilization are found sixty-eight feet below ground level along the banks of the Indus, much below the water table, making archaeological work extremely difficult. Successively higher levels show continuous development from Neolithic beginnings. Unlike Egypt and Mesopotamia, however, where much of our knowledge comes from written records, the Indus civilization must be reconstructed from other evidence. (Although a system of writing developed in the Indus valley, the longest surviving inscription is only twenty-five words; most specimens of Indus writing are short pictographic inscriptions averaging five words, carved on little seals about one inch square or in diameter. The carvings likely were used as stamps to mark ownership of merchandise; they probably represent personal or company names, or short prayers. Most seals also have carved animals or deitylike figures. Thousands of seals have been found throughout the Indus valley and also in Mesopotamia, but no Indian equivalent of a Rosetta Stone has been discovered that unlocks the secrets of the language.) Pottery shards predating the Harappan era of the culture bear cruder versions of the pictographic seals, indicating that the script was an indigenous invention. In any case, the messages on the seals are too short to allow meaningful glimpses into the Indus culture. Because so little written evidence has survived and because what has survived is still undeciphered, the Indus civilization continues to be classified as prehistoric.

Because we do not know the language, we must rely chiefly on archaeological evidence for our knowledge of this civilization. Well over a thousand Indus sites have been identified, covering an area of approximately 300,000 square miles, larger than the state of Texas and twice as large as the area occupied by ancient Egypt and Mesopotamia. The geographic boundaries of the civilization stretch beyond the Indus valley to include all northwestern India to Kashmir in the north, Delhi in the east, and the entire northern shore of the Arabian Sea. The three largest cities excavated bear the modern names Harappa, in Punjab; Mohenjo-Daro, in Sind, 400 miles to the southwest beside the Indus in present-day Pakistan; and Lothal, on the coast in present-day India. Many features, such as the size of bricks and the urban plans, including an elevated mound in each city center, were uniform throughout the area. Hence, archaeologists refer to the civilization as the Harappan culture or the Indus Empire.

An Urban Culture: Mohenjo-Daro

Since Mohenjo-Daro is the best preserved and one of the most systematically excavated cities of the Indus culture, it stands as the prototype for other cities in the region. Mohenjo-Daro was centered around an artificial mound, about fifty feet high, which was fortified by a brick wall with towers. Stores of ammunition stones indicate that this was a citadel. The citadel also has a great bath or tank, thirty-nine feet by twenty-three feet, flanked by a large pillared hall and small cell-like rooms. Archaeologists guess that the pool and hall served a religious or ritual purpose. Since no palace that might have housed royal rulers has been found, archaeologists further deduce that a high priest or a college of priests may have ruled the city. Scholars also surmise that the ritual tanks found alongside Hindu temples in later India may have had their origin in the great bath of the Indus cities. A magnificent granary of brick and timber, with loading platform and ventilation holes, completes the structures on the citadel.

Below the citadel spreads a well-laid-out city, perhaps the earliest example of urban planning. The main broad avenues were oriented north-south; they were intersected by lesser east-west lanes in a grid system. Certain parts of the town were designated for shops; other areas were used by other occupational groups. All buildings were made of baked bricks of uniform size, suggesting a powerful centralized authority.

Merchants' houses in the prosperous residential districts were substantial; the ground floor was about thirty feet square on average, and many had second and third stories. No windows faced the street; instead the rooms opened on a central courtyard. This style of house is found in India today and throughout tropical and temperate areas from China to North Africa. On both the ground and second floors were bathrooms with drains flowing to underground sewers that ended in soak pits (like our septic tanks). Some houses had private wells, but public wells at street intersections provided water for those without them. These features, the state granary, and the sentry boxes found scattered throughout the city could only have been maintained by a highly sophisticated government.

The workers' living quarters also indicate a prosperous economy. They lived comfortably by the standards of the era (and even by present-day living standards of Indian workers) in two-room cottages, with bathrooms with bathing platforms and toilets lined with brick supports for seating, each unit being about twelve feet by twenty feet in Mohenjo-Daro and even bigger in Harappa.

Society and Economy

Anthropologists who have studied the skeletal remains of the Indus people conclude that several racial groups were represented among them. Adults ranged between five feet five inches and five feet nine inches in height. The average life span was around thirty years (the norm for Indians until the early twentieth century). Then as now, most of the noncity dwellers farmed. The main food crops were wheat, barley, peas, sesame, melon, and dates. We cannot be certain whether they irrigated their crops, but we do know they were the first people in the world to grow and weave cotton. Their domestic animals included humped cattle, horses, goats, sheep, pigs, and fowl. Elephants figure in the seals, but we do not know whether they had been tamed; in any case, their ivory was widely used.

Trade flourished. Boats carried goods along the Indus River and the seacoast to West Asia. Lothal, a major seaport, had the world's oldest scientifically designed docks in an artificial basin that took into consideration the water level of high and low tides. Land routes connected the Indus valley with other parts of India. A bead factory found at Lothal has ten rooms and measures 5,380 square feet. Indus artists made jewelry from lapis lazuli (a semiprecious stone possibly from Afghanistan), gold, turquoise from Iran, conch shells from the Arabian Sea, and locally mined carnelian. Perishable items such as textiles and woods may also have been exchanged. Numerous Indus seals and pottery items found in Mesopotamia testify to trade between the two civilizations. Sumerian and Akkadian cuneiform documents from about 2400–2000 B.C.E. mention a land called Dilmun or Telmun in the east with which there was organized trade; these documents may have referred to the Indus civilization.

Indus artisans displayed talent in a large number of basic crafts. They used the wheel to make pottery vessels of many shapes and sizes for food, drink, cooking, and storage.

Randy Olson/NGS Image Collection

An Archaeological Dig in Progress. The Indus people built with bricks. Workers here have uncovered an ancient drainage channel that once carried waste water out of the city.

They also created utensils of stone, ivory, copper, bronze, and silver. They used the lost-wax method, as did the ancient Greeks, to cast metal ornaments and tools, in contrast to the piece mold method of the ancient Chinese. Some ivory combs, copper mirrors, beads made from a variety of materials, and gold and silver jewelry show very fine workmanship and artistry. The many toys and games, such as miniature terra cotta animals, whistles, rattles, and bird cages, show the loving care that adults must have lavished on their children. From excavations in other parts of northern India, it is clear that the Indus culture had a wide influence beyond its immediate region.

Indus Religion

In the absence of written documents, it is difficult to write definitively about the religion of the Indus people. As we observed, archaeologists speculate that they used the Great Bath and the adjoining Assembly Hall in Mohenjo-Daro for religious and ritual purposes, and that a college of priests lived in the rows of small rooms nearby. Excavations have revealed neither temples nor monumental sculptures nor large religious statues such as those in Egypt. However, "fire altars" were found, suggesting the practice of fire worship, perhaps similar to that practiced by later, Vedic peoples. Many terra cotta figurines have been discovered, like those found in sites from Egypt to Iran. The pregnant-looking female figurines, often molded together with children, may represent the Great Mother or nature goddesses. Analogous female nature deities were widespread in the Eastern Mediterranean. There are also nude male figurines; the best example is a three-faced horned figure, nude except for his jewelry, seated with crossed legs in the yoga position and surrounded by four animals—an elephant, a tiger, a rhinoceros, and a buffalo. This image has been called a prototype of Shiva, the later three-faced Hindu god of death, destruction, and fertility, and the lord of beasts.

Indus people may also have worshiped trees and animals, including the bull, which is very common on the seals and in later Hinduism is strongly associated with Shiva. The cow, however, though a nearly universal symbol of later Hinduism, is absent from Indus imagery. The dead were carefully buried in cemeteries, laid out with their heads to the north. Grave goods, though not elaborate, include painted pottery jars, occasionally weapons, and sometimes a sacrificed sheep or goat. We do not know the significance of the burial practices.

The End of Indus Civilization

Civilizations rise and fall for complex reasons. No single cause can account for the decline of the widely distributed Indus civilization, nor can a definite date be assigned to its end. One apparent cause was extensive flooding, likely a result of deforestation and overgrazing. But even more important were major geological changes in the beginning of the second millennium B.C.E. These included coastal uplifts in the northern shores of the Arabian Sea that moved several Indus-era ports as much as thirty-five miles inland. Such dramatic changes ruined the lives and economies of the people in the lower Indus region but left unscathed the life of Harappa farther upriver. We may deduce the interruption of long-distance trade from the almost complete disappearance of seals in the late levels of Mohenjo-Daro and Lothal. The uplift prevented the river's water from reaching the sea and created huge shallow lakes upstream—a condition that probably persisted for decades. Flooding would explain the layers of silt as much as seventy feet deep around Mohenjo-Daro, and the huge embankments, some twenty-five feet high, and other community projects built to keep out the floodwaters. Since such flood-control mechanisms are major undertakings, smaller towns and settlements were no doubt simply abandoned to the floodwaters. In time the floodwaters spilled over the natural barriers and the river resumed its course to the sea. The people of Mohenjo-Daro were then left with the massive task of reinforcing or replacing flood-damaged structures.

This process was repeated at least five times at Mohenjo-Daro. The people, worn out and impoverished by the repeated efforts to fight the floods, endured declining living standards, evidenced in the shoddier construction of later houses, built on the ruins of their predecessors or on artificial platforms raised to avoid flood crests. Economic decline and population pressures are visible everywhere as shanty towns superseded spacious residences and rabbit warrens overspread once neatly laid out streets. Around 1900 B.C.E. the Indus River changed course and a parallel river, the Saravasti, dried up, further contributing to the economic ruin.

Then invading barbarian settlers from the west, descending on the Indus plains through the passes of the Hindu Kush, brought additional pressures to bear. Defensive measures are evident in the last centuries of the Indus cities. Mohenjo-Daro's great citadel was fortified by a brick wall with towers, and Harappa's massive turreted walls were forty feet wide at the base and thirty-five feet tall; its western gate was wholly blocked up to repel invaders from the west. In the centuries after 2000 B.C.E., newcomers settled in villages in outlying areas. Their crude pottery was coarser than the vessels made by the Indus peoples. Fleeing refugees must have streamed into the walled cities for protection, causing further economic and social strains. A potter's kiln built in the middle of a street indicates collapsing municipal standards. Caches of hoarded jewelry speak eloquently of the breakdown of law and order.

Before the end came, most of the inhabitants of Mohenjo-Daro had fled. Several groups of skeletons have been found in dead-end streets, strewn helter-skelter with axe and knife wounds in the skulls, or huddled by wells, then covered by debris. These remains vividly suggest how the last stragglers met their doom. Fires probably destroyed the sacked city. The bodies must have been burnt or buried to prevent contamination.

Harappa and other nearby settlements, which had not suffered previous decline, were abruptly and permanently abandoned. The inhabitants either fled at the threat of invasion or were expelled. At Chanhu-Daro, farther downriver, Indus inhabitants were replaced by squatters, whose huts had fireplaces, a feature unknown to Indus architecture, suggesting that the owners had come from colder climates. Among the scattered remains of the newcomers are copper axes and swords with reinforcing midribs superior to anything the Indus people possessed.

By about 1500 B.C.E., the Indus civilization had perished. While scholars still debate the precise individual causes, it clearly succumbed to a combination of factors. Deforestation

Bronze Figurine of a Man Driving a Chariot. Accompanied by his dog, which sits on the shaft, a man drives a pair of oxen yoked to a chariot. This piece dates to approximately 1500 B.C.E. and was found outside the immediate region of the Indus River valley, showing the widespread diffusion of the civilization.

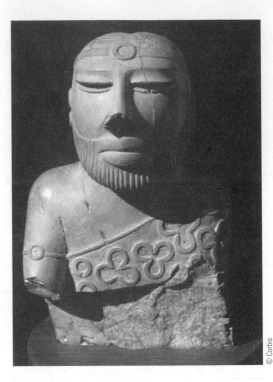

Bearded Man Found at Mohenjo-Daro. Very little statuary from the Indus civilization has been discovered. We do not know whether this figure was a deity or a man.

© Corbis

and degradation of the environment and natural catastrophes first weakened both the morale and the economy of the Indus peoples. Then, from the north and west, came waves of dynamic and warlike invaders and settlers called Aryans, wielding superior weapons and riding swift and terrifying horse-drawn chariots.

The Aryan Invasion and Early Vedic Age

To Indra
I will declare the manly deeds of Indra, the first that he
*   achieved, the thunder-wielder.*
He slew the dragon, then disclosed the waters, and cleft
*   the channels of the mountain torrents.*

He slew the dragon lying on the mountain; his
*   heavenly bolt of thunder Tvashtar fashioned.*
Like lowing kine in rapid flow descending the waters
*   glided downward to the ocean.*

Impetuous as a bull, he chose the Soma, and in three
*   beakers drank the juices.*
The Bounteous One grasped the thunder for his weapon,
*   and smote to death this first born of the dragons.*

When Indra, thou hadst slain the dragon's first born,
    and overcome the charms of the enchanters,
Then, giving life to sun and dawn and heaven, thou
    foundest not one foe to stand against thee.

Indra with his own great and deadly thunder smote into
    pieces Vritra, worst of Vritras,
As trunk of trees, what time the axe hath felled them,
    low on the earth so lies the prostrate dragon.

He, like a mad weak warrior, challenged Indra, the
    great impetuous many-slaying hero.
He, brooking not the clashing of the weapons, crushed—
    Indra's foe—the shattered forts in falling. *

*Robert O. Ballou, ed., The Bible of the World (New York: Viking, 1939), pp. 5–6.

These six verses of a hymn to Indra are from the Rig-Veda, the holiest book of the Aryans who settled in India and also of Hinduism, a religion that developed out of the beliefs of the Aryans and the indigenous Indian peoples. For generations the Aryan priests memorized the songs of praise in a language that was Indo-European and closely related to Greek and Latin. About 1000 B.C.E., these songs were written down in Sanskrit, an alphabetical script of the Indo-European family. Indra was an important god in the Rig-Veda. This hymn portrays him as a hard-drinking warrior who killed dragons and demolished forts. He was also the god of thunder and the bringer of rain.

The word *Aryan* is the Anglicized form for *Aryas* in Sanskrit. It means "noble of birth and race," as the fair-complexioned invaders described themselves, in contrast to the natives whom they called *dasas*, meaning dark skinned, or of "dasa color." *Dasa* in Sanskrit came to mean "slave." Sometime after 2000 B.C.E. the Aryans pushed through the mountain passes that separate Afghanistan from northwestern India. The movement spanned several centuries and included many tribes that sometimes fought each other. Tools and weapons of bronze and copper discovered in northwestern India in association with the early Aryans are very similar in type and date to those found in south Russia, the Caucasus, and Iran. They suggest that the Aryan invaders of India were closely related to the Indo-Europeans who spilled over Europe and Iran in equally dynamic migrations in about the same period.

In material development, the Aryans were less advanced than the people of the Indus civilization. They were not city dwellers, and after conquering the Indus cities, they abandoned them to ruin. There were no significant cities in India for the next 1,000 years, and the remains of the villages with houses of wood and other perishable materials have long since vanished. Thus India from 1500 to 500 B.C.E. is almost an archaeological blank; knowledge about it comes mainly from literary sources.

Early Vedic Society and Economy

The earliest literary sources for the history of India are the hymns and prayers of the Rig-Veda, the literature of the Aryan invaders. These hymns are primarily addressed to male deities. They were memorized by the priests for recital at religious ceremonies, as they are to the present day. After about 1000 B.C.E. and the appearance of writing, the hymns were compiled and written down. Although primarily religious and metaphysical in character, the Vedas and other early writings do contain some historical reference points that supply information about the life of the community during the 1,000-year period of the Vedic Age.

The Aryans were organized according to tribes, each ruled by a hereditary chief, called a *raja* (related to the Latin word *rex,* or "king"). The main function of the raja was to lead his people in war. He was not absolute and had to consult a tribal assembly before making decisions. He had no religious function, except to order sacrifices and provide support for the priests, who were important because they composed, memorized, and passed down to succeeding generations of priests the hymns of the Rig-Veda and other sacred works. They also presided at ceremonies and conducted sacrifices to maintain cosmic order and ensure tribal prosperity in peace and victory in war.

Aryan society was already divided into social classes before the invasion. As the Aryans settled in India among dark-skinned indigenous people, they put more stress on purity of bloodline and class divisions. By the end of the early Vedic period, society had been divided into four great classes; children were born into their father's class and could not change it. This division was given religious sanction. The groupings were based on function and on skin color, called *varna* in Sanskrit. Thus the old tribal class structure was expanded to include people of different skin complexion. In English the word "caste" or "class" is commonly used to refer to these groups. They were, in descending order, the priests (*brahmans*), the warriors (*kshatriyas*), the landholders and artisans (*vaisyas*), and the serfs and servants (*sudras*). The first three castes included the fair-skinned Aryans, while the fourth consisted of the dark-skinned natives. In later centuries the originally intended racial distinctions became blurred as the religion of the Aryans outpaced their physical penetration of India. Thus in South India where there were few Aryans, members of all castes tended to be non-Aryans. These basic divisions, with many subdivisions, survive to the present.

The Aryan social unit was the patrilineal and patriarchal family. Marriages were usually monogamous and apparently indissoluble. Although the wife and mother enjoyed respect, a woman was definitely subordinate to her husband. Daughters were less desired than sons. The Rig-Veda describes unmarried young men and women mixing freely and does not indicate that married women were secluded, as became normal in later times.

The Aryans practiced a mixed pastoral and farming economy. They prized cattle for status and wealth; they valued horses as well, though mainly for military reasons. Domestic animals included sheep (for wool), goats, and dogs. Cows did not have the sacred status of later times, nor were there strictures against eating meat. Most people were farmers and lived in villages. Arable land appears to have been privately owned, but grazing land was probably held in common and manuring and irrigation were practiced. Artisans such as carpenters, metalworkers, and tanners formed subcastes, plied their specialties, and lived in both towns and villages. Most trade was by barter, but cattle were also used as currency in important exchanges. There is no information about

Hymn of the Primeval Man

From that all-embracing sacrifice
were born the hymns and chants,
from that the metres were born,
from that the sacrificial spells were born.

Thence were born horses,
and all beings with two rows of teeth.
Thence were born cattle,
and thence goats and sheep.

When they divided the Man,
into how many parts did they divide him?
What was his mouth, what were his arms,
what were his thighs and his feet called?

The Brahman was his mouth,
of his arms was made the warrior,
his thighs became the vaisya,
of his feet the sudra was born.

The moon arose from his mind,
from his eyes was born the sun,
from his mouth Indra and Agni,
from his breath the wind was born.

From his navel came the air,
from his head there came the sky,
from his feet the earth, the four quarters from his ear,
thus they fashioned the worlds.*

    The preceding verses from a hymn in the Rig-Veda describe how the universe and all within it were created and justify a social order in which humans were divided into four major categories, each with its function. These four divisions are called "castes" in English (*varna,* meaning "color" in Sanskrit). Each caste is subdivided into occupational or geographic groups called *jati,* which remain the foundation of Hindu society.

*A. L. Basham, The Wonder That Was India *(New York: Grove Press, 1954), pp. 240–241.*

international trade in the Vedic Age as there was in the Indus era, and no Vedic Age artifacts have been discovered outside India.

Religion

Our knowledge of early Aryan religion comes from the Rig-Veda. By the time its hymns were written down hundreds of years after they had been composed, many of the words used in them had become archaic and their meanings unclear. The hymns therefore represent an amalgamation of the beliefs of several different Aryan tribes and are not systematic. Nevertheless, hymns from the Rig-Veda are still recited at weddings and funerals and in the daily devotions of brahmans, and they remain part of the living Hindu tradition.

    The objects of Aryan worship were the devas, a Sanskrit word related to *deus,* which means "god" in Latin. Foremost among the gods was Indra, who in some respects resembled the Greek god Zeus, a successful warrior who killed the dasas and demolished their forts. Agni was the fire god (compare Latin *ignis,* which means fire), also god of the hearth and home. He accepted the sacrifices offered by humans and carried them to the other gods, and as such was an intermediary between gods and humans. Soma was both a god and a hallucinogenic drink made from a hemp-type plant and drunk at religious ceremonies. Yama was the lord of the dead. Rudra was the archer god, who was feared and avoided because his arrows brought disease; but he was also the healer god and gave good health to those he liked. Varuna was the ethical god and guardian of the moral order who abhorred sin and punished sinners by inflicting them with disease, especially dropsy, and by condemning them to a gloomy House of Clay after death. Aryans who had performed the proper rites, however, were believed to feast forever in happiness after they died. The Vedas tell of many other gods, demigods, divine musicians, gnomes, goddesses, and *apsarases,* who were similar to the nymphs of the Greeks. Unfortunately, ancient India never did have the equivalent of a Homer or Hesiod of ancient Greece, so we do not have a clear genealogy of the deities of the Aryans, and their relationships are often unclear.

Aryan religion centered on many kinds of sacrifices, ranging from the daily domestic hearth sacrifices performed by the head of the family to the great sacrifices ordered by rulers and chiefs, presided over by many brahmans, and requiring the slaughter of many animals. The goal in each case was to gain the favor of gods, who were believed to descend to earth, partake of the offerings, and then bless the participants by granting their requests for success in war, health, long life, children, good crops, and so forth. The participants drank soma, felt bigger than life, and were rewarded with a sense of well-being.

Aryan religious ceremonies became more complex with the passage of time. Their correct performance came to be regarded as essential not only to individual and community well-being but also to the maintenance of the cosmic order.

The Appearance of Writing

Sanskrit and all other Indo-European languages are related because they all trace back to the spoken tongue of common ancestors who lived in the steppes of the Eurasian plains around 4,000 years ago. Many key Sanskrit, Greek, and Latin words obviously share the same origin, and many grammatical rules of the three ancient languages are similar. The Rig-Veda, which is written in the earliest surviving form of Sanskrit, bears the same relationship to later classical Sanskrit as Homeric Greek to classical Greek.

By the time the Rig-Veda was written, its language was already archaic. Classical Sanskrit, which developed in the first centuries of the first millennium B.C.E., had a less complex grammar and included new words, many borrowed from non-Aryan languages. Even then it was probably never used by ordinary Aryan peoples, who spoke dialects with simpler grammar. The spoken or vernacular tongues were called Prakrits, which literally means "unrefined" or popular languages, as opposed to the "perfected" or "refined" or "Sanskrit" of the scholars. Because Sanskrit was used by the priests (and probably by other members of the upper class) and by government officials, it became a universal language for the subcontinent. Even now brahman scholars from different parts of India can communicate with one another through Sanskrit.

Although writing began around 1000 B.C.E., no document from earlier than the third century B.C.E. has survived. By the time the Vedas were written down, classical Sanskrit had evolved so much from Vedic Sanskrit that scholars and priests concerned with preserving the purity of the religious texts developed the sciences of linguistics and grammar. The oldest extant Indian linguistic text dates to the fifth century B.C.E. and explains obsolete Vedic words. Toward the end of the fourth century B.C.E. a great grammar book, entitled *Eight Chapters,* was written. Sanskrit became standardized, and also perhaps fossilized after the completion of the *Eight Chapters*. It ceased to develop, whereas the Prakrits evolved into modern vernaculars.

The languages of south India belong to the Dravidian group. They are unrelated to Indo-European languages although in time many Sanskrit words were incorporated into their vocabularies. The oldest Dravidian written language is Tamil. The earliest literature in the Tamil language dates to the beginning of the common era.

The Late Vedic Age

Satyakama son of Jabala said to his mother: "Mother, I want to be a student. What is my family?"

"I don't know your family, my dear," she said. "I had you in my youth, when I travelled about a lot as a servant—and I just don't know! My name is Jabala, and yours is Satyakama Jabala."

He went to Gautama Haridrumata, and said: "I want to be your student, sir. May I come?"

"What is your family, my friend?" he asked.

"I don't know my family, sir," he answered. "I asked my mother, and she said that she had me in her youth, when she used to travel about a lot as a servant. . . . She said that as she was Jabala and I was Satyakama. I was to give my name as Satyakama Jabala."

"Nobody but a true brahman would be so honest!" he said. . . . "Go and fetch me fuel, my friend, and I will initiate you, for you have not swerved from the truth."

*Robert O. Ballou, ed., The Bible of the World (New York: Viking, 1939), p. 254.

This passage from an Upanishad extols the virtue of honesty. Ethical behavior was one of the qualities given high emphasis in the quest for truth and salvation that characterized the late Vedic age (about 1000–500 B.C.E.), the five centuries between the composition of the Rig-Veda and the age of the Buddha. Old rituals and sacrifices to the Aryan tribal gods had lost their appeal, and the goal of thinking people was to seek truth and understand the nature of the brahman, or the essential divine reality of the universe. In so doing, scholars brought about new philosophical developments within the existing religious pattern and founded new, breakaway religions.

Our sources of the period are still predominantly sacred literature and the Upanishads, essays that deal with religious and philosophical questions. In addition, there are epic tales about the period, though they were written later. The greatest of those epics is the *Mahabharata*, which survives in two versions; both tell the story of a gigantic war that began in a dispute over the dynastic succession in the Kuru tribe and eventually involved all of India. Corroborative evidence shows that between the tenth and ninth centuries a great war did take place, probably centered in modern-day Delhi. The names of many of the heroes in the epic may indeed be those of contemporary chieftains. However, it is not possible to reconstruct an accurate political history from the epic. Since archaeological work on this era of Indian history is far less comprehensive than that done in Greece, the *Mahabharata* is of even less use to the historian of India than the *Iliad* is to historians of ancient Greece. Both epics served the purpose of providing models of heroic behavior to their societies.

Despite the scarcity of sources, it is known that during the Late Vedic period Aryan society expanded across northern India along the Himalayan foothills and the Jumna and

Ganges Plains to the Bay of Bengal. The center of culture and political power in India shifted from the Indus to the Ganges Valley. The earlier conquered land of Sind and the Punjab (which means "five rivers" because of its location on the upper Indus, where five tributaries converge on the main river) were almost forgotten and, when mentioned, were described as inhabited by the impure, that is non-Aryan, people. Tribal groups had formed into territorial states with permanent capital cities and rudimentary administrative systems. The kings, almost exclusively kshatriyas, now wielded judicial as well as military power. The formerly powerful tribal assemblies were discarded, replaced by courtiers who served the kings.

Late Vedic Society and Economy

The Late Vedic Age was more advanced economically and materially than the previous era. As the tribes settled down and cleared forests, agriculture became more important than animal herding. Most people lived in villages, but the texts mention cities; Ujjian, for example, retains its seventh-century name unchanged. Situated in the present state of Vindhya Pradesh, it was then the capital city of a kingdom and a holy city; it is still sacred to Hinduism.

The texts also note many subcastes of craftsmen and new grain crops. While many continued to eat meat, others began to regard meat eating with disfavor, because new ideals of respect for animal life were developing. There is some, but not conclusive, evidence that India once more traded with Mesopotamia in this period. Caste distinctions became more pronounced and rigid; the members of all four castes found their lives more strictly regulated. Brahmans and kshatriyas, however, increasingly enjoyed privileges denied to vaisyas and sudras, and the gap between the top and bottom of society grew wider. At the top, brahmans enjoyed immense power and prestige, for they were indispensable to the conduct of sacrifices and the maintenance of a correct relationship between this world and the cosmic order. At the lower end, the sudras were regarded as impure. The size of the sudra caste grew constantly, as conquered or assimilated tribal people were added to Aryan-dominated society.

Unlike some other ancient civilizations, Vedic society did not have large numbers of slaves, and no caste of slaves as such existed. Slavery existed, however. War captives became slaves to the victors until ransomed. Undesirable work that some societies relegated to slaves was given to people later known as outcastes or untouchables, a group lower than sudras. Outcastes were considered ritually impure; they were assigned menial and unpleasant tasks, served the rest of society, and were excluded from the Aryan social order. Some outcastes were descended from conquered aborigines. Others were descended from men and women who had been "outcasted" because of severe infractions of caste rules. Still others might have been members of professions that came to be considered impure in the new moral scheme.

Indirect evidence warrants the conclusion that in this period the position of women declined from its earlier relatively high level. Child marriages, in which young girls were sent to live under the authority of their husbands' parents, were common, and had the effect of keeping young women subordinated. Another new practice allowed upper-caste men to take concubines or secondary wives from the sudra caste.

Religion

During the Late Vedic period two religious trends emerged. First, brahman religious leaders challenged the kings' pretensions to political absolutism. Second, men not traditionally associated with religious leadership, as well as some brahmans who were dissatisfied with traditional ways, began to offer new religious ideas that challenged the established religious rituals and prescribed sacrifices. One of these ideas was the doctrine of *karma* (literally "deed"), which held that one's position in this life is the result of deeds and actions in past lives, and that one's present deeds will affect future lives as the soul passes from life to life into infinity. This doctrine of the transmigration of souls—that the soul moves from one body to another from life to life—gave an ethical content to one's actions, and it explained and justified the inequalities in Aryan society. It also linked all forms of life into one comprehensive system that included humans, animals, insects, and, according to some, even inanimate matter. The belief in karma, that one's conduct determined one's status in future existences, became fundamental to all religions originating in India.

The political changes discussed earlier and the development of new ethical and religious ideals combined to cause a pessimistic outlook on the world that is characteristic of the Late Vedic period. This mood caused several developments; one was the trend toward asceticism. Ascetics were men, and occasionally women, of any caste, whose

Lessons from the Upanishads

"Fetch me a fruit of the banyan tree."

"Here is one, sir."

"Break it."

"I have broken it, sir."

"What do you see?"

"Very tiny seeds, sir."

"Break one."

"I have broken it, sir."

"Now what do you see?"

"Nothing, sir."

"My son," the father said, "what you do not perceive is the essence, and in that essence the mighty banyan tree exists. Believe me, my son, in that essence is the Self of all that is. That is the True, that is the Self. And you are that Self, Svetaketu!"

"Put this salt in water, and come to me in the morning."

The son did as he was told. The father said: "Fetch the salt." The son looked for it, but could not find it, because it had dissolved.

"Taste the water from the top," said the father. "How does it taste?"

"Of salt," the son replied.

"Taste from the bottom. How does it taste?"

"Of salt," the son replied.

Then the father said, "You don't perceive that the one Reality exists in your own body, my son, but it is truly there. Everything which is has its being in that subtle essence. That is Reality! That is the Soul! And you are that, Svetaketu!"*

The dominant theme of the Upanishads was a search for knowledge or understanding of the mystery of this unintelligible world and one's place in it. These two passages from an Upanishad assert that salvation is found through knowledge of or realization of the individual self (the *atman*) and the absolute self (*brahman*). The wise person realizes that the two are the same, and his highest quest is then to seek a synthesis of the two. When one achieves that, one is freed from transmigration.

*Robert O. Ballou, ed., The Bible of the World (New York: Viking, 1939), pp. 250–251.

quest for wisdom had led them to abandon the material world in favor of a life of wandering and meditation. They also performed mystical exercises requiring great discipline of both mind and body, with the goal of developing their psychic faculties and insights beyond ordinary understanding. Similarly, in classical Greece, Socrates, in the *Phaedo,* said that the true philosopher is in training for death (that is, the final separation of the soul from the body and its distractions). The ascetic way of life had ancient roots in India. Some hymns of the Rig-Veda even mention a class of holy men who, as a result of meditation and the practice of austerities, acquired great wisdom and powers of perception beyond ordinary people's understanding.

By about 600 B.C.E., toward the end of the Vedic Age, asceticism had become very widespread, and it was through the ascetics rather than the orthodox brahman priests that new religious teachings developed. Some ascetics, in groups or alone, wandered the country, teaching and debating with one another. Others lived rather permanently on the outskirts of towns and villages. Some groups were led by a senior teacher. The movement toward asceticism was certainly in part a protest against the pretensions of the brahmans and their sacrificial cult, though some brahmans who felt the traditional cult to be inadequate also became ascetics.

The Upanishads

The greatest creation of the Late Vedic Era was the Upanishads, a collection of 108 essays dealing with ethical questions, written between 800 and 300 B.C.E. Literally, *upanishad* means "sitting near," and refers to students sitting near a teacher to learn esoteric doctrines from him. Not all those essays are important, nor do they teach a consistent point of view. We know the names of some of the authors, but most of the essays were anonymous group efforts. Just as the Greek philosopher Plato and Chinese philosopher Confucius explained their ideas in dialogue form, so many of the Upanishads contain dialogues, questions and answers between students and teachers.

The general tendency of the Upanishads was toward monism, a metaphysical system in which reality is conceived as a unified whole. Ritual and magic were discouraged as futile when applied without enlightenment, and faith and good works were considered inadequate. The goal of the Upanishads was to seek the knowledge and wisdom that the Vedas did not give. Eventually, the ideas explored in the Upanishads found their way into the new orthodoxy of the Hindu religion that emerged from the synthesis of old and new ideas. In this way, the Upanishads became accepted as an orthodox part of the Vedic literature that for more than 2,000 years has formed the basis of Hinduism, the religion that emerged from early Aryan religion and later additions. The strength of the teaching of the Upanishads is its all-embracing approach, which overrides all barriers of caste and every external and internal difference between believers.

The ideas expressed in the Upanishads, however, were so esoteric and complex that they influenced only the small number of people capable of understanding them. They were entirely too difficult for the vast masses of the people and hence did not permeate downward. The most immediate result of the movement was to widen the gap between the intellectuals and ordinary people.

Meanwhile, the common people began to put their faith in hitherto unimportant deities who now seemed to answer their needs. Most important among them were Shiva and Vishnu, who replaced Indra and Varuna, who had been important earlier. Also known as Rudra, Shiva may have become popular because of his identification with a deity often depicted on Indus seals. Shiva was associated with death and destruction, but also with fertility, something everyone desired. Worshippers appealed to Vishnu for deliverance from distress; he was also identified with Krishna, who taught morality and virtue. These two gods continued from late Vedic to modern times as the most popular deities in Hinduism.

Another result of the religious mood of the late Vedic period is the development of two new religions that sought to change and reform some of the prevailing religious ideas and practices. They are Buddhism and Jainism, and will be discussed in Chapter 4.

China from the Neolithic Age to the Shang Dynasty

Examining into antiquity we find that the Emperor Yao was called Fang-hsun. He was reverent, intelligent, accomplished, sincere and mild. He was sincerely respectful and capable of modesty. His light covered the four extremities of the empire and extended to Heaven above and the earth below. He was able to make bright his great virtue, and bring affection to the nine branches of the family. When the nine branches of the family had become harmonious, he distinguished and honored the hundred clans. When the hundred clans had become illustrious, he harmonized the myriad states. The numerous people were amply nourished and prosperous and became harmonious. . . .

[As he grew older Yao searched for a successor from among all his subjects, and found Shun the best qualified.]

The emperor said: "Come you, Shun, in the affairs on which you have been consulted, I have examined your words; your words have been accomplished and capable of yielding fine results for three years; do you ascend to the imperial throne." Shun considered himself inferior in virtue and was not pleased. But in the first month, the first day, he accepted the abdication of Yao in the Temple of the Accomplished Ancestor.*

*William T. de Bary, ed., Sources of Chinese Tradition, vol. 1 (New York: Columbia University Press, 1960), pp. 8–9. Reprinted with permission.

Until the twentieth century, Chinese were taught that Kings Yao and Shun were historic figures who reigned around 2200 B.C.E. They were revered for their sincerity, reverence, and unselfishness, and for the golden age that their reigns brought. Later rulers were exhorted to emulate them. Since there is no proof that they existed, we can only regard them as culture heroes. In this section we will find out how civilization began in China, how traditional Chinese looked at their past, and how modern archaeology has added to our knowledge of ancient China.

The Land of China

China, a country of continental dimensions, today extends some 2,500 miles from the Pamir Mountains in the west to the Pacific Ocean in the east and over 2,000 miles from the Amur River in the north to the Indochinese border in the south. At 3.7 million square miles, it is slightly larger than the 3.6 million square miles of the United States. This area varies greatly in topography, climate, and vegetation, ranging from subarctic taiga (evergreen forests) in the northeast to tropical jungles in the southwest, from the steppes and deserts of Chinese Turkestan in the northwest to the high plateau of Tibet in the west and the temperate river valleys of the east. Although it is possible to cross the broad deserts and scale the high mountains that separate China from the other civilizations of Asia, the length of the journey and the difficulties and dangers associated with such travel have tended to isolate China from other lands. Conversely, the great river valleys and coastal plains make internal communications relatively easy and thus have helped unify the Chinese.

China can be divided into two broad parts, north and south. The Yellow River dominates North China. It brings the water and deposits the layers of silt on which agriculture depends; it has also since the earliest times brought cruel floods that have given it the name "China's sorrow." Hot in summer and cold in winter, the North China plains receive little rainfall. Here barley and millet are the main crops, and the donkey and oxen are the chief draft animals.

The Tsingling Mountains separate the drainage basins of the Yellow and the Yangtze Rivers. The Yangtze valley and the Hsi (West, also called Pearl) River valley farther south constitute South China. A coastal plain of varying width extends along the entire coastline. Southern China receives abundant rainfall and has mild winters and hot summers. It is the land of double and triple crops each year, paddy rice and water buffalo, and canals and lakes. Contrasts abound between the harsh north and the verdant south (see Map 2.2).

Map 2.2 Shang China.
Most archaeological sites of the Shang dynasty are found along the lower reaches of the Yellow River, the heartland of early Chinese civilization, although some are located along the Yangtze and its tributaries. The last Shang capital, Anyang, is located in modern Honan province.

The Study of Ancient China

The Chinese have a tradition and history that have continued unbroken to the present. Unlike the earliest Indian oral traditions and written documents, which dealt with religion and philosophy, ancient Chinese writings were from the beginning concerned with historiography, or the recording of historic events, with an emphasis on socially applicable morals and virtues.

Early records told of ancient culture heroes who ruled in succession starting from 2850 B.C.E. The greatest was Huang-ti (Yellow Emperor), considered the founding father of the Chinese state because he defeated the neighboring barbarians and united the Chinese people throughout the Yellow River plain. To this day Chinese call themselves descendants of the Yellow Emperor. He was followed by others such as Yao and Shun, whom posterity regarded as sage kings.

Another culture hero was Yu, known as the Great, because he dredged channels of the Yellow River, allowing the floodwaters to flow to the sea and solving the problem of recurring floods. He was so devoted to his work that he never returned home in over ten years, even when he passed by his gate and heard his wife and children weeping in loneliness. Yu was made ruler because of his successful flood control work, and was so loved that when he died the people set aside the man he had chosen to succeed him and put his son on the throne. Thus began the first dynasty, the Hsia (c. 2205–1766 B.C.E.). Little is known about the Hsia kings until the last, who was a tyrant. He was overthrown by a subordinate named Tang the Successful, who founded the Shang dynasty (c.1766–1122 B.C.E.). The last Shang king was a debauched tyrant who in turn was deposed by his subordinate, who founded the Chou dynasty (1122–256 B.C.E.). This, in very brief outline, is how early history was taught to Chinese children until the beginning of the twentieth century.

An Idealized View of Antiquity

At the time when men still followed the Great Way, all under Heaven was owned in common. Men were chosen for their ability and talent. Their teaching was reliable and they cultivated harmony. People of ancient times treated not only their nearest relatives as relatives and not only their own children as children. . . . There was employment for the strong and the young were given the opportunity to grow up. Widows, orphans, those left on their own, and invalids were all provided for. Men had their work and women their shelter. They accumulated provisions because they did not wish anything to be thrown away, but they were not supposed to amass goods for themselves. They toiled because they did not wish goods to be anything but the result of their own efforts. But they were not supposed to do this for the sake of personal advantage. Therefore selfish schemes did not arise and robbers, thieves, and rebels were not in evidence. They went out without shutting the door. This was called the Great Harmony.*

Centuries later, Confucius and Confucians viewed the earliest antiquity as a golden age when virtue reigned and selfishness did not exist. They were undoubtedly exhorting the people of their times to live up to high ideals and to encourage them that such ideals were realizable, because they had once been reality.

*Attributed to Confucius, from the Li Chi, vol. 1, trans. James Legge (1885; reprint, New Hyde Park, NY: University Books, 1967), pp. 364–366.

The Rise of the Shang Dynasty, 1766–1122 B.C.E.

The Agricultural Revolution, evident in the domestication of plants and animals and the appearance of pottery, began in China around 7000 B.C.E. Communities existed in isolation until about 4000 B.C.E., when they began to interact with one another, though remaining independent from other emerging civilizations. Although archaeologists have found many remains that corroborate traditional accounts of the Hsia, no written documents of that era have survived. Thus the Hsia dynasty remains prehistoric.

The Shang dynasty was centered in modern-day Honan province (an area south of the Yellow River in northeastern China). We are not sure of the extent of its political power and its relationship with the peoples of other parts of China. Since the systematic excavation of its last capital began at Anyang in 1928, scores of other Shang sites have been found and investigated. Some major sites might have been earlier capitals of the dynasty. For example, Chengchow in north Honan was probably the second Shang capital, called Ao in ancient records. Excavations have been in progress in Chengchow since the 1950s, and study of the findings reveals that the area was continuously occupied since Neolithic times. The city was rectangular in shape, surrounded by a wall of rammed earth estimated to have been over thirty feet in height, over sixty feet thick at the base, and totaling almost two and half miles in circumference. As with the construction of the Great Pyramids in Egypt, a huge labor force was mobilized to build major Chinese public works. Experts calculate that it took 10,000 men working 330 days a year for eighteen years to build the wall around Ao. The Shang government clearly had the organizational skill to supervise monumental projects.

Within the city walls were large palaces, residences for aristocrats, and ceremonial quarters. Pits with the remains of human sacrificial victims have also been unearthed. Artisans and workers lived close to their work in tamped-earth houses. Remains of these houses are found near kiln sites, bronze foundries, and workshop areas, located outside the walls. Scattered farmhouses dot the countryside. Artifacts made of bronze, jade, and other materials abound throughout, but no writing has been found, either here or at the other presumed pre-Anyang capitals. We can therefore only deduce from nonwritten information that Chengchow (Ao) was an important political and ceremonial center. Pottery and other artifacts of the last Shang phase at Chengchow are of poorer quality, which suggests that by then the center of power had moved elsewhere.

The last twelve kings of Shang ruled from Yin, near present-day Anyang, for 273 years until the dynasty fell; hence the last phase of the Shang is also called the Yin dynasty. When the curious purchasers of the inscribed tortoise shells began to inquire as to their place of origin, the trail led to Anyang, where a major archaeological dig began in 1928.

Anyang was an impressive capital. Eleven large tombs that belonged to the kings have been found. Twelve kings had ruled from Anyang, but the twelfth and last king died in his burning palace as his capital fell and was not given a kingly burial. Smaller tombs in the royal cemetery apparently belonged to other members of the royal family. Unlike the Egyptians, whose rulers were buried in pyramids and tombs carved into cliffs, the Shang kings were buried in underground chambers not unlike those found in the royal cemetery at Mycenae. Each tomb was about thirty feet deep, oblong in shape, with a central burial chamber containing a coffin surrounded by objects of jade, bronze, shell, pottery, and other materials. Remains of human sacrificial victims were found interred in the main chamber and scattered in other parts of the grave, as were dogs, and horses harnessed to chariots. Chariot drivers were buried beside their vehicles. Similarities between Shang chariots and those discovered in burial mounds in the Caucasus region in western Asia led to speculation that Shang China might have had contact with cultures to the west.

All the royal graves excavated up to 1975 had been robbed in ages past, but in 1975 a hitherto undisturbed grave was found. This lavish grave belonged to Lady Hao, the powerful wife of a mighty Shang king who reputedly had sixty-four wives. Her name frequently appeared in oracle bone inscriptions. She led troops in war, owned her own estates, and was the mother of some of the king's children. Thus she had merited an elaborate send-off to the next life. Her grave contains the remains of sixteen sacrificed humans and six dogs. It also held more than 1,600 objects, including many bronzes, jades, ivories, pottery, stone carvings, and 7,000 cowrie shells (used as currency). Originally a building had stood over the grave; it was used for ceremonies and sacrifices conducted in her honor.

The key "documents" that give us an understanding of the Shang dynasty are 20,000 inscribed oracle bones buried in Shang government archives. Questions to the gods were written on these bones, and answers from the gods were recorded there as well. Modern Chinese writing evolved from the script incised into the scapula bones of oxen and inner shells of tortoises. Most of the words have been deciphered. We know that Shang scribes kept government records that they wrote down with brush and ink on slips of bamboo or wood that were bound together and rolled up in the fashion of modern slat screens, but these have long since perished. Some Shang bronze ritual vessels also had inscriptions cast into their lids or bases, but they, like the Indus seals, contained only a few characters identifying the vessel and the clan names of the owners. Major excavations in other parts of China that are contemporary with those of the Shang dynasty show cultures

Neolithic Pots. Both pieces, a large earthenware jar and a bowl, were made by Neolithic farmers in northwestern China between 4000 and 3000 B.C.E. Found in graves, they originally contained food and were buried in the belief that people in the afterlife needed the same things they had in this life. These vessels were handmade by the coiling method and painted with abstract designs in red, black, and white.

that are at the same time similar and different from that at Anyang, but without artifacts bearing explanatory inscriptions.

Shang Government

The Shang oracle bones were used for divination, the art of telling future events through consulting the supernatural, a practice found worldwide that was also used by the Neolithic peoples of China. Not until the Anyang period of the Shang dynasty did the bones contain writing. The Shang king's diviner would inscribe a question on the prepared bone or shell, dig a small pit partway through the piece, and then apply a heated metal rod to the pit, which would cause the shell or bone to crack. The nature of the crack indicated the answer. A typical bone or shell contains a date, followed by "The diviner X asks on behalf of the king . . ."; then comes the question, for example, "Is the drought caused by ancestor X?" or "If we raise an army of 3,000 men to drive X away from Y, will we succeed?" The diviner then recorded the answer. A final statement sometimes gave the outcome, which occasionally differed from the first answer. Other oracles were in the nature of reports to ancestors. Since it was believed that the spirits of royal ancestors could influence events, Shang monarchs regularly offered elaborate sacrifices to propitiate those spirits.

The Shang is a historic dynasty because in addition to archaeological evidence, we now possess copious contemporary documentation about it deciphered from the oracle bone inscriptions. The king's relationship to the ancestor who was the object of a sacrifice was important and was always clearly stated, allowing reconstruction of clear genealogies of the royal family. Oracle bone inscriptions also contained information about Shang government, state, society, and economy, as well as insights into the kings' private lives and relationships with their ancestors. The inscriptions have also corroborated much of the information about the Shang recorded in the later historic texts.

The king was the central focus of the Shang dynasty and the succeeding Chou dynasty. A poem written during the early Chou proclaimed:

> Everywhere under Heaven
> Is no land that is not the king's.
> To the borders of all those lands
> None is but the king's slave.

Historians are not sure whether the Shang state and society were based on tribal alliances or a form of feudalism, in which the king delegated power to noblemen who owed him allegiance and responsibilities such as taxes and contribution of troops in war. We do know that from his capital city, the king ruled through a complex and highly stratified governmental network. Numerous offices and titles are mentioned in the oracle bone inscriptions, but we are not sure of the functions of many of them. Only the king could consult and offer sacrifices to his ancestors and other spirits. Although this was an important source of the king's power and its results affected the whole nation, the king himself, unlike the Egyptian pharaoh, was not considered divine. Ancestors and their living descendants had reciprocal obligations; therefore, for the health and safety of the state, the king had to offer the correct sacrifices to the particular ancestor at the appropriate times. A proper offering should secure the desired response from the ancestral spirit. The king should then make another offering to the ancestor in thanksgiving. This concept of reciprocal responsibility is the essence of ancestor worship practiced by the Chinese.

The king was responsible for correct relations with the wider spirit world as well. The most important spirit was the impersonal high god called Ti, who appointed kings to rule on his behalf and demanded moral uprightness and integrity from all kings, a concept called the mandate of heaven. Heaven appointed a worthy man to rule and allowed him to pass the kingship .to his descendants so long as they ruled with justice and compassion and carried out their religious duties. If they failed to do so, heaven would cut its mandate and appoint another ruler.

Shang kings also led their troops in war. Sometimes calling up 5,000 or more men at a time, they conducted campaigns against neighboring groups; those with non-Chinese cultures were referred to as "barbarians." At first the Shang kings made war mostly in North China, but later they expanded south-ward along the coast and probably into the Yangtze region. The king and the nobles rode to battle in horse-drawn chariots. They and the soldiers used a variety of bronze weapons, including axes, spears, daggers, and metal-tipped arrows. Prisoners of war became slaves and victims in sacrificial burials, and were also buried in building foundations. When not warring, the kings and their nobles held large hunts for sport and for food.

Courtesy of the C. V. Sterr East Asian Library, Columbia University

Shang Oracle Bones. Thousands of inscribed tortoise shells and scapula bones have been unearthed in Anyang. Used for divination, they are the earliest surviving examples of Chinese writing and a rich storehouse of information on the Shang dynasty.

Society and Economy during the Shang Era

A great gap existed between the rulers and the ruled in Shang society. At the top of society were the royal and aristocratic families, who were organized according to patrilineal clans and kept careful genealogies. Since the royalty and nobility practiced polygyny (one man with more than one wife), and since the economy could not have supported an ever-increasing leisure class, it is reasonable to assume that some offspring of the nobility must have been regularly demoted to commoner status. Nobles were rewarded with strings of cowrie shells acquired from South China and Southeast Asia, which were probably used for major transactions. There was also an artisan class such as jade carvers and bronzesmiths, who lived in or around the towns. We do not know of their social status, but since they performed services that needed skills, it is reasonable to assume that they were well treated. Most of the trade must have been in barter form, since there was no coinage beside the cowrie shells.

At the bottom of society were the slaves. Some slaves were acquired deliberately in wars against the Shang's non-Chinese neighbors, while others were convicted criminals who were enslaved as punishment. Slaves were often sacrificed in royal burials and other rituals. The vast majority of the people, however, were not slaves. They were farmers, who probably had the status of serfs, meaning that they were tied to the land and had to give part of their crops to the lord.

By Shang times the hunting-herding-farming economy of the Neolithic Age had given way to a predominantly farming one. Where there was arable land, the landscape was dotted with villages of semisubterranean houses of adobe and thatch. Fieldwork was primarily for men; the common word meaning "male" is a pictograph that combines a symbol representing a field and another meaning work. Since bronze was a luxury metal, farming implements were made of wood, bone, or stone. The major crops were millet, barley, wheat, and vegetables. Women did domestic chores. The pictograph for "woman" or "wife" combined a symbol for female and a symbol of a broom. Women also tended silkworms, spun, and wove. Domesticated animals include horses (used for chariot-pulling only, not for riding or field work), oxen, pigs, sheep, dogs, and fowls. Pork was the staple meat. Animal bones and tusks were used for arrow heads, small tools, and ornaments. Animals were sacrificed in ancestral and other rites; their meat was probably later eaten. Animals were also buried with their owners.

There is no indication in Shang times or in later ages that the Chinese used milk or milk products from any of their milk-producing animals. Yet they were in constant contact with nomadic herders living on the northern rim of their world who relied on milk products. In fact, one can observe a contrast in dietary patterns among the peoples of Europe and Asia based on their use or avoidance of dairy products. In East Asia the people of China, Korea, Japan, Indochina, and Malaya do not use milk products, while all Indo-Europeans (including the Aryans of India), the Semites, Scythians, Turks, and Mongols have used them since early times. The reason for this difference is not clear.

Science, Arts, and Crafts

Chinese tradition says that the Yellow Emperor first established the sixty-year cycle as the basis of calculating time and that the Hsia dynasty fixed the lunar calendar of 366 days a year. To the present day the Chinese call the lunar calendar on which their traditional festivals are based the Hsia calendar. Many oracle bones of the Shang recorded solar and lunar eclipses and noted predictions of their occurrences. From this it would seem that the men who cast oracles were also astronomers and mathematicians. Records show that the decimal system originated during the Shang and was in use at least by the fourteenth century B.C.E. The ability to chart the movement of heavenly bodies, predict

LIVES AND TIMES ACROSS CULTURES

Royal Tombs in Bronze Age Greece and China

Many ancient cultures buried artifacts with the dead for use in the next world. Such burials prove belief in a next world and also help posterity reconstruct life in ancient times. Excavated tombs of Bronze Age rulers of Mycenaean Greece corroborate descriptions of the *Iliad,* just as the royal graves of Shang dynasty rulers at Anyang authenticate passages of the *Books of History and Poetry.*

The following passage describes burial objects found by Heinrich Schliemann during his excavation of one of six shaft graves inside the city wall at Mycenae in Greece.

The five bodies in Grave IV had been literally smothered in costly burial offerings.... Among the finds were ... a silver vase in the form of a bull's head ... with golden horns ...; three remarkable and awe-inspiring gold face masks ..., apparently modeled on the actual features of the deceased; two large gold signet rings showing chariot scenes of battle and hunting; a massive gold bracelet; gold breastplates, diadems and a "shoulder-belt"; nine golden goblets and vases, including the famous "cup of Nestor"; ... more than 400 beads of amber; ... thirty-

two copper cauldrons; ... various adornments for armor and weapons; obsidian arrowheads; perforated boar's tusks; forty-six bronze swords and daggers; four lances; three knives; numerous terra-cotta vases.*

The next passage is from an archaeological report listing items found in a Chinese queen's tomb from the Shang dynasty in the fourteenth century B.C.E.

At least sixteen human [sacrificial victims] were buried in the tomb.... There were also six dogs ... more than 1,600 objects in addition to almost 7,000 pieces of cowrie shells [used as large-denomination money]. Of the 1,600 plus buried objects, there were more than 440 bronze pieces, over 590 jade items, over 560 bone objects; in addition there were over 70 stone objects, several ivory carvings, pottery objects, two made from sea shells and one from a large sea shell. After preliminary study of the burial items, and the deciphering of the inscriptions on the bronze vessels, it would seem that most of them had been the accumulated possessions of the owner of the grave; and that a minority of the pieces had been made expressly as sacrificial items of the person buried.**

**William A. McDonald, Progress into the Past: The Rediscovery of Mycenaean Civilization (Bloomington: Indiana University Press, 1967), pp. 61–62.*
***Kaogu Xuebao, 1977, no. 2, Peking Institute of Archaeology, Chinese Academy of Social Sciences, pp. 59–60, trans. Jiu-Hwa L. Upshur.*

eclipses, regulate the calendar, and define the agricultural season became recognized as the prerequisite for rulership. The Shang oracle specialists were probably the predecessors of the Board of Astronomers of the Chinese government of later eras.

The most remarkable products of the Shang dynasty are bronze ritual vessels that art historians consider unequaled in technical excellence and beauty. The art of bronze casting developed around 2000 B.C.E., in the late Neolithic Age. In early west Asia, India, and Europe, bronze was made by the lost-wax method, whereby a wax model of the object is encased in a clay mold; as molten metal is poured in, the wax melts (is lost) and is replaced by the metal. By contrast, the Chinese cast their vessels in ceramic piece molds. This way very large vessels could be made with complex decorations (the largest Shang vessels found weigh about 1,500 pounds). This method of bronze casting came

LIVES AND TIMES ACROSS CULTURES

Feasting in Bronze Age Greece and China

We have considerable evidence of foods consumed by Bronze Age people. Although little documentary evidence about the diet of ordinary people is available, great literary writings from ancient Europe and Asia depict the feasts of rulers, nobles, and heroes.

The following excerpt is from Homer's *Odyssey*. The hero Odysseus has been washed ashore in the land of the peace-loving and somewhat decadent Phaiakians, who show him much hospitality and assist him on his journey home. In the passage quoted here, the Phaiakian king, Alkinoös, has ordered a great feast for his distinguished visitor, complete with musical entertainment by the blind minstrel, Demodokos, who may be a self-portrait by Homer.

[They] made their way to the great house of Alkinoös, and the porticoes and enclosures and rooms were filled with people assembling, there were many men there, both old and young ones, and for them Alkinoös made a sacrifice, twelve sheep, eight pigs with shining tusks, and two drag-footed oxen. These they skinned and prepared and made the lovely feast ready. The herald came near bringing with him the excellent singer. . . . Pontonoös set a silver-studded chair out for him in the middle of the feasters ... and set beside him a table and a fine basket, and beside him a cup to drink whenever his spirit desired it. *

The second quotation, from the Chou dynasty, vividly describes the delicacies and delicious dishes that family members have prepared in hopes of enticing the soul of a departed loved one to share the meal. The Chinese have always prepared elaborate dishes to commemorate special occasions involving beloved deceased family members. After ceremonially entreating the souls to enjoy their offerings, family members sit down to the lavish meal.

> *The Summons of the Soul*
>
> *Oh soul, come back! Why should you go far
>   away?*
> *All your household have come to do you
>   honour; all kinds of good food are ready;*
> *Rice, broom-corn, early wheat, mixed all
>   with yellow millet;*
> *Bitter, salt, sour, hot and sweet; there are
>   dishes of all flavours.*
> *Ribs of fatted ox cooked tender and succulent;*
> *Sour and bitter blended in the soup of Wu;*
> *Stewed turtle and roast kid, served up on
>   yam sauce;*
> *Geese cooked in sour sauce, cassaroled
>   duck, fried flesh of the great crane;*
> *Braised chicken, seethed tortoise, high-
>   seasoned, but not to spoil the taste;*
> *Fried honey-cakes of rice flour and malt-
>   sugar sweetmeats;*
> *Jadelike wine, honey-flavoured, fills the
>   winged cups;*
> *Ice-cooled liquor, strained of impurities,
>   clear wine, cool and refreshing;*
> *Here are laid out the patterned ladles, and
>   here is sparkling wine.* **

*Richmond Lattimore, trans., The Odyssey of Homer (New York: Harper, 1965), pp. 122–123.
**K. C. Chang, ed., Food in Chinese Culture: Anthropological and Historical Perspectives (New Haven: Yale University Press, 1977), p. 32.

naturally to the Chinese, who were already skilled in pottery making. Indeed, the Shang potter made a high-fired, glazed pottery close to stoneware. Shang pottery and bronze pieces often shared the same shapes and forms of decoration. Pottery making was widespread, but bronze foundries were found only at major urban centers close to ore sites, where they constituted large-scale operations with divisions of labor. Bronzesmiths must have been respected artisans.

Art historians have classified over two dozen distinct forms of bronze ritual vessels, which fall into three categories according to use: for storage, food, and liquids, mainly alcoholic beverages. Most pieces were decorated, some elaborately, with stylized images of real or mythological birds and animals, arranged symmetrically. Styles of decoration varied with time and region from abstract to realistic. Many pieces survived because they were buried with the dead, as the practice of ancestor worship dictated. For over 1,000 years, Chinese connoisseurs have collected Shang ritual bronze pieces; early collectors had attributed magical qualities to these unearthed treasures. Such prac-

The Nelson-Atkins Museum of Art, Kansas City, MO (Purchase: Nelson Trust) 41—43

Shang Bronzes. Bronze ritual vessels made by Shang craftsmen are unsurpassed in artistry and technical virtuosity. Most are richly ornamented with stylized animals whose meanings are lost. Many vessels have survived because they were buried with the dead.

tices and superstitious beliefs led to the looting of early tombs. Shang bronzesmiths also made weapons, chariot fittings, horse harnesses, and mirrors.

Women at Work in Ancient China

With the spring days the warmth begins,
And the oriole utters its songs.
The young women take their deep baskets,
And go along the small paths,
Looking for the tender [leaves of the]
    mulberry tree . . .
In the silkworm month they strip the
    mulberry branch of their leaves,
And take their axes and hatchets,
To lop off those that are distant and high;
Only stripping the young trees of their
    leaves.
In the seventh month the shrike is heard;
In the eighth month, they begin their spinning,

They make dark fabrics and yellow,
Our red manufacture is very brilliant,
It is for the lower robes of our young
    princes.*

    Ancient records tell mostly about the doings of kings and the mighty. However, the *Book of Poetry*, an ancient collection of anonymously written songs and poems, is a good source about the lives of the common people. Besides housework, women also tended the silk worms and spun and wove cloth. Common people wore linen cloth woven from hemp, while the rich wore garments of silk.

*The Chinese Classics, vol. 4: Book of Poetry, trans. James Legge (London, 1871), pp. 228–229.

Shang artisans also worked extensively in jade and other materials. Like bronze, jade was a luxury item used in rituals and buried with the dead. The Shang jade carvers improved upon the skills of their Neolithic forebears. Their raw material, nephrite jade, came from present-day northwestern China, a considerable distance from the Shang urban centers. The abundance in Shang culture of jade and cowrie shells, both of which came from lands outside of Shang political control, indicates international trade. Shang artisans also fashioned utilitarian and decorative objects from stone, ivory, and bone. They invented lacquer by extracting sap from a lacquer tree and applying the liquid to a surface such as wood to form a glossy, waterproof coating. They also worked gold and silver. However, gold was not abundant in ancient China, and gold objects did not have the significance there that they did in most other early cultures.

A Pictographic Script

Although signs and symbols are found on pottery as early as 5000 B.C.E., they are isolated and cannot be considered written language. The earliest extant written records date to the fourteenth century B.C.E., by which time the script exhibited a maturity of stylization that presupposes a centuries-long evolution.

Chinese writing is unrelated to other writings. It is a nonalphabetic script, consisting of symbols or graphs. A good modern dictionary will list over 40,000 graphs, most of which have evolved since Shang times. There are three basic kinds of graphs: (1) Pictographs are conventionalized picture symbols of an object such as the sun and moon. (2) Ideographs frequently are formed by combining two or more pictographs, for example, pictographs of the sun and moon placed side by side mean "bright" or "brilliant." (3) Logographs are formed by combining either a pictograph or an ideograph to indicate meaning and a symbol to give a key to pronunciation. For example, the pictograph of a horse is pronounced "ma," but when it is combined with a pictograph for woman the new word is still pronounced "ma" but means mother. The great majority of words in the Chinese vocabulary are logographs. All three kinds of graphs were evident in late Shang writing.

The Chou Dynasty

Now that the king has received the mandate, unbounded is the grace, but also unbounded is the solicitude. Oh, how can he be but careful! Heaven has removed and made an end to the great state Yin's mandate. There are many former wise kings of Yin in Heaven, and the later kings and people here managed their mandate. But in the end [under the last king] wise and good men lived in misery so that, leading their wives and carrying their children, wailing and calling to Heaven, they went to where no one could come and seize them. Oh, Heaven had pity on the people of the four quarters, and looking with affection and giving its mandate, it employed the zealous ones [the leaders of the Chou]. May the king now urgently pay careful attention to his virtue . . . may he not neglect the aged elders. Then he will comprehend our ancient men's virtue, nay, still more it will occur that he is able to comprehend and endeavor to follow Heaven.*

*William T. de Bary, ed., Sources of Chinese Tradition, vol. 1 (New York: Columbia University Press, 1960), p. 11. Reprinted with permission.

Thus the people of China heard their new Chou rulers justify their conquest of the Shang (Yin) dynasty as the will or mandate of heaven. Around 1120 B.C.E. the leaders of the Chou from northwest China overthrew the Shang dynasty and set up their own rule. They then issued a series of proclamations to explain to the people why they had overthrown the Shang and why the people should submit to their rule. Appealing to the mandate of heaven, they told their new subjects that the last Shang king had forfeited his right to rule by his personal immorality and tyrannical government. Ti had then cut off the Shang's mandate to rule and transferred it to the deserving house of Chou. The concept of the mandate of heaven has remained the cornerstone of Chinese political thinking down to the twentieth century.

After the overthrow of the Shang in 1122 B.C.E., the Chou established the longest-lasting dynasty in Chinese history, ending in 256 B.C.E. This long period is subdivided into the Western Chou (1122–771 B.C.E.) and the Eastern Chou (770–256 B.C.E.). During the Chou dynasty, Chinese civilization underwent fundamental changes that brought the end of the formative era and the beginning of the imperial era, whose political and philosophical systems lasted for the next 2,000 years.

The Chou Conquest

Toughened by years of fighting non-Chinese tribes, the Chou people emerged out of the plain of Chou, situated on the northwestern frontier of the agricultural basin of North China. Shang oracle bone inscriptions described them at different times both as enemies and as allies. Although in the twelfth century B.C.E. the Shang looked on the Chou as semibarbarous country cousins, a Shang king had made an alliance with the house of Chou by giving a kinswoman to the Chou leader in marriage and then conferring on him the title Chief of the West (see Map 2.3).

Parts of the earliest texts that have survived, the *Shu Ching* (Book of History) and *Shih Ching* (Book of Poetry) were written during the early Chou and described and justified their destruction of the Shang. The first undoubtedly historic leader of the Chou was

A Lesson in Politics: The Victor's Point of View

"Heaven then greatly ordered Wen Wang [King Wen] to destroy the great Yin [Shang] and greatly received its mandate; its state and people as a result became orderly." In contrast: "He [King Shou, last ruler of the Shang] was greatly excessive in wine. He did not think of ceasing his licentiousness. His heart was malign and he was unable to fear death. Crimes existed in the city of Shang and in the state of Yin, but for the extinction he had no anxiety. . . . Therefore heaven sent down destruction on Yin and had no mercy for Yin, it was due to his excesses. Heaven is not tyrannical, people themselves draw guilt upon themselves."*

Early Chou rulers used this theme frequently when they lectured their newly conquered subject peoples. They insisted that it was heaven's will that the people obey their new masters. In applying a moral dimension to rulership, however, the early Chou kings were also introducing a weapon with a double edge. In other words, heaven could just as easily turn against them if they failed to live up to high standards.

*James Less, trans., *The Chinese Classics: A Translation*, vol. 3.2: *The Book of History* (London: Trubner, 1865)

Map 2.3 Western Chou China, Eleventh to Ninth Centuries B.C.E. The victorious house of Chou divided its territories into fiefs and granted them to relatives, allies, and even surviving relatives of the previous Shang dynasty, while retaining only a core territory that it ruled directly as *chungkuo* or royal (central) domain. During its initial centuries, the Chou royal house was powerful and exercised control over the feudal vassals.

King Wen (the Cultivated or Accomplished), who laid plans to take on the Shang. The *Shu Ching* justified his actions as in obedience to heaven's wishes.

King Wen's son, King Wu (the Martial) defeated and destroyed the Shang. In accounts that clearly show a Chou bias, King Shou, the last Shang ruler, is described as deserving death in his burning palace at Yin as the dynasty fell to Chou troops. Wu died soon after his victory and left the throne to his young son. As the new king was only a boy, his uncle, the Duke of Chou, became regent. The duke completed the conquest of Shang lands and laid down the institutional basis for what became a long-lived dynasty. He lectured his nephew about the duties of the ruler, and the people about bowing to the will of heaven. When his nephew came of age, the duke handed him the reins of government and retired. Chinese have ever since celebrated King Wen, King Wu, and the Duke of Chou as three of their greatest rulers, and the early Chou as a Golden Age.

Several documentary sources contribute to our knowledge of the early Chou. Although Chou rulers also used divination to find out the will of heaven and of their ancestors, their oracle bones did not contain lengthy inscriptions. Instead, they cast long inscriptions on the surfaces of their bronze ceremonial vessels to document and report major events such as victories and the granting of fiefdoms to royal relatives or allies.

In addition to the information provided by the inscribed vessels, some documents in the *Shu Ching,* and some of the poems in the *Shih Ching,* we have also the *Li Chi,* or Book of Rituals, which describes the organization of the Chou government and the rituals, ceremonies, and etiquette of the Chou court. Tradition says that the *Li Chi* was written by the Duke of Chou. Since the duke, his brother, and his father were considered exemplary rulers by later generations, the government structure, rites, and ceremonies of the *Li Chi* are accepted as evidence of a golden age worthy of study and emulation.

Ruling a land approximately the size of modern France, Chou kings were unable to govern the entire kingdom effectively. They therefore devised a political and economic system called feudalism, which worked in the following way. The king ruled a royal domain directly; he also supervised a central government assisted by six ministers, each responsible for an aspect of administration. The king assigned the remaining land as fiefdoms to his relatives and created marriage ties with meritorious nonrelatives to whom he also awarded fiefdoms. These lords administered the king's laws in their domains, assisted by royal inspectors; they were expected to visit the royal court at prescribed intervals as demonstrations of their loyalty, to contribute substantive revenues to the king's treasury as well as symbolic tribute, and provide military contingents when needed. The lords received their titles at investiture ceremonies at the Chou ancestral temple, and their heirs had to be confirmed by the king. Each fiefdom was called a *kuo,* represented by a pictogram of a walled and guarded territory. The Chou royal domain, the heartland of the nation, was called *chung-kuo,* meaning central state. Later *chung-kuo* came to mean the Middle Kingdom or China.

Western Chou Society and Economy

The early Chou kings were city builders. Likewise the nobles built smaller towns from which they ruled their domains. The proliferation of archaeological sites throughout this long dynasty shows population growth and a trend toward urbanization. This trend was especially pronounced during the Eastern Chou; records show that at least seventy-eight cities were built between 722 and 480 B.C.E.

Hao, capital of Western Chou (situated in the Chou homeland), and Loyang, built by the Duke of Chou as a second capital to administer the eastern conquests (and later the capital of the Eastern Chou), would under various names be the sites of China's capital for the next 2,000 years. So many Chou sites have been identified and excavated that a picture of urban life of that time can be reconstructed. Most early Chou towns were administrative and ceremonial centers and were walled and fortified.

As under the Shang, rank and position were inherited, classifying people according to hereditary social classes. Atop the social ladder were the aristocrats, who ranged from members of the royal family downward through a graded nobility to the knights. The aristocrats were polygynous, organized into patrilineal clans, and kept careful genealogies of their families. Farmers were serfs, bound to the land they tilled, and transferred with the land at each investment of land to a new lord.

Late Chou writers recreated an idealized land tenure system that they attributed to the Duke of Chou and called the well-field system. The name comes from the pictograph for a well (for drawing water), which resembles a tick-tack-toe design, with nine components. Supposedly the early Chou villages were divided into units of eight families, each farming a plot. Villagers lived in a central plot, the ninth one, where presumably the well was located, and farmed it in common for the lord. Such a detailed land distribution was probably impossible for an ancient government. Yet the concept is so simple and just that it has inspired every reformer in China down to the twentieth century. It is another reason that later Chinese recall the early Chou as a golden age.

Unlike India, China had no priestly class after the Shang, because the kings and nobles officiated at their own ancestral sacrifices and ceremonies and appealed directly to their ancestors' spirits. Artisans congregated in towns to serve the needs of the governing nobles and lived in their separate quarters. They probably enjoyed a higher status than the serfs. As the population grew, so did trade and a merchant class. Merchants and artisans in Chou China, as in medieval Europe, had no defined place in the feudal hierarchy, as they had in the Indian caste system. Slavery declined and slaves did not play an important role economically. Few excavated Chou tombs contained remains of human sacrificial victims.

As in Shang times, the cowrie shell, strung in decimal units, was the big-denomination currency. Records tell of kings awarding lords ten to twenty strings of cowrie shells for meritorious service, and the notable event would be inscribed in a specially cast bronze vessel. Standard lengths of silk rolled in bolts, jade, pearls, dogs, horses, and measures of grain were other items mentioned as media of exchange. Metal coins did not come into use until the fifth century B.C.E.

By the sixth century B.C.E., a number of major improvements in agriculture had taken place and become widespread: irrigation, animal-drawn plows, crop rotation, and fertilization. During the fifth century, iron farming implements were introduced. These improvements revolutionized agriculture, increased food production, and led to rapid population growth. Chinese began to move into lands hitherto occupied by aboriginal tribes. Scarcity of land also brought about intensive use of what was available, and hunting and herding as a way of life were gradually abandoned in favor of agriculture.

Chou Religion

Religious practices of the Shang continued and evolved during the Chou period. Kings and commoners alike worshiped the spirits of their ancestors. All believed that in the life following death one needed essentially the same things one had needed on earth. Thus people buried food, drink, and other material goods, according to what they could afford, with the dead. Most of the commemorative bronze vessels cast and inscribed by Chou lords contained the following sentence: "May my sons and grandsons forever treasure and use this vessel."

The specialists or priests who had cast and inscribed oracle bones for Shang kings seem to have disappeared, and owing to the dominance of ancestor worship in religious life, they were not replaced by other priests or magicians. From king to commoner, each invoked his own ancestors for blessing and assistance, and every family's life centered on its ancestral temple or shrine. The practice of human and animal sacrifices to serve the powerful in death declined and died out and came to be denounced in later Chou writings.

Ti, the high god of the Shang, in time came to be identified with Tien or heaven, the chief Chou deity. Tien might have begun as the "great man," as its pictograph, clearly that of a man, would suggest. In time, Tien became a "Great Spirit," a vast, impersonal, supreme deity. The Chou ruler bore the title of *wang,* or king, as had the Shang sovereign. However, in accordance with the doctrine that the Chou rulers had inherited the mandate of heaven, the Chou monarch was also called Son of Heaven. This mandate theoretically could only be maintained by the king's descendants if they, too, carried out heaven's wishes. Otherwise, as had happened to the Shang, the mandate could be revoked and transferred to a more worthy recipient.

The king's ancestral temple was the center of affairs for the kingdom. All important state affairs took place there, and all events of consequence were reported to the king's ancestral spirits. Separate altars were constructed, each for a specific purpose; for example, one for worshiping heaven, another for worshiping earth and the soil, and still others in honor of various spirits. It was the king's responsibility to officiate at ceremonies in honor of heaven, the soil, and the various spirits at appropriate times.

The Eastern Chou

During the dynasty's first three centuries, the Chou rulers expanded their realm and united all of North China under their rule. However, with the passing of time, early kinship ties loosened, the kings' authority declined, and the feudal lords began to identify more with their hereditary territories than with the royal court. By the ninth century B.C.E. kings were experiencing difficulties in dealing with warlike barbarians in both the north and south, and regional lords were beginning to ignore the king's orders and to fight among themselves. In 771 B.C.E. the king was killed in a campaign against a northern tribe, and the western capital, Hao, was overrun. The remnant government fled eastward to Loyang, which had been made the second capital of the dynasty by the Duke of Chou.

This flight marked the end of the exercise of real power by the Chou kings, who reigned but no longer ruled; in time they were consulted only on such issues as genealogy and ritual. The period between 770 and 256 B.C.E. is called the Eastern Chou. The royal domain of the house of Chou was now tiny compared with the extent of the larger feudal states.

The Eastern Chou was an unstable and violent age, marked by many wars. Diplomacy was important, as evidenced by the many interstate alliances, often cemented by marriages. After 680 B.C.E. one ruler, but never the Chou king, was always recognized as the hegemon (*pa*), or predominant lord, who maintained some order. So many wars characterized the last 150 years of the Chou dynasty that it was called the Era of Warring States; during the period 132 states were finally reduced to one.

Since chariot warfare was unsuitable in the hilly northwest or in the wet Yangtze Valley, chariots were replaced by massed infantry and cavalry formations. If contemporary records can be believed, some states fielded infantry numbering in the hundreds of thousands. Military leaders who needed to counter the northern horse-riding nomads created cavalry units, which became the standard auxiliary of Chinese armies. By the fifth century more lethal iron weapons had replaced bronze ones. The crossbow, a Chinese invention that had a more powerful and longer draw than the composite bow and was worked by a precisely cast metal trigger mechanism, came into widespread use. Warfare became more destructive as a result.

In 256 B.C.E. King Cheng of the northwestern state of Ch'in eliminated the house of Chou; by 221 he had crushed the other warring states. In unifying all the land that had once been in the Chou domain, he renamed the national dynasty Ch'in, which became China. That story will be covered in the next chapter.

Eastern Chou Society and Economy

The system of family government that had characterized the early Chou no longer sufficed for an increasingly complex society. Hereditary posts declined, replaced by a system in which promotions were determined by merit. For the first time in Chinese history, men of commoner status rose to important political positions. Most of the new bureaucrats, however, were not commoners, but belonged to the lower aristocracy of knights, called *shih*. Others of the shih class who were disappointed in their quest for public office or who felt disaffected by the chaotic conditions became teachers and developed philosophies to correct the evils and problems of the age. Their ideas, too, will be explored in the next chapter.

Whereas early Chou cities were mostly administrative and religious centers created and inhabited by the feudal lords, their retainers, and the artisans who served their needs, many new cities built during the Eastern Chou were industrial and commercial centers.

The large number of cities built during the last centuries of the Chou underscores a growing population and the rise of the merchant class. Whereas the old cities had a wall that enclosed the lords' residences and government buildings, now a second enclosed area sometimes appeared for ordinary residential and commercial quarters. We have one population estimate for a city of the Warring States period: Lin-tzu, capital city of the state of Ch'i, in northeast China, had 70,000 households, or roughly a third of a million people. There are also accounts of Lin-tzu's bustling traffic, amusement quarters, street markets, and wholesale brokers' businesses.

Rulers eager to increase their revenues encouraged commerce. From the fifth century on, metal coinage became widespread. Inscriptions identified the states that issued them, and different sizes and weights distinguished the denominations. Early coins were shaped like miniature spades and knives. A round coin with a square hole in the center suitable for stringing was first issued by the state of Ch'in. After 221 B.C.E. the format became standard throughout China. Such coins strung in units of 1,000 remained the basic Chinese currency until the early twentieth century.

Three significant improvements in agriculture were made during the Eastern Chou. First was water control, vital for bringing land in the upper Yellow River valley under cultivation, controlling floods, and allowing irrigated rice cultivation in the upper

Yangtze plains. Engineers improved diking techniques, and systematic irrigation became widespread. Second was the introduction of fertilization and crop rotation. Third, and perhaps most important, was the introduction of iron farming implements, sharply increasing the amount of land an individual farmer could cultivate. Iron tools also facilitated the clearing of virgin lands. As the Chinese people expanded the area of land under cultivation and more intensely colonized the land they already occupied, the population reached sixty million by the end of the era. As the population grew, the feudal land tenure system of the early Chou was gradually replaced by that of freehold farmers. Rulers discovered that free farmers worked harder and produced more than land-bound serfs and also fought better to protect their interests. The northwest frontier state of Ch'in took the lead in ending the feudal land tenure and in building irrigation works. Both policies were key to the Ch'in's ultimate success in unifying China. By the end of the Chou dynasty, all the essential technological characteristics of traditional Chinese farming had been introduced.

Summary and Comparisons

This chapter has examined the early developments of two great Asian civilizations. Higher civilization in both India and China rose from indigenous Neolithic cultures in large river valleys. Major archaeological work, begun in both countries in the 1920s, has not only verified information from certain ancient texts but also added enormous quantities of new knowledge.

The Indus, or Harappan, civilization began in northwestern India before 2500 B.C.E. and flourished for more than a thousand years. Although a very advanced urban and trading culture, this civilization is classified as prehistoric because its pictographic script remains undeciphered. After a gradual decline caused by extensive flooding and deforestation, the weakened Indus civilization fell around 1500 B.C.E. to Indo-European nomads called Aryans, who came from the steppes of Eurasia. Not being city-dwellers, the Aryans abandoned the Indus cities, settled in the Indus valley, and gradually migrated eastward to the Gangetic plain. They subjugated the darker-skinned indigenous people and developed a hierarchy of conquering and conquered peoples, which we call the caste system. The Rig-Veda, the most sacred text of the Aryans and of later Hinduism, contains hymns alluding to the Aryan conquest. It and other Vedas were written down in an Indo-European language called Sanskrit between 1000 and 500 B.C.E.

The millennium between approximately 1500 and 500 B.C.E. is divided into the Early and Late Vedic Ages because of marked cultural differences between the two periods. Notably, Aryan society became predominantly agricultural during the late Vedic Age, and the economy became specialized and commercial. Religious changes included the emergence of new deities and the ideas of karma and reincarnation. The search for new answers to life's questions led to the writing of the Upanishads, essays on the nature of human destiny. In time the new deities and the Upanishads were incorporated into Hinduism.

CHRONOLOGY

2500 B.C.E.	Urban civilization in the Indus Valley
	Era of Chinese culture heroes
	Mythical Hsia dynasty in China
2000	
1500	Tang the Successful establishes the Shang dynasty
	Aryans and other factors destroy Indus civilization
	Early Vedic Age
	Earliest extant Chinese writing
	Anyang capital of Shang China
	Kings Wen and Wu establish Chou dynasty
	Duke of Chou
1000	Books of Poetry, History, Rites, Change
	Rig-Veda
	Late Vedic Age
	Eastern Chou
	Spring and Autumn era
	Upanishads written in India
500	Iron weapons, crossbow, metal tools, and coins
	Warring States era
	Eight Chapters
200	

China's first dynasty, the Shang (1766–1122 B.C.E.), was centered in the Yellow River valley. Shang civilization is classified as historic because of writing found incised on tortoise shells and scapula bones of large animals used for divination by Shang kings. These written remains tell us much about Shang government, society, and beliefs. The modern Chinese language is directly descended from the Shang script.

The most beautiful objects from the Shang are bronze vessels, used in rites of ancestor worship and buried in royal and aristocratic tombs. They were made by the piece mold method, unique to China. Bronzesmiths and other craftsmen evidently enjoyed higher status than serfs, who farmed the land.

In 1122 B.C.E., the Shang dynasty ended, overthrown by the Chou, who continued beliefs and institutions as they found them, leaving Chinese civilization essentially unchanged. The Chou conquest expanded the Chinese heartland geographically to include all of the Yellow River valley and parts of the Yangtze River valley. The gradual decline of the house of Chou after 771 B.C.E. resulted in political turmoil as powerful feudal lords competed for supremacy and the right to impose a national dynasty on a reunified land.

There are striking similarities between the first great civilizations of India and China. Both were rooted in indigenous Neolithic cultures; both were riverine, urban, literate, and metal working; and both invented pictographic written scripts. However, because the extensive written remains of the Shang have been deciphered, we know much more about this civilization than that of the Indus Valley, where the scanty extant engravings on seals are not yet understood. Our ability to decode Shang documents makes it a historic civilization, while the Indus remains prehistoric. Shang written materials give us key information about Shang kings and their relations to one another, their gods, and their worship. In contrast, we know nothing for certain about the Indus government or religion.

Both the Indus people and the Shang were excellent builders. Because the Indus buildings were constructed with bricks, there are extensive physical remains of Indus cities, while little survives of the wood and tamped-earth structures of the Shang. The Indus people buried their dead carefully in cemeteries, but without elaborate grave goods. The Aryans cremated their dead, a practice that continued in India, leaving archaeologists with few material remains. On the other hand, the Shang and Chou peoples have left tombs that are treasure troves because of the Chinese custom of burying the dead sumptuously with everything they might need in the next world.

Similarly, both peoples traded far afield, the Indus people with the older Mesopotamian civilization, where documents mention people we infer to be from the Indus region. There is no evidence yet that the Vedic peoples carried on international trade. Both the Shang and Chou traded with Southeast and Central Asia, but their preliterate trading partners left no written records.

Social organization differed sharply in India and China. We cannot reconstruct social patterns in the Indus culture without written evidence, but we know that social distinctions in India became sharper as the Vedic Age progressed, apparently owing to racial distinctions between the conquering Aryans and the indigenous dasas. The Chinese, on the other hand, were racially homogeneous, which meant a gradual erasing of hereditary distinctions by the late Chou dynasty.

Both the Indus Empire and the Shang dynasty came to violent ends. While the Indo-Aryan conquerors had a different culture from the conquered Indus people, on whom they imposed a new language, religion, and social organization, the Chou who overthrew the Shang shared the same traditions, beliefs, and written language, which continued to evolve uninterrupted by political change. Chou bronze wares followed the shapes and decorations of pieces made under the Shang, showing shared artistic traditions and rituals. Thus the transition from one dynasty to another was much less disruptive in China than in India.

By the end of the Vedic Age in India and the Chou dynasty in China, each civilization had achieved a degree of homogeneity. Among Indians, homogeneity was based on shared religious beliefs, social organization, and (among north Indians) languages derived from Sanskrit. Among Chinese, a common historical and political tradition, writing, and ancestor worship created cohesiveness. Although India had no tradition of political unity, in China such unity was indelibly rooted in the earliest folk memory.

Selected Sources

Items indicated with an asterisk (*) are available in paperback.

*Basham, A. L. *The Wonder That Was India*. 1954. Many maps and photos and a well-organized text make this book a pleasure to read.

————, ed. *Cultural History of India*. 1969. Numerous experts contributed to this informative book.

*Chang Kwang-chih. *The Archaeology of Ancient China*. 4th ed. 1986. The most authoritative book on the subject. Many photos, illustrations, maps, and charts make it interesting and informative.

————. *Shang Civilization*. 1980. Professor Chang has pieced together a fascinating jigsaw puzzle from archaeological and textual evidence of China's first historic dynasty.

*————, ed. *Food in Chinese Culture: Anthropological and Historical Perspectives*. 1977. A storehouse of interesting information.

Cheng Te-k'un. *Archaeology in China*. Vol. I: *Prehistoric China*. 1986. A concise and clear account, with photos, charts, and maps.

————. *Archaeology in China*. Vol. II: *Shang China*. 1960. Profusely illustrated with drawings and photos, this comprehensive book examines what archaeologists have learned about the Shang.

————. *Archaeology in China*. Vol. III: *Chou China*. 1963. This book is as authoritative as Professor Cheng's other books in the series.

*de Bary, William T., ed. *Sources of Chinese Tradition*. Vol. I. 1960. A source book of readings.

*————, ed. *Sources of Indian Tradition*. Vol. I. 1958. A source book of readings with helpful introductions.

Fairservice, Walter A., Jr. *The Roots of Ancient India*. 1971. A comprehensive survey of India from the earliest humans to the Aryan invasion.

Feuerstein, Georg, Subash Kak, and David Frawley. *In Search of the Cradle of Civilization*. 1995. Provocative new studies and interpretations regarding ancient India.

Gupta, S. P., ed. *The "Lost" Sarasvati and Indus Civilizations*. 1995. Includes very recent scholarship by many experts.

*Hsu Cho-yun. *Ancient China in Transition, An Analysis of Social Mobility, 722–222 B.C.* 1965. A brief, interesting account.

Ke Yuan. *Dragons and Dynasties: An Introduction to Chinese Mythology*. 1993. Good stories, well explained.

Li, Chi. *Anyang*. 1977. Li supervised the first excavation of Anyang, the last Shang capital, during the 1920s and 1930s.

Majumdar, R. C. *Ancient India*. 1968. A clearly written history of India up to about 1200 C.E.

————. *Concise History of Ancient India*. 3 vols. 1977. An authoritative work.

Rawson, Jessica, ed. *Mysteries of Ancient China: New Discoveries of the Early Dynasties*. 1996. The first account in English of over 200 new archaeological discoveries in China. Richly illustrated.

Smith, Brian K. *Classifying the Universe: The Ancient Indian Varna System and the Origins of Caste*. 1994. A scholarly book on the role of caste in ancient Indian religion and culture.

Spear, Percival, ed. *The Oxford History of India*. 4th ed. 1981. An authoritative book written by many experts and updated with new information.

*Temple, Robert. *The Genius of China: 3,000 Years of Science, Discovery and Invention*. 1986. Concise, well-written, and beautifully illustrated, this book summarizes China's scientific contributions.

*Thapar, Romila. *A History of India*. Vol 1. 1968. A good, concise history from the beginning of Indian civilization to the sixteenth century.

Wagner, Donald B. *Iron and Steel in Ancient China*. 1993. Recent archaeological finds have been incorporated into this study of the development of an important technology.

Watson, William. *Early Civilization in China*. 1966. Lavishly illustrated and clearly written, this book traces the evolution of humans in China from Paleolithic times to the end of the Chou.

Wheeler, Mortimer. *The Indus Civilization: Supplementary Volume to the Cambridge History of India*. 3d ed. 1968. Written by the man who supervised the excavation of Harappa and other sites, with many photos and illustrations.

 Additional resources, exercises, and Internet links related to this chapter are available at the Book Companion Web site: http://history.wadsworth.com/upshurcompact4/

Comparative Essay 2
Great Faiths and Philosophies

And the angel of the Lord called unto Abraham . . . and said, "By myself have I sworn, says the Lord, for because you have done this thing, and have not withheld your son, your only son [Isaac]: That in blessing I will bless you, and in multiplying I will multiply your seed as the stars of the heaven, and as the sand which is upon the sea shore; and your seed shall possess the gate of his enemies; And in your seed shall all the nations of the earth be blessed; because you have obeyed my voice."
King James Version of the Holy Bible, Genesis, Chapter 22, with slight changes.

* * * * *

Homer and Hesiod have ascribed to the gods everything shameful and reprehensible among mankind: theft, adultery, and mutual deception. . . .
Xenophanes

* * * * *

Regarding the gods, I can't tell if they exist or not, nor what they look like, for many things preclude such knowledge: the obscurity of the subject, and the brevity of our lives.
Protagoras

* * * * *

We don't know yet how to serve men, how can we know about serving spirits? . . .
    Devote yourself to the proper demands of the people, respect the ghosts and spirits but keep them at a distance—this may be called wisdom.
Confucius

Although all peoples across the globe have believed in some supernatural power over the universe, their conceptions of that power have varied. The passages quoted above show some of these differing attitudes. Thus, in Judaism an all-powerful, monotheistic deity makes a promise to Abraham as the representative of the Hebrew people. In Greek religion, by contrast, polytheistic deities were often depicted as exhibiting the same vices and virtues as mere humans. This led certain Greek philosophers to skepticism about the existence, or at any rate our conception, of such humanlike gods. On the other hand, though the Chinese philosopher Confucius did not question the existence of the gods, he did recommend keeping a safe distance from them.

By the fifth century B.C.E., and even earlier in Palestine, a number of great religious and philosophical systems had evolved. Jews, Greeks, Indians, and Chinese learned from such remarkable thinkers as the Hebrew prophets, Socrates, Gautama Buddha, and Confucius.

What made these beliefs so appealing and durable? The primary function of religions and philosophies is to explain the meaning of human life and death and to find order in the universe. Religion and philosophy follow different paths and answer somewhat different human needs. Religions demand faith and offer supernatural explanations for the human condition in this life and beyond. Philosophies, on the other hand, are concerned with existing life and society and seek explanations through rational inquiry. In some of the cultures discussed in Chapter 3, many religions and philosophies competed for allegiance, and in the crucible of time only the most useful and appealing survived. For example, in China the era between 600 and 300 B.C.E. is called "The Hundred Schools"; out of this competition Confucianism eventually emerged triumphant.

Most early humans were awed by inexplicable occurrences in life and nature. They could not account for such rhythms of nature as the rising and setting of the sun, the cycle of the seasons, meteorological events, the mystery of birth, aging, and death. Unable to explain these events, people attributed them to supernatural powers.

The belief that there was a power or powers beyond human control caused fear and anxiety, and the desire to ensure right relations with that power. The belief systems described here tried to assuage or lessen the anxieties that earlier faiths had failed to dispel. The great religions provided a sense of harmony and spiritual well-being by spelling out the terms for a right relationship with the divine. They taught their adherents to visualize the divine power as a person—for example, Buddha, Vishnu, and Yahweh— amenable to the supplications of human beings. The faithful believed they could communicate with the deity by prayer and ritual to ensure harmony and good fortune. The Jews, for example, codified their relationship with Yahweh through a covenant or pact. In return for obedience to Him, Yahweh promised His worshipers prosperity and protection.

Greek philosophy and Confucian teaching, on the other hand, stressed universal patterns that could be grasped by human reason and understanding. Early Greek philosopher-scientists sought to explain the mystery of the universe and its workings by observation and rational analysis rather than through supernatural explanations. A knowledge of these patterns would allow people to order their lives in accord with them.

The major religions and philosophies survived because they offered codes of conduct and provided workable ethical bases for society. Their teachings were eventually codified in authoritative scriptures or canons. The Hebrew scriptures, the Buddhist canons, the Confucian Classics, the Taoist Tao-te Ching, and the Hindu Upanishads are among such guidebooks for right living. Although no Greek philosophical text attained the status of a sacred book, Greek philosophers were also concerned with questions of ethical conduct, in part because they found that traditional Greek religion lacked moral consistency. The lasting Greek contribution was thus not a code of religious beliefs, but rather a conviction that human reason, exercised in careful observation and logical argumentation, might discover the laws that both govern the order of nature (physics) and provide the key for right living (ethics).

In summary, these religious and philosophical systems gave a strong sense of security and purpose to the men and women who embraced them, and they provided effective guidance for a meaningful existence. Further, each one contained a distinctive mixture of precepts and ethical principles that exerted an especially powerful psychological attraction for its adherents.

We may ask why so many great belief systems arose across two continents in the same general time span. There is no definitive answer to this question. However, during this period, India, China, Greece, and Palestine all experienced profound social, economic, and political changes. These changes and the insecurities they generated stimulated philosophers and religious leaders to revise old, no-longer-sufficient philosophical and religious systems or to develop new ones. The resulting combinations of beliefs, practices, and perspectives obviously met very basic psychological and spiritual needs. Along with two later religions, Christianity and Islam, which shared many of the same characteristics as those discussed here, the belief systems discussed in Chapter 3 continue to be profoundly influential up to the present day.

3

The Flowering of Great Faiths and Philosophies

• Civilization in Palestine and Phoenicia •

• Classical Greek Civilization •

• The Rise of Buddhism and Jainism in India •

• China: Confucianism, Taoism, and Legalism •

• Summary and Comparisons •

Strange, indeed, would be my conduct, O men of Athens, if I who, when I was ordered by the generals whom you chose to command me at [the battles of] Potidaea and Amphipolis and Delium, remained where they placed me, like any other man, facing death—if now, when . . . God orders me to fulfill the philosopher's mission of searching into myself and other men, I were to desert my post through fear of death, or any other fear. . . .

I might justly be arraigned in court for denying the existence of the gods, if I disobeyed the oracle [of Apollo] because I was afraid of death, fancying that I was wise when I was not wise. . . . No one knows whether death, which men in their fear apprehend to be the greatest evil, may not be the greatest good. . . . But I do know that injustice and disobedience to a better, whether God or man, is evil and dishonourable. . . . Therefore if you [were to] let me go now, and . . . if you [were to] say to me,

"Socrates, this time we will not mind [your accusers] and you shall be let off, but upon one condition, that you are not to enquire and speculate in this way any more, and that if you are caught doing so again you shall die," . . . I would reply:

"Men of Athens, I honour and love you; but I shall obey God rather than you, and while I have life and strength I shall never cease from the practice and teaching of philosophy, exhorting any one whom I meet and saying . . .

'You, my friend,—a citizen of the great and mighty and wise city of Athens,—are you not ashamed of heaping up the greatest amount of money and honour and reputation, and caring so little about wisdom and truth and the greatest improvement of the soul, which you never regard or heed at all?'" . . .

And I shall repeat the same words to every one whom I meet. . . . For know that this is the command of God; and I believe that no greater good has ever happened in the state than my service to the God. For I do nothing but go about persuading you all, old and young alike, not to take thought for your persons or your properties, but first and chiefly to care about the greatest improvement of the soul.*

*Plato, Apology (trans. Benjamin Jowett).

In 399 B.C.E., the philosopher Socrates was tried on charges of atheism and of corrupting the youth of Athens. In his speech defending himself against these charges, Socrates offered the justification above for living a life of intellectual inquiry and urging others to do the same.

Elsewhere in this defense speech, Socrates says, "the unexamined life is not worth living." Indeed, Socrates lived his life, and ultimately died, in an unwavering commitment to the principles expressed in his speech. In this chapter, we will consider several cultures across the Eurasian continent during the first millennium B.C.E. that first and chiefly cared about the soul. The Hebrews of Palestine, the Greeks of many city-states, the Indians of the Late Vedic Age, and the Chinese of the Eastern Chou dynasty developed religions and philosophies that influenced future generations both within and well beyond their original homelands.

As stated in the essay "Great Faiths and Philosophies," religions and philosophies based on the archaic past already permeated and gave structure to ancient civilizations. However, during the middle of the first millennium B.C.E., religious and philosophical innovators challenged, and sometimes discarded, old values and beliefs at critical junctures when they proved inadequate or outdated. In the process new religions, philosophies, and systems of government emerged.

This chapter begins with a study of the evolution of the world's first great monotheistic faith: Judaism. The Hebrews' ethical religion was based on a covenant or pact with God that would sustain them through great adversities. Judaism, because of its influence on Christianity and Islam, also represents how a people small in numbers can have more long-term influence in history than many huge empires.

Greek culture flourished with astonishing inventiveness in philosophy, government, the sciences, and the arts among the city-states of mainland and island Greece. In politics, the world is indebted to Greece, above all, for participatory government. Like the Hebrews, the Greeks were not numerous and established no great empires. Again like the Hebrews, their contribution to the human spirit far outpaced their political sway and would guide and inspire much of humanity to the present.

In India, the mid-period of the first millennium B.C.E. not only produced new philosophies that altered the direction of the Vedic religion (discussed in the previous chapter), but also developed two new religions: Buddhism and Jainism. Buddhism became a universal religion and gave ethical meaning and guidance to countless millions across South, East, and Southeast Asia. It challenged Vedism/Hinduism in India, brought higher civilization to Southeast Asia, and was so influential even in a highly civilized land such as China that Chinese civilization can be divided by this encounter into the pre- and post-Buddhist eras.

The centuries that produced Buddhism and Jainism in India produced new philosophies in China. Of the many, or Hundred Schools of philosophies, that developed in China during this era, two have dominated Chinese thought to the present: Confucianism and Taoism. Confucianism sought to instill in people the values of virtue, love, humanity, and duty to bring about a golden age. Taoism taught escape from a chaotic and immoral world. These two philosophies complemented each other. During the closing centuries of the first millennium, it was the amoral philosophy called Legalism that provided the discipline and force that restored unity to divided China.

Civilization in Palestine and Phoenicia

The Lord said to Abram, "Go forth from your native land and from your father's house to the land that I will show you.
I will make of you a great nation,
And I will bless you;
I will make your name great,
And you shall be a blessing.
I will bless those who bless you
And curse him that curses you;
And all the families of the earth
Shall bless themselves by you."
Abram went forth as the Lord had commanded him.*

*Genesis 12:1–4, from *Tanakh: A New Translation of the Holy Scriptures according to the Traditional Hebrew Text* (Philadelphia: Jewish Publication Society, 1985), p. 18.

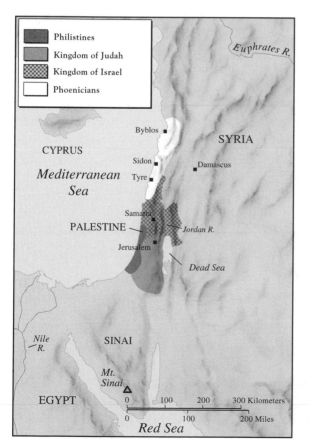

Map 3.1 Ancient Palestine. This map shows the northern and southern kingdoms of the ancient Hebrews and the adjacent areas inhabited by the Phoenicians and Philistines.

Belief in a covenant, or special arrangement with God, pervades Hebrew scriptures and marks a crucial ethical departure from the polytheistic systems of Mesopotamia, Egypt, and Greece. In the developed Hebrew view, one and only one God existed; and this God looked with special love upon the men and women who worshiped him and duly obeyed his laws. Monotheism (belief in only one God) made possible a self-consistent code of ethics. The Hebrew people made their chief contribution to civilization in religion, not in politics or military conquest.

The part of West Asia known as Syria-Palestine and as Canaan was not the center of any major kingdom or empire; it was, however, the midpoint on the route of conquerors from the powerful states of Egypt or Mesopotamia marching to attack each other. Its land was less productive agriculturally than the fertile river valleys that were home to powerful nations elsewhere in West Asia. Nonetheless, two very important cultural groups, the Israelites and the Phoenicians, appeared in this region. The Israelites conceived a religious faith that has exercised a lasting influence on humankind. The Phoenicians created the alphabet and spread it with their trade throughout the Mediterranean world and beyond.

Israelite Political History

In the historical big picture, the Hebrews were neither numerous nor politically dominant. In fact, they were often victimized by powerful neighbors. Their monotheism and their recurrent covenants with God, however, made them uniquely important in the history of civilization.

From about 2000 B.C.E. onward, the Semitic-speaking Hebrews moved from the surrounding deserts of Syria and Arabia, where they had subsisted as nomads, into less desolate regions of West Asia. According to their records, one contingent, led by Abraham, migrated from Ur in Babylonia to Canaan (Palestine). Later, sometime before 1600, certain Israelites (so called from Israel, another name for Jacob, Abraham's grandson) went to Egypt to avoid famine in Palestine; there they suffered oppression and fled in a mass exodus around 1300, under the leadership of Moses, who united his followers in the worship of God. Once again in Palestine, the Israelites exchanged a nomadic for an agricultural mode of existence, engaging in military actions to acquire and defend territory. In time, they intermingled with the original population and adopted various aspects of Canaanite culture, including the institution of private ownership of property. The Israelites succeeded in gaining a hold on territory in Palestine, an area not then controlled by any powerful state. After about 1200, however, another invading people, the Philistines, also entered the region, at first along the coast, but then, by force of arms, farther inland as well. The Philistines were militarily more advanced than their new Canaanite and Israelite neighbors, with better organization and superior (iron) weaponry.

As often happens in history, the Israelites responded to the threat of a strong external opponent by moving toward greater internal unity. During the period 1025–928 B.C.E., the twelve tribes of Israel were joined in a united monarchy under three successive king-generals. The first king of Israel, Saul (reigned 1025–1004), did not attain the needed full cooperation of the various tribes and achieved little before meeting his death in bat-

The British Museum

Relief Sculpture from the Palace of Sennacherib. This sculpture from the royal palace at Nineveh shows captive Israelites being presented to the Assyrian king, Sennacherib (seated on throne), in 701 B.C.E.

tle at Gilboa against the Philistines. His successor, David (reigned 1004–965), gained both victory on the battlefield and political harmony within the united kingdom. He ended the threat posed by the Philistines, ultimately restricting them to the area of five towns in the coastal region near Gaza. David then annexed the remaining Canaanite areas and established a royal capital at Jerusalem, making that city the political, military, and religious center of his realm. He forged strong ties with Phoenicia, thereby giving Israel access to the important ports of Tyre and Sidon, through which Israelite olive oil and grain could be traded for cedar, copper, and various luxury materials such as ivory and gold. The economic and political prosperity continued in the reign of David's son, Solomon (reigned 965–928 B.C.E.), who spent lavishly on public construction projects. He built a magnificent temple and royal palace complex at Jerusalem and enlarged the fortifications begun by David. Such projects necessitated unpopular measures, specifically, heavy taxation and forced labor (already begun in the reign of David). After Solomon's death, the Israelites could no longer endure a West Asian–style royal autocracy, and the kingdom (an area about the size of New Jersey) soon split into two parts: Israel in the north and Judah in the south. Because of the resulting division of resources and manpower, the Israelites eventually lost territories outside Palestine and became increasingly vulnerable to attacks by external foes.

In 722 B.C.E., the expanding Assyrian Empire absorbed Israel, whose people were scattered, being remembered in history as the "ten lost tribes." The Chaldean king Nebuchadnezzar conquered Judah in 597 B.C.E. In 586 Jerusalem was destroyed, and many of its leading citizens were deported to Babylon, marking the end of the period of the

First Temple. Although the Persian ruler Cyrus allowed the Jews (another name for Hebrews, derived from the name Judah) to return to Jerusalem after his conquest in 539, many chose to stay in Babylonia. The returnees completed a new temple—with Persian approval—in 516. This was the beginning of the period of the Second Temple. Palestine remained under Persian control till the conquest of Alexander the Great in 332. It was thereafter absorbed by various Hellenistic kingdoms. Finally, after a last period of independence, it succumbed to the Roman Empire in 63 B.C.E.

Judaism

The religious history of ancient Israel is important out of all proportion to its political history. The various conquerors of Israel and Judah inflicted massacres, destroyed cities and sanctuaries, and imposed the misery of exile. Whatever their condition, however, the Jews gradually managed to formulate and cling to a monotheistic religious tradition that differed notably from the polytheisms of Mesopotamia, Egypt, India, or China.

For this monotheism we have the evidence of a truly remarkable body of literature, the *Tanakh* (the Holy Scriptures, the first five books of which are called the *Torah*), known to Christians as the Old Testament. These writings comprise two-thirds of "the Book" or Bible (Greek *biblos*) that has codified Judaeo-Christian tradition throughout Western civilization. Tanakh is both a religious text and a rich work of literature. It is unique among West Asian documents in giving such a thorough description of its composers' early history and in relating that history to a particular system of religious beliefs.

The most distinctive aspect of those beliefs is monotheism. Hebrew monotheism was characterized by an elaborate code of moral behavior. Unlike the gods of the West Asian and later Greco-Roman polytheisms, the Hebrew God presented men and women with a consistent code of morality and dictated a covenant under which humans would be rewarded for abiding by that code. The Ten Commandments of the Book of Exodus (20:1–17) are only its essence: Orthodox Judaism contains 613 commandments in the Law.

By contrast, the gods of Egypt and Mesopotamia set out no coherently formulated standards of behavior. Whatever ethical imperatives these deities stood for were vague and subject to suspension or cancellation. Thus mortals, even a hero like Gilgamesh, suffered from a deep-seated insecurity, often finding themselves in the double bind of being punished by one god for obeying another. Sometimes, like the polytheistic deities, the Lord God could be vengeful and jealous as well as paternally nurturing. His ways could be hard to fathom, as in the story of the wealthy and virtuous hero of Tanakh's Book of Job, who is overwhelmed by terrible misfortunes that he seems not to deserve. Nonetheless, Judaism normally furnished its followers with a comprehensive code of ethics by which to live their lives. It offered the assurance that the supreme creator looked on human beings as intrinsically valuable, not as mere playthings of the deities. Neither the Greeks nor the Romans, despite their emphasis on the potentials and achievements of humankind, were to formulate a theology that so emphasized the worth of every individual in the eyes of God.

Despite their code, the Jews, both individually and as a nation, broke the Law and disobeyed their God over and over in scriptural accounts. Moreover, in evolving their monotheistic religion, the Israelites were not insulated from the religious influences of their West Asian neighbors. Elijah, for example, had to prove to his people the superiority of their God to the Canaanite god Baal. Other prophets, like Amos, chastised the Jews for their shortcomings and, like Jeremiah, foresaw the coming of divine punishment in the guise of Babylonian conquest. During the exile in Babylon (586–539 B.C.E.), the "second Isaiah" and Ezekiel sang the praises of the one God and of his chosen people, urging repentance and holding out hope for a return to the promised land and a restoration of the temple at Jerusalem.

Judaic scriptures reflect the attitudes of a rigidly patriarchal society. Women's roles were restricted and their moral worth was often suspect. In part, this stemmed from the struggle of monotheistic Judaism against the polytheistic worship of Canaanite deities, especially the popular fertility-goddess Asherah. Judaism mandated the exclusive worship of a male Father-God, a worship eventually organized and administered by a strictly male priestly caste. Women could, of course, pray and study the scriptures, but one of the principal religious responsibilities of parents was to teach the Torah only to sons. When formal education was instituted in ancient Israel, it was limited to males.

The Book of Genesis describes the first woman, Eve, as created from the rib of the first man, Adam. She is thus a secondary creation, somehow inferior to the original

The Return from Babylon: Free at Last

The Israelites . . . celebrated the dedication of the House of God with joy. And they sacrificed for the dedication of this House of God one hundred bulls, two hundred rams, four hundred lambs, and twelve goats as a purification offering for all of Israel. . . . They appointed the priests in their courses and the Levites in their divisions for the service of God in Jerusalem, according to the prescription in the Book of Moses.

The returned exiles celebrated the Passover on the fourteenth day of the first month, for the priests and Levites had purified themselves to a man; they were all pure. They slaughtered the Passover offering for all the returned exiles, and for their brother priests and for themselves. The children of Israel who had returned from exile, together with all who had joined them . . . to worship the Lord God of Israel, ate of it. They joyfully celebrated the Feast of Unleavened Bread for seven days, for the Lord had given them cause for joy by inclining the heart of the Assyrian king [Darius] toward them so as to give them support in the work of the House of God, the God of Israel.*

This passage from the Book of Ezra recounts the joy of those former inhabitants of Judah who had returned from the Babylonian Captivity and restored the destroyed temple at Jerusalem. The theme of exile and return is one of special pathos and power in the history and religion of the Jews. The Passover feast (celebrating the "passing over" of the homes of the Israelites when the firstborn of the Egyptians were slain) was itself a commemoration of another time of exodus or release from foreign captivity (in Egypt). Other exiles, however, like the ten lost tribes, were not so fortunate. And there would be further occasions of dispersal from the promised land, in particular, the great Diaspora ("scattering") after the Roman destruction of Jerusalem in 70 C.E. Still, somehow the God of the Israelites seemed to restore his chosen ones, particularly if they had obeyed his prophets (the word means chiefly "teacher") by repenting their transgressions of his laws. In the passage quoted here, the Lord is credited with controlling the mind of king Darius.

**Ezra 6:16–22, from Tanakh: A New Translation of the Holy Scriptures according to the Traditional Hebrew Text (Philadelphia: Jewish Publication Society, 1985), pp. 1500–1501.*

male. So, too, Eve's role as the first to sin by eating of the forbidden fruit has often been interpreted as owing to the inherent weakness of the female sex. Though the scriptures do contain stories of virtuous and heroic women, such as Deborah, the prophetess and judge who helped deliver Israel from Canaanite oppression in the Book of Judges, the overall tone of Hebrew tradition and scripture is patriarchal.

The canonical (official) books of Tanakh were assembled between 400 and about 150 B.C.E. and constitute one of the most influential legacies of ancient West Asia. In religious thought, the Hebrews far outstripped their materially more fortunate neighbors. Judaism was to survive as a tremendously influential world religion, both in and of itself and as a major element in the evolution of Christianity and Islam.

The Phoenicians: Catalysts of Culture

By the early first millennium, the Phoenicians had emerged in a coastal strip about the size of Connecticut west of the Lebanon mountains and north of Palestine (see Map 3.1). Neither innovators nor originators of culture, the Phoenicians did facilitate its spread, especially between about 1000 and 700 B.C.E. They were the best mariners and traders of the ancient world, with major home ports at Tyre, Sidon, Berytus (modern Beirut), and Byblos. From these, Phoenician sailors and merchants fanned out to all the centers of commerce in the eastern Mediterranean and eventually even as far away as modern Spain and Great Britain (called the Tin Islands after the rich sources of that rare metal mined in Cornwall). This enabled them to maintain their civilized way of life despite the scarcity of fertile soil in their sector of West Asia. Imports included foodstuffs and raw materials such as grain and metals (for example, copper from Cyprus); exported were timber (cedar in particular) and various manufactured goods, including textiles, bronze and ivory artifacts, and a famous purple dye extracted from the shellfish of the region. On the north coast of Africa, in modern Tunisia, they founded Carthage, a prosperous city that later challenged Rome for control of the western Mediterranean.

The most enduring Phoenician gift to civilization, however, was the alphabet. This script, consisting of a small number of easily learned consonant signs, enormously facilitated the spread of literacy and cultural development. The actual characters seem to have descended from a script used at the town of Byblos. They were simpler to learn and to use than, for example, the more cumbersome and difficult Egyptian hieroglyphics. After 1500 B.C.E. the Phoenicians spread alphabetic writing principally through trade contacts. By the eighth century the Greeks had borrowed it, adding signs to represent vowels. They in turn passed it on to the Romans via the Etruscans. The Greek and Roman alphabets were subsequently adopted by virtually all modern European languages.

Classical Greek Civilization

I declare that our city is an education to Greece, and I declare that in my opinion each single one of our citizens, in all the manifold aspects of life, is able to show himself the rightful lord and owner of his own person, and do this, moreover, with exceptional grace and exceptional versatility. . . . Athens, alone of the states we know, comes to her testing time in a greatness that surpasses what was imagined *of her. . . . Mighty indeed are the marks and monuments of our empire which we have left. Future ages will wonder at us, as the present age wonders at us now. . . . For our adventurous spirit has forced an entry into every sea and into every land; and everywhere we have left behind us everlasting memorials of good done to our friends or suffering inflicted on our enemies.**

*Thucydides, History of the Peloponnesian War, trans. R. Warner (Harmondsworth: Penguin, 1954; rev. 1972), pp. 147–148.

In this speech in honor of war dead in 430 B.C.E., the great Athenian statesman and general Pericles patriotically celebrated the civil and military accomplishments of his beloved Athens, assessing with prophetic insight their impression on posterity. The stage for these accomplishments was set earlier, in the Archaic Age, when the Greeks enjoyed freedom from outside interference. Beginning about 500 B.C.E., however, the Greek city-states faced a dire threat from the Persian Empire, which forced the Greek states for once to stand united. Greek victory in that conflict inaugurated a period of brilliant cultural and political achievement, particularly at Athens. Politically, the Persian wars also resulted in the rise and triumph of the Athenian Empire in the era of Periclean Athens. The fifth century closed with the long, debilitating struggle known as the Peloponnesian War, which ended with the triumph of Athens' major rival, Sparta.

The Archaic Revival: New Patterns of Government

In the archaic period (c. 800–c. 500 B.C.E.), renewed contact with West Asia revived Greek architecture, metallurgy, pottery and textile production, and trade. Sea routes linked Greece with many points on the Mediterranean and Black Seas. The Phoenician alphabet was adapted for use in transcribing Greek, and the practice of coining money was adopted from Lydia (a kingdom in Asia Minor); both greatly expedited commercial activities.

In the Greek homelands, however, increasing population and relatively unproductive soil led to starvation, foreclosure, and enslavement for debt. One remedy was to acquire new land. Between 750 and 550 B.C.E., thousands of Greek colonists emigrated to Sicily, southern Italy, southern France, and North Africa, bringing Greek culture to the western Mediterranean. Other Greeks emigrated northward to Thrace, Macedon, and the coasts of the Black Sea. The new settlements were independent states, not units within a unified empire such as the Romans later fashioned.

The Greek city-state, or *polis* (compare English "political"), a city and its immediate rural environs, usually no more than a few hundred square miles, was the setting for momentous experiments in government. Citizen input into domestic and foreign policy set the *polis* off sharply from its West Asian predecessors, where strong monarchies ceded few rights to the common individual. In the early archaic period, most Greek city-states were governed by an aristocratic oligarchy (small ruling elite). After 675 B.C.E., however, changes in military affairs brought changes in government. Greek soldiers now used new advanced, standardized equipment and were carefully drilled and deployed in a phalanx or mass formation of *hoplites* (heavy-armed foot soldiers). The success of this efficient new infantry made all city-states quickly realize that a force of hoplites—the larger the

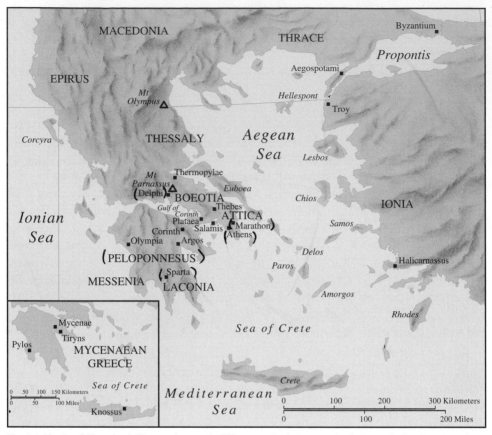

Map 3.2 The Greek Homeland. This map shows major fifth-century Greek city-states, battle sites, and cultural centers in the Balkan Peninsula and on the islands and shores of the Aegean Sea.

better—was indispensable for "national security." Ordinary citizens, mainly farmers, serving in the hoplite army, displaced aristocratic cavalry as the backbone of the military.

Social and political changes rapidly ensued, as the hoplites sought economic advantages and a voice in government befitting their military importance. They often acquired these by backing a tyrant, that is, a usurper-reformer, generally a disgruntled noble. Typically, the tyrant overpowered his aristocratic opponents with a privately conscripted army of hoplite commoners. He rewarded the commoners by canceling debts and redistributing land. Paradoxically, at Athens tyranny led to democracy, when the tyrant abused his powers, became "tyrannical" in the familiar sense, and was overthrown and replaced by an elected leadership.

Full citizenship in Greece was normally confined to adult male landowners. Women could not vote or hold office, nor could they be recognized in law courts without representation by some male, usually a father, husband, uncle, or brother. Women were, however, highly valued as a means of producing citizen children. In most city-states respectable women were carefully supervised and customarily confined to special quarters within the home, to insure that they had no contact with strange males and thus that the children they bore were legitimate. Women were given in marriage by their fathers or other male relatives who verified their citizenship. A substantial dowry accompanied the new wife; although it reverted with her to her family of origin in the event of divorce, while she was married, the dowry money was managed by her husband. Respectable women all followed the same profession: bearing children, keeping house, and making clothing for family members.

Women who were not tied to a single male through a legal marriage were not considered respectable; such women, generally noncitizens or freedwomen, enjoyed greater freedom of movement outside the home and more diversity in occupations, including small-scale selling of clothing, perfumes, and foodstuffs, wet-nursing, and flute playing. Many, however, turned to prostitution, as *hetairai,* sophisticated call girls or "escorts" for males attending drinking parties, or as *pallakai* (concubines), who, though they lived with one male for a length of time, lacked citizenship status and could not bear legitimate children. Pericles himself fell afoul of this legal restriction when he had a child by his long-time companion, the captivating ex-*hetaira* (and noncitizen) Aspasia. He had to secure a special exemption to have his son, also called Pericles, recognized as a citizen.

Much of the labor force in Greek city-states consisted of slaves, acquired through warfare or trade, who had no legal standing even as human beings. The Greeks and the Romans, though more liberal than, for example, U.S. slave owners in freeing individual slaves, never abolished slavery; slaves could no more be given up than tools. Finally,

Athenian citizen

Faking Citizenship: The Case against Neara

Stephanus gave [Phano, the daughter of Neaera] in marriage, as being his own daughter, to an Athenian citizen, Phrastor, together with a dowry of 30 minas [the equivalent of about ten years' wages]. When she went to live with Phrastor . . . she was unable to accommodate herself to his ways, but hankered after her mother's habits and the dissolute ways of that household. . . . Phrastor observed that she was not well-behaved nor willing to be guided by him, and . . . he found out for certain that she was not the daughter of Stephanus, but only of Neaera [allegedly a concubine]. . . . Phrastor was most indignant at all this, and . . . turned the young woman out of his house after having lived with her for a year and when she was pregnant; and he refused to return the dowry.

Stephanus began a suit against him for alimony . . . according to the law enacting that if a man divorce his wife, he shall pay back the dowry. . . . Phrastor also brought an indictment against Stephanus . . . that Stephanus had betrothed to him, an Athenian citizen, the daughter of an alien woman, pretending that the girl was his own daughter, contrary to the following law . . . : "If any person give in marriage an alien woman to an Athenian citizen, pretending that she is related to him, he shall be deprived of his citizen status, and his property shall be confiscated."*

This passage is from a speech delivered in a court case at Athens around 340 B.C.E. At issue is whether Stephanus has given in marriage the daughter of the defendant, a woman named Neaera, whom the prosecution has described as a prostitute/slave, formerly owned by various individuals in Elis, Corinth, and Athens, and now living as the mistress of Stephanus. To recognize the offspring of such a disreputable woman as citizens would threaten the structure of Athenian society and civil law. The harshness of the penalties imposed on offenders shows that this threat was taken very seriously.

*Kathleen Freeman, The Murder of Herodes and Other Trials from the Athenian Law Courts (New York: Norton, 1963), p. 205.

there were intermediate statuses, like that of the *perioikoi* (non-full-blooded) in Sparta and the *metoikoi* or metics (resident non-Athenians, but normally Greeks) in Athens. Both groups had legal protections, served as soldiers, and played a key role economically, but lacked the right to vote or hold office or sometimes even to own land. Political participation in ancient Greece was thus not so inclusive as in modern times.

Athenian and Spartan Social and Political Patterns

Throughout most of Greek history, the most important states were Athens and Sparta. Athens controlled the 1,000-square-mile peninsula of Attica (about the size of Rhode Island) and had the largest population of any Greek city-state (in the mid-fifth century B.C.E., around 300,000, at least one-third of whom were slaves or noncitizens). The lower classes profited when Draco supervised the first written codification of law at Athens (c. 621 B.C.E.). Like Hammurabi's code in Babylonian times, Draco's laws laid down harsh penalties; they were said to have been written in blood (thus the meaning of *draconian*). Still, they did at least distinguish murder from manslaughter and in general shield the lower classes from arbitrary judgments by aristocratic magistrates. At this time, the indispensable hoplite infantry had little control over their personal destinies. Because their land was not very productive, many were deep in debt to aristocratic creditors. They often forfeited their farms or, worse yet, were sold into slavery. The situation grew potentially explosive.

To forestall violent revolution, aristocrats and commoners granted special powers to the chief *archon* (nine archons served as the chief executive officers) in 594. This archon, Solon (c. 640–c. 560), spared the wealthy the radical measure of land redistribution, but canceled debts, forbade debt bondage, and recalled citizens sold into slavery outside Attica. By redefining social status and eligibility for office by wealth rather than birth, and by widening the jurisdiction and composition of juries of citizens, Solon broke the aristocratic monopoly of governmental authority. He also promoted economic development by extending citizenship to immigrant craftsmen, merchants, and traders.

In 508 B.C.E. another reformer, Cleisthenes, ensured more equitable representation of citizens by creating ten large political divisions (tribes) each composed of wards, with residence the chief requirement for citizenship. Each tribe annually elected one archon and chose fifty councilors by lot to serve in a Council of Five Hundred, which managed state finances and foreign policy and determined the agenda for the full assembly of citizens. The latter made the final decisions regarding all weighty matters of domestic and foreign policy and has remained the model of early democratic self-determination. There was also a panel of ten annually elected generals; because, unlike archons, they could be elected repeatedly, the generals came to possess exceptional authority in the Athenian state. Through another innovation, ostracism, the citizenry could vote, using pottery fragments called *ostraca,* to send a dangerously powerful person into a ten-year exile.

Sparta (see Map 3.2) had a government differing in many respects from that of Athens. For example, it retained the archaic institution of kingship; in fact, there were two kings and two royal families. Though these kings were supreme military commanders, civil authority came to be vested in five elected *ephors,* similar to Athenian archons in responsibilities. There was, in addition, a council of thirty elders. An assembly restricted to full-blooded Spartans possessed powers of ratification.

Even more than Athens, Sparta contained a strong class structure. Members of the Spartan ruling elite were called *homoioi* ("equals"). The non-Spartan inhabitants or *perioikoi* ("dwellers around") were free citizens of their own communities but were obliged to serve in Sparta's army and to abide by its foreign policy. The largest population group was the helots or state-owned slaves. The Spartans defeated neighboring Messenia in the seventh century B.C.E. and enslaved its population, forcing them to work on Spartan-controlled land. Freed thus from farm work, full-blooded Spartans made a lifelong, absolute commitment to the most rigorous discipline in education and military training (hence the term *spartan* for living under austere conditions), partly to maintain internal security in the face of a vastly larger subject population. The relationship between Spartans and helots was similar in some respects to that between Aryans and dasas in India. Sparta was the greatest military power in Greece until the fourth century B.C.E., but it paid a high price for this supremacy. The Spartans aborted promising earlier developments in art and poetry to devote their energies exclusively to the code of the soldier. History shows a similar stunting of cultural growth among other excessively militaristic societies (for example, the Assyrians or, in modern times, fascist states).

The Persian and Peloponnesian Wars

In 499 B.C.E., some Ionian Greek cities revolted (unsuccessfully) against Persia. Because Athens had assisted the rebels, the Persians sent a punitive expedition against it in 490. At the plain of Marathon, 10,000 hoplites soundly defeated a Persian force over twice as large. Although King Darius's death in 486 postponed a new assault, his son, Xerxes (reigned 486–465 B.C.E.), planned a much larger invasion with both land and sea forces. He ordered a mile-long bridge to be constructed out of ships cabled together across the Hellespont, which divided Europe from Asia, and a canal built through the Mount Athos peninsula to avoid the risk of storms off its cape.

Fortunately for Greece, the Athenian statesman Themistocles (c. 528–462 B.C.E.) realized that sea power was critical. In 483, when a large new vein of silver was discovered in the state-owned mines at Laurium, Themistocles persuaded the assembly of Athenian citizens to use the bonanza to increase their fleet to 200 triremes and to improve the harbor installations. This democratically adopted decision determined the outcome of the Persian wars.

In 481 Athens, Sparta, and some thirty other states formed a league to defend themselves against the Persians. In 480 Xerxes led about 150,000 troops on the 500-mile march to central Greece. The Persians annihilated King Leonidas' Spartan force at the mountain pass of Thermopylae and pushed on to seize Athens, burning the temples on the Acropolis.

Although the Greeks still possessed powerful forces, victory required coordination of the military and naval strengths of Sparta and Athens, respectively. Themistocles engaged the Persian fleet in the narrow strait between the island of Salamis and Attica. There the Greeks used boarding parties of marines, superior oarsmanship, and effective ramming tactics to win a decisive battle. Xerxes withdrew to Asia Minor, leaving behind a large

The Spartans' Last Stand at Thermopylae

Many of the invaders fell; behind them the company commanders plied their whips, driving the men remorselessly on. Many fell into the sea and were drowned, and still more were trampled to death by their friends. No one could count the number of the dead. The Greeks . . . fought with reckless desperation. . . . They resisted to the last, with their swords if they still had them, and, if not, with their hands and teeth, until the Persians, coming on from the front over the ruins of the wall and closing in from behind, finally overwhelmed them [with arrows and spears].*

For two days, 300 Spartans held the pass at Thermopylae against much larger Persian forces. On the third day, however, the Persians, assisted by a Greek collaborator, brought some of their troops around through the mountains and down to the coast behind Thermopylae. Leonidas and his men, specially chosen from those who had living sons, were thus caught in a slaughterous pincer movement.

*Herodotus, The Histories, trans. A. de Sélincourt (Harmondsworth: Penguin, 1954), pp. 492–493.

force, which Greek forces crushed at Plataea in 479 B.C.E. The victory ensured the independent development of the Greek city-states for another century and a half.

In 478, some 150 Greek cities of Asia Minor and neighboring islands turned to the strongest naval power, Athens, to form and lead a league called The Athenians and Their Allies (known in modern times as the Delian League because its treasury was on Apollo's sacred island of Delos). The league was created to defend the Aegean region and harass the Persians wherever possible. Members contributed either men and ships or money to maintain an allied fleet under Athenian direction. Sparta, which refused an earlier offer to head the league, did not join, but remained the *hegemon* (leader) of the land-based Peloponnesian League. These alliances of Greek city-states resembled those of Chinese states during the late Chou, though on a smaller scale. In both cases, a common culture superficially united member states. Like Athens and Sparta, the hegemonic states of the Eastern Chou (described later in the chapter) tried to control their allies.

At first, the Delian League benefited Greece by rooting out remaining Persian bases in the Aegean and Asia Minor, suppressing piracy, and fostering seaborne mercantile activity, but Athens transformed the Delian League into an Athenian Empire. The treasury at Delos was removed to Athens, which squelched attempts to leave the alliance and interfered high-handedly in the internal affairs of member states. Under Pericles' guidance, Athens became the richest and most powerful Greek city-state and the capital of intellectual and artistic activity. Pericles' mistress, the former Milesian prostitute Aspasia, made his home a social gathering place for the intellectual lights of the era. Pericles' imperialistic foreign policy went hand in hand with the increased prosperity of the lower socioeconomic classes at home. In particular, reliance on the fleet gave a new prominence to the thousands of rowers who were paid for manning the ships. This enabled Pericles to win election to the *strategia* (generalship) so routinely that the historian Thucydides wrote of Athens that "though the system was democratic in name, power was actually vested in the leading citizen."

Sparta and many other Greek states feared the growing power of Athens. When Athens attempted to control supplies of grain, timber, and precious metals at their source, the Spartans declared war and prepared to march on Attica. The Peloponnesian War began in 431 B.C.E. and lasted twenty-seven years. Although the Spartans used severely repressive tactics in maintaining the enslavement of helots in their own country, they painted themselves as champions of Greek liberty in the struggle against Athenian imperialism. Pericles' chief task was maintaining good morale, as may be seen from his speech delivered at the funeral for war dead in 430. A far greater crisis, however, arose when Athens lost perhaps one-fourth of its population, including Pericles, to a virulent plague. Peace was negotiated in 421.

In 415 B.C.E. the volatile, high-living Alcibiades (c. 450–404) persuaded the Athenians to send the finest Greek naval force ever assembled to attack the powerful city of Syracuse in Sicily and add the island, with its rich grain production, to the empire—just the sort of endeavor Pericles had advised against. In 413 the campaign ended in complete victory for Syracuse. Although Athens recovered partially from the Sicilian debacle, Sparta built a formidable fleet of its own, thanks in large measure to Persian subsidies, and shifted the theater of the war to Attica and the Aegean. In 405 a Peloponnesian naval victory severed Athens' grain supply route from the Black Sea. The starving Athenians surrendered unconditionally in 404. Their fortifications were dismantled, and they relinquished the empire and their navy.

Greek Intellectual History: From Myth to Philosophy

Despite political fragmentation, all Greeks shared a religious heritage with roots in the Bronze Age. The images of the Olympian gods, named for their home on Mount Olympus, were already fully formed at the very beginning of the archaic period: Zeus, the supreme deity, sky god, wielder of the thunderbolt; Athena, the warrior-goddess and patroness of intellectual endeavor; Aphrodite, the goddess of erotic love; Apollo, the god of music, prophecy, and medicine; and so on. The gods figured in the tales of poet-singers and in the art of vase painters, sculptors, coin designers, and the like. The mythic stories often answered questions as yet unanswerable by science: What caused thunder? Where did a particularly strange black rock come from? They could convey a moral—treat a guest as you would like to be treated—or simply entertain, as good stories have always done.

Certain religious centers gained exceptional prestige among all Greeks. As was the case among the Chaldeans in West Asia and the Shang dynasty in China, the practice of divination was very prominent in Greece, for example, at Delphi, where the city-states vied with one another in erecting sacred monuments at Apollo's oracular shrine. The Greeks also held athletic contests to honor the gods at various sites, especially Olympia in the western Peloponnese.

The principal occasions for the private citizen to worship in Greece (and indeed throughout the ancient world) were at the numerous festivals throughout the religious calendar. Unlike most modern religious "services," the festivals of the Greek city-states were public, often state-sponsored, events embracing a broad range of activities and spectacles. The farmer and his family left their homestead and spent part or all of a day traveling, generally on foot, to the city, where for a day or perhaps a few days they

The Greek Trireme. *Above:* A cutaway view of a trireme, the standard Greek warship of the classical period. These vessels were about 120 feet long by 12 feet wide, with crews of about 170 rowers seated on benches in three tiers. The ram at the bow was the ship's main offensive weapon; note also the special steering oars at the stern.
Below: In 1987 Greek shipbuilders, working from plans made by a British classical scholar and former chief naval architect of the British Ministry of Defense, completed "the first trireme to be launched in 1,500 years." The *Olympias* was the result of two years' work and the expenditure of $700,000 by the Greek government. With a crew of 130 men and 40 women, mostly college-age Britons, the modern replica achieved a speed of 8.9 knots at forty-six oar strokes per minute.

attended religious events. During the festivals, they watched an impressive, Fourth of July–like parade of religious officials and worshipers wending its way to the shrine of a particular god or goddess. They might also attend athletic competitions, choral performances, poetic recitations, or tragedies and comedies staged to honor the deity. The farmers' visits to the city to pay homage to their gods were thus also civic activities and occasions for popular entertainment. Athenians enjoyed the annual Panathenaic (All-Athenian) festival in honor of the birth of the goddess Athena, with games, musical performances, and recitations of Homeric poetry from "authorized" versions.

As in most ancient religions, including early Judaism, the sacrificial festivals provided the chance for fellow citizens to socialize and, since the core of the actual rites in honor of the many Greek gods was the offering of sacrificial animals and participation in special meals, to consume foods, especially meats, not normally available to them.

The central ceremony took place in the open air; the notion of a church where one sat in quiet, pious, personal devotion to the god was quite alien to the ancient Greeks. The priests and other officials, wearing ornaments and wreaths, led a procession with the sacrificial animal, often a bull, which was also decorated with ribbons or gilded horns, to an altar near a temple or shrine of the god or goddess. A fire blazed on top of the altar; incense often wafted through the air, and typically there was musical accompaniment. The priests or priestesses ritually washed their hands and sprinkled water on the victim. Grains of unground barley (the most ancient agricultural product) were scattered on the ground, the altar, and the victim as prayers were uttered. The officiating priest took a knife and trimmed a few hairs from the animal's head and tossed them in the fire. The victim's throat was then cut, to the accompanying ritual screams of women; care was taken so that the blood fell on the altar, with a bowl sometimes being used to catch and pour the blood.

The sacrificial victim was next disemboweled and carved up. The bones and much of the fat were burned, the savory smoke ascending to the god while the meat itself provided the sacrificial meal for those attending the rite. This was the typical blood sacrifice of the ancient religions. Also, it was the most common form of religious practice in ancient times and is still practiced in some religions today. Thus for the average man or woman, religion meant participating in or witnessing various ritual actions. Unlike the Jews, the Greeks had no sophisticated theology or body of dogma and no sacred book to give moral guidance; they had only "the customs of our ancestors."

Despite frequent, elaborate public rituals, the Olympian gods failed to provide answers to moral and ethical questions or to explain how the physical world worked. Early Greek philosopher-scientists, dissatisfied with simple mythic resolutions of scientific problems, sought to explain the universe by rational inquiry. Some believed that a controlling law (in Greek, a *logos*) underlay the arrangement of basic elements—earth, air, water, and fire; others argued about being and becoming, and the precise nature of appearances and motion. Pythagoras and his followers explored mathematical patterns in the structure of the cosmos and dabbled in theories of the transmigration and reincarnation of souls. In the atomic theory of Democritus, indivisible bits of matter were the basis of all reality. As we will see, in India at approximately the same period, similar questions were being asked by philosophers who wrote their reflections in the Upanishads.

LIVES AND TIMES ACROSS CULTURES

Big-Time Sports in Ancient Greece

As a people, the ancient Greeks were extremely competitive. This is apparent in the nearly constant warfare between city-states, in the court cases that occupied as many as 6,000 jurors a day at Athens, and even in the dramatic festivals at which prizes were given to the best actor, best playwright, best producer.

Perhaps the most prevalent and beneficial outlet for the Greek competitive spirit, however, was provided by public sporting events. Already in the earliest piece of European literature—Homer's *Iliad* (c. 725 B.C.E.)—the heroes compete with each other in athletic contests held to honor the memory of a fallen comrade. But even earlier, in 776, the Greeks had begun to hold great pan-Hellenic games every fourth year at Olympia to honor their supreme deity, Zeus.

The Olympics and three other especially prestigious festivals held at the Isthmus of Corinth and at Delphi were known as "crown" games, because the only prizes awarded were wreaths of olive, laurel, celery, and pine. So too, in the modern Olympics, instituted in 1896, the winners are awarded only medals of nominal intrinsic value. But, in fact, victorious Olympians, then and now, often enjoyed large financial gains: today by product endorsements, personal appearance fees, and professional contracts; in antiquity by such perks as free lunch every day in the dining commons of the town councilmen and automatic qualification at many other meets that did award substantial monetary and material prizes. (By 500 B.C.E., some fifty sets of prize-awarding games were held at regular intervals; by the first century C.E., the number had risen to over 300.)

In reality, Greek athletes—men only, in the ancient world—were professionals who garnered the same sort of spectacular material gains that the Michael Jordans and Wayne Gretzkys of our time have enjoyed. For example, the victor at the one-stade (c. 200-meter) race at the Panathenaic Games held at Athens each year was awarded 100 jars (c. 900 gallons) of olive oil, which could be sold for 1,200 drachmas, the equivalent of four years' wages for the typical skilled laborer. This for less than thirty seconds of "work."

The slate of events at the Olympics and other meets modeled on them comprised five categories of competition:

- Running: Interest was focused especially on sprints of one or two stades. The longest race was twenty-four stades or about three miles (the twenty-six-mile marathon run is a twentieth-century innovation).
- Combat: Wrestlers were required to win the best of five pins. Boxers fought without regard to weight classification and without any division into rounds with rest periods between; bouts continued till one man was unable to continue or "cried uncle." A third combat event, not included in the modern games, was the pankration or "all force" fight, an almost no-holds-barred struggle in which contestants might punch, kick, choke, or strangle their opponents.
- Throwing: Only the discus and javelin were included; there was no shot put or hammer throw.
- Jumping: Only the long jump was included; this was actually some sort of multiple jump, rather like the modern triple jump. An interesting sidelight was the use of "jumping weights" of two to ten pounds that contestants held in their hands and thrust forward as they leapt, evidently to increase momentum (see illustration).
- Horse racing: This included bareback riding and chariot driving with horses, colts, and mules.

The throwing and jumping events were held only as part of the "all-round" competition, that is, the pentathlon or five-event contest (the decathlon is a modern innovation). This comprised the one-stade sprint, long jump, discus, javelin, and wrestling.

By about 450 B.C.E., however, the inconclusiveness of the natural philosophers brought about the Sophists (wise ones), traveling professors who provided instruction, for a fee, in everything from arts and crafts to medicine, philosophy, and oratory. The chief traits of the Sophists were skepticism and relativism. In their opinion, humans would never ascertain absolute right and wrong or good and evil. What was "good" for one might be bad for another. For the Sophists, the only subjects worth pursuing were held to be those that gave individuals the means to achieve their own ends. In Athens, this meant rhetoric—the theory and practice of persuasive oratory. Skill in speaking could even make the worse case appear to be the better; indeed, *worse* and *better* became meaningless terms. As the Sophist Gorgias put it, "The power of speech over the . . . soul can be compared with the effect of drugs on the bodily state: just as drugs by driving out different humors from the body . . . different words can induce grief, pleasure or fear; or again, by means of a harmful kind of persuasion, words can drug and bewitch the soul" (trans. K. Freeman). For the Sophists, it was all a matter of using the appropriate words in the proper situation; ethical questions of absolute right and wrong were both unanswerable and irrelevant.

Socrates (469–399 B.C.E.) extended this questioning of old values. As a young man, he dabbled in natural philosophy, but later shifted his focus to the right conduct of life: What is justice and can it be taught? What is love? Is the soul immortal? Unlike the Sophists, Socrates believed that absolute values did in fact exist and that one could strive to know them through dialectic. He solicited definitions from others and tested them by cross-questioning, a procedure known as the Socratic method of inquiry. Since the definitions nearly always crumbled, he sometimes made enemies, but he never lapsed into the relativistic skepticism of the Sophists.

In 399 Socrates was tried on capital charges of atheism and corruption of the young (he made questioners of them). In defending himself against these charges, as recorded in Plato's *Apology* (defense), he portrayed himself as a victim of old prejudices, wrongly lumped together with the amoral Sophists. He stoutly refused to stop his irksome inquiries, maintaining that the unexamined life was not worth living. Found guilty and sentenced to death, Socrates accepted the decision and, as required, drank a poison called hemlock to show his respect for the laws of Athens, by which he had always abided. He argued on his last day that death—the separation of body and soul—was something not to be feared but desired by the true philosopher, since philosophy was a "training for death." The wise man practices an ascetic way of life, as Socrates had famously done throughout his own life, to reduce the bodily distractions that prevent one's intellectual endeavors from reaching their goal. Death eliminates such distractions altogether. Socrates lived and died by these principles, and bequeathed to humanity a method of inquiry and a style of living and seeking the truth, rather than a body of hard and fast doctrine.

Among the pupils of Socrates was Plato (c. 429–347 B.C.E.), whose philosophy profoundly shaped Western intellectual history. Plato's dialogues present brilliantly dramatic conversations between Socrates and his pupil-friends. Plato sharply distinguishes the reality of the five senses from the world of ideas, which is true and unchanging always and everywhere and thus the only proper source of knowledge.) The philosopher (lover of wisdom) must cultivate the soul, the seat of reason, and suppress the body's misleading sensory experiences. Plato applied this theory of knowledge to such concepts as beauty, virtue, and justice. In his *Republic,* for example, the participants seek to define the "just man" by constructing a detailed model of a perfectly just state, governed by philosopher-kings, whose education is described in detail. The result is an extraordinary mix of philosophy, political science, educational theory, sociology, psychology, and literary criticism. Some modern critics have called the political theory of the *Republic* oppressive and totalitarian, but it must be remembered that Plato aimed to define the just man and not to draw plans for an actual state.

Plato founded a school called the Academy. His best pupil was Aristotle (384–322 B.C.E.), known to his fellow students as "the brain." For a time the tutor of Alexander the Great, Aristotle later founded his own school, the Lyceum. He rejected Plato's emphasis on a separately existing, unchanging reality and based his own general concepts on logical argumentation and observation of natural phenomena. He systematized logic, ethics, political science, metaphysics, the natural sciences, and literary theory. In the Middle Ages, the Scholastics, including Thomas Aquinas, revered Aristotle, and his biological works remained definitive until the eighteenth century. Dante rightly called him "the master of those who know."

In their long tradition of philosophical inquiry, the Greeks succeeded in two major accomplishments. First, they provided an option to "blind faith." Although the old religious views persisted, thinking persons increasingly turned to a more rational, even scientific, way of explaining the world and seeking guidance to right living. While it brought no final answers to the mysteries of life, philosophy did give to human beings a confidence about their capacity to fathom issues of cause and effect, of moral right and wrong, of the origins of things. Second, Greek rationalism established a very durable mind-set, or habit of thinking, for subsequent civilizations.

The Greek Origins of European Literature

The impact of the Greeks on literature was as profound as their contributions to philosophical and scientific thought. The Greeks enriched older literary forms such as the epic and lyric, and the Athenians developed drama and history. Written Greek literature began with Homer's *Iliad* and *Odyssey* in the eighth century. Behind them lay a long oral tradition of epic poetry dating back to Mycenaean times and furnishing a common Greek heritage of heroic myth. Children learned their alphabet with the Homeric epics before their eyes and in their ears. Homer's answers to the great questions of human potential faced by Achilles on the battlefield at Troy and by Odysseus during his journey home influenced the mental outlook of every educated Greek. The aristocratic ideal of *arete* (moral and physical excellence) set a standard of heroic behavior for the whole society.

The Indians and Chinese also had venerable oral traditions and heroic tales that served an educational purpose of transmitting ethical values as did the Greek heroic poems. The oral poetry of the early Aryans in India culminated in the composition of the

Mahabharata and the *Ramayana,* which celebrated the deeds of gods and heroes. Homer's poetry was the closest thing to a Holy Book that the Greeks possessed. Though they were not taken as dogma or as a formal creed, his epics, together with the poet Hesiod's *Theogony,* which recounts the origins and genealogy of the gods, provided an authoritative, early record of the Greek polytheistic system of belief. By contrast, as we have seen, the Rig Veda of ancient India did not present any such clear genealogy of relationships among the gods.

A more down-to-earth, practical strain of Greek literature also emerged in the archaic period. The *Fables* of Aesop normally relate anecdotes from the life of simple folk or animals that carry some moral, often illustrating shrewdness (or lack of it). The fable "Vengeance at Any Price" is typical: "A wasp settled on a snake's head and tormented it by continually stinging. The snake, maddened with the pain and not knowing how else to be revenged on its tormentor, put its head under the wheel of a wagon, so that they both perished together." The moral is that "some men elect to die with their enemies rather than let them live" (trans. S. A. Handford).

The archaic Greeks also developed the lyric, a short poem sung usually to the music of a lyre. The most distinctive aspect of Greek poetry, as compared with that of ancient West Asia, was the prominence of the self-aware individual. The inner life of the poet was appropriate subject matter for serious and not-so-serious writing. Lyric poems were personal, immediate, and flexible in form and content, suitable for recording nearly any experience. The poetess Sappho described the emotional and physiological responses ignited by love:

> . . . *my lips are stricken to silence, under-*
> *neath my skin the tenuous flame suffuses;*
> *nothing shows in front of my eyes, my ears are*
> *muted in thunder.*
> *And the sweat breaks running upon me, fever*
> *shakes my body . . .* (trans. R. Lattimore)

The invention of drama in late sixth-century Athens was one of the most important Greek contributions to civilization. Tragedy evolved from choral lyrics sung at Athenian religious festivals, as singers impersonated gods or heroes and interacted with the chorus in dramatic dialogue. In the fifth century, at the Athenian City Dionysia (festival in honor of Dionysus), three poets each presented three tragedies in competition for prizes. The actors and the chorus of twelve or fifteen singers wore costumes and masks, but there were otherwise few props and little scenery. The theater itself was at first a hillside (the south slope of the Acropolis) with a stage and a circular orchestra in which the chorus danced and sang. Attendance was perhaps as large as 20,000. Admission was inexpensive, and in the time of Pericles the treasury paid for the seats of citizens. Large stone theaters came later, in Hellenistic and Roman times.

For their subjects, playwrights selected and freely modified mythic tales of murder, incest, cannibalism, rape, insanity, parricide, fratricide, infanticide, and suicide. In his *Poetics,* Aristotle said that the crisis of the best plots involved a spectacular coincidence of fall from grace and shocking recognition for the central character, arousing fear and pity in the audience.

Aeschylus (525–456 B.C.E.) wrote plays concerned with major moral and theological issues. In the Oresteian trilogy (*Agamemnon, Libation Bearers,* and *Eumenides*), he wrestled with a thorny question of crime and punishment. Clytemnestra murders her husband Agamemnon, who had sacrificed their daughter Iphigenia to secure safe passage for the Greek expedition to Troy. (Similarly, in Hebrew scriptures, Abraham was willing to sacrifice his son Isaac at the command of God.) Clytemnestra's son Orestes then retaliates by killing her, thereby escaping the Furies (avenging spirits who attack those who kill their kin) of his father but attracting the wrath of his mother's Furies. Orestes escapes the appalling cycle of vengeance only after Athena authorizes a law court to hand down a binding decision. Orestes goes free and vendetta is eliminated, just as it had been historically under such lawgivers as Hammurabi and Draco. Though the human predicament is often painful in the works of Aeschylus, wisdom resulting from suffering ennobles the individual. The Olympian gods ensure ultimate triumph over the forces of darkness and madness.

In the tragedies of Sophocles (c. 496–406 B.C.E.), action arises from personalities subjected to wrenching changes in outlook and fortune. Characters learn not to exceed their limitations or to challenge the gods. Inborn character traits, whether despicable or admirable, may lead to disastrous decisions. In *Oedipus the King,* a man has unwittingly killed his father and married his mother. Oedipus is a conscientious ruler, eager to rid Thebes of a terrible plague by apprehending the murderer of the previous king. Even after he suspects he is the guilty party, Oedipus doggedly pursues the truth. His discovery of that truth destroys his wife/mother and drives him to blind himself. Ironically, the man who at first saw with his eyes but not with his mind later gains inner sight but loses his eyes.

Euripides (c. 485–c. 406 B.C.E.) was attuned to the teachings of the Sophists. His plays are often psychological "thrillers" that question traditional morality. His most powerful works, however, deal with psychological abnormality, with the explosive emotions of men and especially women under stress. The traditional anthropomorphic gods symbolize psychic compulsions. Thus, in the *Hippolytus,* Aphrodite and Artemis represent extremes of sexuality and chastity in Phaedra and her stepson Hippolytus, respectively. Phaedra's supercharged sexual appetite draws her to Hippolytus, who adheres to a cult of virginity, redirecting sexual urges into sadistically obsessive hunting of wild animals. When Hippolytus learns of Phaedra's illicit infatuation and denounces all women with maniacal bitterness, she hangs herself but leaves a note for her husband, Theseus, claiming Hippolytus has raped her. Theseus curses his son, who is trampled to death by his own horses before his father learns the truth.

The Athenians also invented comedy, which, in the Classical period, was strongly satirical. The eleven surviving comedies of Aristophanes (c. 450–c. 385 B.C.E.) are a fantastic mix of serious exposé and uproarious farce, often based on bodily function humor. In *The Clouds,* for example, Aristophanes parodied the Sophists and natural scientists by an outrageous caricature of Socrates, whose eccentric looks and behavior invited such

The Code of the Hero in Homer

And now [Sarpedon] spoke in address to Glaukos,
*   son of Hippolochos:*

"Glaukos, why is it you and I are honored before
*   others with pride of place, the choice meats*
*   and the filled wine cups*

in Lykia, and all men look on us as if we were
*   immortals, and we are appointed a great piece*
*   of land by the banks of Xanthos,*

good land, orchard and vineyard, and ploughland
*   for the planting of wheat?*

Therefore it is our duty in the forefront of the
*   Lykians to take our stand, and bear our part*
*   of the blazing of battle....*

Seeing that the spirits of death stand close about
*   us in their thousands, no man can turn aside*
*   nor escape them, let us go on and win glory for*
*   ourselves, or yield it to others."**

Sarpedon, a son of Zeus and ally of the Trojans during their war against the Greeks, here summarizes the heroic code. The price of nobility and the material advantages it confers is to risk one's life on the battlefield. Humans are inescapably mortal. Death comes for us all, sooner or later. In Homer, the hero seeks to cheat death by winning glory, which will ensure both prestige in this life and continued life in the memories of men and women.

*Richmond Lattimore, trans., The Iliad of Homer (Chicago: University of Chicago Press, 1951), pp. 266–267.

attacks. In *The Knights,* he portrayed the politician and general Cleon, then at the height of his success, as a contemptible demagogue and a blustering, vulgar, stupid upstart. Aristophanes' antiwar sentiments were given free rein in *Lysistrata;* in that play, Athenian women attempt to end the war by a sex strike against their soldier-husbands, who appear in humorously obvious states of agonizing sexual arousal. That Aristophanes could heap blistering abuse on prominent persons and attack their policies without reprisals attests to the remarkable freedom of speech in classical Athens.

Another major innovation of Greek writing was thoughtful narrative and analytical history, as compared to the rote chronicles of ancient West Asia. Herodotus (c. 484–c. 425 B.C.E.), called the Father of History, was born in Asia Minor but lived at Athens and later at an Athenian colony in Italy. His *History* (from Greek *historia,* "inquiry"), though concentrating on the Persian Wars, also compares the cultures of Persia and Egypt with that of Greece; enlivening the narrative are the author's accounts of his own eyewitness experiences and of oral reports collected on his wide travels. The *History* is full of believe-it-or-not tales of amazing happenings, told in a leisurely and enjoyable style. It is also our best source of information about the Persian wars. Herodotus combined the roles of cultural anthropologist, geographer, and naturalist with that of the historian. Yet for all its advance in trustworthiness over Greek mythology, Herodotus' *History* is still often unreliable. He naively accepted stories of oracular pronouncements, inspired dreams, and other divine interferences in human affairs. His chronology and statistics also are often faulty; for example, his number for the army of Xerxes—5,283,220—is ludicrous.

Thucydides (c. 460–c. 400 B.C.E.) came closer to the critical standards of modern historiography. An Athenian by birth, he began his *History of the Peloponnesian War* just after its outbreak, "expecting it to be a great war and more worthy of recording than previous ones." He served as a general, but in 424 was stripped of his command for failing to relieve the besieged city of Amphipolis. His exile for the remainder of the war freed him to work exclusively on his *History*. Thucydides differed from Herodotus by concentrating on political and military events and more carefully evaluating historical evidence. He believed history should chiefly provide an accurate record and analysis of past events as a basis for intelligent decisions in later times. He adopted a sophistic skepticism by giving no place to the supernatural in human affairs. He believed individuals and states acted out of self-interest, not decency or morality; using a tactic sometimes criticized by modern historians, he composed set speeches to crystallize such motivations. He admired Pericles and the Athenian Empire, but realized that growth in the power of any one state inevitably upset the balance between states. Further, he believed that because states with power either used it or ceased to be powerful, war with its unforeseeable turns and brutalizing effects on people was inevitable.

Greek Art and Architecture

Greek achievements in literature, philosophy, and science were matched by progress in architecture and sculpture. A marvelous sensitivity to balance and beauty in form marked the Greek visual arts as "classic" in their perfection.

The worship of the Olympian gods led to the Greek temple, with its encircling colonnade and carefully worked out proportions, probably inspired by Egyptian models. The Parthenon, built in the heyday of Pericles' Athens, was among the finest architectural expressions of the love of symmetrical proportion and an impressive monument to impe-

© Charles O'Rear/Corbis

Parthenon. The Parthenon was built by the architects Ictinus and Callicrates between 447 and 432 B.C.E. to replace the incomplete temple destroyed by the Persians in 480 and to symbolize Athenian imperial might and cultural superiority. The temple was nearly leveled in 1687 C.E. when a Venetian bombardment set off gunpowder stored in it by the Turks. Though it was restored in the late nineteenth and early twentieth centuries, deterioration caused by atmospheric pollutants and rusting iron clamps has necessitated a complete dismantling and re-restoration, currently in progress.

rial strength and religious devotion. Unlike Roman temples or Gothic cathedrals, designed to be approached from one direction, Greek temples dominated their surroundings in all directions. The material was fine marble, hauled, at state expense, from quarries a few miles from the city. Forty-six columns surrounded a two-room inner chamber; the smaller room housed the treasury of the Delian League, the larger a magnificent ivory and gold statue of Athena. On the exterior were sculptures of the goddess's birth and of scenes of warfare. The unique continuous frieze running along the top of the chamber illustrated a Panathenaic procession. A remarkable natural serenity pervades the building.

In free-standing, life-size sculpture the Greeks' restrained realism produces a beautiful nobility in diverse renderings of the human figure. Clear influences from Egypt are visible in the archaic-period *kouroi* of "youth" figures. These present a somewhat stiff, four-square stance, with stylized limbs and details of face and hair. By the fifth century, however, the Greeks were producing sculpture in both stone and bronze, such as the Artemisium Zeus and the Kritios Boy, which exhibit a stunning sense of natural proportion and dynamism. The continuous frieze designed by Pheidias to adorn the Parthenon and illustrating a Panathenaic procession is a triumph of the noble, idealizing, "classical" style.

On a much smaller scale, Greek vase painting attained equally high levels of artistry. The black-figure style, which involved the incising of lines to render details and was predominant in the archaic era, gave way in the classical era to the red-figure style, in which details could be rendered more delicately and precisely by strokes of the painter's brush. The vases, which served utilitarian purposes of storage, mixing, and dispensing of water and wine, often depict scenes and characters from myth and saga: for example, Trojan War heroes and gods or scenes from the *Odyssey* or the careers of Herakles or the Athenian hero-king Theseus. But there are also many scenes of daily life: men reclining at symposia or engaged in drunken revels at after-dinner parties, women bathing or drawing water at the well-head, artisans in their workshops, boys at their lessons in the schoolroom.

Unlike bronze sculptures, which were often lost or melted down in later eras, or architectural monuments ruined by the ravages of time and the elements, the ceramic material of vases—or of their fragments—survives remarkably well. Thus, in many museums around the world, vases provide the readiest access to the art of the ancient Greeks.

The Rise of Buddhism and Jainism in India

The monk Gautama has given up injury to life, he has lost all inclination to it; he has laid aside the cudgel and the sword, and he lives modestly, full of mercy, desiring in compassion the welfare of all things living.

He has given up taking what is not given. . . . He accepts what is given to him and waits for it to be given; and he lives in honesty and purity of heart. . . .

He has given up unchastity. . . . He is celibate and aloof. . . .

He has given up false speech. . . . He speaks the truth, he keeps faith, he is faithful and trustworthy, he does not break his word to the world. . . .

He has given up slander. . . . He unites those who are divided by strife, and encourages those who are friends. . . .

He has given up harsh speech. . . .

He has given up frivolous talk. . . .

He does no harm to seeds or plants. He takes only one meal a day. . . . He will not watch shows, or attend fairs with song, dance, and music. He will not wear ornaments. . . . He will not use a high or large bed. He will not accept gold or silver, raw grain or raw meat. He will not accept women or girls . . . fields or houses. . . . He will not buy or sell, . . . will never bribe, cheat, or defraud. He will not injure, kill or put in bonds, or steal, or do acts of violence.*

*W. T. de Bary, ed., Sources of Indian Tradition, vol. 1 (New York: Columbia University Press, 1958), pp. 114–115. Reprinted with permission.

This passage is part of a long essay praising Gautama Buddha's moral virtues. These attributes, codified as the ten precepts or commandments, became the guiding principles for monks, and, in modified form, for lay persons, too. Gautama founded a world religion called Buddhism. Although it later died out in its original land, India, it remains powerful in East and Southeast Asia.

There was much intellectual ferment in India in the middle of the first millennium B.C.E. It was a transitional period from Aryan tribal states to settled territorial kingdoms, from simple village culture to flourishing towns where artisans and merchants plied their trades and prospered, from old rituals and sacrifices to Vedic gods to new religious ideas and ideals. The previous chapter discussed how asceticism grew and intellectual speculations preoccupied the learned in India during the Late Vedic Age. This section will cover the development of the two new religions that contested the domination of the brahmans—Buddhism and Jainism.

The Life of Buddha

Judged by his posthumous effects on the world, Gautama Buddha, founder of Buddhism, was certainly the greatest man ever born on the Indian subcontinent. Like many great men of ancient times, he was the subject of legends and stories that have become intertwined with the facts of his life. Nevertheless, scholars are reasonably sure about some events. He was born around 566 B.C.E., the son of the chief of the Sakyas, a small tribal kingdom at the foothills of the Himalayas near present-day Nepal, and his consort Maya, who died giving birth. His name was Siddhartha and his clan name was Gautama; in Buddhist literature he is called either Gautama or Sakyamuni, which means "sage of the Sakyas." He was brought up amidst luxury by his father and his aunt (who was also his stepmother), was married at sixteen to his beautiful cousin, whom he won in manly contests (as in Greek mythology, several noblemen competed in archery or other contests for the hand of a noble woman in marriage), and by whom he had a son. Visions of old age, sickness, and death troubled him deeply, however, and made him aware of the hollowness of human pleasures. Then one day he saw a holy man in a yellow robe, was attracted by his serenity, and decided to follow his path.

Now thirty years of age, one night Gautama left his father's household, and in an act called the Great Renunciation, stripped off his fine clothes and jewels, cut off his hair, and donned a yellow robe. For six years he wandered and meditated with five other ascetics, torturing himself to find enlightenment, but in vain. Then he decided to follow the middle path or the way of moderation. Accusing him of backsliding, his companions left him in disgust. One day he seated himself beneath a pipal or bo tree and vowed that he would not leave until he had found the solution to suffering.

For forty-nine days and nights he remained beneath the tree meditating, while demons tempted him with pleasure and power and tormented him with pain, but he was unmoved. On the forty-ninth day he knew the truth, the secret of sorrows and what he must do to overcome them. With this knowledge he was fully enlightened and became a Buddha, the Enlightened or Awakened One. He stayed by the tree, now called the *bodhi* tree (tree of wisdom, the holy tree to Buddhists) for another seven weeks, meditating. Then he journeyed to the Deer Park near Banares (or Varanasi, at a place called Sarnath where later a great monument to Buddhism was erected), and preached his first sermon to his five former companions, thus "setting in motion the Wheel of the Law." They became his disciples.

Buddha spent the remainder of his life teaching. He and his disciples spent approximately eight months each year traveling throughout the Ganges Valley, preaching and organizing Buddhist communities. According to one story, a distraught woman clutching her dead infant approached the Buddha and asked if he could restore its life. Buddha told her to go to the nearest town to obtain a handful of mustard seeds (a common spice), but stipulated that the seeds must come from a family that had not suffered death. She returned at the end of the day empty-handed, but though disappointed, she had learned that all suffer the pain of death. She too became a disciple. During the four monsoon months when travel was impossible, Buddha and his disciples rested and studied in places donated by the pious. As his fame grew, his converts came to include his father and other family members, kings, and humble people. At his stepmother's request, he allowed her to form a community of nuns. Unlike some other holy persons who also appeared to challenge established tradition, he suffered no persecution.

Before his death Buddha admonished his disciples in these words:

> You must be your own lamps, be your own refuge. Take refuge in nothing outside yourselves. . . .
> A monk becomes his own lamp and refuge by continually looking on his body, feelings, perception,
> moods, and ideas in such a manner that he conquers the cravings and depressions of ordinary men
> and is always strenuous, self-possessed, and collected in mind. Whoever among my monks does this,
> either now or when I am dead, if he is anxious to learn, will reach the summit.

His sorrowing disciples gathered to cremate his remains and then divided his ashes among the various Buddhist communities. In accordance with local custom, stupas (mounds) were built over places where the ashes were deposited and bo trees were planted around them. They became pilgrimage sites because they commemorated his death and enlightenment, respectively.

Soon after his death Buddha's disciples gathered together in council to compile his teachings. A second great council held during the fourth century and a third council called by emperor Asoka around 240 B.C.E. further defined and completed the Buddhist scriptures or canons, called the *Tripitaka* (the Three Baskets, because the palm leaves on which they were written were rolled up and deposited in three basket containers according to classification), after the three sections into which they were divided. These sections were: (1) Conduct—rules of behavior for the *sangha,* or orders of monks and nuns; (2) Discourses—a collection of sermons on doctrine and ethics, later enlarged by the birth stories (*Jataka*) that dealt with the previous incarnations of the Buddha; and (3) Supplementary Doctrine—metaphysical elucidations of ideas presented in the Discourses. The canons were written in Pali, a vernacular language of northern India. The canons and commentaries were completed in the second century C.E. Later additions by Buddhist scholars were not considered canonical works.

All Buddhists derive their views from the words of Gautama Buddha. In time, however, different schools of thought arose, based on different interpretations of the canons. Centuries after the master's death it was impossible to be certain what he had meant by certain words, and people interpreted them according to their own emotional needs and the needs of the time. Eventually each branch, and each of the different sects within each branch, developed its own version of the canons.

The Orthodox: Theravada Buddhism

By the time of the Second Council, different interpretations of the canons had led to a schism within Buddhism over monastic discipline. Those who claimed that they correctly followed the original teachings called their way the *Theravada,* or Teaching of the Elders, as opposed to the followers of the minority dissident camp, who called their way the *Mahayana,* which means the Great Vehicle. At the Third Council the Theravada school was proclaimed orthodox and members of the Mahayana were expelled.

Gautama did not question the fundamental premises of Indian thought. He believed that *samsara,* or the transmigration of souls, and *karma,* which determine what we are and what we will be, were basic laws that governed the universe. All Indian philosophies agreed that there were endless rounds of rebirths. However, they differed on what *dharma,* or doctrine, to follow in order to escape *samsara.*

In simple terms Buddha explained that life is transient and painful and that the pain is caused by desires, especially by selfish and sexual desires, for they lead to reproduction, which stretches out the chain of life into new suffering. However, the pain can be ended by cultivating detachment from material things; indifference to material things can be achieved by following the Eightfold Path. The goal was *nirvana,* an indescribable state, which Gautama and Theravada Buddhists equated with "the blowing out" or extinction of craving and consequently of suffering; it was a tranquil state realized by those who are freed from desires. In an ever-changing universe, nirvana is the only constant, for it is not part of the universe. A living person can attain nirvana, and once he does, he will never lose it. When he dies he passes into this state forever in the "final blowing out" that releases him from the cycle of reincarnation.

Gautama did not deny that there is happiness in life; but he argued that on balance sorrows always outweigh joy: "As the ocean has one flavor, the flavor of salt," he reputedly said in explanation. Although he did not deny the existence of gods, he insisted that they too are part of the universe, and cannot help us. Gautama also taught that the universe is soulless and that the world soul or *brahman* of the Upanishads is an illusion. As he explained, nothing passes from one life to another in transmigration. Only a new life arises from a chain of events which includes the old. Thus, the original Theravada Buddhism is a religion without gods, without souls.

The leaders of Buddhism were members of the order of monks and nuns called the sangha. Membership was by avocation, and it was not restricted by caste. Gautama did not attack the caste system directly, but he did not recognize it in his own order. Buddhism and Jainism (which we discuss below) were in part a kshatriya protest against the pretensions and domination of the brahman caste and a rejection of caste restrictions. Undoubtedly Gautama's attitudes and activities weakened the caste system, and when Buddhism declined in India, the caste system reasserted its rigid order.

A person could join the sangha as a novice from age eighteen on, but could not gain full admission as a member until at least age twenty and after a period of satisfactory study. A novice underwent a simple ceremony that involved head shaving, donning a yellow robe, and pronouncing the Three Jewels: "I go for refuge to the Buddha; I go for refuge to the Doctrine (dharma); I go for refuge to the Order (sangha)." The novice also promised to obey the Ten Precepts or commandments. Some of the commandments had their equivalents in the later Christian monk's vows of chastity and poverty, but the Buddhist monk, unlike his Christian counterpart, swore no vow of obedience, for the sangha was essentially a community of free men and women with no central authority or chain of command. The monastic vow was not a lifelong bond (even now all young men in such Theravada Buddhist countries as Thailand and Burma are expected to take vows for a specified short period and then return to lay life). A monk might leave or even reenter the order freely, although backsliding is frowned upon.

Monks spent their time chiefly in study and religious exercises; of the latter, the most important were called the Four Sublime Moods, which required one to sit cross-legged and to fill one's mind with the four cardinal virtues—love, pity, joy, and serenity—and to think of all living things in the light of these virtues. Monks who have reached higher levels meditated on more advanced themes, with the ultimate goal of realizing nirvana. To remind them of their vow of poverty, monks went from door to door every morning to beg for food, which they shared with members of the community. As monasteries became wealthy (poverty is enjoined on the individual, not the community), the requirement to beg was either reduced to a formality or dropped entirely.

In a sermon titled "Address to Sigala," Gautama instructed a young man on familial and other relationships, duties, and responsibilities. It said in part:

Husbands should respect their wives, and comply as far as possible with their requests. They should not commit adultery. They should give their wives full charge of the house, and supply them with fine clothes and jewelry as far as their means permit. Wives should be thorough in their duties, gentle and kind to the whole household, chaste, and careful in housekeeping, and should carry out their work with skill and enthusiasm.

A man should be generous to his friends, speak kindly of them, act in their interest in every way possible, treat them as his equals, and keep his word to them. . . .

Employers should treat their servants and workpeople decently. They should not be given tasks beyond their strength. They should receive adequate food and wages, be cared for in time of sickness

The Sermon That Set the Wheel of Law Turning

1. Now this, O monks, is the noble truth of pain: birth is painful, old age is painful, sickness is painful, death is painful, sorrow, lamentation, dejection, and despair are painful. . . .

2. Now this, O monks, is the noble truth of the cause of pain: that craving, which leads to rebirth, combined with pleasure and lust, finding pleasure here and there, namely the craving for passion, the craving for existence, the craving for non-existence.

3. Now this, O monks, is the noble truth of the cessation of pain: the cessation without a reminder of that craving, abandonment, forsaking, release, non-attachment.

4. Now this, O monks, is the noble truth of the way that leads to the cessation of pain: this is the noble Eightfold Path, namely, right views, right intention, right speech, right action, right livelihood, right effort, right mindfulness, right concentration. . . .*

The quote contains the crux of Gautama's first sermon at the Deer Park. It is the essence of his enlightenment and the central theme of Buddhist teachings. When he preached that sermon, Gautama set in motion the wheel of the law.

Edward J. Thomas, The Life of Buddha as Legend and History, 2nd ed. (New York: Knopf, 1931), p. 87.

and infirmity, and be given regular holidays and bonuses in times of prosperity. They (servants) should rise early and go to bed late in the service of their masters, be content with their just wages, work thoroughly, and maintain their master's reputation.

Unlike the sermon to Sigala, some other sermons and philosophical discourses were difficult for ordinary people to understand, but Jataka stories were not. They therefore became important vehicles for teaching. Like Aesop's *Fables* of ancient Greece, they taught the values of caution and shrewdness in daily life, as well as generosity and self-sacrifice. In the Sibi Jataka, for example, the king of the Sibis (a previous incarnation of Gautama) ransomed a pigeon from a hungry hawk with flesh cut from his own body. Everyone could grasp the moral taught in these stories, which became popular favorites. Through sermons, stories, and examples, Theravada Buddhism taught that all could accumulate merit through individual effort and that all can attain nirvana.

Evolution of the Great Vehicle: Mahayana Buddhism

According to the Pali scriptures, Gautama was not a deity; he had gained his enlightenment by his own efforts after many births, and when he finally entered nirvana, he ceased to affect the universe in any way. The scriptures also taught that there had been other buddhas before Gautama and that there would be others in the future; furthermore, buddhahood was something that everyone could attain just as the holy monks who practiced Gautama's teachings had done. In so doing, a holy monk becomes *arahant* (worthy) and an exemplar for others.

Though inspirational, these teachings also made most people feel inadequate before the challenge of achieving buddhahood. A new interpretation, called *Mahayana* (the Great Vehicle), developed to meet the needs of these believers. In this reinterpreted Buddhism, a great vehicle was found whereby more believers could be carried to nirvana with the help of compassionate beings, called *bodhisattvas*. Mahayana Buddhists called the orthodox school *Hinayana* (Lesser Vehicle), because the self-reliance it demanded of its followers allowed a lesser number to attain nirvana. The nature of nirvana also changed from extinction of the individual soul to a paradise of the blessed. Soon after Gautama's death his followers began to proclaim the phrase: "I go for refuge in the Buddha," as one of the Three Jewels of Buddhism (the other two being dharma and sangha). Mahayana Buddhists interpreted this statement to mean that the master, as distinct from his teaching, was still in some way present and able to help his followers. This point of view led to the deification of Gautama Buddha.

Early Buddhists worshipped outdoors and without statues or images. By the first century B.C.E., however, surviving Buddhist monuments show adoring worshipers honoring symbols of the Buddha, such as his footprint. A little later actual images of the Buddha began to appear as the focus of worship. Although Mahayana Buddhists led the way in this trend, eventually Theravadins followed suit, and Gautama came to be honored in all Buddhist shrines with statues, flowers, incense, and lamps. Bodhisattvas were a hallmark of Mahayana Buddhism. Gautama is portrayed as a bodhisattva in previous incarnations in some Jataka stories. Animals are the heroes of others. One heroic monkey saved his friends from death by making himself a living bridge over the Ganges River so they could escape from hunters by walking over him. Other stories told of wonderfully appealing and compassionate figures who had voluntarily postponed their own buddhahood in order to help other living things achieve the same goal.

Some bodhisattvas had specialized functions, but all answered prayers. Just calling the name of a bodhisattva in sincerity would give merit to the supplicant. Bodhisattvas also became spirits of suffering, taking on the pain and suffering of the world, so that in comparison, the arahants or holy monks admired by Theravada Buddhists seem cold and selfish. By the first century C.E., the idea of a suffering savior, who resembled the Christian idea of a God who gave his life to redeem humanity, became important in Mahayana belief. Scholars agree that the Zoroastrian idea of a savior who will lead the forces of good against those of evil and darkness at the end of the world did influence the Mahayana Buddhist cult of *Maitreya*, or Buddha of the Future, a gentle figure who is worshipped as a bodhisattva.

The Collection of The Newark Museum, Purchase 1965, The Member's Fund

The Nativity of Gautama. Just as Christians celebrate the nativity of Jesus, Buddhists the world over celebrate Gautama's birth. This ninth-century southern Indian stone sculpture shows Queen Maya, flanked by the god Indra, presenting the infant Gautama to the world, while a goddess stands on her left.

Mahayana Buddhism also developed the notion that Gautama had been not a mere man, but rather the earthly expression of a great spiritual being. This being had three bodies, and of these only one, the Created Body, had been on earth. Another, the Body of Essence, eternally permeated the universe; the third, the Body of Bliss (called *Amitabha,* or Immeasurable Light), is the presiding deity of the Happy Land, the most important heaven where the blessed are reborn on lotus buds and live in bliss. Though presiding in heaven, Amitabha continues to take a compassionate interest in the world. Some Mahayana sects believe that calling his name in faith will ensure the faithful's rebirth in this Happy Land.

Thus the Great Vehicle not only created a pantheon of noble and compassionate bodhisattvas but transformed nirvana to a land of joy for the blessed. The faithful no longer sought extinction but participation in a land of bliss. Many Mahayana believers preferred the idea of a suffering savior and compassionate saints who answer prayers to the Theravada notion that all humans must find their own way to salvation. Therefore, while both schools agreed that the world is full of suffering, Mahayana is more socially oriented and optimistic. In both forms, Buddhist teachings were less abstract than the nonviolence and abstinence of the Upanishads and more attainable than the severe self-mortification demanded by Jainism. For these reasons Buddhism is called the religion of the middle way.

Jainism

Mahavira means "great hero." It is the title given to Vardhamana, founder of Jainism, the "religion of the conquerors," which also took shape during the Late Vedic Age. It too challenged Vedism and competed with Buddhism. Much of Mahavira's early life resembled that of Gautama Buddha. Like Gautama, Mahavira belonged to the kshatriya caste. Born about 540 B.C.E., he was the second son of a minor ruler of northern India; he married and had a daughter, but felt spiritually unfulfilled. After his parents' death, he left home at the age of thirty, with his elder brother's permission, to pursue a life of asceticism. When Mahavira started his wandering life, he wore a suit of clothes, but soon he discarded it as an encumbrance, and for the rest of his life, he went in complete nudity. For twelve years he meditated and subjected his body to the severest punishments. In the thirteenth year, Mahavira found full enlightenment and became a *jina,* or conqueror.

Like Gautama, Mahavira spent the remaining thirty years of his life traveling the Ganges Valley with a band of disciples, teaching his new religion. His followers were called Jains, a derivative of the word *jina.* When he died in 468 B.C.E., at the age of seventy-two, reputedly of self-inflicted starvation, he left a disciplined band of naked monks and many lay followers to continue his work. Jain religious canons were codified about 200 years after Mahavira's death, but they did not take final form until the fifth century C.E.

According to Mahavira, the universe is eternal, divided into an infinite number of cycles, each with an up and a down phase. There have already been twenty-three cycles, the era that spanned his life being the twenty-fourth. Universal emperors and other great men lived during each cycle. When the cycle is at its apex, giant people get all they want from wishing trees and have no need for laws and property. During Mahavira's lifetime the world was in decline and would so continue until the cycle reached its nadir, when the tide would turn and things would improve again.

Jainism holds that there are an infinite number of souls in the universe, all fundamentally equal, but differing in the extent to which the accretion of karmic matter from life to life had dulled the originally bright soul. Salvation is to be found by freeing the soul from matter so that it can regain its original pristine purity. Only then can it enjoy eternal bliss in nirvana, atop the universe, above the highest heaven.

Mahavira taught that life pervades the whole world and that all living things belong to one of five classes of life, locked in the process of birth and rebirth. The highest class includes gods, humans, and certain intelligent animals, down through the lower animals, insects, and plants to inanimate objects such as rocks, fire, and water. Only monks (and nuns, according to one Jain sect) have a chance of escaping the process of reincarnation because of their renunciation of the material life and their strict vows and practice of self-denial. Although lay people cannot obtain release from rebirth in this life, they are nevertheless encouraged to lead strictly moral lives, to undertake frequent retreats into monasteries, and to fast often.

Because the five classes are locked together in the eternal cycle of reincarnation, any action that harms life brings adverse consequences. The following verses from the Jain *Book of Sermons* explains this belief:

> Earth and water, fire and wind,
> > Grass, trees, and plants, and all creatures that move,
> Born of egg, born of the womb,
> > Born of dung, born of liquids—
>
> These are the classes of living beings.
> > Know that they all seek happiness.
> In hurting them men hurt themselves,
> > And will be born again among them. . . .
>
> The man who lights a fire kills living things
> > While he who puts it out kills the fire;
> Thus a wise man who understands the Law
> > Should never light a fire.
>
> There are lives in earth and lives in water,
> > Hopping insects leap into the fire,
> And worms dwell in rotten wood.
> > All are burned when a fire is lighted.
>
> Even plants are beings, capable of growth,
> > Their bodies need food, they are individuals.
> The reckless cut them for their own pleasure
> > And slay many living things in doing so.

Hence, Jains are sternly enjoined to practice *ahimsa*, which means behaving in a nonviolent or noninjurious way toward living things. Jains are strict vegetarians and are not allowed to wear silk clothing (because silkworm larvae must be killed before the thread can be unwound) or engage in professions that entail killing living things. This includes farming, which involves accidental killing of living organisms and intentional killing of plant life. Hence, monks must eat only food obtained from begging, because they are forbidden to participate in the killing of life that food preparation entails or to light fires. Since Jains could not follow professions that harmed life, they became merchants, bankers, lawyers, and doctors. They are known for their honesty, hard work, and frugality and are a successful people. Splendid Jain temples, built more than a thousand years ago and still well maintained, attest to the wealth and piety of the community. Down to the present the Jain community maintains many charitable institutions for humans and animals. Their contributions to Indian society are much more important than their present population of 7 million people would lead one to expect.

For two centuries after Mahavira's death the Jains were a small community of monks and lay followers, and they were not persecuted. A schism or split occurred at the beginning of the Mauryan dynasty (third century B.C.E.) over the severity of monastic discipline. Two sects of Jain monks, the Space Clad or Sky Clad (naked) and the White Clad (robed in white cloth), emerged, and the schism has never healed.

Although Jains deny the authority of the Vedas and have their own canons, in time they accepted many Hindu gods, though in subordinate positions to the Jain universal emperors. Their domestic rites at birth, marriage, and death do not differ much from those of Hindus, and brahmans are often called in to officiate on those occasions in Jain households. Hence, some Hindus consider Jainism a sect of Hinduism, and Jains a separate group within the four great orders or castes in Hindu society. Such an attitude is typical of the tolerance Indians have traditionally felt toward people of different religious beliefs and practices. In this way a Jain layman could call on a Hindu priest to perform a ceremony at his house, and also donate to a Jain temple and go there for periodic retreats.

Indian culture owes a debt to Jainism. Many Jain monks were scholars of both religious and secular learning; some were noted mathematicians and astronomers. Great libraries associated with Jain temples have preserved many ancient manuscripts. Their fervent support of nonviolence has undoubtedly helped to spread the ideal among non-Jains as well. In modern times, Jainism had a significant influence on Mahatma Gandhi, who was born and raised in a part of India where Jainism was widespread. Gandhi has written about the deep impression the saintly Jain ascetics made on him in his youth.

China: Confucianism, Taoism, and Legalism

Confucius said: "If a ruler himself is upright, all will go well without orders. But if he himself is not upright, even though he gives orders they will not be obeyed. . . . Lead the people by laws and regulate them by penalties, and the people will try to keep out of jail, but will have no sense of shame. Lead the people by virtue and restrain them by the rules of decorum, and the people will have a sense of shame, and moreover will become good."*

Mencius had an interview with King Hui of Liang. The king said:

"Venerable sir, since you have considered it worth while to journey so far to come here, I assume that you must have brought with you counsels to profit my kingdom—is it not so?"

Mencius replied, "Why must your majesty speak of profit? I have nothing to offer but benevolence and righteousness. If your majesty asks, 'What will profit my kingdom?' then the great officers will ask, 'What will profit our families?' and the lower officers and people will ask, 'What will profit our persons?' Superiors and inferiors will contend with one another for profit and the state will be endangered. But there has never been a benevolent man who neglected his parents, nor a righteous man who regarded his ruler lightly. Let your majesty then speak only of benevolence and righteousness."**

*William. T. de Bary, ed., *Sources of Chinese Tradition*, vol. 1 (New York: Columbia University Press, 1960), p. 32. Reprinted with permission.

**From *The Mencius* I (1), in H. G. Creel, *Chinese Thought from Confucius to Mao Tse-tung* (New York: Mentor Books, 1953), p. 75.

After their deaths, Confucius and Mencius were honored as China's first and second sages. They were concerned with morals and good government and thought that rulers and educated men had an obligation to set good examples and rule by persuasion rather than threats of punishment. Like the Greek philosopher Plato, they had no success in finding a philosopher-king who would be amenable to their advice. Confucius devoted his later years to teaching, and went on to found a philosophy that would be called Confucianism; Mencius, who lived two centuries later, became the greatest Confucian after the master. Around 100 B.C.E. Confucianism became China's state doctrine.

Philosophy flourished in China between approximately 600–300 B.C.E.; indeed, all the classic philosophies that molded Chinese civilization to the present were rooted in this period. The chaotic conditions of the Eastern Chou dynasty (771–221 B.C.E.) inspired many philosophers to offer their ideas, each claiming that he had the solution to reunite the Chinese world. The philosophies ranged from the very abstract to the very concrete, from idealistic to hedonistic. The great variety of views prompted later Chinese to dub this era that of a Hundred Schools, which happened at about the same time that Hebrew prophets were interpreting God's will in Israel, Greek scientists and philosophers were speculating on moral and cosmic issues, and great religious thinkers were teaching in India.

Some of the teachers were not philosophers in the strict sense. For example, Sun Wu, author of *The Art of War*, was a tactician who analyzed the factors involved in total war, including psychological warfare, intelligence gathering, strategy, and mobilization; the work remains useful and even now is often studied in military academies. The three schools that had most influence on China, however, were Confucianism, Taoism, and Legalism.

The Idealist: Confucius and His Teachings

Confucius is the best-known son of China. Few men have so profoundly influenced human lives and history. Confucius (551–479 B.C.E.) was a member of the *shih* (knight) class, the lowest among aristocrats. His family name was K'ung and his given name was Ch'iu, but the Chinese call him K'ung Fu-tzu or Master K'ung, which was Latinized to Confucius by Jesuit missionaries in the seventeenth century. His father died when Confucius was three years old, and he was brought up by a devoted mother in rather humble circumstances. Still, his hobbies were archery and music, which indicate an aristocratic heritage, just as horse riding, music, and the sports of the gymnasium were part of the Greek aristocrat's daily life.

Confucius was ambitious. Because he did not inherit a government position, he had to earn one by his own efforts. Yet he was temperamentally unsuited for a successful career as a politician. His failure to attain responsible public office left him time to study and contemplate, and he finally resigned himself to teaching. He was probably the most learned man of his age. He had a dynamic and revolutionary view of education, which he saw as a means to make government serve the people. Unsurpassed as a teacher, he reputedly imparted his views on life and government to 3,000 students. Soon after his death, about 70 among them, who counted themselves his disciples, compiled his sayings into a book called the *Lun-yu* or *Analects*.

From the *Analects* we know much not only about his views but also about the man, for example:

> In his leisure hours, Confucius was easy in his manner and cheerful in his expression. . . . Confucius fished but not with a net; he shot but not at a roosting bird. . . . When Confucius was pleased with the singing of someone he was with, he would always ask to have the song repeated and would join in himself.

He expressed his love of learning thus:

> At fifteen, I set my heart on learning. At thirty, I was firmly established. At forty, I had no more doubts. At fifty, I knew the will of Heaven. At sixty, I was ready to listen to it. At seventy, I could follow my heart's desire without transgressing what was right.

Confucius believed that human nature was innately good and that it was a moral education that made some people superior, as is reflected in the following sayings by him: "By nature men are pretty much alike; it is learning and practice that set them apart," and, "In education there are no class distinctions."

Confucius wrote a book called the *Chun Chiu* (*Spring and Autumn*), a chronicle of his native state Lu from 722 to 479 B.C.E. The *Chun Chiu*, the *Shu Ching* (Book of History), *Shih Ching* (Book of Poetry), *Li Chi* (Book of Rites), and *I Ching* (Book of Change), which dealt with divination and metaphysical concepts, are called the Five Classics. They are the most important canons of Confucianism and are accepted by all Chinese as the distillation of their heritage from ancient times. Some scholars credit Confucius and his disciples with compiling and editing the earlier classics. In any case, they were conservators who prided themselves on preserving and handing down the heritage of the past.

Confucius taught that people must return to virtue and live the ideal of *jen*, which means "humanity, benevolence, and love." When *jen* is practiced together with *li* (moral and social propriety), society will return to a state of *tao*, or the moral way ordained by heaven and carried out by past sage rulers during the golden age of mythology and the early Chou dynasty.

All individuals exist within society. Moral worth, not birth, makes a person superior. Superior men should devote themselves to public service to bring about general betterment. Leaders should be virtuous and rule by example rather than through fear. When a ruler asked Confucius about government he replied, "If a ruler himself is upright, all will go well without orders. But if he himself is not upright, even though he gives orders they will not be obeyed." To this he added, "Let the prince be prince, the minister be minister, the father father and the son son." He called this concept the rectification of names, meaning that every name carries certain implications. Thus, when a man is called ruler, he should know what is expected of a moral ruler. If he acts according to those ideals, then he is truly a ruler in name as well as in fact. The same holds true for every name in social relationships.

Confucius taught that there are five basic relationships: ruler and minister, father and son, husband and wife, elder and younger sibling, and friend and friend. Each relationship is reciprocal; each person has obligations toward the other. For example, younger siblings should love and respect their older brothers and sisters, who should love and guide the younger ones. The importance of the family is shown by the fact that three of the five relationships are between its members. According to Confucius, the family is the state in microcosm. Older family members give the young ones their first lessons in morality. If the father is kind and just and sets a good example, the family will live in harmony. Likewise if the ruler treats his subjects as a good father does his children, the state will be in good order. Confucius constantly urged filial piety or love and reverence of the young towards the old. What if there is conflict between a son's duty to his father and a higher social duty? Confucius said: "In serving his parents a son may gently remonstrate with them. If he sees that they are not inclined to follow his suggestion, he should resume his reverential attitude but not abandon his purpose. If he is belabored, he will not complain."

Confucius founded a school of moral philosophy, not a religion. He believed in ancestor worship, as did all Chinese, but he shied from speculating about the next world. When asked by a student about the worship of ghosts and spirits, he replied: "We don't know yet how to serve men, how can we know about serving the spirits?" In this he shows a kinship of spirit with Socrates, who similarly was skeptical about conventional notions about life after death.

The Reformer: Mencius and the Confucian Consensus

Confucius had many disciples, who continued his teachings, but the most famous early Confucian was Meng K'o (c. 372–c. 289 B.C.E.), whose Latinized name was Mencius, for Meng Tzu, or Master Meng. Like Confucius, he was born into a *shih* family and lost his father when he was very young. Mencius was raised by his mother, who struggled to give him a good education, moving several times until she found a place near a school. Regretting that he was born too late to know the master, Mencius studied under Confucius's grandson. For a while he traveled from state to state, vainly trying to convice rulers to adopt his ideas, but eventually he settled down to teach. His ideas are set out in a book called *The Mencius,* which became a major Confucian classic.

A brilliant debater, Mencius took on advocates of other schools of philosophy. He also expanded on some ideas not fully developed by Confucius and brought them to their logical conclusion. For example, Confucius said that men should practice jen in dealing

The Continuity of Tradition. These rare volumes are from a twelfth-century edition of the *Book of Mencius,* with annotations and commentary by a famous scholar of the first century C.E. The Chinese invented paper and printing, which made possible the wide dissemination of important books.

National Palace Museum, Taipei, Taiwan, Republic of China

with others, but did not fully explain why. Mencius explained that they should do so because human nature is originally good, so every man has the potential for sagehood, but goodness needs to be cultivated and cannot be achieved through a flash of enlightenment.

Mencius was even more insistent than Confucius that the state should be a moral institution and that the head of state should be a moral leader. He declared that such an ideal state had existed when sage men ruled in the golden age. What if the ruler failed to live up to the ideals? Developing Confucius's theory of the rectification of names to its logical conclusion, Mencius said that such a ruler is no king but a "mere fellow" and that the people have the moral right of revolution. He added that rulers should trust the administration to qualified officials and not interfere with their duties, for to do so would be as foolish as trying to tell a skilled jade carver how to carve jade. It is not enough, he continued, for a ruler merely to set good examples. He should also create an environment that will encourage the people to cultivate high standards of morality. He could do this by providing for the economic well-being of his subjects. This had been done, said Mencius, by the Duke of Chou when he created the well-field system. This land distribution system, so simple in concept, has fascinated reformers from Mencius's time to the present; many see it as the ultimate foundation of social justice in an agrarian society.

Mencius's idealism had a practical base. He argued that it is in the enlightened interest of a ruler to treat his people well, for he cannot expect his subjects to practice morality on empty stomachs. Conversely, Mencius warned that if a ruler abuses his people, they have the right to rise up and overthrow him. These teachings earned Mencius the title of the Second Sage (after Confucius), inspired the love of the people, and established his reputation as a scourge of tyrants.

Confucianism was a practical philosophy that emphasized proper conduct, virtuous life, and humanity, which can be learned through the study of history and the classics. It is also an optimistic philosophy that teaches that human nature is good, that both the individual and society are perfectible, and that life can be harmonious and fulfilling for all. Confucianism faced competition, however, from other schools of thought.

The Mystic: Lao Tzu and Taoism

The word *tao* means "the way." If most philosophers agreed upon one thing, it was that the turmoil of the era was the result of the loss of *tao*, however interpreted. While Confucians, the earnest "do-gooders" who attempted to restore the perceived *tao* of the sage kings of antiquity by moral reforms, others reacted to chaotic times by seeking to rise above the mundane because they regarded the world as beyond saving. The philosophy that these recluses developed to justify and give meaning to their nonaction is called Taoism. Next to Confucianism, Taoism is the most important traditional philosophy in Chinese history. In many ways it is precisely the opposite of Confucianism: paradoxically, though, the two doctrines have acted as necessary counterparts of each other, appealing to different sides of the Chinese character.

Tradition credits Lao Tzu (Old Master) with founding Taoism, but there is no proof that such a man existed. After Taoism had established a following, some Taoists claimed that the Old Master had been a senior contemporary of Confucius from the southern state of Ch'u and had worked as an archivist in the royal Chou court. According to the same tradition, as an old man Lao Tzu had decided to leave China and head west but had been stopped by border guards who asked him to write down his teachings. After doing so, some stories say, he went to India, where he converted the Buddha to Taoism.

The *Lao Tzu* or *Tao Te Ching* (The Canon of the Way and Virtue) is a work attributed to Lao Tzu. Considered the most important canon of Taoism, the *Lao Tzu* is mostly in poetic form and only 5,000 words long. It is a difficult book—terse, deliberately obscure, and thus open to many interpretations. These characteristics have contributed to its appeal through the generations. It begins thus:

> The Tao (way) that can be told of
> Is not the eternal Tao;
> The name that can be named
> Is not the eternal name.
> Nameless, it is the origin of Heaven and earth,
> Nameable, it is the mother of all things.

In another passage the *Lao Tzu* says: "Those who understand don't talk, and those who talk don't understand." Confucians have delighted in throwing this epigram back at the Taoists, saying that in writing this book, Lao Tzu may have proved that point conclusively!

While many passages of the *Lao Tzu* are puzzling, some are not, for example:

Therefore a sage rules his people thus:
He empties their minds,
And fills their bellies;
He weakens their ambition,
And strengthens their bones.
He strives always to keep the people innocent of
    knowledge and desires, and to keep the knowing ones
    from meddling. By doing nothing that interferes with
    anything, nothing is left unregulated.

This passage sums up the Taoist theory of government. Both Confucians and Taoists agree that a sage should rule, but whereas the Confucian sage-ruler should do many things for the people, the Taoist sage-ruler should do nothing at all. Taoists say the troubles of the world are not caused by governments failing to do enough, but by governments doing too much. They claim that before civilization corrupted people, there had been a golden age:

It was when the Great Tao declined,
That there appeared humanity and righteousness.
It was when knowledge and intelligence arose,
That there appeared hypocrisy.
It was when the six relations lost their harmony,
That there was talk of filial piety and paternal affection.
It was when the country fell into chaos and confusion
That there was talk of loyalty and trustworthiness.
Banish sageliness, discard wisdom,
And the people will be benefitted a hundredfold.
Banish humanity, discard righteousness,
And the people will return to filial piety and parental affection.
Banish skill, discard profit,
And thieves and robbers will disappear.

By virtue (*te* in the canon *Tao-te Ching*), Taoists do not mean the virtues achieved through a moral education, but rather the natural, instinctive qualities of virtue, similar to Plato's ideas of the primitive man in the *Laws*. Taoists therefore strive to return to primitive simplicity, to a time before people were corrupted by the follies of civilization. The *Lao Tzu* thus represents an alternative solution to the political chaos and intellectual turmoil of the late Chou. Like Confucianism, Taoism proposes a way of life and philosophy of government for the elite, the only people who could read and who had the leisure to withdraw to contemplate nature.

Chuang Tzu (Master Chuang, c. 369–286 B.C.E.) was the second great figure, and a historical one, of the Taoist school. He reputedly served as a minor official in one of the states; little is known about him, however, for he seems to have spent much time as a hermit. A book of essays called the *Chuang Tzu* is attributed to him. Like the *Lao Tzu*, it does not depend on methodical argument to convince. It is full of whimsy; animals and insects converse philosophically while men speak nonsense. Moralists, especially Confucians, are lampooned with cutting wit. The Chuang Tzu is sprinkled throughout with anecdotes, of which the following is an example:

> Once Chuang Tzu was fishing in the P'u River when the king of Ch'u sent two of his ministers to announce that he wished to entrust to Chuang Tzu the care of his entire domains.
> Chuang Tzu held his fishing pole and, without turning his head, said: "I have heard that Ch'u possesses a sacred tortoise which has been dead for three thousand years and which the king keeps wrapped up in a box and stored in his ancestral temple. Is this tortoise better off dead and with its bones venerated, or would it be better off alive with its tail dragging in the mud?"
> "It would be better off alive and dragging its tail in the mud," the two ministers replied.
> "Then go away!" said Chuang Tzu, "and I will drag my tail in the mud!"

Chuang Tzu agreed with the *Lao Tzu*'s thesis that the Tao is the underlying principle governing all existence. He denied the Confucian concept that man is the measure of all things. To Chuang Tzu, the human mind was clouded by partial understanding; only the Tao was enduring and eternal. He believed that people must free themselves from their own prejudices and their tendency to judge others in terms of themselves. A person who understood and lived in unity with the Tao would be happy and beyond change and death. Chuang Tzu regarded death as a natural step that followed life in an eternal process of cosmic change; therefore it was not to be feared.

Such was the vision of the early Taoist sages. They extolled nature and urged people to attune themselves to it in order to be happy. They offered no governmental programs except that less is better, until people could return to the state of the childlike innocence of ancient times. A true Taoist should not even urge others to follow the Tao because in so doing he was imposing his own value judgment. However, being human, Taoists joined in competition against other schools of philosophy for acceptance.

The Totalitarians: Legalism

Legalism, the other main challenge to Confucianism, was chronologically the last philosophy to emerge from the Hundred Schools period. It had the greatest impact on the political life of the time. Unlike exponents of the other schools who did not hold important public office, Legalist leaders were high government officials with great power; therefore their primary concern was to find solutions to immediate problems and not to devise theoretical approaches. Like busy politicians, they were impatient with the debates of philosophers, which they condemned as "vain talk." Legalism here does not mean jurisprudence; it refers to the theory and method of political organization and leadership. It developed because the state needed a rational social and political organization to enable it to prosper and to unite China by defeating its rivals in war.

The first book expounding Legalist ideas was *The Lord Shang,* written by Shang Yang (d. 338 B.C.E.). Shang Yang (later rewarded with the title of Lord) was chief minister of the northwestern state of Ch'in and was responsible for organizing a system of government that enabled Ch'in to become powerful, overcome its rivals, and unify China a century later. In his book Lord Shang described the policies that he had successfully implemented, such as the abolition of serfdom and the institution of a centralized, bureaucratic administration. He organized all families into mutual surveillance units, imposed harsh punishments, and rewarded informers. Lord Shang also emphasized the importance of rule by law from which the school derived its name.

Han Fei (d. 233 B.C.E.) was another minister of Ch'in. He too left a book named after himself that added to Lord Shang's theories on Legalism. Han Fei later lost a power struggle, was disgraced, and died in prison at the hands of his fellow Legalist and rival, Li Ssu. Li served as chief minister of Ch'in both during its final drive for unification and afterward. Li, who would also be murdered in prison, synthesized the teachings of Lord Shang and Han Fei and brought them to their highest development. Li and Han's deaths reflect the ruthless and violent power struggles typical of the Legalists.

Legalists had no patience with the Confucians and Taoists, who looked back in time for a golden age. The Legalists maintained that people in the present were neither better nor worse than people in the past; only the conditions were different. Rather than long for a restoration of the past, people should solve new problems with new measures. Han Fei's book cited a story to prove this point:

> There was a plow man of Sung in whose field was a tree stump. When a rabbit scampered headlong into the stump, broke its neck, and died, he abandoned his plow and kept watch over the stump, hoping it would get him more rabbits. But he got no more rabbits and became the laughing stock of the whole state of Sung. Now wanting to apply policies of the former kings in governing people in these times belongs in the very same category as watching over the stump!

The idea that the human condition was a changing process was revolutionary at that time.

While Confucians and Taoists were concerned to improve the plight of the people, Legalists believed that human nature was evil, that people were naturally selfish, lazy, disobedient, and reluctant to engage in war. Accordingly, the Legalists sought to defend the state's absolute authority against the demands of the people through stringent enforcement of strict laws. Those who contribute to the state should be rewarded lavishly, while wrongdoers should be punished with exemplary harshness. For example, when the crown prince criticized some laws as too harsh, Lord Shang held the prince's teacher responsible and had him branded. When some people then praised the laws, he ordered them banished for daring to voice their opinions. All learned to keep quiet and obey. Officials should receive job assignments on the basis of talent and not birth, and they should be held strictly responsible for their deeds. No one is above the law, and when the laws are complete, the system is foolproof. The ruler need only retain the authority to reward and to punish, and all else will run automatically.

The ultimate Legalist goal was to establish and perpetuate an all-powerful state, protected by all-embracing laws, impersonally administered. Legalists maintained that there were only two types of useful citizens: farmers and soldiers. The farmers' work created wealth, and good soldiers won wars that made the state powerful. Furthermore, the state should be able to mobilize its able-bodied farmers and use them as soldiers when needed. How does the state convince its citizens that they must fight? Lord Shang answered: "If there is no hope of fame except through service in warfare, the people will be ready to lay down their lives. . . . I would have the people told . . . if they fear harm, it will be only by fighting that they can escape it." He concluded: "A country that directed itself to these two ends [agriculture and war] would not have to wait long before it established hegemony or even complete mastery over all other states." He also observed that "a ruler who can make the people delight in war will become king of kings."

Legalists disdained the classics and moral values such as filial piety, sincerity, and humanity. They feared that these books and values would dissuade the people from the single-minded pursuit of agriculture and warfare. They also wished to eliminate many classes of people: aristocrats because they were born to their privileges; artisans because they produced luxury items that catered to the aristocrats; innkeepers because they served travelers, who were apt to be troublesome and to plot against the state; merchants because of their avarice; moralists (Confucians) because they preached filial piety and loyalty to friends, which might create conflict of interest and militate against total loyalty and obedience to the state; philanthropists because they helped the poor, whose condition was due to their own laziness and extravagance; recluses (Taoists) because they were unproductive and also might teach the people falsehoods; sorcerers (diviners) because they taught the people to rely on divine guidance; and last, swashbucklers because they roamed in bands and used their "private swords" to carry out justice on behalf of the oppressed little folks. Legalists opposed formal education, except in practical fields such as medicine and agriculture. They regarded history and philosophy books as especially dangerous because they taught people to think and question, activities that made people discontented.

Some modern scholars call this school Realism instead of Legalism. They argue that its adherents, who rejected tradition, supernatural guidance, and morality and insisted that government be based on the actual facts of the world as they existed, were realists. Moreover, they maintain, only such unsentimental and hardnosed policies could have succeeded in ending the chaos of the Era of the Warring States and in unifying China.

The Three Ideologies Compared

Although many schools of philosophy competed for acceptance during the late Chou, we can now say, with the benefit of hindsight, that Confucianism, Taoism, and Legalism were the most important.

Confucians were the idealists. They taught that the goal of life should be the pursuit of goodness and that people should be governed by morality and example, not by harsh laws and punishment. Although they looked back in history for the golden age, they did not extol the past for its own sake, rather they praised certain periods and persons in the past for their virtues and accomplishments. In the process, they also reinterpreted old ideas. For example, the ancient texts talked about *li* as rituals and rites of the aristocratic

LIVES AND TIMES ACROSS CULTURES

Military Innovations

Late Chou China shared with classical Greece a high frequency of wars (468 wars were fought in China between 463 and 222 b.c.e.). The continual struggles for survival eliminated the lesser states until one, a frontier state called Ch'in, triumphed and unified China. The constant warfare produced armies of up to a million soldiers, new military tactics, and increased social mobility as success was rewarded by upward mobility and failure punished by a drastic drop in status, even to enslavement.

Wars were at first chivalrous affairs between aristocrats fighting from four-horse chariots in individual combat; witness the question by one ruler to another in 632 before the opening of combat: "Will Your Excellency permit our knights and yours to play a game?" Later, large infantry forces using stronger iron rather than bronze weapons and supported by cavalry had mostly replaced the war chariots. The change was dictated by the expense of maintaining the less maneuverable chariots and the expansion of contested areas to regions unsuitable for chariots. Chinese states near nomadic lands had adopted cavalry when fighting the horse-riding nomads; once in use, cavalry forces became common in all wars. Innovative military tactics also became important, leading to the rise of career tacticians. The most famous was Sun Tzu (also known as Sun the Cripple), whose work *The Art of War* is still studied in military academies throughout the world.

In ancient Greece, too, the style of warfare changed dramatically in the archaic era (c. 800–500 b.c.e.). At the beginning of the period, cavalry was the backbone of the military. Since only very wealthy, aristocratic families could afford to allocate precious land for the raising of horses, the nobility was as predominant in the military as it was in civic affairs. In Homer's epic poems, too, we see great kings and heroes conveyed into battle by chariots; they then fought mostly champion against champion in single combat, like Achilles and Hector at the climax of the *Iliad*.

Then, in the seventh century b.c.e., there was a shift toward reliance on infantry. State security came to rest on the special training of large numbers of citizen foot soldiers (much more numerous than aristocrats), uniformly equipped with bronze and iron defensive armor and weaponry. Small-farmer militiamen and later professional infantrymen were the decisive factor in all the major land battles fought during the remainder of ancient Greek and Roman history. Commanders like the Spartan Pausanias, the Athenian Pericles, the Macedonian Alexander the Great, and the Roman Julius Caesar were gifted strategists with the remarkable ability to solve the logistical and tactical problems of mobilizing, moving, and deploying the tens of thousands of men in large infantry forces. Not surprisingly, Caesar's *Commentaries* on his wars in Gaul were the favorite reading of a later military genius—Napoleon Bonaparte.

class. Confucius and Mencius gave li a moral dimension and insisted that it be applied to all people. They also insisted that the aristocracy should be based on merit and not on the accidents of birth. Many centuries later, two of the founding fathers of the United States, John Adams and Thomas Jefferson, advocated a similar concept of the "natural" aristocracy of talent. These reinterpretations of traditional values made Confucians revolutionaries.

Taoists taught that humans were originally innocent but were corrupted by civilization. They believed in a return to nature and innocence, and that less is better, especially in government. They valued passivity and individual freedom and shunned worldly power and position. Although Taoism resembles a recent idea of government called laissez-faire, no government has tried to put Taoism into action as a philosophy.

Legalists were cynical realists. To them the individual had worth only if he could serve the state, whose primary functions were war and expansion. Morality was irrelevant. Like Confucians, they believed there should be no privilege by birth; but instead of raising the common people to a higher standard of conduct by teaching them moral values, Legalists demoted the aristocrats to ordinary people, discarded li and subjected all to harsh impersonal laws. They were amoral technocrats and efficiency experts.

The Brief Rise and Fall of the Ch'in

Although the Era of Warring States produced great philosophies, it was a difficult period for most Chinese. Many yearned for the reestablishment of a strong dynasty that would once again bring peace and order. In the rise of Ch'in, their hopes were both realized and turned into a nightmare. As a national dynasty, Ch'in was short lived, but its importance cannot be measured by its duration, for it left its imprint on the next 2,000 years of Chinese history.

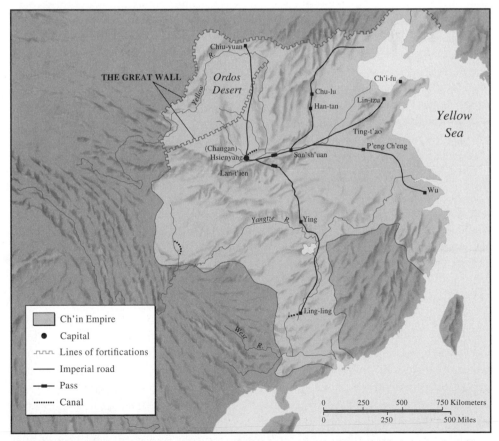

Map 3.3 The Ch'in Empire, 221–206 B.C.E. China was unified in 221 B.C.E., when the Ch'in crushed its rival states. An ambitious program of roads and canals linked the outlying provinces to the capital, Hsienyang, while the Great Wall protected the northern frontiers against nomadic tribes.

Ch'in was located in northwest China, in what had been the Chou homeland. Its rise in some ways was a repeat of the rise of the Chou almost 1,000 years earlier. Because they were tough frontier people, the Ch'in were looked upon by the more advanced Chinese of the heartland as semibarbarous country cousins. Though their location had exempted the Ch'in from most of the wars with other Chinese states, they were nevertheless experienced in war through frequent fighting with nomadic tribesmen from the steppes.

To its original homeland in modern Shensi, Ch'in had early added Szechuan in the southwest along the upper Yangtze Valley. Both lands were rich in agricultural potential if irrigated. Ch'in engineers produced large-scale irrigation and flood-control works (the systems they created in Szechuan are still in use). Despite harsh laws, Ch'in's abolition of serfdom attracted immigrants to settle and farm. Its location on the edge of the Chinese world also saved it from the ravages of the almost continuous warfare that disrupted the economies of the more centrally located states. As a result of economic prosperity, Ch'in built up huge grain reserves, which allowed it to divert manpower from farming into the army in its final push for unification. Its strategic location made Ch'in territories easy to defend from invaders from the east (where most of the Warring States were), while the same mountain passes that protected it were easy staging points to invade the eastern states. Quick to adopt new advances in knowledge and technology, Ch'in soldiers even anticipated the mustard gas used in the trenches in World War I. They used bellows to pump toxic gas generated from burning mustard seeds and other material into the tunnels of their enemies who were besieging Ch'in cities. Ch'in mapmakers drew relief maps that showed the contours of the land and were therefore useful in warfare. A relief map of his entire realm was reported to have been buried in the tomb of the first Ch'in emperor who later unified China.

Ch'in rulers welcomed talented men from other states. In 356 B.C.E., Lord Shang entered into the service of Ch'in from another state and held the office of chief minister until his death in 338. His Legalist policies made Ch'in the most efficiently run state in its time. Officials were chosen on merit and promoted or demoted on their performance, and free men and women worked as tax-paying and land-owning peasants; men also fought as conscript soldiers. Lord Shang was followed by other technocrats; like him, many were born in other states but had been attracted to Ch'in because of the opportunities it offered.

In 247 B.C.E., King Ch'eng, a vigorous and ambitious young man, succeeded to the Ch'in throne, with Li Ssu his chief minister. They completed the conquest and unification of China in 221. Ch'eng decided that he needed a title greater than "king" to match his prestige. With supreme confidence, he called himself *Shih Huang-ti; shih* means "first" and *huang-ti* means "emperor," a title until then used only for high gods. He further decreed that since his house would rule China for all time, his successors would be designated only by numerals, as second, third emperor, and so on. Although his family did not rule beyond the second emperor, the title *huang-ti* was retained by rulers down to the end of the imperial age, in 1911.

Shih Huang-ti and chief minister Li Ssu formally abolished feudalism in the whole empire and instituted a centralized government. The country was divided into

LIVES AND TIMES ACROSS CULTURES

Slavery and Volatile Social Status

During the late Chou (772–222 b.c.e.), the breakdown of the feudal order led to social mobility. For example, out of 713 persons mentioned in important historical works describing this period, over one-third or 34% rose from obscure social origins, proving that there were many opportunities for upward mobility. Others lost status. Prisoners of war, especially captured "barbarians," often became slaves and were presented as rewards to victorious generals. For example, in 594, as a reward for adding territory to the state, a Ch'in general was awarded the families of 1,000 defeated barbarians. Nobles and officials from defeated states could also be enslaved: a former official of a state named Kuo was sold as a slave for five pieces of sheepskin, and another source dated to 655 noted that a defeated ruler and his minister were enslaved and given as part of the dowry of a princess of the victor state. An inscription cites the use of horses, silk, and slaves in lieu of money in commercial transactions. Other sources mention the freeing of slaves who had fought well in battles. Men convicted of certain crimes and their family members were enslaved; people could also be enslaved for indebtedness. All these examples indicate the volatility of social status in the wars that culminated in the Ch'in unification of China.

In both Greece and Rome, slavery was an enduring institution throughout antiquity. In Greece, warfare was the most common source of slaves. Defeated enemies, if not put to the sword or ransomed, were enslaved. This is well-attested in the Bronze Age Linear B tablets and in the epic poems of Homer (c. 725 b.c.e.). Later, the Spartans were able to concentrate on being soldiers because they conquered a neighboring territory—Messenia—and made its inhabitants into state-owned serfs. In ancient Greece, citizens could be stripped of their rights and sold into slavery for nonpayment of debts. The Athenian statesman Solon (594) enacted legislation to prevent the enslavement of Athenian citizens for debt, but he did not abolish the institution of slavery itself. Thus, after taking the island of Melos by siege during the Peloponnesian War, the Athenians put all the males to death and sold all the women and children into slavery. Indeed, slavery was so commonplace that the philosopher Aristotle speaks as if a natural law consigned some people to the status of slaves and others to freedom.

The Romans, too, capitalized on the manpower made available by slavery. Success in warfare resulted in the development of a flourishing trade in slaves and bustling slave markets throughout the empire. So many slaves were employed in farm work by the second century b.c.e. that Rome suffered a series of "servile" revolts in which huge armies of runaway slaves defeated Roman legions in battle.

In the following letter, the Stoic philosopher Seneca (c. 4 b.c.e.–65 c.e.) reflects on the vicissitudes of fortune that made one person a master and another a slave.

"These people are slaves." No: they are human beings.

"These people are slaves." No: they are those with whom you share your roof.

"These people are slaves." No: when you consider how much power Chance can exert over you both, they are fellow slaves.

That's why I find it ludicrous that there should be people who think it shameful to have dinner with their slave. . . .

Each time you remember how much you are entitled to do to your slave, you must remember also just how much your own master is entitled to do to you. "But I don't have any master," you object. The world is still young: perhaps there will come a time when you do have one. *

*Trans. R. Campbell, in Thomas Wiedemann, Greek and Roman Slavery (Baltimore: Johns Hopkins Univ. Press, 1981), pp. 233–235.

commanderies (provinces), which were subdivided into counties. All offices were non-hereditary, and officials were ultimately responsible to the emperor. Uniform laws, weights, measures, coinage, and written script applied to the whole land. The First Emperor ordered roads built to link parts of the country and to facilitate administration and military movements, in much the same way that the Persian emperors Darius and Xerxes had done and that the Roman government would do later. Carts using the roads were required to have axles of standard length, so that the ruts they made would be uniform. His engineers dug a canal linking a tributary of the Yangtze River with the Pearl River in the extreme south to make it easier to supply an army campaigning in the area. The army conquered and annexed lands that today make up southern China and northern Vietnam. In the north, existing walls built by the feudal states against the nomads (and sometimes against one another) were linked together to form a single defense system called the Great Wall. This monumental engineering project was built with conscript and convict labor; although its construction caused enormous hardships, it provided security along a long and vulnerable frontier.

Shih Huang-ti also built a magnificent capital near the first Chou capital, Hao. Because of good surrounding agricultural lands and strategic location, this general vicinity would continue to be China's capital for the next thousand years. Very little remains of the Ch'in capital, but the huge mound, more than 150 feet high, enclosing the tomb that Shih Huang-ti started to build for himself soon after he unified the country is still a major landmark. Records state that tens of thousands of men spent years building the tomb and that it was furnished with fabulous treasures. Nearby, archaeologists have recently excavated three huge underground pits containing over 7,000 life-size terra cotta horses and men, an army to guard him in death.

Despite his real achievements, the First Emperor has been universally reviled in Chinese memory. Popular folk tales denounce his cruelty and tyranny. Millions were conscripted and many died building his walls, canals, palaces, and tomb. Many more paid crushing taxes to support the projects. Scholars abhorred his attempts at thought control. With the Ch'in unification, the Hundred Schools came to an end. Legalism prevailed; all other schools were outlawed. The government prohibited all intellectual discussions; to question the government's policies became treason. In 213 B.C.E., a law ordered all books other than the history of the House of Ch'in and works on agriculture, medicine, and divination confiscated and burned; the penalty for disobeying was death. Scholars were appalled; many, especially the Confucians, spoke out in protest. The emperor had 460 of them arrested and executed. Even the crown prince was not exempt; when he protested the harshness of the punishment, he was banished to duties along the Great Wall. The book burning destroyed forever many ancient texts, creating gaps in our knowledge of the pre-Ch'in eras. Such techniques of totalitarianism and thought control have been used by other tyrants in other eras throughout the world, attesting to the power of the written word. After the fall of the dynasty, when it was again legal to engage in intellectual activities and to write books, accounts were written of the Ch'in dynasty; most of them had little good to say about the First Emperor and his policies.

A Terra Cotta Army. Ranks of life-size infantrymen, horses, and chariots made of pottery are drawn up in battle formation in underground pits that flank the tomb of the First Emperor of the Ch'in. They were intended to protect him in death as his flesh-and-blood forces had in life.

Since all decisions came from the all-powerful emperor, he toiled long hours to do his work. In 210 B.C.E., while on an inspection tour that had as its second goal a search for the elixirs of long life, the First Emperor suddenly died at age fifty, probably from overwork and other excesses. A power struggle followed. Li Ssu and the chief eunuch (eunuchs were castrated males who served in the households of monarchs) destroyed the emperor's will and forged an order commanding the crown prince to commit suicide, which he did. Li and the eunuch put a weakling younger son of the emperor on the throne as Second Emperor so they could rule in his name. Soon these two men fell out and Li was murdered. The eunuch then murdered the Second Emperor and put a son of the late crown prince on the throne. The new ruler had the eunuch executed. By then revolts had broken out everywhere. Loyal generals rushed hither and yon trying to put them down, and many defected when they could not, for failure was a crime punishable by death. In 206 B.C.E., the third Ch'in ruler surrendered to the rebels, thus ending the dynasty.

Summary and Comparisons

This chapter examined the story of several major cultures that flowered in the first millennium B.C.E. and shared a concern with religion and morals. Soon, new developments in religion and philosophy led to the abandonment or modification of previous traditions in favor of new systems of belief.

In Greece, India, and China, intellectual speculation did not evolve in the direction of monotheism. The Hebrews, therefore, were the originators of the first true monotheistic faith, one of the most durable and influential in history. Although the political and mili-

CHRONOLOGY

1300 B.C.E.	
	Moses
1000	
	King David
	First Temple at Jerusalem
	Separate kingdoms of Israel and Judah
650	
	Solon's reforms at Athens
	The Babylonian captivity
	The *Lao Tzu*
	Gautama Buddha, Mahavira
500	Hundred Schools of philosophy in China
	Confucius, *Spring and Summer* and *Analects*
	Theravada Buddhism
	Greek-Persian Wars
	The Parthenon
	Pericles
	Sophocles, *Oedipus the King*
	The Peloponnesian War
	First five books of Tanakh codified
	Jain canon
400	
	Trial and death of Socrates
	Plato, *The Republic*
	Mahayana Buddhism
	Mencius, *The Mencius*
	Tripitaka
	Shang Yang, *Lord Shang*
	Aristotle
	Chuang Tzu, *The Chuang Tzu*
300	
	Chou dynasty ends
	Ch'in, Shih Huang-ti, Li-Ssu
200	The Great Wall of China

tary triumphs of the ancient Hebrew state were short-lived and had little impact outside Palestine, the Hebrew people nevertheless made a momentous contribution to the future of the human spirit through their religion. Judaism furnished its followers with an elaborately formulated and self-consistent ethical code.

The achievements of the Phoenicians were pragmatic. Their sophisticated ports and expert sailors linked West Asia with distant parts of the Mediterranean. Their sailors and merchants also carried an innovation on which no price could be put—a writing system based on an alphabet.

In the archaic period, the Greek world rebounded materially and culturally from the Dark Age. Male citizens increasingly participated in the affairs of their city states. Pericles broadened the basis of democracy and made Athens a focus of economic and artistic activity. The growth of Athenian power, however, led to the Peloponnesian War and ultimately to the dismantling of the Athenian Empire and the hegemony of Sparta and its allies.

Greece was the center of philosophical investigation into the nature of the universe. Greek commitment to the highest intellectual ideals laid the groundwork for philosophical inquiry and the writing of the first factual histories.

Greek literature and art explored the physical and intellectual potentials of human beings. Within a century of their invention, both tragedy and comedy reached the highest levels of artistry, thanks to the city-states' commitment of time, energy, and money to cultural activities. In architecture and the figural arts, also, the Greeks delighted in balance and symmetry of structure and put human beings and society at the center of focus.

In India during the Late Vedic Age (c. 1000–500 B.C.E.), Aryan culture spread eastward to the Ganges Valley and southward to the Deccan Plateau and peninsular India, adapting to contacts with native peoples and experiencing economic transformations. In this era the Upanishads explained the human experience and the relationship with the ultimate. Buddhism and Jainism emerged to play an important part in the future of India and many other parts of Asia.

Despite some differences, the basic views of Jainism, Buddhism, and orthodox Vedism (and Hinduism, a later outgrowth of Vedism) do not disagree: life was governed by universal law or *dharma,* and *karma* or deed determined reincarnation with its painful results; all had as the final goal release, resulting in *nirvana.* However, both of the new faiths deny the validity of the Vedas, the authority of the Brahmans, and the caste system. Similarly, in Greece, Pythagorean teaching about transmigration of souls abandoned traditional religious thinking and offered new, alternative beliefs about the next life.

Gautama Buddha taught the middle way in his Four Noble Truths and Eightfold Path. The greater gains of Buddhism compared with Jainism were due to Buddhism's moderation and more attainable lifestyles, and especially to the popular doctrine of Mahayana Buddhism.

Mahavira, founder of the extremely demanding Jainism, taught a rigorous ethical system that gave special emphasis to the ascetic way of life and to self-denial. So too, in classical Greece, Socrates had sought true knowledge in part by reducing or overriding the physical demands of his body.

Just as political and social ferment in India and Greece around 500 B.C.E. had led to important intellectual and religious developments, similarly, in China, the increasing political chaos of the Eastern Chou (771–256) brought in a period of intellectual turmoil known as the Hundred Schools of Philosophy. Most Chinese philosophers dealt with human relationships in this world, as had the Greek Sophists. The only exception was the school known as Taoism, which advocated passivism, renunciation of civilization, and return to an innocent primitive past. In its advocacy of simplicity and asceticism, Taoism may be likened to Buddhism.

Like the itinerant Greek Sophists, who sought pupils in different city-states, many Chinese philosophers traveled from state to state and attempted to persuade rulers to accept their point of view. Confucius and his disciples were foremost among such dedicated men; they believed that the practice of morality, family responsibility, and virtuous government would bring about a return to the golden age. Confucians were ridiculed by Taoists, who maintained that activism was counterproductive and that the way to achieve peace with oneself was to rise above worldly concerns.

Although Confucianism and Taoism later became the twin mainstreams of Chinese thought, Legalism had an immediate impact on the time. Legalists were cynics about human nature and the nature of power, and were interested only in efficiency and results. Their final goal was an all-powerful state ruled by harsh and impersonal laws. So too, the perfectly just state in Plato's *Republic* was marked by an authoritarianism that rigidly determined all the social, political, military, and educational aspects of life. With Legalism as its guiding ideology, the Ch'in triumphed over the other Warring States and unified China in 221 B.C.E. Between 221–206, the Ch'in ruled China ruthlessly and by terror, obliterating many old institutions. As a system of ruling, however, Legalism was intolerable, as the speedy collapse of the Ch'in empire proved.

All of the major Eurasian civilizations examined in this chapter took great strides in developing important new religious and philosophical systems. All fostered remarkable innovations in religious and ethical thought that had a profound influence on many aspects of life both at the time and through later centuries.

Selected Sources

Items indicated with an asterisk (*) are available in paperback.

*Baldry, H. C. *The Greek Tragic Theater.* 1971. Especially valuable on the social context of the dramatic festivals and on the mechanics of mounting productions.

*Basham, A. L. *The Wonder That Was India.* 1954. A long chapter deals with religions and includes quotations.

Ben-Sasson, H. H., ed. *A History of the Jewish People.* 1969; trans. 1976. A very thorough account from earliest times down to the mid-twentieth century, by several eminent historians.

*Boardman, John. *Greek Art.* 4th ed. 1996. A good basic introduction to ancient Greek art and architecture from the archaic period to the Hellenistic. Many fine illustrations.

Cook, J. M. *The Persian Empire.* 1983. A good, readable, up-to-date introduction to the political and cultural history of ancient Persia. Nicely illustrated.

Cotterell, Arthur. *The First Emperor of China.* 1981. Makes full use of recent excavations of the terra cotta army to bring to life the life and times of the First Emperor.

Creel, H. G. *Confucius the Man and the Myth.* 1949. Creel first gives a biographical account, then explains the development of the myth, the triumph of Confucianism, and its worldwide relevance.

——. *Chinese Thought from Confucius to Mao Tse-Tung.* 1953. Concise, well written, and easy to read.

*de Bary, W. T., ed. *Sources of Indian Tradition.* Vol 1. 1958. Good, short introductory passages explain readings in Buddhist and Jain canons.

*Doody, Margaret. *Aristotle Detective.* 1978. A highly entertaining detective story in which the great philosopher solves the mystery of the violent murder of a prominent Athenian citizen. Realistic background detail.

Edward, J. Thomas. *The Life of Buddha as Legend and History.* 1931. An account of the man and his teachings, the growth of Buddhism, and the myths that surround it.

*Fantham, Elaine, et al. *Women in the Classical World: Image and Text.* 1994. This very current collection of essays by a number of experts includes material on the representation of women in literature, the arts, science, and philosophy throughout Greek and Roman history.

*Hesse, Hermann. *Siddhartha.* 1922; Eng. trans. 1951. A novel about one man and his search for enlightenment.

Hirakawa, Akira. *A History of Indian Buddhism: From Sakyamuni to Early Mahayana.* Ed. and trans. Paul Groner. 1990. Good, comprehensive book.

Hornblower, Simon, and Antony Spawforth, eds. *The Oxford Classical Dictionary.* 3rd ed. 1996. The most comprehensive, one-volume resource for all aspects of the world of ancient Greece and Rome. Includes contributions from hundreds of leading specialists.

Jaini, P. S. *The Jain Path of Purification.* 1979. Good summary of Jain teachings.

Lange, Nicholas de. *Judaism.* 1986. A recent account of the characteristics and importance of this world religion.

Levi, Jean. *The Chinese Emperor.* 1987. A novel on the life and times of the First Emperor; describes the murderous intrigues and horror of life in a Legalist state.

*Mazar, Amihai. *Archaeology of the Land of the Bible: 10,000–586 B.C.E.* 1990; rev. 1992. Simply the best available work on the topic; thorough and attractively presented.

Moscati, Sabatino. *The World of the Phoenicians.* 1968. A good, readable history by the Director of Semitic Studies at the University of Rome.

*Pomeroy, Sarah, et al. *Ancient Greece: A Political, Social, and Cultural History.* 1999. An extremely well-written narrative history, enriched with illustrations and frequent excerpts from primary sources.

Potok, Chaim. *Wanderings: Chaim Potok's History of the Jews.* 1978. A riveting account of 4,000 years of history by the noted American Jewish novelist, scholar, and rabbi.

*Powell, Barry B. *Classical Myth.* 2nd ed. 1998. A wonderfully thorough treatment, founded on ample selections from ancient sources.

*Renault, Mary. *The Last of the Wine.* 1956; reprinted 1975. One of the best of Renault's excellent historical novels; set in the time of the Peloponnesian War.

Robinson, Richard H., and William L. Johnson. *The Buddhist Religion: A Historical Introduction.* 1982. Covers the development of Buddhism in India and elsewhere.

Schwartz, Benjamin. *The World of Thought in Ancient China.* 1985. A comprehensive exposition of Chinese classical philosophies.

*Starr, Chester G. *Individual and Community: The Rise of the Polis, 800–500 B.C.* 1986. A good, recent presentation of the cultural, economic, and political achievements of the citizens of the Greek polis.

Twitchett, Dennis, and Michael Loewe, eds. *The Cambridge History of China.* Vol. 1: *The Ch'in and Han Empires, 221 B.C.–A.D. 220.* 1986. Definitive treatment by many experts; Chapter 1 deals with the Ch'in Empire.

Vaux, R. de. *The Bible and the Ancient Near East.* 1972. A useful assessment of biblical narratives within the context of the history of the Near East.

*Waley, Arthur. *Three Ways of Thought in Ancient China.* 1939. A short, lucid study of Confucianism, Taoism, and Legalism, with many quotes from original writings of the three schools.

Additional resources, exercises, and Internet links related to this chapter are available at the Book Companion Web site: http://history.wadsworth.com/upshurcompact4/

COMPARATIVE ESSAY 3
The Defining Characteristics of Great Empires

Most noteworthy by far and most marvelous of all is the grandeur of your concept of citizen-ship. There is nothing on earth like it. For you have divided all the people of the Empire . . . into two classes: the more cultured, better born, and more influential everywhere you have declared Roman citizens . . . the rest vassals and subjects. . . . Everything lies open to everybody; and no one fit for office or a position of trust is an alien. There exists a universal democracy under one man, the best princeps [emperor] and administrator.

Aelius Aristides, in N. Lewis and M. Reinhold, eds., *Roman Civilization, Sourcebook II: Roman Empire* (New York: Harper, 1966), pp. 135–136.

Several great empires—the Hellenistic kingdoms, the Roman Empire, and the Mauryan and Han Empires—flourished between about 300 B.C.E. and 200 C.E. Each unified under one government diverse and often previously antagonistic peoples and states. Each was maintained by huge resources of manpower and materials. The quotation above praises the Roman imperial achievement and the many benefits the empire brought to its citizens.

Empires were secured by powerful military forces, effective bureaucracies, and diplo-matic alliances that often included the exchange of hostages and arranged marriages between ruling families. A poem by a homesick Han princess attests to the high individ-ual human cost of dynastic marital affiliations:

My family sent me off to be married on the other side of heaven;
They sent me a long way to a strange land, to the king of Wu-sun.
A domed lodging is my dwelling place, with walls made of felt;
Meat is my food, with fermented milk as the sauce.
I live with constant thoughts of my home, my heart is full of sorrow;
I wish I were a golden swan, returning to my home country.

Princess Hsi-chun, in James P. Holoka and Jiu-Hwa L. Upshur, eds., *Lives and Times: A World History Reader*, vol. 1 (Minneapolis/St. Paul: West Publishing, 1995), p. 173.

Although they varied considerably in size and longevity, each empire controlled much more territory and larger populations than a single city or group of settlements. Each of the empires discussed in Chapter 4 controlled lands at least the size of the United States east of the Missis-sippi. Each had populations numbering in the tens of millions and endured for at least two cen-turies. Other empires had appeared earlier in history (for example, the Egyptian, Assyrian, and

Persian), while others would form later (for example, Aztec, Inka, Ottoman, and Mongol). *Although each was distinct, most great empires shared numerous common characteristics.*

Successful empires were stable and durable for the following reasons: each had centralized leadership and an efficiently run government. Empires were often headed by a more or less stable hereditary dynasty, bolstered by a social and political elite like the Roman patricians or the great families in Han China. Most successful imperial administrations also recruited at least some officials on the basis of merit and not birth. This was true of the Hellenistic states, Rome under the emperors, and Han China. In fact, many empires relied on their schools to fill administrative positions; the successful ones also gave efficiency ratings and on-the-job training to promising officials, and based promotions on performance. In Han China, administrators were chosen from a pool of formally educated men through recommendation, examination, and efficiency ratings. An imperial university for training bureaucrats had over 30,000 students at its peak. In the Hellenistic states, literacy in Greek was essential for successful advancement in both public and private sectors.

Great empires had uniform currencies and standards of weights and measures that simplified tax collection, government finance, and trade. Rulers issued coins that publicized themselves and their political programs. Reasonable fiscal and tax systems generated sufficient revenues to run the government without overburdening the population. When greed or overwhelming needs caused extortionate taxation, disaffection or rebellion often resulted, presaging eventual decline and fall. The maintenance of an adequate military force always took up the largest share of tax revenues and much manpower.

All empires also required service from their citizens, either as soldiers or as laborers. For example, in Rome all male citizens were obligated to serve in the army, initially without pay. Likewise, the Han government demanded military and corvée service (compulsory, unpaid labor) from its adult males. In time, in both China and Rome, long-term, professional forces superseded inadequate part-time citizen soldiers. Successful empires possessed weapons and military technology superior to those of their enemies; they also supplemented this technological superiority with defensive installations such as the Great Wall in China and Hadrian's Wall in Roman Britain. Vital empires were almost invariably aggressive, often attacking and absorbing their weak or hostile neighbors. Military strength and wealth from booty brought safety and provided the preconditions for further economic expansion and technological innovation. The resulting prosperity contributed to social harmony and political stability. However, the great expense of garrisoning vast territories with professional soldiers also imposed huge financial burdens that drained treasuries.

Empires had uniform legal codes, which the governments enforced. Examples were Rome's Twelve Tables (and the later Justinian Code) and the Mauryan code engraved on stone pillars. The Roman legal system became the foundation for many later European codes. Similarly, later Chinese and other East Asian legal systems were based on the Han legal code. Muslim empires often based their legal systems on the Qur'an.

All great empires built elaborate public works. Although often constructed by forced labor, the roads, aqueducts, granaries, and irrigation works generally had long-term benefits for all inhabitants, often outlasting the states that built them. The Persians, Romans, and Inkas were especially good civil engineers. Their roadways expedited troop movements, domestic commerce, and international trade. Even today, many Roman highways are still in use. An international overland route, called the Silk Road, linked the Roman and Han Empires. Safe trade and travel along this 6,000-mile route was possible because of the Pax Romana and Pax Sinica. Such domestic and international peace maintained over long periods promoted well-being for millions of people. The mapping and policing of sea lanes and the building of harbors and lighthouses also promoted both domestic and international trade. All empires built lavish public monuments, especially in capital cities. Temples, tombs, and palaces, which had no tangible benefits for ordinary people, nevertheless provided spiritual consolation and inspired pride. Even in ruin, the Roman Colosseum, Asoka's pillars, and the monuments at places like Copán in Central America still inspire awe and admiration.

Great imperial governments also patronized learning, expressed in literature, art, and philosophy. In Han China, the government-sponsored writing of history set the example for succeeding generations. In Ptolemaic Egypt, the government supported research in the sciences and a great library in Alexandria. The emperor Augustus's encouragement of writers resulted in masterpieces of Latin literature such as Vergil's *Aeneid*. The political integration of vast imperial territories also brought about linguistic integration. Latin became the universal language of western Europe, Greek of the eastern Mediterranean, and Chinese of East Asia.

Successful empires instilled a sense of strong allegiance and a spirit of public service in their people. Even after such empires fell, the memories of their grandeur continued to capture the imaginations of later generations. For centuries, western Europeans longed to resurrect the glories of the Roman Empire. The very name of Rome, the eternal city, led Constantinople to be called the "Second Rome," and after Constantinople's fall to the Muslim Ottoman Empire, Russian rulers designated Moscow as the "Third Rome." So too, the Chinese have continued to call themselves the Han people. Asoka's lion serves as the national symbol for modern India.

In Chapter 4 we shall examine several of the world's earliest great empires: the Hellenistic, Roman, Indian, and Chinese. Each had many of the characteristics outlined in this essay.

The Age of Great Empires

•

• Macedonian Conquest and Hellenistic Empires •

• The Rise and Decline of Roman Power in the Mediterranean World •

• The Emergence and Disintegration of the Mauryan Empire •

• China's First Imperial Age: The Han Dynasty •

• Summary and Comparisons •

When Pausanias [a former favorite and now aggrieved bodyguard of King Philip of Macedon] asked [his teacher] how he could become most renowned, the sophist answered: "by slaying the man whose achievements were the greatest, for the assassin's fame would endure as long as the great man's." Pausanias took this opinion as applicable to his own situation. He immediately resolved to revenge himself during the distractions of the wedding festival [of Philip's daughter]. Having readied horses at the city gates, he went to the entrance of the theater carrying a concealed Celtic dagger. Philip on his arrival bid his companions to enter ahead of him, and with his bodyguard ordered to keep their distance, was by himself. Pausanias darted forward and stabbed the king through his ribs, killing him instantly. Then he made a dash for the gates and his getaway horses . . . . Pausanias nearly made it to the waiting horses, but his shoe caught in a vine and he fell. As he was getting up, Perdiccas and the others overtook him and slew him with their javelins.*

Hsiang Yu invited Liu Pang to stay for a banquet [at the former's military camp]. . . . [During the banquet] several times Fan Tseng [Hsiang Yu's supporter] shot Hsiang Yu meaningful glances, but Hsiang Yu did not respond. Finally Fan Tseng rose and went out. Summoning Hsiang Chuang [another supporter of Hsiang Yu], he said:

"Our lord is too kindhearted. Go in, drink a toast, and offer to perform a sword dance. Then strike the lord of Pei [Liu Pang] down where he sits. If you don't do this, we will all end up his captives."

Hsiang Chuang went in to offer a toast, after which he said, "Our prince is drinking with the lord of Pei, but we have no entertainers in the army. May I perform a sword dance?"

"Very well," said Hsiang Yu.

Hsiang Chuang drew his sword and began the dance . . . [but] Hsiang Po [a supporter of Liu Pang] followed suit, shielding Liu Pang with his body so that Hsiang Chuang could not strike him.**

*Plutarch, *Life of Alexander,* trans. James P. Holoka, in James P. Holoka and Jiu-Hwa L. Upshur, *Lives and Times: A World History Reader,* vol. 1 (Minneapolis/St. Paul: West Publishing, 1995), p. 143.
**Ssu-ma Ch'ien's *Shih chi* [Records of the Grand Historian], in K. C. Chang, ed., *Food in Chinese Culture: Anthropological and Historical Perspectives* (New Haven: Yale University Press, 1977), p. 64.

Both successful and failed assassinations have had a great impact on history. The first excerpt describes how a disgruntled bodyguard and lover of King Philip of Macedon picked an opportune moment to kill his master and was himself killed almost immediately afterward. Circumstantial evidence indicates that Philip's son and successor Alexander was implicated in the plot. Alexander had quarreled with his father and was afraid of being disinherited in favor of Philip's son by a new wife. Since Pausanias was killed immediately, we cannot know for certain that Alexander was guilty of patricide.

The second passage recounts a banquet in 206 B.C.E. hosted by Hsiang Yu, the leading candidate to succeed the recently toppled Ch'in dynasty. Liu Pang, his lieutenant and the chief guest at the banquet, was also his main rival. Here the quick reaction by one of Liu Pang's aides foiled an assassination attempt by Hsiang Yu's supporters. Liu Pang went on to destroy Hsiang Yu and founded the successful Han dynasty.

This chapter highlights the principal achievements of four of the greatest empires of the ancient world. Three—the Macedonian/Hellenistic, Mauryan, and Han—were founded by ambitious and opportunistic men who seized the advantages offered by wars, invasions, and assassinations. By contrast, the Roman Empire, though it too saw its share of assassinations, grew by the efforts of many great men building on the achievements of their predecessors.

The Hellenistic kingdoms, unlike the classical Greek city-states, brought Greek culture to large, politically unified territories. The Roman Empire unified the entire Mediterranean basin and spread Greco-Roman culture throughout Europe and much of West Asia. The India of the Mauryan Empire, particularly under emperor Asoka, witnessed unprecedented political and religious unification. In Han dynasty China, a remarkable flowering of culture accompanied military and governmental successes.

A Greek citizen of the Roman Empire, Aelius Aristides, once praised Rome in the following terms:

> *You have surveyed the whole world, built bridges of all sorts across rivers, cut down mountains to make paths for chariots, filled the deserts with hostels, and civilized it all with system and order. . . . Before your rule, things were all mixed up topsy-turvy, drifting at random. But with you in charge, turmoil and strife ceased, universal order and the bright light of life and government came in, laws were proclaimed, and the gods' altars acquired sanctity.*

Though there is some exaggeration in this adulatory account, it is nevertheless essentially true, and similar words could rightly be addressed not only to Rome but to any of the empires examined in this chapter.

Macedonian Conquest and Hellenistic Empires

> *You [Philip] are called to action . . . by your ancestors, by Persian effeminacy, by the famous men, true heroes, who fought against Persia, and most of all by the fitting hour which finds you in possession of greater strength than any previous European, and your adversary in deeper hatred and wider contempt than any monarch in history. . . . What will be the praises sung of you, when it is realized*

that in the political field you have been the benefactor of all Greek states, and in the military the conqueror of Persia? No achievement can ever be greater than to bring us all out of such warfare to unity of spirit.*

*Isocrates, "Philip," in Greek Political Oratory, trans. A. N. W. Saunders (Harmondsworth: Penguin, 1970), pp. 164–165.

The Greek city-states of the fifth century B.C.E. had achieved remarkable triumphs in their economic, cultural, and intellectual life, but they failed to overcome interstate rivalries and to unite their world in a lasting political organization. In the wake of the debilitating Peloponnesian War, no Greek state was powerful enough to control or rally the rest for any length of time. This situation changed forever with the careers of Philip II (reigned 359–336 B.C.E.) and Alexander the Great (reigned 336–323 B.C.E.). The two Macedonian leaders enlarged the Greek world and dramatically changed it both politically and culturally.

In the quotation above from an open letter to Philip II, the Athenian orator Isocrates urges the Macedonian king to lead Greece in a crusade against the Persians. He appeals to long-standing Greek prejudices: freedom-loving, rational, masculine Greeks are contrasted with enslaved, barbarian, effeminate Persians. As usual, however, the Greek states were fatally incapable of united action, and Philip was more interested in gaining supremacy for Macedon than in saving Greece from its chronic internal strife.

By 338 B.C.E. Philip had taken advantage of weaknesses of the old city-state system to establish Macedon as the dominant political and military force in the Greek world. After Philip's death, his son Alexander capitalized on this military superiority to conquer vast territories in Asia and Africa. On his death they were divided into several very large kingdoms, which we designate Hellenistic (the word indicates postclassical Greek civilization from the death of Alexander in 323 into the first century B.C.E.).

The Father: Philip

After the Peloponnesian War, the Spartans for a time maintained a shaky predominance among Greek city-states but lacked the diplomatic and financial savvy of the Athenians; by the mid-fourth century B.C.E., Greece was still a disunified collection of independent city-states. The common folk, disenchanted with endless warfare, lost their patriotic enthusiasm for the polis. Greek soldiers often served as mercenaries for the highest bidder, whether Greek or not.

Before the reign of King Philip II, Macedon was an underdeveloped region in northernmost Greece. Many Greeks thought of Macedonians as hard drinking, backward, and uncivilized. In fact, Macedon was a sleeping giant, with valuable natural resources and huge manpower reserves. Similarly, in China during the Warring States era, the frontiersmen Ch'in people were thought to be uncouth country cousins by the more advanced Chinese of the heartland. Nonetheless, they were able forcibly to unify China as Philip and Alexander subjugated Greece.

Philip first reformed the army, making it fully professional, with the highest standards of discipline and elite units called companions. He increased its size to more than

25,000 men diversified among infantry, light-armed skirmishers, archers, slingers, and cavalry. He also introduced a new, thirteen-foot thrusting spear, better siege machinery, and more effective infantry tactics. Philip funded this crack army by seizing the Mount Pangaeus gold and silver mines. He then defeated the Balkan neighbors who had long plagued Macedon. Philip next unified and modernized his country by redistributing the population into new urban centers and by making better use of arable land. He ushered Macedon into mainstream Greek culture by promoting education and encouraging artists and intellectuals to come to the new royal capital at Pella, where Alexander was born. Philip also dared to aim at political domination of Greece.

The Greek city-states feared this growth of Macedonian power and influence. In a series of speeches known as *Philippics,* the Athenian statesman Demosthenes portrayed Philip as addicted to power. Deciding the time had come for a showdown, the Athenians and Thebans confronted the Macedonians at the battle of Chaeronea in 338 B.C.E., and were crushed by Philip and eighteen-year-old Alexander. Chaeronea ended the tempestuous history of the city-state as the primary Greek political unit. From now on, large empires absorbed the Greek states into new political structures. Greece was only the first of many territories that fell to the expanding power of Macedon.

After Chaeronea, Philip announced his intention to avenge Persian offenses, especially Xerxes' burning of Greek temples 150 years earlier, and envisaged a campaign of glorious conquest in Persia. In 336, however, with preparations for this expedition well under way, he was murdered by a disgruntled member of the royal bodyguard. After the assassination of Philip, the troops proclaimed Alexander king; the chance for glory in the Persian campaign went to the son, not the father.

The Mother: Olympias

Philip's principal instrument of foreign policy was warfare or the threat of it. However, as a means of securing good relations with neighboring states and tribes, he also entered into dynastic marriages—some half dozen altogether. This was his motive in marrying a member of the royal family of Epirus. But his connection with Myrtale, or Olympias as she came to be known, was to be especially important, for she bore him the son—Alexander—who was to succeed him.

Our primary ancient historical sources were composed, virtually without exception, by men. Given the rigidly male-dominated and patriarchal ancient Greek society, it is no surprise that Greek historians often vilified strong-willed women who dared to affect the course of political events or to influence men in positions of power. Olympias is no exception.

The first strike against Olympias was her semibarbaric status: as an Epirote rather than a Macedonian, she was at two removes from the Greek ethnocentric definition of "civilized." She was said to be an enthusiastic devotee of that most foreign-seeming of Greek gods, Dionysus, whose rites involved wild dancing on the mountainsides and the dismemberment and eating raw of sacrificial animals.

The second strike against her was psychological: she was overly sensitive to any slight to her honor and fiercely determined to avenge any such slight. Her relationship to the equally strong-minded Philip was evidently troubled from the outset. And when Philip took a full-blooded Macedonian wife in order to ensure a legitimate heir to his throne, he alienated Olympias irretrievably.

Olympias enjoyed much closer ties to her son than did Philip, who was constantly away campaigning or busy governing Macedon. She and her kinfolk were Alexander's first teachers. In the final rift between Olympias and Philip, Alexander sided with his mother. Moreoever, Alexander's future conception of himself as a latter-day Greek mythological hero was nourished from boyhood by his mother's insistence that his true father was Zeus, not Philip at all.

When Philip was assassinated, Olympias understandably shed no tears for the man who had spurned and humiliated her. Some contemporaries even suggested she had engineered the murder. In fact, it is far more likely that Alexander was behind the murder conspiracy, though this cannot be proven. There can be little doubt, however, that Alexander's extremely forceful and compelling personality owed as much to Olympias as to Philip.

The Son: Alexander

The nineteen-year-old Alexander possessed tremendous determination and an unquench-able thirst for power. As a youth, he underwent thorough training in athletics and weapons use; he was a fast runner and rode a horse almost before he walked. Nor was his intellectual development neglected: Philip hired the philosopher Aristotle to be Alexander's tutor. His education gave him a scientific curiosity about the natural world and a deep love for literature, especially the epics of Homer and the odes of the great Boeotian lyric poet, Pindar. Alexander's military training culminated in his command of the attacking wing of the Macedonian forces at Chaeronea. By the time his father was assassinated, he was a great favorite among the troops.

In 336 B.C.E., as Alexander was putting down invasions by Macedon's semibarbaric neighbors, the Greek city-states saw a chance to regain their freedom. When Thebes revolted (with Athenian encouragement), Alexander marched swiftly into Greece and destroyed the city (except for the house Pindar had lived in) as a horrifying example to other would-be rebels. He treated Athens much more leniently, out of respect for its cultural history and especially its naval power. Alexander now began his campaign against Persia, crossing the Hellespont in 334 B.C.E. precisely where Xerxes had crossed to attack Greece in 480—the symbolism was obvious. Besides his army of 65,000, Alexander brought with him technicians, road builders, surveyors, administrators, financial officers, and secretary-journalists. In addition, geographers, botanists, zoologists, astronomers, and mathematicians collected information that formed the basis of European knowledge of West Asia and India for many centuries afterward.

In the next decade, Alexander conquered the whole Persian Empire (see Map 4.1). While he was in Asia Minor and Syria-Palestine, Alexander ran the risk that the Persian navy might attack Greece or cut his supply lines at the Hellespont, forcing him to withdraw from Asia. The Persians, however, unwisely decided to give battle on land, first at the Granicus River in 334 B.C.E. and then, under King Darius III himself, at Issus in 333.

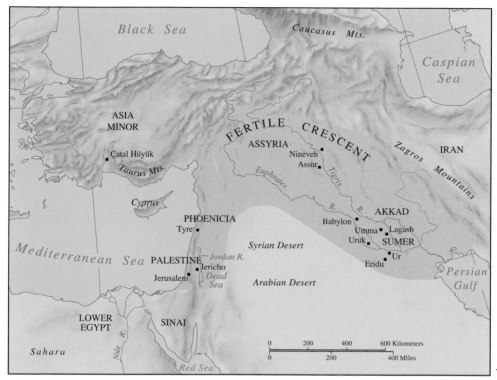

Ancient Mesopotamia
The two great rivers of Mesopotamia flow out of Anatolia (present-day Turkey): in Mesopotamia the Euphrates runs some 800 miles and the Tigris about 440, from northwest to southeast, before they join as the present-day Shatt al-Arab, whose 100-mile course ends in the Persian Gulf.

Western Chou China

Eleventh to Ninth Centuries B.C.E. The victorious house of Chou divided its territories into fiefs and granted them to relatives, allies, and even surviving relatives of the previous Shang dynasty, while retaining only a core territory that it ruled directly as *chungkuo* or royal (central) domain. During its initial centuries, the Chou royal house was powerful and exercised control over the feudal vassals.

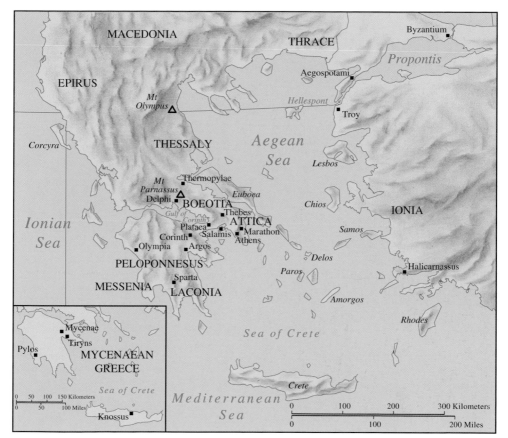

The Greek Homeland

This map shows major fifth-century Greek city-states, battle sites, and cultural centers in the Balkan Peninsula and on the islands and shores of the Aegean Sea.

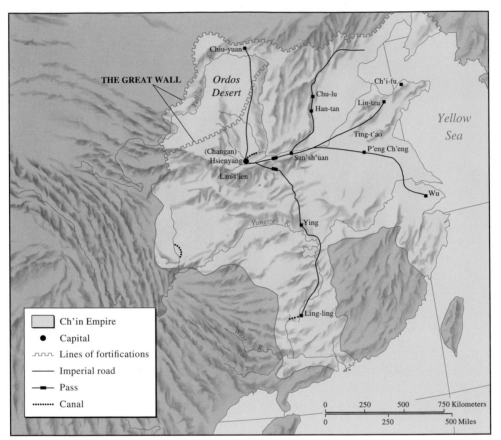

The Ch'in Empire, 221–206 B.C.E.
China was unified in 221 B.C.E., when the Ch'in crushed its rival states. An ambitious program of roads and canals linked the outlying provinces to the capital, Hsienyang, while the Great Wall protected the northern frontiers against the nomadic tribes.

The Boy Alexander and the Black Stallion

Philonicus the Thessalian brought the horse Bucephalas to Philip, offering to sell him for thirteen talents; but when they went into the field to try him, they found him so very vicious and unmanageable that he reared up when they endeavored to mount him, and would not so much as endure the voice of any of Philip's attendants. Upon which, as they were leading him away as wholly useless and intractable, Alexander [about ten years old at the time], who stood by, said, "What an excellent horse they are losing for lack of courage and know-how!" Philip . . . said, "Do you reproach your elders, as if you knew more and could better control him yourself?" "I could manage this horse," replied Alexander, "better than others do." "And if you do not," said Philip, "what will you forfeit for your rashness?" "I will pay," answered Alexander, "the whole price of the horse." Everyone laughed at this; and as soon as the wager was settled between them, Alexander immediately ran to the horse, and taking hold of the bridle, turned him directly toward the sun, having noticed that he was disturbed by the movement of his own shadow.

Then letting him go forward a little, still keeping the reins in his hands and stroking him gently, when he began to grow eager and fiery, he shed his upper garment and with one bound mounted him firmly. When he was astride him, he gradually drew in the bridle and controlled him without blows or spurs. Then, when he was quite relaxed and ready to run, he let him go full speed, urging him with his voice and his heels. Philip and the others gazed in silence and some anxiety, but seeing him return rejoicing in what he had done, they burst into applause. Philip shed tears of joy and kissed the boy as he dismounted, saying "O my son, look for a kingdom worthy of you, for Macedon is too little for you."*

Philip's words were, of course, prophetic. Alexander kept the mighty Thessalian stallion and rode him in most of the major battles of his career. When the great warhorse died, some twenty years later, in the Indus region after the battle of the Hydaspes River, Alexander named a settlement there Bucephala in his honor.

*John Dryden, trans., "Life of Alexander," sect. 6, in vol. 2 of Plutarch's Lives, ed. A. H. Clough (New York: Dutton, 1910), p. 467 (with slight modifications).

Alexander won both battles and added the Mediterranean portion of the Persian Empire to his conquests. He marched into Syria and Palestine, where he took Tyre, a key Persian naval base. In Egypt, where he was proclaimed pharaoh, Alexander founded the city of Alexandria in 331. This later became the principal center of Hellenistic cultural development, the most important port in the eastern Mediterranean, and the second most populous city (after Rome) in the history of the ancient world. Alexander also underwent a decisively important religious experience when he consulted at the oasis of Siwah the oracle of Ammon, whom the Greeks equated with Zeus, the god he may have believed was his true father. Though we do not know the content of the oracle's message, since Alexander refused to disclose it till he had spoken with his mother (he died before seeing her), he henceforth believed himself marked out by the gods for even greater achievements than merely punishing the Persians.

Alexander next set out to conquer the heartland of the Persian Empire—modern Iraq and Iran. He beat Darius decisively at Gaugamela near the Tigris in 331. The beaten king escaped and was shortly thereafter assassinated by dissatisfied allies. Alexander then marched triumphantly into Babylon, Susa, and Persepolis, seizing massive booty in gold and silver. At Persepolis, he burned the great royal palaces and temples, avenging the Persian destruction of Greek temples. Turning his war machine eastward to the Indus Valley, Alexander and his troops ran into winter weather in mountainous terrain and torrential

Map 4.1 Conquests of Alexander the Great and the Hellenistic Kingdoms. After the death of Alexander, his far-flung empire, which had never really been stabilized administratively, was carved up during a long series of struggles among his successors. Three major kingdoms emerged by the third century B.C.E.—the Macedonian, the Seleucid, and the Ptolemaic.

monsoon rains. In the main pitched battle of this part of the expedition, Alexander defeated the Indian potentate Porus at the Hydaspes River in 326. Reluctantly yielding to the wishes of his weary troops, Alexander abandoned his plan to march even farther east. The journey back to Persia proved perilous, as the army encountered heavy fighting and suffered tremendous loss of life during a disastrous trek through the Gedrosian desert region.

During his long campaign of conquest, Alexander assumed many of the trappings of Persian royalty, since he saw himself as the successor of the Great King and had come to admire Persian customs. He married the Sogdian princess, Roxane, and encouraged his officers to marry into Iranian nobility. He also promoted a plan of race fusion of his Macedonians and Persians, without much success. He treated Persians and other Iranians as his subjects rather than enemies and recruited a special corps of Iranian troops into the Macedonian army. He even demanded typically Persian signs of obeisance, specifically, prostration before the king. Since, for Greeks, such actions were associated only with the worship of the gods, many of Alexander's veterans resented the apparent arrogance and inaccessibility of their leader.

Alexander was not one to rest on his laurels or devote his life to the administrative tasks of achieving political and social stability in conquered lands. Instead he planned new expeditions to the Arabian Peninsula, Africa, and perhaps the western Mediterranean. In 323, however, he died at Babylon of a fever of unknown origin, possibly malaria. The long journey, wounds suffered in battle, and probably advanced alcoholism had finally exhausted Alexander's marvelous stamina. Although Roxane bore a son,

Alexander IV, after Alexander's death, both were murdered.

When Alexander was asked on his deathbed to whom he wished to leave his empire, he answered, "To the strongest." The result was ultimately a division of the empire into three Hellenistic kingdoms: Macedon and Greece; the Seleucid Empire, extending from Asia Minor to India; and the Ptolemaic kingdom, embracing Egypt and, at times, parts of Palestine. These kingdoms differed markedly from the classical city-states. Much larger in territory and ethnically more diverse, they were administered by an elaborate hierarchy headed by a remote, godlike king of Macedonian descent who made the laws, owned much of the land, and was deified after death. Private citizens counted for much less politically than had their fifth-century ancestors and consequently felt little patriotic fervor.

The Hellenistic kingdoms endured for about two or three centuries. Macedon and

Silver Tetradrachm. This four-drachma piece shows a divinized Alexander wearing the royal diadem and the ram's horns symbolic of Zeus Ammon, whose oracle he consulted at the oasis of Siwah. For the first time in Western civilization, coins bore the image of human rulers, as well as of gods. The coin, minted after Alexander's death, demonstrates the artistry of Greek coin designers and die cutters.

The Granger Collection

Egypt fell entirely under Roman domination. The overextended Seleucid empire lost territory too, as the culturally Hellenized kingdoms of Bactria and Parthia split off in its central and eastern sectors; in the West, it succumbed to Roman armies. Ultimately, the Parthians would rule from the Euphrates to the Indus and, with superb cavalry, pose an insoluble military problem for the Romans; they also exploited their profitable position as brokers in the trade between East and West.

A Sophisticated, Cosmopolitan Society and Economy

Although wars occurred, an unprecedented level of cooperation among cities and among Hellenistic kingdoms brought stability and prosperity. Greek educators, artisans, merchants, and soldiers moved into recently conquered regions. Trade relations were more secure and extensive, and Greek language and culture pervaded the newly formed kingdoms, at least among the upper classes.

Although most Hellenistic families were farmers, a remarkable growth in manufacturing and international commerce took place. Each region had special commodities, which were exchanged around the Mediterranean and southwestern Asia: grain from Egypt, the Black Sea, and Sicily; olive oil from Attica; wines from Ionia and Syria; salt fish from Byzantium; cheese from Bithynia; prunes from Damascus; glass from Sidon; parchment from Pergamum (in present-day western Turkey), bitumen (used in Egypt for embalming) from the Dead Sea; marble from Paros and Attica; timber from Macedonia and Lebanon; precious purple dye from Tyre; ivory from India and Egypt; gemstones from

A Prenuptial Agreement from Hellenistic Egypt

Apollonia agrees to live with Philiscus in obedience to him, as is appropriate for a wife to her husband, possessing with him the property that they have in common. Philiscus . . . is to provide her with every necessity and a cloak and other possessions . . . at a level appropriate to their means, and Philiscus [may not] . . . bring into the house another wife in addition to Apollonia or a concubine or a catamite nor is he permitted to beget children with another woman so long as Apollonia is alive, nor to set up another household unless Apollonia is in charge of it, and he promises not to throw her out or insult or mistreat her and not to alienate any of their joint property in a way that would be injurious to Apollonia. If Philiscus is shown to have done any of these things or if he has not provided her with the necessities or the cloak or the other possessions as specified, Philiscus must immediately return the dowry of two talents and four thousand drachmas of copper money.

Similarly, Apollonia is not to stay away for a night or a day from Philiscus' household without Philiscus' knowledge, nor is she to live with another man or to cause ruin to the common household or to bring disgrace on Philiscus in whatever brings disgrace to a husband. If Apollonia voluntarily wants a separation from Philiscus, Philiscus is to return her dowry intact within ten days.*

The passage quoted here is from a papyrus found at Tebtunis in Ptolemaic Egypt and dates to 92 B.C.E. By ancient standards, this is an equitable marriage agreement. The basic responsibilities of both husband and wife are stipulated and the disposition of the dowry and other communal property is carefully defined. The woman Apollonia has been well served by the male relatives who negotiated this marriage contract on her behalf.

*Mary R. Lefkowitz and Maureen B. Fant, Women's Life in Greece and Rome: A Source Book in Translation, 2d ed. (Baltimore: Johns Hopkins University Press, 1992), p. 90.

India and Arabia; frankincense (used as a burnt offering in many religions) from Arabia; balsam from Jericho; and slaves from Thrace, Syria, and Asia Minor.

Enhancing our knowledge of the Hellenistic world are many finds of papyrus in the arid soil of Egypt. The papyri record all sorts of official administrative dealings, as well as private communications and documents including wills, receipts, accounts, letters, lists, and memoranda. Others record agreements regarding marriage, divorce, adoption, apprenticeship and employment, and loans and sales of property and goods.

Hellenistic governments promoted and safeguarded these trade relations. Existing road networks, including those of the Persians, were maintained and expanded; water supply along caravan routes was ensured; efforts were made to suppress piracy; and standard monetary systems were adopted. Certain cities—Rhodes, Delos, Corinth, and Ephesus, in particular—grew wealthy as transit depots. With the rise of Rome in the third century and after, new Italian markets further stimulated commerce.

An Age of Scientific Advances

The Hellenistic kingdoms allocated financial support for various cultural enterprises. The Ptolemies of Egypt, for example, built and supported two important facilities, the first of their kind in history: the great Library of Alexandria and the affiliated "think tank" known as the Museum. Eminent librarians presided over the collection of some half-million volumes (papyrus rolls), and the world's first textual critics carefully edited the great works of Greek literature.

The Stoic Mind Is a Citadel

Take me and cast me where you will, for there I shall keep my divine part tranquil . . . if it can feel and act according to its proper constitution. Is this change of place sufficient reason why my soul should be unhappy and worse than it was, depressed, expanded, shrinking, frightened? . . .

If you are pained by any external thing, it is not this thing that disturbs you, but your own judgement about it. And it is in your power to wipe out this judgement now. But if anything in your own disposition gives you pain, who hinders you from correcting your opinion? . . .

Remember that the ruling faculty is invincible, when self-collected it is satisfied with itself, if it does nothing which it does not choose to do, even if it resist from mere obstinacy. . . . Therefore the mind which is

free from passions is a citadel, for humans have nothing more secure to which they can fly for refuge and for the future be inexpugnable.*

In this passage, Marcus Aurelius preaches the Stoic doctrine of self-control. The right-thinking person understood that human suffering was a result of an inner response to an outer occurrence. If the mind was correctly trained and attuned to the true nature of the universe, no accident could harm it. Indeed, "accidents" were entirely neutral—simply things that occurred. The Stoic individual possessed a refuge in reason that offered absolute protection from the seemingly harmful events in the world around us.

*Marcus Aurelius, Meditations, Book 8, sects. 45–48, trans. George Long, in The Stoic and Epicurean Philosophers, ed. Whitney J. Oates (New York: Random House, 1940), p. 550.

The scientific contributions of Hellenistic scholars were especially significant. By 300 B.C.E. Euclid had clearly explained the principles of geometry in his Elements, the basic textbook for the next 2,000 years. The brilliant inventor and mathematician Archimedes of Syracuse (c. 287–212) worked on the geometry of spheres and cones and established the value of pi. Astronomers made surprisingly accurate calculations: a sun-centered theory of the universe was proposed, but the older, earth-centered theory won out, and its formulation by Claudius Ptolemy was not superseded until the work of Copernicus, Galileo, and Newton in the sixteenth and seventeenth centuries. Eratosthenes accurately calculated the circumference of the Earth by comparing the angles of shadow at noon during the summer solstice at two widely separated locations on the same meridian. In biology and medicine, dissection of cadavers and even of living convicts (supplied by King Ptolemy) advanced understanding of anatomy, including the function of the brain and central nervous system and the distinction between veins and arteries.

Hellenistic thinkers showed little interest in applied science and engineering. Under pressure from their rulers and patrons, however, they did produce some new military hardware; Archimedes was as famous for his machines and weaponry as for his mathematical genius; for example, he invented a giant catapult that could hurl 200-pound missiles up to 200 yards.

Escapism and Individualism in Hellenistic Culture

Religion in Hellenistic times was directed more to the spiritual and escapist needs of the individual than to the promotion of civic responsibility. Since the individual was no longer an integral part of a civic group watched over by guardian deities, the old state religion lost its meaning. Needing more immediate emotional satisfaction and assurance of self-worth, people turned to the impressive secret ceremonies of popular new sects known as mystery religions. Cults like those of Dionysus from Greece, Isis from Egypt, and Mithras from Persia offered an escape to a joyful hallucinatory experience of union with a god or goddess, an experience induced by alcohol or drugs, delirious dancing, and sexual frenzy. The promise of immortality was a further attraction. Mystery religions remained popular in the Roman Empire and helped pave the way for Christianity.

For many educated persons, two new philosophical systems—Stoicism and Epicureanism—filled the vacuum left by the waning of the old religion. Zeno of Citium (335–263 B.C.E.) taught in Athens at the Stoa Poikile (painted hall), and his doctrine is thus called "Stoic." Its principal tenets were as follows: First, goodness is based on knowledge. Only the wise person is really virtuous. Second, the truly wise person lives in harmony with nature by means of one's reason, which is part of the divine, universal reason (= God) governing the natural world. It follows that, third, the only good is harmony with nature. External "accidents" like sickness, pain, and death cannot harm the truly good person. Stoicism's emphasis on outwardly directed concepts like duty and civic responsibility later ensured its prevalence in the Roman Empire. Indeed, the Roman Emperor, Marcus Aurelius, was a practicing Stoic whose book of *Meditations* is a masterpiece of Stoic philosophy.

Epicurus (341–270 B.C.E.), who taught at Athens about the same time as Zeno, preached the following principles: First, nothing exists but atoms and void. The soul, like all else, is material and disintegrates like the body; thus it cannot suffer after death. Second, the only good in this life is pleasure, a perfect equilibrium or inner tranquillity, defined as the absence of pain or stress. Third, all our actions should be directed toward the minimizing of pain, that is, toward pleasure. This was an inwardly directed system, recommending withdrawal from society and public life. Its emphasis on pleasure invited charges of vulgar hedonism: Eat, drink, and make merry, for tomorrow you die and will not be held accountable. These perceptions are reminiscent of the charges that some Chinese leveled against Taoists. Despite such accusations and misconceptions, the Epicureans exerted great influence and found their most eloquent proponent in the Roman poet Lucretius.

Stoicism and Epicureanism both offered ethical systems suited to the conditions of life in the Hellenistic world. Rather than focusing exclusively on the search for knowledge about the nature of the universe, they stressed the ability of properly educated individuals to ensure their own happiness. In different ways, each promised release from the psychological and spiritual pain of life in a cosmopolitan world where traditional values were dying.

After the masterpieces of the classical era, literature in the Hellenistic period is disappointing. Menander (c. 342–c. 290 B.C.E.) perfected the New Comedy, whose emphasis, typical of the era, was on private family squabbles rather than the sharp-witted satirical reference to current events and public policy found in Aristophanic Old Comedy. Recent papyrus finds give a clearer impression of this comedy of manners, featuring young lovers, upstart slaves, crotchety old men, and so on. Mistaken identity, contrived or accidental, often motivated the plot. An immensely popular form, New Comedy's influence

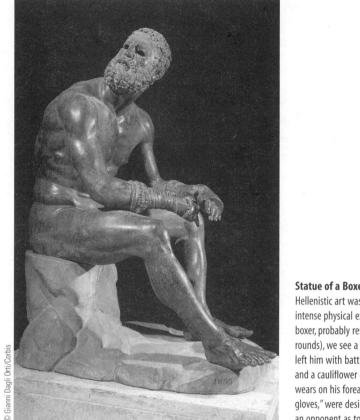

© Gianni Dagli Orti/Corbis

Statue of a Boxer. One of the favorite subjects of Hellenistic art was the human figure in the throes of intense physical exertion or pain. In this statue of a boxer, probably resting between bouts (there were no rounds), we see a veteran of many fights, which have left him with battle scars, including a broken nose and a cauliflower ear. The leather straps and pads he wears on his forearms and fists, known as "sharp gloves," were designed as much to inflict damage on an opponent as to protect the wearer.

extended to the Roman stage, in the work of Plautus and Terence, and later to Shakespeare's comedies. The situation comedies of television are modern analogues.

Hellenistic art, best represented in sculpture, is both more ornate and more individualistic than classical art, particularly in its representation of extreme emotion. Artists could still capture classical Greek nobility of form, as in the superb winged Nike of Samothrace, but the supple sensuality of the Venus de Milo is more typical. Humbler, more naturalistic subjects were chosen too: for instance, a gnarled old boxer waiting his turn to compete, or a little girl holding a pet dove. The famous Laocoön group, showing the Trojan priest Laocoön and his two sons being attacked by two sea serpents, symbolically captures the essence of war's hellish human price. Its style differs markedly from the sublimity of most Classical sculpture. The discovery of the Laocoön at Rome during the Renaissance created a sensation and profoundly influenced Michelangelo (who viewed it within hours of its discovery), Titian, and Lessing.

Hellenistic artists practiced their art at the behest of the royal families or for wealthy private citizens. They did not, like their classical predecessors, create adornments for the greater glory of the beloved city-state or the gods who watched over it. In this regard, they followed the same trend toward individualism and escapism that can be seen in Hellenistic philosophy and literature.

The Rise and Decline of Roman Power in the Mediterranean World

The study of history usefully provides a record of all manner of experiences inscribed as it were on a glorious monument. From that record, the reader may choose examples worthy of imitation by himself and by his nation and examples of behavior that are thoroughly disgraceful and to be avoided. If I am not deceived by my love of the work I have set myself in writing history, no republic was ever greater, more virtuous, or abundant in good examples. Into no state did greed and self-indulgence come so late. In no state was there such respect for so long a time for frugality and an austere way of living.*

*Livy, *Ab Urbe Condita*, Book 1, praefatio (translated by James P. Holoka).

These words of praise come from the historian Livy's preface to his magisterial history of Rome. Writing in the late first century B.C.E., he had witnessed the violent upheavals that attended the political transition from Republic to Empire. It was a time of disillusionment among many Roman intellectuals. But Livy found solace in writing the history of his state from its very beginnings. For he found there the record of great achievements and remarkable moral probity. While we may apply a more critical standard in our assessment of Rome's rise to power, the value of studying its history is assured by the influence Roman examples have exerted in the story of civilizations.

Rome had humble beginnings, however, and Romans were not always masters of the world. To explain Rome's rise, we must consider its origins, the social and political practices that gave it internal strength, and the military exploits by which it overcame external threats and conquered great reaches of land. We will examine the resulting Greco-Roman civilization that so shaped the culture and thought of later ages. Finally, we will consider the factors that led to the collapse of Roman power.

The Early Roman Republic

Centrally located in the Mediterranean, Italy has hot and dry summers and mild winters with moderate rainfall. As in Greece, the mountainous land separated the population into numerous city-states in valleys or coastal plains, but, with abundant timberland and more cultivatable land, Italy could support large populations.

The history of Rome begins in the eighth century B.C.E., when three major ethnic groups inhabited the Italian peninsula. Greek colonists of the archaic period built towns throughout southern Italy and in Sicily. The Etruscans, who had immigrated in the same period, possibly from Asia Minor, occupied the territory between the Tiber and the Arno Rivers and exerted a crucial influence in culture and religion. Constituting an older ethnic strain than the Greeks and Etruscans were the Italic peoples—Latins, Sabines, and others—in whom were combined a Mediterranean people, perhaps from North Africa, and Indo-Europeans from across the Alps. They were a hardy stock, primarily farmers and herders.

The archaeological record shows that Rome in the eighth century was inhabited by shepherd folk: Latins and Sabines. Etruscan influence in the next three centuries brought progressive urbanization. The Tarquins of Roman myth likely reflect a historical period of Etruscan political and cultural domination. Rome's expulsion of its overlords marked the start of a period of government by elected officials, under a republic.

© Betthmann/Corbis

Bronze She-Wolf. This bronze statue (fifth century B.C.E.) represents the most famous city symbol ever devised. The wolf was a kind of totem animal from earliest times: when Romulus and Remus were exposed on the banks of the Tiber by their evil great-uncle, a she-wolf rescued and suckled them. The statue is a fitting symbol of the Roman virtues of warrior prowess and unflinching dedication to family (the twins are a Renaissance addition).

In the early republic, the population of Rome was sharply divided into patricians and plebeians. The patricians were a hereditary aristocracy that accepted high civic responsibility not just for the sake of power but also because of the dignity conferred by public recognition of services rendered. The plebeians, who comprised the great mass of the free population, farmers, shepherds, small merchants, and artisans, suffered from poverty and oppression by aristocrats. By going on strike or threatening secession, however, the plebeians eventually secured certain essential individual rights and freedoms for all citizens, not just patricians. These included the right to vote for magistrates, the right to have marriages between citizens legally recognized, the right to secure legally binding commercial contracts, and the right to due process in any criminal proceedings. Although the plebeians respected the political competence of the patricians, they successfully agitated for the right to intermarry with patricians and for a written code of law. The Twelve Tables (449 B.C.E.) marked the beginning of a distinguished history of Roman law, which extended down to the Justinian code of the sixth century C.E. Though excluded from patrician status, plebeians could rise to the rank of *equites* (knights), if they possessed the financial resources to raise horses and serve as cavalry in the army. They also eventually won the right to serve in the highest public offices. By the early third century, such guarantees of fair play and opportunities for advancement, won by hard struggle, were the inalienable right of every Roman citizen.

The Twelve Tables: The Law in Early Republican Rome

When a debt has been acknowledged . . . thirty days must be the legitimate time of grace. After that, the debtor may be arrested by laying on of hands. . . . The creditor may . . . bind [the defaulter] either in stocks or in fetters . . . with a weight no more than fifteen pounds, or with less if he shall so desire. . . . Unless they make a settlement, debtors shall be held in bonds for sixty days. During that time they shall be brought before the praetor's court in the meeting place on three successive market days, and the amount for which they are judged liable shall be announced; on the third market day they shall suffer capital punishment or be delivered up for sale abroad, across the Tiber.

Quickly kill . . . a dreadfully deformed child.

A child born ten months after the father's death will not be admitted into legal inheritance.

Females shall remain in guardianship even when they have attained their majority . . . except Vestal Virgins.

Persons shall mend roadways. If they do not keep them laid with stone, a person may drive his beasts where he wishes.

It is permitted to gather up fruit falling down on another man's farm.

If any person has sung or composed against another person a song such as was causing slander or insult to another, he shall be clubbed to death.

*If a theft has been done by night, if the owner kill the thief, the thief shall be held lawfully killed.**

The Twelve Tables, Rome's earliest written code of law, represented a victory for the plebeian order. Though the code seems to mete out a rough justice, the very fact that it existed in written form shielded, for example, the poor (plebeian) debtor from completely arbitrary punishment by a patrician magistrate. Also, once the law was written down, it could subsequently be amended and refined to create a more rational and humane system of justice. The Twelve Tables also furnishes invaluable evidence for the human condition in early republican Rome: it was an agrarian world, much concerned with questions of property, debt, law and order, and the various rights of family members.

*Naphtali Lewis and Meyer Reinhold, eds., Roman Civilization, Sourcebook I: The Republic (1951; reprint, New York: Harper, 1966), pp. 103–104, 106–107.

Rome, like Greece, was a slave-owning society. Perhaps one-fourth of the population throughout antiquity consisted of slaves acquired through warfare, piracy, and trade. Slaves provided the bulk of the labor force, performing household tasks and the heavy work of farming and mining. Slavery in ancient Rome was also a mechanism for the assimilation of new peoples. The common practice of freeing slaves as a reward for loyal service gave rise to a class of second-class citizens called freedpersons; such large populations of non-Romans were given their freedom that by the late republic perhaps one-half of the citizenry of Rome had slave ancestry.

Although republican Rome never allowed as much participation of common citizens in key governmental decisions as classical Athens had, it did allow for representation of various elements of its society and adjusted to changing needs. The various magistracies were normally annual in tenure and divided among colleagues. Two consuls, elected annually for a one-year term, were the chief civil authorities within the city and commanders of the armed forces. They were empowered to appoint a dictator for a six-month term in times of dire emergency. Other elected officials had responsibility for administering justice; supervising public works; producing games, races, and contests; maintaining official financial accounts; and conducting the census. In addition to the civic magistracies, the Romans elected for life the *pontifex maximus* (chief priest), who presided over the entire apparatus of the state religion. Finally, the Roman Senate was a key advisory body of ex-magistrates who held membership for life. *Senatus Populusque Romanus* (the Senate and Roman People; abbreviated SPQR) was the logo of Roman jurisdiction.

Roman society was based on "piety," the value system that embraced devotion to the gods and to members of one's family, both living and dead. Romans honored the memory of their forefathers and held to their morality of hard work and self-discipline in service to gods, family, and state. As in the teachings of Confucius, the family was a microcosmic state: the father was effectively king and chief priest of the miniature nation of his family. Roman women were educationally and legally disadvantaged, like their Greek sisters, but they could aspire to be *matronae* (mothers of families). In return for her fidelity, fertility, and domesticity, the Roman woman could expect to be revered within her family and Roman society.

Roman religion, like Greek, was polytheistic and involved civic as well as personal duty. Roman beliefs were shaped by foreign influences. The old Italic agricultural gods were modified to parallel Etruscan and/or Greek gods. Venus was equated with Greek Aphrodite, Jupiter with Etruscan Tinia and Greek Zeus, and so on. The goal of Roman religion was *pax deorum* (peace with the gods). Prayers, vows, sacrifices, acts of purification or atonement were all designed to appease gods who were easily angered and liable to inflict punishment on an entire group, guilty and innocent alike. Divination of various kinds was practiced in an effort to ascertain the will of the gods: soothsayers read the stars and the flight patterns of birds and professional "gut watchers" discerned the future in the entrails of sacrificial animals. In return for observance of religious rituals, Romans hoped for favorable answers to their requests for divine assistance.

The Roman Conquest of Italy and the Mediterranean

After 509 B.C.E. Rome joined, and later dominated, a league of Latin cities that defended its fertile plains against the frequent incursions of neighboring hill peoples like the Sabines. Success against these enemies led ultimately to their political absorption and the replacement of Oscan language dialects by Latin. After the setback in 387 of a shattering defeat at the hands of Gauls, fearsome Celtic invaders from across the Alps, the Romans embarked on campaigns of conquest against Gauls and Etruscans to the north and against Samnites and Latins to the south. By 290, Rome controlled more than half of the Italian Peninsula.

Roman predominance in the Italian Peninsula at the beginning of the third century B.C.E. rested on a shrewdly conceived system of annexations and alliances. Rome also established colonies of citizens or, more often, of allies, thus increasing its territory, available manpower, and military strength. Rome's conquests were achieved by an army of unpaid militia conscripted for each campaigning season. Discipline, obedience to authority, and endurance of adversity combined with first-rate training and drill to make the

LIVES AND TIMES ACROSS CULTURES

Women's Rights: A Test Case in Republican Rome?

During the early part of the second Punic War (218–201 b.c.e.), after a succession of stunning victories by Hannibal (see below), the Roman government passed a special measure to restrict women's possession or display of such luxury items as gold jewelry and expensive clothing. This law remained in force throughout the war and was still not revoked when prosperity returned after its end. As a result, the women of Rome dared to launch a public campaign for its repeal. The historian Livy reports that "the matrons, whom neither counsel nor shame nor their husbands' orders could keep at home, blockaded every street in the city and every entrance to the Forum. As the men came down to the Forum, the matrons besought them to let them, too, have back the luxuries they had enjoyed before, giving as their reason that the republic was thriving and that everyone's private wealth was increasing with every day. This crowd of women was growing daily, for now they were even gathering from the towns and villages. Before long they dared go up and solicit the consuls, praetors, and other magistrates."

One of the consuls for that year, the crusty Marcus Porcius Cato, an arch-conservative and staunch opponent of repeal, delivered a speech attacking the women for their (in his view) outrageous misbehavior and for fomenting a governmental crisis.

I blushed when, a short while ago, I walked through the midst of a band of women. . . . Our ancestors did not want women to conduct any—not even private—business without a guardian; they wanted them to be under the authority of parents, brothers, or husbands; we (the gods help us!) even now let them snatch at the government and meddle in the Forum and our assemblies. What are they doing now on the streets and crossroads, if they are not persuading the tribunes to vote for repeal? Give the reins to their unbridled nature and this unmastered creature, and hope that they will put limits on their own freedom; unless you do something yourselves, this is the least of the things imposed upon them either by custom or by law which they endure with hurt feelings. They want freedom, nay licence (if we are to speak the truth), in all things. . . . If they are victorious now, what will they not attempt? . . . As soon as they begin to be your equals, they will have become your superiors . . . .*

Speaking against Cato and in favor of repeal was Lucius Valerius, one of the tribunes:

From the very beginning—the reign of Romulus—when the Capitoline had been taken by the Sabines and there was fighting in the middle of the Forum, was not the battle halted by the women's intervention between the two lines? . . . After the kings had been expelled,

Roman soldier the best the world had yet seen. The efficiency and preparedness of its military were to stand Rome in good stead during its coming struggles against major powers outside the Italian Peninsula.

In the third century Carthage was the major power in the western Mediterranean. Originally founded as a Phoenician colony (called *Poeni* in Latin, giving the adjective "Punic"), its central position in the Mediterranean, near modern Tunis, and its excellent harbor made it a preeminent trading city. It controlled the exchange of gold, silver, and tin from Spain and Africa for wine, textiles, and manufactured goods of its own or from the Hellenistic East. The rise of Rome to a rival first-class power imperiled that advantage.

when the Volscian legions and their general, Marcius Coriolanus, had pitched camp at the fifth milestone, did not the matrons turn away the forces which would have buried the city? When Rome was in the hands of the Gauls, who ransomed it? Indeed the matrons agreed unanimously to turn their gold over to the public need. Not to go too far back in history, in the most recent war, when we needed funds, did not the widows' money assist the treasury?

Hannibal was in Italy, victorious at Cannae. Already he held Tarentum, Arpi, and Capua. He seemed on the verge of moving against Rome. Our allies had gone over to him. We had no reserve troops, no allies at sea to protect the fleet, no funds in the treasury. . . . Widows and children were donating their funds to the treasury.

Shall it be our wives alone to whom the fruits of peace and tranquillity of the state do not come? . . . When you, a man, may use purple on your clothes, will you not allow the mother of your family to have a purple cloak, and will your horse be more beautifully saddled than your wife is garbed? . . . They cannot partake of magistracies, priesthoods, triumphs, badges of office, gifts, or spoils of war; elegance, finery, and beautiful clothes are women's badges, in these they find joy and take pride, this our forebears called the women's world. When they are in mourning, what, other than purple and gold, do they take off? What do they put on again

when they have completed the period of mourning? What do they add for public prayer and thanksgiving other than still greater ornament? Of course, if you repeal the . . . law, you will not have the power to prohibit that which the law now forbids; daughters, wives, even some men's sisters will be less under your authority—never, while her men are well, is a woman's slavery cast off; and even they hate the freedom created by widowhood and orphanage. They prefer their adornment to be subject to your judgment, not the law's; and you ought to hold them in marital power and guardianship, not slavery; you should prefer to be called fathers and husbands to masters. *

Although Cato and Lucius Valerius hold opposing views on the repeal of the wartime emergency legislation, both speak from a patriarchal bias. Cato blatantly resists the granting of any rights or freedoms that might incite the "unbridled nature" of women. Lucius Valerius recognizes the sacrifices women have historically made in the state's interest and appears to sympathize with their deprivation of signs of status and position. But, while he recommends a more enlightened and kindly exertion of control, all power will remain firmly in the males' hands. In this particular instance, the women prevailed and the offending legislation was revoked.

*Livy, History of Rome, 34.1, trans. Maureen B. Fant, in Mary Lefkowitz and Maureen B. Fant, Women's Life in Greece and Rome: A Source Book in Translation, 2nd ed. (Baltimore: Johns Hopkins University Press, 1992), pp. 143–146.

When Carthage began to expand in Sicily (see Map 4.2), Rome decided in 264 to send troops to the island, thus starting the first Punic War. After Rome built a fleet to match that of the Carthaginians, final victory came in 241 at the high price of 200,000 men and 500 ships lost. Rome's Italian allies and colonists had supplied the needed reserves of manpower and material. The fruits of the hard-earned triumph were sweet. Carthage paid an indemnity of 3,200 talents (200,000 pounds in weight) of silver over the next ten years and ceded its territory in Sicily and, eventually, in Corsica and Sardinia. Rome had acquired its first overseas possessions, and the long process of adapting their government to the requirements of a far-flung empire began in earnest.

Initial hostilities in the second Punic War were ignited by friction in Spain, where members of the Barca family—Hamilcar and later his son Hannibal (247–183)—had been directing the creation of Carthaginian colonies. In 219 Hannibal took by siege the Spanish town of Saguntum, which had contracted an alliance with Rome. War broke out the following year.

Hannibal surprised the Romans by leading men, horses, and combat elephants across the Alps into the Po Valley. By his tactical brilliance and his superior cavalry, he defeated Roman troops sent to stop him, but could not take Rome itself, for the allied cities of central Italy held firm. Instead, he established himself in southern Italy, devastating the territory of those cities that resisted and accepting the cooperation of others.

The tide turned in Rome's favor with the appointment of a brilliant general, Publius Cornelius Scipio (236–183). He succeeded in taking the New Carthage, the nerve center of Punic power in Spain, in 209. Later, Scipio carried the war to North Africa and, after Hannibal was recalled by Carthage, defeated the great general at Zama in 202. In 201 Carthage capitulated, surrendering Spain and agreeing to pay an indemnity of 10,000 talents. The once mighty city survived, only to be razed in 146, after the third Punic War. Rome, now the foremost power in the western Mediterranean, was ready to turn to the Hellenistic East.

As Cicero later said in his *Republic,* "Our people, by defending allies, have become masters of the entire world." When Rhodes and Pergamum appealed to Rome, its armies defeated the Macedonian king in 197. Rome later went to war with the Seleucid kings, again with Macedonia, and with a confederation of Greek states called the Achaean League. The result in each case was Roman victory and the creation of new provinces or puppet states from formerly independent Greek territories. Attalus III (reigned 138–133), the last king of Pergamum, bequeathed his kingdom to Rome, and Rome possessed its first province in Asia.

Between 264 and 133 Rome had won important victories because of the bravery and discipline of the loyal legionary soldiers, and the competence, and sometimes brilliance, of its generals. Rome's military success cost its opponents dearly, as Roman soldiers hunted down and butchered or enslaved Spaniards, Gauls, and Sardinians. Nor were civilized adversaries spared plunder, enslavement, rape, and extortion. As the historian Tacitus cynically said, "Plunder, murder, theft, these they misname empire; and where they make a desert, they call it peace."

By 133 B.C.E., empire building had become Rome's chief industry, a source of glory for the Roman nobility and of profits both for the state and for entrepreneurs, businessmen, publicans (tax collectors), and provisioners of the army. New trade routes and markets proliferated in the Mediterranean region. However, many had little share in these profits of empire. The small farmer who had been the mainstay of the early republican state began to disappear. Devastation by Hannibal's army and long neglect of farms caused by military service in the second century ruined many farmers, forcing them off their land. Wealthy senatorial aristocrats bought up the holdings of failed farmers and combined them into vast estates worked by the plentiful slaves obtained through foreign conquests. Dispossessed free men drifted to Rome in search of work or handouts, swelling the ranks of a restless urban population.

For the citizens of Rome, the downside of the greatly enlarged slave labor force was the threat of revolt. Although many literate and skilled slaves from the Greek east found a comfortable life in the homes of wealthy Romans, the great majority of slaves were consigned to hard labor in the fields and mines. Runaways turned to banditry in the Italian countryside and posed a problem of national security: for example, 100,000 rebellious slaves led by the gladiator Spartacus were crushed in 71 B.C.E., but only after two years at large, during which they inflicted several defeats on Roman legions.

Provincials, too, often suffered from the predations of Roman governors, who were often less interested in fair administration than in enriching themselves through excessive taxation. Inclusion in the empire was thus a mixed blessing.

The Breakdown of the Republic and the Rise of Augustus

By 133 B.C.E., Rome had long since outgrown the makeshift constitution that had served well in early phases of its history. The vast territorial expansion of the empire and the tremendous powers wielded by generals and politicians finally strained the whole framework to the breaking point. Roman history became a tale of power seizures, assassinations, mob violence, political collusion, and, in general, an utter disregard for republican habits of government.

After 133 the political atmosphere in Rome was charged by tension between *populares,* both patrician and plebeian, whose policies generally favored the common people, and *optimates,* again both patrician and plebeian, whose policies generally favored the entrenched senatorial elite. Gaius Marius (157–86 B.C.E.) solved Rome's recruitment problem and acquired a private army by transforming farmer-militiamen into paid professional soldiers. Land grants to discharged veterans accelerated Romanization of outlying parts of the empire and shifted soldiers' allegiance from the civil authorities to the military commander.

Marius's former subordinate Sulla now set the precedent of using military force to achieve his own political ends. Beginning in 83 B.C.E., he fought a bloody civil war against his *populares* opponents and had himself appointed dictator. Because Sulla needed land and money to reward his troops, he set forth proscriptions, lists of public enemies who could be murdered for a reward, including many whose only offenses were their political opinions or their wealth.

In the next thirty years, three new strongmen accumulated fantastic military and political power. Gnaeus Pompeius (106–48 B.C.E.), called Pompey the Great, Marcus Licinius Crassus (c. 112–53 B.C.E.), and Gaius Julius Caesar (100–44 B.C.E.) cooperated for a time to subvert the republican system in favor of their own personal goals, but the uneasy balance of mighty egos finally collapsed.

Julius Caesar had family connections to important *populares* and had served in various high offices. The phenomenal success of Caesar in the Gallic wars of 58–50 B.C.E. upset the tripartite balance of power. He gained for Rome the territory from the Alps to the Atlantic and the North Sea. He also won tremendous booty, shared liberally with his devoted army, which grew from two to thirteen legions. Meanwhile, Crassus's dream of military glory died with him and most of his seven legions on the plains of Mesopotamia, near Carrhae, in 53 B.C.E. The Parthians proudly displayed the captured legionary eagle standards (and Crassus's head on a pike) as trophies. Events now swiftly brought Caesar to supreme power. When the Senate voted that Caesar should lay down

Map 4.2 The Roman World at the Time of the Late Republic. Shown here is the territory under Roman control by about 133 B.C.E. The inset map shows the routes of Hannibal's army and important sites during the second Punic War.

his command before returning to Italy, Caesar chose rebellion. He forced Pompey and an army loyal to the Senate to withdraw to Greece. Caesar defeated him in 48 at Pharsalus. Escaping to Alexandria, Pompey was stabbed to death.

Caesar settled matters from one end of the Mediterranean to the other. He established Cleopatra (69–30 B.C.E.) as queen of Egypt, where he remained almost a year. At Rome, Caesar reduced the number of grain dole recipients, carried out public works programs, and revised the calendar, making it solar rather than lunar. Caesar spared Roman citizens who had fought against him in the civil war and even secured offices for former aristocratic opponents, but continued to monopolize power, becoming in 44 *dictator perpetuus* (dictator for life). This angered jealous aristocrats and alarmed true republicans, including Marcus Junius Brutus (85–42), who murdered Caesar at a meeting of the Senate on the Ides (fifteenth) of March 44 B.C.E.

After Caesar's assassination, no one individual leader was able to consolidate all his powers. Caesar's grandnephew, Gaius Julius Caesar Octavianus—"Octavian" (63 B.C.E.–14 C.E.)— used his vast inherited riches to raise armies and buy influence. After the group responsible for assassinating Caesar was eliminated, Octavian persuaded the western provinces, Italy, and most of the surviving Roman aristocracy that Marc Antony, a colleague of Julius Caesar's who was in control of the eastern provinces of the empire, meant to make Cleopatra joint ruler and shift the center of empire to Alexandria. In 31 Octavian crossed to Greece and defeated Antony and Cleopatra at the naval battle of Actium. At Alexandria the following year, Antony committed suicide to avoid capture, as did Cleopatra, last Hellenistic ruler in the Ptolemaic line from Alexander's day.

Octavian, now left as the single all-powerful ruler, inaugurated the imperial period of Roman history, an epoch that witnessed a fusing of West Asian, Greek, and Roman cultural traditions. He accepted the name Imperator Caesar Augustus (*augustus* means "venerable" or "majestic") and announced his intention to restore republican institutions. However, the next forty-one years brought instead a steady, calculated implementation of a new monarchy, as Augustus's shrewd outward show of respect for republican institutions disguised his monopoly of power. Actually, Augustus genuinely respected most Roman traditions and tried to revive a society demoralized by civil strife.

The emperor's powers were virtually unlimited. He kept exclusive control of the military, which meant ultimate civil authority as well. Augustus's stupendous personal wealth allowed him to win and maintain the people's favor. He built new forum areas, renovated temples, improved roads, and, to keep the urban poor from growing restive, financed public games and kept grain prices artificially low, thereby setting the precedent for later emperors.

Unlike Alexander the Great, Augustus engaged in conquest not for its own sake but to secure borders and to promote the arts of government within them. He succeeded both by his own administrative skills and by those of the men he selected for positions of power. As an economic result of this stability of government, commercial and manufacturing activity flourished during the *Pax Romana* (Roman Peace). Augustus also reopened and made secure trade routes both inside the Mediterranean and outside it, for example, with Arabia, India, and China, via the Red Sea and Indian Ocean.

Cleopatra, Last of the Hellenistic Queens

When [Cleopatra] first met Antony she sailed on a golden barge, dressed like Aphrodite. She was not so beautiful as some earlier Macedonian queens, but she possessed a magical charm and a beautiful voice. She was well educated and spoke many languages including Egyptian (unlike many male Ptolemies). . . . Since Antony did not have intellectual aspirations, Cleopatra entertained him as he desired. The two of them enjoyed Oriental luxury, Cleopatra playing the exotic companion to Antony's pleasure, though the debauchery and drunkenness ascribed to her are not in keeping with the traditions of Hellenistic queens, and, as far as we know, she had sexual liaisons with only Caesar and Antony. Legends built up by her enemies are doubtless the source of unflattering accounts, since Cleopatra's competence as a ruler was never questioned, and Egypt remained loyal to her. . . .

She resembled Alexander the Great in her ability and quest for world empire. She posed a major threat to Octavian and Rome. . . . When Octavian finally declared war after Antony had formally divorced Octavia [Octavian's sister], he declared war on Cleopatra alone. . . .

After being defeated by Octavian, Antony committed suicide and died in Cleopatra's arms. Rather than grace Octavian's triumph, Cleopatra killed herself by allowing an asp to bite her breast. . . . She dominated Antony, and, if she loved him, she certainly never let emotion divert her from her schemes. The Romans feared her as they had feared only Hannibal, and they created a legend that survives to this day.

More than any other woman of the ancient world, Cleopatra has captured the imagination of biographers, historians, and creative writers. Shakespeare, in particular, in his tragedy *Antony and Cleopatra,* made famous the story of this Hellenistic queen. Whatever the romantic embroidery on her life, as lover of Julius Caesar and wife of Marc Antony, she played a major role in the turbulent last years of the Roman Republic.

*Sarah B. Pomeroy, Goddesses, Whores, Wives, and Slaves: Women in Classical Antiquity (New York: Schocken, 1975), pp. 187–188.

Roman Cultural Developments

Roman military conquest of the Greek east was paralleled by Greek cultural conquest of Rome in the third and second centuries B.C.E. Greek ways of living and thinking so penetrated Roman society that, as the poet Horace put it, "Captive Greece captured its crude conqueror and brought the arts to hayseed Latium."

Their service in campaigns in the Hellenistic kingdoms gave Roman armies a taste for things Greek. They admired magnificent temples and elaborate festivals, enjoyed dramatic performances in splendid theaters and athletic exercises in palestras. They indulged in the creature comforts of public baths, of luxurious mansions adorned with works of art, of sumptuous meals skillfully prepared by master chefs. In imitation of what they had seen in the Hellenistic kingdoms, Roman aristocrats beautified their homes with sculptures and vases and their bodies with jewelry and fabrics from the Greek east. Slaves trained as barbers, doctors, painters, personal secretaries, and tutors brought high prices. Bakeries and taverns began to dot the streets and served imported wines as well as domestic varieties. Dates, peaches, apricots, lemons, plums, cherries, and spices were introduced to Italy from the east.

Also in the second century B.C.E., Epicurean and Stoic philosophers brought their teachings to Rome. Mystery cults, too, like that of Bacchus (in Greek, Dionysus) and of the great mother-goddess Cybele, imported from Asia Minor, first began to make inroads in the traditional beliefs. These alarmed Roman authorities because of their particularly strong appeal to the downtrodden members of society. Bacchus's worshipers were often women seeking to satisfy religious feelings and perhaps to register a disguised protest against male social dominance.

Epicurus and the Human Triumph over Religion

When human life lay prostrate on the earth oppressed by the heavy burden of religion which seemed to show its head in the heavens, threatening human beings with a terrifying face, it was a Greek who first dared to lift his head and resist its power. He feared neither the tales of gods nor their lightning bolts nor their thunder in the heavens. All these things only spurred his brave spirit to break through the constricting boundaries of nature's gates. The vital force of his intellect carried him past the flaming walls of the universe as he traversed that immense realm in his mind and soul. In triumph he returned to us with knowledge of all that can or cannot come to be, of how each thing has its potentials defined and regulated. In this way, religion was cast down in subjection and we human beings raised to the heavens by his victory.*

Lucretius believed that humankind lived in a benighted and unreasonable state of religious fear before Epicurus developed his philosophy. In particular, men and women lived their lives badly, committing crimes like human sacrifice or unjust war, because they feared reprisals by gods who made contradictory and often irrational demands on them. The typical polytheistic belief in vengeful, fickle, and immoral gods had too long kept people in ethical and intellectual darkness. Epicurus freed humankind from such fears by daring to shed light on the universe with the power of his intellect, which revealed that the gods, if they existed, in fact played no part in our lives and thus posed no threats of punishment.

*Lucretius, De Rerum Natura, Book 1, lines 62–79; translated by James P. Holoka.

Under the influence of Greek culture, Roman literature made its debut in the late third and early second centuries B.C.E. Plautus (c. 254–184 B.C.E.) and Terence (c. 190–159 B.C.E.) produced the first Latin masterpieces by their adaptations of the Greek comic drama of social mores. The treasure house of Greek literature entered the school curriculum and soon nearly every educated Roman was bilingual and well versed in Greek classics.

Roman literature came of age in the late republic and reached its zenith in the early empire. The first truly great master of Latin language and style was Cicero (106–43 B.C.E.). Among his best-known speeches are the verbal cannon blasts of the *Philippics,* directed against Marc Antony. In a lighter vein are the treatises *On Friendship* and *On Old Age,* delightful reflections on ethical living by a man wise in experience. So great was Cicero's authority as a Latin stylist that, centuries later, one Christian prelate found himself unable to refer to the Holy Spirit in a Latin sermon because there was no word for it in Cicero.

The greatest Roman poet of the republic, Lucretius (c. 94–c. 55 B.C.E.), wrote the *De Rerum Natura (On the Nature of Things),* presenting the central axioms of Epicurean philosophy with consummate artistry and fervent commitment. Lucretius especially admired Epicurus for dispelling the terrors of conventional Greco-Roman religious belief.

Another interesting poet, Catullus (c. 84–c. 54 B.C.E.), was a member of a chic group of avant-garde writers called New Poets. Many of his poems were inspired by his love (and later hatred) for the woman he called Lesbia:

> Let's do some living, my Lesbia, and loving,
> and not give a damn for the gossip
> of all those stern old moralists;
> suns can set and then rise up again,
> but our brief sunburst goes out just once,
> and then it's curtains and the big sleep.
> Gimme a thousand kisses, then a hundred,
> another thousand, another hundred,
> then still another thousand and hundred,
> then let's make so many thousands
> that we lose track, no counting 'em at all,
> so those envious fools can't jinx us
> by toting up our kisses.

(Poem 5, translated by Lawrence Smith and James P. Holoka)

According to various sources, this intriguing woman was beautiful, aristocratic, witty, ultrafashionable, nymphomaniacal, adulterous, and perhaps murderous. Other poems relate practical jokes, a visit to the distant grave of a beloved brother, a mock funeral lament for a pet sparrow, and the delight of homecoming after a long absence.

An important aspect of literary production in this period was the influence of the emperor himself. Augustus possessed an exceptional ability to induce the best literary talents to restore the morale of Romans by writing poetry and history that advocated

Rome's Mission

Others will cast more tenderly in bronze
Their breathing figures, I can well believe,
And bring more lifelike portraits out of marble;
Argue more eloquently, use the pointer
To trace the paths of heaven accurately
And accurately foretell the rising stars.
Roman, remember by your strength to rule
Earth's peoples—for your arts are to be these:
To pacify, to impose the rule of law,
To spare the conquered, battle down the proud.*

In these lines, Vergil identifies the distinctive Roman achievement in history as the art of government: the manifest destiny of the Romans was to unify the earth's peoples into a peaceable order. In Vergil's eyes, this was something to be proud of, surpassing even the artistic and scientific achievements of those "others," the Greeks.

*Virgil, The Aeneid, trans. R. Fitzgerald (New York: Random House, 1983), Book 6, lines 847–853

nationalistic ideals of patriotism and morality. Maecenas, the great literary patron of Vergil and Horace, was an indispensable aide to Augustus in this area.

Between 30 and 19 B.C.E., the greatest Roman poet, Vergil (70–19 B.C.E.), created the *Aeneid*, a masterpiece of world literature. The epic describes the exploits of the hero Aeneas after the fall of Troy. The gods choose Aeneas to lead a band of Trojan refugees on a perilous journey to Italy, where his descendants are to mingle with native Italians and found Rome. Since the gods in the epic gradually disclose the manifest destiny of the Roman Empire, the poem was both foundation myth and mission statement for the Roman people. Without being jingoistic, it gave the Roman world its national epic. The self-effacing Aeneas is unlike Homer's more egocentric heroes. He follows the commands of the gods, even when it means he must leave the homeland he loves or a woman who loves him. The placing of duty above personal interest was precisely the ideal Augustus wished to hold up as a model of patriotic devotion in troubled times.

Another first-magnitude poet of the Augustan period was Horace (65–8 B.C.E.). His *Odes* are compact poems on such universal subjects as love, pleasure, the brevity of life, and art and nature. They are filled with memorable gemlike phrases like *carpe diem* (seize the day) and with patriotic sentiments ("sweet and fitting it is to die for one's country"). Horace also extolled the blessed security and social regeneration of the Augustan age.

Livy (59 B.C.E.–17 C.E.) wrote a massive history of Rome from the founding of the city down to his own day. The *History*, like the *Aeneid*, furnished models of patriotic heroism and morality. Although Livy was less critical in his judgments and handling of sources than, for example, Thucydides, the *History* was both an immediate popular success and influential in later ages.

The greatest Roman historian, however, was Tacitus (c. 56 C.E.–c. 120), whose *Histories* and *Annals* are our best and most extensive narrative of the period from 14 to 96 C.E. Tacitus wrote from the perspective of a man disgusted with both the emperors' abuses of power and the subservience of the aristocratic classes. In his pages, we meet the mistrustful emperor Tiberius listening to the charges of informers and indulging in sexual perversions at his villa on Capri; the genial but naive emperor Claudius, manipulated by scheming wives and freedmen; and, of course, Nero with his uncontrolled passions and delusions of artistic grandeur.

As Tacitus attacked the political impotence of the aristocratic class, the satirist Juvenal (c. 60 C.E.–c. 135) trained the powerful weapon of his biting criticism on its social and moral degeneration. He mercilessly denounced those he felt were corrupting Roman society, especially the immigrant "Greeklings" who excelled in unsavory jobs while seducing the wives and children of native Romans. The satires attack, among others, upper-class married women, Egyptians, homosexuals, soldiers, hypocritical philoso-phers, and the evil emperor Domitian. Juvenal's transformation of painful moral indigna-tion into literary art has made him the archetypal satirist.

Roman sculpture and painting derived almost entirely from Greek models. Indeed, the thousands of exact Roman reproductions are often our best source for the lost Greek originals. Roman artistic innovation was confined to the ultrarealistic depiction of actual persons, warts and all, particularly in the busts of worthy Romans that adorned homes and tombs. In architecture, however, the Romans did advance beyond Greek models. In particular, they used concrete to alter traditional building types in momentous ways. Roman architects were able to create curvilinear forms—the arch, the vault, the dome—while respecting Greek aesthetic norms of balance and symmetry. These distinctively Roman designs strongly influenced the architecture of later times, particularly the Romanesque.

Huge public baths, sports arenas, and temples were the most typical structures of the new imperial architecture. The amphitheater—essentially a 360-degree version of the Greek theater—first appeared in southern Italy, but the most famous was the Colosseum. It accommodated some 50,000 spectators and was the site of gladiatorial contests, wild animal "hunts," executions of Christians, and even mock sea battles.

The most durable and impressive example of the new imperial architecture was the Pantheon (Temple of All Gods). Unlike Greek temples, which impress by stunning exte-rior views, the Pantheon depends on its huge enclosed space for its effect. Its dome was the world's largest till the building of St. Peter's in Vatican City. The Pantheon strongly influenced Renaissance architects and, through them, Thomas Jefferson, in his design for the library rotunda at the University of Virginia.

The Roman spirit emphasized stability, order, and smooth practical function. Although much earlier the Indus people (see Chapter 2) and of course the Greeks (see Chapter 3) had practiced urban planning, Roman civil engineers operated on a much larger scale throughout the vast empire. Every significant town and city in the Roman Empire possessed walls, paved streets, efficient water supply and waste disposal systems, facilities for the preparation, storage, and distribution of food, centers for political, administrative, and judicial functions, temples and associated structures, commercial shops, and recreational and cultural complexes.

Roman engineers built the most durable roads in the world, providing vital trans-portation and communication arteries throughout the empire. The huge Roman imperial highway system was some 50,000 miles in extent. Construction was done by soldiers or forced labor (slaves and prisoners of war), always with careful attention to good foundation,

© Roger Ressmeyer/Corbis

View of a Roman Town. This photograph shows the forum or "downtown" area of the typical Roman town of Pompeii, which was buried by the volcanic eruption of Mount Vesuvius in 79 C.E. The forum includes a central open space and various surrounding commercial, civic, and religious buildings.

choice of material, smooth paving, and proper drainage. The Romans were also excellent hydraulic engineers. Large reservoirs situated on high ground fed fountains, baths, and private residences. A constant flow of water through public latrines carried waste out to the sea through the sewer system. When sources were lacking nearby, water was diverted, sometimes over long distances, by aqueducts. At Rome, more than a dozen aqueducts kept 1 million people plentifully supplied, and an extensive underground drainage system emptied into the Tiber.

Politics, Society, and Economics in the Early Empire

Although the immediate successors of Augustus, like him members of the Julio-Claudian family, could not match his managerial skills, they nonetheless maintained stability in domestic and foreign policy. This was despite the eccentricities and even mental aberrations of some of the emperors themselves. Caligula (reigned 37–41) and Nero (reigned 54–68) were psychopaths who committed incest and murdered close family members, Nero even his own mother. Despite such problems at the top, the system Augustus installed was remarkably resilient and durable.

By the second century C.E., succession based on the support of the army and the accident of birth into the imperial family was replaced by one in which each emperor selected and legally adopted his own successor, usually a capable and experienced administrator and/or general. Trajan (reigned 98–117) pleased the masses in Rome by

Map 4.3 The Roman Empire from 14 to 117 c.e. Shown here is the Roman Empire in the reign of the emperor Augustus and, a century later, in the reign of the emperor Trajan, when it had reached its greatest extent.

his major building programs and gifts of money. He also enlarged the empire by the addition of Dacia (modern Romania). Hadrian (reigned 117–138) tirelessly traveled throughout the provinces of the empire, personally attending to military security along borders. He everywhere indulged his strong interest in the arts and architecture through the construction and renovation of magnificent temples (including the Pantheon), markets, and other facilities. The general prosperity in the empire continued until 165, when an epidemic (possibly smallpox) caused great loss of life. This severely compromised Rome's military strength, as decreasing Roman manpower and increasing Germanic pressure along the Rhine-Danube frontier overtaxed a defensive system designed to repel one border incursion at a time.

During the early empire, the Roman world was a vast cosmopolitan collection of more than 5,000 towns (see Map 4.3) and their surrounding hinterlands inhabited by a population of 50 to 60 million. Commercial activity flourished because of a uniform currency system, the suppression of piracy, the highway network, and the maintenance of harbors and dockyards. Roman ports saw a constant flow of textiles, grain and other foodstuffs, metals (gold, silver, copper, tin, lead, iron), manufactured goods (glass, pottery, jewelry, paper), and luxury items (silk, ivory, precious gems, spices) from all over the Mediterranean world as well as from Arabia, India, and China.

Besides material advantages, Roman intellectual culture also became widespread in the empire. The Latin language was learned by citizens in the western part of the

LIVES AND TIMES ACROSS CULTURES

"The Going Rate": Wages and Prices in the Roman Empire and China

In 301 C.E., the emperor Diocletian attempted to control the rampant inflation plaguing the late Roman Empire by issuing an "Edict on Maximum Prices," which stipulated limits on wages and prices. Although the edict failed to have the desired effect, it provides modern students with valuable insights into personal income and the cost of goods and services. We can, for example, get an idea of the relative earnings of people in various professions by comparing their wages. Sewer cleaners, camel and mule drivers, shepherds, and farmhands made 25 denarii per day. Scribes made that same amount for 100 lines of fair copy. Wall painters made 75 denarii per day, a sum that arithmetic teachers made per month for each pupil they instructed. Rhetoric or public speaking teachers made 250 denarii per pupil each month. Barbers made 2 denarii per head. Tailors made 60 denarii for a cut-and-finished-hooded cloak of first quality.

While it is impossible to convert ancient Roman monetary units into present-day dollar equivalents, we can get some sense of the real cost of specific items by restating prices in terms of a day's wage. According to Diocletian's Edict, for example, a carpenter or a baker earned up to 50 denarii per day; on that basis, the following prices obtained:

Item	Cost (in days' wages)
20 lbs. wheat	2
20 oz. best-quality wine	.6
20 oz. cheap wine	.2
20 oz. beer	.1

Item	Cost (in days' wages)
20 lbs. salt	2
20 oz. honey, best quality	.8
1 lb. pork	.25
2 chickens	1.2
1 lb. best-quality fish	.5
100 oysters	2
1 pr. soldier's boots	2
1 pr. women's boots	1.2
1 lb. wool, best quality	3.5
1 lb. wool, 2nd quality	1
1 lb. white silk	240
1 lb. silk, dyed purple	3,000
1 lb. gold	1,000

There were no equivalents of Diocletian's price regulations for China during a similar period. There is nevertheless information on wages and prices for Han China, where a poll tax, which together with the land tax constituted the chief source of revenue, the former at 120 coins per head for adults and 23 for each child between seven and fourteen years old. A Han inscription of 90 C.E. says that a ten-yard roll of undyed silk cloth weighing thirteen ounces had a value of 618 coins. We may compare this with the monthly stipend of between 360 and 3,000 coins paid to officers serving in the northwestern frontier guard. In one case, an officer whose monthly stipend was 900 coins was paid two rolls of silk. Another document from northwestern China during the Han stated that 20,000 coins could purchase two adult female slaves, twenty ox-carts, or ten draft horses.

empire. The modern Romance languages (French, Italian, Spanish, Portuguese, Romanian) are direct descendants of Latin. In the east, Greek persisted in preference to Latin, while in the west educated people were generally bilingual, as the literature and philosophy of both Greece and Rome were transmitted to succeeding generations. Rome showed special originality by creating law schools and recognizing medicine as an important specialization.

Decay and Temporary Recovery in the Later Roman Empire

After 180 a time of troubles set in for the Roman Empire. The era of Roman imperial peace and tranquillity was over. Armed conflict among would-be successors effectively militarized the civil authority of the emperor. Between 235 and 284 more than twenty emperors assumed power, as mutinous legions or imperial guards deposed or murdered the same claimants they had earlier conspired to put on the throne.

Rome also faced increasing defense problems. In the east, the Persians, under the Sassanid dynasty, pushed back Roman legions in the area. The capture of an emperor, Valerian (reigned 253–260), by Persian forces was a conspicuous blow to Roman self-esteem. Elsewhere, Germanic tribes made incursions along the Rhine-Danube border and in Britain, and the Dacians frequently broke into the Balkans.

The chaos of the third century was temporarily checked by the reforms of the emperor Diocletian (reigned 284–305). Diocletian staffed the imperial bureaucracy with the best available talent, reorganizing provinces into smaller districts supervised by more officials. In light of the frequency of barbarian invasions, Diocletian believed that the empire had become too large for one man to rule and split it into four administrative sectors. In each, a tetrarch (one-fourth ruler) held supreme authority. Rome was not one of the four imperial capitals and thus faded farther into the background. To meet the defense needs of the empire, Diocletian enlarged the army from 300,000 to 500,000, in part by enlisting barbarians. After Diocletian's resignation in 305, the tetrarchy soon disintegrated in a complicated series of civil wars fueled by personal ambition and the reversion to dynastic inheritance.

By 324 Constantine (reigned 306–337) had emerged as the sole ruler of the Roman Empire. In general, Constantine followed the governmental policies of Diocletian, ruling autocratically and consulting only a few trusted appointees. Constantine prepared the way for the empire's split into eastern and western halves by founding a new imperial capital, Constantinople, on the site of Byzantium. Constantinople (modern Istanbul) commanded a peninsula on the European shore of the Straits of Bosporus, convenient for the direction of military operations along the Danube to the north and against Persia to the east. For over a thousand years, this "second Rome" preserved a residue of Greco-Roman civilization (see Chapter 5) until its fall to the Ottoman Turks in 1453.

The troubles of the third and fourth centuries exerted a powerful disintegrative force on Roman society, economics, and culture. The emperors were forced to siphon wealth from the more prosperous eastern half of the empire to sustain the overburdened west. Increases in spending on defense and the ever-growing imperial bureaucracy led to dire economic difficulties, as imperial tax collectors tightened the screws on a shrinking population of taxpayers. Debasement of coinage caused rampant inflation. Efforts at wage and price controls were no help. Individuals had to be forced to remain in certain essential, but now much less profitable, occupations; these included soldiering, farming, and grain shipping, among others. The nobility retained only honorific titles; true power was in the hands of thousands of petty bureaucrats. Well-to-do landowners, who had in the past voluntarily put their skills and funds at the disposal of government, were now taxed to their limit and laid under legal obligations of public service. The ultimate collapse was near.

The Emergence and Disintegration of the Mauryan Empire

But this last combat with Porus [king of northwest India] took off the edge of the Macedonians' courage, and stayed their further progress into India. For having found it hard enough to defeat an enemy who brought but twenty thousand foot and two thousand horses into the field, [the Greeks] thought they had reason to oppose Alexander's design of leading them on to pass the Ganges too, which they were told was thirty-two furlongs broad and a hundred fathoms deep, and the banks on the further side covered with multitudes of enemies. For they were told the kings of the Gandaritans and Praesians expected them there with eighty thousand horses, two hundred thousand foot, eight thousand armed chariots, and six thousand fighting elephants.*

*Aubrey Stewart and George Long, trans., Plutarch's Lives, vol. 3 (London: Bell, 1925), p. 73.

Alexander's incursion into India in 326 B.C.E. was an epoch-making event for both sides. His soldiers were shocked by the formidable heavy cavalry of war elephants the Indians used in battle, the very size of India, which seemed to stretch on endlessly, and the prospect of determined Indian resistance. They refused to march any further and forced their king to turn back. After Alexander's retreat and later death, northwest India was thrown into chaos, but his feats inspired an ambitious young Indian to found the first great Indian empire.

Alexander's invasion had another important and lasting consequence. It opened up direct land and sea communication between India and the Hellenistic kingdoms that Alexander's generals founded in western Asia. Hellenistic artistic traditions influenced Indian art, especially Buddhist art in later centuries. Some scholars believe that contact with Greek gods modified some Indian Buddhist teachings. Indian astronomy was indebted to Hellenistic astronomy and borrowed many terms from Greek.

This section will begin with Alexander's conquest of northwestern India and continue with the Mauryan Empire, the first great Indian empire, and its successor states. It will also explore some of the cultural interactions between India and lands to the west, relying on archaeological remains, coins, inscriptions, and the accounts of foreign (Greek and Chinese) observers. It ends with the successor states that followed the fall of the Mauryan Empire.

Persian and Greek Precursors

Major upheavals culminated in the founding of the Mauryan Empire around 313 B.C.E. As we have seen in Chapter 3, an economic and social revolution had produced Buddhism and Jainism in the sixth century. These religions offered their followers new ethical and social standards that emphasized the individual rather than tribes or castes.

Persian and then Macedonian invasions of northwest India also added to the trauma of the period. In 518 B.C.E., King Darius of Persia had conquered a part of northwest India and made it the twentieth satrapy (province) of the Persian Empire, ruled by Persian appointees. One of the wealthiest in the empire, it paid substantial taxes and supplied numerous soldiers, some of whom participated in the Persian invasion of Greece. Persian power gradually weakened, and the empire fell to Alexander.

In 326 B.C.E., Alexander's conquering army reached northwest India and found many warring states in what had once been the Persian satrapy. Some states submitted to him, others he subdued. He then confronted King Porus (also called Puru), the most powerful ruler in the upper Indus Valley. After a hard-fought battle Porus was brought captive before Alexander, who was so impressed that he confirmed him as a vassal king, restored his lands, and even added to them. After Alexander died in 323 B.C.E., his successors, fighting one another to partition his empire, withdrew from newly conquered northwest India. Local revolts broke out, and by 317 the last Greek general had left India.

The Rise of Chandragupta Maurya

Taking advantage of Alexander's death, Chandragupta Maurya, an Indian who may have known the Macedonian conqueror, drove out the remaining Greek forces. He then subdued the tribes in the northwest, marched east, and overthrew a kingdom located along the Ganges. Taking over its capital city, Pataliputra, he proclaimed himself ruler around 313 B.C.E.

Alexander's general Seleucus Nicator succeeded to his empire in Asia. In 305 B.C.E., he set out to reconquer India, failed, then agreed to a treaty in 303 in which Seleucus gave up his claim to India and ceded the Kabul Valley in present-day Afghanistan to Chandragupta in return for 500 elephants. The agreement was cemented by a marriage; perhaps a Seleucid princess was sent to India. Seleucus also sent an ambassador, Megasthenes, to reside at Pataliputra. Chandragupta also exchanged ambassadors with the Ptolemies in Egypt and with other Hellenistic rulers.

Megasthenes wrote a detailed account of India and of life at Chandragupta's court that became the standard source for later classical accounts on India. Although not always accurate, it is nevertheless valuable because it was the first authentic and lengthy account of India by a foreign observer. Another source on this period is the *Arthasastra (Treatise on Polity)*, a book reputedly written by Kautilya, a minister to Chandragupta, who some think was the real architect of the Mauryan Empire. The *Arthasastra* is a detailed book that dealt with the theory and practice of government and the laws and administration of the Mauryan Empire.

The *Arthasastra* described a highly organized and thoroughly efficient autocracy. The ruler was assisted by a council of ministers and an elaborate bureaucracy. He was supreme in military and civil affairs and the final arbiter of justice. As in Persia, a network of spies reported to the ruler directly. If accounts can be believed, Chandragupta's army had 600,000 men, 9,000 elephants, chariots, and a naval auxiliary. All were paid directly by the royal treasury.

The capital city Pataliputra (modern Patna), situated at the confluence of the Ganges and Son Rivers, was a grand place. Megasthenes described it as enclosed by a wooden wall approximately nine miles long by two miles wide with 570 towers and sixty-four gates, all protected by a moat. The palaces and other buildings were also made of wood, a good precaution against earthquakes, but highly perishable. Archaeological excavations have confirmed the Greek ambassador's claim that the opulence of the palaces rivaled that of the Seleucid palaces at Susa.

We learn from the *Arthasastra* that a council of thirty men governed the capital city, administering its finances, sanitation, water supply, public buildings, and gardens. The council was divided into six committees, each with a clear-cut function; for example, one supervised industries and another took care of foreigners and pilgrims.

Chandragupta ruled for twenty-four years. Megasthenes wrote admiringly of his energetic administration of justice. Kautilya's account of the Emperor's busy schedule tells us that his days were divided into ninety-minute segments, spent in meditation, meetings with ministers, and receiving reports. His rare public appearances were occasions of pageantry and grandeur as he rode in a golden litter or an elephant-drawn chariot, dressed in embroidered robes of gold and purple, and surrounded by a bodyguard of women. His favorite diversion was the hunt in the royal game preserve, where he shot arrows at game driven before him by beaters. Elaborate precautions were taken to protect him from assassins; he reputedly slept in a different bedroom every night. We know little about his family life or of his end. Jain tradition of doubtful authenticity says he abdicated the throne, became a Jain monk, and fasted to death in the manner of Jain saints.

Bindusara, a son of Chandragupta, succeeded him around 297 B.C.E. and ruled until around 272. He was known as the Slayer of Foes, which suggests that he was a successful warrior. Stories say that he had sixteen wives and 101 sons; the latter may be an exaggeration, since the names of only four sons are known.

Emperor Asoka

Asoka was not Bindusara's eldest son, but while still young, he was given major responsibilities as governor of two strategically located provinces in the northwest, at crossroads of international trade. His first wife was a devout Buddhist; they had a son and a daughter. Buddhist sources tell of a war of succession in which Asoka defeated his inept elder brother, and then had all his other brothers and possible rivals killed. That Asoka was not crowned until four years after his father's death does strongly suggest a disputed succession.

By 269–268 B.C.E., Asoka was firmly in control of the largest empire to that date in Indian history, a realm that included most of modern Afghanistan and all of India except the extreme south. Little is known of the first eight years of his reign. Presumably he spent his time in governing, in family life, and in the accepted pastimes for royalty, including lavish entertaining. As he later said: "Formerly in the kitchen of King [Asoka], many thousands of [animal] lives were daily slaughtered for [making] curries."

Asoka's conquest of Kalinga in southeast India later filled him with such remorse that he changed the direction of his government, and his personal life. He gave up eating meat and commanded his kitchen staff to prepare only vegetarian dishes for everyone. He replaced hunting with pilgrimages to places associated with the life of the Buddha. He also labored hard as king, declaring: "At all times and in all places, whether I am dining or in the ladies' apartments, . . . official reporters should keep me informed of the people's business. . . . At any hour and at any place, work I must for the commonweal." He devoted the rest of his reign to the realizing of Buddhist teachings in laws and deeds.

His enthusiastic espousal of Buddhism contributed to its spread in India and beyond. He was to Buddhism what the Roman Emperor Constantine would be to Christianity.

We know much about Asoka's rule because he had his laws and pronouncements carved on stone pillars and on rock surfaces throughout the empire, many of which have survived. He ordered his officials to read these edicts at public gatherings so that ordinary citizens would learn of his commands.

"All men are my children," said Asoka, and although he tolerated all religions, he nevertheless attempted to reform his "children" according to the teachings of Buddha. In application, this meant replacing some traditional practices with the ethics of Buddhism. He relaxed somewhat the stern laws that applied to criminals, although he did not abolish the death penalty. Those condemned to death were given three days' grace to settle their affairs before their sentences were carried out. He prohibited animal slaughter in religious ceremonies, declared many species protected, and encouraged people to become vegetarians, or at least to abstain from eating meat on certain days. Asoka also enjoined his people to cultivate such virtues as obedience to parents, kindness to servants, generosity to friends, and respect to holy men. He told them to be honest and to speak the truth and to give to charity.

Asoka was even ready to hand down disagreeable orders if he believed certain popular pastimes contravened Buddhist ideas. Thus he banned certain festivals where people had a good time eating, dancing, drinking, and watching performances, because he thought they were immoral. He created a new category of officials called morality officers to ensure that his officials conformed to his ideals and lived up to his code of behavior. The morality officers were allowed to pry into people's private lives, even those of the emperor's brothers and sisters. Similarly, Augustus saw moral exhortation and legislation as one of his duties as ruler of Rome.

Asoka also worked in practical ways to improve the people's daily lives. He set up botanical gardens to cultivate medicinal plants and erected hospitals for both people and animals. He constructed highways and built and maintained rest houses and wells along the routes. He also had fruit and shade trees planted for the benefit of all users.

Many grand religious edifices and new cities were built during Asoka's reign. According to Buddhist literature, he had the Buddha's remains further divided and enshrined in great mounds (*stupas*) throughout his empire to serve as pilgrimage destinations. A Chinese Buddhist pilgrim who visited India in the seventh century C.E. recorded more than eighty *stupas* and other structures associated by tradition with Asoka. That so many had survived or were still remembered a thousand years after his time certainly testifies to his munificent patronage of Buddhism.

Asoka also supported Buddhist missionary activities outside India. Two of his children entered the Buddhist order and are credited with bringing Buddhism to Ceylon (modern Sri Lanka). They took with them cuttings of the pipal tree under which Gautama had meditated and achieved enlightenment. Some ancient pipal trees on the island reputedly are descended from those cuttings. At a great rock fortress at Sigiriya in Ceylon, surviving frescoes of Buddhist heavenly nymphs from the sixth century C.E. resemble the wall paintings of the Ajanta caves in India (see Chapter 6), an indication of the close cultural

Asoka Transformed by the Horrors of War

Eight years after his coronation King Devanampiya Piyadasi [of Gracious Mien, and Beloved of the Gods—a title by which Asoka was addressed] conquered the Kalingas. In that (conquest) one hundred and fifty thousand were deported [as prisoners], 100,000 were killed [or maimed] and many times that number died. Thereafter, with the conquest of Kalinga King D. P. [adopted] the practice of morality, love of morality and inculcation of morality. For there arose in King D. P. remorse for the conquest of Kalinga. For this purpose this rescript on morality has been written that my sons and great grandsons should cease to think of new conquests and in all the victories they may gain they should be content with forbearance and slight punishment. For them the true conquest should be that of morality; all their delight should be delight in morality for benefit in this world and the next.*

Deeply remorseful over the suffering his conquest of Kalinga in southeast India had brought about, Emperor Asoka renounced war as an instrument of policy for himself and his successors. He had this statement carved on a rock pillar as a public confession and manifesto. He also converted to Buddhism and would devote much of his remaining years to the propagation of morality and righteousness according to Buddhist teachings. This fascinating man is revered by Indians as the greatest ruler in their history. Indeed, he ranks as a great ruler in the pageant of humanity.*

*Edict 13, trans. B. G. Gokhale, Asoka Maurya (New York: Twayne Publishers, 1966), Appendix.

(and sometimes political) ties that linked southern India and Ceylon. Recent archaeological studies show that Indians dominated maritime trade in South and Southeast Asia between 200 B.C.E. and 300 C.E.; Buddhist missionaries from India and Ceylon were instrumental in spreading religion as well as Indian commerce and culture throughout the region. They were the forerunners of Indian settlements that would flourish in many parts of Asia in later centuries. Asoka also ordered his ambassadors at the courts of Egypt, Macedonia, the Seleucid Empire, and other states in the west to spread Buddha's message, but with no apparent results.

Around 240 B.C.E., Asoka convened the Third Buddhist Council at Pataliputra. It dealt with differences within the monastic order and completed the compiling of the canons. He then appointed special officers to enforce the monastic discipline and had disobedient monks expelled from their orders. The Roman Emperor Constantine later did much the same thing in dealing with disputes among Christians.

Although an enthusiastic Buddhist, Asoka was tolerant of other faiths. As one of his edicts instructed: "All sects deserve reverence for one reason or another. By thus acting a man exalts his own sect and at the same time does service to the sects of other people." In another edict he advised all to honor brahmans and ascetics. A story about his father Bindusara illustrates the Mauryans' cosmopolitan outlook on religions and philosophies. Bindusara had sent an ambassador to the court of King Antiochus Soter of Syria to request figs, grapes, and a good Greek philosopher, for whom he said he would pay a high price. Antiochus sent him the exotic edibles but said that he could not find a philosopher for sale.

For all his commitment to humanitarian ideals, Asoka was nevertheless the ruler of a mighty empire. Thus, despite renouncing war, he did not disband his army. He warned primitive tribal people on the borders of his empire that if they failed to be persuaded by his *dharma* (moral duty) and infringed on his empire, he had the force to punish them. In other words, like any astute ruler, he continued to maintain a large military for its deterrent effect. His renunciation of war as an instrument of state policy was in itself a great innovation, unique among successful rulers. Some scholars, however, attribute the rapid decline and fall of the Mauryan Empire after Asoka's death in part to his pacifist policy, which they suggest weakened the military.

Although Asoka's edicts are couched in Buddhist terms, they show no interest in theology. Thus, it is possible that Asoka used Buddhism as an instrument to unify his heterogeneous empire. Nevertheless he imbued statecraft with high moral aims. That he was also tolerant of other faiths is proof of his realism as well as of his magnanimity. His reign laid the foundations for one of the greatest conquests in history—Buddhism's peaceful conquest of India, central Asia, Ceylon, Southeast Asia, China, and Japan.

Little is known of Asoka's last years. Some sources say that he became reclusive toward the end and was succeeded by his son, while others say that he was deposed by a grandson. In any event, soon after Asoka's death around 232 B.C.E., his sons and grandsons divided the empire. The last king of the main branch of the line was killed in 185, but several minor families that claimed Mauryan descent ruled parts of India for centuries.

Culture of the Asokan Age

Asoka's long reign, the wide extent of his empire, and contacts with Persia and the Hellenistic world brought about an unprecedented flowering of culture. Buddhist art also began in this period.

The artistic achievements of the Asokan age, however, can only be understood against the background of what had preceded it. The history of art in India between the Indus civilization and the third century B.C.E. is very sketchy. Whereas the Indus people had built with enduring materials, mainly brick, their successors had built with wood, which quickly perished in the humid Indian climate. Likewise sculptures of wood and clay and paintings in perishable media have all vanished. While the Mauryan palaces and even the city wall of Pataliputra continued to be made of wood, India's first stone monumental sculptures date to Asoka's reign.

Thirty spectacular stone pillars, some engraved with inscriptions, were erected at sites throughout the Mauryan Empire under Asoka. Ten have survived in almost perfect condition, others are damaged, still others have disappeared. They are between thirty and forty feet high and each weighs at least forty tons. They are made from hard gray sandstone polished to a lustrous shine. Each pillar is surmounted by a capital and topped by animal sculptures, either singly or in groups, carved in the round. The animals have symbolic importance to Buddhism. They are the lion, whose roar compares with the Buddha's preaching; the horse, which stands for Buddha's renunciation of the world; the elephant, which symbolizes his conception by his mother; the bull, representing strength; and the goose, because a legend says Buddha was the king of geese in an earlier incarnation. The wheel, which represents the sacred law or dharma, is also found on the pillars, placed below the animals. When India gained its independence from Great Britain in 1947, the four-lion Asokan capital was chosen as the nation's emblem and the wheel of law became the centerpiece of the national flag. That leaders of secular and

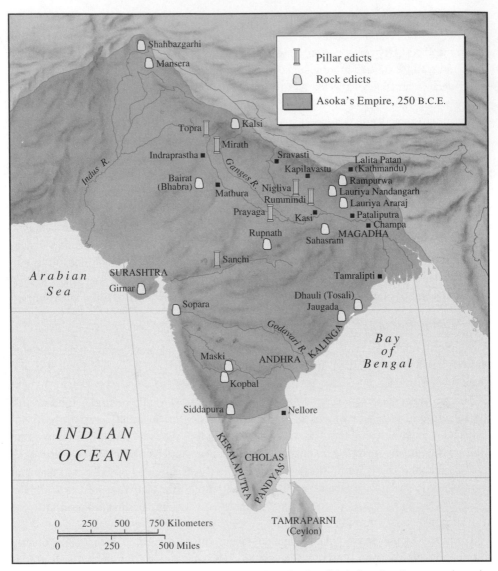

Map 4.4 The Empire of Asoka. Asoka expanded the empire he inherited so that all the Indian subcontinent except the southern tip and part of modern Afghanistan were incorporated into one administration. India was prosperous, and the capital, Pataliputra, was a grand city.

predominantly Hindu modern India would choose these Buddhist emblems as national symbols bespeaks the powerful memory of Asoka and his association with a great past.

Asoka erected and inscribed his pillars to announce major events in his reign, proclaim laws, and state his Buddhist ideals. He also used them to proclaim the grandeur and extent of his empire. The artistic inspiration for these monumental pieces is difficult to trace. A case can be made for indigenous roots for the bull, lotus, and elephant motif, which were frequently found in the Indus civilization seals. The lion and horse motifs, on the other hand, have a long history in Persian and West Asian art and are probably imported.

The high quality of the sculptures can only have resulted from generations of technical and artistic experience with the medium. We do not know who the stone sculptors were. But since no Indian stone sculptures have been found prior to the Asokan period, and since this art form vanished at the end of his reign, the Asokan monuments were probably made by Hellenistic artists invited by the court of Asoka or by Indians influenced by them.

The earliest cave shrines and dwellings also date to Asoka's reign and continued under his successors. For centuries, ascetics had taken shelter in caves during the monsoon season. But the sudden acquisition of skills in stone working, which led to the enlarging of natural caves and to polishing and decorating their surfaces, again suggests Persian and West Asian inspiration, because these techniques already had a long history in Persia and West Asia.

Asoka continued the Vedic and early Buddhist custom of erecting mounds to enshrine the funeral remains of great people. Gautama's disciples had divided his ashes at the first Council and enshrined them under stupas. As Buddhism grew it became a meritorious act for the pious to worship at such sites. Asoka is credited with a further division of the Buddha's remains so that more people could benefit spiritually from visiting them. We know little of the original decoration of Asoka's stupas, since they have been built over in later ages. They were probably hemispheric mounds set on platforms, with flights of steps from four directions that lead to the base. Later on, railings, gateways, and arches were added to enclose and decorate the sites, and these were profusely ornamented with scenes from the Buddha's life and from Jataka stories.

The earliest extant examples of writing since the Indus civilization also date from the reign of Asoka. They survived because they were engraved on stone rather than written on perishable materials. They are his edicts, proclamations, and sermons engraved on rocks, pillars, and cave walls throughout the Mauryan Empire. Persia and Mesopotamia are again the likely sources of inspiration and examples because Indians were first introduced to official proclamations and panegyrics engraved in stone by King Darius I. The language and lettering of the rock edicts varied, indicating that several languages were current in different parts of the Mauryan empire. Most of the inscriptions were written in the Old Brahmi script, from left to right. It is the parent of most of the scripts now current in India. However, those found in the western part of the empire were written in Greek or Aramaic, while those found in the northwest were written in a script then current in Iran. As with ancient Egyptian hieroglyphics, the characters' meanings were lost, and they were not deciphered until 1837, by an Englishman, when modern scholarship on ancient India, called Indology, began.

Extant Buddhist and Jain canons and commentaries were substantially completed during Asoka's time. Nonreligious works, such as the early versions of the epics *Mahabharata* and *Ramayana,* also date from approximately this period, although both were added to and reworked later. In its final form, the *Mahabharata* is seven times as long as the *Iliad* and the *Odyssey* combined. Like the *Iliad,* it is a tale of an epic war fought by gods and men; stories of knightly chivalry, love, piety, duty, and devotion are interwoven with violence and gambling. Written in verse form and narrative style, the following passage tells how princess Damayanti chose as her husband her true love Nala, even though four gods had taken on his appearance in the hope that she would pick one of them by mistake. The theme of competition for a beautiful, royal woman is familiar from the Greek stories of Helen's betrothal and, in the *Odyssey*, the contest for the hand of Penelope.

Then, when the right time had come,
*   at the auspicious day and hour,*
King Bhama invited
*   the lords of earth to the bride-choice.*

When they heard, the lords of earth,
*   all sick at heart with love,*
in haste assembled,
*   desiring Damayanti.*

Like great lions the kings entered
*   the hall firmly founded,*
with its splendid porch
*   and shining golden columns.*

Then on their several thrones
*   the lords of earth sat down*
all decked in fragrant garlands,
*   with bright gems on their ears.*

      . . .

Then fair-faced Damayanti
*   entered the hall,*
stealing with her splendor
*   the eyes and thoughts of the kings.*

When the glance of the noble
*   spectators fell on her limbs*
there it was fixed,
*   and never wavered.*

Then, while the names of the kings
*   were being proclaimed,*
the daughter of Bhama saw
*   five men of the same form.*

Whichever of them she looked at
*   she recognized as Nala.*
Wondering in her mind,
*   the fair one was filled with doubt.*

      . . .

Thus thinking over and over,
*   and pondering again and again,*

*she resolved that the time had come
   to take refuge in the gods.*

*"I heard from the mouth of the swans
   that Nala had chosen me as his bride,
and so, if that be true,
   may the gods show him to me!*

    . . .

*May the great gods, the world-protectors
   take on their own true form,
that I may recognize
   the king of men, of good fame!"*

*When they heard Damayanti,
   mournful and piteous
they did as she had asked,
   and put on their true forms.*

*She saw the four gods
   sweatless, not blinking their eyelids,
their garlands fresh and free from dust,
   not touching the ground with their feet*

*But the king of Nisadha had a shadow,
   his garlands were withered,
his body bore dust and sweat,
   and he blinked his eyelids.*

*The modest long-eyed girl
   seized the hem of his garment,
and on his shoulder she placed
   the loveliest of garlands.*

*She chose him for her lord,
   she of the fair complexion,
and suddenly all the kings
   together shouted and cheered.*

*And all the gods and sages
   thereupon cried bravo.
and shouted at the wonder,
   praising Nala the king.*

Krishna, an incarnation of Vishnu, and beloved of millions in later Hinduism, is a hero in this great poem. Woven into it is the *Bhagavad-Gita,* a lofty philosophical poem through which Hindus have since learned lessons about morality and religious law. Here Krishna teaches the ideal of duty and action to fulfill one's function in society without personal desire or ambition.

The briefer *Ramayana* resembles the *Odyssey* in that it tells about the hardships and wanderings of the hero, and his faithful wife who waits patiently for his return. The couple's cause triumphed, and they were reunited with the help of the monkey king and his monkey soldiers (hence Hindus revere the monkey and there are temples to Hanuman, the monkey god and Rama's helper). Hindus revere Rama and Sita, the hero and heroine of the *Ramayana,* as the ideal man and woman.

Life under the Mauryans

The Mauryan Empire was richly diverse. In addition to the capital city, Pataliputra, there were several other sizable cities surrounded by strong walls punctuated by lofty watch-towers and pierced by gates. Texts mention city streets lit by torches at night, pleasure parks, assembly halls, and gambling places as well as trading booths and artisans' quarters.

As in the Roman Empire, rulers often sponsored public entertainments for city people. They were usually associated with religious festivals and consisted of singing, dancing, dramatic presentations, chariot races, jousts of arms between men, and animal combats. Asoka was offended by the violence and immorality associated with the festivals and sought to restrict them. Girls and boys from upper classes amused themselves with music, singing, and dancing, and boys and men in addition gambled with dice, and played a game like hockey and a board game that later became chess.

Most people lived in the countryside as farmers, herders, and hunters. Most farmers were sudras and lived in simple mud and thatch houses in villages. Land was owned either by the government or privately. Slavery existed, but the number of slaves was not large. Villages were largely autonomous but paid taxes and dues to the government, customarily one-sixth of the harvest. Agriculture was highly regarded and farmland was supposed to be spared from ravages during wars. Farmers organized themselves for communal projects such as digging irrigation ditches, but were exempted from military and other government services. Then as later, farmers suffered from periodic famines brought on by natural disasters and by locusts. The *Arthasastra* enjoined rulers to store extra food for emergencies and to distribute seeds and food during hard times.

The herdsmen and hunters, also mostly sudras, often lived in tents beyond the pale of the villages. Cattle were always important for their milk, but were rarely butchered for meat. The hunter and trapper were responsible for getting rid of pests and sometimes also for providing food. There was large-scale land clearing for agriculture and the building of irrigation works during the Mauryan dynasty.

Most artisans were vaisyas, an important group living in both cities and villages. Pataliputra's municipal government had a board that supervised artisans in that city. Some villages specialized in one craft, and specialties tended to be passed from father to son. The artisans included ivory and stone workers, painters of frescoes, metal smiths, jewelers, textile weavers, embroiderers, oil-millers (who extracted oils from seeds), bamboo workers, tool makers, and potters, each specialty organized into a guild. Each guild was headed by a foreman or elder who supervised the workers; guilds also performed some of the functions of modern banks. The textile industry employed many women; some worked in shops while others worked at home. New subcastes of artisans were recorded during this time, proof of the proliferation of manufacturing.

Transportation by water was highly developed. Seagoing ships sailed as far away as Burma, the Malay Peninsula, Ceylon, and the Persian Gulf. They navigated by the stars. Most water trade was along north India's well-developed waterways, along the Indus and Ganges Rivers, and their tributaries. The Mauryan government even established a bureau that built ships and leased them to merchants.

The chief items of trade were silk and cotton textiles, ivory, jewelry, and gold. Some trade was by barter, but it was being replaced by silver and copper coinage. Pataliputra had a special board that supervised trade and commerce. It regulated weights and measures and placed a stamp on items it had inspected. Later, as trade with the Roman Empire flourished, gold and silver coins from Rome became plentiful in India, supplementing locally minted coins. Romans from Pliny the Younger (61–c. 113 C.E.) on regretted their people's appetite for Indian luxuries, especially fine cotton textiles, bought with precious metals. From the west, Indians imported sweet wines, exotic fruits, luxury handicrafts, entertainers, and beautiful girls for the harems of the rich.

Marriages were monogamous for most, polygynous for rulers and aristocrats. There were a few communities that practiced polyandrous marriages (one wife with several concurrent husbands). Most men and women were expected to marry, some of both sexes (fewer women) became ascetics and lived celibate lives and were honored for it. Although some uppe-class women and female ascetics were well educated, most women were not literate, but neither were most men. *Sati,* or the custom of widow immolation on her late husband's funeral pyre, was practiced by a few. Both men and women wore adornments; upper-class women were especially noted for the richness of their clothing and jewelry.

Successor States to the Mauryan Empire

Jawaharlal Nehru, late prime minister of India, described the confusing state of India after the collapse of the Mauryan Empire in 185 B.C.E. in the following words:

> The Maurya empire faded away and gave place to the Sunga dynasty, which ruled over a much smaller area. . . . In central Asia the Shakas or Scythians had established themselves in the Oxus Valley. The Yueh Chih, coming from farther east, drove them out and pushed them into north India. These Shakas became converts to Buddhism and Hinduism. Among the Yueh Chih, one of the clans, the Kushans, established their supremacy and then extended their sway over northern India. They defeated the Shakas and pushed them still farther south, the Shakas going to Kathiawar and the Deccan. The Kushans thereupon established an extensive and durable empire over the whole of north India and a great part of Central Asia. . . . This borderland state, called the Kushan empire, with its seat near modern Peshawar, and the old university of Taxila near by, became the meeting place of men from many nations. There the Indians met the Scythians, the Yueh Chih, the Iranians, the Bactrian Greeks, the Turks, and the Chinese, and the various cultures reacted on each other.*

*Jawaharlal Nehru, *The Discovery of India,* ed. Robert Crane (New York: Doubleday, 1960), pp. 89–90.

As in Europe after the collapse of Rome, a loose structure of government with less central control emerged. Civil wars became endemic as military adventurers ousted one another in quick succession. In this situation the borderlands became victim to invaders of varying backgrounds and levels of civilization. However, compared to western Europe after the fall of Rome, intellectual and artistic life in India suffered less extensive damage. Some of the invaders who settled in northwestern India were the Bactrian Greeks, Parthians (Iranians or Persians), and Scythians, who introduced Roman, Hellenistic, Persian, and central Asian art, which enriched Indian artistic traditions to form a new synthesis. Mauryan power had never been strong in southern India, and the region remained unaffected by the invasions that disrupted the north during the succeeding centuries.

The Yueh-chih, strongest of all the invading groups, entered India toward the end of the second century B.C.E. They had earlier been driven westward from China's northern border by more powerful nomads, the Hsiung-nu, ancestors of the Huns that later ravaged Europe and invaded the Roman Empire. By 60 C.E. one of the Yueh-chih tribes, the Kushans, had established an empire that stretched from northern India westward to the Caspian Sea. They converted either to Hinduism (mostly to a sect that chiefly worshipped Shiva) or to Buddhism. Kanishka (reigned c. 78–111 C.E.), the greatest Kushan king, was a patron of Buddhist religion and art. After the death of Kanishka, decline set in and the empire broke up during the third century, with remnants surviving until the sixth century.

The reasons for the fall of the Kushan empire remain shrouded in mystery. It may have been due in part to the loss of Afghanistan to Persian control, and with it fresh sources of manpower for the army. Kushan rule, however, left a rich cultural legacy.

Kushan Culture: Buddhism in a Cosmopolitan Setting

The chaos of the post-Mauryan era had no adverse effect on the spread of Buddhism within and beyond India. From northwest India missionaries traveled the Silk Road west to Persia and central Asia and east to China (see the next section). The large number and high quality of Buddhist temple remains in communities in the Kushan realm and along the Silk Road, rich even in ruin, show both the devotion of the believers and the prosperity brought by this international trade in luxuries.

King Kanishka was revered by some Buddhists almost as a second Asoka, and indeed there are many parallels. Like Asoka, he ruled a prosperous and powerful empire and waged victorious wars early in his reign, annexing additional lands. Although a Buddhist, he tolerated other religions, as coins from his reign that include the Hindu god Shiva, the Roman god Hercules, and Persian deities, show. Like Asoka, he patronized Buddhism by building and repairing shrines and encouraging missionary work. About the year 100 Kanishka called the Fourth Buddhist Council at his capital city, near modern Peshawar on the present-day Pakistan-Afghan border. Five hundred monks attended the council to settle disputes in Buddhism and to collect and compile commentaries on the Tripitaka. He also lavishly patronized Buddhist art.

By the first century, many Buddhists favored community worship of the Buddha as a savior god and some aspired to be saintly bodhisattvas who delayed their own entrance to nirvana to help suffering living beings achieve enlightenment. Many of the devout, however, wished there was an image of Buddha to assist them in their prayers.

The first images of the Buddha date to Kanishka's time, although the origins of the Buddha images are in dispute. Some scholars argue that the likenesses of the Buddha evolved from images of *yakshas,* or earth spirits of Hinduism, and therefore are Indian in origin. Others point out that the Kushans were a non-Indian dynasty and that early Buddhist images show strong Greco-Roman influences. Evidence supports both sides. The two artistic sources express the same subject matter: the image of the Buddha and the stories of his life and previous lives, along with bodhisattvas and other deities associated with Buddhism, including Vedic gods.

Large numbers of the Gandharan, or Greco-Roman-influenced, Buddhist sculptures have been found in the ruins of Taxila, a north Indian center of international commerce and art, and at various sites in Afghanistan and Pakistan. Most are statues that depict the Buddha and bodhisattvas, or are reliefs that describe the Buddha's life or scenes from Buddhist texts. They are characterized by realistic moldings of the human body and accurate delineations of muscles. Many of the stone and stucco (painted plaster) statues and relief carvings of the Buddha and others in Gandhara are so beautifully robed and coifed that they would not have been out of place in imperial Rome. They are distinguishable from their secular counterparts only by their halos (a western import) and their religiously significant hand gestures.

Later Gandharan artists were especially fond of stucco as a medium. This was perhaps due to close sea contacts with Alexandria in Egypt, where at that time the art of working with stucco was well developed. Apparently, a continuing influx of artists and artisans from Roman provinces arrived in India throughout the Kushan period. The imported artists must also have trained local people in their media and styles. It is not surprising then that deities of Greece and Rome are sometimes found in Buddhist scenes.

In the prosperous Bamiyan valley in Afghanistan, at the crossroads of the Silk Road, monks in the fifth century honeycombed a towering cliff wall of the Hindu Kush with grottoes and cells, and crowned the complex with three colossal Buddha statues carved from the cliffs. The tallest stands at 175 feet high in its own niche. They were finished with lime plaster and decorated with paintings. The site gave inspiration to pious Chinese pilgrims as they approached India in their long journey and inspired Chinese Buddhists to excavate similar rock grottoes in their homeland. After the eighth century, Bamiyan and other Buddhist sanctuaries in Afghanistan were desecrated by Muslim invaders. They have stood since then amid empty ruins, pockmarked by artillery shells of later Muslim cannons, for which they served as targets. Even in ruin, they stand witness to the energy and creativity that marked the Buddhist centuries in Afghanistan and northwest India.

Mathura was already an art center when the Kushan empire took over. The red sandstone religious statues that its artists produced would adorn Buddhist, Hindu, and Jain holy places for centuries to come. Whereas the Gandharan Buddhas had faces of the Greco-Roman god Apollo and wore togas, those from Mathura are dressed like Indians in thin *dhotis* (loin cloths); *yaksha* spirits became bodhisattvas, surrounded by *nagas* (anthropomorphic serpent figures of ancient Indian lore) and other symbols of Indian mythology. The Mathuran art style survived the fall of the Kushan empire to reach its ultimate development in the following Gupta era. At both centers, Kushan art mirrored social life. Scenes of drunken orgies abound; Gandharan ladies' dresses could have been worn by matrons in any city of the Roman world, while nudity or scanty dress in the Indian fashion is conspicuous in Mathuran figures. Later, when Buddhism spread to China, Korea, and Japan, Greek, Roman, and Persian art forms were introduced to the farthest shores of East Asia.

Coins provide much information and a great deal of the chronology of post-Mauryan dating, since there is very little reliable chronological record otherwise. The Greeks popularized coinage as the medium of exchange, and Indian rulers followed suit. They usually carried images of the issuing ruler on one side and of a deity on the other, along with an inscription. The large quantity of Roman coins found in India supports the contention that India enjoyed a favorable balance of trade against Rome, a circumstance Roman leaders bemoaned. Roman coins were probably circulated as an international currency, which might explain why gold coins issued by Kanishka conformed to the Roman standard. An interesting gold coin bears the image of Buddha on one side, and of Kanishka on the other. Kanishka wears the baggy trousers and tall boots of central Asia, suggesting his nomadic heritage. Although a Buddhist, he is pouring an offering on a fire altar, a Persian religious practice. These coins suggest that initially the conquering rulers worshipped their Hellenistic and Persian deities. But since they were numerically few, they were in time assimilated and became Indianized.

Several centuries of contacts with the West left other legacies. A number of words in Sanskrit and modern Indian languages are borrowed from Greek, especially in the sciences and in astrology, where Indian scholars were very alert to new information. A work titled *Questions of Melinda* (an Indianized name of a minor Hellenistic king, Menander, who converted to Buddhism), though Buddhist in content, shows the stylistic influence of the philosophical dialogues of Plato.

China's First Imperial Age: The Han Dynasty

"Gentlemen, for a long time you have suffered beneath the harsh laws of Ch'in. . . . I hereby promise you a code of laws consisting of three articles only: 1) he who kills anyone shall suffer death; 2) he who wounds another or steals shall be punished according to the gravity of the offense; 3) for the rest I abolish all the laws of Ch'in. Let the officials and people remain undisturbed as before. I have come to save you from injury, not to exploit or oppress you. . . ."

*He sent men to go with the Ch'in officials and publish this proclamation. . . . The people of Ch'in were overjoyed and hastened with cattle, sheep, wine, and food to present to the soldiers, but Liu Chi declined all such gifts, saying: "There is plenty of grain in the granaries. I do not wish to be a burden to the people." With this the people were more joyful than ever and their only fear was that Liu Chi would not become King of Ch'in.**

*William T. de Bary, ed., *Sources of Chinese Tradition*, vol. 1 (New York: Columbia University Press, 1960), pp. 154–155. Reprinted with permission.

In victory Liu Chi (also known as Liu Pang) displayed the essential qualities of compassion and justice that were in sharp contrast to the oppression and tyranny of the govern-

Courtesy of Richard Edwards

Colossal Buddha. This enormous Buddha statue stands 175 feet high in a niche shaped as a body halo. Located at a crossroads of international travel, it made an indelible impression on all who passed and was a prototype for similar monuments in China. In 2001 the fanatical Muslim rulers of Afghanistan ordered this statue and thousands of smaller Buddhist statues and figures in museums in that country destroyed.

ment that he had rebelled against. A poor commoner with little education, he was nevertheless a profound psychologist, identifying with the common people and soldiers. These qualities won him the support and respect of the people and explain his success against both the Ch'in and other contenders for power. Liu became the first commoner to found a dynasty. Known as the Han, it was one of the longest lived and most successful in Chinese history. This is the reason why 95 percent of Chinese up to now call themselves the Han people and their language the Han language. Likewise, the Japanese and Koreans call Chinese the Han language. Thus the Han dynasty is to China and East Asia what the Mauryan dynasty is to India and Buddhists throughout Asia. The following pages will explore Han history, achievements, and legacy.

The Han Dynasty, 202 B.C.E.–220 C.E.

Several contenders sought to fill the vacuum created by the fall of the Ch'in dynasty in 206 B.C.E. The winner was Liu Chi, who was proclaimed emperor of the new Han dynasty in 202. History knows him as Han Kao-tsu or High Ancestor of the Han. He was the first commoner to ascend the throne, an event made possible because of the Ch'in abolition of feudalism and the opportunities created by the wars of the preceding centuries. The Han dynasty is divided into two halves; the earlier part was in retrospect called the Western or Former Han, the later part the Eastern or Later Han.

Kao-tsu and his supporters had suffered through the harshness of Ch'in rule and were well aware of the feelings of the people. Establishing his capital at Changan (near the Ch'in capital Hsienyang), Kao-tsu retained the basic structure of the Ch'in government but removed its abuses. For example, he moderated the cruel Ch'in penal code, lifted the ban against intellectual activities, and lightened taxes from two-thirds of the farmer's crop under Ch'in to one-fifteenth. To give the people a chance to rest and recover from years of war, Kao-tsu pursued a foreign policy of conciliation and appeasement toward the powerful northern nomads called Hsiung-nu. In the third century these nomads had formed a powerful confederacy and had menaced China across the entire northern frontier. The Great Wall had not kept out these horse-riding raiders from the steppes. After a disastrous war against the Hsiung-nu, Kao-tsu was forced to bribe them with large annual "gifts" of gold, grain, and silks, and a princess as bride. Kao-tsu died prematurely, in 195 B.C.E. Soon afterward the king of the Hsiung-nu had proposed marriage to his widow, Empress Lu, with the following letter:

> I am a lonely widowed ruler, born amidst the marshes and brought up on the wild steppes in the land of cattle and horses. . . . Your Majesty is also a widowed ruler living in a life of solitude. Both of us are without pleasures and lack any way to amuse ourselves. It is my hope that we can exchange that which we have for that which we are lacking.

Although furious, she was forced to refuse him politely:

> My age is advanced and my vitality is weakening. Both my hair and teeth are falling out, and I cannot even walk steadily. The shan-yu [title of Hsiung-nu king] must have heard exaggerated reports. I am not worthy of his lowering himself. But my country has done nothing wrong, and I hope he will spare it.

Empress Lu ruled ably for the next fifteen years and continued Kao-tsu's policies, as did her successors. With peace and frugal government, the economy expanded and production soared, so that despite a further tax cut to one-thirtieth of the crop, the state treasury was full and granaries bulged.

When Emperor Wu (the Martial, reigned 141–87 B.C.E.) ascended the throne, the Chinese people, now fully recovered and confident, were willing to support a new vigorous and aggressive foreign policy. Wu campaigned in the south and regained control of the Pearl River valley and the Red River valley in modern Vietnam, both of which had seceded at the fall of the Ch'in. Another campaign brought southern Manchuria and Korea into the Han Empire. Wu then established a Chinese-style government in the newly annexed regions. He also sponsored Chinese immigration, which gradually resulted in the assimilation or Sinicization (from the Latin Sinica, meaning "China") of the local people.

These early wars were preparation for a showdown with the Hsiung-nu; however, Wu needed an ally. Much earlier, the Hsiung-nu had defeated the Yueh-chih, an Indo-European nomadic group north of China. Fleeing westward, the Yueh-chih finally settled in Bactria, in modern Afghanistan and northern Pakistan, converted to Buddhism, and founded a state called Kushan.

In 138 B.C.E., Emperor Wu sent a young courtier named Chang Ch'ien to find the Yueh-chih and offer them an alliance against the Hsiung-nu. Chang's journey was one of the most daring travel epics in antiquity. To reach the Yueh-chih, he had to cross Hsiung-nu territory; he was captured, given a Hsiung-nu wife, and made to settle among them and raise a family. Chang escaped after ten years, continued his quest, and finally found the Yueh-chih, but they had no desire to cross swords with the Hsiung-nu again. En route home, Chang was recaptured by the Hsiung-nu, and again escaped, finally returning to Changan in 126, with only two of his original staff of a hundred.

Even though he failed in his primary assignment, Chang Ch'ien's account of this trip and his later diplomatic mission to central Asia opened the Chinese to new horizons, peoples, cultures, and products. His information brought about further explorations and trade by land and sea between China, India, Persia, and other lands. His report of "blood sweating" horses (actually, the horses were bleeding, from the bites of tiny mites) later sent Chinese armies campaigning across central Asia to obtain them.

In 133 B.C.E., Wu launched an eighteen-year campaign that evicted the Hsiung-nu from an area bounded by a southward dip of the Yellow River. In 129 they were cleared from the entire Chinese northern border from Inner Mongolia across Turkestan. Some 700,000 Chinese colonists were sent out to settle the conquered lands, and the Great Wall was extended westward. Beyond it, a string of fortified outposts stretched into Central Asia, which the Chinese called the Western Regions. Chinese protectors-general were

The Flying Horse of Kansu. The Han government waged wars, used diplomacy, and traded to obtain these fast horses bred in central Asia. This bronze horse, found in the tomb of a Han general in Kansu in northwestern China, epitomized the qualities of strength and speed the Chinese prized in these "blood-sweating" horses.

The High Cost of Empire

1. Lament of Hsi-chun

   My people have married me
   In a far corner of Earth;
   Sent me away to a strange land,
   To the king of the Wu-sun.
   A tent is my house,
   Of felt are my walls;
   Raw flesh my food
   With mare's milk to drink.
   Always thinking of my own country
   My heart is sad within.
   Would I were a yellow stork
   And could fly to my old home!

2. To His Wife, by General Su Wu, c. 100 B.C.E.

   Since our hair was plaited and we became man
       and wife
   The love between us was never broken by doubt.
   So let us be merry this night together,
   Feasting and playing together while the good
       time lasts
   I suddenly remember the distance that I must
       travel;
   I spring from bed and look out to see the time.
   The stars and planets are all grown dim in the sky;
   Long, long is the road; I cannot stay.
   I am going away on service, away to the battle-
       ground,
   And I do not know when I shall come back.
   I hold your hand with only a deep sigh;
   Afterwards, tears—in the days when we are
       parted.

   With all your might enjoy the spring flowers,
   But do not forget the time of our love and pride.
   Know that if I live, I will come back again,
   And if I die, we will go on thinking of each other.

3. Parting from Su Wu by Li Ling

   I came ten thousand leagues
   Across sandy deserts
   In the service of my Prince,
   To break the Hun tribes.
   My way was blocked and barred,
   My arrows and swords broken.
   My armies had faded away,
   My reputation is gone.
   My old mother is long dead.
   Although I want to requite my Prince
   How can I return?*

Individual men and women paid a high price for the nation's military and diplomatic successes. Three poems illustrate this point. The first is by princess Hsi-chun. Around 100 B.C.E., she was given in marriage to a client king of Wu-sun, whose land supplied Han with fine horses. Her husband was already an old man and the couple had no common language, so during their occasional meetings they only drank a cup of wine together. The second was by General Su Wu, who wrote it for his wife, before he set out to campaign against the Hsiung-nu. He was captured during the war and held for nineteen years before being released. While Su Wu returned home, a fellow captive chose to stay. In the third poem he explains why.

*Arthur Waley, Translations from the Chinese (New York: Knopf, 1941), pp. 18, 52, 53.

appointed to supervise local vassal kings, who were required to pay homage and tribute by coming to Changan and to leave their sons there to be educated and to serve as hostages in a pattern similar to Rome's arrangements with its client states. In return, vassal kings received Chinese titles, lavish gifts, and the right to trade. These conditions were so attractive that rulers in regions like Kashmir in India, which had not been conquered by the Han, voluntarily enrolled themselves as vassals. No more Chinese princesses were sent as brides to Hsiung-nu chieftains. Wu's successors continued his policies against the Hsiung-nu, shattering their power. In 51 the southern branch of the Hsiung-nu submitted to Han rule, while another branch was defeated by the Han in Samarkand and fled westward. The flight of the Hsiung-nu set off a vast westward migration as numerous people were pushed west in a domino effect that continued until the fourth century C.E., when some of them reached the borders of the Roman Empire.

Between 9 and 23 C.E. a usurper attempted and failed to establish his own dynasty. A descendent of the house of Liu reestablished the Han dynasty in 23 C.E. and moved his capital eastward to Loyang, hence the name, Eastern Han, for the era. Loyang is strategically situated at the bank of the River Lo, a tributary of the Yellow River. It had been the capital of the Eastern Chou dynasty.

Restored to power and prosperity, Chinese arms again overawed much of central Asia, and trade and culture flourished. General Pan Ch'ao campaigned all the way to the Caspian Sea, and his vanguard units reconnoitered the shores of either the Persian Gulf or Black Sea. Chinese protectors-general continued to supervise kingdoms across central Asia in the farthest extension of power in its history. Caravans carrying the international luxury trade traveled in safety. The Pax Sinica in the east matched the Pax Romana in the west; together the two empires dominated most of the ancient world.

In the second century, minors on the throne, power struggles between powerful consort families, and economic inequities led to rapid dynastic decline. The upper class became hedonistic, dabbling either in escapist Taoism or the new foreign religion, Buddhism. Ground-down peasants revolted and generals sent to quell them seized power, ending the dynasty in 220. Nevertheless, four centuries of Han rule had firmly established the foundations of traditions and institutions that would continue to the present century and spread the Sinitic civilization across eastern Asia. To later dynasties the Han became the yardstick against which they all measured themselves.

Han Government

Han emperors presided over a centralized, bureaucratic government headed by a prime minister. Ministries and bureaus had clearly defined functions such as fiscal and judicial affairs, imperial rituals, and the metropolitan police force. The basic local government unit was the county (there were between 1,000 and 1,400 counties); ten to twenty counties formed a commandery (later called a province), headed by a governor. The three-tier government system remains in effect in China to the present and is similar in organization to the three tiers of county, state, and national government of the United States. Governors had to submit detailed annual reports to the central government with statistics on economic conditions, finance, education, justice, and other matters in his commandery. Inspectors sent from the capital regularly investigated local affairs and checked on local officials in a manner similar to the special officials who acted as the "eyes and ears" to the Persian kings.

Kao-tsu had partially restored feudalism by creating a number of principalities and lesser fiefdoms for imperial relatives, in-laws, and meritorious officials. However, the recipients received revenues rather than political power from their fiefs, and their domains were subject to the inspectors and other officials of the central government. Wu's reforms virtually wiped out the princely and noble domains. This separation of government positions from family prerogatives was a great advance in political institutions.

Kao-tsu and his successors failed to control the ambition to power of their wives, mothers, and in-laws. An empress could be powerful because she assisted the emperor

LIVES AND TIMES ACROSS CULTURES

Mathematical Problems in the Ancient World

Although the Han schoolboys' curriculum consisted mainly of the classics and history, they were also given some training in mathematics and exercises related to everyday affairs. Here are examples:

1. A fast horse and a slow horse set out together on the 3000 li [900 kilometers] long journey from Changan to Ch'i. The first day the fast horse travels 193 li, thereafter increasing his speed by 13 li each day. The slow horse covers 97 li on the first day, thereafter reducing his speed by $\frac{1}{2}$ li each day. After reaching Ch'i the fast horse starts his return journey and meets the slow horse. When does the meeting take place and how far has each horse traveled? Answer: After $15\,^{135}/_{191}$ days; the fast horse has traveled $4534\,^{46}/_{191}$ li, and the slow horse $146\,^{145}/_{191}$ li.

2. A man is hired as a salt porter. If he is paid 40 cash for carrying two measures of salt for a distance of 100 li, how much will he be paid for carrying 1.73 measures for a distance of 80 li? Answer: $27\,^{11}/_{15}$ cash.

During his school days in the third century B.C.E., Eratosthenes of Cyrene (in North Africa) was known to his fellow pupils as "Beta" because he excelled in so many subjects as to be nearly (or "second") best in each. In his later life, he was an astronomer, mathematician, poet, and chief librarian at the famous Library of Alexandria in Egypt. The most famous mathematical problem he solved had to do with the circumference of the earth. Eratosthenes had noticed that during the summer solstice, the sun's rays fell vertically at Syene (modern Aswan) some 500 miles up the Nile, but at an angle of 7° at Alexandria to the north, near the mouth of the Nile. Applying basic Euclidean geometrical principles to this observation, Eratosthenes calculated the circumference of the earth. While the precise equivalent in feet or meters of his unit of measure (the stade) is not known, it is nonetheless clear that his computation was amazingly accurate. He also measured the degree of obliquity, or tilt, of the earth's axis.

in performing rituals and was considered the "mother of the empire," but she was legally subordinate to her husband and could be demoted. Dowager empresses (mothers and grandmothers of reigning emperors) were infinitely more powerful, however, because filial piety required sons to obey their mothers. Empress Lu set the precedent by presiding over the government after Kao-tsu's death, making her son ruler in name only. He could not stop her domineering ways and her extreme cruelty to her husband's concubines and their children, which caused him to suffer a nervous breakdown shortly after ascending the throne. He later abandoned himself to drinking, dying young after a seven-year reign. Dowager Empress Lu then appointed, dismissed, and killed several stepsons in succession; she also appointed members of her family to powerful posts and ruled for fifteen years until her death. Seven other dowager empresses ruled as regents while their sons were minors; some continued to rule even after their sons became adults. As regents they appointed and dismissed emperors and officials, often appointing their relatives and eunuchs to powerful positions, and issued laws. When there was more than one dowager empress (for example, when a mother and grandmother were both alive), feuds between them and their families resulted in coups and battles.

Han government was administered by a professional civil service rather than by hereditary nobles. Men were assigned to positions based on their education, merit, and ability to deal with people effectively. The first requirement for an aspiring official was an education. This requirement favored the rich, because books, which were copied on silk, wood, or bamboo slips, were expensive and rare. Since public service was rewarded with honors and riches, a popular saying held that it was better to bequeath books than gold to one's sons. Local officials were annually required to recommend educated young men of good moral character and send them to the capital city for written and oral exams. Those who passed were then given posts. They served on probation during the first year, and received permanent appointments if they acquitted themselves satisfactorily. Every sixth day was a day of rest, and leaves were granted for illness and for mourning the death of parents. In 124 B.C.E., a national university was established at the capital to prepare young men in the Confucian classics for the civil service. Enrollment was based on a geographic quota so that all areas of the empire were represented; from an original fifty students, their number had grown to 30,000 by the second century. Along with the Ch'in edict that unified the written language, this massive national educational network for training officials proved invaluable in holding together a huge and diverse empire.

Every third year each official received an efficiency rating and report from his superior and was either promoted, demoted, transferred, or dismissed according to his rating and the recommendation of his superior. Aged officials received pensions on retirement. A law of avoidance forbade a man to serve in his home area, to ensure that there would be a national rotation of the civil service and that no one built a power base that might challenge the throne. This rule remained in force until the twentieth century. Subordinate officials in each unit of local government, however, must come from that area to ensure that local voices and interests were heard.

Girls did not attend schools, nor could they take the official exams. However, girls from well-to-do families often received a private education, which included the womanly arts of weaving, embroidery, music, and painting, as well as the classics and poetry. A lady wrote of her education in these lines:

> At thirteen I could weave silk,
> At fourteen I learnt to cut a garment,
> At fifteen I played Kung Hou (a musical instrument),
> At sixteen I finished the Book of Odes and other classics,
> At seventeen I married thee.

The Han ideal, as in Rome, was the citizen soldier. Adulthood began at twenty, and every male was liable for one year of military service at twenty-three; the three-year delay was intended to allow the citizen time to accumulate savings so that he could serve without pay. Every year after the harvest, until they were fifty-six, men were liable for one month of reserve military duty. Actually, the citizen-soldier concept was impractical for a country the size of China, given the need to defend distant frontiers. Therefore, draft-eligible men who did not wish to serve could pay substitute money that was used for paying draftees and volunteers for longer-term service.

Ruins of hundreds of Han outposts, fortresses, watchtowers, walls, and ramparts across the entire northern frontier testify to the enormous burden of maintaining the Pax Sinica. Frontier garrisons protected the agricultural settlements and horse stud farms for cavalry horses, delivered the mail, and made secure the trade and diplomatic links between China and countries to the west. Because northwestern China had a dry climate, many reports, inventories, regulations, and personal accounts of the Han period have survived. They tell of a rigorous and disciplined life of military duty and farming that kept the empire secure and its prestige high. A fragment of silk from an officer's letter said plaintively: "the distance is long; contacts are rare; my rank is low and my person is humble; exchanges of letters are difficult." Most infantry soldiers carried a 40-inch-long steel sword, twice as long as and much stronger than the bronze sword blade of an earlier time. Iron was also used for javelin tips and arrowheads, knives, and chainlink and fish-scale armor. Throughout world history, camp followers accompanied soldiers on the march and at military encampments. Emperor Wu formally enrolled and supervised prostitutes as a category of camp followers for his far-flung military units.

The cavalry, essential for fighting the Hsiung-nu, supported the infantry in battle; in one campaign 130,000 horses participated—fewer than 30,000 returned. Thus the government gave top priority to obtaining good horses from friendly nomads and to controlling horse-breeding country. The powerful central Asian breeds, unlike the smaller ones native to China, could carry a fully armored soldier into battle. Horses for riding and pulling carriages became a status symbol for the rich. The combination of superior iron weapons, leadership, organization, martial spirit, and cavalry enabled the Han to triumph over the nomads and preserved the peace. Around the end of the Han dynasty, the Chinese first cast stirrups from metal. This important invention gave the rider greater control over his horse, freed his hands, and made mounting and dismounting easier. Nomads spread this Chinese invention westward until it was universally used.

The Land and People

The census of 1 C.E. counted the Han population at 60 million; it was 56.5 million in 157, perhaps more populous than the Roman Empire of the same period. Most Chinese were farmers. Land was privately owned and could be bought and sold. The typical farm family consisted of husband, wife, and three children, working about seventeen acres. In the north, millet, wheat, and barley were the grain crops; in the south, rice. Pigs and fowl were the common meat animal. Fish and tortoise raised in ponds also provided protein.

Wind-powered bellows lowered the cost of making cast-iron tools, now used everywhere; plows were now made entirely of iron. Other technical innovations include a three-legged seeder that could plant three rows of seeds simultaneously, an iron harrow, and a leveler. Paired or singly yoked oxen pulled the plow and other farm machinery; by using the nose ring, an innovation, one man could control an oxen team. Archaeologists have found some giant plowshares thought to be ditch diggers. Iron tools enabled the government to build large irrigation projects. Old reservoirs were enlarged and new ones built to hold water for irrigation. Han engineers built the world's first canals that were

Soldiers' Orders. This wooden slip came from a Han military outpost in northwestern China along the Silk Road. It gives instructions for signaling between posts as follows: "The order will be put up where it can be seen by the soldiers of the section of each post so that all may know it by heart and understand it; a close watch is to be kept and as soon as there is a fire signal the section of the post shall light one in turn...."

The British Library

designed to follow the contour of the land as a way around or over hills. Wells with winches to draw the water and brick-lined spill troughs to funnel water for irrigation became common.

The government encouraged widespread planting of mulberry trees and sericulture (raising silkworms and spinning and weaving silk cloth). Silks were China's most desired export commodity, and bolts of silk were used as currency and given as state gifts. To ensure China's monopoly in silk production, the government prohibited exporting silkworm eggs. Tending silkworms and carding and spinning silk was women's work, and each family in silk-producing areas was required to pay a tax in silk floss and fabric.

Everyone paid a poll tax, and cultivators paid a small land tax. During many years when the state treasury was full, the tax was remitted altogether, once for as long as eleven years. Adult males also spent one month a year in corvée labor, mostly on public works projects after the harvest season.

Despite the general prosperity, the small farmers, as in Rome at this time, found themselves in trouble. Without reserves to tide them over difficulties, farmers often went into debt, and if they could not pay their debt, they lost their land and had to work as sharecroppers, paying 50 percent of their yield to the landowner. Some left the land to become laborers, and the most unfortunate, like poor Athenian farmers before Solon's reforms, had to sell their children or themselves into slavery to pay off their debts. Government attempts at direct relief and schemes to resettle the dispossessed on virgin lands did not solve the fundamental problem of inequity in a free land-tenure system. Those with capital to invest, like wealthy contemporary Romans, accumulated great estates worked by tenants and slaves. The rich estate owner who also enjoyed political connections often could evade taxes. That put a greater strain on the remaining small freeholders. Just as in Rome, the fall of the free peasantry had its corollary in the rise of great families. Individual great families rose and fell, and the government tried to limit the size of estates, but as a class the landowning magnates continued to prosper.

Land ownership thus became an acute social issue. As the dynasty declined, the power of great families increased unrestrained, until some fielded private armies that challenged the government. The worsening economic crisis led to large-scale peasant revolts in the second century, which precipitated the dynasty's downfall.

Cities, Manufacturing, and Commerce

Large urban centers were a characteristic of Han China. Enclosed by a wall sixteen miles in circumference, the capital city Changan was one of the largest in the world, and like Rome, was cosmopolitan and luxurious. It was a planned city of palaces, temples, markets, and private residences; the widest avenues measured 150 feet across. Whereas the Greeks and Romans built in stone, the Chinese (and Indians) used mainly wood, a highly perishable material. Thus not much remains standing from Han times except the tomb mounds for rulers and aristocrats, portions of city walls, and foundations of buildings.

Loyang was smaller, with a maximum total population of half a million. In 131 the state university campus at its outskirts had 240 buildings that housed classrooms and dormitories for 30,000 students. Then as now, citizens complained that many students spent their time boisterously having fun rather than studying. Many towns had specialized functions, such as manufacturing silk or iron, and others were noted for trade, or as garrison and administrative headquarters.

Both manufacturing and commerce flourished, and merchants made fortunes dealing in grain, iron, and salt. The iron industry produced not only weapons and agricultural tools but also common household items such as cooking pots, knives, scissors, and needles. One government-owned mine was allotted 100,000 corvée laborers each year to mine iron ore. Blast, reduction, and "steel puddling" furnaces were all in use.

Debates over proper government economic policy raged through much of the period. Confucians agreed with Legalists that merchants were social parasites; both scorned the profit motive as unworthy. Thus they put merchants at the bottom of the social order, below the scholars, farmers, and artisans. Emperor Wu promulgated sumptuary laws that forbade merchants to flaunt their wealth and regulated their other activities. He also nationalized the iron and salt industries and established a liquor licensing system, setting up a pattern that persisted to the twentieth century. He also set up state granaries to stabilize grain prices and to discourage speculation. State-owned factories and workshops were formed in many other fields. Despite these state actions, merchant princes continued to amass fortunes.

Crafts also flourished, as artisans created an extensive array of beautiful objects. Excavated tombs reveal that the metropolitan styles of Changan and Loyang were copied as far afield as Lolang in Korea and central Asia. Gorgeous Han silks were prized throughout the ancient world, and the beautiful articles of lacquer have not been surpassed since. Potters made a wide range of vessels for daily use, some covered with rich green and amber glazes. They also made scaled-down models of houses, animals, and tools that were buried in tombs for "use" by the dead in the spirit world. These grave goods enable us to reconstruct much of Han life.

Bronzesmiths made articles for ritual as well as daily use and decoration that even the middle class could afford. Bronze mirrors were especially prized; thousands have been excavated, even in Korea and Japan, some still with their prices marked on them. Some mirror makers advertised their wares by casting words of praise on them, for example: "The substance of this mirror is pure and bright; the rays it radiates could be compared to those of the sun and moon," and "The mirrors made by the Ye family are handsome and great. They are as bright as the sun and the moon; indeed they are rare to find."

Jade was another ritual as well as luxury item. The securing of the northwest, where nephrite jade was found, made for a steady supply. Because popular superstition had it that jade could preserve the body from decay, royalty had jade burial suits made for themselves. Archaeologists have recovered several jade suits from princely tombs.

The Silk Road: Link between East and West

As the centuries passed, the great civilizations of Eurasia came into increasing contact with one another. Contacts between China and the West resulted from Emperor Wu's victory over the Hsiung-nu, who had blocked access. He then exchanged ambassadors with King Mithridates II of Parthia (modern Iran), giving presents of silk to Mithridates and receiving acrobats and ostrich eggs in return. Trade between China and Parthia followed. Roman descriptions of Crassus's defeat at Carrhae in 53 B.C.E. told of the gleaming silk banners that preceded the Parthian soldiers. Less than ten years later, when Julius Caesar entered Rome in triumph, his procession also had silk banners.

During the early Roman Empire, wealthy women developed an almost insatiable demand for silk fabrics, to the disgust of Roman moralists. The Roman political leader and philosopher Seneca said: "I see garments in which there is nothing to cover either the wearer's body or her shame." Emperor Diocletian's "Edict on Maximum Prices" in 301 rated raw white silk by weight at one quarter the value of gold; if dyed purple, raw silk was rated at triple the value of gold.

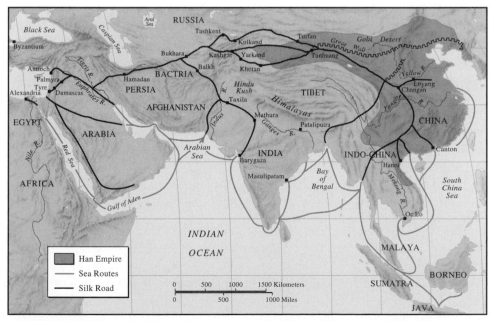

Map 4.5 The Han Empire and the Silk Road. In addition to controlling China, northern Korea, and Vietnam, Han outposts and garrisons dominated central Asia, allowing trade to cross the Silk Road to India, Persia, and the Roman Empire.

The Silk Road that connected the Chinese and Roman Empires and the lands in between began in the Han capital Changan and proceeded westward to Tunhuang, the last Chinese settlement. After crossing mountains and deserts and stopping at oases, it ended at a port of the eastern Mediterranean, where the goods were shipped to Rome. The transshipping made many trading stations en route prosperous. With the Han and Roman Empires in control of most of the route, roads were kept open and secure. Silk, both woven and raw, was China's major export; although skins, iron, lacquer, and spices were also exported. From the Roman Empire, China imported wool and linen fabrics, amber, coral, Syrian glass, Egyptian papyrus, wines, and acrobats and entertainers—the latter were status symbols in aristocratic Han households—but above all gold coins and bullion.

In the first century C.E., the Romans developed a sea route to the east, which had a twofold advantage over the land route: ships carried more than draft animals, and they bypassed territory controlled by the difficult and often hostile Parthians. During the reign of Augustus, as many as 120 Roman ships sailed from Red Sea ports for south India every year. Mostly Indian ships carried Roman wares to Southeast Asia and Canton in southern China. They also carried Indian and Southeast Asian products such as ivory, tortoise shell, gems, pearls, precious woods, and spices. Romans were alarmed by their unfavorable balance of trade, which caused a drain on the empire's precious metal reserves. As Emperor Tiberius complained, this outflow paid for "articles that flatter the vanity of women. . . . In exchange for trifles our money is sent to foreign lands and even to our enemies." In the second century, Pliny the Younger claimed that annually this trade drained the Roman treasury by 55 million sesterces paid to India and 45 million to China and Arabia. For comparison, a Roman soldier was paid about four sesterces per day.

The great distance precluded direct communications between the Chinese and Roman governments. Trade dropped off after the third century when political conditions deteriorated first in China and then in the west.

Religious and Intellectual Life

Emperor Kao-tsu and his immediate successors were practical men and had no professed philosophical preferences. Nevertheless, they realized that Legalism had become a liability because of its association with the hated Ch'in dynasty. But they needed dedicated men to help run the government and to dignify it with proper rituals. Enter the Confucians, whose conviction that the place of a scholar was in government and that li or rituals were important in human relations made them natural allies of the imperial system. In 136 B.C.E., Emperor Wu declared Confucianism the official state philosophy and banned students of Legalism from government service. Wu also established a state university with a curriculum based on Confucian works and an embryonic examination system. These measures ensured the dominance of Confucians in the bureaucracy. Without a comparable approach for recruiting officials, the Mauryan dynasty fell quickly. Paradoxically, once in government, the Confucians found that they needed to put into effect certain Legalist techniques and concepts.

Tung Chung-shu (c. 179–c. 104 B.C.E.) was largely responsible for creating an examination system that became the institutional basis of Confucianism as the state ideology.

He reinterpreted Confucian teachings and added to them current ideas to make Confucianism the theory of the unified empire. The universe, Tung explained, consisted of heaven, earth, and humans. The emperor was the highest representative of humanity, and it was up to him and the government to interpret the will of heaven and, by moral and beneficent government, help people develop their potential for goodness and maintain harmony. It was the emperor's duty to set a good moral example, to take care of the economic needs of the people, to make it profitable for them to become virtuous, and to help them achieve moral fulfillment.

If he failed to exercise his power properly, the emperor would disrupt cosmic harmony and forfeit the mandate of heaven. To prevent such disasters, Confucians counseled rulers to seek their advice and to take warning from natural portents, which they reported and interpreted. Seasonable weather and abundant harvests meant that heaven was satisfied, while droughts, floods, and strange happenings portended heaven's displeasure. The ruler or son of heaven indeed had heavy responsibilities.

Although a reinterpreted and eclectic Confucianism became the state ideology, other schools were not suppressed. Confucius was exalted as a sage, not a god or king. The spirit of his teachings influenced laws; he was not a lawgiver. Philosophical Taoism had a revival during the Han. Taoist ideas of cultivating self-contentment and seeking harmony with nature provided an outlet from Confucian strictures and allowed a degree of individualism to prevail.

Religious or popular Taoism also enjoyed popularity. Rooted in folk beliefs and superstitions, it was concerned with drugs and potions to prolong life and attain immortality, and with using alchemy to produce gold from base materials. These interests led to experiments and new knowledge in chemistry, pharmacology, and other sciences and to the discovery of the compass, which greatly helped navigation, and of gunpowder later. Many persons may have achieved premature immortality from taking the drugs and potions, but that did not disillusion the true believers, who asserted that the immortals, men and women who had found the secret of everlasting life, had merely pretended to die in order to confound those of little faith. Others participated in group worship and believed in salvation. In late Eastern Han, one religious Taoist group spread so fast that the government, fearing its political implications, acted to suppress it. Thereupon its adherents rebelled, donning a yellow head scarf for identification. The Yellow Turban uprising of 184 C.E., which capitalized on peasant discontent, precipitated the fall of the Han dynasty.

Buddhism had begun to take root by the first century C.E. It spread overland via the Silk Road and by sea from the south. In the second century a number of monks from Persia, central Asian kingdoms, and India were translating Buddhist canons into Chinese, assisted by Chinese monks. Buddhism introduced new concepts such as *karma* and reincarnation, and reinforced existing ideas about compassion. Buddhist meditation and yoga were akin to Taoist practices, leading some Chinese at first to think that Buddhism was a Taoist sect. Buddhist translations freely borrowed Taoist vocabulary. Many Taoists claimed that Lao Tzu had gone to India and converted Gautama to Taoism. Thus second-century Han emperors saw no contradiction when they placed deities of both faiths on the same palace altar and worshipped them together.

In retrospect, the introduction of Buddhism was one of the greatest events in Chinese civilization. After several centuries of assimilation and accommodation, Buddhism would be accepted as one of the three teachings of China, alongside Confucianism and Taoism. As a result, it had a major influence on Chinese thought, art, and literature.

The greatest literary glory of the Han was the writing of history. We have already noted in the previous chapter that the prestige of historical writing is deeply rooted in Chinese civilization. Han historians contributed two great works. The first was the *Shih Chi (Records of the Historian)*, a comprehensive history of the world as then known to Chinese, from the era of the culture heroes to the first century B.C.E. It was written by a father and son team, and its format and elegant prose were held up as a model for succeeding historians. It was divided into five sections: basic annals (narrative of important events), chronological tables, monographs (analytical essays on topics of special interest such as music, astronomy, and economic affairs), histories of great families of the past, and biographies (which included lives of statesmen, notable women, thinkers, rogues, and assassins).

This multifaceted approach to history set the standard for later dynastic histories that continued to the present century. Ssu-ma Ch'ien, the son and more famous of the duo, believed that history had two purposes: to give information and to provide moral instruction. Like the Athenian historian Thucydides, he invented speeches and dialogues that he felt fitted the historical characters and their situation and brought persons and events to life.

The second great work was titled *The History of the Former [Western] Han Dynasty*. It was begun by Pan Ku (32–92 C.E.), brother and uncle of the great generals, father and son conquerors of central Asia, and finished by his equally famous sister Pan Chao, who also wrote a book of moral instructions for upper-class women. Another famous woman author wrote a multivolume work titled *Lives of Famous Women* that recorded the lives and deeds of over a hundred famous and infamous women up to that time.

Other literary works of the Han dealt with philosophy, poetry, and fiction. In the bibliographical section of the *History of the Former Han Dynasty*, Pan Ku listed 1380 works of fiction, but none has survived.

Summary and Comparisons

This chapter covered the development of several great empires that, after periods of prolonged intellectual ferment and political turmoil, succeeded in imposing unity and order.

The fragmented and weak Greek city states allowed backward and semi-Greek Macedon to rise to ascendancy under Philip and his son, Alexander the Great. Alexander conquered the Persian Empire and controlled territory from Egypt to northwestern India. After his early death, that empire broke up into three Hellenistic states, which were, in their turn, finally absorbed by Rome. Alexander's conquests and the successor Hellenistic states accelerated the spread of Greek culture throughout the eastern Mediterranean and western Asia.

Further west, on the Italian Peninsula, Rome rose to dominance by outstripping neighboring Greek, Etruscan, and Latin cultures. After ousting their Etruscan monarchs

CHRONOLOGY

550 B.C.E.	
	Beginning of Roman Republic
350	
	Demosthenes
	Alexander the Great
	Chandragupta Maurya
	Kautilya, *Arthasastra*
	Euclid's *Elements*
	Stoicism and Epicureanism
	The *Mahabharata* and *Ramayana*
	Emperor Asoka
	Third Buddhist Council
	Scipio defeats Hannibal at Zama
200	Han Kao-tsu founds the Han dynasty
	Tung Chung-shu
	Emperor Wu
	Travels of Chang Ch'ien
	Confucianism becomes the state ideology in China
50	Extensive trade along the Silk Road
	Cicero
	The assassination of Julius Caesar
	Cleopatra
	Emperor Augustus
	Ssu-ma Ch'ien, *Records of the Historian*
1 C.E.	Buddhism spreads in China
	Eastern Han dynasty
	Pan Ku, Pan Chao, *History of the Former Han Dynasty*
	King Kanishka
	Fourth Buddhist Council
100 C.E.	
	Plotinus and Neoplatonism
	Emperor Constantine
	Compilation of the Talmud
400	

and forming a republic, the Romans first dominated the entire peninsula, then, between 264 and 30 B.C.E., wrested control of the Mediterranean from Carthage and the Hellenistic kingdoms. The Roman Empire reached its zenith during the first two centuries C.E., then declined dramatically during the third, when autocratic rulers postponed total collapse by dividing the empire into eastern and western halves.

Alexander's brief incursion into the Indus Valley inspired Chandragupta Maurya to found a dynasty and begin the conquest of an empire that would embrace nearly the entire Indian subcontinent under his successors. The Mauryan Empire reached its zenith under Asoka, who converted to Buddhism, giving it impetus to spread beyond India. Northwest India suffered many invasions by Greeks and Persians after the fall of the Mauryan Empire; the most successful invaders, however, were nomads from China's northwest called Yueh-chih by the Chinese and known as Kushans after they entered India. Kushan power and culture reached its zenith under the great monarch Kanishka around 100 C.E.

Further east, the Han dynasty (202 B.C.E.–220 C.E.), founded by a commoner named Liu Pang, unified the Chinese peoples after a long era of warfare. The Han leaders ended feudalism, adopted Confucianism as a state ideology, and established an educational and examination system that endured in China for two thousand years. Han military success affected Korea in the east, Vietnam in the south, and central Asia in the west.

All four major empires treated in this chapter enjoyed outstanding leadership by great founding leaders and their heirs. Although they did not achieve the same degrees of success or durability, each left a rich legacy to billions of people up to the present day. Alexander the Great, for example, died young, but his powerful generals partitioned his empire and established states that shared many cultural traditions and endowed the eastern Mediterranean world with a degree of cohesion, including a common language for the educated.

Although the Mauryan Empire collapsed soon after the reigns of its three founding rulers, its cultural and religious gains survived and spread far beyond India's frontiers. Despite scholars' knowledge of Sanskrit and Prakrit, languages of Buddhist literature, the Mauryan Empire failed to bequeath a common language to India. This hindered its quest for unity throughout subsequent history.

The Han Empire endured for four centuries, gave its name to most Chinese to the present, left an indelible mark on all east Asian civilizations, and bequeathed a common writing system.

The Roman state lasted longest, in part because it underwent many internal transformations, from monarchy to republic and finally to empire. It, too, left indelible marks on the language, laws, and religion of much of Europe.

Patronage of the arts and other cultural activities under all four empires fostered sacred scriptures, poetry, literature, and philosophy that still exert powerful influences today.

Each of the empires assimilated and civilized disparate peoples and created a common heritage for them. The geographic extent of the Mauryan Empire expanded the notion of India and brought Indian civilization even into southern India and Ceylon (present-day Sri Lanka). Similarly, the Han Empire absorbed many less advanced peoples as heirs of a common Chinese heritage. International trade, travel, and missionary activities made each empire more cosmopolitan, and extended the influences of hitherto insular cultures across continents.

Finally, the political needs of the states and the emotional and spiritual needs of their peoples led to the formation or development of great religions and philosophies. Reinterpreted Confucianism became the moral foundation of the Chinese empire, as Christianity became the official religion of the late Roman Empire (see Chapter 5). New philosophies such as Stoicism and Epicureanism in the Hellenistic states and the further evolution of existing Taoist philosophy in China helped the elite cope with an impersonal world. Higher religions such as Buddhism, Jainism, and Christianity offered moral grounding and spiritual comfort to both the elite and ordinary people, while mystery cults in the Roman Empire and magical Taoist practices in China both consoled and empowered the masses.

The great achievements of the Roman, Mauryan, and Han Empires have left a lasting legacy both within and beyond the borders of Europe, India, and China.

Selected Sources

Items indicated with an asterisk (*) are available in paperback.

Balsdon, J. P. V. D. *Life and Leisure in Ancient Rome*. 1969. Based on a critical assessment of literary, inscriptional, and archaeological evidence.

Begley, Vimala, and Richard D. De Puma, eds. *Rome and India: The Ancient Sea Trade*. 1991. By many experts on different topics.

*Boardman, John, et al., eds. *The Roman World*. 1988. This volume of the Oxford History of the Classical World contains essays by leading authorities on all aspects of Roman civilization; excellent illustrations.

*Bryher, Winifred. *The Coin of Carthage*. 1963. An entertaining historical novel about the fortunes of two Greek traders trying to make their way in a world convulsed by the second Punic War.

Ch'u, T'ung-tsu. *Han Social Structure*. 1972. Jack L. Dull, ed. Comprehensive in scope and full of human interest and anecdotes.

Erdosy, George. *Urbanism in Early Historic India*. 1988. On the development of cities between 1000 B.C.E. and 300 C.E.

Frye, Richard N. *The Heritage of Central Asia: From Antiquity to the Turkish Expansion*. 1996. This book shows how central Asia connected all the ancient cultures of Europe and Asia.

Gokhale, B. G. *Asoka Maurya*. 1966. A good biography of the man and his age.

Green, Peter. *Alexander the Great*. 1970. This engaging and superbly illustrated biography of Alexander is well-balanced in its assessment of his accomplishments. Covers the career of Philip II also.

Langguth, A. J. *A Noise of War: Caesar, Pompey, Octavian, and the Struggle for Rome*. 1994. A riveting account of a turbulent era by a popular biographer.

*Le Glay, Marcel, et al. *A History of Rome*. Trans. Antonia Nevill. 2d ed. 2000. This comprehensive history of ancient Rome is equipped with excellent graphics: chronologies, illustrations, maps, plans, and a glossary.

Loewe, Michael. *Everyday Life in Early Imperial China*. 1968. Many pictures and drawings help bring back life in China 2,000 years ago.

*Long, A. A. *Hellenistic Philosophy*. 2d ed. 1986. This very helpful study covers Epicureanism, Skepticism, and Stoicism.

*McCullough, Colleen. *The First Man in Rome*. 1990. *The Grass Crown*. 1991. *Fortune's Favorites*. 1993. *Caesar's Women*. 1996. *Caesar*. 1999. These five richly detailed historical novels in the author's "Masters of Rome" series trace, with considerable fictional embroidery, the careers of Marius, Sulla, Pompey the Great, and Julius Caesar, among others.

Pirzzoli-t'Serstevens, Michele. *The Han Dynasty*. 1982. A beautifully illustrated volume with easy-to-read text.

*Plescia, Joseph. *The Bill of Rights and Roman Law: A Comparative Study*. 1995. A fascinating and concise comparison of the development of citizens' rights in ancient Rome and in the U.S. Bill of Rights.

*Pomeroy, Sarah. *Women in Hellenistic Egypt*. 1984. A fascinating account of the lives of women on all social levels during the period.

Power, Martin. *Art and Politics in Early China*. 1992. On interactions between the government and art in Han China.

*Renault, Mary. *Funeral Games*. 1981. A vivid fictionalized treatment of the bloody and chaotic struggle for power by Alexander's successors after 323 B.C.E.

*Scarre, Chris. *The Penguin Historical Atlas of Ancient Rome*. 1995. Contains, in addition to excellent full-color maps and illustrations, a quite detailed, topic-by-topic history of ancient Rome.

Soren, David, et al. *Carthage: Uncovering the Mysteries and Splendors of Ancient Tunisia*. 1990. The best general account of ancient Carthage and its civilization from the ninth century B.C.E. to the sixth century C.E.

Soucek, Svat. *A History of Inner Asia*. 2000. A comprehensive look at the peoples of a region important to Indian, Chinese, and other civilizations.

*Southern, Pat. *Augustus*. 1998. The best recent account of the life and times of the first Roman emperor and the system of government he instituted.

*Stoneman, Richard. *Alexander the Great*. 1997. The best brief biography of the Macedonian conqueror.

*Walbank, F. W. *The Hellenistic World*. 1982; rev. ed. 1993. A concise, accurate, up-to-date presentation of political and cultural developments of the era.

Yu Ying-shih. *Trade and Expansion in Han China: A Study in the Structure of Sino-Barbarian Economic Relations*. 1967. Deals with interaction between politics and economics.

Additional resources, exercises, and Internet links related to this chapter are available at the Book Companion Web site: http://history.wadsworth.com/upshurcompact4/

Comparative Essay 4
The Decline and Fall of Empires

At Pei-mang how they rise to Heaven,
Those high mounds, four or five in the fields!
What men lie buried under these tombs?
All of them were Lords of the Han world. . . .
When the dynasty was falling, tumult and disorder rose,
Thieves and robbers roamed like wild beasts. . . .
They have gone into vaults and opened the secret doors.
Jewelled scabbards lie twisted and defaced:
The stones that were set in them, thieves have carried away,
The ancestral temples are hummocks in the ground:
The walls that went round them are all levelled flat.
Over the tombs the ploughshares will be driven
And peasants will have their fields and orchards there.
They that were once the lords of a thousand hosts
Are now become the dust of the hills and ridges.

Arthur Waley, *Translations from the Chinese* (New York: Knopf, 1941), pp. 76–77 (poem by Chang Tsai, third century C.E., lamenting the desecration of Han imperial tombs after the fall of the dynasty).

Dynasties [Empires] have a natural life span like individuals . . . as a rule no dynasty lasts beyond the life span of three generations. . . . In a dynasty affected by senility as the result of luxury and rest, it sometimes happens that the ruler chooses helpers and partisans from groups not related to the ruling dynasty but used to toughness. He uses them as an army which will be better able to suffer the hardships of wars, hunger, and privation. This could prove a cure for the senility of the dynasty . . . but only until God permits His command regarding the dynasty to be executed.

Ibn Khaldun, The Muqaddimah: An Introduction to History, trans. Franz Rosenthal (Princeton: Princeton University Press, 1967), pp. 135–136.

Why do great empires crumble away or die? Are their deaths inevitable? The Chinese poem above from the third century C.E. describes the robbed and desecrated Han imperial tombs after the fall of that once glorious dynasty. Like empires around the world, the Han Empire had once seemed almost invincible, but it too had fallen into decline and had finally collapsed. Over the centuries, historians have put forth numerous reasons for the demise of empires. For example, Chinese scholars accepted a cyclical theory of history, namely, that growth and prosperity are inevitably followed by decline and fall. Chinese writers also accepted the proposition that periods of unity are followed by disunity and chaos, which in turn give way once more to unity. The great fourteenth-century Arab historian Ibn Khaldun shared these views. Judeo-Christian historians, on the other hand, believed that historic progression served God's purpose, and that history would end when God's kingdom was established on earth. In the nineteenth and twentieth centuries, modern theories range from the Marxist view that all history is the result of class struggle based on economic causes to Arnold Toynbee's hypothesis that empires rise when they meet the physical and spiritual challenges of the people and time and fall when they no longer do so.

The problem with broad theories such as these is that they may lead their exponents to bend, distort, or use facts selectively to prove their case, while ignoring or dismissing important factors that fail to serve their thesis. In fact, the rise and fall of great empires result from many complex reasons, some of which are shared, while in other instances they are specific and unique. Therefore it is difficult and unwise to force the explanation for the fall of empires into a uniform framework. As we shall see in the chapter that follows, empires have characteristically declined and collapsed as a result of a combination of factors.

1. *Dynastic succession.* To paraphrase the great twentieth-century British statesman and historian Winston Churchill, although democratic governments are imperfect, they are nevertheless superior to all other forms of government. In particular, constitutional democracies built on the rule of law have clear rules concerning acquiring, holding, and relinquishing power. No major ancient empire was democratically governed. All were hereditary dynasties, ruled most of the time by men, but sometimes by women. Succession to power was often based on primogeniture or some other form of selection within the ruling family. Inevitably, after some generations, ruling families produced weak heirs due to wine, song, sexual excess, mental deficiency, or other causes, or they left heirs too young to govern capably. Ineffectual leaders and disputed successions generally brought about revolts, usurpations, and civil wars that toppled the ruling dynasty and contributed to the decline and fall of the empire. For example, the lack of an adult male heir spelled the breakup of Alexander's empire. A disputed succession broke up the Mongol empire two generations after its founding by Genghis Khan. Inferior rulers and minor rulers manipulated by relatives and eunuchs brought about the end of the Mauryan and Han Empires. Disputed succession led to coups that severely undermined the strength of the Roman and Inka Empires, and ended the unity of the Muslim Empire a generation after Muhammad's death.
2. *Bureaucratic corruption.* All effective empires relied on an honest bureaucracy and created checks and balances to ensure it. For example, the Romans emphasized the duty of the upper class to set moral examples and to devote their lives to public service.

Han China created state universities and an examination system to educate and select men of integrity and ability for public service. In time, however, all bureaucracies succumbed to corruption, and corrupt governments provoked rebellions; for example, a peasant revolt called the Yellow Turban rebellion contributed to the fall of the Han Empire.

3. *Inequitable economic burdens.* Successful empires depended on sufficient revenues to support the military, bureaucracy, and other arms of government. Sufficient revenues depended on a prosperous population engaged in agriculture, trade, and industries. Those who could evade taxes, however, generally the powerful, often found ways to do so, thereby enhancing their incomes and becoming richer. The resulting shift of the tax burden to the poor and powerless inevitably led to decreased revenue for the government and aroused anger among the taxpayers. A resentful population often revolted, and impoverished governments frequently lacked the resources to put down such revolts, or to secure defenses against outside enemies. A vicious cycle of decline and fall resulted. For example, the rise of large plantations and the concomitant fall of a free farming citizenry contributed to the fall of both Rome and the Han. The inability of the Gupta Empire in India to collect revenues to pay its officials contributed to its collapse, while the system of farming out tax collection to corrupt officials led to the decline of the Ottoman Empire.

4. *Regional, racial, or ethnic tensions.* Great empires were usually composites of numerous racial, ethnic, and religious groups who resisted full integration. The Hellenistic empires never fully integrated the ruling class of Greeks and the subject Egyptians, Persians, and other ethnic groups. In India the reversion to regional states divided by language and ethnicity demonstrates how difficult the Mauryan task of attempting to unite the subcontinent had been. A major weakness of the Aztec Empire was its tenuous control over restless subject peoples, who were often ready to join outsiders against their current masters. Widely disparate regional interests led Emperor Diocletian to divide the Roman Empire into four administrations with four capitals and four leaders. In time the division solidified into two separate empires, each with its official language, traditions, and culture.

5. *Decline of martial spirit.* The existence of a will to fight, or, put another way, the willingness of a populace to sacrifice property or life itself to defend the state, is an intangible but important factor in the rise and fall of many empires. The success of the Roman Empire was in part due to its male citizens' pride in military service. When that spirit declined, Rome was forced to recruit unreliable mercenaries. The need to pay mercenaries drained the treasury. This was also true of the Han and T'ang Empires in China. When the T'ang government needed to recruit barbarian units for the army, the result was a rebellion that almost toppled the dynasty. According to some, the Indian emperor Asoka's emphasis on pacifism and moral persuasion, as state policies sapped the martial spirit of the Indians, contributed to the fall of the Mauryan Empire.

6. *Costly technology.* All successful empires created engineering wonders that helped to sustain them. From China to India, West Asia, the Mediterranean world, and South

America, imperial governments built and maintained roads, harbors and waterways, irrigation projects, defensive walls, and other installations. They maintained granaries to provision troops defending their borders, to relieve famine, and to enhance their economies. The Great Wall of China, the Roman roads and aqueducts, the enormous granary complex of the Inka, and Ptolemaic irrigation works along the Nile River are major examples of the energies expended to maintain safety and enhance the economies of those empires. Whatever their intrinsic merit, however, the expense of initiating and maintaining projects of such magnitude often impoverished the governments that supported them, turning what was originally an advantage into a liability.

7. *Moral decline.* This is an intangible factor. Nevertheless, from Augustus on, Roman leaders decried the decline of their citizens' moral fiber and their increasing self-indulgence and hedonism. Similarly in Han China, the hedonism and extravagance of the upper classes were blamed for the decline of the dynasty. Emperor Asoka of India appointed morality officers to uphold high moral standards, with dubious results.

8. *Escapist or otherworldly religions.* The eighteenth-century historian Edward Gibbon blamed Christianity, which stressed heavenly rather than earthly rewards, for declining civic spirit and other ills of the Roman Empire. He also blamed religious strife among Christians for the increasing chaos of Rome. Likewise many upper-class Han Chinese indulged in otherworldly Buddhism or escapist philosophical Taoism. Emperor Asoka's encouragement of pacific pursuits and the nonviolent teachings of Buddhism and Jainism may also have contributed to weakening the Mauryan Empire.

9. *External enemies.* All successful empires were forged through conquest and maintained through military strength. While defeated enemies schemed for revenge, the wealth generated by powerful empires inspired envy, especially among less affluent neighbors. Thus outsiders awaited opportunities to breach the defenses of the Han and Roman Empires, to loot, settle, and rule the lands they coveted.

5

Disruption and Renewal in West Asia and Europe

•

I saw how the Northmen had arrived with their wares, and pitched their camp beside the Volga. Never did I see people so gigantic; they are tall as palm trees, and florid and ruddy of complexion. . . . Every one carries an axe, a dagger, and a sword, and without these weapons they are never seen. Their swords are broad, with wavy lines, and of Frankish make. From the tip of the finger-nails to the neck, each man of them is tattooed with pictures of trees, living beings, and other things. The women carry, fastened to their breast, a little case of iron, copper, silver, or gold, according to the wealth and resources of their husbands. Fastened to this case they wear a ring, and upon that a dagger, all attached to their breast. About their necks they wear gold and silver chains. . . . Their most highly prized ornaments consist of small green shells, of one of the varieties which are found in [the bottom of] ships. They make great efforts to obtain these . . . , stringing them as a necklace for their wives.

They are the filthiest race that God ever created. They do not wipe themselves after going to stool, nor wash themselves after a nocturnal pollution, any more than if they were wild asses.

They come from their own country, anchor their ships in the Volga, which is a great river, and build large wooden houses on its banks. In every such house there live ten or twenty, more or fewer. Each man has a couch, where he sits with the beautiful girls he has for sale. Here he is as likely as not to enjoy one of them while a friend looks on. At times several of them will be thus engaged at the same moment, each in full view of the others. Now and again a merchant will resort to a house to purchase a girl, and find her master thus embracing her, and not giving over until he has fully had his will.

Every morning a girl comes and brings a tub of water, and places it before her master. In this he proceeds to wash his face and hands, and then his hair, combing it out over the vessel. Thereupon he blows his nose, and spits into the tub, and, leaving no dirt behind, conveys it all into this water. When he has finished, the girl carries the tub to the man next him, who does the same. Thus she continues carrying the tub from one to another, till each of those who are in the house has blown his nose and spit into the tub, and washed his face and hair. . . .

If one of their number falls sick, they set up a tent at a distance, in which they place him, leaving bread and water at hand. Thereafter, they never approach nor speak to him, nor visit him the whole time, especially if he is a poor person or a slave. If he recovers and rises from his sick bed, he returns to his own. If he dies, they cremate him; but if he is a slave they leave him as he is, till at length he becomes the food of dogs and birds of prey.*

*Albert Stanburrough Cook, "Ibn Fadlan's Account of Scandinavian Merchants on the Volga in 922," Journal of English and Germanic Philology 22 (1923), 56–63.

Civilized life was transformed in the first millennium C.E., a period that spanned the end of the ancient Greco-Roman world and the beginning of the Middle Ages. The civilizations of Europe, West Asia, and North Africa that are examined in this chapter were both the destroyers and the inheritors of Roman culture. In many places, civilization either had never attained or actually receded from the standards of classical Greece and Rome, but in others, equally advanced cultures arose in the aftermath of Rome's fall. In the passage quoted above, Ibn Fadlan, an emissary of the Abbasid caliph Al-Muktadir (reigned 908–932), recounts the strange and revolting habits he observed among the Vikings, a Scandinavian people who had settled along the Volga River (in present-day Russia) in 922 C.E. It vividly portrays the reactions of the sophisticated Arab to the crude and vigorous Vikings, exposing the very different sensibilities of members of two divergent cultures in the Middle Ages.

As noted in the preceding comparative essay, the reasons for the fall of empires are many and varied. Although scholars disagree over the precise reasons for the fall of Rome or Constantinople, there is no doubt that the rising power of the Germanic tribes in Europe and the emergence of a dynamic new Muslim Empire in Arabia first threatened and then overtook the older Roman Empires. After first describing religious and social conditions in first-century Palestine and the spread of Christianity throughout the Roman Empire, this chapter will trace the long decline and destruction of the western, Roman Empire and the gradual disintegration of the eastern, Byzantine Empire.

As we shall see, Germanic peoples and Eurasian nomadic invaders made massive incursions into Europe and western Asia, destroying the western portion of the Roman Empire. This opened the way for a new civilization of the Franks in western Europe during the Carolingian era and the Middle Ages. At the same time, in the eastern portion of the Roman Empire, the Byzantines fashioned a durable imperial government and a distinctive tradition in art and literature. Eventually, however, their empire also manifested the symptoms of internal decay.

Beginning in Arabia in the seventh century, Islam rose to prominence among the major religions of the world. Unlike the Huns and other destructive invaders, the Muslims were agents of constructive change. Like Christianity, Buddhism, and the other great faiths, Islam shaped not only the spiritual but also the temporal lives of its millions of adherents, from India to Spain. In the process Muslims spread their own culture and assimilated elements of Greco-Roman culture, which they later transmitted to western Europe.

Political, Religious, and Social Unrest in Palestine: 63 B.C.E. to 73 C.E.

What has become of that great city, the metropolis of the Jewish people, with its protective walls and forts and towers, bursting with war materials and thousands of defenders? The city we thought God had founded? It has been destroyed root and branch, and now the only sign of its existence is the camp of the enemy that destroyed it. A few hapless old men sit and weep by the ashes of the temple precinct; a few women kept alive to sate the lust of the enemy. Who among us in this situation could bear to look on the sun's light any longer, even if he could himself live in safety? Who among us is such an enemy of his fatherland, such a coward, such a lover of life, that he does not regret being alive to see all this? We should all have died rather than see that holy city sacked by enemy hands, that sacred temple so ruined and profaned. We cherished the noble hope of avenging the city. Since that hope has now left us, let us hurry to die honorably. Let us show mercy to ourselves, our wives, and our children, while it is still in our power to do so. For we and our children were fated to die; even the fortunate cannot escape death. But nature does not impose on men the necessity of bearing disgrace, slavery, and the sight of our wives and children shamefully treated; such things come to those who refuse to avoid them by seeking death. . . . Let us die unenslaved; as free men with our children and wives, let us depart this life together. *

*B. Niese, ed., *Flavii Iosephi opera*, vol. 6: *De bello Judaico libri vii* (Berlin: Weidmann, 1895; reprinted 1955), trans. James P. Holoka.

This is a passage from a speech given to Jewish rebels by their leader Eleazer in 73 C.E. at the fortress of Masada, where the besieging Roman army is about to break through its defenses. Eleazer encourages his men to cheat the Romans of their victory. Some 960 rebels and their families committed suicide rather than be killed or enslaved by Roman soldiers the following day. This stunning act of defiance marked the last gasp of a revolutionary movement intended to throw off Roman overlordship.

This section will examine the remarkable political, social, and religious conditions of life in Palestine during the century and a half leading up to the failed revolt. This was a crucially important era both for the subsequent history of the Jews and Judaism and for the new world religion—Christianity—which now entered the stage in Palestine.

Palestine under Roman Rule

The direct Roman control of Palestine that Pompey the Great had instituted in 63 B.C.E. was loosened during the reign of King Herod the Great. With Rome's backing, Herod seized power from a rival claimant to the throne and held it throughout a long reign (37–4 B.C.E.), during which Palestine enjoyed peace and prosperity. His new port city of Caesarea Maritima and his lavish project to reconstruct the Temple of Solomon are symbols of the affluence the small Jewish nation enjoyed under Herod. In the latter part of his reign, however, Herod was preoccupied with issues of dynastic succession that led him to monstrous acts such as the execution of members of his own family and the slaughter of the infants after the birth of Jesus (Matthew 2:16–18).

After Herod's death, the Roman authorities divided his kingdom among his sons. This arrangement, however, did not last long, and beginning in 6 C.E. the various parts of the Jewish state again began to come under the direct authority of Rome as the province of Judaea. Roman prefects, including Pontius Pilate (governed 26–36), familiar from the

New Testament, and then imperial officials known as procurators ruled the province. These Roman administrators often behaved brutally toward the Jewish population and tolerated massacres of Jews by Greek-speaking inhabitants of the province. These abuses led to uprisings by various militant Jewish groups who used guerrilla tactics in hopes of regaining their freedom.

The subversive and terrorist activities of political resistance groups, especially the Zealots and the Sicarii or "dagger-men," as the Romans called them, eventually caused Rome to take decisive action. The Roman generals (and later emperors) Vespasian and his son Titus led a force of 60,000 troops into the province and crushed the rebellion in a bitterly fought war that resulted in the capture of Jerusalem and the destruction of its great Temple in 70 C.E. Some few pockets of resistance, such as the fortress of Masada near the Dead Sea, were rooted out by 73.

The failure of their revolt and the loss of their temple as a central religious and political focus caused Jews to be scattered around the eastern Mediterranean and even farther afield in a dispersal known as a Diaspora. The character of Jewish life had altered profoundly. In these new circumstances, Jewish leaders called rabbis began to place greater emphasis on observance of religious and social customs in Jewish communities. Essential to preserving and teaching these customs was the Talmud, a multivolume encyclopedia of Jewish religion. It had been orally accumulated over several centuries in Palestine and Babylonia, receiving final codification early in the sixth century C.E.

Religious Ferment

Reflecting in part these dramatic changes in political life in Palestine under Roman rule, various religious factions within Judaism emerged or became more sharply defined. These groups are familiar from the Christian Gospels and from the writings of the historian Flavius Josephus (born Joseph Ben Matthias), a Jew and Pharisee who became the protégé of the Flavian emperors Vespasian and Titus.

The Pharisees were mainly lay people of various social classes and occupations. They espoused adherence to the Torah (law) in every aspect of life, though they allowed for some flexibility in interpretation of the law. They also stressed prayer, fasting, and the paramount importance of ritual purity. They believed that a savior or Messiah would come to lead their nation against the forces of unbelievers and looked forward to an afterlife with God after the resurrection of the dead.

The Sadducees were a much more socially exclusive party; they belonged to aristocratic families whose members often served as priests. They did not, however, have the same degree of popular approval as the Pharisees, from whom they differed in several key doctrinal matters. For example, the Sadducees did not accept the comparatively new doctrines of resurrection of the dead and an afterlife. Along with the Pharisees, they had a prominent voice in the Sanhedrin (supreme religious and judicial council of the Jews). This theologically conservative party sought accommodation and peaceful coexistence with the Roman political authorities.

The Zealots were a group that advocated revolutionary overthrow of the Roman authorities so that they could establish a free nation based on their religious teachings.

Like present-day fundamentalist Muslim revolutionaries, they espoused a very literal reading and strict application of the law. The Zealots and other radical groups, such as the Sicarii, escalated their acts of resistance to the point of open revolt in 66 C.E., with ultimately disastrous results for Judaea, as we have seen.

The preservation and transmission of the Jewish religious doctrines embodied in Mosaic law were the specific responsibility of a class of teachers and legal experts known as scribes. This very honored (though unpaid) occupation drew its practitioners from all social classes and included Pharisees, Sadducees, and Zealots.

A Noble Social Experiment: The Essenes

Amid the factionalism among the Jews under Roman rule, various groups had sought to opt out of the doctrinal strife and bitter political conflicts altogether. These groups withdrew to deserted corners of Judaea to form new communities where they might live according to their own utopian social and religious practices.

One of these separatist groups—the Essenes—is especially well known to us because of a sensational archaeological discovery. In 1947 an Arab shepherd came upon a cave in the hills at Qumran, a mile or so from the northwest coast of the Dead Sea. In it and several others excavated later were hundreds of scrolls written in Hebrew and Aramaic, a related dialect. The Dead Sea Scrolls and extensive archaeological remains at Qumran reveal a monastic community that had its own set of theological tenets and that pursued a simple, self-sufficient existence.

The founder of the community, called the Teacher of Righteousness in the scrolls, probably lived in the mid or late second century B.C.E. Theologically, the Essenes were similar to the Pharisees in their emphasis on the law of Moses, ritual purity, and scrupulous observance of the Sabbath. Unlike the Pharisees, however, they did not believe in the resurrection of the dead. They also considered the Pharisees and other traditional Jewish groups to be corrupt and depraved and saw their own group as the one true Israel, called upon to fight, under the leadership of a Messiah, in an apocalyptic battle of Light against Darkness.

The scrolls indicate that initiation into the community was a three-year process, culminating in an oath that bound members to be just in their dealings with others, to be truthful, to show piety to God, and to discharge the other duties stipulated by the leaders of the sect. Baptism marked the repentance of initiates and entry into the fellowship of "God's Elect."

By the time of Roman rule in the first century C.E., the Qumran community had built an aqueduct and large reservoirs to supply water, a pantry and large kitchen with five fireplaces, a pottery workshop, flour mills and ovens, living quarters, and cemeteries holding the remains of over a thousand people. Another room, where a bench, three tables, and two inkwells were found, appears to have been a writing room—a forerunner of the scriptorium of medieval monasteries. This is likely where the famous scrolls were transcribed.

New Testament scholars have studied the Essene community at Qumran in comparison with elements of Christian doctrine and the communal style of life of early Christian

The Community Rule of Qumran

These are the rules by which they shall judge at a Community Court of Inquiry . . . :

If one of them has lied deliberately in matters of property he shall be excluded from the pure Meal of the Congregation for one year and shall do penance with respect to one quarter of his food. . . .

If any man has uttered the Most Venerable Name even though frivolously, or as a result of shock or for any other reason whatever, while reading the Book or praying, he shall be dismissed and shall return to the Council of the Community no more. . . .

Whoever has deliberately lied shall do penance for six months. . . .

Whoever has borne malice against his companion unjustly shall do penance for . . . one year; and likewise, whoever has taken revenge in any matter whatever.

Whoever has spoken foolishly: three months.

Whoever has interrupted his companion while speaking: ten days.

Whoever has lain down to sleep during an Assembly of the Congregation: thirty days. . . .

Whoever has spat in an Assembly of the Congregation shall do penance for thirty days.

Whoever has been so poorly dressed that when drawing his hand from beneath his garment his nakedness has been seen, he shall do penance for thirty days.

Whoever has guffawed foolishly shall do penance for thirty days. . . .

Whoever has gone about slandering his companion shall be excluded from the pure Meal of the Congregation for one year and shall do penance. But whoever has slandered the Congregation shall be expelled from among them and shall return no more.*

This passage from the Dead Sea Scrolls illustrates the rigorous rule the Qumran community lived under. Like Calvin's followers in sixteenth-century Geneva (see Chapter 9), members of the sect believed that those chosen to be among the elect by God had to live up to much higher standards than those of other, more conventional factions of believers. The regulations laid down here would have satisfied the strictest monastic orders of medieval Christianity (discussed later in this chapter).

*Geza Vermes, The Dead Sea Scrolls in English, 2d ed. (Harmondsworth: Penguin, 1975), pp. 82–84.

groups. We do not know whether the community had ties to the Zealot groups whose theological outlook was rather like their own. Though they do not seem to have shared the Zealots' enthusiasm for armed insurrection and terrorism, the Essenes suffered the same fate as other Jewish settlements, and the Qumran community was destroyed by Vespasian's legions in 68 C.E.

Palestine in the first century C.E. was a hotbed of religious ideas—reactionary, revolutionary, and conservative. In an atmosphere of political oppression, thinking Jews were wrestling with the question whether their religious convictions could be accommodated to life under Roman rule. Some thought cooperation was the best path; others, like Eleazer's rebel band on Masada, preferred death to despotism. And for many, the best hope for salvation—both political and spiritual—seemed to lie in the coming of a savior or Messiah. Christianity was born in these conditions.

Early Christianity

Two cities have been formed by two loves: the earthly by the love of self, even to the contempt of God; the heavenly by the love of God, even to the contempt of self. The former, in a word, glories in itself, the latter in the Lord. For the one seeks glory from men; but the greatest glory of the other is God, the witness of conscience. . . . In the one, the princes and the nations it subdues are ruled by the love of *ruling; in the other the princes and the subjects serve one another in love. . . . The one delights in its own strength, represented in the persons of its rulers; the other says to its God, "I will love Thee, O Lord, my strength."**

*Augustine, The City of God, trans. M. Dods (New York: Random House, 1950), p. 477.

Augustine wrote these words in the final days of the Roman Empire in the West. From the vantage point of an eminent Christian man of learning, he contrasts the earthly city of humanity—most fully realized in Rome itself—with the heavenly city of the Christian God. As the empire of Rome began to show signs of its mortality, many of Augustine's contemporaries also turned their eyes toward visions of more enduring, timeless realms of spiritual truth and divine love. The following section describes the rise and ultimate victory of the Christian religion within the Roman Empire.

The Origins of Christianity

The old Greco-Roman polytheism continued as the official creed of the state during the imperial period. Beginning with the deification of Julius Caesar, the ruler cult expanded the roster of deities, as the Roman Senate voted divine honors for successful and popular emperors after their deaths. In fact, however, a conglomeration of religions had begun to replace the traditional Roman religion during the late republic. As we have seen, mystery religions in honor of Bacchus and Cybele had won enthusiastic followings in Italy by the second century B.C.E. By 100 C.E. the cults of the Persian god Mithras and the Egyptian goddess Isis, among others, had attracted many believers and begun to replace the old religion in the hearts of Roman citizens. Though new to the Roman world, these mystery religions had roots in the distant past of ancient West Asia; their elaborate initiation rituals satisfied deep-seated desires for unity with the deity. The worn-out rituals of Greco-Roman polytheism could not match such powerful inducements to belief.

Amid the Jewish religious fragmentation of the first century C.E., an itinerant Jewish preacher, Jesus of Nazareth (c. 6 B.C.E.–c. 29 C.E.), inaugurated a new religion, Christianity. Many Jews who embraced this faith believed that Jesus was the Messiah (anointed one or savior) whose coming was frequently alluded to in the Old Testament. The Book of Ezekiel, for example, prophesied that a future prince of the house of David would bring salvation to the Jews at the time of the final destruction of the world. Under first Seleucid and then Roman rule, many Jews looked with great expectancy for the coming of an earthly savior who would destroy their oppressors and establish the preeminent power of Israel.

Jesus, however, directed his followers' hopes away from this world toward an otherworldly realm. His teaching emphasized the imminent "coming" of the kingdom of God, a new age of love and justice under God's reign. To prepare for God's kingly rule, men and women were enjoined to love God and their fellow human beings. Like Buddha, Jesus was an "enlightened one." As Buddha had spent forty-nine days and nights in meditation and temptation by demons (see Chapter 3), so Jesus spent forty days and nights in the wilderness, where he fasted and was tempted:

Jesus was then led by the Spirit into the wilderness, to be tempted by the devil. For forty days and nights he fasted, and at the end of them he was famished. The tempter approached him and said, "If you are the Son of God, tell these stones to become bread." Jesus answered, "Scripture says, 'Man is not to live on bread alone, but on every word that comes from the mouth of God.'". . .

The devil took him next to a very high mountain, and showed him all the kingdoms of the world in their glory. "All these," he said, "I will give you, if you will only fall down and do me homage." But Jesus said, "Out of my sight, Satan! Scripture says, 'You shall do homage to the Lord your God and worship him alone.'" Then the devil left him; and angels came and attended to his needs. (Matthew 4:1–11, Revised English Bible)

Although Jesus respected the Jewish scriptures, he opposed the Pharisees on matters of Sabbath observance, food laws, and ritual purity. He also believed the priestly Sadducees had corrupted the Jerusalem temple for personal gain. Jesus' popularity with the masses, who "heard him gladly," and his ties with some Zealots made him seem threatening to Roman authority in Judaea, only recently established. When Jesus arrived in Jerusalem, Roman and Jewish officials arrested, tried, convicted, and crucified him as an agitator.

After the death of Jesus, his followers announced he had risen from the dead and was the long-awaited Messiah (in Greek, *Christos,* "anointed one"), adding large numbers to their ranks by their dynamic preaching. Converts underwent ritual baptism; this rite and the common meal of bread and wine (the Eucharist or Lord's Supper) became central ceremonies of Christian observance.

A Jewish convert to Christianity, Paul (c. 3–c. 67 C.E.) of Tarsus carried the new faith to Greek-speaking non-Jews in a series of extensive missionary journeys in Asia Minor, Greece, and Rome. He represented Jesus as a dying and resurrected savior-god who taught that sin so alienated humans from God that only God's grace could save them. According to Paul, God had offered that grace through the life, death, and resurrection of Jesus the Christ.

Paul, who has been aptly called "the apostle to the Gentiles [non-Jews]," was the only first-century partisan of the Christian faith to leave a substantial written legacy. His letters constitute one-fourth of the New Testament, and the Book of Acts is a detailed account of his career. Paul also established numerous Christian churches in Asia Minor and the eastern Mediterranean. He was executed by the authorities in Rome in the time of Nero.

As the new religion attracted large numbers of adherents, Roman authorities abandoned their usual policy of religious toleration. The first recorded persecution of Christians took place after a terribly destructive fire in the city of Rome in 64, when Nero tried to curb rumors blaming him for the disaster by pinning responsibility on the Christians in the city. He imposed horrible penalties, including burning people alive, a common punishment for arson. Before the third century, however, there was no consistent empire-wide policy of persecution. Provincial governors only sporadically enforced the laws against Christianity. For instance, when Pliny the Younger wrote to ask Trajan what should be done about persons accused of being Christians in his province of Bithynia, the emperor answered, "No hard and fast rule may be set down. They are not to be hunted down; if they are brought before you and convicted, they should be punished. Nevertheless, anyone who denies he is Christian and verifies it by supplicating our gods should be pardoned accordingly, however suspicious his past life" (Pliny, *Epistulae,* book

A Christian Woman Accepts a Martyr's Fate

After these [executions in the amphitheater], on the final day, they brought in Blandina and a boy named Ponticus about fifteen years old. These two had been made to watch the torments of the other martyrs on previous days. The authorities tried again to constrain them to swear allegiance to their idols, and the mob was enraged by their stubborn refusal to do any such thing. Thus, they ignored the tender years of the boy and did not balk at torturing a woman. They proceeded to put them through the whole course of brutal torments, but could not make them swear allegiance to their gods. Encouraging and assuring Ponticus was his sister, as the pagans [believers in traditional Greek and Roman deities] all witnessed; thus strengthened, he coura-geously bore the torture and surrendered his spirit in death. Blessed Blandina, kept to the last, counseled her children like a virtuous mother and sent them tri-umphant to meet the Lord their King. She then eagerly went forth to the same torments her children had suf-fered, actually glorying in her death as if she were attending a wedding feast and not herself being feasted on by wild animals. She was whipped, torn by beasts, burned by iron, and finally put in a basket and gored by a bull, which savaged her for some time, though she was now unconscious and quite impervious to the pain, thanks to her faith and adherence to her instruction and her communion with Christ. Thus when Blandina was sacrificed, the pagans all granted that no woman had ever endured so many and such awful torments.*

This passage from the Church historian Eusebius describes a particularly savage persecution that took place at Lyons in Gaul in 175–176 C.E. The Roman Empire had been suffering from barbarian invasions and an outbreak of a virulent plague; consequently, a kind of mass hysteria, uncontrolled by an incompetent provincial governor, may explain the brutality of the attacks on Christians. The amazement and sometimes even sympathy of pagans who witnessed the uncanny poise and staunch faith of their Christian victims is a common motif in many biographical accounts of early martyrs. As the Christian writer Tertullian (c. 160–c. 240) put it, "the blood of the martyrs [those killed for their faith] is the seed of the church."

*Eusebius, Ecclesiastical History, vol. 1, ed. Kirsopp Lake (Cambridge: Harvard University Press, 1926), book 5, chap. 1, trans. James P. Holoka.

10, no. 97, trans. James P. Holoka). With few exceptions, this rather enlightened policy of Trajan's was adhered to until the mid-third century. Whatever persecutions did occur tended to enhance Christianity's appeal.

Christianity competed effectively with the mystery religions in the Roman Empire in part because of its literature and its organization. Certain lives of Jesus (the Gospels or "good news"), letters by missionaries like Paul, and accounts of Christian teaching were eventually collected in the New Testament, which was joined to the body of Jewish scriptures, termed the Old Testament, to create the Christian Bible. Christian organiza-tion early showed a remarkable diversity of specializations, including prophets, teachers, healers, and administrators. Committees composed of elders—members distinguished for their faith and maturity—regulated the activities of each local congregation, whereas its religious services were conducted by a presbyter (priest or minister). Where several congregations existed in the same city, they came to be supervised by a higher official, the bishop.

The Triumph of Christianity

By the late third century, Christianity had become an increasingly divisive factor in the Roman world. While many were attracted to Christianity for its apparent stability, order, and morality, others blamed it for sapping the empire of its strength by diverting the interest and loyalty of its citizens away from their civic responsibilities. Persecutions became more frequent and widespread. The most notable was begun by Diocletian in 303 and accelerated by his successor, Galerius (reigned 305–311). Churches were destroyed and Christians, especially bishops and other leaders, were hunted down and executed. Sacred scriptures were burned and church holdings seized.

The status of Christianity in the Roman Empire changed with startling suddenness during the fourth century. In 311, on his death bed, Galerius recognized the failure of his religious policy and issued an Edict of Toleration, permitting Christians to practice their faith and rebuild their churches. Constantine, influenced by his mother's devout Christian faith and a prebattle vision of a Christian cross ("In this sign you will conquer"), confirmed this toleration by his Edict of Milan in 313, restoring confiscated Christian properties. He also granted the Christians special favors such as lands and buildings, tax exemptions for their clergy, and permission for their bishops to act as imperial judges. Constantine perhaps envisaged Christianity as a new imperial ideology that could provide unity to a sadly battered empire. Later emperors followed and extended his pro-Christian policies, until by the end of the fourth century Christianity and Judaism were the only legal religions in the empire.

Besides the crucial factors of sincere belief in the Christian God and imperial encouragement of that belief, we may note four reasons for Christianity's final victory over competing faiths and fearsome persecution. First, it was simple in its demand for absolute allegiance, brushing aside the welter of alternative religions and requiring a single, irreversible commitment to one creed. It offered permanent values at a time when political and spiritual absolutes were fast disappearing from the Roman horizon.

Second, it was equalitarian. Like the Hindu Upanishads, which ignored barriers of caste and other differences among believers (see Chapter 3), Christianity stressed the value of every individual soul. It was open to any and all, from the lowest slave (even female slaves) to the emperor. Every soul could be saved, regardless of ethnic origin or social status: "There is no question here of Greek and Jew, circumcised and uncircumcised, barbarian, Scythian, slave and freeman; but Christ is all, and is in all" (Colossians 3:11, Revised English Bible).

Third, Christianity held out the hope of a better life in the world of the heavenly city. This was a compelling enticement when the foundations of the earthly world of the Roman Empire were shaking. Though various mystery cults similarly promised immortality, in the case of Christianity the courage and equanimity of martyrs who endured torturous deaths lent credence to the notion that true believers would gain eternal bliss in the presence of their God. "I am the resurrection and the life. Whoever has faith in me shall live, even though he dies; and no one who lives and has faith in me shall ever die" (John 11:25–26).

Finally, Christianity satisfied the universal need to belong. Founded on the injunction to "Love thy neighbor," the Christian community shared a value system and manner of living as well as a body of ritual. Persecution only strengthened this bond, as the church assumed the responsibility of caring for its own in a hostile environment, ministering to the indigent and sick, supporting orphans and widows, and supplying a source of self-

LIVES AND TIMES ACROSS CULTURES

Women and the Medical Professions in Late Antiquity

As with most other professions in the ancient world, medicine was formally practiced at its highest levels almost exclusively by men. Men performed surgeries, wrote the medical textbooks, instructed students in the medical schools. But on the level of day-to-day attention to patients, women—then as now—were the chief hands-on caregivers, and in much larger numbers than men. One historian has described the circumstances under which women practiced medicine as follows:

Medicine was part of the lives of ordinary women. They were agents as well as patients, the first line of defense against illness. Hospitals were available from the late fourth century [C.E.], as one form of Christian charity, but sick people who had homes were usually nursed there: women supervised diet and tried out traditional remedies. Some women were acknowledged experts on illness and medicines generally; others specialized in childbirth and problems associated with reproductive life, including "female complaints" and sexual difficulties. It was easier and cheaper to call on them than to employ a doctor with a professional training....

Some women described themselves, or were described by others as medica ["doctor"]. . . . These women could not attend university lectures or train with doctors, but midwives and nursing attendants could work with doctors, and women caring for the sick could listen as the doctor explained the case to his trainees. According to Soranus [a second-century physician and prolific medical author]..., the "complete midwife" understood all the branches of medicine: dietetics, pharmacy, and cheirourgia—that is, the "manual work" which includes massage and manipulation as well as the use of instruments. *

The expertise of such women did not go unappreciated, as may be seen from the following epitaph inscribed in the second century C.E.:

Farewell, lady Panthia, from your husband. After your departure, I keep up my lasting grief for your cruel death. . . . You guided straight the rudder of life in our home and raised high our common fame in healing—though you were a woman, you were not behind me in skill. In recognition of this your bridegroom Glycon built this tomb for you. **

*Gillian Clark, Women in Late Antiquity: Pagan and Christian Lifestyles (Oxford: Clarendon Press, 1993), pp. 63, 67.
**Mary R. Lefkowitz and Maureen B. Fant, Women's Life in Greece and Rome: A Source Book in Translation, 2d ed. (Baltimore: Johns Hopkins University Press, 1992), p. 265.

respect in the lives of thousands of urban poor. Such activities, which were foreign to Greek and Roman religious expression, made the believer's earthly life more tolerable and meaningful, even in the face of adversity, quite apart from the prospect of a life after death.

As the Christians became preeminent in the empire, they devoted increasing attention to defining their beliefs. Ironically, efforts to make simple and clear formulations of the tenets of Christian belief often produced only complexity, confusion, and conflict. Special councils were held to resolve disagreements. From the Council of Nicaea in 325 there emerged the distinctive Christian doctrine of the Trinity and a definitive statement of essential beliefs of Christian faith, the Nicene Creed.

The writings of the church fathers also helped to clarify Christian dogma. Jerome (c. 348–420) mastered Greek and Hebrew and produced a translation into Latin of the whole Bible known as the Vulgate (common or ordinary), because it used an everyday style of language. His translation remained standard for a thousand years.

The greatest church father was Augustine (354–430). As a teacher of rhetoric, he had explored most Roman beliefs and enjoyed many of life's pleasures before embracing Christianity. His *Confessions* recounted the sinfulness—particularly sexual sins—of his earlier life and the importance of God's grace to his rehabilitation. In his *City of God,* written shortly after the Visigothic sack of the city of Rome in 410 (see below), Augustine argues that destruction of the Roman Empire may be part of God's plan and that humans ought to give their permanent allegiance not to the empire but to the city of God.

Some Christians practiced a rigorously disciplined religious life called monasticism and formed communities of monks and nuns, in much the same way as the Buddhist *sangha* was organized, though with greater hierarchic stratification and centralized control than in Buddhist orders. Typically, they vowed themselves to poverty, sexual abstinence, and obedience to superiors. Their day was divided into periods for physical needs such as eating and sleeping, prayer and meditation, study, and, in the Latin West, work. Such communities speeded the Christianization of the countryside, contributed new models for spiritual leadership, and preserved much of classical civilization while transforming it to serve Christian purposes.

The papacy also developed during the period 300–500. Archbishops in the empire's major cities became known as patriarchs. Although there were several patriarchs in the East, in the West there was only one, the patriarch of Rome, also called pope (from Latin *papa* or "father"). The Roman popes asserted that Jesus had granted jurisdiction over the whole church (Matthew 16:16–19) to the apostle Peter, later the first bishop of Rome. The popes claimed that they, as successors of Peter, were the heirs of that authority. This claim caused bitter conflicts in the Roman Empire's Greek-speaking eastern portions. In the Latin-speaking West, however, where no other patriarch existed, papal claims to authority were enforced by a decree that required all bishops in the western Roman Empire to accept them. The following section will describe how, as the Germanic migrations nullified the political power of the Roman emperor in the West, the papacy became a symbol of Christian unity in that area.

Upheaval and Transition in Western Europe

"*Waiting for the Barbarians*"
What are we waiting for, packed in the forum?

The barbarians are due here today.

Why isn't anything going on in the senate?
Why have the senators given up legislating?

Because the barbarians are coming today.
What's the point of senators and their laws now?
When the barbarians get here, they'll do the legislating.

Why did our emperor set out so early
to sit on his throne at the city's main gate,

Because the barbarians are coming today
and the emperor's waiting to receive their leader. . . .

Why have our two consuls and praetors shown up today
wearing their embroidered, their scarlet togas? . . .

Because the barbarians are coming today
and things like that dazzle barbarians.

And why don't our distinguished orators push
forward as usual
to make their speeches. . . ?

Because the barbarians are coming today
and they're bored by . . . public speaking.

Why this sudden bewilderment . . . ?
(How serious everyone looks.)
Why are the streets . . . rapidly emptying,
everyone going home so lost in thought?

Because . . . the barbarians haven't come.
And some people just in from the border say
there are no barbarians any longer.

Now what's going to happen to us without them?
The barbarians were a kind of solution. *

*C. P. Cavafy, *Selected Poems*, trans. E. Keeley and P. Sherrard (Princeton: Princeton Univ. Press, 1972), pp. 6–7.

In this poem, the Greek author Constantine Cavafy (1863–1933) imagines the state of mind of Romans in the twilight of their empire, as ancient ways of living were giving way before the force of new peoples and new patterns of life. It was, of course, a frightful process, but the Roman Empire had, by the fifth century, lost its strength and its ability to guarantee a secure life for its inhabitants. In this sense, the "barbarians" were, as Cavafy's poem suggests, "a kind of solution" both politically and culturally in the history of western Europe. The present section will describe the fall of Rome and the rise and triumph of the various states that replaced it in western Europe, in particular the Carolingian Empire.

The Fall of the Roman Empire in the West

The Roman Empire after the death of Constantine in 337 struggled unsuccessfully to resist the submersion of its western half under waves of Asiatic and Germanic invaders and immigrants. The Huns, fast-moving horsemen from the steppes of Asia, provided one catalyst of change. Related to the Hsiung-nu who harassed Han China and the Huna or "White Huns" who invaded India, they pushed into central Europe to the north of the Roman Empire, and later, under their king Attila, raided into the empire itself. In the process they displaced many of the German tribes living outside the empire; the Germans in their turn, desiring a more settled existence in the fertile cleared land to the south, poured into the Roman Empire. Emperors perished in battle, large tracts of land were successively ceded or stripped away, and finally Rome itself was sacked in 410. In

Map 5.1 German Invasion Routes. This map shows the avenues of invasion and immigration followed by the various Germanic tribes that finally overwhelmed the Roman Empire's defenses, beginning in the late fourth and early fifth centuries.

476, the last Western emperor was deposed by the German leader Odoacer, who became the first barbarian king of Italy (reigned 476–493). The once brilliant light of Roman power in the West flickered out as Visigoths and Ostrogoths, Franks, Burgundians, Vandals, and others divided the territories of the old western empire.

Ancient and present-day scholars have offered various responses to the question of what caused the fall of Rome. Those who emphasize a decay from within point to economic crises caused in part by the bloated imperial bureaucracy and the financial strain it placed on an empire whose inhabitants were unfairly overtaxed and decimated by plagues, poverty, and declining birth rates. Some believe Christianity, with its emphasis on the heavenly Kingdom of God, discouraged the patriotic virtues that had sustained Rome in earlier days; similarly, the later Han Chinese dabbled in escapist Taoism and otherworldly Buddhism. Others cite a loss of traditional Roman moral values as non-Italians and even barbarians gained prominence within the society, the civil administration, and the ranks and officer class of the army. Soil exhaustion, protracted drought, the gradual poisoning of the aristocracy by lead water pipes and lead-containing food storage and cooking vessels, and slavery as an impediment to technological advance are still other causes of decline that scholars have suggested, some more plausibly than others. However, many of these weaknesses also affected the eastern half of the empire, which did not collapse.

The best explanation for the fall of the Roman Empire in the West is the intensified barbarian pressure directed against defense forces spread thin by the great length of the Rhine-Danube frontier. This pressure had been felt since the second century, but as Germanic migration steadily increased in the late fourth and throughout the fifth century, insupportable demands were placed on the military and financial resources of the western half of the empire, where the economic and social structure had long been crumbling.

The Germanic States of Western Europe

In contrast to the Byzantine and Islamic institutions of imperial government and urban life, Germanic society featured family and tribal structures in a rural setting. German families who owned or held land were subject to military service and tax assessment. They sometimes lived in isolated farmsteads, but were more often grouped together in villages. The tribe or people was the aggregate of all persons who lived under the same law, fought in the same army, and recognized a common king. Germanic tribes were patriarchal, and women, on all levels of society, had subordinate roles.

Tribes contained free persons, slaves, and half-free persons later known as serfs. Slaves became less common as settled life replaced migration and reduced slave-raiding activity. Also, many individuals rose out of slavery to become half free, while free persons fell to half-free status under the protection of noble lords. The half-free had to remain on the land they worked, but were not another's personal property. The merchants, clergy, and nobles became the only fully free persons. Nobles maintained their status by intermarrying and collected benefits and privileges from Germanic kings.

Most Germans depended on agriculture for their livelihood. In the great plains of northern Europe, where rainfall was generally plentiful and the seasons moderate, the heavy, wet soil produced two crops per year. However, poor, locally made tools and the

The Roman Tax Collector—"Like a Wild Beast"

What a terrifying individual [the tax-collector] could be is nicely illustrated in . . . the Life of St. John the Almsgiver, . . . The Saint is represented as thinking about the dreadful monsters he may meet after death, and the only way he can adequately express the appalling ferocity of these wild beasts is to say that they will be "like tax-collectors." Certainly, tax collection from the poor in Roman times was not a matter of polite letters and, as a last resort, a legal action: beating-up defaulters was a matter of routine, if they were humble people. . . . In [Roman-controlled] Egypt . . . local officials would seize taxpayers whom they alleged (rightly or wrongly) to be in default, imprison and ill-treat them, and, with the aid of soldiers and local levies, burn down their houses. . . .

According to [the historian] Ammianus [Marcellinus], an Egyptian in the late fourth century would blush for shame if he could not show on his back scars inflicted by the tax-collector's whip.

One aspect of the economic crisis of an empire that had to support a bloated bureaucracy and a huge military machine was an unfair system of taxation. The rich were often able to evade taxes, while the poor were at the mercy of relentless government officials and tax collectors. In this respect at least, the replacement of Roman authority by Germanic states actually brought relief to many of the empire's inhabitants.

*G. E. M. de Ste. Croix, "The 'Decline and Fall': An Explanation," in Donald Kagan, ed., The End of the Roman Empire: Decline or Transformation? *3d ed. (Lexington, MA: Heath, 1992), p. 58.*

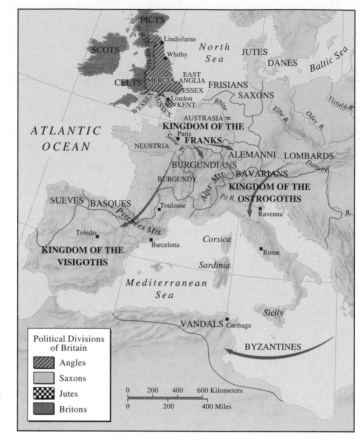

Map 5.2 Germanic States in Europe. Major German states about 500 are shown here; arrows indicate important German advances after that date.

lack of fertilizer kept crop yields low, until a heavy plow came into wider use after the sixth century. Because their only method of restoring soil fertility was to let land lie idle, the Germans needed large areas to support relatively few people. They usually settled in small, densely populated communities widely separated from one another, in which all members cooperated in necessary agricultural activities.

The rulers of these scattered peoples retained and modified traditional features of Germanic kingship. Kings moved beyond the status of tribal chiefs by becoming successful war leaders who conquered and ruled territories, not merely people. They gave gifts to loyal followers, as war bands formerly divided booty. The kings maintained the tribal laws and settled disputes between free persons, whereas lords judged disputes among their serfs and slaves. The kings now embodied the tribe's common origin and history, and their succession came to depend on dynastic (family) right rather than individual right.

Germanic rulers also incorporated Christian and Roman elements into their government structure. They used Latin in royal documents and law codes and adopted the biblical practice of anointing the king at accession. Under the church's guidance, kings regarded their subjects as Christians and defense of the faith as one of their royal tasks.

By contrast with the Byzantine and Islamic Empires described later in this chapter, the Germanic peoples of western Europe had difficulty controlling their own territories and were harassed by warlike neighbors. Large landed estates dominated agricultural activity and sought economic self-sufficiency. While trade dwindled and towns decayed, the only significant international institution, the church, became the heir of much of the Roman cultural tradition.

The Triumph and Disintegration of the Carolingian Empire

Out of the preceding patterns of Germanic life, one people, the Franks, rose to prominence under the leadership of a dynamic ruler, King Clovis (reigned 481–511). Instead of separating Romans and Germans, Clovis chose to merge them by requiring both peoples to do military service and permitting intermarriage. Clovis's baptism as a Roman Catholic Christian shortly before 500 separated the Franks from the other Germans, who were Arian Christians. The Franks championed Roman Catholic orthodoxy against the Arians and won the support of the Christianized Roman aristocracy of Gaul. The Roman Catholic clergy supplied Frankish kings with educated advisers and other benefits, such as the flattering legend that the Holy Spirit had descended directly from heaven for Clovis's baptism. The Byzantine emperor later designated Clovis an honorary consul.

The German custom of dividing property among all of a deceased father's sons meant that the sons of Frankish kings often fought among themselves to gain control of all the territories of their father. Successive generations of the descendants of Clovis followed this process, weakening the monarchy and allowing the Frankish nobles to augment their political power and to assimilate royal lands and wealth.

In the eighth century, the Carolingian family (from the Latin *Carolus*, for "Charles") took control of the Frankish monarchy. Under King Charlemagne the Carolingian Empire was transformed into a restored Roman Empire. On Christmas Day in the year 800, the pope crowned Charlemagne (or Charles the Great; reigned 768–814), deliberately using the Roman titles emperor and Augustus, together with the Byzantine procedures of patriarchal coronation and popular acclamation. Charlemagne, rising from prayer and crowned by God, probably reminded many of Constantine, the first Roman emperor to become a Christian, by whose authority the pope claimed to act. The idea of Rome as the model of a universal state persisted in the notion of a Holy Roman Empire down to 1806.

At its maximum extent under Charlemagne, the Frankish Empire included most of present-day France, Belgium, the Netherlands, and Luxembourg, and portions of Germany, Italy, Switzerland, and Spain. Most of this territory had been wrested from the Frankish Empire's German neighbors and some of it from Muslims in Spain (see the Islamic section of this chapter) and Asiatic tribes from central Eurasia.

At the center of the Carolingian state was a reorganized royal household that included officials supported by the extensive lands held by the royal family. Lacking money, the kings paid those officials with land grants and exemptions from taxation and from visits by royal administrators. Such grants were also made in return for military service, especially by mounted warriors who required land to maintain themselves and their horses.

As deteriorating clan and tribal organizations ceased providing customary protection and services, many became personal and economic dependents of noble landowners.

Carolingian dukes had the responsibility for governing large frontier areas known as marches. Counts (controlling territories called counties) became the essential personnel of Carolingian administration; they were required to make frequent public declarations of loyalty and to live in areas where they had no personal connections, administering smaller regions in accordance with local custom. The monarchs sent inspectors to review and when necessary correct the counts' activities. The kings strictly prevented the counts from passing on their offices to their children. Each count served as the king's governor and military commander in one province, assisted by a viscount and one or more judges. Hampering royal control, however, was an insufficiency of counts or supervisors and slow long-distance communications. Strong kings could crush rebellions of counts and dukes, but under weak kings, the nobles sometimes became independent. Nevertheless, Carolingian administration was fairly stable. Although there were differences, the political system established by the Carolingians in many ways resembled the feudal order reputedly established by early Chou kings of China.

In addition to reforming their administration, the Carolingian rulers beginning with Pepin III created the most effective armed forces in western Europe. Usually enjoying a

Map 5.3 The Carolingian Empire. Shown here are the boundaries of the Frankish kingdom before 768 together with surrounding territories acquired during the reign of Charlemagne. The inset shows the division of the Carolingian Empire among Charlemagne's grandsons.

decisive numerical advantage over opponents, their armies consisted primarily of well-armed and highly disciplined infantry, together with smaller groups of cavalry, wearing helmets and mailed coats and armed with swords and spears.

The cooperation of the Carolingian dynasty with the church continued as Charlemagne returned the pope to Rome and restored him to power after his enemies had hounded him from the city. It was mainly in gratitude for this that Pope Leo III crowned Charlemagne Emperor of Rome, thus bestowing prestige beyond that of any other German ruler.

Pepin III and his son Charlemagne owed their success to broad support from church leaders and laity, an effective army, and the weakness of their enemies. However, only a powerful ruler able to enforce loyalty and obedience could manage the weakly unified Carolingian state. Charlemagne's successors lacked that ability, and during the ninth century the Frankish empire disintegrated. Charlemagne's son, Louis, divided his empire and the crown lands among his sons upon his death in 840, thus precipitating a series of civil wars that broke up the Carolingian Empire. Out of the collapse emerged what became a French monarchy and a German monarchy. The nobles, however, increasingly disregarded any central authority and enlarged their own power by in effect dividing the kingdoms into large territorial principalities, further eroding the remnants of Carolingian royal government. Such developments were reminiscent of what had happened in China during the late Chou dynasty.

Giraudon/Art Resource

The Coronation of Charlemagne. According to some contemporary writers, the coronation was an unwelcome surprise to Charlemagne, although it clearly required advance preparation and apparently had the monarch's approval.

Religious and Cultural Developments in Early Western Europe

In an increasingly Germanized western Europe, the Christian church faced numerous problems as it assumed the moral, spiritual, and cultural leadership formerly exercised by the Roman Empire. Disappearance of Roman rule in the West deprived the church of imperial support, and the expansion of Islam reduced the territory of Christendom. Furthermore, Greek and Latin churches developed differences in belief, practice, and organization. Superstition, violence, and immorality characterized popular life; most people only vaguely understood or followed Christian teachings. Religious leadership frequently fell to uneducated and morally lax priests, and to bishops better qualified to wield political power than to provide spiritual guidance.

The church responded to these problems on a number of fronts. It infused its ideas of justice and mercy into codes of law, maintaining schools and hospitals, and assisting widows, orphans, and slaves. Monasticism, although introduced to the West before 500, was reformulated by Benedict of Nursia (480–547). He wrote a moderate and humane rule of life for monastic communities based on study, prayer, and physical labor.

To counter the luxury, sexual laxity, and disregard for authority that afflicted some of the clergy, Benedict required vows of poverty, chastity, and obedience, and submission to the absolute authority of an abbot. Pope Gregory I (reigned 590–604) wrote a *Life of Benedict* and promoted the spread of Benedictine monasticism in Europe. Monks and

LIVES AND TIMES ACROSS CULTURES

Food for Buddhist and Christian Monks

Buddhist monks and nuns were strictly forbidden to eat meat. In addition, on specified days they had to fast after the noonday meal. On special occasions such as the Buddha's birthday and other days of religious significance or secular celebrations, vegetarian banquets were held at temples for both clerics and laypeople.

Between 838 and 847 a Japanese monk named Ennin traveled and studied in China and kept a detailed diary of his stay. Ennin described a feast for about 750 participants, including monks, nuns, men, women, and children at a famous temple at Mount Wutai. All received equal portions, with seconds given on demand. Although he did not describe the dishes, we gather from other sources that some of them were fashioned to resemble the forbidden meat dishes. Even today Buddhist restaurants among Chinese communities serve "chicken," "meat," and "fish" made from soybeans.

At about the same time, in the Europe of Charlemagne, monasteries complying with the Benedictine rule of life also featured a menu that seems rather ascetic by modern standards. Monks took only one daily meal in winter and two in summer. Although meat (especially pork, beef, mutton, venison, and poultry) was eaten in some monasteries on special feast days, for the most part the menu was vegetarian. The typical meal consisted of three dishes of dairy products, such as cheese, vegetables, and bread or a kind of grain porridge that served as the principal staple of the diet. The members of more austere monasteries restricted themselves to barley bread (often mixed with ashes), gruel, and vegetables, with even poultry and fish forbidden. On Sundays the great treat consisted of a little cheese thinned with water.

nuns following the Benedictine rule won converts to Christianity and instructed those converts in basic Christian belief and practice.

The other prominent Christian institution, the Roman papacy, gained increasing significance, primarily through the efforts of Gregory I. By adroit land management and shrewd negotiations with Byzantines and Lombards, Gregory made the papacy financially and politically independent. His *Book of Pastoral Care* helped the clergy perform their duties effectively. He also worked to convert German kings from Arianism and sent missionaries to England in 597, which in 664 agreed to follow the Roman observance. The Roman hierarchy was aggressive in converting the German and Slavic peoples of central Europe and the Irish, providing western Europe with religious unity.

Ireland became an important center of early medieval cultural and religious activity. Its conversion to Christianity, traditionally attributed to Patrick (389–461), a Roman citizen educated in Gaul, opened the island to continental influences. Irish monasteries became centers of intellectual activity; each had its *scriptorium* (writing room) for the essential work of copying both Christian and classical manuscripts in excellent, clear handwriting and elaborate decorative calligraphy. The Irish copyists also developed the art of illumination (painting brightly colored pictures on manuscripts).

England's conversion to Roman Catholic Christianity stimulated an outburst of literary productivity. The Old English epic of the eighth century, *Beowulf*, recounts the hero's slaying of monsters and a fire-breathing dragon. Although composed in the Germanic heroic tradition, the poem is altruistic in spirit, and it may have been intended as a Christian allegory.

As part of their responsibility for the Christians in their realm, the Carolingian rulers reorganized the administration of the Frankish church, restored old bishoprics and established new ones, and vigorously upheld Latin Christian theology against its challengers. Pepin III and Charlemagne enriched Frankish monasteries and restored them to compliance with the Benedictine rule. The monasteries in turn provided scribes and advisers for royal service. Charlemagne also presented a broadly conceived program for peacefully introducing Christianity among the pagan Saxons and Slavs.

Believing that the quality of the clergy determined the quality of spiritual life, Charlemagne promoted both classical and Christian education, mandating, for example, a teacher of grammar for each cathedral and a teacher of theology for each archbishop's cathedral. Monastic schools concentrated on the liberal arts, and a special palace school was established for educating the sons of Frankish nobles. Scholars whom Charlemagne recruited for this school built a collection of classical writings that preserved and made available earlier knowledge.

Charlemagne stimulated monasteries to become active centers for producing accurate, hand-copied manuscript books, including the Bible, manuals for the conduct of worship services, and the Benedictine rule for monks that was to form the basis of monastic reforms during the next several centuries. The monks also produced manuscripts of classical writers as well as of church fathers. More than 8,000 Carolingian manuscripts still exist, and over 90 percent of surviving Roman literature was passed on to later ages in Carolingian manuscript form. This outburst of intellectual and literary activity is sometimes termed the Carolingian Renaissance (rebirth).

Magical Practices in the Carolingian Era

Maleficia [sorcery/witchcraft] appeared in many forms. It could impede the growth of another's grain by magic powers . . . or incantations. It rendered a neighbor's cattle sterile or brought harm on others through making knots in a dead person's girdle. Love potions to excite a husband's passion or attract a lover were made from sperm, menstrual blood, and aphrodisiac plants. . . . Bones of the dead, cinders and ashes, hair, pubic hair, different colored strings, various herbs, snails and snakes were used in maleficia, sterilizing potions, and abortifacients.

By far the most popular magical practices were those designed to protect and cure. Prisoners seeking to be free of their bondage, or peasants who feared that their horses would injure themselves, all recited the formulae preserved in Germanic texts. Sick children were carried to the peak of the roof while medicinal herbs were cooked to the recited incantations. Amulets and phylacteries [protective charms] endowed with particular characteristics were sold to anyone who wanted their protection. . . . Models of human limbs were hung from trees or placed at crossroads to procure the healing of an arm or leg. . . . Divination was practiced . . . by . . . paying heed to the direction of smoke, or examining the excrement or liver of animals, climbing to the rooftops, interpreting dreams or opening books at random. . . . Some of the manuscripts which the monks copied carry the magical squares which predicted the course of an illness by combining the letters of the victim's name and the number of the day on which he fell ill.*

The belief in the efficacy of magic or sorcery is both ancient and stubborn. Even in the face of official disapproval (and sometimes active persecution) by civil and religious authorities, many people have always tried to mobilize magical powers to their own benefit or to the detriment of others. The Carolingian Empire, despite its Christian allegiance, was no exception to this sort of activity.

*Pierre Riché, Daily Life in the World of Charlemagne, trans. Jo Ann McNamara (Philadelphia: University of Pennsylvania Press, 1978; orig. 1973), pp. 184–185.

Carolingian art, like literature and education, evolved from religious activity and employed late Roman and contemporary Byzantine models and techniques. For example, books priests used to conduct worship services were beautified by illuminations; that is, separate pictures, elaborately decorated book or chapter titles, or large initial letters using traditional Germanic art forms of animals and interlaces. Builders of Carolingian churches usually followed the Roman basilica style, occasionally roofing the atrium to form a porch or adding an enclosed prayer room above the atrium. The architects of Charlemagne's chapel at his capital city of Aachen copied Byzantine imperial models to produce an octagonal building symbolizing the emperor's divinely aided joining together of earth and heaven; Justinian's church of Hagia Sophia at Constantinople served a similar symbolic purpose. Painting on church walls generally made little use of scriptural themes and human forms in order to avoid the appearance of idolatry.

Europe under Siege: A New Wave of Invaders

As the Carolingian Empire disintegrated in the late ninth century, the face of Europe was transformed by new waves of invaders. The Magyars and Vikings produced widespread destruction and disrupted existing institutions and patterns of living. Amid the resulting disorder, successful resisters to those attackers began to establish new social, economic, and political patterns and to form new centers of European development.

Invited from western Asia by the Byzantines to aid in war against the Bulgars, the Magyars, nomadic ancestors of modern Hungarians, occupied the Hungarian basin of the Danube by 900, and soon were raiding Italy, Burgundy, and other Frankish and Germanic territories.

Another group of invaders, Vikings from Scandinavia, raided widely throughout Europe. Their motives included a desire for plunder; dislike of increasing royal authority in Denmark, Norway, and Sweden; overpopulation; climate change; and sheer love of adventure. The Norwegians raided and established settlements in western England and Ireland. Danish Vikings attacked lands on both sides of the English Channel. They conquered the eastern half of England and also seized land at the mouth of the Seine River in Francia, which became the nucleus of the Duchy of Normandy. Well might western Europeans pray, "From the fury of the Northmen, O Lord deliver us." Swedish Vikings crossed the Baltic and worked their way southward across Russia on the extensive north-south river systems, reaching Persia and Constantinople via the Caspian and Black Seas, respectively. They became so numerous that the Latin name *Rus* (for ruddy) that distinguished them from the resident Slavs became applied to the entire land and all its people.

The Vikings also sailed westward across the North Atlantic and in 874 settled in Iceland, establishing the oldest continuously functioning democratic community. Erik the Red, an exile from Iceland, landed on the island of Greenland, and settlements of Europeans soon followed. In 1000, Erik's son Leif sailed farther west and briefly occupied Vinland, probably northern Newfoundland. As royal authority and Christianization increased in Scandinavian lands during the tenth century, the great age of Viking expansion ended.

The absence of effective imperial power in the disintegrating Carolingian Empire left local leaders to develop their own responses to the invaders of the ninth century. In England, Viking raids and English resistance combined to produce a united monarchy. The Danes destroyed all the Anglo-Saxon kingdoms except Wessex, whose king, Alfred the Great (reigned 871–899), effectively opposed them by combating the Vikings at sea and fortifying and garrisoning towns as defensive strongholds. Gradually, Alfred gained authority over Anglo-Saxon lands in the west of England that had escaped Viking rule. By gathering scholars from various lands, he revived literature and learning in England, creating a solid basis for its future development.

In Italy, independent towns, grown prominent as Carolingian authority waned, led the resistance to Magyar and Muslim invaders. Within these towns, bishops became the principal leaders, building town fortifications and collecting tolls and other monies to pay for them. They secured powers and privileges from kings and exercised control of urban defenses, revenues, and courts. Powerful bishops and strong, independent cities continued to play important roles in subsequent centuries of Italian history.

In the eastern regions of the empire, where Carolingian rule was recent, earlier German tribal divisions reemerged in five large duchies, areas dominated by dukes who seized royal lands and powers and controlled the churches in their districts. When the last Carolingian ruler died in 911, the dukes chose one of their number as king to validate their rights and titles to land and to coordinate common defense measures. In the face of persistent Magyar invasions, an able, new dynasty of Saxon rulers (919–1024) emerged to reassert royal authority over the land, which became known as Germany.

In the Carolingian Empire's western areas, the invasions accelerated decentralization of government, as counts and other nobles offered the only meaningful opposition to the invaders, acquired lands and goods, and usurped royal authority. Although Carolingian kings continued to rule until 987, when the last of the line died without heirs, political followed sexual impotence. In the place of the monarchy, aggressive local lords exercised warfare and defense responsibilities and managed royal courts and revenues.

Feudal Relationships

As Carolingian government deteriorated, nobles seeking to provide protection and administer justice combined two well-established Carolingian practices—the personal relationship of vassalage and the landed relationship of benefice or fief—in a set of relationships, new in the west, called feudalism (from Latin *feudum,* "fief"). In vassalage a free man (the vassal) proclaimed his dependence on and faithfulness to another free man (the lord) and promised to serve him, usually militarily. The lord, in return, granted the vassal useful possession, but not ownership, of land called a benefice or fief. Similarly, in China under the Chou dynasty, lords contributed both revenues and homage to the kings and received in return confirmation of their social status and of their fiefdoms.

Counts and dukes held their lands as fiefs of the king, lesser nobles held their estates as vassals of counts or dukes, and they in turn granted smaller fiefs to their own vassals. Hence the same person might be the vassal of a greater lord and the lord of lesser vassals. Thorny complications arose when vassals held fiefs from different lords who became enemies. A woman had no property rights and if, as sole survivor, she inherited lands or money from her father, the property became her husband's.

The personal pledges and obligations between lords and vassals theoretically ended when one of them died, but in practice sons normally assumed the loyalties and duties of their fathers. Typically, a vassal owed not only his own personal military service, but often also that of additional knights from his own estates. In addition, he was expected to serve in the lord's court of justice and to feed and house the lord and his traveling companions when required. Vassals also helped to raise a ransom if their lord was captured and gave the lord money on the occasion of the knighting of his eldest son, the marriage of his eldest daughter, and the succession of a son to his father's fief. In return, the lord provided the vassal with military protection and justice through his court.

At first, nobles held large estates whereas lesser vassals, often termed knights, held few if any lands; the nobles led armies into battle whereas knights followed and obeyed. As time passed, knights gradually gained extensive lands, privileges, and jurisdictional rights and married into old noble families, eventually forming a single aristocracy.

Lesser lords and vassals were armed and trained as warriors to preserve the privileges of communities and maintain the safety of the church, but most fought to acquire land and wealth or for the sheer joy of fighting. The armed and mounted knight dominated offensive warfare. Defensive warfare centered on castles, the nobles' fortified homes, which had evolved by the twelfth century into structures built of stone.

Europe in the Middle Ages

Society is divided into three orders. The ecclesiastical order forms one body. The nobles are the war-
riors and the protectors of churches; they defend all the people, great and small. The unfree is the
other class. This unfortunate group possesses nothing without suffering. Supplies and clothing are pro-
vided for everyone by the unfree because no free man can live without them.

Therefore the city of God which is believed to be one is divided into three; some pray, others fight,
and the others work. These three groups live together and could not endure separation. The services of
one of them allows the work of the other two. Each, by turn, lends its support to all. *

*Adalberon, "Carmen ad Rotbertum regem," in Robert Boutruche, *Seigneurie et féodalité* (Paris: Aubier,
1959), pp. 371–372, trans. in Norton Downs, ed., *The Medieval Pageant* (Princeton: Van Nostrand, 1964),
p. 93.

This description, written about 1000, reflects the traditional medieval view of European
society as an unchanging interrelationship of three orders or estates. (The terms *medieval*
and *Middle Ages* refer to the conventional western division of history into ancient,
medieval, and modern.) While this view accurately described many aspects of medieval
society, it did not take into account a number of important changes that were under way,
changes that would dramatically move Western society away from this three-class division. The present section examines developments in Europe in the period between 900
and 1350.

Economic and Social Changes in the Countryside

From 1000 to 1300, the economy of Europe developed and prospered. Available farmland tripled, and the food supply increased notably, bringing up the population. Europeans resettled lands that had been depopulated by the ninth- and tenth-century invasions and also opened new lands for farming, especially forested and marginal areas,
those east of the Elbe River in central Europe, and lands conquered from the Muslims in
the Iberian Peninsula. To ensure productivity, medieval farmers adopted the three-field
system of cultivation in which only a third (rather than a half) of the land lay fallow (to
restore fertility) during the year. Technological improvements like the heavy plow, the
shoulder collar for horses, metal horseshoes, and more efficient water and windmills
contributed to the jump in food supply. Between 500 and 1300 Europe's population
grew from 25 million to more than 70 million.

During the fourteenth century, however, Europe's increasing economic and demographic growth took a sharp reverse. The climate became colder and rainier, causing harvests to shrink and prices to soar. This was a warlike period in which ravaging armies
destroyed crops, barns, and mills. Famine became a fact of life. Adding to these troubles,
bubonic plague (the "Black Death") ravaged the population. Between 1348 and 1354,
perhaps one-third of all Europeans died as the plague spread, in the words of one contemporary, "like fire when it comes in contact with large masses of combustibles." The
population did not recover fully till about 1600.

Whether times were easy or hard, peasant farmers and their life pattern constituted
the core of medieval society. Most of the farming people of Europe lived in villages ranging

from ten to several hundred peasant families, located in manors, units of political governance and economic exploitation controlled by ecclesiastical establishments or by secular
nobles. The manors were organized so that they would contain enough villages to produce nearly everything needed by their lords.

The workforce on a manor consisted primarily of families of serfs, semi-free persons
linked to the lord and to the land who could not be sold away from their lands. Their
village was a cluster of huts surrounded by fields. Each family was assigned several plots
or strips, some on the more fertile and some on the less fertile land available to the village. On these plots each family produced food that it used for its own consumption,
barter, payment of tithes to the church, and dues to the lord. There was also pasture
where plow animals, sheep, and cattle grazed and a wooded area on which the peasants
gathered fuel and building materials and where pigs foraged. Usually there was a stream
that supplied fish and powered the water mill. Typically there were none of the schools,
hospitals, or other amenities sometimes found in medieval towns. The parish church was
the center of activity, where villagers celebrated religious holidays, baptisms, and marriages; in the churchyard they found their final resting place. Church bells provided the
only timekeeping most people knew, and feast days marked the year's seasons.

Each farm family retained about half its own produce after paying the lord a percentage of the crop for the use of the pasture and woods and fees for the use of the lord's
mill and oven. The lord also collected payments when a serf's son inherited his father's
holdings or when a serf's daughter married outside the manor. Moreover, the church collected its tithe (10 percent). Serfs also performed labor services for the lord, working his
land and repairing roads or carrying firewood.

By 1300 some lords, seeking to attract workers to bring new lands under cultivation,
offered milder terms of service to peasants and improved the working conditions of their
serfs. Some freed them from labor obligations in return for cash payments and allowed
them to pay rent in money rather than crops. On occasion, lords granted peasant communities charters that freed them from performing the obligations of serfs and permitted
them to pay their dues collectively rather than individually. As wages and prices rose in
the West during the fifteenth century, manorial lords sought to increase their cash
incomes by raising cattle or sheep or growing commercial agricultural products such as
dyestuffs, which required fewer laborers and gave high returns for low costs. Thus by
1500, most western European peasants were no longer serfs owing labor and goods to
their lords but renters who had traded the security of serfdom for the freedom to earn or
to lose money and livelihood. The gradual waning of feudalism in western Europe
resembled what had happened in China during the late Chou dynasty.

While western European peasants were enjoying greater freedom, eastern European
peasants were losing what freedom they had. The lords in that area preferred to grow
grain for export to western Europe and took advantage of fourteenth- and fifteenth-
century wars and other upheavals to acquire large landholdings. They enforced manorial
obligations and imposed serfdom even upon formerly free peasants.

In the West, meanwhile, freedom proved to be a mixed blessing, as lords sought to
wring maximum rents from their tenants. Moreover, the ravages of war and the taxes of

monarchs fell most heavily on peasants, since clergy and nobles were largely exempt from royal taxation. Peasant discontent with the status quo sometimes exploded into rebellions, which were easily defeated by regular armies. Still, the peasants' grievances persisted, and reappeared to trouble later lords and rulers.

The Growth of Trade and the Development of Towns

European commercial activity expanded dramatically from the tenth through the fourteenth century. Whereas early medieval trade had been conducted by local merchants who exchanged perishable items and local commodities for salt, wine, and metals in village markets, by the eleventh century long-distance trade had begun to revive.

Descendants of Viking raiders now traded across the northern seas, bartering furs, timber, fish, and wax for textiles, grain, and wine. To the east, they established commercial relations with the Byzantine and Islamic Empires via the Baltic Sea and the river routes of Russia, trading for Islamic silver or Byzantine gold. By the thirteenth century, Germans had replaced Scandinavians as the primary merchants of northern Europe. The northern trade was primarily in staples: grain, butter, cheese, fish, timber, metals, and salt. German trading towns united in a Hansa (confederation) to preserve their dominant position in commerce.

In the ninth and tenth centuries, Italian port cities, particularly Venice, revived the Mediterranean trade. Byzantine merchant citizens in some Italian port towns traded easily

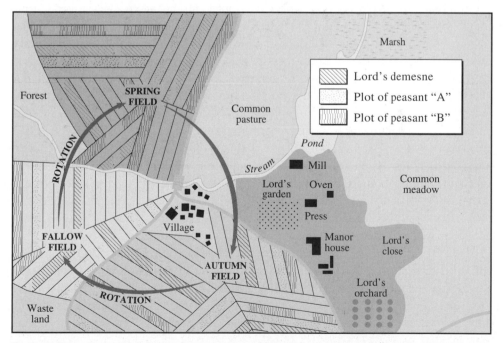

Map 5.4 A Manor. The noble lord dominated the manor; he controlled the best land and the essential services of oven, mill, and press. The operation of the three-field system and the division of land into strips prompted villagers to work together at common tasks.

with both the Byzantine Empire and the Muslims; religious differences between eastern and western Christians and between Christians and Muslims posed no obstacles when it came to commercial relations. During the eleventh century, Genoa and Pisa wrested control of the western Mediterranean from the Muslims, but by the late fourteenth century Venice had taken control of the lucrative trade with the East.

The eastern Mediterranean trade was based upon a sophisticated intercontinental commercial network. Venetian merchants exported slaves, timber, iron, and tools to the lands east of the Mediterranean and imported furs, silks, spices, and perfumes from the Byzantines and Muslims, who had brought them from India and China. For a brief time the Mongols permitted Europeans to bypass Islamic middlemen (see Chapter 8) and to trade directly with East Asia. The Venetians sold the Asian luxuries to the upper classes in western Europe, often investing the proceeds in new manufacturing establishments (see below) that were beginning to spring up in Italy.

From the northern and southern seas, trade quickly expanded inland, and by the late twelfth century merchants were moving continuously along Europe's rivers and roads, and commerce was fast displacing agriculture as the most dynamic force in European economic life. During the disastrous fourteenth century, European commercial activity faltered, as population decline diminished markets and wars interfered with commerce.

Manufacturing came later than trade in European economic development. Medieval "manufacturers" were typically craftsmen who produced goods in their own shops and sold them directly to the public. Early manufacturers employed individuals in building construction and textile making, which developed during the medieval period using complex systems of organization. Members of the building trades found employment erecting churches and public buildings in growing towns and cities. As many were wage earners and owned neither the materials nor the tools they used, they resembled factory laborers. Some entrepreneurs used a "domestic" system in which they distributed raw materials to and collected finished products from workers who labored in their homes rather than in a factory.

Enlarged agricultural productivity and increasing commercial activity sparked a growth of town life. Various forms of the German word *Burg* ("fortress")—burg, burgh, bourg, or borough—came to apply to the town, whose inhabitants were called burghers, later known as the bourgeoisie. Compared to the countryside, towns displayed a volatile juxtaposition of individuals and groups in close quarters. Besides merchants and artisans, there were free peasants, runaway serfs, and ambitious younger sons of lesser nobles, as well as masters and students at schools or universities.

Medieval cities and towns were small by present-day European standards. A substantial eleventh-century trading city, such as Bruges, might have only 5,000 inhabitants. Towns grew with commerce, and by 1300 several Italian cities had 100,000 inhabitants each, and Venice held 200,000 persons. Elsewhere, Paris had a population of 80,000, London half that. The Black Death struck cities exceptionally hard, killing up to half their inhabitants.

As the new elements in medieval society, town-dwelling merchants and manufacturers had to struggle to obtain acceptance for their activities, which did not fit the traditional

Map 5.5 Medieval Trade Routes. By the end of the thirteenth century, trade routes covered most of western and central Europe. Vikings in early centuries and the German Hansa later controlled commerce in the northern seas. In the south, the Italian cities of Genoa and Venice dominated Mediterranean trade. Overland routes used rivers whenever possible to reduce transportation costs. In eastern Europe, however, trade routes were few, and the economy remained primarily agricultural.

concept of the three estates. To obtain freedom from servile and burdensome tax obligations, they sought charters from the local lord of the land. A lord might grant a charter for a money payment, but sometimes towns had to defeat lords in battle to obtain such documents. A charter usually provided the town's inhabitants freedom from servile obligations, typically permitting them to hold land and buildings for a money rent and forbidding the arbitrary seizure of their property. It also allowed burghers to maintain courts and make laws.

Burghers in northern Italy, whose towns were under the jurisdiction of the Holy Roman Emperor, went still further, seizing control of the cities' defenses, revenues, and courts, and extending their authority over the surrounding countryside. City leaders began to develop important aspects of a new political order: corporate authority, delegated power, and representative government.

To regulate economic activity, craftsmen and merchants formed "guilds." Merchants' guilds protected their members' interests against outsiders and secured each member a share in the trade available, generally by regulating prices and competition. Similarly, artisans set up craft guilds that supervised wages, prices, labor conditions, quality standards, and methods and amounts of production. Socially, guilds conducted banquets and sponsored religious festivals. They also saw to the proper burial of deceased members and cared for widows and orphans.

Women as well as men found economic opportunities in craft guilds. By 1300, at least 15 of 100 Paris guilds, including garment makers and workers in silk and embroidery, were entirely female. After 1300, however, economic activities for women were increasingly restricted or eliminated. The economic decline of German towns in the period between 1300 and 1500 was due in part to the suppression of flourishing female industries and the replacement of skilled women by unskilled men.

The Theory and Practice of Christianity

Like kings and princes who strove to create stable and effective governments, medieval religious leaders endeavored to centralize the organization and improve the quality of the medieval church. Although by 1000 the rulers of most European peoples had adopted Christianity for themselves and their subjects, the problems of ordering Christian society remained formidable. Viking and Magyar invasions had destroyed not only churches and monasteries but also ecclesiastical institutions, as monarchs converted bishops into vassals with fiefs and diverted the resources of the church to private, family, and "state" purposes.

Significant religious abuses arose from the feudalization of the church and the accompanying lay domination of church offices. Christians frequently decried the ineptitude and immorality of the clergy, who were often ill-educated and appointed for political rather than spiritual reasons. Such appointees sought personal advancement and the control of ecclesiastical property, while showing a shallow, mechanical attitude toward religious life. Many ignored the church's rule of celibacy and either married or had sexual partners, creating further possibilities for the diversion of church lands.

By 1000, efforts to reform the church to eliminate such abuses were under way. As an alternative to local lords controlling the church, eleventh-century reformers created a centralized church bureaucracy under papal control, with its own officers, law, and resources. By the early thirteenth century, the popes directed an extensive bureaucracy through the papal Curia, which was staffed by well-trained clerics in specialized departments handling correspondence and records, finances, judicial cases, and the application of church law. Popes directly asserted their authority over lower levels of church administration either through correspondence or by special emissaries.

A formidable tool for eradicating error in this period was the judicial process known as the Inquisition. Twelfth-century popes ordered bishops to conduct inquests concerning heretics within their dioceses and to punish the guilty by excommunication. Pope Innocent III added confiscation of goods and property to the punishment of heretics. The accused were denied legal counsel, interrogated by torture, and required to prove their repentance by identifying accomplices. Although some found guilty were sentenced to penances or prison terms, the Inquisition was less bloodthirsty than has been presumed; most convicted heretics were in fact put to death by governments, not by the church.

As in earlier centuries, the regimen of the stricter monastic orders, such as the Cluniacs, revitalized monastic discipline. Another monastic group, the Cistercian order, popularized the role of Mary, the mother of Jesus, who became the object of special devotion and veneration as the Blessed Virgin. Important religious feasts were established in her

The Growth of a Town

After this, because of the work or needs of those living in the chateau, there began to stream in merchants—that is, dealers in precious goods—who set themselves up in front of the gate, at the chateau's bridge; then there followed tavern-keepers, then inn-keepers to provide the food and lodging for those who came to do business in the presence of the prince, who was often there. Houses began to be built and inns to be made ready, where those were to be lodged who could not be put up inside the chateau. ... So many dwellings accumulated there that right away it became a large town.*

These words of a contemporary observer describe the beginnings of Bruges (originally Brugge, "the bridge"), one of northern Europe's foremost medieval towns. In central and eastern Europe, outside the territories of the old Roman Empire, new towns were usually founded by colonies of merchants who settled around a fortified stronghold, such as a castle or monastery, strategically located on a major trade route or at the intersection of two or more routes. Such settlers needed services that others came to provide, and settlements quickly grew into towns.

*Documents relatifs à l'histoire de l'industrie et du commerce en France, *ed. Gustave Fagniez,* Collection de textes pour servir à l'étude et l'enseignement de l'histoire, *Vol. I (Paris: Picard, 1898), pp. 54–55, trans. Carolly Erickson,* The Records of Medieval Europe *(Garden City: Doubleday, 1971), pp. 152–153.*

honor and churches and cathedrals were dedicated to her. Jesus Christ's love and compassion could be secured through Mary, who would intercede on behalf of all sinners. The series of prayers known as the rosary deepened popular devotion to Mary.

Pressing religious needs in towns and cities and the threat of heresy prompted the development of mendicant (begging) orders during the early thirteenth century. Mendicant friars rejected life in monasteries and worked in the world while living under a spiritual rule. Relying on donations for the necessities of life, they preached and, by performing charitable deeds, made Christianity relevant to the lives of town dwellers. Dominican friars were broadly educated and specialized in preaching and teaching; they subsequently joined university faculties. Dominicans energetically preached the Gospel to non-Christian Europeans and sought conversions in eastern Mediterranean lands and India.

The Franciscans, founded by Francis of Assisi (1182–1226), espoused a world-embracing joyousness; they spread rapidly throughout Europe, and some became missionaries in Syria and North Africa. They engaged in scholarship and university teaching, forming notable centers of theological study in Paris and Oxford.

Many women, too, found religious withdrawal from the world attractive. Besides professed nuns, lay sisters from peasant or artisan families performed many menial tasks. Nunneries gave their residents both self-esteem and the respect of society. They also offered women good education and the chance to use organizational and management skills that might otherwise be wasted.

By the thirteenth century, Roman Catholicism was widely prevalent among Europeans, and the beliefs of medieval Christians formed a coherent and integrated system. They believed God was one, almighty, all-knowing, just, and merciful. The universe, created by God, was orderly, and in it human beings had a special place and destiny. By sinning, people had disobeyed God and thus had lost their original righteousness and God's supernatural grace, forfeiting their hope of heaven. Sin rendered men and women incapable of doing good by their own efforts. Therefore, God had sent Jesus Christ to redeem humans and qualify them for heaven. As the custodian of God's grace, the

Execution of Heretics. Frequently, as in this thirteenth-century painting, heretics were executed by burning. At left, King Philip II of France sits on his horse. Note the scaffold (upper right) for mass hangings.

church was an essential intermediary between God and the faithful. By the seven sacraments, the church claimed to bring God's grace to all members at critical junctures of life. Baptism cleansed individuals of original sin and initiated them into the Christian fellowship. At puberty, confirmation reaffirmed a person's membership in the church and gave one additional grace for adult life. Two people might unite their lives in the sacrament of Holy Matrimony, or a person might "marry" the church in holy orders. Extreme unction (anointing with consecrated oil) prepared one for events after death. Christians could receive forgiveness from sin's consequences through the sacrament of penance. They could even receive Jesus Christ's body by partaking of the Eucharist, in which bread and wine were miraculously changed by means of the sacrificial mass into Christ's body and blood.

Saints, too, were believed to intercede with God on behalf of humans. Each town, each trade, even each disease, had its appropriate saint, and prayers and devotion to them were supposed to be especially efficacious. A lively traffic in holy relics (remains of saints) developed. A pilgrim to Venice about 1400 reported seeing there the arm of one saint, the staff of another, the ear of St. Paul, and a tooth of Goliath.

Pilgrimage, journeys to holy sites, although arduous and dangerous, also became increasingly popular acts of devotion and a means to secure grace. Geoffrey Chaucer's *Canterbury Tales,* written in the 1390s, vividly describes the members of such an expedition. A pilgrimage combined religious duty and holiday relaxation; hence pilgrimage routes came to be carefully arranged. Rome and Jerusalem attracted pilgrims from throughout Christendom.

The extent of popular piety, however, should not be exaggerated. The illiterate masses remained uninstructed about basic Christian beliefs and minimally involved in religious observances. Pre-Christian religious practices persisted in many places. Demons and mysterious powers were thought to fill the world and to require appeasement. Persons skilled in "white" magic, knowledgeable in healing by judicious use of herbs and "home remedies," and able to "see" what the future had in store were in great demand.

Jews in Medieval European Life

After Rome had dispersed the Jews in the first and second centuries C.E., they settled throughout West Asia and around the Mediterranean. Life in Christian lands, certainly as compared to Islamic Spain, was difficult and often dangerous for Jews. They were excluded from most occupations, except trading and moneylending; the latter was forbidden to Christians by the church. For self-serving reasons most Christians unreasonably believed that Jews were collectively responsible for Christ's death, that they were active servants of Satan, that they murdered Christian boys and used their blood for secret rituals, and that they poisoned wells and spread disease through the land. Christians executed, lynched, and banished large numbers of Jews. The warriors of the First Crusade massacred Jews in several Rhineland towns. The Third Lateran Council (1179) forbade Christians to live near Jews, thus spurring the growth of the ghetto, a walled section of a city in which Jews were compelled to live. European rulers in need of money exploited popular feeling by expelling Jews and seizing their abandoned property.

Beginning in the ninth and tenth centuries, the ongoing Christian reconquest of Spain forced many Jews to leave Spain in flight from both Muslim and Christian persecution. They joined meager groups of their coreligionists in the north to establish vigorous centers of Jewish life in southern and northeastern France and in the German Rhineland. Other Iberian Jews found refuge in North Africa and Turkey. As persecutions continued in western Europe, many Jews migrated into Poland and Lithuania, forming a major new Jewish population center there.

Feudal Monarchy in Western Europe

During the period from 900 to 1300, kings in some parts of Europe managed to replace the severely decentralized political order of the ninth and tenth centuries with more organized political structures known as feudal monarchies. The office of the king was endorsed by church and scripture, the person of the king was considered sacred, and kings continued to receive honor and prestige. Their primary functions were to provide justice and enforce the king's peace within their realms and to raise and lead national armies to resist external foes.

In addition, as previously discussed, feudal monarchs were overlords of the greater and lesser nobles within the system of feudal relationships, a system they exploited to extend their controls. Feudal kings had the right not only to demand various services and dues in return for their grants but also to recover possession of fiefs forfeited by unfaithful vassals or lost by a vassal's failure to produce heirs.

Despite many rights and responsibilities, feudal monarchs did not have direct authority over the mass of their subjects. Under the feudal structure, monarchs had contact primarily with their chief vassals and the inhabitants of the royal family's own domains. Between the kings and the remainder of their subjects were various levels of lesser vassals, many of whom exercised the rights to wage war, coin money, and dispense justice. Feudal kings thus exercised overlordship while sharing power, rather than wielding unlimited direct authority.

Diffused government was another distinctive aspect of feudal monarchy. In the autocratic and centralized Roman and Byzantine Empires, the ruler used an extensive military and civilian bureaucracy to carry out government services. In contrast, medieval European feudal monarchs, like the Chinese feudal monarchs of the Chou era, governed through a series of relationships in which both they and their vassals personally performed essential public services, administered justice, and waged war.

Feudal monarchies lacked the resources to provide more than limited services. The king derived income primarily from the royal domains and estates he personally owned, feudal payments from vassals, fines, and monies paid by certain churches and monasteries. A council composed of the king's great vassals formally recognized a new king, furnished him with advice and counsel, and judged certain important cases in his name. Between meetings, a smaller body of officials carried on council functions. The great vassals administered local government theoretically in the name of the king but in fact often quite independently.

Feudal monarchy had a varied history. The Holy Roman Empire, inheriting the eastern areas of the former Carolingian Empire, was an example of a feudal monarchy that failed. In the late Middle Ages, the empire was headed by a succession of German kings who engaged in a shifting power struggle with the popes. Although early German rulers succeeded in creating a strong feudal monarchy, their additional imperial responsibilities complicated the task of their successors. Emperors had duties in both Italy and Germany, but usually lacked the resources to make their power truly effective in both places.

The Holy Roman Empire had little significance in European political and religious developments after the death of Frederick II (reigned 1212–1250). Although it eventually expanded to embrace an area as large as that ruled by Charlemagne, the empire itself was merely a loose union of principalities and states. The medieval ideal of an earthly empire peaceably cooperating with the church's dominions remained illusory.

On the other hand, by combining features of Anglo-Saxon and Norman society, England initially became an extremely successful feudal monarchy. During long years of struggle against the Danes, Anglo-Saxon institutions gained strength and maturity, while the descendants of the Danes in Normandy developed efficient feudal governing arrangements there. William of Normandy fused the two sets of institutional relationships by conquering England in 1066. England's small size, its lack of internal divisions, and the swiftness and thoroughness of William I's conquests made its experience unique.

During the twelfth century, England's royal administration became more elaborate and efficient as Henry II (reigned 1154–1189) made England Europe's best-governed state. He closely supervised royal officials and established some government departments at a permanent royal capital at Westminster, near London. Under Henry, royal law replaced a previous patchwork of local laws and customs with a common law governing all English subjects and made justice uniform as well as equitable throughout England.

Throughout most of the thirteenth century, Henry's successors exhibited neither his ability nor his interest in government, and royal authority diminished. The barons forced King John (reigned 1199–1216) to issue in 1215 a Great Charter (*Magna Carta* in Latin). This committed kings to obtain baronial consent before levying new taxes, to administer justice according to established procedures rather than in an arbitrary and capricious manner, and to recognize and permit subjects to enjoy various rights and liberties. Later generations viewed the Magna Carta as a guarantee of fundamental human rights for all.

The reign of Edward I (1272–1307) saw the development of the English Parliament. Edward summoned barons, prelates, royal judges, administrators, shire knights, and members of town governments to parliaments, or formal conferences, to obtain advice on important issues and to support him in times of crisis. The knights and town representatives began to meet separately from the barons, and thereby laid the basis for the division into a House of Commons and a House of Lords. Through the English common law and the operations of Parliament, English kings and their subjects defined their respective rights and responsibilities and forged elements of a national unity.

In France, feudal monarchy developed more slowly than in England, but eventually became a model for other European lands. The reign of Philip IV (1285–1314) brought the development of the medieval French monarchy to its apex. Philip brought additional territories under royal control and consolidated the royal system of justice by making the court of appeals (the Parlement of Paris) its center. The success of his move to tax the French clergy convincingly demonstrated how powerful and secure the French monarchy had become.

To obtain public support for his opposition to the pope, Philip created the Estates General, a parliament-like body composed of members of the three great social classes, or estates: the clergy, nobles, and townspeople. French monarchs used the body as a sounding board for royal policy and a means of stirring up support for royal decisions. However, the Estates General was never permitted to gain the authority that the English Parliament possessed. It had no power base from which to bargain with the king, and never became an integral part of the French government. In France, the crown remained the one great unifying concept, and nobles retained provincial or regional rather than national interests.

The failure of feudal monarchy in the Holy Roman Empire long postponed the development of national unity in Germany and Italy. By contrast, in England and France, the success of feudal monarchy led in varying degrees to strong national states at a comparatively early date.

The Spiritual and Intellectual Life of the Later Middle Ages

During the eleventh and twelfth centuries, expanding royal bureaucracy, an increasingly complex ecclesiastical organization, and reviving commercial activity created a growing demand for educated persons to perform clerical and administrative tasks. Before 1000, most education in Europe had taken place in schools set up in cathedrals or monasteries. In response to the new demand, schools revised their curricula to stress study of the seven liberal arts derived from Greco-Roman civilization: grammar, logic or dialectic, rhetoric, arithmetic, geometry, astronomy, and music. By this time, a flood of new knowledge, primarily from the classical Greeks but transmitted and enlarged by Muslim and Jewish scholars, had become available. As artisans and merchants had done previously, scholars organized themselves into guilds known as universities (from Latin *universitas,* meaning "guild" or "society").

The term *university* came to mean a group of scholars working in close proximity and providing a basic program of instruction in the seven liberal arts and in one or more of the higher disciplines of theology, law, or medicine. By completing the six- to eight-year program, a student obtained a master's degree and a license to teach. Bachelor's programs of four to five years' duration developed later, but did not authorize their holders to teach. Universities were highly mobile, and relations between them and their hometowns were frequently strained and occasionally violent. Sometimes students and masters left town and established separate universities elsewhere. Gradually, wealthy patrons endowed

---

Piety and Pleasure in Latin Poetry

Nigher still, and still more nigh
Draws the day of Prophecy,
Doom'd to melt the earth and sky

Oh, what trembling there shall be,
When the world its Judge shall see,
Coming in dread majesty!

Now the books are open spread;
Now the writing must be read,
Which condemns the quick and dead.

Now, before the Judge severe
Hidden things must all appear;
Nought can pass unpunish'd here.*

In the third place, I will speak
Of the tavern's pleasure;
Nor shall I find it till I greet
Angels without measure,
Singing requiems for the souls
In eternal leisure
In the public-house to die
Is my resolution;
Let wine to my lips be nigh
At life's dissolution:
That will make the angels cry,
With glad elocution,
"Grant this toper, God on high,
Grace and absolution!"**

Both poems treat the theme of life's end, but in markedly different manners. The first, part of the majestic *Dies Irae (Day of Wrath),* presents the somberness of the Last Judgment in words, meter, and rhyme. The second presents a very different attitude toward life, which the poet's technique helps to emphasize. Both moods were part of medieval life.

*F. J. E. Raby, A History of Christian-Latin Poetry from the Beginnings to the Close of the Middle Ages, 2d ed. (Oxford: Clarendon Press, 1953), p. 443.
**John Addington Symonds, ed. and trans., Wine, Women, and Song: Medieval Latin Students' Songs (1884; rpt. New York: AMS Press, 1974), pp. 65–66.

colleges and universities with buildings and funds to pay for housing, feeding, and instructing students.

In northern Europe, the focus of study was theology, and scholars labored to improve their understanding of the Christian faith. During the eleventh century, some investigated the value of human reason in comprehending religious truth. Anselm of Bec (1033–1109), who later became archbishop of Canterbury, emphasized the use of logical reasoning in theology, even as a method to prove God's existence. Still, he ultimately subordinated reason to faith: "I do not seek to understand that I may believe, but I believe that I may understand; for this I also believe, that unless I believe I will not understand." By contrast, Peter Abelard (1079–1142) insisted that "by doubting we are led to question, and by questioning we arrive at the truth."

Scholars called "Scholastics" (because they worked in the medieval schools) responded to a challenge posed by the work of Aristotle. The most influential Scholastic thinker was Thomas Aquinas (1225–1274), who, in his massive *Summa Theologica (Summary of Theology)*, recognized theology and philosophy as separate realms of knowledge and maintained that properly conducted rational inquiry would support the principles of revelation.

As works of Jewish, Islamic, and Greek philosophy were translated into Latin after their piecemeal recovery from Byzantium and formerly Islamic lands in the twelfth century, studies in logic expanded. Aristotle's *Organon,* with its emphasis on syllogism and deductive and inductive logic, provided Scholasticism a much-needed tool; but Aristotle's rationalism also challenged scholars to harmonize the findings of natural knowledge with the conclusions of religious faith.

Science became another prominent area of medieval intellectual activity, especially with the translation of Greek and Arabic scientific works during the eleventh and twelfth centuries. During the thirteenth century, Roger Bacon (1214–1294), among others, made Oxford a major center of scientific studies. Bacon promoted an inductive investigation method involving observation and experimentation with appropriate instruments and methods. He described the nerve system of the eye, made magnifying glasses, and proposed high-technology warfare employing gigantic mirrors to focus the sun's rays and incinerate opponents.

Medieval Literature, Art, and Architecture

In addition to numerous scholarly writings, medieval writers composed a great quantity and variety of imaginative literature. Several Latin hymns from this period, such as the *Dies Irae (Day of Wrath),* are still sung in churches today. Secular writers also used Latin to produce nonreligious poetry about all aspects of life.

In both quantity and artistic quality, poetry in vernacular languages such as French, German, and English became more important than Latin poetry. During the eleventh century, northern French minstrels began to compose *chansons de geste* (songs of great deeds) and to sing them for audiences of nobles. These action-packed narratives vividly described battles, usually against non-Christian foes, and praised bravery in battle, loyalty to the lord, and generosity to all (including the minstrel!). In French, the *Song of*

Roland related with much fictional elaboration a bloody battle between Saracens (Spanish Muslims) and a detachment of Charlemagne's army ambushed in the pass at Roncevaux in the Pyrenees mountains. Its heroic characters became as well-known as those of the *Iliad* and the *Aeneid.* Epics soon appeared in other languages: the Spanish *Song of the Cid,* for example, told of the noble deeds of the eleventh-century heroic "Lord Champion" in the golden age of medieval chivalry. Although these poems and the music of the minstrels often glorified Christian victories against the Muslims, they were often based on forms and images copied from Islamic societies, particularly in Spain.

Meanwhile, minstrels known as troubadours composed lyric poetry in the Provençal dialect of southern France. Troubadour lyrics elaborated an entire art of love that emphasized a lover's good manners and refinement rather than skills in battle and induced nobles to acquire some knowledge of music, poetry, and history. The idea of selecting a marriage partner on the basis of love and serving her faithfully for years made the marriages of some nobles more than business transactions.

A third literary form, the romance, grew from the interaction of troubadour and *chanson de geste* traditions. Romances generally started from a theme or a person of the remote past, but completely disregarded historical accuracy in their treatments. A promi-

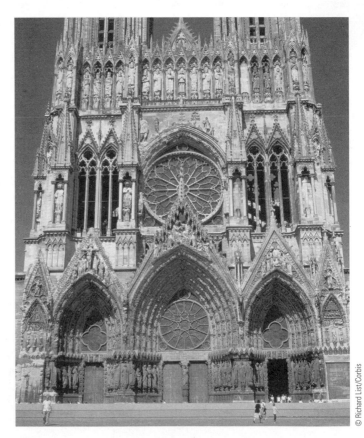

Façade of Rheims Cathedral. Elaborate decoration was a typical feature of Gothic architecture and sculpture; note especially the magnificent stained glass window above the central doorway.

© Richard List/Corbis

nent figure in the romances was Arthur, a semilegendary sixth-century English king who, by the twelfth century, had become a literary archetype of the ideal monarch. Arthur's court at Camelot, full of charming ladies and chivalrous knights, became the imaginary setting for religious sentiment and romantic love.

In addition to epics, lyrics, and romances for noble audiences, medieval writers produced fables, fabliaux, and dramas for town dwellers. Fables were brief moralistic stories featuring animals that symbolized people and their characteristics. Many popular fables came from France and related the exploits of Reynard the Fox, a wily character who consistently outwits his moral but stupid adversaries. *Fabliaux* were satirical poems depicting lives of ordinary people with vigorous and coarse humor while ridiculing conventional morality. In these forerunners of the modern short story, all priests and monks are gluttons and lechers, all women are lustful and easily seduced, and praise goes to those who outwit others.

Medieval drama developed from performances in church during religious ceremonies, illustrating in particular events associated with Christmas and Easter. In time, new scenes and incidents were invented, stock characterizations and crude scenery developed, and guilds assumed responsibility for play production. By the thirteenth century, such morality plays emphasized three distinct subjects: saints' lives, biblical stories, and the personification of correct behavior.

Although French and German remained the leading vernacular literatures into the thirteenth century, an Italian, Dante Alighieri (1265–1321), produced the greatest medieval literary masterpiece, *The Divine Comedy*. It describes a journey through hell, purgatory, and paradise, concluding in the awesome presence of God. Dante's guides for that journey were, respectively, Virgil, a spokesman for classical rationalism, Beatrice, an object of romantic and unconsummated but now spiritualized love, and St. Bernard, the epitome of Christian sanctity. The result is a majestic vision of the entire medieval universe.

The artists and artisans of the medieval era created impressive works of architecture, sculpture, and painting that matched the accomplishments of the scholars and writers. So many churches were built (more than 1,500 in France alone during the eleventh century) that a writer shortly after 1000 remarked that the earth was being covered with a white robe of churches.

· The architectural style of the eleventh and twelfth centuries is called Romanesque because it used Roman-type building materials and architectural features. Medieval builders employed the Roman basilica plan with certain alterations; it featured a large open rectangular area, called the nave, for accommodating worshipers, and a semicircular apse for the altar and the conduct of religious services. Intersecting aisles were arranged in a cross-shaped floor plan. A continuous barrel-vault roof was supported by massive piers and arches and thick walls with few windows and doors. The atmosphere was one of mysterious darkness but also of castlelike protection.

The twelfth century saw a major innovation in Romanesque architecture, the Gothic style. Influenced by the emphasis of contemporary writers on illumination through prayer and meditation, Gothic architects featured space, light, and height. They unified interior space by replacing the rounded Romanesque arch with the pointed arch, which raised roofs higher above the floor. External buttresses replaced the thick walls of Romanesque churches; this permitted large stained glass windows to flood the building's interior with multicolored light. Sculptors decorated Gothic churches with secular and biblical subjects. The Gothic style remained the dominant European art style into the sixteenth century except in Italy, where interest in classical artistic forms led to the distinctive art style of the Renaissance.

The cathedral became the town's religious center. It was, both physically and spiritually, an ordered unity like that of Thomas Aquinas's *Summa Theologica* or Dante's *Divine Comedy*, combining several distinct but related elements into a structurally coherent whole.

The East Roman or Byzantine Empire

As the inner part of the temple was seen, and the sun lit its glories, sorrow fled from the hearts of all. . . . And when the first gleam of light, rosy-armed driving away the dark shadows, leaped from arch to arch, then all the princes and peoples with one voice hymned their songs of prayer and praise; and as they came to the sacred courts it seemed to them as if the mighty arches were set in heaven. . . . Whenever anyone enters the church to pray, he realizes at once it is not by any human power or skill, but by the influence of God that it has been built. And so his mind is lifted up to God, and he feels that He cannot be far away, but must love to dwell in this place He has chosen.*

**Procopius, *Buildings*, trans. H. B. Dewing and G. Downey (London: Heinemann, 1940), pp. 11–17, 25–29.*

So wrote a Byzantine in contemplation of the magnificent church of Hagia Sophia (Holy Wisdom) in Constantinople. Like the Gothic cathedrals in western Europe, the Hagia Sophia was a symbol of the Byzantine Empire's glorious cultural achievements. As we have seen, Germanic peoples had destroyed the Roman Empire's Mediterranean unity by 500 and ruled large portions of Rome's former domain in the west. However, far from these militarily threatening outside enemies, most of Rome's former eastern territories survived intact as the Byzantine Empire ("Byzantine" referred to an old Greek town Byzantium, incorporated in the imperial capital, Constantinople). Containing the richer and more populated half of the old Roman Empire, the Byzantine state retained Rome's political and social structures and preserved its cultural heritage for a thousand years (476–1453). In the empire, Justinian I (reigned 527–565), perhaps the greatest Byzantine emperor, combined the cultural heritage and political order of classical Greece and Rome with the vitality of the Christian religion. In so doing, he foreshadowed many Byzantine contributions to civilization that rival the work of the architects of Hagia Sophia. This section examines Byzantine accomplishments during the period from 500 to about 1400.

Life in the Byzantine Empire in 500

Freed of heavy expenses for military defense and economic development of the west, the Byzantine Empire prospered economically while remaining socially and ethnically diverse. A top layer of Greek aristocrats ruled over a majority population of Slavs, Arabs,

Armenians, Jews, and others. In rural areas, aristocratic nobles held large landed estates, worked by free tenant renters (sharecroppers) called *coloni*. Although the coloni were technically free, they were actually tied to the land by economic necessity.

During the eighth to eleventh centuries, the empire enjoyed relative economic prosperity and agricultural plenty. The government controlled the prices of the staples of the Byzantine diet, bread and olive oil, and manipulated the currency to maintain stability. As in earlier empires from Asia to Europe, the authorities in the Byzantine Empire supervised the upkeep of roads and ports to facilitate trade. Industries, especially the manufacture of brocaded textiles, flourished. In a manner similar to guilds in the west, guilds held monopolies over some manufacturing specialties like textiles, and foreign merchants were encouraged to establish businesses.

The capital, Constantinople, was one of the biggest cities of the age and at its zenith may have had a population of one million. The main street, a sweeping thoroughfare, was lined with shops and a terraced promenade decorated with statues of emperors and popular actresses. An enormous hippodrome or stadium, with seating for 60,000 spectators, was the site of spectacular and exceedingly popular chariot races. Betting on favored teams such as the "blues" or "greens" was a popular pastime and when teams did poorly,

© Vanni Archive/Corbis

Hagia Sophia. Byzantine rulers were justifiably proud of the Church of Hagia Sophia (Holy Wisdom) with its towering dome. This architectural achievement remains a major monument in present-day Istanbul; the needle-shaped minarets were added by the Ottomans. The Byzantine builders created a huge open space by placing the principal dome atop two half domes. This arrangement so astounded sixth-century contemporaries that they asserted the dome had been let down from heaven.

it was not uncommon for their supporters to come to blows. These fights sometimes developed into full-scale riots that occasionally threatened the survival of the government.

The wealthy frequently owned slaves to work in their private homes. Large numbers of merchants, artisans, educators, and administrators lived lives of great luxury in large cities or seaside villas located in the European and West Asian sections of the empire. Although members of the ruling elite lived well and reaped the benefits of empire, most people lived on the margin of starvation in one-story city tenements or village huts. As in earlier Greek traditions, men dominated society, and the lives of most women centered on their families and homes; few held any position of political, cultural, or economic importance.

Throughout its long history, the empire steadfastly maintained its identity as the living embodiment of the Roman Empire, but its culture, language, and lifestyle became increasingly Greek. The state paid the instructors at the university of Constantinople, and students often received low or free tuition. Students learned classical Greek writings and followed classical educational traditions taught in classical Greek. However, the coloni and workers spoke a different, common vernacular Greek.

Although Christianity was the official religion, the empire's Christians were divided by theological differences. The church leaders and elite were notoriously disputatious and constantly debated the smallest point of Christian theology, particularly questions involving the nature of Christ and the Trinity. The Orthodox upheld the conclusions of religious councils regarding the Trinity and the nature of Christ, but many non-Orthodox churches, branded as heretical by the Byzantine rulers, differed widely in their beliefs. For example, in eastern Europe (as well as in most of the German states of western Europe) most Christians believed that Jesus was not equal to God. Syria and Egypt, where the populations retained their own rich cultural traditions and local languages and

Theodora, Empress of Many Talents

Theodora, the belly-dancer whom Justinian defied convention to marry . . . was possessed of no ordinary beauty, charm and intelligence. She was a born actress and enjoyed being the centre of attraction as the great lady of the imperial court; and in contrast to her austere husband she revelled in the luxury, pomp and elegance of life in the Great Palace at Constantinople. She shared to the full his conception of the majesty of the Roman Empire. But whereas Justinian belonged to the Latin world and thought like a Roman, Theodora was a Greek or perhaps one may say a Byzantine. But as man and wife they complemented one another. Justinian was devoted to her, and her death in 548 marked a turning-point in his career.*

The wives or mistresses of eminent rulers have often exerted great influence on the course of history. The first Roman emperor, Augustus, found in his wife Livia a source of strength and dependably good advice. By contrast, Agrippina, the wife of the emperor Claudius, ruthlessly manipulated (and finally murdered) her husband in his doddering last years, even inducing him to prefer Nero, her son by a former marriage, to his own direct offspring. Justinian's Theodora, like Pericles' Aspasia, was one of those forceful personalities who overcame a dubious background to capture (and more than repay) the attentions of an important leader.

*Donald M. Nicol, "Justinian I and His Successors, A.D. 527–610," in Byzantium: An Introduction, *ed. Philip Whitting (New York: Harper, 1973), p. 18.*

scorned their Greek-speaking rulers, were also strongholds of nontrinitarian Christianity. From Egypt, the Coptic Christian church spread into Ethiopia in eastern Africa, where it established a Christian society that survives until the present day (see Chapter 7).

Centered around the eastern Mediterranean, the Nestorians believed that Christ had two separate natures, while the Monophysites argued that Christ's divine nature had absorbed his human nature. Some of these communities still live in present-day Syria, Iraq, and Lebanon. Nestorian missionaries also converted tens of thousands in southern India and China. Some authorities claim that by the ninth century, the Nestorians were the single largest Christian group in the world. Although many of the eastern Christians in western Asia ultimately converted to Islam, theological disputes about the nature of Christ have continued up to the present throughout the Christian world.

Within the Byzantine Empire, the emperor exercised absolute authority over both religious and political matters. He appointed and dismissed officials, issued edicts, sat as the final court of judicial appeal, commanded the military and naval forces, and conducted foreign policy, often seeking to avoid war with rulers and peoples outside the empire. Initially, emperors were chosen from the imperial family by the army and confirmed by the Senate in Constantinople; the mothers and wives of the emperors also often played a key role in the selection of successors. By the fifth century, the patriarch of Constantinople, representing both the people and the church, crowned and consecrated the emperor.

Justinian I

Justinian I, the greatest Byzantine emperor, was an able and active ruler. He was responsible for keeping harmony in what he regarded as a Christian Roman state. He saw his duties as both ecclesiastical, ministering to spiritual needs, and political, attending to earthly affairs. His able and courageous wife, Theodora (c. 500–548), assisted him in those tasks. She restrained his religious zeal and eased tensions between governmental authorities and heretics. Early in his reign, a riot between supporters of rival chariot racing teams spread throughout the city, prompting Justinian and his advisers to consider fleeing the capital, but Theodora urged them instead to stay and fight. When they did, the riot was quelled and the throne secured.

Justinian beautified Constantinople by a large-scale building program, ensuring employment for laborers and also for artists, who added mosaics, sculptures, and icons (pictures of religious figures) to many buildings. Byzantine art became nearly as important as the Greek language in defining Christian faith.

Justinian also systematized Roman law: he directed a committee to compile all Roman legislation and legal commentaries of jurists and to produce a standard textbook for students. The new code, the *Corpus Juris Civilis* (Collection of Civil Law), made Orthodox Christianity the law of the land. Although essentially conservative, it improved the lot of freemen, slaves, and women, and encouraged charitable gifts to the church. The code later become the basis for the civil law of many European and Latin American nations.

In addition, Justinian sought to complete the Christianization of the empire. In 529 he closed the ancient, pre-Christian philosophical schools in Athens. He also restricted the civil rights of so-called heretics; for example, Jews, other non-Christians, and non-Orthodox

Christians were prohibited from living within the walls of Constantinople and were barred from many public offices and teaching positions.

Under Justinian, Byzantine literature and learning flourished. Christian teachers stressed the best elements of classical moral training, philosophical thought, and literary craftsmanship. They taught the classical tradition from the Christian viewpoint and wrote on both classical and Christian topics, producing epigrams in the classical Greek manner, poems in elegant Homeric verse, and histories in the style of Herodotus and Thucydides. The subject matter of most literary output, as well as the style, tended to focus on the past; Byzantine writers and artists were not noted for innovation or experimentation.

The Empire's Neighbors

Although he devoted enormous energy to internal matters, Justinian spent most of his reign and much of the empire's wealth on the reconquest of the western Mediterranean, particularly the German-occupied territories in North Africa, the southern coast of Spain, and Italy. Following his death, the Visigoths reconquered southern Spain and a new Germanic group, the Lombards, moved from the Danube Valley to seize much of northern and central Italy. As a result, the Byzantine presence in the west was reduced to North Africa, Sicily, and some regions on the Italian coast, with Ravenna serving as the imperial administrative center.

Justinian's warfare in the west weakened the empire's eastern and northern defenses and created serious problems for his successors. To the north, the Slavs, an Indo-European agricultural people, moved southward through the Danube Valley, now vacated by the Lombards. They entered Macedonia and Greece by 600 and soon thereafter attacked Constantinople. To counter the Lombards and Slavs, seventh-century Byzantine emperors placed civil and military authority in the hands of regional military commanders, and the region's civilian population became the defending army. This ensured the survival of the empire but changed it into a society mobilized for continual warfare. The Byzantines also long enjoyed naval supremacy, thanks in part to "Greek

Scala/Art Resource

Theodora. This spectacular mosaic depicts Theodora arrayed in a jewel-encrusted gown and robe. Dynamic and resourceful, Theodora was a trusted adviser to her husband, the Emperor Justinian I, and became a powerful political figure in her own right.

Map 5.6 The Mediterranean in the Time of Justinian. Around 525, after the Germanic migrations into western Europe, the Byzantine Empire occupied only the limited area shown. Justinian I expanded the empire by recovering territories from Goths and Vandals, but some of these gains were lost soon after his death.

Fire," a petroleum-based incendiary substance that could be discharged from tubes and was not extinguishable by water.

Farther east, Justinian's successors went to war with Persia soon after 600. The Persians, under the Sassanian dynasty that had replaced the Parthians, enjoyed early successes, quickly conquering Syria and Egypt and attacking Constantinople. However, the Byzantines countered by invading Persia and occupying its capital, Ctesiphon (in present-day Iraq). By 628, the Persians were forced to seek peace.

The war with Persia, which brought the Byzantines no long-term territorial gains, exhausted it economically and made it vulnerable to attacks by vigorous new foes. The Arabs, newly united under Islam, seized Syria and Egypt from the Byzantine Empire and Mesopotamia from the Persians shortly after 630. Two Arab sieges of Constantinople, in 674–678 and 717–718, were unsuccessful; thereafter, the Taurus Mountains dividing Asia Minor from Syria became the Byzantine-Arab frontier. Another Asiatic people, the Bulgars, entered the Balkans from the north late in the seventh century, gaining control of the lower Danube Valley. They integrated the local Slavic peoples into a Bulgar-dominated state. Thus the outer fringes of the empire were lost to increasingly powerful rivals.

Religious Issues

Byzantine wars had religious as well as political dimensions. Justinian fought the Germans as much because they were Arians as because they were occupiers of imperial territory. His successors similarly opposed Slavs and Bulgars as non-Christian pagans. Following

Zoroastrianism and Islam, respectively, the Persians and Arabs easily conquered Syria and Egypt in the seventh century, in part because non-Orthodox and Orthodox Christians failed to mount any collective opposition to the invading forces.

Arab and Persian conquests removed Jerusalem, Alexandria, and Antioch from the empire, leaving Constantinople and Rome as the major Christian centers. As time passed, leaders in those two centers often disagreed on religious issues. Believing it was their duty to maintain orthodoxy, Justinian and his successors tried to reestablish doctrinal unity. The bishops of Rome (popes), however, claimed headship of the church and regarded the definition of Christian faith as their responsibility. Doctrines acceptable in the east and proclaimed by bishops in councils under the direction of the patriarch of Constantinople often encountered papal opposition, whereas eastern Catholics often rejected doctrines the west could support. Church councils in the sixth and seventh centuries failed to resolve such conflicts.

In the eighth century, Emperor Leo III (reigned 717–741) created a new rift among Christians. He believed that many of the empire's bright and able men were diverted from state service because they were interested in monastic practices that involved the worship of icons (images of sacred Christian figures). Leo accordingly tried to discredit monasticism by attacking the misuse of icons in eastern churches as idolatrous and by prohibiting their use. This sharply divided the empire's population into iconoclasts (image breakers) and iconodules (image users). Many of latter fled to monasteries or to western imperial territories in south Italy and Sicily. Because the popes opposed the iconoclasts, Leo retaliated by transferring many rich papal lands in Italy to the patriarch of Constantinople. Iconoclasm polarized Latin and Greek Christians and divided the Byzantine Empire even after the ecumenical Council of Nicaea in 787 restored relations between Rome and Constantinople. The dispute over icons was eventually resolved by the Empress Irene (reigned 780–802), who required priests to provide instruction to parishioners on the appropriate use of icons. Irene ruled by brute force and succeeded in imposing her son as successor. For her service to Christianity, the Church subsequently declared her a saint.

Decline of Empire

During the ninth century, the Byzantine Empire gradually regained some of its former power; emperors reestablished use of icons and restored the empire's financial and military resources. In 867 an ambitious son of Armenian peasants assassinated the reigning emperor and seized the throne as Basil I. Basil established the long-lived Macedonian dynasty (867–1054), which ably led the empire for nearly two centuries.

Byzantine cultural and religious life flourished under the early Macedonians. Literary output grew, while educational activity and interest in classical authors revived. Poems and hymns in praise of saints and prose accounts of their lives were published, while histories and lexicons attested to the Byzantine fascination with the classical past. The emperor Constantine VII (reigned 912–959) patronized scholarly activity and authorized important works describing the administration of the empire and Byzantine court ceremonies. Out of the recurring border wars with Muslims came the *Epic of Digenes Akritas* ("the border warrior born of parents from different ethnic groups"), which resembles western European works such as the *Song of Roland* and the *Song of the Cid*.

In art, the iconoclastic controversy triggered interest in the forms of Greek art popular during Alexander the Great's time, in the historical and secular rather than the ecclesiastical and spiritual, and in Islamic art and its use of ornament. This second golden age of Byzantine art was characterized by the pursuit of dignity, grace, restraint, balance, and refinement.

Under the Macedonian rulers, Byzantine artistic and literary developments continued to copy classical Greek models in which secular taste often contrasted with religious sensitivity. In the decorations of aristocratic homes and in manuscript illuminations, classical themes and mythological or allegorical scenes were popular. The exploitation of their classical inheritance gave the Byzantines superiority over Latin Christianity in literary and artistic achievements in the ninth and tenth centuries.

Byzantine vitality also contributed to cultural and religious expansion. Byzantine emperors considered the late ninth-century conquests and subsequent conversion of Serbians and other Slavs to Orthodox Christianity to be one of their greatest accomplishments. The Bulgars negotiated with both Latin and Byzantine Christians, but the work of Byzantine missionaries and the diplomacy of Byzantine emperors and patriarchs induced the Bulgar ruler to adopt Eastern Orthodox Christianity. By the tenth century, the Bulgar capital of Preslav became a center for training Slavic clergy. They were taught in Old Church Slavonic, a literary language devised by Byzantine missionaries that became a means by which Byzantine culture was infused into eastern and southeastern Europe.

During the tenth century, Kievan Russia began to move into the Byzantine cultural orbit. As trade with the Byzantines grew, Kievan rulers sought closer ties with Constantinople. Prince Vladimir (reigned alone 977–1015), a baptized Christian, married Anna, sister of the Byzantine emperor Basil II (reigned 976–1025). The Bible, saints' lives, and

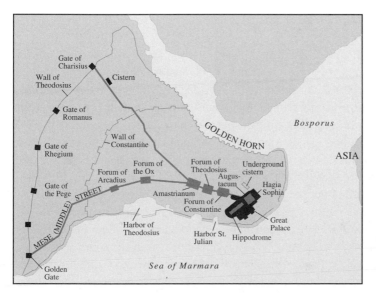

Map 5.7 Constantinople. The capital of the Byzantine Empire, Constantinople was a large city with a lavish complex of imperial buildings and churches. Its location astride the Bosporus provided it with natural defenses that were further strengthened by a series of walls around the city. This map also shows the Hippodrome, where the famous games were held, Hagia Sophia, and the Mese, or middle, street.

religious service books translated at Preslav from Greek into Old Church Slavonic formed the earliest Russian Christian religious literature.

In southeastern Europe, the Byzantine Empire declined rapidly. Although a series of vigorous emperors from 1081 to 1185 asserted imperial authority, increased commercial connections with Italian cities, and restored Constantinople as a leading cultural center, a subsequent rapid succession of short-lived rulers weakened the empire. By 1200 rebellions in Serbia and Bulgaria led to the establishment of independent states. In 1204 Latin crusaders sacked the capital of Constantinople and made most of the Byzantine Empire a Latin Empire until 1261. Although the Paleologi dynasty (1261–1453) was able to destroy the Latin Empire and recover Constantinople and much of northern Greece, from 1300 onward the Byzantine Empire increasingly became, like central Europe, politically fragmented. Like the Greek and Roman Empires before it, the Byzantine Empire, which had persisted for more than a millennium, disintegrated and finally disappeared. Byzantium was to be replaced during the fifteenth century by a new, non-Christian power, the Ottoman Turks, who, like the Byzantines, had a tradition of absolute rule (see Chapter 8).

Islam and Islamic Empires

The apostle of God became a young man. God protected him from the loose behavior of the pagans. He was the most generous of his people . . . kind to his neighbors, courteous, faithful. . . . He was the bravest of men.

[Muhammad's reactions when he had his first vision as he meditated in a desert cave:] "One came to me with a written scroll, while I was asleep, and said 'Read!' I said 'I cannot read. . . .' He pressed me with it, until I thought death must be nigh. . . . And he said, 'Read in the name of thy Lord who created; He created man from a sensitive drop of blood' [Qur'an 96.1–2]. And he departed. . . .

And I awoke. . . . And it was as if the scripture were written on my heart."*

*Emel Esin, *Mecca, the Blessed; Madinah, the Radiant* (New York: Crown, 1963), pp. 70, 76.

Thus did the prophet Muhammad's Arabian contemporaries describe the prophet and his first revelation of what was to become one of the world's major religions. Just as Buddha and Jesus had gone to meditate in remote areas, so too, did the prophet Muhammad. There he experienced a series of revelations that were then transmitted first to converts in Arabia and then to growing numbers in Africa and eastern Asia.

Although the peoples in pre-Islamic Arabia were predominantly tribal nomads, Mecca and Medina had been major centers for religious pilgrimages and trade, particularly of frankincense and myrrh from Yemen, for generations. A few Jewish and Christian communities were also scattered about the peninsula; these communities continued to maintain some commercial and cultural ties with the Byzantine Empire, which controlled most of the eastern Mediterranean. Merchants and city dwellers enjoyed a fair degree of prosperity, but most of the population in the Arabian Peninsula lived in either scattered desert oases, where they eked out a subsistence livelihood growing grains, vegetables, and date palms, or as nomads who traveled with herds of camels, goats, and sheep from one life-giving watering hole to the next. The majority of these *bedouin* (tribal people) were animists (believers that inanimate objects like stones, trees, and animals possess spirits or souls), living in what Islamic society would term ignorance.

Muhammad: A Religious and Political Leader

The prophet Muhammad, who came from the Hashim family or branch of the Qurash tribe, was born in Mecca around 570 or 571. He was raised by his grandfather and as an adult married an older widow, Khadijah. Muhammad rapidly gained a reputation as an honest and successful businessman. When he was around forty years old, Muhammad became increasingly religious and began to spend longer periods of time in deep meditation. As early as 610, Muhammad began to have revelations from Allah (God), which were transmitted through the angel Gabriel. Muhammad began to preach the word of Allah and slowly gained adherents to the new religion, Islam (submission to God). The believers in Islam were known as Muslims, or those who submit to the will of God.

Muslims believe in one God and in the prophets of the Old and New Testaments; they include Christ as a prophet. They also believe in progressive revelation, the existence of angels, and the doctrine of the day of judgment. Islam, like Christianity, is a universal religion in which all people who accepted the belief in one God and in Muhammad as his prophet were seen as equal before Allah and within the community. For Muslims, Islam is the perfection of all previous religions, including Judaism and Christianity. As Islam spread and attracted converts around the world, its universal nature and its equal treatment of all believers proved to be two of its major strengths.

The revelations from Allah received by Muhammad were set down in the *Qur'an (Koran),* which contained instructions governing all aspects of human life. As the Islamic community grew in numbers and expanded over vast territories, the Qur'an was supplemented by the *Hadith,* which is a collection of the sayings and traditions of the prophet Muhammad. Muslims accept six authoritative collections of the Hadith. In addition, a complex body of law, the *Shari'a,* gradually evolved. The Qur'an, Hadith, and Shari'a provide the guidelines for the conduct of Muslim societies. Over several centuries, differing interpretations of the Qur'an, the Hadith, and the Shari'a led to the formation of several different schools of Islamic law.

A large percentage of Islamic law deals with family matters. In Arabia, where women had previously enjoyed no legal status, Islamic injunctions were a major improvement. As the prophet was known to have said, "Paradise is at the foot of the mother." Under Islamic law, a widow was guaranteed a portion of her husband's estate and could own and dispose of property; women also had the right of divorce in specific instances. These legal rights were granted in Islam centuries before most women in the Christian west obtained such rights. However, in keeping with traditional practice in western Asia, Islamic societies remained patriarchal, the oldest male acting as the leader, provider, and final authority in the family. Muslim law permitted polygamy, which was common in Arabia and much of the rest of the world at the time. A Muslim male could have four wives at any one time if each wife were treated equally. In actual practice only the wealthy could generally afford more than one wife.

LIVES AND TIMES ACROSS CULTURES

People of the Book

The three major monotheistic religions—Judaism, Christianity, and Islam—emerged from western Asia and built on many of the same traditions. They are based on belief in one and only one God, creator of the universe and humankind. All three accept Abraham and Moses as important teachers and prophets. Christians believe Jesus was last in a long line of prophets and, in addition, was the son of God. Jews do not accept Jesus as the son of God and continue to await the Messiah's arrival. Although Muslims accept Jesus as a prophet and the virgin birth by Mary, they do not believe in the resurrection. They view Muhammad as the last and greatest of the prophets.

All three stress the written word, each having a sacred text: the Torah for Jews, the Bible for Christians, and the Qur'an for Muslims. These texts provide the basic theology of the religion as well as guidance for daily life, including dietary regulations, religious practices and rites, and a host of instructions for proper behavior. Judaism and Islam also share a common emphasis on law and the duties of believers. The texts provide guidelines for proper daily behavior and the path to salvation after death. They are also rich sources for poetry, stories, and histories of, for example, the creation of the world and early human history.

Although women played important roles in the early history of each religion, such as Sarah in Judaism, the Virgin Mary and Mary Magdalene in Christianity, and Khadijah and Aisha in Islam, all three were organized along patriarchal lines. Men were the religious leaders and interpreters of the sacred texts and law. Rabbis in Judaism, priests and ministers in Christianity, and imams in Islam were traditionally men; indeed, women were frequently barred from holding these positions. Although a few women have become rabbis and ministers in the contemporary era, men continue to dominate the leadership, particularly in conservative branches, of all three religions.

These and other commonalities created a Judeo-Christian-Islamic tradition that had a major impact around the world.

In eras when religious tolerance was generally unknown, Islam enjoined believers to grant safe havens to people of the book (Jews and Christians) and usually to Zoroastrians and not to force conversions or to persecute these communities unless they waged war against Muslims. This tolerance, however, was not extended to animists or polytheists such as Hindus.

The Qur'an also provides regulations for marriage (including divorce); loaning of money (interest is forbidden); diet; the treatment of women, orphans, and slaves; and the behavior of government. Muslim theologians and legal experts who interpreted and explained Islamic canons were known collectively as the *ulema*. Importantly, Islam, in contrast to early Christianity, did not separate church from state.

Every true Muslim was instructed to follow the five basic pillars: belief in Allah and Muhammad as his prophet, prayer five times a day, the giving of alms, fasting from sunrise to sunset during the month of Ramadan, and the *hajj* or pilgrimage to Mecca once in a lifetime. The observance of these five pillars still serves as the principal means of salvation for Muslims, and nonobservance is believed to lead to eternal suffering in the afterlife.

The hajj commemorates the *hijrah* (flight) in 622 of Muhammad and his followers from the merchants of Mecca, who feared the new religion would threaten both their preeminent political and social status and the wealth they enjoyed from pilgrims coming to worship in the city. The hajj centers on the *Ka'bah,* a cube-shaped shrine in Mecca, which had long been a place of pilgrimage for tribal peoples in the Arabian Peninsula. In addition to its spiritual meaning, the hajj has also enabled diverse and widely scattered Islamic peoples to exchange ideas and goods while maintaining a cohesive structure.

The new Islamic community took refuge in Medina, became the dominant political and social force, and attracted more and more converts. Worried over the growing political and financial power of Muhammad and his followers, the leaders in Mecca launched several armed attacks to destroy the new community. When the Muslims successfully defeated these attacks, they gained more converts. By 629, the Muslims led by Muhammad were strong enough to mount a force of more than 1,000 believers to march on Mecca; by 632 Muhammad had successfully incorporated the city within the new and growing Muslim community. Just a few months after his return to Mecca, however, Muhammad died of a fever. Because Muhammad had left no specific instructions regarding a successor, the community of the faithful immediately gathered together and by consensus selected the first caliph, or leader.

The First Four Caliphs and Islamic Conquests

The first caliph, Abu Bakr, had been one of the original converts to Islam. As Muhammad's faithful friend, Abu Bakr was known for his devotion and was widely respected for his wisdom and good humor. Following Muhammad's death, a number of the Arabian tribes had broken with the Islamic community. Abu Bakr immediately appointed loyal chiefs to subdue these revolts. Subsequently, many of the tribal leaders participated in the military conquests of the entire Arabian Peninsula and in expeditions into Syria and Iraq.

After Abu Bakr's death in 634, the Islamic community selected the energetic Umar as the second caliph. Umar's administration was marked by a period of military conquest, as Muslims assimilated widely different areas and peoples into an Islamic Empire. In the east, the Iraqi territories of the old Sassanid Empire were conquered, and in 637 the capital at Ctesiphon fell to Arab/Islamic domination. These military victories brought vast wealth, which was lavishly bestowed upon the soldiers. With promises of military victories and booty, the Islamic armies had little difficulty in attracting recruits.

In following years, Muslim armies met with similar military successes against the Byzantine Empire. Damascus fell to Khalid's forces in 635, and at the decisive battle of Yarmuk in 637, the forces of the Roman emperor were decisively defeated. Jerusalem was incorporated into the Muslim Empire in 638. The Muslims then turned their energies toward Egypt and Africa; in 639 they reached the banks of the Nile, taking Alexandria in 641. Two years later most of Persia had fallen.

Arab women and children accompanied the armies on military campaigns, and women frequently joined the fighting. The Byzantine soldiers, accustomed to women remaining secluded at home, were shocked to see Arab women on the battlefields. At Yarmuk, when the Arab army moved to retreat, women seized swords and tent posts and

The Sacred Mosque and Ka'bah at Mecca. This photograph shows the holiest site in the Muslim world during the time of pilgrimage. Although the courtyard can hold a half-million pilgrims, in recent years it has been too small to contain the crowds, which can exceed 4 million worshipers.

© AFP/Corbis

urged the soldiers to rejoin the battle; some also joined the frontlines on horseback. The result was a complete rout of the Byzantine army.

The extremely rapid expansion of the Muslim/Arab Empire was attributable in part to the weaknesses of the Sassanid and Byzantine Empires. More important to the Muslims' success, however, were their fervent religious belief and the equalitarian nature of the religion, which treated converts as equals within the community. The Muslims' treatment of their new subjects also contributed to their success. In contrast to leaders of earlier empires in Egypt and China, for example, Umar did not attempt to force the conquered peoples to assimilate or to adopt Arabian customs. Umar's decision to interfere as little as possible with the conquered peoples was perhaps his most important contribution to the continued success and endurance of the Islamic Empire. During Umar's caliphate, provincial governors were appointed to administer the new territories; their major job was to collect taxes, which, in many cases, were far lower than those collected by the Byzantine or Sassanid Empires. Hence, many peoples actually welcomed the new rulers and were rapidly absorbed within the Islamic society. Non-Muslims were not forced to convert and were allowed to maintain their own laws, as well as to practice their own religions. They were not permitted to bear arms, however; nor, for example, could their church towers be taller than the highest minaret in a town. In contrast to other societies of the age, which often forced conversions and persecuted or killed people of differing beliefs, the Islamic Empire became known for its relative tolerance of minorities and non-Muslims.

Similarly, Islamic law strictly regulated the treatment of slaves. Muslims could not enslave other Muslims, and the freeing of slaves was encouraged. In contrast to many other societies, particularly in the Western Hemisphere, slaves in the Islamic world were not generally used as agricultural labor on huge plantations, but were kept only as workers and protectors for domestic households or as soldiers in the army.

As the "second founder of Islam," Umar also established a single authoritative version of the Qur'an; all other copies were destroyed, and the Qur'an has remained unchanged since that time. Unfortunately, while praying in Medina, at the very peak of his power, Umar was fatally wounded by a disgruntled slave. On his deathbed Umar appointed a committee of six prominent merchants to select the next caliph.

After some debate the committee chose Uthman, from the powerful Umayyad family, as the third caliph. An elderly man in his seventies, Uthman was not as forceful a leader as his predecessors, and he was widely criticized for favoring members of his own family over the rest of the *umma* (Islamic community). For example, Uthman appointed his cousin Mu'awiyah governor of the flourishing province of Syria. Mu'awiyah proved an able ruler and military strategist, however, ordering the building of the first Islamic fleet, which immediately conquered the islands of Cyprus and Rhodes. With his army and

Map 5.8 The Expansion of Islam. Most of Islam's early territorial gains were at the expense of the Persian and Byzantine Empires. The former was entirely absorbed, the latter, already diminished by German gains, lost Syria, Egypt, and all of its North African possessions. Muslims then advanced into the Iberian Peninsula and France in the west and toward the banks of the Indus River in the east.

The Death of a Caliph

The people rushed upon him, some striking him with their scabbards, others striking him with their fists. A man came at him with a broad iron-tipped arrow and stabbed the front of his throat, and his blood fell on the Koran. Yet even when they were in that state they feared killing him. Uthman was old and he fainted. His wife Na'ila and his daughters wailed loudly. Al-Tujibi came, drawing his sword to thrust it into his belly. When Na'ila protected Uthman, he cut her hand. Then he leaned with his sword upon his chest; and Uthman, Allah bless him, was killed before sundown.*

This emotional description of Caliph Uthman's assassination has all the hallmarks of an eyewitness account. The assassination marked a major turning point in Islamic history after which leadership for the community would be hotly contested.

*From Ibn Jarir al-Tabari (d. 923), "The History of Prophets and Kings," in The Islamic World, ed. William H. McNeill and Marilyn Robinson Waldman (New York: Oxford University Press, 1973; reprint, Chicago: University of Chicago Press, 1983), p. 76.

fleet, which made him the dominant military force in the eastern Mediterranean, Mu'awiyah emerged as a powerful leader in his own right.

The Caliph Uthman's leadership was increasingly opposed by faithful Muslims in Medina and in provincial towns on the eastern frontier. An open revolt began in Kufah in Iraq in 655 and soon spread to Medina. In 656 the rebels broke into the caliph's home and assassinated him. Political assassination has often triggered unrest and accelerated changes in the course of history. For example, the assassinations of Uthman and Julius Caesar both sparked struggles for power that ended with the emergence of able administrators and founders of dynastic lines (Mu'awiya and Augustus).

After Uthman's death, once again, the Muslim leaders gathered to select a leader; after a week, the notables agreed to appoint Ali, Muhammad's son-in-law, as the fourth caliph. From the very beginning of his reign, however, Ali met with widespread opposition. So many in Medina were against him, including some who believed he had been implicated in Uthman's death, that Ali fled the city and established his capital in Kufah (in present-day Iraq). Nevertheless, the discontent continued. Aisha, Muhammad's favorite wife, disliked Ali, who had once accused her of infidelity. Astride a camel, Aisha led her supporters into a bloody battle against Ali in 656. Defeated at the so-called Battle of the Camel, in which many of the original followers of the prophet were killed, Aisha was forced to retire to Medina where she died of natural causes several decades later.

Mu'awiyah was to prove a much more dangerous opponent to Ali's supremacy. He refused to resign as virtual ruler of Syria, and he had the support of the powerful Umayyad family. In 657 he challenged Ali's leadership at the battle of Siffin, in northern Syria. Although the battle was essentially a standoff, more and more provinces aligned with Mu'awiyah, who clearly held the preponderance of power. Some of Ali's original followers now turned against him. Known as *Kharijites* (seceders), they were against any sort of compromise and now opposed both Ali and Mu'awiyah. The Kharijites considered themselves to be the only true revolutionaries within the Muslim world. In 661 a Kharijite murdered Ali. His death ended the age of the "rightly guided" caliphs—the first four caliphs, all of whom had either been related to Muhammad or had been his close compatriots.

The Glorious Umayyads

Our Caliph, successor of God, is the most fortunate; his good omen brings down rain showers from above. He belongs to the most prestigious clan of Quraysh, no other tree can parallel his glorious branch. Following the right and refraining from wrong, his people always endure when tragedy strikes. Their enemy does not dare to fight them, for their resolve is always strong.

They continue to fight till they win;
 yet, in peace they are the most magnanimous.
In times of drought they race the winds
 to feed and shelter the stricken ones.

Sons of Umayya, your favors are very generous;
 you give without any spite or drudgery.*

These excerpts from a poem in praise of Caliph 'Abd al-Malik by the noted Umayyad poet al-Akhtal (d. 722) reveal the esteem in which many Umayyad Caliphs were held. Writers also sought to win the favor and patronage of the court by penning highly flattering, if not always factually correct, descriptions of the rulers. Writers and poets were similarly supported in the Chinese and other empires.

*Wilson B. Bishai, Humanities in the Arabic-Islamic World (Dubuque, Iowa: W. C. Brown, 1973), p. 79.

The Umayyad Caliphate

After Ali's death, Mu'awiyah declared himself caliph in Jerusalem in 661 and established Damascus as the new capital of the Islamic Empire. He granted a substantial pension to Hasan, Ali's eldest son and possible rival; Hasan retired from politics and spent the rest of his life in Medina. Mu'awiyah generally appointed able and vigorous governors to oversee the far-flung empire and engaged in lively discussions on governmental policies with the notables in Damascus. Many of the officials were Syrians or had been administrators in the Byzantine Empire. Thus many Byzantine traditions and cultural achievements were assimilated within the Umayyad caliphate. Commanding the strongest army within the empire, Mu'awiyah launched a series of attacks against the remaining territories of the Byzantine Empire in present-day Turkey and, as previously noted, tried but failed to take Constantinople, the Byzantine capital.

Simultaneously, Muslim forces in Egypt and northern Africa continued to extend their influence. With Berbers from North Africa and other new African recruits from the sub-Saharan regions, they succeeded in moving across the Strait of Gibraltar in 710 and 711. From there, Tarik, the Berber commander, smashed the Visigoths and incorporated half of Spain under his command. The Muslims called the territory Al-Andalusia, Land of the Vandals, and proceeded to create in Spain a vibrant civilization that was to last for nearly eight centuries. The Muslim forces, known as Moors in western Europe, also made continual forays across the Pyrenees, reaching as far as Tours, only 234 miles south of Paris. Although they remained a military threat for decades, they never succeeded in incorporating France into their empire. As a result, the rest of Europe remained predominantly Christian, while Islamic governments prevailed in the Iberian Peninsula, across North Africa, and in western Asia, excepting for those parts of the Anatolian Peninsula (present-day Turkey) still held by the Byzantine Empire.

During the Umayyad Caliphate, similar expansions occurred in central Asia. Al-Hajjaj, viceroy in the eastern provinces, conquered Samarkand and surrounding territory in central

Asia. Simultaneously, Muslim forces marched into northern and western India, conquering the lower Indus Valley (Sind) in 712. The majority of the populations in these territories gradually converted to Islam, and the areas became part of the Islamic world.

The Split between Sunnis and Shi'i

Before his death, Mu'awiyah had his son, Yazid, accepted as his heir and thereby instituted the procedure of hereditary accession to the caliphate. Yazid was a better warrior than administrator, and during his reign a major schism of immense importance to the future Islamic world occurred. After the death of Ali's eldest son Hasan, his younger brother Husayn became the leader of those who had continued to support Ali's cause and to oppose Umayyad rule. Husayn refused to recognize the legitimacy of Yazid. With a small, poorly equipped force, he advanced against Yazid's army. The two rival sides clashed on the field of Kerbala, a city south of contemporary Baghdad on the tenth of Muharram (October 10, 680). Husayn and his badly outnumbered supporters were killed. Husayn's head was cut off and presented in a triumphal display to Yazid.

Husayn's martyrdom became the rallying point for opponents of the Umayyad Caliphate throughout the empire. Their opposition was based on a political division over who should rule, rather than on spiritual differences. The Shi'i or party of Ali maintained that the line of leadership should follow directly through the prophet's family. The Sunni, or Orthodox majority, contended that leadership could be bestowed on any able believer.

Kerbala, where Husayn was buried, became a major point of pilgrimage for the Shi'i, who marked his death in the month of Muharram with passion plays and ceremonies of self-flagellation. Ultimately, the Shi'i would become predominant in present-day Iran, which already differed from the Arabian Peninsula owing to its largely Farsi-speaking population and its unique cultural and historical identity. Shi'i also make up a sizable portion of the populations in present-day Iraq, Lebanon, the eastern Arabian Peninsula, and some other areas of the Islamic world.

The Shi'i ultimately split into a number of different sects, the most important of them being the Twelvers. They recognized the Imams (leaders) through Husayn's children and believed that the twelfth Imam, Muhammad al-Muntazar, disappeared into a cave in 878. According to Twelver Shi'i belief, Muhammad al-Muntazar did not die but went into occultation, a state in which other religious leaders could commune with him while he remained invisible. Twelvers believed that Muhammad al-Muntazar would return as the Mahdi (the rightly guided one) to save the world. As a result, the *mullahs* (clergy) assumed a special role within the Shi'i communities, which continued to look to the clergy for direction and leadership. The Shi'i clergy also established a hierarchy in which particularly knowledgeable and esteemed mullahs became known as *Ayatollahs*. In contrast, the orthodox, or majority, Sunni Muslims had neither an established clergy nor a hierarchy of religious notables.

In addition, a number of other splits developed among the Shi'i. Some argued that the fourth Imam, Zayid, was the last real Imam; they became known as Zayidis and in the contemporary era are found mostly in Yemen. Others held that Isma'il, the seventh in line, should have been recognized as the last infallible Imam. They ultimately established communities in Tunisia and India. From Tunisia their leaders, the Fatimids, established an independent Fatimid Caliphate in Cairo in 969. Cairo subsequently became a rival for power and glory to the eastern capital in Baghdad. (These dynasties are described in Chapter 8.)

The Establishment of the Abbasid Caliphate

The Umayyad Caliphs in Damascus had increasing difficulties keeping the diverse and widely scattered peoples of the empire under their sole control. From the onset, the provinces in North Africa, Spain, and Egypt had been largely self-governing under the local provincial governors.

Meanwhile, the growing wealth and increasingly secular behavior of the Umayyad rulers caused mounting opposition, even in Syria and Arabia. The rulers' lavish lifestyles had also corrupted many within the ruling circles, and it became increasingly difficult to attract recruits to fight for the Umayyads. Rumors that the Umayyad Caliphs drank wine, expressly forbidden to Muslims, and that one caliph even swam in a pool filled with wine, were all used by the Umayyads' opponents to gain adherents from among the devout Muslim/Arab communities.

Rebellions became increasingly frequent. One group, the Abbasids, who were led by the great-grandson of the Prophet Muhammad's uncle, gathered support from the Shi'i and from disgruntled groups in Iraq and Iran. In 747 the Abbasids called for an open revolt against the Umayyad caliphate and within three years had defeated the Umayyads at a decisive battle near the Tigris river. In 750 Damascus fell and the Abbasids promptly attempted to eliminate all members of the Umayyad family. One, Abd al-Rahman I, fled to Spain, where he established a new dynasty that lasted for nearly 300 years. The Abbasid leader, Abu al-Abbas, was proclaimed caliph at Kufah in 749 and proceeded to establish a new caliphate (see Chapter 8).

Summary and Comparisons

As the Roman Empire declined, the Christian church effectively replaced the collapsing political system as the temporal ruler. In Europe, Christianity swept aside all other competitors and outlived the Roman Empire.

In the fourth and fifth centuries, barbarian invasions finally overwhelmed the defenses of the Western Roman Empire. In contrast to China, where one dynasty led to another with a continuation of most cultural and political institutions, the collapse of Rome led to sharp changes in European institutions and society. Although internal deficiencies of the type discussed in the comparative essay preceding this chapter played a part in its collapse, Rome perished more from assault than from senility. From this point on, the distinctive Greco-Roman civilization was modified at the hands of the Germanic kingdoms of western Europe and the Byzantine Empire to the east, both already on the scene by 500. Another heir, the Islamic Empire, was emerging just over the horizon.

In the Latin west, Germanic peoples practiced subsistence agriculture in tribal societies under weak kings; many African societies were organized along the same lines. In

CHRONOLOGY

30 B.C.E.	Crucification of Jesus
73	Masada
	The Gospels
400	
	Augustine, *City of God*
	Attila the Hun
	Last emperor of Rome
	Justinian I
	Hagia Sophia
600	Islam: Muhammad
	The Qur'an
	Battle of Yarmuk
	Byzantines use "Greek fire"
	Split between Shi'i and Sunnis
	Umayyad Calipahte
	Abbasid caliphate
	Islam spreads to East Indies and Iberian Peninsula
	Umayyad predominance in Spain
800	Charlemagne and the Carolingian Renaissance
	Olga, princess of Kiev
1000	
	al-Cid
	Romanesque architecture
	Vernacular literature begin in Europe
1100	
	Gothic architectural style begins
1200	Francis of Assisi
	The Magna Carta
	Beginning of universities in Europe
	Philip II, "The Fair"
	Thomas Aquinas, *Summa Theologica*
1300	
	Dante Alighieri, *The Divine Comedy*

Europe, one people, the Franks, became prominent. By adopting Roman Catholic Christianity and requiring Romans and Germans to work together, King Clovis provided a basis for new political and cultural development. Creative individuals preserved elements of the classical heritage, and innovative religious leaders gave new directions to western European life.

During the period 750–1000, Carolingian rulers unified the Frankish kingdoms and dominated western Europe. They created an adequate, if loosely organized, governmental administration and used an effective army to expand their territories. They also stimulated a modest, mostly religious, literary and artistic activity, sometimes called the Carolingian Renaissance. Charlemagne, the greatest Carolingian ruler, was crowned Holy Roman emperor by the pope in 800. During the ninth century, however, Carolingian rulers engaged in civil wars, and the empire disintegrated into small, weak states, just as similarly organized central powers in western and eastern Asia had disintegrated in earlier centuries.

During the ninth century, Muslim, Magyar, and Viking invaders completed the breakup of the Carolingian Empire and local warlords rose to prominence. Different European regions responded by creating a variety of social and political relationships. Feudalism, a system of mutual obligations between lords and vassals, was the most notable of these new relationships. Kings struggled with popes and the nobility and in many cases increased their political control.

During the medieval period, western and central Europe underwent important economic and cultural changes. The population doubled, agriculture expanded, and town life, trade, and manufacturing grew. Christianity remained vigorous; in particular, monasteries met the religious needs of a generally pious population; however, religious minorities generally were not well treated; and Jewish communities, especially in western Europe, suffered increasing discrimination.

A lively cultural life emerged in Europe during this era. The first European universities were founded during the late Middle Ages, encouraging philosophical and theological studies. The rudiments of the modern scientific method and outlook were also established, thanks in part to the translation of Greek and Arabic scientific works. In the late Middle Ages, literature, art, and architecture also reached great heights.

Despite the German conquest of the western portions of the Roman Empire by 500, the eastern Roman or Byzantine Empire continued to prosper. Its rulers retained Rome's political and social structure and fostered both Christianity and secular Greek culture. Justinian I, the greatest Byzantine ruler, codified the law and promoted intellectual and artistic activity.

Just as Rome, weakened by domestic problems, succumbed to outside conquerors, the Byzantine Empire ultimately did, too. By 1200 rebellions in the Balkans had led to the creation of independent states and the growing Arab/Islamic Empire took large pieces of territory in western Asia. In the thirteenth century, Latin crusaders propped up the Byzantine state for a short period of time, but the state never regained its former vitality. This left the way open for its final overthrow by the rising power of the Ottoman Turks.

While the history of the Byzantines was one of gradual decline, that of the Muslims was one of explosive expansion. Islam proved to be not only a dynamic new religion but also a force for political and economic unity. From 622 to 632, under the leadership of the prophet Muhammad, Islam was accepted by most of the tribes in the Arabian Peninsula. The first three caliphs following Muhammad's death initiated a series of military conquests that had established Islamic societies from the Indus River in the east to Spain in the west by 750. Like earlier centrally organized empires in Asia and the Western Hemisphere, the Umayyad caliphs at Damascus fostered a vibrant new culture by encouraging the arts and education. Islamic universities in Cairo and North Africa flourished. Like universities in Christian Europe, Islamic institutions of higher education also emphasized theology and philosophy, albeit from a differing religious and world viewpoint. All in all, Islamic expansion from West Asia to Africa and East Asia was one of the most rapid and far reaching in human history.

Eventually, the Muslim community, like the earlier Byzantine, Mesopotamian, and Egyptian Empires and some Chinese dynasties, also fell prey to open civil strife. This ultimately fragmented the Islamic world into a number of competing political centers. In addition, the community of Muslims split between the Sunnis, who thought the right to rule could be exercised by any believer, and the Shi'i, who maintained that rule should follow through Muhammad, Ali, and their successors. This schism was the major cause for the collapse of the Umayyad Caliphate in Damascus and the emergence of the rival Abbasid Caliphate in Baghdad. Similar divisions in Christianity would later threaten the hegemony of the Catholic church and fragment political leadership in Europe.

Selected Sources

Items indicated with an asterisk (*) are available in paperback.

*Abu-Lughod, Janet L. *Before European Hegemony: The World System* A.D. *1250–1350*. 1990. An intriguing discussion of the patterns of cultural and commercial interaction across Eurasia in the period covered.

Akkad, Mostapha, dir. *The Message*. A historically correct and spectacular epic film about Muhammad and the early converts to Islam. Also available in videotape.

*Amt, Emilie, ed. *Women's Lives in Medieval Europe: A Sourcebook*. 1993. A valuable collection of primary documents.

*Angold, Michael. *The Byzantine Empire, 1025–1204*. 1997. This political history provides a fine overview of the empire during a key period of change.

Armstrong, Karen. *Islam: A Short History*. 2000. A good, concise overview by a leading theologian.

*Bayard, Tania, ed. and trans. *A Medieval Home Companion: Housekeeping in the Fourteenth Century*. 1991. A handbook of instructions written for his fifteen-year-old bride by an elderly citizen of Paris around 1393.

Benjamin of Tudela. *The Itinerary of Benjamin of Tudela: Travels in the Middle Ages*. Rev. ed. 1987. This twelfth-century travelogue, by a Jewish native of Navarre, contains fascinating descriptions of hundreds of cities: Baghdad, Constantinople, Alexandria, and Jerusalem, among others.

*Benko, Stephen. *Pagan Rome and the Early Christians*. 1984. A good account of the collision of paganism and Christianity in the Roman world.

*Brown, Peter. *The World of Late Antiquity: A.D. *150–750*. 1971. Especially valuable for its coverage of religious and cultural developments and of the transition from antiquity to the Middle Ages.

"The Byzantine Empire." Insight Media. Two-part video (thirty minutes each) tracing the empire's glory and long decline.

Chuvin, Pierre. *A Chronicle of the Last Pagans*. Trans. B. A. Archer. 1990. A recent account of the momentous changes in religious life in the Roman Empire as seen from the pagan vantage point.

Clark, Gillian. *Women in Late Antiquity: Pagan and Christian Life-styles*. 1993. An engaging and highly informative treatment of women's lives, based on an intimate familiarity with the primary sources.

*Davis, R. H. C. *A History of Medieval Europe: From Constantine to Saint Louis*. 2d ed. 1988. A thorough, highly readable, and up-to-date history.

*Endress, Gerhard. *An Introduction to Islam*. 1994. A balanced reference work on the basics of Islam and Muslim practices.

"The Five Pillars of Islam." Films for the Humanities. Video on Islamic faith in historical context.

Fleischer, Richard, dir. *The Vikings*. 1958. An adventure story treatment of Viking activities; filmed on location in Norway and Brittany.

*Gardner, John. *Grendel*. 1971. An enthralling short novel that retells the Beowulf story, but from the point of view of the monster!

*Gottfried, Robert S. *The Black Death: Natural and Human Disaster in Medieval Europe*. 1983. An engrossing account of the causes, course, and consequences of the great plague.

*Gregory of Tours. *The History of the Franks*. Trans. Lewis Thorpe. 1976. In this work, a sixth-century bishop describes the history and illuminates the life of his people.

*Hinks, Roger. *Carolingian Art*. 1962. Provides a useful insight into the ideas and values of the period as expressed in painting and sculpture.

*Hourani, Albert. *A History of the Arab Peoples*. 1991. Splendid chapters on social development, demographic movements, and historical issues.

"Islam and Christianity." Films for the Humanities and Sciences. This thirty-minute video explores the long and often hostile relations between two major world religions.

*Kaegi, Walter. *Byzantium and the Early Islamic Conquests*. 1992. A military history of the early clashes between the Byzantine and Muslim Empires.

*Kagan, Donald, ed. *The End of the Roman Empire: Decline or Transformation?* 3d ed. 1992. A good anthology of essays constituting a helpful, brief survey of major theories.

*Kennedy, Hugh. *The Prophet and the Age of the Caliphates*. 1986. An excellent introduction to the rise and growth of Islam to the eleventh century.

*Mattingly, Harold. *Christianity in the Roman Empire*. 1967. An extremely concise and cogent account of the subject; originally a series of lectures.

Medieval Epics. Trans. William Alfred et al. 1963. Includes *Beowulf, The Song of Roland, The Nibelungenlied,* and *The Poem of the Cid*.

Momigliano, Arnaldo. *Essays on Ancient and Modern Judaism*. Ed. S. Berti, trans. M. Masella-Gayley. 1994. The essays on the Jews in ancient Greek and Roman society are especially valuable.

*Moriarty, Catherine. *The Voice of the Middle Ages in Personal Letters, 1100–1500*. 1989. This compendium of 200 letters includes selections from Petrarch, Dèrer, Da Vinci, and Eleanor of Aquitane.

Nicol, Donald MacGillivray. *The Byzantine Lady: Ten Portraits, 1250–1500*. 1994. Fascinating account of women within the empire.

Norwich, John J. *Byzantium: The Decline and Fall*. 1996. A thoughtful analysis, particularly of the schism between the Roman Catholic and the Eastern Orthodox churches.

Reynolds, Susan. *Kingdoms and Communities in Western Europe, 900–1300*. 2d ed. 1997. An excellent, very current study that stresses both social and political history.

*Riché, Pierre. *Daily Life in the World of Charlemagne*. Trans. Jo Ann McNamara. 1978; reprinted 1988. A fascinating survey of the topic; gives an engrossing account of the activities, values, and preoccupations of people on all strata of society.

———. *The Carolingians: A Family Who Forged Europe*. 1983; trans. M. I. Allen. 1993. A thorough investigation of the Carolingian era in medieval history.

Todd, Malcolm. *The Early Germans*. 1992. An account of the changes brought by the migration of Germanic tribes throughout Europe and North Africa between 400 and 600.

*Tuchman, Barbara W. *A Distant Mirror: The Calamitous 14th Century.* 1978. A riveting account, with a focus on the life of a French knight.

Vermes, Geza. *The Complete Dead Sea Scrolls in English.* 1997. This is the best and most complete edition of the scrolls published to date.

Williams, Marty, and Anne Echols. *Between Pit and Pedestal: Women in the Middle Ages.* 1993. Features lively, accurate recreations of the everyday lives of women of many social classes and occupations.

*Wilson, David M. *The Vikings and Their Origins: Scandinavia in the First Millennium.* 1989. An excellent recent treatment of the subject; good illustrations.

*Winston, Richard. *Charlemagne: From the Hammer to the Cross.* 1954. A lively biography of the emperor by a modern popular writer.

Ziegler, Philip. *The Black Death.* 1969. A useful discussion of the social and economic consequences of the plague that swept through Europe in the fourteenth century.

 Additional resources, exercises, and Internet links related to this chapter are available at the Book Companion Web site: http://history.wadsworth.com/upshurcompact4/

6

Disruption and Renewal in South and East Asia

•

• India from the Guptas to the Muslim Dynasties •

• Indianized Southeast Asia •

• China's Second Imperial Age •

• China Partitioned: The Sung and Nomadic Dynasties, 960–1279 •

• Two Sinicized States •

• Japan: The Merging of Chinese and Native Cultures •

• Summary and Comparisons •

Then Amaterasu . . . commanded the heir apparent saying:

"Now it is reported that the pacification of the Central Land of the Reed Plains has been finished. Therefore, descend and rule it, as you have been entrusted with it."

Then the heir apparent replied saying:

"As I was preparing to descend, a child was born; his name is Ninigi. . . . This child should descend."

Hereupon, she [Amaterasu] imparted [unto Ninigi] the myriad Maga-Tama beads and the mirror which had been used to lure, as well as the sword . . . and said:

"This mirror—have [it with you] as my spirit, and worship it just as you would worship in my presence."*

On September the ninth the decree was given. Henceforth the T'ang Imperial Dynasty was abolished, and the new one was to be called Chou. . . . [Empress Wu] assumed the audacious title "Holy Spirit Emperor." It was an advance from "Holy Mother Divine Sovereign" [a title she had earlier assumed]. At last her ambition was realized. She was a "female emperor," not an empress only. The term "Holy Spirit" constituted also an advance toward divinity.**

*Kojiki, trans. Donald L. Philippi (Princeton: Princeton University Press; Tokyo: University of Tokyo Press, 1969), pp. 137–140.

**James P. Holoka and Jiu-Hwa L. Upshur, eds., *Lives and Times: A World* History Reader (Minneapolis/St. Paul: West Publishing, 1995), vol. 1, p. 183.

Anthropologists and historians speculate that early human societies were matrilineal. Evidence supports this thesis in Japan, where the Shinto founding myth tells how the Sun Goddess Amaterasu began Japan's imperial line. The items that Amaterasu gave to her grandson became the three imperial treasures that symbolize sovereignty to this day. Early Chinese travelers corroborate the matrilineal thesis with accounts of a Japanese ruler called the sun princess, and a number of empresses in fact ruled during Japan's first historic centuries.

In China, a patrilineal society, with a sharp division between male and female spheres, has prevailed throughout recorded history. Daughters were denied the right of political succession, although mothers and wives often exercised great power in both the government and family. Empress Wu of the T'ang dynasty has the unique distinction of deposing and killing her own sons to succeed her dead husband as female emperor. She gave herself titles that were unprecedented in Chinese history and attempted to establish her own dynasty. Ill health, however, forced her to retire at age eighty and her experiment came to an end.

In both India and China, a period of invasions and upheavals followed the first great imperial age. As in western Europe after the Roman Empire collapsed, when imperial restraints crumbled and new peoples arrived, India experienced an age of innovation and creativity.

The Gupta dynasty reunified northern India in the fourth century C.E.; during its two-century rule, Indian culture reached its golden age. Hinduism began the evolution that has continued to the present day while Buddhism began its irrevocable decline. Islam became a force on the Indian subcontinent from the beginning of the eighth century, and by 1000 C.E. Muslims from central Asia controlled all northern India. Although unable to ward off the invaders, Hinduism and Hindu culture survived. Buddhism, however, vanished from India. The Gupta and post-Gupta period saw the expansion of Indian culture throughout a great part of island and mainland Southeast Asia through a peaceful transmission by Indian traders, missionaries, and immigrants.

China fragmented soon after the collapse of the Han dynasty in 220 C.E.; nomadic invaders ruled the North for three centuries while weak native dynasties ruled the South. Buddhism now became the dominant religion, enriching Chinese civilization with its teachings and the Greco-Roman-Indian artistic traditions. China was reunified in 581 and entered a grand second imperial age under the T'ang dynasty. China was powerful and cosmopolitan under the T'ang, absorbing from other cultures and passing on its great achievements. The following Sung dynasty refined many earlier traditions but failed to continue the diplomatic and military successes of its predecessor. Cultured, urban, and refined, the Sung suffered repeated military reverses before its ultimate conquest by the Mongols in the thirteenth century.

Chinese political power expanded Chinese civilization to Korea and Vietnam starting around 100 B.C.E. Japan voluntarily accepted most aspects of Chinese civilization and sinicized Buddhism. In Southeast Asia, Korea, and Japan, distinctive cultures emerged from the fusing of Indian and Chinese influences with indigenous traditions.

This chapter will explore the forces of disruption and renewal that shaped India and China and their enduring legacies at home and abroad.

India from the Guptas to the Muslim Dynasties

The people are numerous and happy; they have not to register their households, or attend to any magistrates or their rules; only those who cultivate the royal land have to pay a portion of the gain from it. . . . Throughout the country the people do not kill any living creature, nor eat onion or garlic.*

He caused distress to no man in the city, but he chastised the wicked.

   Even in this mean age he did not fail the trust of the people.

   He cherished the citizens as his own children and he put down crime.

   He delighted the inhabitants with gifts and honours, and smiling conversation, and he increased their love with informal visits and friendly receptions.**

*H. H. Gowen, *History of Indian Literature* (New York: Appleton, 1931), p. 336.
**A. L. Basham, *The Wonder That Was India* (New York: Grove Press, 1954), p. 104.

The first passage was written by Fa-hsien, a famous Chinese pilgrim who traveled and studied in India during the Gupta period. The second, which was found on a contemporary rock inscription, describes the exemplary provincial administration under an early Gupta king. Both accounts describe a well-governed land under the Gupta dynasty, which had succeeded in uniting northern India. The Guptas and Harsha were the last of the Hindu/Buddhist monarchs to rule over a united and flourishing northern India. Soon after Harsha's death, the region was subjected to centuries of Muslim invasions that permanently changed the religious composition of the subcontinent.

The Gupta Empire, Harsha, and the Rajputs

With the breakup of the Kushan state, northern India was once again fragmented into numerous petty states. Early in the fourth century, a minor prince named Chandra Gupta rose to power in the Delhi region where the Jumna and Ganges Rivers converge. Around 320, after victories in war and marriage to the princess of a powerful tribe, he crowned himself "Great King of Kings," an act that began the Gupta era. By the time he died in 335, the Gupta dynasty ruled the Ganges River valley, the heartland of the earlier Mauryan Empire.

In several respects the early reigns of the Gupta dynasty seemed a reenactment of the Mauryan era. Chandra Gupta I was followed by his son, Samudra Gupta (reigned 335–376). Most of the information about him comes from a eulogy inscribed on an Asokan pillar, praising him as a great warrior who had "violently uprooted" nine kings in northern India, an act that won him the title of "exterminator of all other kings." Samudra Gupta added large parts of northern India to his direct rule and made vassals of the remaining rulers. He was also a cultured man, a capable administrator, tolerant of different religions, and a patron of the arts. The reign of his son Chandra Gupta II (reigned 376–415) was the high-water mark of the Gupta Empire, to which he added the Deccan region.

The early Gupta dynasty is India's classical age because it established the standards in culture and the arts that later eras looked to for inspiration and example. Just as the Greek ambassador Megasthenes' observations provided insights into the Mauryan Empire, another foreigner, the Chinese Buddhist pilgrim Fa-hsien, supplied information about life in the reign of Chandra Gupta II. Fa-hsien traveled widely in India between 405 and 411 and spoke glowingly of the efficient and benevolent government and a merciful justice system, the rarity of crime, and the generally peaceful state of the land. He marveled that one could travel from one end of India to the other without fear of molestation and without need of passports. On social customs and mores Fa-hsien said: "In this country they do not keep swine or fowls, and do not deal in cattle; they have no

Map 6.1 The Gupta Empire.
The great early Gupta rulers conquered most of northern India and gave that area an extended period of peace and prosperity. But even at its height, the Gupta Empire did not control southern India.

shambles [butcher shops] or wine-shops in their market places. In commerce they use cowrie-shells. The Pariahs alone hunt and sell flesh." He also recorded the grandeur of the capital city, Pataliputra, its great religious processions, and the charitable institutions maintained by people of means. Considering the conditions in a divided China and the problems besetting the contemporary late Roman Empire, India under the early Guptas was without doubt the best-governed and most prosperous empire in the world.

The later Guptas, who reigned after 415, were mostly undistinguished rulers, and northern India once again came under attack by invaders. The White Huns, called Huna in India, were nomads from central Asia, who may have been related to the Huns who threatened Europe in the same period. The Huna invaded India repeatedly in the fifth century; much of northwestern India, especially Buddhist establishments in the region, suffered enormous damage from their depredations. Some historians claim that the earlier Chinese defeat of the Hsiung-nu and Gupta resistance of the Huna led other Hunnish tribes to move further west and eventually penetrate the Roman Empire. Resistance to the repeated invasions weakened the Gupta Empire, which disappeared by 550. It was replaced by minor rulers who had once been Gupta vassals and by Hunnish and related tribal states.

The Roman Empire from 14 to 117 C.E.

Shown here is the Roman Empire in the reign of the emperor Augustus and, a century later, in the reign of the emperor Trajan, when it had reached its greatest extent.

Germanic Invasion Routes

This map shows the avenues of invasion and immigration followed by the various Germanic tribes that finally overwhelmed the Roman Empire's defenses, beginning in the late fourth and early fifth centuries.

Medieval Trade Routes

By the end of the thirteenth century, trade routes covered most of western and central Europe. Vikings in early centuries and the German Hansa later controlled commerce in the northern seas. In the south, the Italian cities of Genoa and Venice dominated Mediterranean trade. Overland routes used rivers wherever possible to reduce transportation costs. In eastern Europe, however, trade routes were few, and the economy remained primarily agricultural.

The Expansion of Islam

Most of Islam's early territorial gains were at the expense of the Persian and Byzantine Empires. The former was entirely absorbed, the latter, already diminished by German gains, lost Syria, Egypt, and all of its North Africa possessions. Muslims then advanced into the Iberian Peninsula and France in the west and toward the banks of the Indus River in the east.

In 606 a sixteen-year-old young man named Harsha ascended the throne of a petty state in the Jumna-Ganges valley. He ruled for the next forty-one years and nearly succeeded in restoring the glory days of the Guptas. Two contemporary sources provide information about Harsha (reigned 606–648). One is the *Life of Harsha,* a biography by a protégé named Bana; the other is the journal of Hsuan-tsang, a celebrated Chinese pilgrim who spent fifteen years on the subcontinent, eight of them in Harsha's dominions, and kept a voluminous account. According to Bana, Harsha upon becoming king "went from east to west, subduing all who were not obedient." He was so busy that "the elephants were not unharnessed, nor the soldiers unhelmeted." In six years he had subdued all northern India, but was not able to gain control of the Deccan and the south. He then reigned in peace for thirty-five years.

Harsha was a gifted and energetic ruler. He traveled constantly to render justice and to supervise the government. Although inclined toward Buddhism, he nevertheless patronized all religions. A distinguished scholar and patron of learning, he was also the author of three plays. Harsha was a lavish sponsor of charities and built many hospitals to dispense free medical care to the poor and travelers. According to Hsuan-tsang, on one occasion for seventy-five days Harsha and his retinue distributed the wealth of the treasury and his personal possessions to half a million people, until nothing remained "except for the horses, elephants and military accouterments, which were necessary for maintaining order and protecting the royal estate, nothing remained."

Soon after witnessing Harsha's remarkable largess, Hsuan-tsang, who had been away from home for sixteen years, decided to return to China. He refused all Harsha's gifts except for a fur cloak and money for his traveling expenses. But he was laden with the treasures for which he had come to India. They included 651 manuscripts and numerous relics and images of the Buddha and Buddhist saints. Harsha's escort accompanied the Chinese pilgrim to the frontier of his realm. When Hsuan-tsang arrived at Changan, the Chinese capital, in 646, he was welcomed as a great celebrity by the Chinese emperor, his court, and thousands of ordinary people.

Thanks to the bond established by Hsuan-tsang, Harsha exchanged ambassadors with the Chinese emperor T'ai-tsung. When T'ai-tsung's third envoy arrived in India, however, he found Harsha had been assassinated and his throne usurped. In a remarkable demonstration of Chinese power, the ambassador rushed to Tibet, where T'ai-tsung's son-in-law was king, raised an army, and returned to defeat the usurper, who was arrested and taken to China as prisoner. Nevertheless, Chinese intervention could not save Harsha's kingdom from disintegration.

Superficially there were many similarities between the Gupta administration and that of the Mauryans. The great accomplishment of the Mauryans had been the creation of a highly centralized empire of continental proportions. The Guptas, however, failed to reduce their local administrators to total obedience. The town and village councils and the professional guilds also remained largely autonomous. Inadequate revenue compelled the Guptas to pay official salaries partly in land grants, with the result of a rise of local power. Thus the king's authority was limited to those areas under his direct control.

When the Mauryan Empire fell, the people of the Deccan and southern India had freed themselves and established independent kingdoms. The inscriptions that have survived,

Life during Harsha's Reign

With respect to the ordinary people, although they are naturally light-minded, yet they are upright and honourable. In money matters they are without craft, and in administering justice they are considerate. They dread the retribution of another state of existence, and make light of the things of the present world. They are not deceitful in their conduct, and are faithful to their oaths and promises. In the rules of government there is remarkable rectitude, whilst in their behaviour there is much gentleness and sweetness. With respect to criminals and rebels, these are few in number, and only occasionally troublesome. . . . As the administration of the government is founded on benign principles, the executive is simple. The families are not entered on registers, and the people are not subject to forced labour. The private [holdings] of the crown are divided into four principal parts; the first is for carrying out affairs of state and providing sacrificial offerings; the second is for providing subsidies for the ministers and chief officers of state; the third is for rewarding men of distinguished ability; and the fourth is for charity to religious bodies, whereby the field of merit is cultivated. In this way the taxes on the people are light, and the personal service required of them is moderate.*

These comments about India by the Chinese Buddhist pilgrim Hsuan-tsang paint a picture of good government and contented people under Harsha. They agree with observations of other Chinese pilgrims who had visited India somewhat earlier during the Gupta dynasty. In this way Harsha's reign forms the finale of the Gupta era.

*Si-Yu-Ki Buddhist Records of the Western World, *translated from the Chinese of Hiuen Tsiang* (A.D. 629) *by Samuel Beal (London: Truther, 1884), pp. 83, 87.*

the remains of cave temples, and the records of Chinese pilgrims agree that Buddhism flourished throughout the region in the post-Mauryan centuries. South India was prosperous because it produced spices and precious stones desired by the Romans and other peoples. Since the first century C.E., increased knowledge of the winds and currents brought about a flourishing sea trade between south Indian ports and the Persian Gulf, the Red Sea, Southeast Asia, and China.

Harsha was assassinated in 648. Amidst the political anarchy that followed in northern India, the first of many Muslim armies crossed the mountains in the northwest and appeared at the plains of the Indus in 712. While some Muslims raided and then retreated, others came to stay. In these actions they were no different from earlier invaders, but, whereas the Greeks and central Asian tribal raiders that preceded them had been rapidly assimilated, the Muslims, with their rigidly defined religion, largely retained their separate identities.

Religious Developments: Hinduism and Buddhism

Modern Hinduism gradually emerged during and after the Gupta era. The intellectual basis of Hinduism was revitalized as the brahmans expounded the philosophy of the Upanishads and debated Buddhist theologians. At the same time, in response to the challenge of Buddhist and Jain teachings, ways of life for the ordinary Hindu also began to evolve. They were called the Way of Worship and the Way of Works. All Hindus believed in the law of karma, that deeds had their consequences; they hoped by following dharma or the sacred law, they could finally attain *moksha* (release from the round of reincarnations). While some brahmans and ascetics studied the philosophy of the Upanishads and thus followed the Way of Wisdom, most men and women followed the more attainable Way of Worship or the Way of Works.

In the Way of Worship, a devotee chose a personal deity and did his or her bidding, attended temple ceremonies, and took pilgrimages. While the Vedic gods receded in importance, three earlier obscure gods emerged to the forefront. One was Brahma, the creator god and the personified universal spirit of the Upanishads. The primary objects of worship, however, were Vishnu (patron god to many Gupta rulers), the benevolent preserver god, and Shiva, the fearsome god of death and fertility. Myths about the gods were collected in the Puranas, the equivalent of the Bible of popular Hinduism. As the Puranas told believers, Vishnu has been reincarnated nine times, and each time he saved the world from demons and evil forces. His early incarnations, or *avatars,* were in animal form—for example, the Fish, who saved Manu, the father of the human race, from the Cosmic Flood. The seventh incarnation was Rama, the perfect man, the deified hero of the epic *Ramayana,* who is worshipped together with his faithful wife Sita, the ideal woman. The eighth incarnation was Krishna the "dark [skinned]," probably originally a non-Aryan god of the south. Stories about Krishna's pranks as a youth, his popularity with ladies as a young man, and his championship of moral duty as a mature man are known and loved by all Hindus. His ninth incarnation was Gautama Buddha. The admission of Gautama into the Hindu pantheon blurred differences between Hindus and Buddhists and hastened the absorption of Buddhists into the orthodox Hindu fold. After the twelfth century, with the destruction of the remnants of the great Buddhist establishments in northern India by Muslim conquerors, Buddhism finally vanished from the land of its birth. The tenth reincarnation of Vishnu is yet to come. Vishnu was worshipped with his wife Lakshmi, the goddess of good luck; the two are frequently depicted together in affectionate poses.

While millions worshipped Vishnu, other millions, mainly in southern India, called themselves devotees of Shiva. In addition to death and fertility, Shiva was identified with the Vedic storm god Rudra and was also patron god of ascetics, lord of the dance, and the embodiment of cosmic energy. Shiva's wife

T. Richard Burton, Hindu Art; courtesy of The British Museum

Shiva. This eighteenth-century painting shows the male and female aspects of the god of destruction with the Bull of Nandi, Shiva's mount and a fertility symbol, below them.

manifested herself in different forms, often as the fertility goddess, perhaps the mother goddess of the Indus civilization. As Durga and Kali, she was bloody and terrible and demanded sacrifices. (Among those who worshipped Kali were members of a small sect called Thuggees, from which the English word "thug" derives. Thuggees specialized in robbing and killing travelers as acts of devotion to Kali.) Their pot-bellied and elephant-headed son Ganesha was the patron god of learning.

The gods and goddesses are represented by statues and pictures and are worshipped at home, in temples, and at special ceremonies with offerings of flowers, food, dance, and incense. Sites associated with them were also the destination of pilgrims. Fertility cults that worshipped the mother goddess and other symbols were popular throughout the land.

While worshipping their personal deities, Hindus were also encouraged to follow the Way of Works. It taught that all persons were born and reared in their respective castes and must follow caste rules. As an inscription of the Gupta dynasty says, good rulers should "keep the castes confined to their respective spheres of duty." In addition, all must repay their debts to parents and ancestors through the proper discharge of duty and responsibility to family, to seers through diligent study and proper respect, to the gods through worship, and to humanity through charity and kindness. In living up to the demands of the Ways of Worship and Works Hindu men and women hoped to acquire good karma and either in this life or future incarnations be able to follow the Way of Wisdom. These essential teachings and practices of Hinduism persist to the present.

The Guptas and Harsha patronized both Hinduism and Buddhism. Leaders of both religions held frequent theological debates. Jewish and Christian communities also appeared in India during this era. Some Jews came to India as refugees after the Great Dispersion of 70 C.E. Their descendents still live in Kerala on the southwestern coast of India, and are divided into two groups: the "white Jews," who claim to have retained their Semitic racial identity, and the "black Jews," who have intermarried with Indians. Most Indian Christians also lived in Kerala. They claimed descent from converts of the apostle Thomas, who had reputedly come to proselytize in India. They professed the Syrian branch of Christianity; many are prominent in modern India.

Art, Architecture, Life, and Culture

Indian art is inextricably linked with religion. Both Buddhist and classical Hindu art reached their peaks during the Gupta era, which saw the synthesis and climax of previous tendencies and produced the classic style that inspired much of the art of the entire Buddhist and Hindu world throughout Asia.

The goal of religious art, in India as elsewhere, was to express devotion and to make religious and philosophical ideals intelligible to all people. The greatest contributions of Gupta artists are their classical representation of the divinities of India. These works combine vigor, refinement, and sublime idealism with a sense of rhythm and movement. In sculptures of the Buddha, the ideal of serenity found its noblest expression and became the standard.

The most impressive surviving Buddhist sites are the cave temples. The grandest is Ajanta, located in the Deccan in an isolated hillside by a river valley. Although the caves were excavated more than a thousand years between the first century B.C.E. and the ninth century C.E., most were built during a great burst of artistic activity in the mid-fifth century. Each of the twenty-nine cave temples is entered through a portal into the main hall where two rows of columns divided the interior into a central nave and side aisles, in much the same way as the interior of Christian basilica churches is divided. At the far end of the hall is either a giant image of the Buddha or a stupa that commemorates his nirvana. A typical hall is sixty-five feet square, with a fourteen-foot-high ceiling. Beyond the halls and cut still deeper into the cliffs are the monks' quarters. Intricately carved columns and capitals, sculptures in the round, and friezes decorate the caves. The Ajanta caves can be compared with the Acropolis, built in Athens a thousand years earlier. Both exemplify the highest artistic accomplishments of their respective culture's classical periods, and both were built to honor the gods and the achievements of the people.

A remarkable number of fresco paintings have survived in Ajanta; they are hailed as among the greatest wall paintings anywhere in the world. Although the subject matter is Buddhist, many scenes are drawn from contemporary life. The depictions of voluptuous ladies and sumptuous scenes illustrate Indian reconciliation of the sensuous and worldly with the spiritual and religious.

Revitalized Hinduism, already strong in the Gupta period, was represented in cave and free-standing temples. In addition to several Ajanta caves that were Hindu, other contemporary cave temples were dedicated exclusively to Hindu deities. Shiva and Vishnu were most often represented in these Hindu shrines. In contrast with the serenity exhibited by Buddha statues, Vishnu and Shiva are often shown in poses full of dynamic energy; they frequently appear in association with their female counterparts. A remarkable eighth-century Hindu temple dedicated to Shiva is located near Ajanta. The immense structure is actually not a building in the conventional sense. It was literally carved out of the rock of a hillside, a rare technical feat.

Metal casting also reached its apogee. The castings range from an eighty-foot-tall copper image of the Buddha at Nalanda to the huge wrought Iron Pillar of Delhi that would have been a feat for even the best foundries of the modern age. The rich variety of gold coins of the Guptas also showed artistic excellence. The highly developed aesthetic sense and excellent mastery of execution of Gupta sculptures made them the ideal and despair of artists of later generations.

Literature and scholarship in India always depended in part on court patronage. The Guptas patronized many genres of the arts. Literature ranged from refined court poetry to popular fairy tales and fables. "Sinbad the Sailor" and several other stories popularized in *A Thousand and One Nights* originated in India.

Whereas Egyptians wrote on papyrus and the Chinese invented paper, the first surviving Indian books that date to the fifth century were written on birch bark and specially prepared leaves. The resurgence of Hinduism resulted in the revival of Sanskrit, now used in Hindu as well as Buddhist and Jain writings. Other works from this period dealt with law, medicine, and the sciences. Indian scholars devised a sign for zero and worked out a decimal number system, knowledge that was transmitted to the Arabs and later adopted by the rest of the world, which called it the Arabic numeral system. India also led other cultures in knowledge of algebra and is largely credited with founding modern mathematics. Astronomy became a separate discipline. Astronomers found out that the earth was round and rotated on its axis and calculated the length of the year to almost the exact length we know today.

Formal education for men was offered at both brahmanical and Buddhist institutions. The curriculum resembled that in medieval European universities and included theology, grammar, rhetoric, logic, metaphysics, prose and verse composition, and medicine. Interestingly, the first works on veterinary medicine date to Gupta India and dealt mainly with horses and elephants, probably because of their value in the army. The famous university at Nalanda had an international student body that included men from China, Ceylon, and Southeast Asia. Students received free board and tuition from the revenue of lands that had been donated to the monastery. There were no schools for girls, though upper-class girls were taught at home. The only women with a life independent of the family were Buddhist nuns, actresses, courtesans, and prostitutes. The courtesan was a cultured female companion, like the hetaera of ancient Greece and geisha of Japan.

Towns grew, many with specialized functions or crafts for domestic consumption or export. Many towns were planned with streets that were oriented to cardinal points, with drains and wells. The rich lived in brick houses, the poor in houses made with wattled bamboo. Public parks provided places for recreation and musical performances. Popular culture flourished. Frequent religious festivals lent color to daily life. People participated in processions and elaborate religious festivals at richly decorated temples, the dwelling places of gods and goddesses.

The family was patriarchal, land was owned jointly by the extended family, and women were subordinate to men, but children were taught to obey both parents. Marriages were arranged by parents and took place when both parties were very young. Except for those of princes, unions were monogamous. Because of the hot climate, clothing tended to be scanty and loose fitting, except in the cold north, where people wore close-fitting jackets. Men often wore only a loincloth, sometimes with another piece of fabric thrown over the body. Women wore a *sari* or a long piece of cloth wound around the waist in folds, falling to the feet, and draped across the shoulder. Both sexes wore long hair, loose or braided, and both, especially women, adorned themselves with jewelry and flowers.

Hsuan-tsang described Indians as clean and fastidious in manners. He said of their eating habits:

> Before every meal they must have a wash; the fragments and remains are not served up again; the food utensils are not passed on; those which are of pottery or of wood must be thrown away after use, and those which are of gold, silver, copper or iron get another polishing. As soon as a meal is over they chew the tooth-stick and make themselves clean. Before they have finished ablutions they do not come in contact with each other.

At death the mighty and humble alike were cremated. The virtuous upper-caste widow committed *suttee,* or suicide at the funeral pyre of her husband.

India under the Impact of Islam

In 712, two generations after the death of Harsha, an Arab army conquered Sind, in northwest India, an event heralding the powerful role that Islam would soon play in the history of India. Earlier attackers had been assimilated over time, but these Muslim invaders would not be, because their iconoclastic monotheism was incompatible with Hinduism and Buddhism. Although the zeal of some early Muslim conquerors embittered relations with Hindus, some lower-caste Hindus found dignity in the religious equality that Islam accorded to all believers and converted voluntarily.

The Arab invaders of 712 did not penetrate beyond Sind and generally lived in amity with their neighbors. Meanwhile, the Arabs conquered and converted the Turks of central Asia. Ferocious warriors, now on behalf of Islam, the Turks at first enlisted as bodyguards of their Arab rulers but in time asserted their independence and established their own states. Some Turkic slave bodyguards even established slave dynasties. In 1023 Mahmud of Ghazni, in present-day Afghanistan, rode into India with 30,000 mounted warriors, pillaging and killing as they went. Mahmud called himself the "image-breaker," because he delighted in destroying Hindu and Buddhist places of worship and killing "nonbelievers." His soldiers boasted that they massacred 50,000 Hindus in one Hindu shrine city alone.

Turkish conquerors after Mahmud continued to wreak havoc on Buddhist and Hindu institutions and places of worship. Countless Hindu, Buddhist, and Jain shrines were demolished; some of their stones were recycled to build mosques and monuments to commemorate Muslim power. The Qutb Minar (victory tower) in Delhi was partly built with stones from demolished Hindu and Jain temples. The great Buddhist university at Nalanda, its library filled with priceless manuscripts, was destroyed. Buddhism never recovered from those blows. Hinduism survived in northern India, but without the state patronage that had allowed it to blossom intellectually it turned inward. The caste system became more rigid, and, in compliance with Muslim standards, women became more secluded and wore the veil in public.

Some Indians, most notably the Rajputs of northern India, fought the invaders bravely. *Rajput* means son of a king. Rajputs were kshatriyas (warrior caste), and according to their genealogies they belonged to thirty-two clans that descended from the sun, the moon, and the stars. Modern scholars think that they were descended from the Huna and other previous invaders who had become assimilated and had created fake genealogies to lend themselves greater dignity. Like the knights of medieval Europe and the *samurai* of Japan, they were fiercely proud hereditary warriors. The young Rajputs were brought up on epic stories of old. On reaching puberty, boys went through a ceremony called the binding of the sword, which bound them to a code of honor that included respect for women. The men disdained manual labor; they either fought or hunted and played manly sports. Women enjoyed considerable freedom; they hunted and even went to war with their husbands. On the other hand, when her husband died

A Rajput Lady's Creed

"Boy, tell me, ere I go, how bore himself my lord?"

"As a reaper of the harvest of battle! I followed his steps as the humble gleaner of his sword. On the bed of honour he spread a carpet of the slain, whereon, a barbarian his pillow, he sleeps ringed by his foes."

"Yet once again, oh boy, tell me how my lord bore himself?"

"Oh mother, who can tell his deeds. He left no foe to dread or to admire him." She smiled farewell to the boy, and adding, "My lord will chide my delay," sprang into the flame. *

The Rajputs loved epics about heroic deeds in battle and the hunt. The stories, sung by bards, celebrated the heroism of both men and women. In this tale, the widow asked her fallen husband's page about his death at the Muslim siege of Chitor; then she sacrificed her life to honor him. Other tales told of Rajput ladies committing mass suicides at the news of their husbands' deaths in battle, rather than surrender to the Muslims. They built a huge funeral pyre and leapt into the flames.

*H. G. Rawlinson, India: A Short Cultural History, p. 202, quoted in James Tod, Annals and Antiquities of Rajasthan (London: H. Mitford, 1920), vol. 1, p. 246.

in battle, a Rajput woman was expected proudly to mount his funeral pyre and commit suicide. When not fighting Muslim invaders, Rajputs often fought among themselves. Indian bards composed and recited epic poems that celebrated the brave deeds of Rajput lords and ladies in customs similar to those of the ancient Macedonian chieftains and medieval European knights.

The Rajputs never became a united force and were defeated by the conquering Muslims. Since Hindu society clearly demarcated functions, only the kshatriyas had a duty to fight. On the other hand, when Muslims subjugated ever larger territories, the social cohesiveness of the caste system enabled the Hindus to persevere and thus preserve their way of life.

During these centuries, politically divided southern India escaped Muslim conquest and the ravages suffered by the north. Temple building, culture, and art flourished in the south, and, with northern India under Turkish Muslim rule, it was here that Indian styles and trends in art and architecture persisted. Southern Indian culture also inspired and influenced the Indianized states of Southeast Asia.

Indianized Southeast Asia

The city is twenty li [three li equals a mile] in circumference and is pierced by five gates, each with two portals. . . . A huge moat protects the wall spanned by massive bridges. Fifty-four stone carved warrior deities stand guard on either side of each bridge, looking huge and fierce. All five gates are similar. . . .

The city wall is twenty feet tall and made of stone, so well fitted together that grass cannot grow in the crevices. There are no crenellations. . . . On the inside of the wall there is a sloping earthen rampart over a hundred feet wide, pierced by gates that are open during day hours and closed at night, and watched by guards. . . .

In this country most trading is done by women; that is why as soon as a Chinese man arrives in the country he marries a local woman, to help him in business. Every day the market opens at six and continues until noon. Trading is not done in shops, but by displaying the goods on a mat spread on the ground. Each merchant has an allotted space. . . .

I do not think gold and silver are found in this country, and that is why they desire above all gold and silver from China. Next in demand are lightweight and heavyweight textiles, tin wares, lacquered dishes, celadon glazed ceramics, and mercury, vermilion, paper, sulphur, saltpeter . . . linen, yellow grass cloth, umbrellas, iron pots, copper trays, fresh-water pearls, tung oil, bamboo nets, baskets, wooden combs and needles. . . .*

*James P. Holoka and Jiu-Hwa L. Upshur, eds., *Lives and Times: A World History Reader,* Vol. 1 (Minneapolis/St. Paul: West Publishing, 1995), pp. 278–280.

This description of Angkor Thom, the splendid capital city of the Khmer kingdom, was written by Chou Ta-kuan, a Chinese member of the embassy sent by the Mongol ruler Kubilai Khan to demand Khmer's submission to the Mongol Yuan dynasty in 1296. Chou also described the desirability of many types of Chinese goods and the important role of Khmer women in local commerce, which made them useful wives to Chinese merchants who wished to succeed in business locally.

Indian Economic and Cultural Expansion

Although the nature and extent varied from region to region, Indian influence assumed a major role in the development of Southeast Asia during the first millennium C.E. For this reason Southeast Asia is often referred to as Greater India or Indianized Asia. Similarly, Asia Minor, southern Italy, and Sicily were called Magna Graecia or Greater Greece because the ancient Greeks migrated to those areas where they introduced important elements of Greek culture. Since the beginning of history, Southeast Asia's natural resources had been a magnet for international trade. Indian traders were the first to come; along with brahmans and Buddhist monks, they settled throughout Southeast Asia. Trade and settlement were vehicles for the spread of Indian culture, especially among the elite. Local chiefs modeled themselves on Indian rajas and invited brahmans to perform their court rituals in accordance with the Vedic traditions.

Once the resources of Southeast Asia became known, trade developed on a large scale. Skilled Indian mariners developed seaborne trade routes that carried exotic goods throughout much of Asia and as far as the eastern provinces of the Roman Empire. The early Indian traders ventured to Southeast Asia, where many of the items that the Romans wanted, such as spices, gold, resins, and scented woods, were found. When the Parthians (Iranians) cut off the gold supply from Siberia and declining trade with Rome cut off India from the gold of the Roman Empire, Indians sought an alternative source in Southeast Asia. Some Buddhist *jataka* stories told of princes and nobles sailing abroad to make their fortunes; others mention the Island of Gold to the east of India.

Trade led to settlement that developed into colonies. Local peoples, especially the elite, who admired the sophisticated Indian way of life emulated it. India's cultural influence in Southeast Asia was achieved entirely by peaceful means and continued for over a millennium. No military expeditions were launched from India to maintain Indian power in the lands where its cultural influences held sway. After the fall of the Roman Empire ended the Indian role as middlemen, the increasing demand in India for the

Courtesy of Margot Duley

Buddha's Nirvana. This colossal stone image of the reclining Buddha from Polonnaruwa, Sri Lanka (formerly Ceylon), is forty-six feet long. It dates to the twelfth century, when Buddhist missionaries from Ceylon continued to exert great influence in Southeast Asia.

products of Southeast Asia supported continued trade. Indian trade served as conduit for religion, as Buddhists and Hindus introduced their faiths throughout the regions, especially in present-day Burma, Thailand, Cambodia, and Java. This direct influence waned after the thirteenth century, however, when Hindu and Buddhist Indian merchants and missionaries were replaced by Indian and Arab merchants of Muslim faith, who also spread Islam.

Except for northern Vietnam, which was a Chinese cultural and political satellite, Chinese contacts with Southeast Asia were mainly mercantile and technical. The Chinese treasured the ivory, pearls, hardwoods, and other products of Southeast Asia, and a small number of Chinese merchants settled in the region, as the opening document of this section showed. China also adopted a strain of early-ripening rice from Champa in present-day southern Vietnam. Although most of the merchandise brought by Chinese traders to Southeast Asia has perished, large quantities of Chinese ceramics dating from the Han dynasty and later have survived. Some local peoples called china pots "singing jars" because they made a resonant sound when struck. The ceramics were buried in graves or handed down and preserved as treasured heirlooms. Local potters in Thailand, Vietnam, and other lands learned the technology and art of ceramic making from Chinese potters. Some of their products were modeled after Chinese originals, whereas others reflected local taste. Other Chinese inventions and innovations in agriculture and metallurgy were also passed along to Southeast Asian lands.

Mainland Southeast Asia

Although geographically closest to India, Burma (recently renamed Myanmar) did not come under Indian influence until the Gupta period. Around 500, Theravada Buddhist missionaries arrived from Ceylon and converted the people of Burma to their branch of Buddhism, to which they have remained faithful to the present.

Abundant rice grown with irrigation made Burma prosperous. Pious rulers and people contributed lavishly to build thousands of Buddhist shrines at Pagan on the Irrawady River, the political and cultural center of Burma. Many Burmese monks went to Ceylon for study and ordination. Just as in Ceylon, Pagan shrines were usually stupas, which stood on stepped terraces that symbolized the sacred mountain of the Buddhist cosmos. The Pagan stupa was tall and highly ornate, with a bell-shaped dome.

By the late thirteenth century the dynasty that ruled from Pagan was in decline. In 1271 Kubilai Khan, the Mongol ruler of China (see Chapter 8), sent envoys to Pagan,

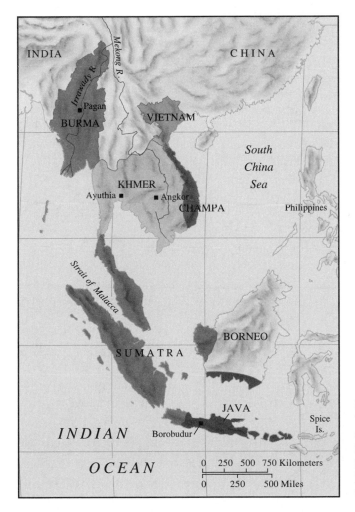

Map 6.2 Southeast Asia in the Twelfth Century. No one empire dominated either mainland or island Southeast Asia. On the mainland, the Khmer state was at its height; in the islands, various Indianized states warred against each other.

demanding submission and tribute. The Burmese king refused to receive them. Two years later, when another mission from Kubilai made the same demands, the Burmese king had the envoys executed. This meant war. The victorious Mongols annexed north and central Burma and devastated Pagan. Eventually the Burmese king acknowledged Mongol overlordship, but shortly after these events, Mongol power began to wane and Burma regained its independence. After a period of civil wars, Burma was reunified in the second half of the fourteenth century, but Pagan never regained its ancient glory and never became the capital again.

At the same time that the Buddhist religion and culture flourished in Burma, Indian influences inspired the Khmer people to build magnificent monuments and decorate them with beautiful sculpture and friezes. A Chinese chronicle of the third century described a kingdom called Fu-nan in the Mekong delta in present-day southern Vietnam, which had been founded in the first century by an Indian brahman who married a local princess. Indian culture was thus introduced to southern Indochina. In the seventh century, Fu-nan was conquered by its vassal state, Cambodia, which gave its name to the region.

The full flowering of classic Cambodian (Khmer) civilization between the ninth and the fifteenth centuries was the result of the blending of Indian civilization with Khmer ideas and ideals. At its height, the kingdom of Cambodia ruled present-day Cambodia, Laos, Thailand, parts of Burma, Vietnam, and the Malay Peninsula. Numerous Sanskrit inscriptions engraved in stone give many details of these centuries.

Hinduism and Buddhism came to Cambodia at the same time; Hinduism was preeminent till the twelfth century, Buddhism thereafter, although features of both remain to the present. Both Indian religions merged with local beliefs into a state cult of the god-king. Thus, although temples and statues were dedicated to Vishnu, Shiva, or Buddha, they were really funerary shrines for the divine king who commissioned them and who believed himself to be the earthly incarnation of that god. The art of Cambodia blended and integrated Indian concepts with traditional elements. The facial and physical features depicted in the statues and friezes are Cambodian. Using a folk style that incorporated many elements, Cambodian artists not only integrated Hindu and Buddhist themes but also depicted stories that celebrate Cambodian history and the glory of Khmer rule.

Between the tenth and twelfth centuries, the kings of Cambodia built a capital at Angkor Wat, which even in ruin is one of the architectural wonders of the world. For more than two centuries, each god-king built temples and decorated them with statues and reliefs to outshine those of his predecessors, just as Egyptian pharaohs had done in ancient times.

The most magnificent monument in Angkor Wat was built in the twelfth century as a temple for Vishnu and as a sanctuary of the divine king who identified with him. Here a series of terraced structures culminates in the central shrine 213 feet above the ground. The walls and galleries are decorated with narrative relief carvings of Hindu legends and Khmer history. They depict dancing angels and stories of Vishnu's different incarnation, together with military and other scenes that celebrate the power of the Khmer kings.

In 1177 Angkor Wat was sacked by the forces of Champa, another Indianized state located in present southern Vietnam. After repelling the attackers, the Khmer rulers built a new capital nearby called Angkor Thom, a magnificent square-shaped city surrounded by an eight-mile-long stone wall, and a wide moat (as the Chinese ambassador described in the passage at the beginning of this section) and provided with a remarkably complex drainage and irrigation system. The greatest monument in Angkor Thom is called the Bayan, a Buddhist shrine dedicated to a popular bodhisattva and the king who identified with him. The Bayan is a shrine with a forest of towers; the central one, which dominates the rest, is 150 feet high. All the towers are decorated with giant heads of the bodhisattva-god-king. Miles of friezes portray religious and secular scenes, among them the Khmer army and navy in action against the forces of Champa. The huge expense of building Angkor Wat, Angkor Thom, and other monuments at sites still unexcavated sapped the state's economy and contributed to its eventual decline.

Starting in the fourteenth century, the Khmer kingdom was increasingly threatened by Thai invaders from the west. In 1431 the Thais captured and looted Angkor Thom and carried off many prisoners. Without the bureaucracy to supervise and maintain the complex irrigation system, Cambodia's political power, art, and culture went into long decline after this disaster. Those Khmer leaders who survived fled south and established themselves in a new capital called Phnom-Penh, which is still the capital city of Cambodia.

The Thai or "free people" came from the borderlands of Burma, Tibet, and southwestern China. The advancing Chinese, and later the Mongols, had gradually pushed them south. By the twelfth century, the Thais had formed a united government. They were Buddhist converts, having established close ties with Ceylon and Burma and accepted Theravada Buddhism before arriving in Thailand around the twelfth century. Ayuthia, Thailand's first capital, was named after Ayodhia, capital of the legendary kingdom of Rama of the Indian epic *Ramayana*. Although Thais are Buddhist, they were also influenced by Hinduism, as evidenced by their decision to name their capital after a legendary city of Hindu epic. Even today Shiva and other Hindu deities are honored in Thai Buddhist temples and the Thai royal court maintains brahmans to perform religious ceremonies.

Pali, the language of Buddhist scriptures, became Thailand's sacred language, and an alphabet based on Sanskrit became the writing system and remains so today. The Khmer prisoners who settled in Thailand influenced their captors; Thai art and culture showed a heavy debt to Khmer models.

Although the iconography of Thai art, like that of most Southeast Asia, derived from Indian sources, in time it became uniquely Thai and no longer dependent on Gupta or Khmer models.

Island Southeast Asia

In the Gupta and post-Gupta period, Indians brought Mahayana Buddhism to Sumatra, Java, and Malaya. Indian writing systems, art, and architectural styles prevailed throughout the region. When the Chinese Buddhist pilgrim Fa-hsien returned to China from

Pictures of Life from Stone Reliefs

Two of these [reliefs] show us ploughing.... The plough is drawn by a pair of bulls, the yoke resting on the shoulder in front of the hump, with a collar round each beast's neck. The plough itself is the ordinary primitive square shape, by which one side scrapes along the ground and forces the ploughshare into the earth; the other side sticks up with the top bent over to the back and guided by the hand of the ploughman who walks behind and directs it with his left hand, holding a stick in his right....

Another example of work . . . is the potter's. . . . On one side we see the jars already made, on the other side the potter is at work, using a flat stick to get a good shape. Bearers with carrying-poles are bringing large round balls, it may be clay or gourds with water. Women and children are looking on....

In a goldsmith's [shop] the purchaser, seated opposite to the merchant, is holding a pair of scales, in one scale there is a ring and in the other there seems to be a bag of money.*

Although very little written material has survived describing life in ninth-century Java, the miles of reliefs of Borobodur, some depicting daily life, give vivid pictures of all classes of people in their daily pursuits. They give substance to the saying that a picture is worth a thousand words.

*N. J. Krom, Barabudur: Archaeological Description, vol. 2 (The Hague: M. Nijhoff, 1927), pp. 227–229.

Ceylon by sea in 410 C.E., he sailed on a ship that carried over 200 passengers. Such ships regularly plied the route between Ceylon and the islands in Indonesia where Buddhism had become a thriving religion. In the seventh century, another Chinese pilgrim studied Sanskrit in a monastery with more than 1,000 monks on Sumatra (an island of present-day Indonesia) and wrote that "many kings and chieftains of the Southern Ocean admired and believed in Buddhism."

Java, Sumatra, and other islands attracted traders from China and India, for gold, tin, ivory, camphorwood, and, above all, spices were much in demand in China and India; Indian sailors also carried these items to West Asia for shipping to Europe.

The growing world demand for spices, especially pepper, which was used for preserving meat, had a powerful influence on the history of all Southeast Asia, especially the islands. Two factors outside Southeast Asia played key roles in the economic development of the region: the Crusades and the policy of the Chinese government. The Crusades aroused demand for Asian products in Europe and thus trade between the two continents, much of which either originated in or passed through Southeast Asia. Indian Muslims became middlemen in trade between East Asia, island Southeast Asia, and West Asia, from which the goods were transshipped to the Mediterranean. These merchants were also instrumental in the Islamization of Malaya and the Indonesian islands after the thirteenth century.

The trade policy of Southern Sung China also contributed to the region's economic development. Always in need of revenue to appease or fight its northern nomadic neighbors, the Chinese government encouraged the export of porcelains and other products to Southeast Asia, which stimulated economic development of the region.

The Sung government lacked the power and the desire to dominate Southeast Asia politically, but its successor, the Mongol Yuan dynasty under Kubilai Khan, demanded submission of the petty states on the island of Java. When some Javanese states refused, Kubilai sent a large naval expedition of 1,000 ships and 20,000 men in 1292 to conquer the island. It was a costly failure.

The art of the islands of present-day Indonesia is heavily indebted to India. Some of the greatest examples of Buddhist art are in fact found on Java. Around 800, Mahayana Buddhists at Borobodur on Java built the single largest Buddhist monument. Conceived as a representation of Mount Meru, the World Mountain, it is a succession of terraces. As pious pilgrims climb the terraces, they are symbolically leaving behind the world of desire and moving upward toward spiritual perfection and ultimate union with the cosmic Buddha who dominates the central stupa that crowns the whole edifice. Although the sculpture here follows closely the Gupta style, it also shows characteristics that are uniquely Javanese. The racial type portrayed is Malay rather than Indian, the figural style is softer than that of India, and the scenes depicted are uniquely Javanese. Moreover, the ten miles of relief sculpture of *jataka* stories and of scenes from the life of the Buddha show a narrative tradition that was more developed than in India. Many Hindu temples contemporary with Borododur have also survived on Java. They show the wide range of Indian cultural influences that prevailed on the island.

From the ninth century until the final triumph of Islam after the fourteenth, Hinduism replaced Buddhism as the predominant cultural force on Java and Sumatra. Great shrines were built to worship Shiva, Vishnu, and other deities of the Hindu pantheon. Ganesha, Shiva's son, the elephant-headed and pot-bellied god of learning, was especially popular. He was represented in two aspects, as the benevolent and protective deity and as a fierce god whose throne is ornamented with human skulls.

An extensive literature, written in a Sanskrit-derived alphabet, also date to the Hindu period. The *Ramayana* and *Mahabharata* epics were widely loved throughout the islands. To this day, their stories, modified by Javanese legends, are told in the popular shadow-puppet plays called *wanyang* and in dance and theatrical performances. Thus, although Hinduism survived only on the island of Bali, the influence of Hindu India remains strong in the culture and language of Indonesia to the present day.

Although Chinese ships had traded with the present-day Philippine islands since the beginning of the common era, as Chinese coins and pottery excavated there prove, the islands remained largely isolated and politically fragmented. No stable states emerged, and despite the introduction of Indian writing, few written materials survive. Thus the Philippines did not fully enter the historic era until their conquest by Spain in the sixteenth century. Four centuries of Spanish rule made the Philippines culturally, politically, and socially closer to Latin America than Asia.

China's Second Imperial Age

At this time in the city of Ch'ang-an there were not more than one hundred families. Weeds and thorns grew thickly as if in a forest. Only four carts could be found in the city. The officials had neither robes of ceremony nor seals. Instead they used tablets of mulberry wood on which their names and rank were inscribed. *

Outside the inner doors, the two court ladies with flowing purple sleeves,
Now turn to the throne to lead the procession from the audience chamber.
The spring wind blows the swirling smoke of incense in the hall,
The sunlight plays across the dazzling robes of the thousand officials.
We hear the striking of the hour from the clepsydra in the high tower,
*As a servitor standing near, I note that the Heavenly Countenance is joyful.***

*Charles P. Fitzgerald, *China: A Short Cultural History* (New York: Praeger, 1961), p. 260.

**Poem by Tu Fu, quoted in *Cities of Destiny*, ed. Arnold Toynbee (New York: McGraw-Hill, 1967), p. 147.

The first excerpt depicts Changan during the fourth century after the once-great capital of the Han Empire had been sacked and plundered by nomadic invaders. The city's desolation symbolizes the ruin of northern China during the age of disunity. The second is a poem by a famous T'ang poet describing a court ceremony of the rebuilt and once-more cosmopolitan Changan during the height of China's second imperial age.

As after the end of the Roman and Mauryan Empires, the dissolution of the Han dynasty was followed by three and a half centuries of disruption, wars, and invasions. Just as Christianity and the Latin language eventually built bridges between conquerors

Map 6.3 China in the Age of Disunity. China was partitioned between 317 and 580 C.E. While Hunnish and other nomadic groups called Tartars ruled North China, Chinese dynasties controlled the Yangtze Valley and lands to the south, with a disputed area between. While repeated invasions devastated North China, the south became developed for the first time.

and conquered in western Europe and became the basis of a common culture, Buddhism and the Chinese language and culture ultimately united the Chinese and their nomadic rulers. China, however, was more successful in restoring unity and rebuilding an empire than either Rome's successors in western Europe or the Guptas in India.

Political Turmoil and Barbarian Invasions

The age of disunity began in 220 when the ineffectual last emperor of the Han was forced to give two of his daughters to a powerful general in marriage and then to abdicate in favor of his son-in-law. The usurper's heirs soon met the same fate he had meted out to the emperor. The chaos in the Chinese world allowed the regrouped Hsiung-nu to renew their attack. They destroyed Loyang in 311 and burned the imperial library, causing irreparable loss, and in 316 also laid waste to Changan.

North China would be ruled by many groups of nomadic conquerors until the end of the sixth century. The Chinese peasant was reduced to serfdom or to slavery, working for a tiny class of alien rulers. Some of the elite fled to southern China and established a new capital at Nanking on the lower Yangtze. The mountain range that divided the Yellow

---

Northern and Southern Chinese Chauvinism

"Though the Wei [T'o-pa] Dynasty [that ruled north China] is indeed prosperous, it is still one of the Five Barbarians. The correct New Year's Day [i.e., the calendar] has been passed down from one generation to the next, and this surely exists only south of the Yangtze. The jade seal of the First Sovereign Ch'in Emperor [seal of legitimate rule] now belongs to the Liang Dynasty [that ruled south China]."

So said the rather drunken guest of honor at a banquet. He was from the southern court sent to the northern capital on a diplomatic mission. To this a northern nobleman replied:

"You are only using the area of the lower Yangtze as a temporary refuge, and there you live meanly in a corner of the empire.... Among your close-cropped gentry, there are none with strong and healthy looks, and your tattooed people [the aborigines] are endowed with bodies that are small and weak. They float about on your three rivers, row about on your five lakes—unaffected by ritual or music, not to be improved by laws and ordinance. Although the prisoners transported to the South under the Ch'in and Han dynasties brought in and intermixed the true Chinese speech [of the north], still the difficult southern languages of Min and Ch'u

*were not changed for the better.... You are steeped in these inherited ways; you have never felt the transforming effects of proper ritual; you are like the people of Yang-t'i [a notorious goiter area] of whom it is said that they don't know that a tumor is a deformity."**

The above exchange is interesting for several reasons. First, it shows that the northern nobleman, a man of nomadic roots, had become entirely Sinicized by the sixth century. By then intermarriage between Chinese and nomads had become so common that few pure bloods could be found any more. Second, it shows that after several centuries of partition, distinct cultures, with different dialects and ways of life, had developed that distinguished northerners from southerners. Third, it reveals the chauvinistic attitude northerners and southerners had toward each other. Each group claimed superiority, regarded itself as the true heirs of the Han, and accused the other of being tainted by lower cultures, whether that of the nomads of the north or that of the aborigines of the south. China would eventually be reunited by a northern nobleman of mixed Chinese and nomadic descent.

*Arthur Wright, The Sui Dynasty: The Unification of China, A.D. 581–617 (New York: Knopf, 1978), pp. 32–33.

from the Yangtze drainage basins became the boundary between the northern and southern kingdoms. Short-lived dynasties followed one another in both north and south. By the time China was once more reunified, southern China had built up its population and was fully acculturated. The refugee governments in southern China claimed, with some legitimacy, to be the true successors of the Han and attempted to keep alive ancient traditions. The shift of the center of gravity from northern to southern China would continue after the end of the era of disunity.

Given their small numbers and lack of experience in administering a sedentary people, the conquering rulers of northern China were forced to employ the remaining Confucian officials in their government. The new masters found themselves in a dilemma. To exercise effective control and to enjoy fully their new power, they needed to be located in the Chinese heartland. Thus in 494 the king of the T'o-pa—a Turkic tribe and the most successful and long-lived nomadic dynasty in North China, moved his capital from Tatung, in the frontier between agricultural China and the steppe grasslands, to the former Han capital Loyang. But in moving into China they risked losing their ethnic and cultural identity. In time the T'o-pa rulers became so Sinicized that they banned continued use of T'o-pa tribal names, clothes, and customs. They soon also lost their martial ardor. Since their rule was based on conquest, the softened T'o-pa were soon ousted by other nomads and became merged into the general population. Thus, even in northern China, Chinese culture survived to triumph, assimilating and absorbing the conquerors.

Buddhism in China

Ages of bloodshed are often ages of faith; so it was during the age of division in China. The most important intellectual trend in China during this disruptive period was the growth of Buddhism and its adaptation to Chinese conditions. In the process both Buddhism and China were changed.

Buddhism appealed to members of the upper class in southern China because as exiles from their ancestral homes in the north they needed the consolation of religion. Being literary men, they discussed and studied Buddhist teachings, contacting Buddhist centers in India and Ceylon by sea to obtain original texts. Buddhism reached a high point under Emperor Wu (reigned 502–549) of the southern state of Liang, who compared himself with Asoka by giving up eating meat, forbidding animal sacrifices, convening religious assemblies, and building temples. To honor his father he built a monastic complex of thirty-six buildings that stretched for over two miles and housed a thousand monks. He encouraged people to join the *sangha* (Buddhist religious community) and did so himself several times. Also reminiscent of Asoka, Wu lost control over the government in his later years, and his dynasty quickly declined after his death.

In North China, where chaos frequently prevailed, Buddhist missionaries attached themselves to the ruling princes, who exercised control over the church and sought the monks' advice in return for protecting them. Missionaries from India and central Asia were welcomed in the courts of the nomadic rulers, who found the universalist teachings of Buddhism more congenial than the ideals of Confucianism. Buddhism exerted a civilizing influence on the nomads and also offered consolation to the oppressed peasantry.

Until the end of the fourth century, religious movements had gone one way, as missionaries traveled from India and central Asia to China. Fa-hsien was the first recorded Chinese Buddhist monk to travel to Gupta India to study and collect the canons and then return to China. He set off for India by the overland route in 399, studied at all the sites holy to Buddhism, and finally returned to China via Ceylon and the sea route, arriving in 413. He spent his remaining years translating the sutras (scriptural writings) that he had brought back from India into Chinese. Fa-hsien's journals gave valuable information on the history and geography of India and other lands where he had traveled and lived.

Fa-hsien's pathfinding journey started a movement that would continue for three centuries. Pilgrims who traveled to India and the lands in between brought back information and ideas that made Buddhism a vital intellectual force. It was a perilous journey, as a passage from Fa-hsien's journal narrated the real and imagined terrors of crossing the desert indicates:

> *In the desert were numerous evil spirits and scorching winds, causing death to anyone who would meet them. Above there were no birds, while on the ground there were no animals. One looked as far as one could in all directions for a path to cross, but there was none to choose. Only the dried bones of the dead served as indication.*

Shoshoin Treasure House, Nara, Japan

Five-String Lute. This Chinese-made musical instrument, shown front and back, probably originated in India, and its mother-of-pearl and tortoise shell decoration shows Persian inspiration. Musicians playing lutes and other instruments participated in T'ang court and religious ceremonies. This lute was taken to Japan, where it had similar functions. From the collection of a seventh-century emperor, it now forms part of Japan's national treasures.

Dedicated Buddhist missionaries and translators made their religion dominant throughout China; even sporadic government persecution did little to hinder its growth. Similarly, Christianity had triumphed in the Roman Empire despite periodic persecution. Nevertheless, it would be misleading to equate the triumph of Buddhism in China with that of Christianity in the Roman Empire because, unlike Western monotheistic religions (Judaism, Christianity, and Islam), Buddhism, Taoism, and Confucianism did not demand total loyalty from their followers. Most Chinese found no incompatibility in simultaneously honoring Confucius, worshiping Buddha, and practicing Taoist rites. To express this ideal, the Chinese coined a phrase: "Three ways to one goal," which reflects both Chinese religious tolerance and Buddhism's adaptability.

Classical Greco-Roman-Indian art entered China with Buddhism. Its progress eastward can be easily traced from surviving Buddhist monuments and works of art. The oases of central Asia were the furthest outposts of the classical Greco-Roman world and were also the melting pot where several cultures and peoples met and where merchants, missionaries, pilgrims, and local peoples mingled. Buddhist sculptors were at work at the oasis at Miran on the southern branch of the Silk Road in the third century, and their art, preserved by the dry desert air, shows a definite classical inspiration.

East of Miran, images of Buddha turn up next at Tunhuang, the westernmost Chinese settlement on the Silk Road. Beginning in the fourth century, pious Buddhists excavated cave temples in the cliffs at Tunhuang. Over several hundred years, they honeycombed a whole mountainside with the "Caves of the Thousand Buddhas," decorating them with frescoes that show the gradual fusion of Chinese and imported styles.

Between 460 and 494, an escarpment near the Great Wall outside Tatung (then capital of a northern Chinese dynasty ruled by nomads called T'o-pas), was carved with twenty caves and adorned with Buddhist frescoes and sculptures, the largest image of the Buddha being seventy feet high. The concept of the cave temples was Indian in origin. Stylistically the works were Greco-Roman-Gandharan, reminiscent of the Buddhist cave temple at Bamiyan in Afghanistan, modified to suit Chinese ideals of formalism and stylization.

When the capital of the T'o-pa dynasty was moved east to Loyang, a new series of cave temples was begun outside that city at a site called Lungmen, where work continued with interruptions until the eighth century. According to a recent count, 142,289 Buddhist sculptures still survive at Lungmen. The Lungmen sculptures show a fusion and synthesis of Greco-Roman, Indian, central Asian, and Chinese styles. Many lengthy carved inscriptions that accompany the sculptures also tell of the Sinicization of Buddhism. For example, many of the statues were commissioned by monks and nuns, who dedicated them to benefit the souls of their parents and ancestors. This shows that even in joining the sangha, Chinese monks and nuns retained their family loyalty. People from all social classes participated in commissioning statues and other works of art at Lungmen; they even formed societies that took up donations in order to accumulate funds for that purpose. Many inscriptions expressed the hope that all living things attain salvation, a clearly Mahayana message.

According to one account, Loyang around the year 500 had a population of 500,000 to 600,000 people and 1,367 temples. Built of wood, they have all perished. The cave temples at Tatung, Loyang, Tunhuang, and other sites, however, have survived to testify to the religious fervor of the period and the cosmopolitan nature of its art.

China Reunified: The Sui and T'ang Dynasties

The year 581 was a decisive one in Chinese history: in that year a northern nobleman named Yang Chien proclaimed himself emperor and established the Sui dynasty. Although it lasted only four decades, the Sui dynasty laid the foundation for the great and long-lived T'ang dynasty that followed.

Yang Chien was assisted by his able wife, the Empress Tu-ku. Like many other northern aristocrats at the time, both were of mixed Chinese and nomadic ancestry. Yang wisely used everything at his disposal—military force, diplomacy, religion (Buddhism and Taoism), and philosophy (Confucianism)—to forge an empire of continental proportions. He succeeded more completely than the Guptas in India and Charlemagne in western Europe, because China more than India and western Europe enjoyed the legacy of a unified language, written literary and historical traditions that extolled the ideal of unity, and an experienced bureaucracy that was shaped in Confucian learning and dedicated to public service.

The Sui dynasty did not long survive its frugal and wise founder because Yang Chien's son and heir was an unstable megalomaniac who reputedly murdered his father to gain

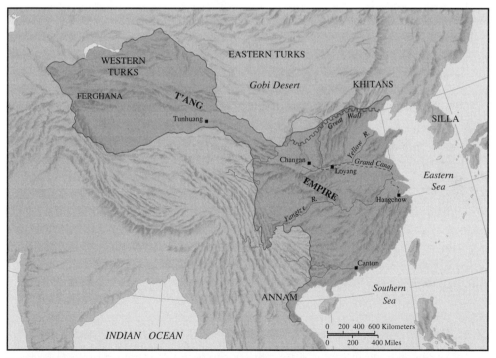

Map 6.4 T'ang China. The T'ang Empire at its height was more extensive and populous than the Han. The Pax Sinica, maintained by T'ang armies, allowed merchants, missionaries, and pilgrims to travel freely across central Asia to India, Persia, and points west.

University of Pennsylvania Museum (neg. #58-62844)

A Famous Battle Charger. The six horses that the T'ang emperor T'ai-tsung rode to his victories are commemorated in relief sculptures. This one and five others guard his tomb outside Changan.

the throne, as Alexander the Great reputedly had also done. But unlike Alexander's, his foreign military expeditions were costly failures. His overly ambitious public works projects and luxurious court life exhausted the treasury and angered the people. Revolts broke out everywhere, and chaos reminiscent of conditions at the end of the Ch'in again threatened to overtake China.

The chaos was short lived, however, because one rebel named Li Yuan (as the Duke of T'ang, he was a high official in the Sui government) quickly established a new dynasty. The Li family traced its genealogy to a famous Han general, and more fancifully to the mythical Lao Tzu (to whom later Taoist followers had given the surname Li). Most of the credit for Li Yuan's success is due to his second son, Li Shih-min. Then aged seventeen, he persuaded his timid father to revolt, fought to make his cause triumphant, and later succeeded him as emperor T'ai-tsung (the same ruler who sent his ambassador to the court of Harsha). The T'ang dynasty ruled from 618 to 907, an epoch that is remembered as one of the most brilliant in Chinese history. T'ai-tsung is revered as the most heroic ruler of all Chinese history. His generals were deified in popular lore; statues of the six horses he rode in campaigns guard his tomb and were remembered in ballads. Unlike Alexander the Great, who named a city after his favorite horse Bucephulus, T'ai-tsung did not name cities after his horses.

T'ai-tsung (reigned 626–649) established Chinese authority across Mongolia, Tibet, Afghanistan, and central Asia. In submitting, the Turks and Mongols acknowledged him their Grand Khan, the first Chinese ruler to be so honored. He was also an able administrator and valued the advice of honest critics. At the death of a minister who was also an outspoken critic, Wei Cheng, he said: "With bronze as a mirror one can correct his improper appearance; with history as a mirror one can understand the rise and fall of nations; with good men as a mirror, one can distinguish right from wrong. I lost one mirror with the passing of Wei Cheng." He tolerated all religions, promoted Confucianism in government and education, patronized Buddhism, and welcomed Nestorian Christians.

T'ai-tsung's son and successor, Kao-tsung (reigned 649–683), was best remembered for his infatuation with Lady Wu, his father's young concubine. At T'ai-tsung's death she was sent to a Buddhist convent. Kao-tsung paid a visit to the convent on the first anniversary of his father's death; when he left, he took Lady Wu with him. She later became her stepson's empress, and then killed and deposed her own sons to become China's only woman "emperor." Empress Wu ruled until she was eighty. She even attempted, but failed, to establish her own dynasty. Old and ill, she was forced to abdicate in favor of one of her surviving sons. Historians criticized the means she used to gain and maintain power (she killed and imprisoned many of her own children, stepchildren, in-laws, and officials who opposed her usurpation) and her scandalous private life—she took numerous young lovers (as did eighteenth-century Russian Empress Catherine the Great). When in her seventies she heard reports that her grandson and granddaughter made fun of her affairs, she ordered them to commit suicide. Nevertheless, she was a capable ruler, who brought Manchuria under Chinese rule and compelled the kings of Korea to acknowledge Chinese overlordship. This relationship between China and Korea continued until the late nineteenth century. She was also a devout Buddhist and endowed many temples.

T'ang prestige and prosperity reached its peak during the reign of Wu's grandson, Ming-huang, or the Brilliant Emperor (reigned 712–756). Ming-huang worked hard for most of his reign and was also a patron of the arts. The most celebrated poets of the age lived in his court and immortalized his reign with their unsurpassed poetry. But Ming-huang lived too long for his own or China's good. At age sixty he fell under the spell of Lady Yang, a young concubine of one of his sons. He took her into his own harem and abandoned himself to the pursuit of pleasure. She was famous for her plumpness and briefly made obesity fashionable; she was also immensely extravagant, which the doting and aged emperor allowed. Ming-huang's neglect of his duties and his elevation of her greedy and incompetent relatives and favorites to power had disastrous results: defeat by an Muslim army, which ended Chinese control of central Asia and destroyed Buddhism in that region, and a major rebellion led by Lady Yang's favorite, a general of Turkic origin and commander of "barbarian" mercenary soldiers. Ming-huang had to sacrifice Lady Yang to appease his angry loyal troops who blamed her for the rebellion and would not fight for him until she had been killed. His sacrificing her and subsequent abdication in humiliation became the subject of a famous romantic poem. Although the rebellion was

LIVES AND TIMES ACROSS CULTURES

Cultural Borrowing and Adaptation—The Chair

Although the chair was a part of life in ancient Egypt, Greece, and Rome, it did not exist in East Asia in antiquity. Until 1,000 years ago, the Chinese sat on mats placed over the floor, as do many Japanese even now. Their nomadic neighbors, and the Persians and Arabs with whom Chinese established contact about 2,000 years ago, also sat on rugs or mats. By the eleventh century, however, the Chinese had changed entirely to sitting on chairs and had altered their domestic architecture, the interior arrangements of rooms, and clothing styles to suit the new furniture.

Historian Charles P. Fitzgerald has studied the introduction of chairs in China and determined that a large folding camp stool, which the Chinese called a *hu-ch'uang* (barbarian bed), was introduced in the second century from the eastern provinces of the Roman Empire. It became popular for informal seating because it elevated the sitter from the sometimes damp and drafty floor, but he still curled his legs on the seat. Fitzgerald further established that by the mid-T'ang dynasty, around 800, the frame chair had been introduced, probably from the Byzantine Empire. The T'ang dynasty was a cosmopolitan period in China when many foreign customs were adopted. The Japanese monk Ennin, who spent many years traveling in China, noted that T'ang officials sat on chairs, but with their legs curled on the seat. Fitzgerald concluded:

In the more sophisticated Sung period which soon followed, the break with the old tradition gathered swift momentum. In A.D. 960 the great officials were furnishing their houses with chairs and tables; in the next century they were even designing their own furniture; by the dawn of the twelfth century the whole nation had given up on the floor and taken to chairs and benches.*

Interestingly, the Koreans and Japanese, who had always modeled their cultures on China, did not follow it in this important transformation.

*Charles P. Fitzgerald, Barbarian Beds: The Origin of the Chair in China (Canberra: Australian National University, 1965), pp. 49–50.

put down, the central government never fully recovered its authority, nor the dynasty its prestige and vitality. Slow decline set in; the final end came in 907.

An Enlightened Government and a Prosperous Economy

The key to the T'ang dynasty's success was the restoration of a stable central government, aided by the revival of schools and the examination system. The T'ang rulers reinstated and enlarged the Han system of examinations based on Confucian classics as the basis for selecting government officials. The government established a school system from the country up to the imperial university, open to most young men of talent. It administered examinations at regular intervals on several levels, recruited successful candidates into the civil service, and later rated them to determine promotions and dismissals.

Since bright young men were trained in the same curriculum in order to qualify for the examinations and public service, a uniform educational system emerged. Because Confucian ideology was the basis of the examinations, the schools produced a ruling class imbued with the same ethical principles and values. Even Buddhist schools offered a Confucian curriculum that helped poor boys realize their potential. The widespread use of paper, invented in the first century, made books cheaper. However, although printing was invented during the T'ang period, its general use, which would make books still cheaper and more widely available, did not happen until a later era.

The competitive examination system strengthened the T'ang state by turning men of intellectual ability into strong supporters of the government. It created an elite dedicated to government service and to the consensus that the learned and morally worthy should lead and represent public opinion. The perfection of the examination system and the bureaucracy of merit that it produced in T'ang and later eras was one of the greatest achievements of the Chinese civilization and a major reason for its stability and endurance. Their absence was detrimental to the Gupta and Carolingian dynasties' success.

The T'ang era was one of great economic prosperity. International trade flourished, and more caravans plied the Silk Road than during the best Han days. Meanwhile, the Yangtze valley had experienced enormous growth and development and had become the breadbasket (or rice bowl) of China. Realizing this, the Sui rulers built an extensive system of waterways, called the Grand Canal, to link up the Yangtze and lands further south with the Yellow River valley. The enormous drain of manpower and resources required by this project contributed to the popular discontent that ended the Sui dynasty. The Grand Canal allowed the T'ang to tap the abundant resources of the south.

T'ang prosperity was partly based on an ambitious land policy called the "equal field" system. It was an adaptation of the "well-field" system, supposedly instituted by the Duke of Chou, that had helped make the early Chou a golden age. Under the equal field system, all land theoretically belonged to the emperor or the state, which distributed about eighteen acres to every able-bodied man between twenty-one and fifty-nine years of age. Other categories of people—for example, widows who headed families and the elderly—received somewhat smaller allotments. The government then assessed taxes as well as labor on public works projects on the basis of the land allotment. It exempted certain able-bodied males from taxes in return for military service. This complex and largely equitable land and tax policy worked well for over a century. It was made possible by a capable bureaucracy that kept careful census and detailed land survey records.

China and the World Beyond

China was at its most cosmopolitan during the T'ang dynasty. Not until modern times would it again be so open to foreign influences. Two million people lived in Changan and its environs, making it the largest and most populous city in the world (for comparison, Constantinople around 600 had a population of about 1 million). The market places of Changan and other large cities bustled with life; Chinese mingled with people from Japan, Korea, Southeast Asia, India, and the many lands of central and western Asia. Some had come freely to trade, settle, or offer their services; others were brought as slaves. The rich vied with one another to include foreign grooms, entertainers, dancers, and musicians in their entourage. Foreign fashions became fads and foreign ways such as drinking grape wines and playing polo became fashionable.

A burgeoning middle class competed with the court and nobility for luxury goods. Central Asian horses were great status symbols. Judging from the numerous models of horses found in tombs, many people owned them. People loved expensive and exotic items, such as jewelry and gems from India and gold and silverware from western Asia, for their non-Chinese shapes and decorative motifs, their foreign ideas, and the foreign persons represented on them. Much of T'ang life can be reconstructed from the numerous pottery replicas of people, animals, and objects buried to serve the dead in the next world.

T'ang cosmopolitanism hinged on the dynasty's military power and the increase in international trade. Skillful military strategists, the early T'ang generals subdued the nomads from Manchuria westward to central Asia and posted garrisons at important points in the interior to maintain peace and secure trade. A strong martial spirit drew recruits to the army. The T'ang also produced several famous female warriors. T'ai-tsung's sister commanded troops and campaigned alongside him. Another young woman, Hua Mu-lan, disguised herself as a man and answered the call to arms for her aged father. According to tradition, she revealed her identity only years later at an audience before the emperor. A famous ballad celebrated her going to war:

> In the eastern market she bought a fine horse,
> In the western market she bought saddle and blanket,
> In the southern market she bought bridle and reins,
> In the northern market she bought a long whip.
> At dawn she set out from her parents' house,
> At dusk she camped at the Yellow River shore.
> She did not hear her father and mother calling to their daughter;
> She only heard the hissing voice of the Yellow River's flowing waves.
> At sunrise they set off and left the Yellow River,
> At dusk they camped beside the Black Water.
> She did not hear her father and mother calling to their daughter;
> She only heard the Hunnish horsemen shout across the hills of Yen.
> Ten thousand li she rode on many duties,
> Borders and mountains crossed as swift as flight.
> Through the northern night there sounded out the kettle-drum,
> In the winter daylight soldiers' armour gleaming. . . .

The flourishing international trade also contributed to the prevailing cosmopolitanism. The increased volume of trade and the need for a more efficient medium of exchange than metal coins brought about money drafts, the precursor of paper money. Invented in 811, they had the picturesque name of "flying cash."

T'ang international relations were of two kinds. One was between powerful China, under the Son of Heaven, and its dependent and subservient vassal states, particularly the various kingdoms of Korea, the many tribal states of the north and northwest, and Tibet. The presence of Chinese garrisons and the advantages of trade no doubt helped to maintain the overlord-vassal relationship between China and its small neighbors. China maintained equal relations with India, Persia, and the Byzantine Empire. T'ai-tsung and Harsha exchanged ambassadors, and China had diplomatic relations with the Sassanian dynasty of Persia for several centuries. The western limit of the Chinese world was the Byzantine Empire—Fu Lin to the Chinese. T'ang histories recorded four embassies from

Byzantium, probably sent to enlist Chinese military aid against rising Muslim power. No Chinese embassies were sent to Byzantium.

The Chinese government first heard about Islam in 638, when T'ai-tsung received an appeal for help from the king of Persia for aid against the advancing Arab Muslims. T'ai-tsung did not deliver military assistance, because of the distance and because at the time he had barely consolidated his own empire. Early in the eighth century, as Muslim armies advanced on central Asia and Afghanistan, the Buddhist states, which were sometimes Chinese vassals, sent urgent appeals to China for help. From the Muslim side, Caliph Walid also sent an ambassador to the T'ang court to urge against intervention. China did nothing to hinder the Arab advance. In 751 a Chinese garrison was routed by the army of Caliph Abul Abbas of the Abbasid caliphate in a battle near Tashkent, the only time the Chinese and the Arabs were engaged in hostilities. Soon afterward, Lady Yang's favorite began a rebellion, and the remaining T'ang garrisons were recalled from central Asia. The caliph even sent an army to help the Chinese defeat the rebels. Although the rebellion was crushed, the weakened T'ang government could not reassert its power in central Asia, and Muslim rule was established there.

The Apogee of Buddhism

Buddhism came of age in China during the early T'ang. Patronized by the court and supported by all elements of society, it served the ordinary people with festivals, lectures, and charitable activities. After the greatest Buddhist pilgrim, Hsuan-tsang, returned to China from India laden with precious manuscripts, he spent his remaining years translating them into Chinese. He was an indefatigable worker who alone was responsible for translating works equivalent to twenty times the volume of the Bible. The outpouring of religious works won Buddhism the respect of intellectuals. Hsuan-tsang also brought back many "genuine relics" of the Buddha, which became objects of veneration for millions of the faithful, in the same way that "relics" associated with Jesus, the prophets, and saints were venerated by Christians.

As Chinese Buddhist leaders studied the voluminous religious writings, several distinctively Chinese Mahayana Buddhist schools emerged. Three remained most important. T'ien-t'ai, begun about 600 and named after a famous monastery, reflected the Chinese tendency toward synthesis and harmony in the way it organized the vast body of Buddhist literature and recognized the validity of each sutra in its place. In this way, T'ien-t'ai muted the conflicts that had risen between different Indian schools of interpretation. This sect appealed primarily to the educated.

The Pure Land sect was named after the "Pure Land" or Western Paradise that the masses of Mahayana believers strove to achieve. It taught that salvation, or rebirth in the Pure Land, could be attained by faith, expressed through calling the Buddha's name. It appealed mostly to the common people, and thus had many followers.

The Ch'an (Zen in Japan) sect began in China in the sixth century. It was introduced by a semilegendary Indian missionary, Bhodidharma, who reputedly meditated for nine years facing a blank wall before he achieved enlightenment. Ch'an's antischolastic emphasis and stress on meditation and intuitive enlightenment derived at least in part

Buddha Is Highly Overrated

Now Buddha was a man of the barbarians who did not speak the language of China and wore clothes of a different fashion. His sayings did not concern the ways of our ancient kings, nor did his manner of dress conform to their laws. He understood neither the duties that bind sovereign and subject, nor the affections of father and son. If he were still alive today and came to our court by order of his ruler, Your Majesty might condescend to receive him, but it would amount to no more than one audience in the Hsuan-cheng Hall, a banquet by the Office for Receiving Guests, the presentation of a suit of clothes, and he would then be escorted to the borders of the nation, dismissed, and not allowed to delude the masses. How then, when he had long been dead, could his rotten bones, the foul and unlucky remains of his body, be rightly admitted to the palace? Confucius said: "Respect ghosts and spirits, but keep them at a distance!"*

Han Yu (786–824) was the author of this diatribe. He was a famous scholar-official and a staunch defender of Confucianism. He vehemently opposed Buddhism as an alien faith inimical to both Confucianism and Chinese society. The quotation was part of a memorial he presented to the emperor to oppose a planned ceremony in the palace to honor a supposed relic of the Buddha. Han Yu's rhetoric shows that he was opposed to Buddhism both because it was superstitious and because it originated outside China (he also opposed Taoism). The emperor, who was a devout Buddhist, was so enraged by the memorial that he exiled the author. Later Chinese hailed Han Yu as the early leader of the Confucian revival, and the memorial just quoted as the opening salvo of that movement.

*William T. de Bary, ed., Sources of Chinese Tradition (New York: Columbia University Press, 1960), vol. 1, p. 373. Reprinted with permission.

from philosophical Taoism, as did its love of nature and simplicity. Together with Taoism, Ch'an Buddhism was a major inspiration to artists and poets.

Buddhism reached its high-water mark in the early T'ang. Persecution in the midninth century marked the beginning of its decline. Confucians criticized Buddhism on several scores: it promised people what they could not have; it encouraged people to make donations they could ill afford; and its encouragement of celibacy undermined the social order and teachings of filial piety. Confucians also attacked the Buddhist church for its wealth, its tax-exempt status, and the unproductive life of its monks and nuns. Some of the criticisms were justified, but others were xenophobic and nationalistic, as Han Yu's memorial illustrated.

Rivalry between Buddhism and Taoism on occasion led to persecution of one faith or the other; in one instance, both religions were targeted at the same time. The most severe persecution of Buddhism occurred between 841 and 845, under a pro-Taoist emperor. The persecutions, however, were chiefly aimed at religious property and members of the clergy, and unlike religious persecutions in Christian Europe, they seldom bothered individual believers.

Buddhism's decline during the later T'ang was also attributable to competition from revitalized Confucianism. International developments also contributed. After the eighth century, Muslim armies seized territories from northwest India through Afghanistan and central Asia—lands that had hitherto been Buddhist. As a result, Chinese Buddhists were no longer able to maintain their contacts with their fellow religionists in India. Intellectually isolated, Chinese Buddhism ceased to be a vital religion.

In restoring the examination system, the T'ang monarchs gave emphasis to Confucian political ideology at the expense of Buddhism. Thus Confucianism became the basis of education and once again began to dominate intellectual life. Ironically, Buddhism contributed to its own intellectual decline by endowing Confucian schools to educate poor boys.

Zoroastrianism and Islam also entered China during this period; the former through Persian traders and later refugees from Muslim invaders. The son of the last Sassanian king was given a commission in the T'ang army. However, unlike the larger Persian refugee community in India, whose members retained their faith and remained a distinct group called the Parsees, the Persians in China were soon assimilated. Reputedly, many Muslim troops sent by the Caliph to assist in putting down the rebellion against Minghuang did not return home. They married local women and settled down in northwest China, founding the Muslim community there. Similarly, in the Roman Empire soldiers stationed in such far-off provinces as Dacia (Romania) and North Africa had settled and intermarried with local women. Before the end of T'ang, sizable settlements of Muslim traders had also been established in southern Chinese ports, most notably Canton. The Chinese government allowed them to elect their own leaders and to live by their religious laws.

The Golden Age of Poetry and Sculpture

The T'ang was a great creative epoch. Many fields of art flourished, but above all it was remembered as a golden age of poetry. About 3,000 poets from this period are known to us, and several of them are considered unsurpassed. One of the best loved was the romantic Li Po, who relished good wine with or without company, as he wrote in "Drinking Alone by Moonlight":

> *A cup of wine, under the flowering trees;*
> *I drink alone, for no friend was near.*
> *Raising my cup I beckon the bright moon*
> *For he, with my shadow, will make three men.*
> *The moon, alas, was no drinker of wine;*
> *Listless, my shadow creeps about at my side.*
> *Yet with the moon as friend and the shadow as my slave*

> *I must make merry before the Spring was spent.*
> *To the songs I sing the moon flickers her beams;*
> *In the dance I weave my shadow tangles and breaks.*
> *While we were sober, three shared the fun;*
> *Now we are drunk, each goes his way.*
> *May we long share our odd, inanimate feast,*
> *And meet at last on the Cloudy river of the sky (The Milky Way).*

According to popular legend Li drowned as he leaned out of a boat to embrace the moon during a drinking party with his friends. Great portraitists and painters of landscape also distinguished the age, but few of their works on paper and silk have survived.

Buddhist art and sculpture also reached maturity under the T'ang. Many consider this the great age of sculpture, which until the flourishing of Buddhism had been a relatively

Buddhist Cave Temple. The giant Buddha and attendants are part of a cave temple complex that dates to the T'ang dynasty and is located near the capital city, Loyang. The figures show Greco-Roman-Gandharan influence.

minor art form in China. In addition to monumental sculptures preserved in the rock cave temples, artisans also produced small metal images of the Buddha and bodhisattvas, thousands of which survive. The T'ang Buddha images reflect Chinese humanistic interest—they are lifelike and intimate and mirror contemporary concepts of beauty.

Because of the power and prestige of the T'ang, their artistic forms became an international style that spread to Korea, Japan, and other lands. The imperial ambitions of the early T'ang, which led to Chinese control of central Asia, also caused Chinese Buddhist art to move westward, back along the same routes into central Asia. In the early twentieth century, at Tunhuang and further west, Western scholar-explorers discovered long-sealed Buddhist cave temples that had been forgotten or buried for centuries in sand. The paintings and sculptures show that for a thousand years this area was a melting pot where Gandharan, Indian, central Asian, and Chinese styles met and synthesized. Archaeologists have coined the name Serindia for this now desolate area.

Secular sculpture also flourished. The most spectacular are the monumental human and animal figures that lined the path to the artificial earthen mounds that covered the imperial tombs. More than a thousand years later, they are vivid reminders of the power of the ruling house. The six relief sculptures of T'ai-tsung's battle chargers that guarded his tomb, with inscriptions that recount their deeds and wounds, tell poignantly of the close relationship between the man and his horses. T'ang tombs yielded tens of thousands of ceramic sculptures of horses, camels, grooms, officials, and entertainers that are minor masterpieces of the anonymous sculptors of the age. The countless other artifacts excavated from tombs, made of silk, jade, bronze, and other metals and materials all testify to the great prosperity and high artistic standards of that era.

China Partitioned: The Sung and Nomadic Dynasties, 960–1279

The [enemy's] heavy soldiery is entirely concentrated in the eastern capital. Having repeatedly suffered severe defeat, their morale has been destroyed. Within and without they are shaken and in alarm. According to intelligence reports I have heard, the enemy intends to abandon his baggage and hastily flee across the river. Moreover, now the loyalist guerrillas are responding to the changed situation. The officers and men are obeying orders. Heaven determines the course of human affairs in its own time . . . success is within our grasp. [Such] a time will not come again. The opportunity was hard [to come by] and can be lightly lost. . . . It is only for Your Majesty to desire it.*

**Edward Kaplan, "Yueh Fei and the Founding of the Southern Sung" (Ph.D. diss., University of Iowa, 1970), pp. 434–435.*

So urged Yueh Fei, the most successful general of the Sung dynasty and one whose memory as a great patriot is revered by Chinese to the present. Yueh was hoping to stiffen the ruler's resolve and win support for his successful campaign to oust nomadic invaders from North China and regain lost lands. The emperor responded as follows:

From the moment military operations began, We knew things must end with peace negotiations. . . . Military force was unavoidable, [but] how could we gain pleasure from offensive warfare? During this dynasty, [Emperor] Chen Tsung kept the peace with the Khitan for over one hundred years and the people did not know soldiers. Though [Emperor] Shen Tsung [the predecessor of the emperor who wrote this reply] talked of war and trained soldiers, actually he never used them. From the beginning until the present, We have thought only of peace. As We loved the people of north and south equally, We have taken the road of accommodation to defend them. (Kaplan, pp. 557–558)

Map 6.5 The Sung and Its Neighbors. The Sung dynasty never ruled the entire Chinese world. During the first part of the dynasty (960–1125), called the Northern Sung in retrospect, powerful nomadic states, the Liao and the Hsi Hsia, constantly menaced China.

Yueh Fei failed to win his emperor's support, and all the military advantage his army had gained was lost. The emperor's speech characterized the policy of the entire Sung dynasty toward the nomadic invaders—avoid war almost at any cost and buy peace whenever possible. The Sung was the most pacifist dynasty in Chinese history. Its love for peace and abhorrence of war were in part responsible for the loss of North China to several nomadic groups and later South China to the Mongols.

A Checkered History

The closing decades of the T'ang dynasty were wracked by civil wars brought on by power struggles between ambitious generals and mutinous troops. They continued for half a century after the T'ang ended in 907. While China was fragmented, much as it had been after the fall of the Han, the nomads once again began moving southward and attacking Chinese lands.

The Sung dynasty was born out of a mutiny. In 960 an adventurer who had recently proclaimed himself emperor in North China appointed a capable young general named Chao K'uang-yin commander-in-chief of an expedition against the nomads. His officers and men did not like their assignment and felt no loyalty toward the government, particularly after the emperor died and left an infant on the throne. They mutinied and hailed Chao their emperor; thus a new dynasty, the Sung, was born. Such "elections" of emper-

Chao K'uang-yin, Founder of the Sung Dynasty. Although this portrait shows him wearing civilian clothes, Chao K'uang-yin still looks the part of a powerful general. Most of his successors, however, showed no military aptitude and let the army decline.

National Palace Museum, Taiwan, Republic of China

ors by rebellious troops had been frequent in the Roman Empire and in post-T'ang China; they had usually led to more violence and bloodshed. The Sung was an exception, for soon after unifying the country the new emperor removed from their military commands those officers that had raised him to the throne. He did it, however, with tact and generosity, rewarding them with titles and pensions.

Domestically the Northern Sung enjoyed peace and prosperity. Even in its smaller territory, the population, over 100 million in 1114, surpassed peak Han and T'ang figures. Cities grew, as did an urban middle class. The printing press, now in wide use, made books cheap and commonly available, and literacy became widespread. For the first time, many men of middle class or humbler origins could afford to study for the examinations and realistically aspire to join the civil service.

The Sung government, pacifist and humane, was dominated by civilians. The two political parties, called the Conservatives and Innovators, settled their differences on social and economic policies through political and philosophical debates. The losers lost their jobs but never their heads. Kaifeng, a city south of the Yellow River, became the Northern Sung capital. Changan and Loyang, despite their fine strategic locations, would never be capitals of China again. Centuries of wars and invasions had so depleted the economy in their vicinities that they could no longer support a central government, and lack of good water transportation made it too difficult and expensive to provision those cities. In contrast, Kaifeng was located in a rich agricultural plain and was easily reachable by canal from the south. However, it lacked natural defenses and was vulnerable to cavalry attacks from the north.

Although the dynasty was founded by a general, it produced no distinguished warrior rulers. Sung emperors were instead known for their patronage of the arts and connoisseurship, and several were accomplished artists. Such cultured and art-loving rulers were ill-equipped to deal with the military and diplomatic needs of the time. In 1127 nomads captured Kaifeng and carried the artist emperor, his heir, and 3,000 members of his court into captivity in the steppes, where they were subjected to numerous indignities, as this victor's account relates:

> The two commoners [of the Sung, former Emperor Hui-tsung and his son Emperor Ch'in-tsung] were presented [to the Court of the nomadic Chin state, whose emperor] bestowed the title of Duke of Stupid Virtue to the father and the title of the Marquis of Double Stupidity to his son. . . . On the xxx day of the sixth month of the eighth year [1134] . . . the Imperial Decree ordered the six daughters of the Duke of Stupid Virtue to be the wives of members of the Imperial Household.

In 1127 Sung loyalists put another son of the captive emperor on the throne in South China and set up the Southern Sung (1127–1279), with Hangchow south of the mouth of the Yangtze river, as capital city. Marco Polo later described Hangchow as far superior to Venice. In retrospect, the earlier period when Kaifeng was the capital city is called the Northern Sung. The new Sung emperor abandoned his captive relatives, made peace with the northern invaders, and agreed to the watershed of the mountains that divided the Yellow and Yangtze Rivers as their boundary. Everyone then settled down to enjoy the pleasures of peace, and culture flourished as never before.

How to Prevent Coups d'état

In the first year of his reign [960] the new Emperor summoned all his military officers—the men responsible for the mutiny to which he owed his throne—to a banquet. When the company had drunk deeply and were in cheerful mood, the Emperor said:

"I do not sleep peacefully at night."

"For what reason?" inquired the generals.

"It is not hard to understand," replied the Emperor. "Which of you is there who does not covet my throne?"

The generals made a bow and all protested:

"Why does Your Majesty speak thus? The Mandate of Heaven is now established; who still has treacherous aims?"

The Emperor replied: "I do not doubt your loyalty, but if one day one of you is suddenly roused at dawn and forced to don a yellow robe [official robe of an emperor], even if unwilling, how should he avoid rebellion?"

The officers all declared that not one of them was sufficiently renowned or beloved for such a thing to

happen, and begged the Emperor to take such measures as he thought wise to guard against any such possibility. The Emperor, having brought them to this point, promptly made his proposal known:

"Life is short. Happiness is to have the wealth and means to enjoy life, and then to be able to leave the same prosperity to one's descendants. If you, my officers, will renounce your military authority, retire to the provinces, and choose there the best lands and most delightful dwelling places, there to pass the rest of your lives in pleasure and peace until you die of old age, would this not be better than to live a life of peril and uncertainty? So that no shadow of suspicion shall remain between prince and ministers, we will ally our families with marriages, thus, ruler and subject linked in friendship and amity, we will enjoy tranquility."*

All carried out their parts of the bargain. There never was a mutiny during the Sung dynasty.

*C. P. Fitzgerald, China: A Short Cultural History, 3d ed. (New York: Praeger, 1976), p. 382.

Soon the fearsome Mongols rose over the steppes and began to cast a dark shadow over the Southern Sung. It was only a matter of time before the Sung, along with everyone else in the way, were swept away by Mongol power. Sung strategists even invented a new weapon—gunpowder-filled bamboo tubes launched rocket-fashion—to defend against Mongol attacks. The Mongols proved to be good students of military science, however, and soon incorporated the gunpowder rockets into their arsenal. The Sung were pushed ever southward, until the last emperor drowned off the coast of Canton in 1279 as his few remaining ships were being overwhelmed. By this time Kubilai Khan, grandson of the feared Genghis Khan and himself a great warrior, was well established in Peking as emperor of the new Yuan dynasty.

Difficulties in the Pursuit of Peace and War

Since antiquity, Chinese statesman had debated the merits of a defensive versus an offensive strategy against the nomads. The Sung opted for defense for two reasons. First, there had been a decline in martial spirit among the Chinese. The great aristocratic families of the Han and T'ang eras who had played a prominent part in the military had been decimated by the wars of the later T'ang period. By contrast, Sung leaders were literati with distinctly unmartial tastes and interests, and the ideal gentleman was an unathletic scholar. Whereas T'ang ladies rode, hunted, and played polo, Sung court ladies began to bind their feet because small, dainty feet became fashionable.

The second reason for the Sung's defensive stance was the ruling house's deliberate strategy of subordinating the military to civilian control and reducing the feeling of esprit de corps among the soldiers. Thus officers were rotated among different units to prevent them from developing a spirit of camaraderie. The Sung rulers also discouraged respect for military service. This disdain was evident in a saying coined at that time: "You don't use good iron to make nails, you don't use good men to make soldiers." Indeed, soldiers were often used like prisoners to perform manual labor, and were sometimes tattooed on the face to prevent desertion. The objective of the Sung's military policies was to prevent mutinies, and in that sense the policies were successful. No mutinies or revolts occurred under the Sung, but their army was also too weak to protect the empire.

Not surprisingly, the Sung produced few great generals. The most famous general was Yueh Fei, who lived in the twelfth century. Operating mainly on his own, Yueh achieved impressive successes in recovering recent territorial losses to the nomadic Chin dynasty in North China. The peace party at court, however, fearful and jealous of his popularity, had Yueh arrested and then murdered in prison. The court quickly concluded a treaty with the Chin, conceding the entire Yellow River valley.

The Sung strategy for survival was to rely on diplomacy. Whereas nation-states that were equals in international status developed in Europe after Charlemagne, no similar evolution took place in East Asia. Under the powerful Han and T'ang dynasties, the tradition of a single powerful state surrounded by satellites had evolved. But the Sung rulers were compelled to share with other states territories that had formerly been part of the Han and T'ang Empires. After early efforts failed to recover sections of North China

Map 6.6 The Southern Sung. After the loss of North China, the Sung government moved its capital to Hang-chow, south of the Yangtze River. It was pushed ever southward and destroyed by the Mongols in 1279. The period between 1127 and 1279 is called the Southern Sung.

from a nomadic state called the Liao, the Northern Sung government concluded a peace treaty with it that not only acknowledged its loss of territory, but also agreed to pay the Liao an annual tribute or "brotherly gift" of 100,000 ounces of silver and 200,000 bolts of silk. After several decades, the Liao demanded an increase of 100,000 units in each category and the Sung government gave in rather than risk a military confrontation.

Anxious to share such good fortune, the Tibetan rulers of Hsi Hsia, another border state in an area once part of the Han and T'ang Empires, also threatened war and ended up getting annual gifts of 200,000 units each of silver and silk from the Sung. These agreements left no doubt who was the "younger brother" or the lesser nation in the relationships. Likewise, the Southern Sung paid a tribute in silver and silk to the Chin, successors of the Liao in North China, and formally acknowledged the Chin's status as overlord. In another reversal from the Han and T'ang model, the Sung emperor addressed the nomad ruler as his "uncle." By accepting such treaties, the Sung rulers had submitted to terms that Han and T'ang emperors would have regarded as shameful and intolerable. Yet the Sung considered the payment of tribute or bribe the lesser evil than war. Thus they were in no position to help in the last decades of the eleventh century when three embassies from the Byzantine Empire sought military help against the invading Turks.

Because of its constant need to raise money to pay tribute and maintain the army, the Sung government encouraged international trade and taxed it for revenue. Chinese ceramics, desired everywhere from Japan to Egypt, was exported in large quantities. Assembly-line techniques were developed to speed up ceramic production, and different types of wares were produced to suit the tastes of various customers, as determined by market research. Since hostile nomadic states blocked access to the west by land, Chinese traders worked to develop sea trade with Japan and Southeast Asia. Trade with western Asia was conducted through the Arabs, who dominated the Indian Ocean.

Dynamic Neo-Confucianism and Stagnant Buddhism

Buddhism, already in decline during the late T'ang, continued to wane as an intellectual force among the ruling classes of China. A reason was the collapse of Buddhism in India during the eleventh century, owing to the Muslim invasions. Denied intellectual stimulus from India, Chinese Buddhists created no new schools and produced no additional translations of the scriptures.

Sung governmental policy also contributed to the decline of Buddhism. To address the perennial budget crunch caused by tribute payments and the cost of maintaining a large standing army, the government raised revenue by selling ordination and other priestly certificates. Prior to this, governments had insisted that the sangha (monastic community) maintain its standards by examining candidate monks on their understanding of the scriptures before issuing them ordination certificates. The end of the religious exams and the sale of ordination certificates not only corrupted the priesthood but also contributed to a decline in the doctrinal vitality of Buddhism. Although the Ch'an sect, which emphasized intuitive enlightenment, and the Pure Land sect, which stressed faith and prayer, remained popular, neither was interested in points of doctrine. Neither offered an intellectual counterpoint to revived Confucianism.

The only noteworthy development in this period was the metamorphosis of Maitreya, the Buddha of the Future, into the fat Laughing Buddha, surrounded by many children, commonly found in temples and domestic shrines. He came to embody all that was to be desired—prosperity (represented by a fat belly), many children, and contentment. As a poem commonly associated with him says:

The big belly is capable to contain, it contains all
  the things under Heaven which are difficult to contain.
The broad face is inclined to laugh, to laugh at the
  laughable men on earth.

The Confucian revival begun in the late T'ang reached its high point during the Sung period, when the best minds turned to the classical literature of antiquity. Although several Confucian schools emerged, the Neo-Confucian school led by Chu Hsi (1130–1200) eventually prevailed and was acknowledged as orthodox. Neo-Confucianism remained the official interpretation of the master's philosophy in China, Japan, and Korea until the late nineteenth century. Chu Hsi and his followers claimed that earlier Confucians had misunderstood the real meaning of the master, which they had rediscovered.

Neo-Confucianism was the great intellectual contribution of the Sung. Its distinctive feature was its ethical character. It condemned the otherworldliness of Buddhism and insisted that human fulfillment in this life is possible through self-cultivation. It accepted a supreme controlling force in the universe and believed that this force is expressed through the five chief virtues, namely, benevolence, righteousness, reverence, wisdom, and sincerity. It accepted the goodness of human nature and explained that evil resulted from the neglect of this nature. However, Neo-Confucianism failed to provide an answer to the problems of injustice, nor did it explain why humans were born with varying fortunes. This is perhaps why Buddhism, which did explain such matters, continued to have a mass following.

Since Chu Hsi and other Neo-Confucians came from the ranks of scholar-officials, it is not surprising that much of their writing dealt with political philosophy and with policies intended to bring about the well-being and moral betterment of the people. As one famous Sung scholar-official put it: "The true scholar should be the first to become anxious about the world's troubles and the last to enjoy its happiness." Neo-Confucians advocated a benevolent and paternalistic government where morally upright officials advised the hereditary monarch. From late Sung to the end of the nineteenth century, the school curriculum and examinations were based on Chu Hsi's interpretation of Confucianism. The triumph of Neo-Confucian orthodoxy during the last 700 years of imperial China largely explains the stability and conservatism of Chinese society until the twentieth century.

Age of Refinement in Culture and the Arts

The Sung period was noted for its cultural refinement. From emperor down, great and powerful men patronized the arts. The Sung ideal gentleman was a scholar-statesman, and most distinguished scholars and artists were also officials. Their output in historical,

Ceramics for Export. Chinese ceramics were widely exported during the Sung and were treasured from Japan to Egypt. Green glazed wares, called celadon, were especially prized in the Middle East, where people believed that poisoned food could be detected if served on them.

Courtesy of the Minneapolis Institute of Arts

literary, and philosophical writing was prodigious. The printing press made their works, along with encyclopedias and other multivolume books, widely available.

Religion no longer dominated art in Sung China. No new monumental Buddhist shrines comparable to those undertaken during the T'ang and earlier eras were constructed during the Sung. Artworks were enjoyed for their aesthetic and not religious worth. Some of the greatest painters in Chinese history worked during the Sung period. Landscape painting flourished, and while some artists represented nature as a whole, others made intimate studies of a branch of flowers, a bird, or a spray of bamboo to depict nature in microcosm. Ceramics ranked highest among the minor arts. The technique of high-fired, hard-glazed porcelain was fully developed and the words *porcelain* and *china* became synonymous. From this time ceramic wares replaced lacquer and metal articles for daily household utensils. New glazes and forms were invented, ranging from the refined and sophisticated pieces produced for the court to various folkware pieces for ordinary use. Potters also turned out sturdy items that would withstand the sea or land journey to Japan, Southeast Asia, the Middle East, and North Africa.

In the daily life of all classes, tea drinking, which had begun in the T'ang, became more common. The tea bush grows in the temperate climate of southern China, and the development of that region resulted in the spread of tea cultivation and drinking. With the completion of the Grand Canal during the Sui dynasty, cheap waterborne transportation brought tea and other southern commodities to the north. Teahouses sprang up in all towns and cities as social gathering places. The Sung court consumed 60,000 pounds of many varieties of tea annually for various purposes, including official gifts. Government offices served tea, and officials attending meetings were served teas of their choice. Tea often replaced alcoholic drinks at social occasions, and the well-to-do vied with one another to serve tea in the most attractive porcelain cups.

The peace of the Sung period was purchased at a high price, and this perhaps explains why so many people were determined to enjoy it at all levels. Hangchow and other cities were famous for their restaurants, tea and wine houses, and pleasure quarters. There was a mood of resignation even as people pursued their pleasures. As a poet of the Southern Sung wrote:

Beyond the hills, more blue hills; tall buildings are backed by taller.
When, here on the West Lake, does singing and dancing cease?
    So heady is the warm breeze that pleasure-seekers, quite drunk,
Forget their southern exile, and take Hangchow for Kaifeng.
    [Hangchow, capital of the Southern Sung, was built around the shores of the scenic West Lake.]

LIVES AND TIMES ACROSS CULTURES

Companionable and Bossy Wives

Educated Sung families emphasized the training of daughters as well as sons, and the biographies of the era feature many accomplished literary women. Educated girls were desirable wives because they were intellectually compatible with their husbands and good teachers to their children. While some marriages achieved this ideal, others did not, as the two following contemporary accounts show. The first is from the autobiography of Li Ch'ing-chao (1081–1140). Both her parents were distinguished scholars and she herself was famous for her prose and verse. In the second excerpt, a man writes about his sister-in-law.

When we were married in 1101, my husband was twenty-one and was still a student at the National University. Both our families being poor, we lived a very frugal life. On the 1st and 15th of every month, my husband had leave of absence from the university to come home. He would very often pawn his belongings to get 500 cash, with which he would walk to the market at Hsianag-kuo Monastery and pick up rubbings of ancient stone inscriptions. These, together with some fresh fruits and nuts, he would carry home and we would enjoy together the edibles and the ancient rubbings, forgetful of all our troubles in the world. . . .

When my husband became prefect of two prefectures, he spent practically all his income on books and antiques. When a book was bought, he and I would always read it together, mending the text, repairing the manuscript, and writing the captions. Every evening we studied together till one candle was burned up. In this way our collection of books surpassed all other collections in the country because of this loving care which my husband and I were able to give to it. We were resolved to grow old and die in such a little world of our own.*

Tsung-shu was quick-witted from youth and knew how to read. When she came of age, she married the scholar Tung . . . . Tung was weak and timid, Shu arrogant and overbearing. She bossed him around as though he were a servant. Unsatisfied with him she became depressed and fell ill. In the winter of 1126 . . . Tung died. In the following year Shu followed her mother to Nanyang, where she ate, drank, and amused herself without any sign of grief. . . . [Later her father proposed a new marriage for Shu] mentioning Wang Yueh as a possibility. Shu said, "I've already been troubled once in my life by a literary official and have no desire to repeat the experience. I'd be satisfied with a military officer." So she married Mr. Hsi.**

*Hu Shih, "Women's Place in Chinese History," in Li Yu-ning, ed., *Chinese Women through Chinese Eyes* (Armonk, NY: M. E. Sharp, 1992), pp. 9–10.
**Patricia Buckley Ebrey, *The Inner Quarters: Marriage and the Lives of Chinese Women in the Sung Period* (Berkeley: University of California Press, 1993), pp. 160–161.

As the Mongol forces advanced inexorably southward during the thirteenth century, the impending end must have been apparent. As a T'ang poet had written:

> The last glow of sunset, for all its boundless beauty,
> Portends the fast approach of darkness.

Two Sinicized States

At daybreak each morning, with the beating of a drum, the headmaster and the instructors of the academy assemble the students in the courtyard. After making a bow to the instructors, the students enter the hall, where lectures and discussions on the classics take place. They study, deliberate, and counsel and assist one another to reach a full understanding of the relationships between ruler and minister, father and son, husband and wife, elder brother and younger brother, and friend and friend. For days and months, they work and rest together as one body to train themselves until they become new men. It is from these students that the future loyal ministers and the future filial sons are produced in prolific number to serve the state and their families. Indeed, never before in the history of our country have we witnessed such a splendid success in nurturing loyal officials and filial sons as we see now.*

*Peter H. Lee and William T. de Bary, eds., Sources of Korean Tradition, vol. 1: From Early Times through the Sixteenth Century (New York: Columbia University Press, 1997), p. 298.

This passage, written in the early fifteenth century, describes the curriculum for the young men studying at the Korean government-run Royal Confucian Academy, located adjacent to the Shrine of Confucius in the capital city, Seoul. Like the state university established by the Han Chinese government in the second century B.C.E., the academy trained civil servants by teaching them the Confucian classics, with emphasis on moral teachings, especially the five cardinal human relationships.

Korean culture fused Chinese learning with its own native traditions. This is apparent even in Korea's founding myths. In one myth, Kija (Chi-tzu in Chinese), a relative of the last king of the Shang dynasty, fled his native land with 5,000 followers in the twelfth century B.C.E., when the Shang ended; he then founded a new state in Korea. This story parallels Aeneas's flight from burning Troy and later founding of Rome. A second influx from China came during the end of the Chou dynasty in the wars that preceded unification by the Ch'in. The first Korean state was created in the second century B.C.E., in northwestern Korea, where Chinese influence was strongest. It was called Chosen, the name still often used for present-day Korea. The second founding myth tells about the mating of a tiger and a bear, which produced a human son called Tan'gun, who founded the Korean state and taught the people the arts of civilization.

The dichotomy between Chinese influence and indigenous Korean traditions persists. Despite Korea's transformation into a Sinicized state, it retained distinctive cultural characteristics, and Koreans resisted Chinese political domination. For example, written Chinese was the only script used in Korea up to the thirteenth century, even though spoken Korean belongs to the Altaic linguistic group, which is related to Japanese but not to spoken Chinese. A phonetic alphabet suitable for transcribing spoken Korean was invented in the thirteenth century; yet such was the prestige of written Chinese that the Korean alphabet was not adopted officially until the mid-twentieth century. Chinese vocabulary is so integral a part of Korean that even now Koreans must learn written Chinese. The number of Chinese characters Koreans know remains the measure of the level of their education. It is not possible to distinguish a Korean from a Chinese by personal names.

Korea

Situated on a peninsula on the northeastern tip of mainland China adjacent to Manchuria but separated from China by a mountain range and the Yalu River, Korea is about the size of Minnesota. The ancestors of Koreans migrated to the peninsula from Manchuria and North Asia starting around 2000 B.C.E.; the migration of peoples continued well into historic times. A wave of Chinese immigrants, fleeing the wars of the late Chou era, brought knowledge of bronze and iron making and other advanced technologies to the peninsula. By the third century, a northern Chinese state had extended some control over northern Korea. In 194 B.C.E., Koreans under Chinese influence established the first Sinicized state, called Chosen, in northern Korea, with its capital near modern Pyongyang.

Northern Korea was conquered by Emperor Wu of the Han dynasty in 108 B.C.E., and was organized into four commandaries (provinces) within the Han Empire. By 75, however, only one commandary, called Lolang, remained under Han control. Lolang prospered as a flourishing outpost of Han civilization and remained a part of the Han and its successor states until 313 C.E.

The Han conquest was important to Korea for both cultural and political reasons. Many Han-era tombs excavated near Pyongyang (then capital of Lolang, now the capital of North Korea) show strong Chinese influence. The Han conquest also stimulated the

Map 6.7 Early Korea and Japan. Both came under the cultural influence of China.

Koreans to organize regional states, which emerged during the first century B.C.E. The three largest ones contended for mastery until one unified the entire peninsula in the seventh century.

Sinicization in all three states had proceeded rapidly, all adopting Chinese-style governments, legal codes, tax systems, state universities to teach Confucianism and Chinese history, and Buddhism as the officially favored religion. All three kingdoms also became tributary states of China. However, because Korean society was more tribal and aristocratic than Chinese, government positions were determined by one's "bone rank," or birth. Thus schools and examinations were limited to the elite few, and the closely knit aristocrats monopolized power for centuries.

The reunification of China in the sixth century had a strong impact on Korea. The confident founders of the Sui and T'ang dynasties, hoping to emulate their illustrious Han predecessors, attempted to reconquer Korea. It would also allow China to outflank the nomads to the north. For these reasons the Chinese governments launched successive campaigns to conquer Korea between 589 and 659. Chinese threats speeded Korean unification under the Silla dynasty, which offered determined resistance to China and compelled the Chinese to withdraw in 668. Although the Silla kings accepted the status of vassals to the T'ang empire, they nevertheless enjoyed autonomy in their government.

The Silla dynasty was overthrown by the Koryo dynasty (918–1392), from which the name Korea derives. The Koryo remained vassals to the Sung and to the nomadic dynasties that ruled North China. The same nomadic groups who raided and conquered China raided and made vassals of Korea, the most ferocious being the Mongols. In one raid alone in 1254, the Mongols reportedly carried off 206,800 male Korean captives. In 1258 Korea surrendered completely to Mongol rule. The Mongol overlords retained the Koryo kings as puppets, married them to Mongol princesses, and frequently required them to live in the Mongol capital Tatu (Peking). Mongol exactions in wealth and human resources, including the lost Korean lives among those forced to serve in Kubilai Khan's two failed attempts to conquer Japan, took a cruel toll on the population. It is no wonder then that when the Mongols were driven out of China, their Koryo henchmen were ousted from Korea as well.

From the seventh to the seventeenth century, unified Korea increasingly resembled China. Korean governmental, legal, financial, and educational systems were all modeled after the Chinese. Thousands of Koreans continued to study in China, so that intellectual trends and styles in the two countries remained indistinguishable.

Vietnam

Like Korea, Vietnam is a close neighbor of China. It is separated from the southern Chinese province of Kwangsi by low mountains and jungles. Because the earliest Vietnamese histories were written by Chinese, and because of China's influence in the making of Vietnamese civilization from early times, Vietnamese history and culture must be looked at against a Chinese background.

As in Korea, the historic period for Vietnam began toward the end of the first millennium B.C.E. At that time a people called the Yueh lived in coastal China from the south-

Movable Type: Korea's Contribution to the World

In the third year [1403], King T'aejong remarked to the courtiers around him: "If the country is to be governed well, it is essential that books be read widely. But because our country is located east of China beyond the sea, not many books from China are readily available. Moreover woodblock prints are easily defaced, and it is impossible to print all the books in the world by using woodblock prints. It is my desire to cast copper type so that we can print as many books as possible and have them made available widely. This will truly bring infinite benefit to us." In the end, the king was successful in having copper type cast with the graphs modeled after those of the Old Commentary on the Book of Odes [one of the Confucian classics] and the Tso Commentary [a book explaining one of the classics], and that is how the typecasting foundry became established in our country.**

Movable, metallic type was first developed in Korea in the thirteenth century. This was a great improvement on the woodblock method of printing developed earlier by the Chinese. The fifteenth-century Korean king described here is sponsoring book printing because a Confucian state had an obligation to promote scholarship, and concomitantly good government. Movable type spread from Korea to Japan and China, and thence westward from China.

*Peter H. Lee, and William T. de Bary, eds., Sources of Korean Tradition, Vol. 1: From Early Times through the Sixteenth Century (New York: Columbia University Press, 1997), pp. 305–306.

ern bank of the Yangtze River southward to the Red River valley of northern Vietnam. They practiced slash-and-burn agriculture and made bronze artifacts. Toward the end of the third century B.C.E., the newly unified China under the Ch'in dynasty conquered and annexed what is now South China and the Red River valley in northern Vietnam. The Chinese called the Red River region Nan-Yueh (South Yueh) and governed it from Hanoi. Turned around and pronounced in the local manner, Nan-Yueh became Vietnam.

When the Ch'in dynasty fell, northern Vietnam came under a secessionist Chinese state centered at Canton. In 111 B.C.E., shortly before conquering Korea, emperor Wu of the Han dynasty reconquered and annexed northern Vietnam up to roughly the seventeenth parallel and organized the region into three commandaries (provinces). They remained part of China until 939 C.E.

Upper-class Vietnamese assimilated Chinese culture, but some resisted Chinese rule. When the Chinese governor killed a troublesome lord as an example to others in 39 C.E., his widow and her sister (called the Trung sisters) took up his cause, proclaiming themselves queens and leading a revolt that lasted for three years. Later Vietnamese honored them as national heroes. Before the tenth century, twelve separate Vietnamese uprisings against China occurred, propelled by nationalistic or anti-Chinese feelings, and fueled by local grievances. During the T'ang dynasty, China renamed Nan-Yueh An-nan, meaning the "pacified south." Pronounced An-nam in the local dialect, this remains the name for northern Vietnam.

In 939 Vietnamese forces defeated the Chinese army and established an independent dynasty. Except for short intervals of Mongol invasions in the thirteenth century and Chinese control for several decades in the early fifteenth century, Vietnam has retained its own government since that time, although like Korea it acknowledged China as overlord until 1885. At home the Vietnamese ruler called himself emperor, but when he addressed the Chinese ruler, whom he called lord, he referred to himself as subject and vassal king.

Under Chinese rule, Vietnam benefited from rapid progress and technological innovation. Chinese-designed irrigation works made possible intensive rice culture in the Red River valley. China also introduced efficient bureaucratic administrative machinery that replaced the rule of old feudal chieftains. Confucianism became the foundation of the governmental, educational, and moral systems, and Mahayana Buddhism became the influential religion. The Chinese administration collected taxes, demanded corvée labor from Vietnamese males, and drafted them for the military.

Upper-class Vietnamese, like their Korean counterparts, meticulously copied Chinese social customs and cultural norms. The Vietnamese adopted the same surnames and given names as the Chinese and wrote in the same language, although in time they created new words that were different from Chinese. They wore similarly styled clothing, used chopsticks in eating food of a cuisine closely related to that of southern China, made ceramic wares similar to those of China, and built and decorated their houses in like manner.

Despite Chinese cultural influence, a Vietnamese self-consciousness and national identity emerged, due to several factors. Ancient cultural patterns from prehistoric times linked Vietnam to Southeast Asia. Vietnam's distance from the center of China's political power and its strategic insignificance to China made Chinese intervention less likely than in the case of Korea. Vietnam's frontier location between the Chinese world to its north and the Indianized states to its south and southwest allowed it to draw from two major cultures and sharpened its self-consciousness. This national consciousness was strengthened by struggles against Chinese domination and by Vietnam's southward expansion against the Indianized Champa and Khmer states.

Japan: The Merging of Chinese and Native Cultures

Because We had heard of the great Sui empire of propriety and justice located in the west, We send tribute. As barbarians living in an isolated place beyond the sea, We do not know propriety and justice, are shut up within Our borders, and do not see others. . . .

Our queen has heard that beyond the ocean to the west there is a Bodhisattva sovereign who serves and promotes Buddhism. For that reason, We have been sent to pay her respects. Accompanying us are several tens of monks, who have come to study Buddhist teachings.

. . .

The emperor of China greets the Wo [another name for Japan] empress.

Your envoys . . . have arrived and made their report.

Having been pleased to receive the command of Heaven to become emperor, We have endeavored to extend virtue everywhere, irrespective of distance.

We are deeply grateful that the Wo empress—residing in the seas beyond—bestows blessings on her people, maintains peace and prosperity within her borders, and softens manners and customs with harmony. *

*Delmer M. Brown, ed., *The Cambridge History of Japan*, vol. 1: *Ancient Japan* (Cambridge: Cambridge University Press, 1993), pp. 182–183.

These are two early accounts of the first Japanese embassy sent to China in 607 by Prince Shotoku, regent of Japan, acting on behalf of Empress Suiko. The first is from the official history of the Chinese Sui dynasty and tells the event from the Chinese point of view. The second is from *Nihonji*, an official history of Japan written in 720, and represents the Japanese perspective. Both accounts agree that it was Japan that took the initiative of seeking knowledge from China.

Geography and Early History

The four main islands of Japan and the many smaller islands are located in northeastern Asia, separated from the mainland by the Sea of Japan and the East China Sea. Japan is roughly the size of California, is larger than Great Britain, and only slightly smaller than France.

There are several similarities between the British Isles and Japan. Both are separated from the continent by sea, which gave them comparative freedom from the wars and invasions that periodically swept the mainland. Compared with the English Channel that separates Britain from France, the seas that separate Japan from China and Korea are much more formidable, being 250 miles wide at the narrowest crossing point. Thus, historically, the Japanese were more isolated from mainland Asia than the British were from Europe.

Only about 20 percent of the land surface, mostly along the coast and river valleys, is level enough for cultivation. The rest of the land consists of mountains covered with forests. Scenes of natural beauty abound; one of the most beautiful is Mount Fuji, whose peak is a perfectly shaped, snow-covered volcanic cone more than 12,000 feet high. Although arable land is scarce, Japan has temperate weather and abundant rainfall, allowing intensive agriculture, with double-cropping in the southern islands. The main cereal crop is rice, grown in irrigated fields. The surrounding seas are rich in fish, shellfish, and edible seaweed, which provide protein in the diet.

Japanese written records date from about 500 C.E., but archaeological evidence and Chinese written records indicate that Japanese culture had been evolving for several millennia prior to that time. By the third century C.E., the Japanese were building huge earthen mounds up to 120 feet high, surrounded by moats and guarded by clay figures of animals and warriors, some riding horses. Those mounds were burial places for important people. We can infer from the size of the mounds and from artifacts they contain that society was highly aristocratic and that mounted aristocrats wielding iron weapons could mobilize the large workforce that was necessary for building the impressive mound tombs. The people of this tomb culture, as the era was called, in increasing contact with peoples on mainland Asia, would last into the seventh century and develop into the fully historic civilization of Japan.

The earliest Japanese written records pertaining to its origins are two works called *Kojiki (Records of Ancient Matters)* and *Nihonji (Chronicles of Japan)*, written in 712 and 720 C.E., respectively. Both open with the mythological "age of the gods," a dimly remembered past reshaped to glorify the ruling family and to create a false picture of long-centralized rule and antiquity so the Japanese might enhance their self-image vis-à-vis

China and its much older culture. As the *Nihonji* described in the opening passage of this chapter, Amaterasu, the Sun Goddess and founder of the sun line, sent her grandson, Ninigi, from heaven to rule the southern island of Kyushu with the imperial regalia. All three items in the regalia had special significance in early Japan. The bronze mirror was a symbol of Amaterasu, but in general mirrors, many imported from China, were treasured and frequently found in the burial mounds. The iron sword was a symbol of power to the warrior aristocrats, and swords are also found in the burial mounds. The curved jewels probably derived from the shape of bear and other animal claws and were used as amulets; such jewels have also been found in burial mounds in Japan and Korea.

According to the same creation myth, Ninigi's great-grandson overcame other deities and founded the Japanese state in Yamato around the Nara plain, not far from present-day Osaka, in 660 B.C.E. This part of the myth is probably a glorified account of how the Yamato sun-worshipping clan fought and defeated other clans and their patron deities and expanded its power. If so, the Japanese rulers are similar to the Greek heroes of the Trojan War or the chiefs of the Aryan invaders of India, who were also deified by posterity. Chinese records indicate that the Yamato state subdued areas hitherto dominated by "hairy men" (presumably the proto-Caucasian first inhabitants of the islands called Ainu) and became increasingly powerful. Although the Yamato clan dominated Japan at the beginning of its historic period, the islands were actually ruled by semiautonomous clans, each worshiping its own deified ancestors but acknowledging the supremacy of the sun goddess and her descendants.

This body of myths was later given the name of Shintoism (Way of the Gods) to distinguish it from Buddhism and Confucianism. Shinto myths thus reflected the political supremacy of the sun goddess clan and the subordination of other local cults. The deified ancestors of the subordinate clans were given less important places in the pantheon. Ancestors, awe-inspiring objects, and emperors, called *kami,* were all considered superior and were objects of reverence and worship.

Primitive Shinto, like other shamanistic beliefs, emphasized harmony with nature but had no philosophy, theology, or clear moral code. Most rites involved reverence to the memory of dead family members and clan ancestors. Shrines were simple structures made of wood and frequently rebuilt. Worshippers who attended rites at the shrines bowed, clapped their hands to arouse the spirits' attention, and joined in processions. They also offered wine, food, the first catch or fruit of the season, and the firstborn child (symbolically). Shintoism had no notion of guilt or sin, but stressed ritual purity. Association with birth, death, sickness, and the like brought on ritual impurity, which could be removed with exorcism and cleansing ceremonies. Ritual cleansing involved bathing, which might explain the Japanese preoccupation with bathing and physical cleanliness since early times. Similarly, the official religion of ancient Rome stressed the observance of rituals such as purification and expiation and offered little ethical instruction.

The Adoption of Chinese Civilization

Japanese life was greatly altered by Chinese culture between the sixth and ninth centuries. Much impressed by the might of the Sui and T'ang dynasties, Japanese aristocrats cultivated a strongly Chinese style of life, built a powerful Chinese-style state, and absorbed Chinese art and learning. The year 552 is the traditional date for the formal introduction of Buddhism and the start of the heavy influx of Chinese culture in Japan. Buddhism, then at its height in China and already Sinicized, served as the vehicle for the introduction of many aspects of both Indian and Chinese culture that would transform Japan. Chinese influence spread at a rapid pace for the next three centuries and transformed Japan from a primitive to a sophisticated culture.

Three factors explain the great eagerness of the Japanese to learn from the continent beginning in the sixth century. First, the Yamato rulers had found the existing hereditary clan government, which resembled that of the Germanic tribes of Roman times, inadequate for their expanded needs. They were therefore anxious to learn about more advanced concepts and methods from the continent. Second, by the sixth century the Japanese had attained a cultural level that enabled them to appreciate what China had to offer. Third, starting late in the century, China was again unified and entering a great era under the Sui and T'ang dynasties, thereby offering a successful model worthy of emulation.

Although an empress occupied the Japanese throne at this important time, the actual ruler was her nephew and regent, Prince Shotoku (ruled 573–621). This remarkable man was the chief architect of the great changes that would transform Japan. Legend says that Shotoku was born holding a statuette of the Buddha. He was not only a devout Buddhist, but also a learned theologian. By the time he came to office, many Chinese and Korean Buddhist missionaries were already at work in Japan, and their activities had provoked a heated controversy among the ruling aristocrats. Some were faithful to the traditional Shinto beliefs, while others enthusiastically converted to Buddhism. In 592 Prince Shotoku's pro-Buddhist faction won control of the court, and with their victory, Buddhism was established as the official faith.

Buddhism was an attractive new force in Japan. Some, like Prince Shotoku, studied its teachings, but most early converts were attracted more by Buddhism's elaborate rituals and ceremonies and magnificent art and architecture than by its theology. They were also impressed with the supposed magical powers of the new religion, or the prospect of gaining personal salvation. The eagerness of many to embrace Buddhism must have been inspired, at least in part, by the desire to partake in the material benefits it brought to Japan.

Early Japanese Buddhism was an extension of T'ang Chinese Buddhism. This was evident in temple and monastic architecture (the best extant examples of the T'ang style are found in Japan) and in the early Japanese Buddhist sects. Those architects and craftsmen who built the early temples were probably Chinese and Korean immigrants, and some of the sculptures and decorations they used to adorn the temples were imported from China or Korea. In time Japanese artisans would imbue their works with a uniquely Japanese spirit. All six Buddhist sects in early Japan were Chinese in origin. The most popular, the Tendai sect (T'ien-t'ai in China), appealed to well-educated upper-class Japanese, just as it had to a similar class in China.

Though a devout Buddhist, Shotoku turned to Confucianism for organizing the government. In 604 he issued a document called the Seventeen Article Constitution, which contained guidelines on morals and ethics for the government and society. An important goal of the constitution was to transform Japanese government into a centralized monarchy by stripping power from the hereditary clans. Except for Article 2, which enjoined all to respect the Three Jewels of Buddhism, the articles embraced Confucian principles and Chinese governmental practices. Article 16 enjoins in part:

> Let the people be employed [in forced labor] at seasonable times. This is an ancient and excellent rule. Let them be employed, therefore, in the winter months, when they are at leisure. But from Spring to Autumn, when they are engaged in agriculture or with the mulberry trees, the people should not be so employed.

This passage refers to the ancient Chinese practice of levying able-bodied males to labor on government projects. The implementation of such a practice on a national level was new to Japan (no one knows precisely how labor was recruited and organized to build the mound tombs).

Prince Shotoku also adopted the Chinese calendar. In doing so he was also embracing the Confucian world order and indicating his acceptance of Confucian ideas about the relationship between heaven, earth, and humans. China required all vassal states to accept its calendar, but Japan did so voluntarily and did not become a Chinese vassal state. He also copied the Chinese court rank system and established Chinese-style government offices.

Shotoku also broke ground in another area. In 607 he organized an embassy to China to learn from the Chinese; later he sent two more. Thirteen more embassies were sent after Shotoku's death, making a grand total of sixteen between 607 and 838. These embassies were major undertakings; each was equipped with four ships carrying between 500 and 600 promising and eager young men chosen from good families. They included junior government officers, Buddhist monks, scholars in Chinese literature, painters, and musicians, among others. These youths remained in China, some for ten years or more, to learn as much as they could in their chosen fields. After returning to Japan, they worked in important positions or taught their skills to others. The voyages were also full of hazards because sailing ships had to cross open seas with no compasses. (The Chinese had invented the first magnetic compass in the fourth century B.C.E., but did not use it in navigation until between 850 and 1050; subsequently, the instrument was widely adopted by other peoples.) The sustained commitment to send numerous embassies showed remarkable farsightedness on the part of Japan's government leaders. The embassies were extremely successful and helped to bring about one of the greatest technology transfers in premodern times. In addition to the officially sponsored students, others were sent by Buddhist monasteries or went under private auspices with trading ships.

In 645 Chinese-trained officials with the goal of transforming Japan into a miniature T'ang China pushed Prince Shotoku's policy to its logical conclusion. A new set of laws, called the *Taika* (Great) Reform, made the ruler, now titled *tenno* (meaning heavenly emperor, a Chinese-sounding title), head of a theoretically centralized empire. The Taika Reform abolished private land ownership, made the emperor the theoretical owner of all land as in T'ang China, and instituted a Chinese-style tax system. Officials with Chinese titles assisted the emperor in administration, using Chinese bureaucratic practices, rituals, and ceremonies. Like China, the country was divided into provinces and counties, which were given Chinese-sounding names. The officials also promulgated a law code, sections of which were copied verbatim from the T'ang code.

Japanese women lost ground as a result of the Taika Reform. In compliance with Chinese notions of propriety, women were gradually barred from the imperial succession. As a result Japanese society was transformed from one based on a mixture of matrilineal and patrilineal principles in which both men and women could succeed to political power (Amaterasu, a goddess, was the founder of the sun clan), to an exclusively patriarchal one. Whereas between 592 and 770 half the rulers were women, after 770 women were shut out from the succession. A desire to conform to Chinese standards was one reason for the change. Another was the behavior of the last reigning empress, who virtually handed over the reins of government to her favorite, a Buddhist monk, rumored also to be her lover. He became so powerful that people feared he planned to usurp the throne. After she died, government leaders determined to forestall a repetition of her disastrous reign by barring women from the succession.

Until 710 Japan had no permanent capital city. This was partly due to the rudimentary nature of the government and to Shinto notions of purity, that death was defiling; so that at the death of an emperor, his residence was abandoned or destroyed, and the residence of his successor became the new seat of government. Thus buildings, including Shinto shrines, were simple and impermanent. These ideas did not apply to Buddhist temples and monasteries, which were grand, beautiful, and built to last.

To symbolize the adoption of T'ang-style centralized government and display the grandeur of the court, a capital city was laid out at Nara in 710. A number of beautiful Buddhist temples already stood in the vicinity. Two and a half by three miles square, Nara was conceived as a scaled-down Changan, capital of T'ang China; its streets were laid out in a grid pattern with a magnificent palace at the northern end and many temples scattered throughout. The most spectacular temple in the city was called the Todai-ji (Great Eastern Temple); its main hall, built in the eighth century, was the largest wooden building in the world. It housed a fifty-three-foot bronze statue of the Buddha that weighed over a million pounds. In 752 when the temple was formally dedicated, 10,000 monks, including some from China, Korea, and India, attended the celebration. Neither the grand Buddha hall nor the great Buddha statue has survived. Many other great temples were built in the eighth and ninth centuries with the support of the court and aristocratic families.

Nara ceased being the capital after 794; as a result, few buildings were added after that date. Thus it remains a T'ang period city, more so than any city in China. The emperor built a new capital called Heian some distance away in order to escape the domination of the powerful Buddhist monasteries at Nara. It was later called Kyoto (which means capital city) and remained the imperial capital until 1867. Somewhat larger than Nara, it, too, was planned as a scaled-down version of Changan. The four centuries between 794 and 1185 are called the Heian Age, which was characterized by refined and sophisticated culture.

Departures from Chinese Models

Even as the Japanese struggled to duplicate Chinese culture, many things remained different. The Japanese economy was less developed than that of China. Shintoism continued to be important despite the popularity of Buddhism, because even a devoutly Buddhist emperor remained a Shinto high priest and carried out a heavy schedule of Shinto rituals, assisted by the Office of Shinto Deities.

Japanese society also remained sharply differentiated according to hereditary class. Thus, while Japan duplicated China's state university and examination system, both institutions were reserved for the sons of the aristocracy, as they were in Korea. Government posts remained hereditary despite their Chinese-sounding titles.

Some of the ambitious measures of the Taika Reform were abandoned or modified after a trial period, because conditions in Japan did not allow their operation. The most drastic reform had been over land ownership and taxation. The reformers had attempted to adopt the T'ang "equal-field" system. Judging by surviving records, Japanese leaders during the Nara and early Heian periods made heroic efforts to carry it out, with considerable success in some areas. Even in T'ang China, with its considerable bureaucratic machinery and experience, the equal-field system had broken down after a hundred years; small wonder it could not be sustained in Japan.

The Heian period was one of general economic expansion, but the central government did not benefit. Aristocratic families evaded taxes and Buddhist institutions did not pay them. Possessing the capital and manpower to bring new lands into cultivation, the aristocrats gradually gained control over increasing tracts of land. While they thrived and grew rich, the revenue-starved central government became steadily poorer, and its remaining officers had less and less work to do. Meanwhile the remaining small landowners and free peasantry were saddled with the entire burden of the land tax. To escape the crushing taxation, many peasants placed themselves and their land under the protection of a lord or monastery, working for their patrons for a fee less than the tax bite.

By about the tenth century, ceremonial duties were all that were left for the emperor and atrophied central government to perform. But whereas a Chinese royal house that had become irrelevant would be overthrown, such was the prestige of the imperial line and respect for hereditary rights in Japan that no one attempted to replace the dynasty.

Instead of supplanting the imperial family, the most powerful and wealthy court family in Heian, the Fujiwara, simply married into it. The period between the ninth and twelfth centuries is called the Fujiwara centuries because that clan dominated the government through having a monopoly of supplying empresses and consorts to the emperors and princes. In this way, the imperial government became a sham headed by emperors who were puppets of the Fujiwara family. When a child emperor ascended the throne, his maternal uncle or grandfather, a Fujiwara, naturally became regent. When the emperor grew up and married, his empress and concubines were also Fujiwara women, perhaps the daughters of his mother's brother, the regent. Thus there was no reason for the regent to give up his power, even after the emperor became an adult. As soon as the son of a Fujiwara empress was old enough to sit through state ceremonies, the emperor was prevailed upon to retire so that the regency cycle could begin once again.

The Fujiwara were very wealthy because they owned numerous tax-free estates, but by the twelfth century they became decadent and their power faded. Other clans rose to power but let the Fujiwara continue to dominate the imperial family through the web of intermarriage between the two clans.

Language and the Arts in the Nara and Heian Periods

The court and nobility dominated culture and the arts during the Nara and Heian periods. Since Japan had no written language, it borrowed Chinese writing. This posed problems since Chinese and Japanese belong to separate linguistic families, Sinitic and Altaic, respectively, with quite different grammar and syntax. Eventually, the Japanese incorporated Chinese words into their vocabulary and invented a system of syllables that permitted them to reflect the Japanese grammatical structure and to write Japanese words that had no Chinese equivalents. Initially, however, the Japanese were forced to read, write, and compose entirely in Chinese, and Chinese was used exclusively in all early books by Japanese authors, as well as in all government records and documents. However, mastery of written Chinese gave educated Japanese a distinct advantage, for it enabled them to draw on the entire corpus of Chinese literature, the treasures of a 2,000-year-old civilization. Similarly, educated Romans' knowledge of Greek gave them access to the literature of ancient Greece.

Since the Chinese were keenly conscious of the importance of history, the Japanese naturally adopted the same attitude; like the Chinese they preserved historical records and compiled dynastic histories. The Japanese also honored the Confucian moral code, looked up to Chinese sages and heroes as role models, and revered learning.

After the ninth century the Japanese were mature enough to innovate and depart from Chinese models. At this time a distinctly Japanese style began to emerge. A phonetic script, *kana,* was developed for writing Japanese. While men of the upper classes continued to write in Chinese according to Chinese conventions, noble ladies, who did not have to pursue an equally strict educational curriculum, learned to write in Japanese, using *kana.* The result was a flowering of Japanese literature written by women. Lady Sei Shonagon's *Pillow Book* was a journal of court life that painted a picture of sophisticated people preoccupied with good taste and manners even in religion. The outstanding work of the period was Lady Murasaki's *Tale of Genji.* It portrayed a decadent court society of cultivated but effete men and women from the emperor down who followed an elaborate dress code and valued the ability to write poetry more than government.

Such literary works indicate the growth of a native culture. They suggest a parallel with medieval Europe, where the clergy and government officials wrote in Latin, while popular literature was written in vernacular tongues. While Heian Japan and medieval Europe owed their cultural heritage to China and Rome respectively, each developed distinctive characteristics. In its gradual evolution of feudalism, Japan was definitely departing from the contemporary Chinese model of the Sung dynasty and evolving its own unique culture.

Early Feudal Japan

In contrast to Europe, where feudalism declined with the rise of national monarchies, in Japan feudal institutions replaced national institutions after the eleventh century. The emperors reigned but no longer ruled. They were replaced by the provincial lords, some of whom were descended from the old clan aristocrats, while others came from court families who had earlier left the capital. These lords managed the estates, supervised the peasants, and fought local wars against one another or the retreating Ainu. Some still acknowledged vassalage to great court families such as the Fujiwara and remitted part of their income to them, but less so with time since they no longer needed protection from the imperial government.

Mounted warriors dominated Japan's feudal society. Each aristocratic warrior was attended by small retinues of squires, clad in light armor made of metal, fabric, and leather, which was superior to that worn by contemporary European knights. Armed with bows and arrows and curved swords made of the finest tempered steel in the world by Japanese smiths, they resembled the knights of medieval Europe. A Japanese knight was called either a *samurai,* which means a "servant" (to a lord), or a *bushi,* which means "noble warrior." A feudal relationship, also resembling that in Europe, existed between lord and samurai and often continued for generations. The lord provided his knights

Elegant Court Life

A preacher ought to be a good-looking man. It is then easier to keep your eyes fixed on his face, without which it is impossible to benefit by his discourse. Otherwise the eyes wander and you forget to listen. Ugly preachers have therefore a grave responsibility. . . . If preachers were of a more suitable age I should have pleasure in giving a more favorable judgement. As matters actually stand, their sins are too fearful to think of.*

About the twentieth day of the second month the Emperor gave a Chinese banquet under the great cherry-tree of the Southern Court. . . . The guests [royal princes, noblemen, and professional poets alike] were handed the rhyme words which the Emperor had drawn by lot, and set to work to compose their poems. It was with a clear and ringing voice that Genji read out the word "Spring" which he had received as the rhyme-sound of his poem. [After the party Genji spent the night with a lady of the court.] Suddenly they saw to their discomfiture that dawn was creeping into the sky. . . ." Tell me

your name," he said. "How can I write to you unless you do? Surely this is not going to be our only meeting?" She answered with a poem in which she said that names are of this world only and he would not care to know hers if he were resolved that their love should last till worlds to come. It was a mere quip and Genji, amused at her quickness, answered, "You are quite right. It was a mistake on my part to ask." And he recited the poem: "While I still seek to find on which blade dwells the dew, a great wind shakes the grasses of the level land."**

Lady Sei Shonagon and Lady Murasaki were contemporaries who lived around 1000; both came from the Fujiwara clan and moved in court circles. The former wrote a book of sketches about court life, manners, and morals and the latter a novel about the romantic life of a prince. Both works are masterpieces of prose written in kana, and both paint clear, wonderful pictures of the refined and effete life of the court in Heian.

*Lady Sei Shonagon, The Pillow Book, quoted from W. G. Ashton, History of Japanese Literature (New York: D. Appleton, 1899), p. 116.
**Lady Murasaki, The Tale of Genji, trans. Arthur Waley (New York: Modern Library, 1960), pp. 210–214.

with income derived from his agricultural estates. In return, the samurai was expected to serve his lord with absolute loyalty and die in his cause.

The samurai code of conduct, called *bushido* (way of the warrior), did not idealize samurai women, who were expected to be brave and to die rather than submit to shame, but they could inherit property, and some were quite successful in managing estates. Samurai also took pride in their ethic of living a hard, Spartan life. They shunned luxury and were expected to face pain and death with indifference.

The feudal period in Japan was punctuated by many small conflicts between competing warrior cliques. In the twelfth century these culminated in two major wars between rival clans, both descended from junior branches of the imperial line. They had early left Kyoto to make their fortunes in the provinces. Tales from these wars have provided materials for countless plays and stories popular to later generations.

The final victor was a lord named Minamoto. He had the emperor appoint him "Barbarian-Quelling Generalissimo" and delegate to him supreme military authority. In Japanese, the shortened version of the title was *Shogun,* a name the hereditary military dictators used until the mid-nineteenth century. The Minamoto chose Kamakura, a seaside town near present-day Tokyo, as the seat of the Shogunate. Kamakura was located in the productive Kanto plain, where many Minamoto estates were located. The shogunal dynasty called its government the *bakufu,* which means "tent government," that is, a military administration in contrast to the civil government in Kyoto and theoretically subordinate to it.

The Kamakura Shogunate lasted for a century and a half, outlasting the Minamoto line that had established it. In a typically Japanese fashion, another feudal clan, the Hojo family, married a daughter to the Minamoto Shogun and then eliminated the Minamoto line. It then installed a nonentity as Shogun and ruled the country as shogunal regents. By the thirteenth century, Japan had a very confusing government structure, with an emperor who was the puppet of the Fujiwara clan. That clan supervised a sham government in Kyoto, while in Kamakura a puppet Shogun presided over the bakufu, which was really ruled by the hereditary shogunal regent, a man of the Hojo clan.

In the mid-thirteenth century, for the first time in its history, Japan was faced with a terrifying foreign threat: the Mongols who had conquered much of Asia and Europe and intimidated the rest. In 1266, Kubilai Khan sent envoys to Japan demanding submission. The bakufu refused, and it meant war. In 1274 an invasion force of 25,000 Mongols and their Korean subjects landed at Hakata Bay in northern Kyushu. The Mongols were accustomed to massed cavalry tactics, while the samurai fought in individual combat. After an inconclusive battle, the Mongols reembarked in the face of a coming storm and sailed back to Korea, suffering heavy storm-inflicted losses en route; total casualties amounted to a third of the invading force.

Certain that the Mongols would return, the bakufu assembled a large force and erected a wall around Hakata Bay. When the Mongols returned in 1281 with 140,000 men and a huge armada, the wall restricted the Mongol cavalry, while small, and easily maneuverable Japanese crafts inflicted heavy damage on the large Mongol ships in the confined space of the bay. In the same way, Athenian ships had the advantage over those

LIVES AND TIMES ACROSS CULTURES

Japanese Adaptations

Japan owed many of its cultural developments to China and to India via China. The transformation of the Indian Dhyana school of Buddhism to Ch'an in China, then to Zen in Japan is a good example. Tradition says that in 520 C.E. the Indian master Bodhidharma came to China to preach a religious discipline aimed at tranquilizing the mind of the practitioner so that he can devote himself to exploring his own inner consciousness. The goal is to attain serenity and peace amid a turbulent world. As it developed in China, Ch'an was influenced by philosophical Taoism, with its emphasis on spontaneity and naturalness.

Ch'an's introduction to Japan coincided with the establishment of military-dominated regimes called the shogunate. In Japan, the sect became known as Zen, a variant pronunciation of the Chinese word. The shoguns patronized Zen partly because it was not dominated by the old court aristocrats as the other Buddhist schools were. In addition, its teachings could be adapted to the culture and code of conduct of the warriors who formed the backbone of the shogunate. Its close association with the military class infused Zen with a martial spirit, and it became especially influential with the Japanese military. During the strife-filled feudal period, however, people in many other walks of life were also attracted to Zen.

The rise of Japanese feudalism brought an increasing segregation of the sexes and sequestration of women. Thus the easy social intermingling between men and women described in Lady Murasaki's and Sei Shonagan's books became history. With the seclusion of respectable women, men could only socialize freely with entertainers and courtesans. This situation had a parallel in ancient Athens, where respectable women were practically cloistered in their own homes, and professional "companions" (*hetairai*) provided physical and intellectual stimulation for men at dinner parties.

Like everyone else in hierarchically structured Japan, the courtesans were segregated in the *Yoshiwara* or "Flower District" of town and were strictly ranked. The *geisha*, which means "art person," stood on top. Like an Athenian hetaira, a geisha spent a long apprenticeship learning literature, song, dance, conversation, and the art of pleasing men. She was a fashion setter in her gorgeous clothes and jewelry and was waited on by maids. She entertained at lavish parties for her male customers, rarely granting her sexual favors except by arrangement. Some eventually became concubines to important men, others retired to teach young aspirants.

of the invading Persians in the Bay of Salamis in 480 B.C.E. Then a devastating typhoon struck, wrecking the Mongol fleet and marooning their soldiers. The invading force lost between 60 to 90 percent of its men. The Japanese attributed their salvation to divine intervention in the form of *kamikaze*, or "divine wind," just as the English later thanked God for the storm that destroyed the Spanish Armada. The Mongols never returned, although the bakufu continued the mobilization for two decades just in case.

The strain of the Mongol invasion and the cost of preparedness sapped the strength of the bakufu. The joy of deliverance soon evaporated, and since there were no spoils to share, many of the samurai faced financial hardship. In any case, after several generations the personal bonds that had tied the samurai to the bakufu were wearing thin. The end came in 1333, with the extermination of the Hojo family by a rebel force. With that came also the end of the first phase of feudalism in Japan.

Religion and Social Life during the Early Feudal Era

During the twelfth and thirteenth centuries, cultural changes were also reshaping Japan. The Japanese began to alter Buddhism to reflect the outlook of their feudal society. While the Buddhist sects of the Nara and Heian eras survived and continued to serve the elite, new sects imported from China or formed in Japan emerged that better served the needs of the warriors and the ordinary people. One new sect was the Pure Land, introduced from China in the twelfth century. By offering salvation to the faithful in the blissful Pure Land of Amida Buddha (Japanese shortened form for Amitabha Buddha), it gave hope to the masses and became immensely popular among them. It allowed the faithful to acquire salvation simply by repeating Amida Buddha's name in faith and sincerity. In the thirteenth century, a Japanese priest began an offshoot called the True Pure Land, which discarded most of the scriptures and appealed to ordinary people by repudiating clerical celibacy and encouraging priests to live among the congregation. The True Pure Land went so far as to assert that a single sincere act of calling the Buddha's name was sufficient for salvation. Its simplicity contributed to its popularity, making the True Pure Land the largest branch of Japanese Buddhism, followed by the Pure Land sect.

The Zen sect, which is the Japanese pronunciation of the Chinese word Ch'an (meditation), was introduced to Japan at the end of the twelfth century. It especially suited the needs of the samurai because it emphasized simplicity and discipline, rather than scholastic studies, and reinforced the idea of physical discipline and mental toughness extolled by the bushido code. Thus Zen became the sect of the warrior caste of feudal Japan; and with their support, it achieved great prestige and influence.

Zen also helped shape the Japanese aesthetic sense and to synthesize the refined artistic vision of Sung China with the Japanese love of the simple and tranquil. Tea drinking, newly popular in China, was introduced to Japan at this time, at first for medicinal use. As in China, tea soon became a national drink, and in the hands of Zen aesthetes, it evolved into the tea ceremony, which became an art and a unique style of social intercourse. Imported Sung ceramic ware was favored for the tea ceremony; surviving specimens are among Japan's loveliest cultural treasures.

A monk named Nicheren (1222–1282) founded a popular Buddhist sect, named after himself. A fiery street preacher who militantly opposed the other Buddhist sects, he chauvinistically insisted that Japan was the land of the gods and that Japanese Buddhism was the only true Buddhism. Nicheren's sectarianism and nationalism, as well as his emphasis on congregational worship and reading the scriptures in Japanese translation, in some ways resembled Protestant Christianity that later developed in Europe.

Buddhist religious fervor, so strong at this time, was reflected in many new temple buildings and religious sculptures; the most famous is the monumental bronze Kamakura Buddha, cast in the mid-thirteenth century. The temples that still stand show strong Sung influence, a reflection of the pervasive cultural contacts that continued between China and Japan. Many translations of Buddhist works were written in kana, reflecting the popularizing of Buddhism.

The peasants lived in simple two-room huts, clustered in villages. A few could afford wooden floors, but most simply covered the dirt floor with straw mats. They wore clothes made from the fiber of a perennial hemp plant called ramie; less frequently, they wore clothes made of silk. Cotton cloths were first imported from Korea in the fifteenth century. By the sixteenth century, cotton was grown, spun, and woven in Japan. Although rice cultivation was widespread, most of the crop was turned over to the lord. Peasants ate inferior grains such as millet, roots, and wild grass seeds.

While the medieval peasant was largely self-sufficient, he did trade his surplus and items he made such as vinegar and wines for salt, pottery, and iron tools in the local markets, usually held three times a month. Peasants with the same skills formed guilds. Metal coins, mostly minted in China, were increasingly used in trade; in time peasants began to commute their dues in cash also.

Farm women did most of the planting, threshing, and milling and took goods for sale in the markets. They also formed guilds for recreation and for work associated with festivals. Religious festivals, organized around local shrines, provided villagers with plays and dance performances.

Summary and Comparisons

This chapter discussed the second imperial age in India and China. The Gupta dynasty and later King Harsha brought much of northern and central India under their rule during the fourth, fifth, and early seventh centuries. Under their rule, India enjoyed unprecedented prosperity and cultural advancement; it is the classical era of Indian art and architecture. Buddhism reached its apogee and began to show signs of decline, while a revived Hinduism began to assume its final form. Disunity again prevailed in India after Harsha's death in 648; divided India could not resist the waves of Muslim invasions that began in 712. Muslim rule now prevailed in most of northern India. Southern India, though divided, escaped Muslim invasions.

The Gupta era also saw the peaceful spread of Indian religions and culture throughout most of mainland and island Southeast Asia, from Burma to present-day Indonesia. Buddhist and Hindu missionaries and Indian merchants ushered most of the region into the historic era, as Indian influences blended with local traditions to form distinctive cultures.

After three centuries of divisions and nomadic invasions, China's second imperial age was politically successful and enduring. During the Sui and T'ang dynasties, Buddhism, entering via the Silk Road, became fully Sinicized. Although the Sung dynasty was militarily weak and unable to rule all Chinese-popluated lands, it continued the cultural growth of the preceding era. Unfortunately, the pacifist Sung succumbed to formidable nomadic invasions. Muslim invasions severed the close link between India and China contributing to the decline of Buddhism in China.

Chinese political and cultural influence spread to Korea and Vietnam beginning with the Han dynasty and accelerated in the second imperial age. The Korean and Vietnamese civilizations at this time were scarcely distinguishable from the Chinese, but in time, both merged foreign influences with native traditions.

CHRONOLOGY

1 C.E.	Ajanta and other cave excavations begin in India
	Buddhism arrives in China
	King Kanishka calls Fourth Buddhist Council
	Gandharan and Mathuran art styles
	Paper invented
	Three Kingdoms and era of disunity in China
	Spread of Buddhism
	The Gupta dynasty
	Revival of Hinduism in India
	Buddhist cave temples begin in China
500	
	Yang Chien reunifies China, Sui dynasty
	Grand Canal in China
	Harsha rules in India
	Founding of T'ang dynasty
	Hsuan-tsang goes to India
	Confucian revival
	Muslims invade India
750	
	Golden age of Chinese poetry: Li Po
	Printing invented
	Northern Sung dynasty
	Liao, Chin, Hsi Hsia states in North China
	Neo-Confucianism gains; Buddhism declines in China
	Chinese examination system fully developed
1000	Turkish Muslims conquer North India; Rajput resistance
	Southern Sung dynasty
	Porcelain manufacture perfected
	Gunpowder invented
	Mongols conquer the Southern Sung
1300	

Japan entered its historic age around 500 C.E. under heavy Chinese and Sinicized Buddhist influence. Unlike Korea and Vietnam, Japan was not under Chinese political dominance but freely emulated China's more advanced culture. It too, in time, combined native and imported traditions to form a refined culture and combine titular imperial rule with warlord dominance and feudal institutions.

In both India and China, northern regions suffered invasions after the fall of their respective first empires, and, in both, invasion brought new ideas. The Greeks who settled in Afghanistan and northwestern India introduced their artistic styles to adorn Buddhist worship sites while the Greek-influenced Buddhist missionaries introduced Greco-Indian art to China. Both cultures were enriched as a result. The Muslim invaders that entered India after 712 brought monotheistic religious ideas irreconcilable with Hinduism and Buddhism; their invasions therefore caused fissures that persist on the Indian subcontinent to this day. In contrast, although China's post-T'ang nomadic invaders were unstoppable, they were culturally backward; unlike the highly advanced Arab and Turkic Muslims who invaded India, they were not literate and lacked higher religions. Moreover, their small numbers made them easily assimilable. Each group eventually lost martial prowess, failed to sustain a distinct identity, and ultimately added little to the Chinese civilization that absorbed it.

Though Indian culture had penetrated Southeast Asia in earlier times, its greatest impact in the region occurred during and after the Gupta period. Likewise, while China began its rule over parts of Korea and Vietnam during the Han dynasty, the gradual absorption of China's culture continued under the more advanced T'ang and Sung eras. Japan accepted Chinese culture just as Southeast Asia absorbed that of India; in both cases, the process was voluntary, not the result of political control.

Selected Sources

Items indicated with an asterisk (*) are available in paperback.

Arthaud, J., and B. Groslier. *Angkor.* 1957. A richly illustrated book on Angkor, with good text.

*Brazell, Karen, tr. *The Confessions of Lady Nijo.* 1973. This memoir of a Japanese court lady, long lost and rediscovered in 1940, recreates aristocratic life of the fourteenth century.

"Buddha in the Land of Kami." Films for the Humanities. Video on interactions between Buddhism and Shintoism in Japan between the seventh and twelfth centuries.

Carter, T. F. *The Invention of Printing in China and Its Spread Westward.* Rev. ed. 1955. Chronicle of an event of vast world importance.

*Chang, K. C. *Food in Chinese Culture: Anthropological and Historical Perspectives.* 1977. Fascinating and entertaining account of Chinese food and eating habits from antiquity to the present.

*Ch'en, Kenneth. *Buddhism in China: A Historical Survey.* 1964. A comprehensive and readable survey of the evolution of Buddhism in China to the twentieth century.

China Central T.V. and Central Park Media. *The Silk Road.* 1982. A series of six 55-minute films, each devoted to a portion of the ancient Silk Road.

*Coedes, G. *Indianized States of Southeast Asia.* Ed. Walter F. Vella. Trans. Sue Brown Cowing. 1968. Deals with the multifaceted influences of India on the region through 1,500 years.

Deuchler, Martina. *The Confucian Transformation of Korea.* 1992. On Korea between the tenth and fourteenth centuries.

Devahuti, D. *Harsha: A Political Study.* 1970. A detailed study of India in the sixth and seventh centuries and of Harsha's accomplishments.

Ebrey, Patricia B. *The Inner Quarters: Marriage and the Lives of Chinese Women in the Sung Period.* 1994. A recent study of women and domestic life.

Ebrey, Patricia B., and Peter N. Buckley, eds. *Religion and Society in T'ang and Sung China.* 1993. A useful collection of articles by nine experts in this period of Chinese history.

Farris, William W. *Heavenly Warriors: The Evolution of Japan's Military, 500–1300.* 1991. On the early phase of Japan's warrior culture.

Gernet, Jacques. *Daily Life in China on the Eve of the Mongol Invasions, 1250–1276.* Trans. H. M. Wright. 1962. A good book on an often overlooked subject.

Hall, D. G. E. *A History of South-East Asia.* 2d ed. 1964. A comprehensive and authoritative book.

Hansen, Valerie. *Changing Gods in Medieval China, 1127–1276.* 1990. Interesting look at religion, especially folk religion.

Jaschid, Sechin, and Van Jay Symond. *Peace, War, and Trade along the Great Wall: Nomadic-Chinese Interaction through Two Millennia.* 1989. Pathbreaking study of interactions between China and Inner Asia.

Lane-Poole, Stanley. *Medieval India under Mohammedan Rule (A.D. 712–1764).* Reprinted 1979. A comprehensive account of Muslim conquerors and rulers.

Lo, Kuan-chung, or Shih Nai-an. *All Men Are Brothers.* Trans. Pearl S. Buck. 1933. A popular Chinese novel about a band of Robin Hood–like men and women during the Sung dynasty who took the law into their own hands for just causes.

*Lady Murasaki. *The Tale of Genji.* Trans. A. Waley. 1935. Japan's greatest novel on courtly life.

Packard, Jerrold M. *Son of Heaven: A Portrait of the Japanese Monarchy.* 1987. Traces the world's longest-reigning royal house from its beginning to the present.

Puri, B. N. *India under the Kushanas.* 1965. A good survey of the Kushan era.

Quaritch Wales, H. G. *The Making of Greater India.* 1951. A concise but comprehensive treatment of the spread of Indian culture throughout Southeast Asia.

Reischauer, Edwin O. *Ennin's Travels in T'ang China.* 1955. T'ang China as observed by a Japanese Buddhist monk.

*Samson, George. *A History of Japan to 1334.* 1954. First of a three-volume work on Japan by a recognized authority.

Sato, Hiroaki, trans. and ed. *Legends of the Samurai.* 1995. This book deals with the Japanese military elite from earliest times to the eighteenth century.

*Schafer, Edward H. *The Vermilion Bird: T'ang Images of the South.* 1967. An interesting account of southern China and Southeast Asia.

*——. *The Golden Peaches of Samarkand: A Study of T'ang Exotics.* 1983. An interesting book about the unusual things most history books leave out.

Sinor, Denis, ed. *The Cambridge History of Early Inner Asia.* 1990. This work by a number of specialists has several chapters on China's nomadic neighbors.

Smith, Vincent A. *The Oxford History of India.* 4th ed. Ed. Percival Spear. 1981. A part of this authoritative book deals with the period this chapter discusses.

Steinhardt, Nancy C. *Chinese Imperial City Planning.* 1990. A comprehensive survey through the ages.

Stierlin, Henri. *The Cultural History of Angkor.* 1979. Profusely illustrated, this short but interesting text deals not only with the Khmer culture, but also those of Burma, Thailand, and Champa.

Swann, Peter. *Art of China, Korea, and Japan.* 1963. A good, short, and well-illustrated book that integrates history and art.

*Tinker, Hugh. *Southeast Asia: A Short History.* 2d ed. 1990. Good, short introduction.

Twitchett, Denis, and John K. Fairbank, eds. *The Cambridge History of China.* Vol. 3: *Sui and T'ang China, 589–906.* Part 1. 1979. Many experts contributed to this authoritative volume.

Waley, Arthur. *The Poetry and Career of Li Po.* 1958. Waley brings to life a wonderfully eccentric man and his great work.

Whitfield, Susan. *Life along the Silk Road.* 1999. Recreates lives of people, from princesses to laborers, along the greatest trade route in history.

*Wriggins, Sally H. *Xuanzhang, A Buddhist Pilgrim on the Silk Road.* 1996. An engaging account of the travels of China's most famous pilgrim to India and back.

Wright, Arthur F. *The Sui Dynasty: The Unification of China,* A.D. *581–617.* 1978. Excellent portraits of two men who ruled China around 600 C.E.

———. *Buddhism in Chinese History.* 1959. A good book for both students and specialists.

*Wu, Cheng-en. *Monkey.* Trans. Arthur Waley. 1943. A sixteenth-century novel of how a supernatural monkey and other beasts helped Hsuan-tsang get Buddhist scriptures from India. Chinese children love it as fairy tale and adults as satire.

Additional resources, exercises, and Internet links related to this chapter are available at the Book Companion Web site: http://history.wadsworth.com/upshurcompact4/

COMPARATIVE ESSAY 5
Cultural Borrowing and Cultural Isolation

There are three religious groups here, the panc-h'i *[pandits or brahmans] or learned men, the Buddhist monks or* ch'u-ku, *and the Taoists or* pa-ss'u.
James P. Holoka and Jiu-Hwa L. Upshur, eds., *Lives and Times: A World History Reader*, vol. 1 (St. Paul: West Publishing, 1995), p. 278.

Cavalry warfare in Eurasia came about through a long process of historical evolution. . . . Horsemanship was practiced by Indo-European peoples of the Ukrainian steppes as early as 4000 B.C.E. . . . It is likely that the horse had been domesticated in China during the Neolithic era (circa third millennium B.C.E.) when it was harnessed to the chariot as well as used as a draft animal. . . . Chinese records indicate that the Di [a nomadic people living to the northwest of China] rode horses as early as the Spring and Autumn era (722 to 481 B.C.E.). By the time of the Warring States (403 to 221 B.C.E.), the nomadic use of mounted men had become a form of warfare so powerful as to inspire emulation.
Adam T. Kessler, *Empires beyond the Great Wall: The Heritage of Genghis Khan* (Los Angeles: Natural History Museum of Los Angeles County, 1993), pp. 17–18.

The first cultures evolved and advanced in isolation mainly through independent invention. For example, agriculture appeared in three widely separated parts of the world (West Asia, China, and the Western Hemisphere) at about the same time, each based on different crops (grain/rice, maize/potatoes). Likewise many early cultures independently invented the technique of firing utensils made of clay to make pottery.

With the passage of time, travel, trade, and warfare brought peoples of different cultures together. Diffusion—the passing of ideas, technologies, and languages from one culture to another—became increasingly frequent. The two passages quoted above prove this point. The first was written by a twelfth-century Chinese visitor to Angkor, capital of ancient Cambodia. Situated in Southeast Asia, ancient Cambodia (also called the Khmer state) was ideally located to benefit from traders, missionaries, and settlers from China to the north and India to the west. Although the writer remarked on the presence of Taoist priests from China, Hinduism and Buddhism became the primary religions of that land, with Buddhism finally triumphing. The second passage shows the importance of warfare in affecting technology transfers. When the Di, a nomadic neighbor of the Chinese, learned horse riding, they were able to menace the Chinese more powerfully, compelling them to adopt cavalry in warfare in self-defense.

Another example of war as an important catalyst of diffusion can be seen in the spread of iron weapons. The Hittites were the first people to use iron weapons and became feared widely as a result. In self-defense their neighbors and victims hastened to learn the new technology and make their own iron weapons. Eventually, the technology of making weapons and agricultural implements from iron spread throughout Europe, Asia, and Africa, and iron replaced bronze as the primary metal.

Wars and conquest also spread cultures and ideas. For example, through conquest, the more advanced Chinese spread their culture to Korea and Vietnam. On the other hand, the less cultured Roman conquerors became admiring students of the sophisticated Greeks they subjugated. The Mongols eventually adopted the religions, written languages, and technologies of their different victims, and as a result lost their homogeneity and unity.

Commerce and group migration have also been important vehicles for the spread and diffusion of cultures. In the case of commerce, Greeks trading with the Phoenicians in the eastern Mediterranean adopted the Phoenician alphabet. Chinese traders and Buddhist teachers brought the Chinese writing system to Japan. The Silk Road, a major commercial route across Eurasia, introduced new religions, crops, technologies, art forms, raw materials, and finished products to different cultures across two continents. Indian merchants and other travelers by sea brought the sciences, mathematics, and writing of India's ancient civilization to the peoples of Southeast Asia. Oceans prevented dissemination from Eurasia to the Amerindian civilizations until the end of the fifteenth century. Iron-working was not independently invented in the Americas.

Group migration is another important means of diffusion. From earliest times, people have moved from one region to another in search of land and resources, as conquerors, or in flight from enemies. In Italy, the immigration of the Etruscans from Asia Minor around 900 B.C.E. and of the Greeks after 700 resulted in rapid advances in technology and art throughout the peninsula. In Africa, when the Bantu migrated into the central and southern part of the continent, they brought their own language and customs, which in time were adopted by local peoples. The spread of the Indo-European languages is another example of this type of diffusion. This language system originated in the steppe heartland of Eurasia; the migrating tribes who moved into other parts of Europe and Asia spread their language. As a result, nearly all the languages from northern India to Ireland belong to the Indo-European family and are related.

It is important in studying world history to understand that most civilizations were the amalgamation of indigenous and borrowed elements. Chapters 6 and 7 prove how true this was throughout classic Mesoamerica, the Amerindian empires, the early African kingdoms, Southeast Asia, and Japan. During more recent centuries, as means of transportation and communication have expedited contact between societies, diffusion has increasingly become the predominant mode of cultural change. As the world becomes more interconnected, so too the speed and extent of cultural borrowings and exchanges will increase.

7

Developing Civilizations

•

• Mesoamerican Civilization •

• Andean Civilization •

• African Cultures •

• Summary and Comparisons •

At the same time that the city [Cuzco] was being peopled, our Inca [Manco Capac] taught the Indians those occupations which appertain to a man, such as breaking up and cultivating the ground, and sowing corn and other seeds, which he pointed out as fit for food and useful. He also taught them to make ploughs and other necessary instruments, he showed them the way to lead channels from the brooks which flow through the valley of Cuzco; and even instructed them how to prepare the sandals which we now wear. On the other hand, the Queen employed the Indian women in such work as is suitable to them, such as to sew and weave cotton and wool, to make clothes for themselves, their husbands, and children, and to perform other household duties. In fine, our princes taught their first vassals everything that is needful in life. . . .

The Inca Manco Capac, in establishing his people in villages, while he taught them to cultivate the land, to build houses, construct channels for irrigation, and to do all other things necessary for human life; also instructed them in the ways of polite and brotherly companionship, in conformity with reason and the law of nature, persuading them, with much earnestness, to preserve perpetual peace and concord between themselves, and not to entertain anger or passionate feelings toward each other, but to do one another as they would others should do to them, not laying down one law for themselves and another for their neighbours. He particularly enjoined them to respect the wives and daughters of others; because they were formerly more vicious in respect to women, than in any other thing whatever.*

*Ynca Garcilaso de la Vega, First Part of the Royal Commentaries of the Incas [1609], ed. and trans. Clements R. Markham, vol. 1 (London: Hakluyt Society, 1869), pp. 65–69.

This passage belongs to a foundation legend centering on the achievements of the first Inka, Manco Capac. Especially notable is the concern shown for the status and equitable treatment of women, something not evident in any of the patriarchal societies contemporary with the Inka around the world.

This chapter returns to Amerindian civilizations and African cultures taken up in Chapter 1. It is instructive in looking at these non-Eurasian civilizations to consider the concepts of cultural isolation and cultural borrowing discussed in the previous Comparative Essay

The Amerindian civilizations that had already been established in Mesoamerica and the Andes continued to develop on an increasingly sophisticated course, particularly in engineering, mathematics, astronomy, and the decorative arts. Down through the years some scholars have claimed that Egyptians or Phoenicians or early Japanese or Chinese or some other Eurasian group had somehow crossed the ocean and created these civilizations. A few even professed to find evidence of extraterrestrials landing in Peru. However, most scholars view the Amerindian civilizations as completely indigenous.

In comparison with the Amerindian civilizations, the cultures of sub-Saharan Africa, although separated from Eurasia by an ocean of sand, showed some signs of Eurasian influence. East Africa had close relations with Egypt because of the Nile, and proximity to commercial traffic on the perimeter of the Indian Ocean meant more substantial contacts in general with Eurasia. On the other hand, cultural diffusion into western Africa before the advent of Islam was slight. The Bantu culture that spread into southern Africa showed the least evidence of diffusion.

Mesoamerican Civilization

Our first father-mothers . . . were simply made and modeled, it is said; they had no mother and no father. . . . No woman gave birth to them, nor were they begotten by the builder, sculptor, Bearer, Begetter. By sacrifice alone, by genius alone they were made, they were modeled by the Maker, Modeler, Bearer, Begetter, Sovereign Plumed Serpent. And when they came to fruition, they came out human:

They talked and they made words.
They looked and they listened.
They walked, they worked.

They were good people, handsome. . . . Thoughts came into existence and they gazed; their vision came all at once. Perfectly they saw, perfectly they knew everything under the sky, whenever they looked. The moment they turned around and looked around in the sky, on the earth, everything was seen without any obstruction. . . .

They understood everything perfectly, they sighted the four sides, the four corners of the sky, on the earth, and this didn't sound good to the builder and sculptor. . . .

And so the Bearer, Begetter took back their knowledge: . . . They were blinded as the face of a mirror is breathed upon. Their eyes were weakened. Now it was only when they looked nearby that things were clear.

And such was the loss of the means of understanding, along with the means of knowing everything. . . .*

*Popol Vuh, trans. Dennis Tedlock (New York: Simon & Schuster, 1985), pp. 165–167.

This Maya creation story resembles explanations of the origins of humankind in other cultures. Unlike many of these other accounts, however, there is no "fall," as in the Judeo-Christian tradition, nor are men and women created as limited toys for the gods to enjoy, as in several Asian traditions. In the Maya version, human beings are made perfect and through no lapse of their own are later made imperfect. The stress on knowledge and on perception is also notable and well suits a people who made great innovations in mathematics, astronomy, and engineering.

In Chapter 1 we discussed the Olmec, the parent culture of Mesoamerican civilization. After 400 B.C.E. Olmec society began to lose its vigor, and other cultures arose. The three most notable were the large urban culture centered on Teotihuacán, the mathematically and astronomically sophisticated Maya culture, which lasted almost 2,000 years, and the Aztec state, Mesoamerica's culminating Amerindian empire.

Urban Splendor: Teotihuacán

Teotihuacán arose in an arid valley approximately thirty miles northeast of present-day Mexico City. In 100 B.C.E. the area was a cluster of villages; by 200 C.E., massive public buildings had been laid out. Centuries of prosperity followed, and by 500 Teotihuacán, now a grid-shaped metropolis of 200,000, had become one of the largest urban centers of the world. One reason for Teotihuacán's preeminence was a reliable water supply. Although located in an arid climatic zone, the city was centered on a dozen large, permanent springs in an area of rich volcanic soil. Like the inhabitants of the Tigris-Euphrates valley earlier, the Teotihuacanos used terracing, canals, and other water-saving methods to produce abundant food crops that supported a large population.

The reconstructed center of the city gives some idea of its size and shape. Ceremonial buildings, ball courts, and two great pyramids, the largest almost 600 feet square, sit along a central avenue extending almost three miles. Less dramatic, but equally important to archaeologists, are the remains of some 3,000 other structures within the city. Most of these were multifamily dwellings; typically, each structure featured a patio and a cement foundation with an elaborate drainage system.

Another factor in Teotihuacán's rise to prominence was its control of the obsidian trade between highland Mexico and the gulf coast. Teotihuacán built up a substantial industry for producing obsidian tools, and its artisans also manufactured pottery and other items for large-scale export.

It is unclear how far the Teotihuacanos extended their rule from their valley. Some authorities claim that it expanded hundreds of miles to the east into Maya territory; others maintain that Teotihuacán's influence was commercial and cultural, but that political control reached only into neighboring valleys.

For many Mesoamericans, Teotihuacán was a focus of pilgrimage and worship, for it was there that their ancestors emerged from the underworld. Much of Teotihuacán religion was directed to worship of a "Great Goddess," a female divinity who provided the springs of water. Her images depict her gesturing outward, with water, seeds, and flowers issuing from her body and her clothing. Another powerful symbol of water and fertility was the Feathered (or Plumed) Serpent, the fanged, feather-collared serpent who is depicted undulating on seashell beaches. The Serpent was also a manifestation of the planet Venus, the morning and evening star, the Teotihuacán deity of warfare and blood sacrifice.

Teotihuacanos, living in a generally barren wasteland, were undoubtedly anxious about the permanence of their existence, and devised practices to help the Great Goddess keep

Map 7.1 The Development of Mesoamerican Civilization. Present-day Mexico and Central America were home to several advanced civilizations. The architecture, art, and religion of Teotihuacán influenced the region for centuries. The Maya civilization added greatly to the sophistication of Mesoamerican architecture, mathematics, astronomy, and the calendar.

Teotihuacán well-watered. Mesoamerican astronomers for many centuries carefully recorded the appearance of Venus as the morning and evening star. Calculating that Venus had a 584-day cycle and that five of these cycles corresponded to eight 365-day years, they formulated an almanac of 2,920 days. Apparently, a warrior cult found in Teotihuacán and other Mesoamerican cultures used the phases of Venus to find the most propitious times to undertake what some modern investigators have termed "star wars," campaigns conducted to secure sacrificial prisoners. These prisoners were executed in great public ceremonies, providing the blood "soul" that turned into water, thus sustaining Teotihuacán; Teotihuacán paintings depict red drops of blood from dead and dying prisoners literally turning into blue drops of water.

Although early Teotihuacán art rarely depicted military themes, after 500 C.E. there were more and more allusions to warfare, and archaeologists have found the remains of a great wall. At this same time, the Teotihuacán trading area began to contract. The population of Teotihuacán declined dramatically, and by 800 C.E. people had abandoned the city and settled in the outlying villages. Scholars have proposed many reasons for the end of Teotihuacán civilization, including environmental degradation, revolt, and invasion. When the Mexica (Aztecs) came wandering into the valley centuries later, only the crumbling mounds of the great city remained; so impressive were even the ruins, however, that the awed visitors said it must be Teotihuacán, in their language "the Abode of the Gods."

The Integration of Mesoamerican Civilization: The Maya

More is known about Maya civilization than about either the Olmec or Teotihuacán cultures. Maya culture survived, even if somewhat transformed, until after the Spanish conquest, and four million persons still speak Maya today. Although scholars have deciphered Maya writing, overzealous Catholic missionaries, trying to annihilate the pagan past of the Maya, left only three preconquest Maya books intact, together with fragments of a fourth. Several postconquest Maya books, among them the *Popol Vuh,* are also of great value in understanding the Maya. Glyphs (inscriptions on rocks) have survived in great numbers. Archaeologists at first thought that most of them did little more than depict stylized human figures, list names and dates, and make a brief reference to some important event. New discoveries, especially tombs containing murals, pottery, and jewelry, now make it clear that the Maya artisans often portrayed individual Maya rulers realistically.

The Maya lived in dense rain forest lowlands in present-day northern Guatemala and in neighboring Belize, Mexico, and Honduras. Their staple food was maize, and it had long been thought that they practiced exclusively slash-and-burn agriculture, a technique that wasted land and produced a relatively low yield, thus supporting only a small population. However, aerial surveys have revealed "unnatural" tracts of land under the jungle canopy. On-site investigation proved that the Maya in fact had employed a second type of agriculture. They built canals in swampy areas alongside raised plots of earth, which drew moisture from the canals by capillary action. The maize and vegetables were fertilized with swamp lilies (depicted on many Maya statues and monuments) dredged from the drainage ditches. The high yield of the raised-field system could support a population of millions.

By 700–800 C.E.—the approximate era of Muhammad, Charlemagne, and the T'ang dynasts—Mayan civilization was at its height. It was composed of about twenty-five independent city-states led in size by Tikal and Copan with perhaps 30,000 inhabitants each. Each city had a number of satellite towns and villages. These city-states traded with—and made war on—each other via a complex river system supplemented by roads built by forced labor. The city-states were characterized by a highly stratified society in which royal dynasties supported by priests and warrior nobles ruled over farmers, artisans, and traders.

Compared to their Mesoamerican predecessors, the Maya had easy access to an enduring building material—limestone. They built colossal tomb-pyramids, some 250 feet high, topped by temples and palaces made of limestone. In the larger Maya cities, these impressive buildings, interspersed with walled ball courts, were surrounded by hundreds of smaller mounds supporting thatched private dwellings. The tops of the great pyramids were often connected by wide causeways, over which marched sumptuous royal and religious processions, watched by the massed populace far below. The huge city of Tikal was thirty-two square miles in area, spreading out from six temple complexes.

Unlike their Olmec predecessors and the Andean Amerindian cultures, the Maya developed a written language, one that was so difficult to translate that it eluded experts for generations. Some have claimed the decipherment of Maya writing is a feat that ranks with the unraveling of the "double helix," the DNA code. Steles recording the triumphs of Harvest Mountain Lord between 143 and 156 C.E. are the earliest dated writing so far deciphered in the Western Hemisphere. Unfortunately, surviving Maya writing is limited mainly to astronomical almanacs and to glyphs on steles proclaiming genealogical and political propaganda about each city's royal dynasty. The bark books that might have furnished evidence about the economic, legal, and literary aspects of Maya civilization have perished through natural decay or by destruction from European invaders.

The crowning glory of Maya civilization was the full development of a mathematics-calendar system that was among the most advanced in the world at that time. This complex calendar was initially devised about 600 B.C.E. by the Zapotecan and Olmec cultures in south-central Mexico, and spread across the region. The Maya used a base-20 mathematics system, with a dot for units and a bar for fives. It included a sign for zero, a mathematical tool of enormous power. Chinese, Indian, and Muslim mathematics all made use of the zero, while the Romans, in contrast, had no zero, which made their calculations cumbersome at best.

The Mesoamerican calendar, as the Maya fully developed it, was extremely complicated: a 260-day year (thirteen twenties) ran parallel to a solar year (eighteen twenties plus five days that were considered ill-omened). Once every 18,980 days, almost exactly 52 years, the 260-day year and the solar year coincided and the cycle began again; that date was one of great ceremony. Of greater significance in dating and understanding Mesoamerican civilization is the Long Count, a Maya linear calendar. The Maya believed that, after several earlier creations and destructions, a new creation had occurred on August 13, 3114 B.C.E. that was to end no earlier than 4772 C.E., and according to some extremely advanced Maya calculations, perhaps not for 142,000,000,000,000,000,000,000,000,000,000,000 (nonillion) years.

The Maya needed an elaborate calendar because the extensive astrological observations and mathematical calculations on which it was based helped them propitiate the gods who demanded appropriate recognition every day of the year. The Maya pantheon contained a host of gods, many of whose functions are not well understood at present. Each day had a name associated with two gods, one from the 260-day ritual calendar and one from the 365-day solar calendar. The pairings of these gods changed daily throughout the fifty-two years it took the two calendars to come back to their starting point. The attributes of each god determined the characteristics of the day. It was no simple matter for an individual to get safely through a given day. He had to know not only the names of the two gods controlling the day but also the relations between the gods and thus what had to be done to placate them. The Maya were obsessed with "good" and "bad" days; according to one of the surviving guides to good and bad days, the bad far outnumbered the good, and on those bad days special care was required in the performance of daily labors.

The religious mainstay of the Maya people was the ruler, who performed the key ceremonies that perpetuated the order of the universe, visible and invisible. The lord, usually male but occasionally female, was divine, or descended from gods. The lord, especially in the role of chief priest, bound together the nine levels of the underworld, the earth, and the three levels of heaven and made it possible for the people to communicate with their ancestors and the gods. Upon the lord's death, elaborate state ceremonies prepared for his journey into the underworld. At the same time, intense ceremonies marked the ascension of the new lord, because the people of the city-state were in terrible danger until a lord was in place to maintain the universal order.

Like many premodern cultures, the Maya believed that their gods required humans to practice rituals of sacrifice, thereby feeding the gods and recognizing their role in maintaining the universal order. A key sacrifice was human blood. In many cultures, such as those of the ancient Hebrews, the Greeks, and the Romans, the gods were satisfied by the blood of animals.

It was not so in Mesoamerican civilization. The key sacrificial act of Maya culture was the frequent shedding of royal blood to properly connect the people of the state with the gods. In public ceremonies the lord pushed a sting-ray spine through his penis or scrotum, while his consort pulled a thorn-embedded rope through a hole in her tongue. Maya nobility also shed their blood. This bloodletting not only fed the gods, but

© British Museum

The Life-Giving Blood of Monarchs. This carving illustrates a Maya ceremony in which rulers gave their blood to ensure divine favor for their kingdom. Here, a queen pulls a rope braided with thorns through her tongue.

also enabled the practitioner to hallucinate, bringing forth the Vision Serpent. The Serpent in turn brought forth such images as Venus warriors and ancestors, who answered questions about the future. Hallucinogenic enemas were another way to contact one's ancestors.

Although Maya city-states waged wars of conquest against each other at times, often Maya wars were ritualistic, designed to capture the rulers of another state rather than destroy the adversary's city. The Maya had adopted from Teotihuacán the Venus warrior cult, which specialized in securing captives for sacrifice in Maya religious and political rituals. The blood of these captives apparently played a supplemental role in the rituals of the Maya. Some were tortured for years to give blood at many ceremonies, and a captive of high standing, perhaps a ruler, was killed at the accession ceremonies of the Maya monarchs. The number of victims was quite low, however, compared to the mass butchery of the Aztecs (see below).

The Maya version of the sacred ball game appears to have become more complex and deadly compared to Olmec practice, although the rules are still not known. Clad in protective padding, Maya rulers are often depicted playing ball against a captive leader in a T-shaped court flanked by steep temple walls or stone bleachers. Apparently the captive leader, after losing the ritual ball game, was bound to a rubber ball and dropped from the high temple walls or bounced down the stone steps.

The Maya looked on the afterlife as a dangerous, but survivable, experience. The souls of living humans, nobles and commoners alike, were portrayed as being transported in huge dugout canoes across the water of life, paddled by the gods. As death approached, the dugout slowly sank, dropping the souls into Xibalba, a fearsome underground realm with the overwhelming stench of rotting corpses and disease, peopled with death gods, creatures with overpowering putrid breath and stupendous farts, out to kill human souls. Many souls never returned from that dread place, but the Maya had hope. Previously, ball-playing Hero Twins had fooled the not-too-bright death gods and had been reborn and returned as ancestors. Reigning monarchs claimed their predecessors had returned; ordinary Maya hoped their souls, too, would outwit the demons and return as ancestor spirits to advise their descendants.

As archaeological discoveries in the last few years have shown, not all Maya cities centered on astronomy, religion, and war. At Cancuen ("Place of Serpents"), in the jungles of Guatemala, archaeologists have uncovered the splendid palace of King Tah ak Chaan, covering the area of two football fields with 170 high-ceilinged rooms arranged around eleven courtyards. The surrounding city was apparently a prosperous center of commerce and crafts located on a navigable river. There is no evidence that the city's rulers engaged in major wars with neighbors.

Between 800 and 900 Maya civilization in the heartland of Guatemala began to decline. About 1100 there was a revival, mixed with outside influences, centered at Chichen Itza and Uxmal in drier Northern Yucatan, reaching its peak about 1300. After 1400 decline again set in, hastened by plagues, disastrous weather, recurrent warfare, and the lack of an effective central authority. When the Spanish arrived in 1517, Maya civilization, now almost 2,000 years old, was in a state of collapse.

Mesoamerican Imperialism: The Aztecs

As Maya civilization was fading in Guatemala and the Yucatan, a new Mesoamerican group, the Aztecs, became dominant in the highlands of central Mexico, scene of the Teotihuacán culture. The Aztecs, who usually called themselves Tenocha or Mexica, were a nomadic tribe from the north that straggled into the Valley of Mexico and tried to find a place to settle on the shore of Lake Texcoco. For several generations the Aztecs led miserable lives as mercenaries or provided cheap labor for the settled tribes. Then, in 1345, fleeing from an enemy, the Aztecs took refuge on several marshy islands in the lake. According to their legends, when they arrived on the largest island they saw an eagle perched on a cactus with a serpent in its mouth. The eagle commanded the Aztecs to build temples and to feed the sun with the blood of sacrificed victims.

From their island base, the Aztecs created a formidable empire. At first they continued to serve as mercenaries, but in 1428, allied with two other towns, they destroyed their former employers and seized a base on the mainland to supplement their main island, Tenochtitlán. The Aztecs soon dominated their allies and moved into the areas that offered the greatest economic rewards.

By 1500 the Aztec Empire stretched from the Pacific Ocean to the Gulf of Mexico, controlling 28 million people. By then Tenochtitlán and other nearby islands had fused into one great capital city, with an estimated population of 400,000. Another million Amerindians lived in fifty or more city-states in the surrounding Valley of Mexico.

Tenochtitlán was an engineering marvel. The Aztecs built a dam to control the lake level and constructed two aqueducts to bring fresh water from the mainland to supplement the springs on the islands. To supply food for Tenochtitlán, the Aztecs expanded upon the Maya system of hydraulic agriculture, draining swamp land and creating artificial islands to grow food for the city. Three great causeways, the longest more than five miles long, linked Tenochtitlán to the mainland. The city itself had wide avenues, imposing temples and other public buildings.

Tenochtitlán could not be fed from its islands alone, and the Aztecs waged war to secure tribute in both food and luxury goods, as well as to obtain victims for their sacrificial rites. They carried on substantial trade with states that were still independent; merchants were an essential part of the Mesoamerican economy, as they had been since Olmec times. The Aztec language, Nahuatl, became the standard language of the area they controlled, probably from commercial convenience.

Despite this economic reliance on other areas, the Aztecs never completely centralized their government. The Aztec state combined direct control over Aztec areas with indirect control over nearby vassal states. At the center was the emperor, a reincarnation of the sun god, who lived in opulence surrounded by a harem of concubines, a bevy of servants, and a battery of state officials. His governors, who administered the city of Tenochtitlán and the incorporated provinces, acted as rulers themselves as they held court, conducted religious ceremonies, collected taxes, and imposed regulations.

The rest of the empire was essentially a league of tribute-paying city-states. Although the Aztecs built strong fortresses here and there, they generally did not maintain garrisons in conquered territories. If the flow of required tribute diminished, the Aztecs sent out their army composed of imperial troops and allied forces, sometimes accompanied by local militia, and subdued the territory again.

In its exploitative aspects, the Aztec Empire resembled the Roman Empire; but whereas the Roman Empire provided the subject people with many benefits, the Aztecs gave their subjects few benefits and many burdens. Consequently, Aztec vassals were constantly looking for a way to topple their overlords.

With such restless subjects, and since war was essential to their economic system and religion, Aztec society stressed the virtues of the warrior, and the Aztec nobility was one of military service. Although the son of a noble had many advantages, and it was certainly easier for him to rise than it was for the son of a commoner, he did not inherit his father's position or distinctions, which had to be earned. As in Republican Rome and imperial China, but unlike most premodern cultures, it was possible for commoners to earn distinction in war and rise to power.

Aztec society was not entirely organized on a military basis. Priests, who could be female as well as male, had a separate hierarchy, as did those merchants who engaged in long-range trade. The commoners, of course, formed the bulk of the population, and they owned their personal possessions but not the land they worked. Beneath them was a large group whose legal status was about halfway between an indentured servant's and a slave's. For some, this status was temporary, until some debt was paid or some criminal punishment worked off; for others, it might be permanent. In either case, children born to members of this class were free commoners.

Women traditionally had respected status in Aztec society. The early Aztecs had stressed matrilineal descent, and women could own and inherit property, make contracts, sue in court, divorce their husbands, and under certain circumstances, remarry. Motherhood was honored.

As the Aztecs became more imperialistic, however, patrilineal concepts began to emerge, and female roles began to alter. The Aztecs brought in polygamy among the upper classes to balance the excess of male over female mortality brought about by war. Aztec women were encouraged to bestow sexual favors on warriors, and women captured on campaign were given to the victorious soldiers.

An Aztec Poet Sings

I, the singer, I make a poem
That shines like an emerald
A brilliant, precious and splendid emerald.
I suit myself to the inflexions
Of the tuneful voice of the tzinitzcan....
Like the ring of little bells,
Little golden bells....
A scented song like a shining jewel,
A shining turquoise and a blazing emerald,
My flowering hymn to the spring.*

This poem not only provides a great deal of information about Aztec technology, but it also suggests the continuing fascination with colors that is a mark of modern Mexican esthetics. On the technological side it shows the use of metals to make bells, and even more, it shows that the Aztecs knew how to make an alloy that would produce a bright, cheerful sound, which is far more difficult than simply casting the metal. A *tzinitzcan* was probably some sort of xylophone.

**John H. Cornyn, "Aztec Literature," in XXVIIe Congrès International des Americanistes (Mexico, D.F., 1939), vol. 2, pp. 328–331.*

Aztec religion focused on nourishing the sun, which in return furnished the light necessary for life. The food for the Sun God was human hearts, extracted from the living chests of sacrificial victims. As was true at Teotihuacán and in the Maya culture, the need for human victims spurred the Aztecs to make war in order to obtain captives, but the Aztecs took this practice much farther than their predecessors. They not only gathered captives from war, but also forced vassal states to pay tribute in the form of human beings. Precise numbers of those sacrificed are notoriously unreliable, but there is evidence that the Aztecs sacrificed as many as 20,000 victims in one celebration, and Moctezuma II claimed that when he came to the throne in 1502, he sacrificed 40,000 persons. Other gods, hundreds of them, controlled other facets of the world and received a diversity of offerings. To honor the god of planting and springtime, for example, the priests flayed sacrificial victims and then wore the newly removed skins for their rituals. Other offerings, however, might include flowers, music, and dancing.

Like the Maya, the Aztecs were obsessed with good and bad days, signs, portents, and divination. In their mind, the world was in delicate balance, and only continual human sacrifices at their religious ceremonies kept the universe operating and prevented the dark forces from destroying everything.

The Aztecs rewrote history to mask their barbarian origins and their ignominious first century in the Basin of Mexico. They claimed kinship to the Toltec, a culture that preceded them. They promoted some of the Toltec gods—especially the plumed serpent god, Quetzalcoatl, and the storm god, Tlaloc.

Aztec metalwork was primarily artistic, not utilitarian. The Aztecs used gold, copper, silver, tin, and alloys, including bronze, and their metalwork, based on Toltec models, was superb. The main Aztec concentration in their art was the carving of massive stone statues, bigger than those of their predecessors, intended to last for eternity. Their literature, too, mostly in the form of poetry, was extraordinarily rich.

Andean Civilization

In districts where the quantity of water for irrigation was small, they [the Inka] divided it proportionately (as they did with everything they shared out) so that there would be no dispute among the Indians about obtaining it. This was only done in years of scanty rainfall when the need was greatest. The water was measured, and as it was known from experience how long it took to irrigate a fanega [1.6 acres] of land, each Indian was accordingly granted the number of hours he needed for the amount of land he had, with plenty to spare. Water was taken by turns, according to the order of the plots of land, one after another. No preference was given to the rich or the nobles, or to favorites, . . . or to royal officials or governors.*

*Garcilaso de la Vega, Royal Commentaries of the Incas, and General History of Peru, trans. Harold V. Livermore (Austin: University of Texas Press, 1966), vol. 1, p. 248.

In this passage Garcilaso de la Vega depicts the essential justice of Inka rule in Peru. De la Vega, through his mother, was a second cousin of the last two Inka rulers.

The Inka Empire was the last, and by far the greatest in population and extent, of a series of Amerindian cultures that had flourished in Peru and the Andes for more than

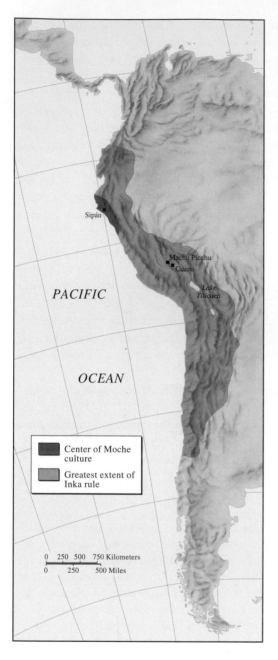

Map 7.2 The Development of Andean Civilization. Over the centuries, highly developed but nonliterate cultures evolved in the area of present-day coastal Peru, Ecuador, Bolivia, and Chile. The Moche culture featured monumental architecture and intricate work in precious metals. After 1200, the Inka, from their capital at Cuzco, began to dominate the Andes region; within about three centuries they had conquered a vast domain underpinned by a centralized administration, state socialism, and an extensive, well-engineered highway network.

3,000 years. In Chapter 1 we discussed the Chavin culture, the first civilization to appear in this area. Many cultures followed the Chavin in this area in the centuries after 200 B.C.E. In this section we will discuss the Moche, a culture just now coming to the attention of the world through a number of archaeological projects. We will then turn to the Inka, whose engineering skills and thoroughgoing economic and political restructuring programs were unique to Amerindian experience.

The Artistry of the Moche Culture

The Chavin culture that faded out in the last centuries B.C.E. was succeeded by the Moche society, which dominated the Peruvian coast and the nearby hill country between 100 and 700 C.E., the same time as Teotihuacán and the apex of Maya culture. In Eurasian terms, the Moche were active from the height of the Roman Empire to the height of the Carolingian Empire, and from the end of the Han to the beginning of the T'ang dynasty. Little was known about the Moche until the past decade, when archaeologists made a series of important discoveries bearing on this major Amerindian group.

As in Mesopotamia, the Moche maintained their population in their arid coastal climate by inheriting and expanding an elaborate irrigation system that provided food supplies sufficient to support cities of more than 50,000. Their diet consisted of maize, beans, avocados, squash, peppers, potatoes, and peanuts, along with llamas, guinea pigs, and fish, a diet more nutritious than that of many modern South Americans. Their society, like most of the others in Andean and Mesoamerican civilization, was apparently rigidly hierarchical, in which warrior-priest kings, a warrior-priest nobility, and male and female priests lived in splendor while the masses worked. The newly discovered tombs of the elite are crammed with splendid artifacts demonstrating advanced techniques in textiles, pottery, and jewelry and depicting elaborate religious ceremonies. No examples of writing have come to light; it appears that the Moche, like all Andean civilizations and early Mesoamerican cultures, did not have a written language.

As in Mesoamerica, Moche art and architecture centered on religion. Like Mesoamericans, the Moche based their religion on waging war to obtain prisoners whose blood sacrifice was needed to ensure fertility of their land. Warrior-priests, assisted by other priests, conducted these rituals on immense pyramids and platforms that were the center of urban complexes. There is considerable evidence that the Moche warriors relied heavily on bluster and on jangling noises to intimidate their enemies. The Pyramid of the Sun was among the world's largest buildings; built from over 100 million adobe bricks, it was 135 feet tall and covered 12.5 acres. It served as an administration building and a mausoleum as well as a temple.

The Moche culture is notable for the skills of its artists. Although few textiles have survived, those that have are of high quality. Moche potters produced a variety of ceramics,

LIVES AND TIMES ACROSS CULTURES

Women and Religious Rituals

*I*n 1991, after the three royal tombs at Sipán had been excavated, the tomb of a woman who served as the Priestess of the Sacrifice Ceremony was excavated approximately fifty kilometers south of Sipán . . . [at] San José de Moro. . . . It had a room-sized burial chamber . . . which contained multiple individuals and great quantities of associated grave contents.

The woman was buried with a metal goblet the size and form of the one used in the Sacrifice Ceremony, and she had a pair of large plumes made of a silver-copper alloy, which were identical to those that characterize the headdress of the Priestess. . . .

The fact that the Sacrifice Ceremony was so widespread in both time and space strongly implies that it was part of a state religion, with a priesthood in each part of the kingdom composed of nobles who dressed in prescribed ritual attire. When members of the priesthood died, they were buried at the temple where the Sacrifice Ceremony took place, wearing the objects they had used to perform the ritual. Subsequently, other men and women were chosen to replace them, and to perform the same ceremonial role.*

Like the priestesses of classical Greece or the Vestal Virgins of Rome, women in Moche society held positions of authority and prestige within the system of religious observances and rituals, as the evidence of wall paintings and goods found in graves of priestesses show.

*Walter Alva and Christopher B. Donnan, Royal Tombs of Sipán, 2d ed. (Los Angeles: University of California Press, 1994), pp. 223, 225.

including ritual goblets for religious ceremonies. They created pottery and three-dimensional clay sculptures that depict the life of commoners as well as kings; one can see the misery of tortured captives and the joys of sex and of chewing coca leaves. These potters also worked with low-relief designs and painted complex scenes of important rituals on their pottery.

The Moche were especially skilled and imaginative jewelers, working with smelted gold, silver, and platinum and with jade and turquoise. They used the lost-wax method to create three-dimensional metal castings with interchangeable parts. The artists also employed imaginative gilding techniques to make nonprecious metals, especially copper, look like gold. To adorn the bodies of the elite, Moche crafts workers created necklaces of gold and silver beads shaped like human heads with inlaid mother-of-pearl jaguar teeth, gold ear and nose plugs, gold protective plates for buttocks and chest, silver-copper alloy ritual masks, and hammered gilded copper masks and helmets. Many other objects such as scepters and spearheads were also cast in precious metals or copper.

Moche political power faded about 700, and for several hundred years various empires dominated sections of the Andean uplands, extending their power down to the adjacent coast. Meanwhile, urban states continued to flourish on the north coast of Peru. Chan Chan, the capital of a secondary state, had over 50,000 inhabitants. Its wide, straight streets divided the city into ten districts, each of which had massive protective walls thirty to forty feet high and ten feet thick and its own ceremonial center, an unusual and unexplained design for a city. The era of political fragmentation ended abruptly in the fifteenth century, however, when a highland people, the Inka, burst upon the region.

Amerindian Social Engineering: The Inka

The Inka came late to the Peruvian scene. Because they, like their predecessors, were nonliterate, little is known of them before the Spanish came, and what is known generally concerns the period after 1438. Inka oral tradition, which the Spanish recorded, went back to a king who ruled about 1200. All that is certain is that the Inka started their rise to power from the city of Cuzco, in the Andean highlands northwest of Lake Titicaca. For two hundred years, they expanded slowly at the expense of their neighbors.

Then under their Inka (ruler) Pachacutec (reigned 1438–1473), the Inka people flashed like a meteor across Andean civilization. Within two decades Pachacutec and his son, Thupa Yupanki, conquered dozens of other peoples in the Titicaca Basin and the adjacent highland river systems. The more the Inka prevailed, the more manpower and supplies became available to them. Success bred success, and the Inka conquered to the north as far as present-day Quito, Ecuador, and took control of the older cultures on the Peruvian coast. After Thupa Yupanki (reigned 1471–1493) came to the throne, he smashed uprisings in some of the newly acquired territory and then moved south, adding much of present-day Bolivia and the northern part of Chile to the empire. Wayna Qhapaq (reigned 1493–1525) spent much of his reign consolidating the empire, marching his army from Chile to the rain forests of the upper Amazon and on to Ecuador to put down rebellions, extending the northern limits of the empire slightly in the process.

Photo by Susan Einstein, UCLA Fowler Museum of Cultural History

Moche Warrior Ear Ornament. This piece of jewelry, made of gold and blue-green mosaic pieces, depicts a warrior holding a war club in his right hand. It was found in one of the royal tombs at Sipán.

The new empire, essentially acquired in fifty-five years, dwarfed any state hitherto created in the Andes and Peru. Inka emperors ruled some 12 million people patchily distributed in a domain stretching about 3,000 miles from north to south. They had done this without wheeled transport, draft animals, a system of writing, and with only occasional use of copper tools and weapons. Ruling from the highland capital at Cuzco, the Inka called their empire *Tawantinsuyu,* the Land of the Four Quarters, in reference to the four major divisions of their realm.

The Inka had an empire, but with it came a major problem. How, as a tiny minority of perhaps 70,000, could they rule millions of recently conquered peoples scattered across a difficult terrain? To accomplish this, Inka authorities carried out a comprehensive restructuring of much of Andean society. They relocated populations, reordered the economy, constructed an extensive transportation network, and inculcated a state religion. This program was carried out most thoroughly in the older parts of the empire in the central Andes and on the Ecuadorian and Chilean frontiers was influenced by the sophisticated cultures along the Peruvian coast.

Inka planning began with their campaigns of conquest. Inka leaders saw to it that ethnic Inka males were not wasted in nonmilitary tasks or unnecessary combat. In the early days, as much of the military supplies as possible were carried by llamas and Inka women; later, members of conquered groups hauled the goods. The Inka took over other peoples as much as possible by negotiation and bravado, massing their men in a show of force to overawe their opponents and get their peaceful submission. If a group held out in a siege or in other ways fought back, the Inka, like the Mongols or Alexander the Great, massacred the population or deported them as a warning to others. To garrison the frontiers and to watch areas considered likely to rebel, the Inka settled groups of soldiers conscripted from other parts of their empire to remain as alien watchdogs.

The Inka needed reliable stocks of food and other materials to supply their armies, a difficult proposition considering the patchy pattern of settlement and production in their empire. Upon conquering a territory the state claimed control over all its resources, including human labor. In each locality, Inka authorities divided the land into three portions, one each for the sun (the state religion), the state, and the community. Laborers from the community worked Inka state and sun agricultural land as they had worked the lands of their former rulers. The state, with many construction projects on its agenda, wanted the general population to be well fed and self-supporting so they could produce healthy youngsters for the labor force; accordingly, the Inka sometimes gave back part of the conquered land to the community in exchange for *mit'a,* special labor for road building and other state projects.

To increase food production the Inka, combining economic sophistication with military prudence, carried out a massive resettlement program. Before the Inka conquest, local feuds in many areas had forced the local populations to stay out of the more fertile, but more dangerous, valleys where maize could be grown. They lived and fortified themselves on the more defensible ridges, raising potatoes. Having brought peace along with their conquest, Inka authorities moved families from the fortified ridge-top towns—thus reducing the chance of effective revolt—and settled them in new, smaller villages down in the nearby valleys, in order to expand the production of maize. Thus most agricultural families retained their households and remained in a familiar neighborhood near their old town, but became more productive. Some women in the agricultural communities wove cloth from wool supplied by the state; other individuals made rope or utilitarian pottery or collected honey and feathers.

With staple food production stabilized, even increasing, the Inka then designated certain families or groups in every locality to specialize in producing other sumptuary products such as fine textiles, elaborate metalwork, and imperial Inka pottery. Other groups were relocated to the eastern slopes to raise more cotton, cacao, and coca. The alien military colonies that watched the unreliable groups and garrisoned the frontiers were usually held responsible for producing special products. Some young women were selected to reside at the ceremonial centers in the new Inka towns in segregated quarters out of public sight. They wove cloth and brewed beer for religious ceremonies, and were later married to men designated by the state. Other individuals were taken to Cuzco to be servants or concubines for the royal and noble families; some of these individuals rose to positions of prominence.

Like the Persians and Romans, the Inka developed an elaborate road system to move military forces quickly around the empire, transport their food supplies where needed, and in general tie their widespread domains together. Using the forced labor of their subjects the Inka supervised the construction of two main roads, one on the coast and one in the highlands, that ran the length of their empire. With only humans and llamas to traverse them, the roads were only twenty-five feet wide, but well engineered. They were built upon strong foundations and laid along efficient gradients, passing across suspension bridges, through tunnels, and over mountains. Those north-south trunk roads were connected with lateral east-west main roads at major cities; a network of secondary roads tied many villages in the empire to the system. Forced labor gangs built almost 20,000 miles of roads and thousands of rest stations a day's walk apart. Runners stationed at convenient intervals carried government messages throughout the breadth of the empire. In their engineering prowess the Inka were typical of Andean culture, which had already developed an elaborate system of irrigation canals along the coast.

To tie supplies and the road network together, the Inka, directing masses of special mit'a labor, built a series of new towns on the new transportation grid and built hundreds of warehouses outside each town. They reserved the land nearest town for the production of state-owned food, storing it in the warehouses. These storehouses did much more than feed the armies. The Inka used the stored food to support local officials, mit'a laborers, persons traveling on government business, those attending state ceremonies, special craft workers, areas suffering from crop failures, and other projects. Although Inka storage facilities were built along the highways, they were intended mostly for local or regional use. With transport limited to humans and llamas, it was impossible to bring a steady supply of goods from long distance to Inka armies in garrison or on campaign. The Inka could only hope that if they were efficient in producing supplies and storing them in large amounts everywhere in the realm, their armies could be fed and their empire preserved.

As might be expected, the elaborate Inka system of economic and social controls was administered by an extremely hierarchic and bureaucratic government. As in other cultures, the choice of a new Inka was no easy decision. Since each reigning Inka had several wives and a number of concubines, the path to the succession was sometimes disputed by rival claimants. Oral tradition told of crimes and civil wars as rival claimants battled for the throne, until a new divine Inka, Son of the Sun, established his claim. The deceased rulers were believed to be intermediaries with the gods, and their mummified remains were brought forward to partake in religious ceremonies and be consulted by priests on important matters. The male relatives of each departed Inka were entitled to all the wealth that ruler had accumulated during his reign, in part to support that royal corpse in imperial style for eternity. As time went by, the number of royal households supporting imperial mummies had, naturally, increased, and each new Inka was faced with a need to accrue riches during his reign so that his descendants could maintain his corpse with becoming grandeur. This need for each Inka to find new wealth was one of the motives for Inka expansion.

Beneath the eccentric world of the Inka royalty, the machinery of government ran fairly smoothly. The upper nobility, composed of the Inka's blood and adopted relatives; administered the four quarters and the provincial subdivisions of the empire. In much of the Inka domain, local bureaucracy was set up on a numerical rather than a geographic basis. The top local official administered 10,000 families; under him ten officials administered 1,000 families, and so on down to the most minor official, who administered five families. To supply the huge number of officials necessary to run such an elaborate governmental system, the state employed some lesser Inka nobility, but it drew most of these officials (as had ancient Rome) from the traditional leaders of the group to be governed. The cooperating elite received honors and valuable state goods from the Inka. They could pass their office and status on to their children if the Inka found them sufficiently efficient and trustworthy. This practice of having the local elite carry out Inka authority among their people was another method designed to hold the loyalty of conquered peoples and their leaders.

Inka local authorities strictly regulated the private lives of their subjects. They tried to impose their language, Quechua, on their subjects and did not allow individuals to travel far from their homes. Even marriage, which was obligatory, was, in theory, arranged by the government.

The lack of a written language did not handicap the government because the census and storehouse records vital to proper administration were kept on *khipus*. A khipu was a rope from which hung a collection of strings with knots tied into them to record numbers. Different knots and different textures and colors of the strings coded the data to various subjects and purposes; one khipu could very well have recorded as much information as a modern ledger.

The Inka used religion as another means to unify the state. Cuzco and the new towns built by the Inkas were used to stage elaborate ceremonies that indoctrinated their subjects in the state religion while also allowing their subjects to worship their traditional gods. The Inka encouraged, perhaps required, the people of the nearby communities to come to the new towns for religious ceremonies that sometimes lasted for days. While in town the attendees were housed, fed, and provided with beer, and sometimes given clothing and sandals—all at state expense.

The Inka religion contained a creator god, and in its early stages sparingly featured human sacrifice. The primary focus of public worship, however, was the Sun God, along with the god of rain and thunder. Inka religion included animism as well, with practically every geographic feature having resident spirits and each family and each individual having a guardian spirit. The Inka religion had doctrines of sin and confession and taught a belief in personal immortality. The Inka had oracles, looked for omens, and practiced divination, but unlike the Maya were not obsessed with lucky and unlucky days. The wealthy sacrificed grain or killed llamas in the ritual, and the poor sacrificed guinea pigs. Human sacrifice took place at times, although they never attained anything like the Aztec volume of victims.

Despite their elaborate administrative and engineering systems, the Inka had major problems. Given the primitive level of transport and communication available to them, Inka rulers still found themselves too far from the extremities of the empire to rule effectively. Some scholars maintain that the cumbersome state bureaucracy employed by the Inka retarded economic development, as compared to a money-based market economy.

Perhaps the greatest problem in the Inka state was its capricious system of succession. Under the rule of the three great Inka monarchs the empire was spared strife over the succession, but in 1525, when Wayna Qhapaq died, two of his sons claimed the throne.

For seven years, civil war ravaged the empire, while a plague caught from the Europeans spread throughout the Inka world, killing many. When the Spanish arrived in 1532, they found the Inka state already in advanced decline.

African Cultures

The king . . . was naked, wearing only a garment of linen embroidered with gold from which hung four fillets on either side; around his neck was a golden collar. He stood on a four-wheeled chariot drawn by four elephants; the body of the chariot was high and covered with gold plates. The king stood on top carrying a small gilded shield and holding in his hands two small gilded spears. His council stood around similarly armed and flutes played.*

I, 'Ezana, king of Axum . . . made war upon Noba [Nubia], for the peoples had rebelled and had boasted of it. Twice and thrice they had broken their solemn oaths, and had killed their neighbors. And as I had warned them, and they would not listen, I made war on them. They fled without making a stand, and I pursued them for 23 days, killing some and capturing others . . . burnt their towns, both those built of bricks and those built of reeds, and my army carried off their food and copper and iron . . . and destroyed the statues in their temples, their granaries, and cotton trees and cast them into the Seda [Nile]. And I planted a throne at the place where the rivers Seda and Takkaze join.**

*Robert W. July, *A History of the African People* (New York: Scribner's, 1970), p. 48.
***The Horizon History of Africa* (New York: American Heritage, 1971), p. 80.

The preceding passages give glimpses into the wealth and power of the King of Axum (in present-day northern Ethiopia) where a large empire of enormous military and commercial power flourished contemporaneously with the Roman Empire around 350 C.E. The account of King 'Ezana's military victory over Nubia was inscribed on a stele (carved stone pillar) at his capital in Axum. Axum was one of many empires that emerged in Africa, some of which dated from early historical times. These states were as varied in organization as the landscape from which they arose. The following section will give a general overview of the geographic and social diversity in Africa. Then, a number of the cultural and political systems that existed from approximately 900 to 1600 will be described; the discussion will begin with the civilizations in North Africa and Ethiopia and will continue geographically from western to central, then from eastern to southern Africa.

Geographic and Social Diversity in Africa

The continent of Africa, an area more than three times larger than the continental United States, exhibits enormous geographic and cultural diversity. Scholars estimate that there may be as many as 1,000 different ethnic groups speaking almost as many languages in Africa. Linguists have classified this multitude of languages into four major phyla or categories. Although human life probably first emerged in Africa, climatic extremes and infertile soil have kept human societies from prospering in much of the land area. Sitting directly on the Equator, much of central Africa is subtropical, and there are vast arid areas in the north and in the south. Sparse rainfall, droughts, and resulting famines have

LIVES AND TIMES ACROSS CULTURES

Folk Wisdom

Throughout history, riddles and proverbs have been popular forms of "folk wisdom" in Africa and the rest of the world. Folk wisdom amuses, teaches moral lessons, and tests mental quickness. Among the Yoruba of West Africa, storytellers often asked riddles to attract the attention of audiences before a performance. For example, a storyteller might pose the following riddle:

Question: We call the dead—they answer.
          We call the living—they do not answer.
Answer: Dry, dead leaves; fresh tree leaves.

Proverbs are also popular in most African societies. As the wisdom of proverbs is often universal, it is not surprising that many African proverbs have equivalents in the Arab and Western worlds. Some examples of African proverbs and their equivalents from other cultures are:

Mouth not keeping to mouth, and lip not keeping to lip, bring trouble to the jaws. (Yoruba-West Africa)

Talk is silver, silence is gold. (Western)

He fled from the sword and hid in the scabbard. (Yoruba)

Out of the frying pan, into the fire. (Western)

The tar of my country is better than the honey of others. (Moroccan North Africa)

There is no place like home. (Western)

An old cat will not learn how to dance. (Moroccan)
You can't teach an old dog new tricks. (Western)

If music changes, so does the dance. (Hausa—Central Sudan)

What is written on the forehead, the eye must see. (Arabic)

Keep up with the times, or what must be, must be. (Western)

been common in Africa since the beginning of recorded history. For example, along the 1,200-mile Niger River in West Africa rainfall averages between eight and twenty inches in a good year; the lack of rain has impeded population growth in many areas. Deforestation and overuse of the soil since ancient times have contributed to making much of the terrain inhospitable.

Save for the tropical rain forests, the central sections of the continent receive the most rainfall and are therefore the most conducive to agricultural development; however, these areas are infested with the tsetse fly. The fly carries the trypanosomiasis parasite, deadly to both humans and cattle, the main source of livelihood for many African societies. Humans, especially those living along fertile river banks, must also cope with other debilitating and often deadly diseases, including river blindness, malaria, and bilharzia (a parasitic disease transmitted to humans by river snails). African societies have generally adjusted to these diseases and climatic conditions by living within the constraints imposed by nature; or as one Swahili proverb put it, "Do not borrow off the earth, for the earth will require its own back with interest."

Owing to these basic ecological problems, some African peoples led a nomadic existence based on herding sheep, goats, or cattle. In many herding societies, such as the Masai in present-day Kenya, the number of cattle he owned determined a man's status within the community. Cattle were also used as a medium of trade and given as a "bride price" to a young woman's family upon her marriage. Although herding societies often looked down upon the settled, farming communities, economic exchanges of goods (animals, hides, or ivory for sugar and other commodities) between the two were nonetheless commonplace.

In some areas, specific ethnic groups monopolized professions; for example, in landlocked present-day Mali, the Fulani, who are herders, use the banks of the Pondo River as pasture, while the Bambara farm along the river and still others are fisherfolk. However, most African peoples worked in mixed economies as both farmers and herders. As in Central and South America, traditional farmers in Africa frequently used the slash-and-burn technique to clear plots of land. They then cultivated the plots for several years; after the soil ceased to be productive, they abandoned the fields and the entire cycle was repeated elsewhere. The slash-and-burn technique contributed to the nomadic existence of many African peoples and also led to further degradation of the soil.

Kinship relationships were extremely important in African societies, and high value was placed on marriage and children. Lineages, or lines of descent, determined crucial matters such as inheritance and identity. As in Indian and Arab societies, marriage involved the entire extended families, not just two individuals as in much of the West. Most African societies were polygamous and patrilineal (descent follows through the father); however, some were matrilineal (descent follows through the mother).

Although the organization of living space, building materials, and architectural styles found in Africa were as diverse as its climate, African villages and homes reflected the high value and emphasis placed on communal relationships. In contrast to the rather private closed-in buildings and rooms found in much of West Asia or Europe, many African homes and public buildings were tightly grouped in circular or irregular patterns and were circular in shape. Circular, communal storage granaries were often clustered around the villages, and were often built beside or on top of homes or on stilts to protect them and to keep out the damp, insects, and vermin. Whereas the centralized governments of ancient Egypt and many Asian empires controlled the collection and storage of basic foodstuffs, in most of sub-Saharan Africa food storage was organized on a local level. The villagers constructed and maintained collectively owned granaries; in some areas separate granaries were built for men and women.

Most Africans used mud brick, straw, clay, and wood to build their homes, generally reserving stone construction for public or monumental buildings. Clay gave artists greater freedom for artistic expression and ease in constructing contoured, free-form designs than did stone or brick; clay was also resistant to the extremes of temperatures, particularly heat, found in much of Africa. Great care was lavished on the upkeep of the clay walls. As early as the fourteenth century the famous traveler Ibn Battuta remarked on the beauty of the decorative ornamentation on the buildings of African towns and villages. Decorative shapes and designs varied tremendously. The one-story, one-room circular homes grouped around larger communal buildings in much of Mali were fairly typical, but homes with straw roofs and monumental entrances were also found in Mali and the Cameroons. In Mauritania and East Africa stone buildings with elaborate interior designs were common.

Historically, the region above the Sahara Desert, extending from present-day Morocco in the west to Egypt in the east, was Mediterranean in orientation. The great Carthaginian Empire flourished in present-day Tunisia, and much of North Africa had been part of the empires of Egypt and later of Rome. Farther south, however, the historical ties with Mediterranean cultures became tenuous.

Islamic North Africa

Western and northern Africa and Egypt, however, had also been connected by trade routes with Saharan and central African societies. The Berbers, who since ancient times have lived in large areas of North Africa, generally controlled these caravan trails. Their origin is unknown, and they speak their own distinct language. As the Muslims spread across Egypt and all of North Africa in the seventh century, the Berbers converted to Islam, but maintained their own language and ethnic identity.

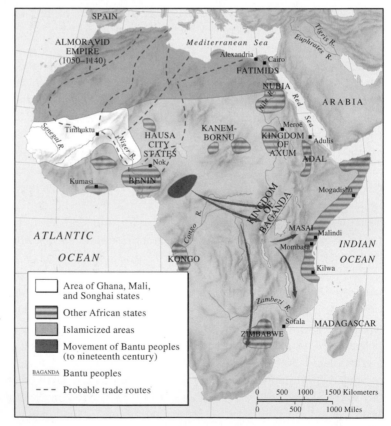

Map 7.3 Africa, 900–1500. Many great empires or kingdoms, such as Ghana in West Africa, Axum in the east, and Zimbabwe in the south, flourished throughout the African continent from 900 to 1500. In North Africa, the majority of the population converted to Islam.

Except for Morocco, the Islamic societies that had been established in North Africa were all incorporated into the Ottoman Empire in the sixteenth century. Governors who were either appointed directly by the sultan or were local rulers who pledged their loyalty to Istanbul ruled these North African provinces. Although trade continued with sub-Saharan states, the northern sectors of Africa remained tied culturally, religiously, and politically with the Arab world and the Ottoman Empire.

The Berber rulers in Morocco, meanwhile, resisted most Portuguese and Spanish territorial onslaughts and at the same time expanded southeastward. In 1590, under Sultan Mansur, Moroccan forces armed with cannon attacked the declining Songhai Empire (present-day Mali), whose soldiers were equipped only with spears and bows and arrows; the power and wealth of that once great state came under direct Moroccan control.

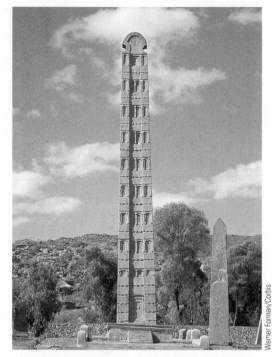

Axum Stelae in Ethiopia. This is only one of the more than 1,300 stelae found at Axum in Ethiopia. Although most of the inscriptions have not yet been translated, the monoliths indicate that the Axum architects were well advanced and that the city must have had elaborate stone palaces and public buildings.

Werner Forman/Corbis

Thus, despite its ties with the Mediterranean world, North Africa also retained links with central and southern portions of the continent by exchanges of goods, peoples, and ideas. Similar interrelationships existed between the great kingdoms in Egypt, the Sudan, and Ethiopia.

Christian Ethiopia

In keeping with the patterns noted in the comparative essay on empires, the most sedentary populations, and ultimately the most highly advanced empires in Africa, tended to develop around the major rivers that provided consistent sources of water and fertile land. As noted in Chapter 1, the early empires of Egypt and the Kushites in the Sudan both arose along the banks of the Nile.

From 300 B.C.E., however, the Kushite kingdom with its capital at Meroë (in present-day Sudan) began to decline. As Egypt declined in military and economic importance under Roman rule, the demand for iron ore from the Kushite kingdom dropped, and its economy suffered. The Kushite kingdom was also weakened by attacks from surrounding desert tribes and, most crucially, by Axum, a new rival economic and military power based in Ethiopia.

In 700 B.C.E. Semitic tribespeople from Yemen, in the southern Arabian Peninsula, moved across the Red Sea to the eastern coastal regions of Africa. They gradually migrated to the Ethiopian highlands, possibly to escape the malaria-infested coast. The new immigrants intermarried with the indigenous population and transmitted their skills in dry stone building and hillside terracing.

From the assimilation of the Semitic and indigenous populations came a unique society with its own language, Ge'ez, though Ethiopians issued documents in Greek as well. The synthesis of African and Arabian peoples in Ethiopia is analogous to the assimilation of peoples in the Hellenistic world and the emergence of Swahili culture along the coast of East Africa.

The new Ethiopian kingdom, with its capital, Axum, in the highlands, and a port, Adulis, on the Red Sea, was in an advantageous position to benefit from increased sea trade in the region. As trade along the Red Sea prospered, Axum emerged as a major trading center for eastern Africa, the Nile, and southern Arabia. To protect both the sea and land trading routes, Axumite kings conquered large sections of Ethiopia, and by the fourth century C.E. had overwhelmed the Kushite kingdom's capital city of Meroë.

Although the early Axum rulers were animists, the empire became Christian in the fourth century, after decades of contact with the Christian world through Byzantium and the Coptic Christians in Egypt. A Syrian Christian was instrumental in converting King 'Ezana, who, like other imperial rulers in Rome and Asia, encouraged or forced the religious conversion of his subjects. Thus, the empire became predominantly Christian many years before much of Europe. However, the decline of Byzantium and the Muslim conquest of Egypt and North Africa in the mid-seventh century cut off Axum from the Mediterranean world, and the Christian kingdom gradually lost its importance as a trading center and became increasingly isolated.

As the commercial power of Axum faded, people migrated to the nearby high plateaus intersected with mountains and deep gorges, which provided ideal terrain for well-defended fortresses. Here in Ethiopia they created a Christian kingdom under the *negus* or emperor, and Ge'ez remained the language of the Coptic (Christian) Ethiopian church.

The series of spectacular churches carved into solid rock at Lalibela are monuments to the artistic energy and religious fervor of the people. Constructed about 1181 by King Lalibela, the churches attested to his deep-seated religious devotion. Ethiopian tradition holds that one of the most remarkable of these churches was built in one day by fervent believers assisted by angels. In many ways these monuments are reminiscent of the Gothic cathedrals produced during an era of similar fusion of church and state in Europe. The development of the Ethiopian Christian kingdom in relative isolation from outside forces was made possible by its unique terrain and was in marked contrast to the extensive exchanges and assimilation of peoples in central and southern Africa.

By the sixteenth century, Muslim armies from Arabia, which already controlled most of the coastal regions of the Horn of Africa, began to attack Christian Ethiopia. Early in the sixteenth century, a local military ruler, Ahmad ibn Ghazi (reigned 1506–1543), organized forces that threatened the very survival of Ethiopia. Known as Gran, or left-handed, Ahmad instilled his forces with a fervent belief in *jihad* (holy war) and brought most of Ethiopia under his control. To save his government, the Ethiopian emperor Lebna Dengel (reigned 1508–1540), who claimed direct descent from King Solomon and the Queen of Sheba some 2,500 years earlier, appealed to the Portuguese for help.

The emperor's appeal fell on receptive ears. The Portuguese and Ethiopian cultures were both headed by devoutly Christian absolute monarchs hostile to the Muslims. In addition, the Portuguese had long been fascinated with Ethiopia, which they believed might house the famed realm of Prester John. The myth of this fabled Christian kingdom and the mystery of its exact location had created lively debate in Europe; Mongolia, China, and India had been suggested as possible locations. When these possibilities had been discarded, Portuguese adventurers began to search for Prester John's mythical kingdom in Ethiopia. Most were initially disappointed by the poverty of Ethiopia and dismayed by many of its religious customs. Nevertheless, the riches of Ethiopian religious art and architecture impressed the Portuguese missionary Father Alvarez. Alvarez's books on Ethiopia described these finds and excited even more interest among Europeans in the remote African kingdom.

In response to Emperor Lebna Dengel's appeal, Portugal sent an expeditionary force under the command of Dom Christoval da Gama to rescue the Christian kingdom from its many enemies. In 1529, however, da Gama was surrounded by Muslim forces, taken captive, and decapitated. Da Gama's death marked the apex of Muslim power in Ethiopia, which waned after the death of Ahmad the Grand. In the remote mountains of northern Ethiopia, the emperors attempted to continue their absolute rule, but internal political rivalries, religious disputes, and Muslim opposition weakened their power. Although Ethiopia's relative isolation prevented it from keeping pace with the commercial and political growth of other, wealthier kingdoms in central and western Africa, its difficult terrain made it almost impossible for outside forces to conquer it.

The Bantu

As early as 200 B.C.E., peoples from the present-day Nigeria-Cameroon border began a migration that was to change central and southern Africa. Like other groups around the world, these people called themselves simply "the people," or Bantu. Although scholars disagree as to the exact size and chronology of the Bantu migrations, they followed along the northern and eastern edges of the tropical forest and then south along the western coast. Future linguistic and anthropological studies will provide additional information on the Bantu origins.

Originally fisherfolk, the Bantu also grew crops such as yams and sorghum and hunted small game. In East Africa cattle were and, in many regions, still are the basis of the social-economic organization. Some Bantu groups like the Tutsi adopted cattle as the basis of their economic livelihood but did not worship the cattle or consider them sacred. While many Bantu peoples specialized as either agriculturalists or pastoralists, most practiced a mixed economy based on agriculture and herding.

In spite of the enormous diversity of the Bantu peoples throughout central and southern Africa, Bantu societies manifested certain common characteristics, and along with languages based on common linguistic roots, they shared folklore and oral historical traditions and similar pottery-making techniques. Lacking a written language, Bantu elders, like Greek epic poets before Homer, passed on long, involved stories of the history and culture from generation to generation.

Iron implements came into use among the Bantu by 300 B.C.E. The Nok, who lived in the region between the Benue and Niger rivers in present-day Nigeria, were apparently the first people in West Africa to use iron-making technology. As noted in Chapter 1, the Bantu peoples may have gained their knowledge of iron working and the lost-wax process for bronze casting from the Kushites, who migrated west from the Nile valley as their empire declined. It is also possible that ironworking among the Bantu occurred spontaneously through independent invention; archaeological exploration in western Africa may yield more answers to these questions in the future.

As Bantus put iron spears and hoes to use, they increased their food supply, thus creating larger, healthier populations. The increase in population undoubtedly put additional strain on the available arable land, which was quickly exhausted by the slash-and-burn technique of the Bantu farmers. In addition, the influx of migrants seeking relief from the growing aridity of the Saharan regions put pressure on the Bantu. With plenty of available land southward, they began to migrate into central Africa along the Congo River. From there they apparently moved along the Zambezi and ultimately reached the eastern African coast and southern Africa, perhaps as early as the third or fourth century C.E.

These migrations, each of which may originally have numbered only a few hundred people, continued over hundreds of years. A superior iron technology enabled the Bantus to dominate groups in central and southern Africa. Temperatures of above 1,500 degrees Celsius are needed to melt iron ore, and the Congo, with hardwoods that burned very hot, allowed for the production of particularly fine high-grade iron. The Congo became a leading center for iron production. Numerous smelting furnaces remain scattered throughout central and southern Africa, but as caches of iron ingots have not been found, it appears that the crude iron metal was immediately made into hoes, other implements, and weapons.

With a few exceptions, such as the Pygmies in the equatorial forest, the Bantus successfully assimilated with other indigenous peoples. As a result, the Bantu language, like Indo-European in Eurasia or Nahuatl in Mexico, became the prototype of hundreds of central and southern African languages. Similarly, Bantu cultural and social mores spread throughout the territories, much as Olmec cultural innovations spread throughout Mesoamerica. The Bantu diffusion was based not so much on military or even technological superiority; rather it emerged from their creation of settled agricultural communities, which attracted and culturally overwhelmed the nomads and hunters of central and southern Africa. These numerous Bantu societies were the direct ancestors of the multitudinous ethnic groups that the Europeans encountered in the nineteenth century and are scattered from Nigeria in West Africa, north into the forest and south to the Congo, and to the Indian Ocean in East Africa.

Bantu societies had a complex system of belief in the supernatural and an extremely wide range of means of worship and of ways of dealing with the supernatural. Many believed in nature spirits and in the power of the ancestors, who gave identity and onward movement to life. The ancestors were believed to be responsible for transmitting the accumulated wisdom of the society; for example, passing on the knowledge of iron smelting.

Many Bantu societies, as well as other West African ethnic groups, had a belief system based on a supreme god or higher deity. Some in West Africa, such as the Yoruba, who belong to a Bantu-related linguistic group, had an extremely complex cosmology with a pantheon of gods and goddesses. The Yoruba believed that the God Oduduwa sprinkled sand on water and then released a chicken that scratched the sand, thereby creating the first land on earth; the Yoruba city of Ife, founded about 850 C.E., was believed to have been built on the site of creation. According to Yoruba history, Oduduwa had sixteen sons from whom the Yoruba royalty and *oni* (king) were descended. Building on the Nok knowledge of carving, Yoruba artists at Ife created elaborate bronzes and carved stone sculptures of the royal rulers.

In many Bantu societies, worship involved the use of highly sophisticated and finely wrought carved masks or fetishes, used in a complex system of rituals that often involved dance. Just as some Christians considered icons as aids for spiritual devotion, so, too, did many Bantu peoples consider masks and other carved objects as a means of approaching the supernatural. Specialized experts, or medicine men and women, and diviners often assisted in these rituals and were viewed as intermediaries between the supernatural and the physical world. Many Amerindians had similarly complex cosmologies and ceremonial rites.

The family was the basis of Bantu societies and economies. As one proverb taught, "A man outside his clan is like a grasshopper without wings." Nuclear clusters of related families formed villages and clans. Much as Amerindian societies did, Bantu societies lived in balance with nature; when the population grew too large or the arable land was exhausted, Bantu clans had to migrate elsewhere. Most Bantu societies were organized around the village and were patriarchal and polygamous, although a few were matriarchal.

Many Bantu societies were organized along age sets or age grades in which work, social life, and political responsibility were meted out on the basis of age. Age grades were divided along gender lines from the youngest boys and girls, to those who had reached puberty, to the elders, who had the most responsibilities and authority. When they reached puberty, young boys and girls often underwent extensive rites of initiation to mark their membership in the adult community. The Kikuyu in Kenya divided the male population among boys, warriors, and elders. Work was strictly defined along gender lines, with farming and cooking often considered "women's work" and hunting and martial arts "men's work." The elders in Bantu societies were highly respected for their knowledge and experience.

Bantu societies were often extremely democratic in that adult men had rights of full participation in the governing of the societies. Bantu governmental systems lacked uniformity and ranged from the highly organized monarchy of the Baganda to the decentralized systems of the Kikuyu. The non-Bantu speaking Igbo in southern Nigeria were organized into councils that conducted affairs of state and made political and economic decisions on the basis of consensus. The Igbo placed high value on the work ethic, rewarding those who prospered and contributed to the society. The Ganda had a highly institutionalized monarchy in which the kings were viewed as divine in the same way that the ancient Egyptians and Romans, among others, had deified their rulers. Many of the centralized monarchies established a feudal system of patron-client relationships with other groups who paid tribute or were treated as vassals or held as slaves. In contrast, the Kikuyu never had kings or even chieftains, but lived in scattered homesteads in the Kenyan highlands and relied upon the extended family to act as the major governing force.

As in India, the extremely damp and humid climate of central Africa has militated against the preservation of wood and straw architecture and carvings, and the lack of good building stone limited stone architecture. Nevertheless, some stone constructions—like those of Zimbabwe—do remain as evidence of the Bantu achievements; these will be described later in this section.

Successor States: Kingdoms of Gold and Salt

Less accessible to the Mediterranean civilizations were the states of Ghana (flourished 500–1250), Mali (1250–1450), and Songhai (1450–1600). These wealthy and elaborately organized kingdoms are often referred to as successor states because each built on the ruins and contributions of its predecessor. Located on savannas (grassy plains with scattered trees), these states were originally based on wealth secured from the trade of salt and gold.

Published memoirs in Arabic by Muslim travelers, various works by Europeans, oral traditions, and archaeological and anthropological studies have all contributed to our knowledge about these kingdoms. Firsthand written accounts by contemporaries tend to be more common in the kingdoms under Islamic rule, where literacy in Arabic was fairly widespread among the elite. Many of the non-Muslim kingdoms, lacking written languages, relied on oral traditions to transmit knowledge of historical and social events; recent scholarship indicates that many of these oral traditions are as accurate and detailed as the written records. Like written accounts, oral renditions often exaggerated the glory and power of victorious, successful rulers.

Muslim traders referred to ancient Ghana as the Land of Gold. The gold was mined in Upper Volta and in parts of present-day Guinea and Mali; the salt came from remote regions of the Sahara, where in some places it was so common that it was used as building blocks for houses. The rulers of Ghana, Mali, and Songhai became rich as the middlemen for this vast trade. They had the valuable gold and salt brought to central depots where the goods were loaded on camels in huge Berber-run caravans that traversed the Sahara to the Mediterranean coast. The salt was then sold around the Mediterranean.

The Ghanaian kingdom rose to power by 500 C.E., reaching its peak in 1050. Its founders were the Soninke people, but because all Ghanaian kings took the name "Ghana," little has been ascertained about individual leaders. Oral traditions held that there had been twenty-two kings before the rise of Islam in 622. By the eighth century Muslim writers were already describing the richness of the kingdom. By 1000 the

The Epic of Askia Mohammad

A man came who was wearing beautiful clothes.
He was a real man, he was tall, someone who looked
good in white clothes, his clothes were really
beautiful.
One could smell perfume everywhere.
He came in to sit down next to Kassaye.
They chatted with each other, they chatted, they
chatted.
He said to her, "It is really true.
"Kassaye, I would like to make love with you.
"Once we make love together,
"You will give birth to a boy,
"Whom Si will not be able to kill.
"It is he who will kill Si and will become the ruler."
Kassaye said to him, "What?"
He said, "By Allah."
She said, "Good, in the name of Allah."
Each night the man came.
It is during the late hours that he came,
Each time during the coolness of the late evening,
Until Kassaye became pregnant by him.
Kassaye carried her pregnancy.
Kassaye had a Bargantche captive.
It is the Bargantche woman who is her captive, she lives
in her house, and she too is pregnant.
They remained like that.
Kassaye kneeled down to give birth.
The captive kneeled down to give birth.

So Kassaye, Kassaye gave birth to a boy.
The captive gave birth to a girl.
Then Kassaye took the daughter of the captive, she took
her home with her.
She took her son and gave it to the captive.
So the people left for the palace.
They said to Si:
"The Bargantche captive has given birth."
He said, "What did she get?"
They said, "A boy."
He said, "May Allah be praised, may our Lord give him
a long life and may he be useful."
Then they were thoughtful for a moment.
They got up and informed him that Kassaye had
given birth.
They asked, "What did she get?"
They answered, "A girl."
He said, "Have them bring it to me."
They brought it to him, he killed it.
It is the boy who remained with the captive and Kassaye.*

This is a portion of the long, oral epic tracing the history of the great Songhai ruler, Askia Mohammad Touré. By the trick described here, Askia Mohammad was saved from death; he ultimately surmounted his humble upbringing, defeated his family's enemies, and became ruler over a vast empire in West Africa. At its zenith, this kingdom covered over 400,000 square kilometers of territory.

*The Epic of Askia Mohammed, narrated by Nouhou Malio, in John W. Johnson, Thomas A. Hale, and Stephen Belchers, eds., Oral Epics from Africa: Vibrant Voices from a Vast Continent (Bloomington: University of Indiana Press, 1997), pp. 127–128.

Ghanaian kings ruled over extensive vassal states that paid tribute and were controlled by an army at least 200,000 strong, recruited from among those same vassal states. Ghana was a classic trading state, and its cities, like Kumbi Saleh, Gao, and the fabled Timbuktu, became exceedingly rich. As in similar feudal kingdoms elsewhere, internal strife and uprisings by vassal states undermined the central authority of Ghanaian rulers, who by 1250 succumbed to the Mali kingdom founded by Sundiata (reigned 1234–1255).

By this time, Islam had already begun to make a profound impact on the West African kingdoms. As Islam had spread across northern Africa during the eighth century, traders and nomads had brought the new religion with them to West Africa. In general, throughout Africa, Islam made the greatest impact in urban areas, where Muslim traders often resided. Islam had a wide appeal because of its relatively direct theological precepts and its openness to all converts. There were also undeniable commercial benefits to be derived from alliances with the rest of the Muslim world. As a result, the ruling black aristocracy often converted to Islam, while the people in rural areas generally remained committed to the religions of their ancestors. However, converts to Islam often maintained many of their old religious and cultural practices along with their Islamic beliefs.

With the conversion of the ruling elites, Islamic and Arabic cultural and religious beliefs were gradually merged with the indigenous cultures of West Africa. The ties with Islam provided the elites with further commercial and intellectual contacts with the vast and, at that time, powerful Islamic world. As in Europe, the conversion of a feudal leader often meant the ultimate conversion of the people under his rule; as Christianity spread with the conversion of key leaders, so did Islam and Islamic culture in Africa.

Mansa Kankan Musa (reigned 1312–1337) was the best known of the powerful leaders of Mali; Muslim historians were lavish in their praise of his leadership. In 1324–1325, he made a famous pilgrimage to Mecca with an entourage of five hundred slaves, each with a golden staff; the slaves drove hundreds of camels loaded with some four tons of gold. According to contemporaries, Musa and his entourage spent gold so freely that they depressed the price of gold on the Cairo exchange for decades. Mali, however, soon fell to the same sorts of internal rivalries and uprisings that had destroyed the Ghanaian kingdom. The nomadic Taureg attacked and finally occupied Timbuktu in 1433–1434.

By the mid-fifteenth century, the growing Songhai kingdom, founded by Sunni Ali (reigned 1469–1492), had largely supplanted Mali. Ruling from the city-state of Gao, in present-day Mali, the Songhai spread their authority far across western Africa and into the Sahara. Sunni Ali extended and consolidated the empire, dividing it into provinces under appointed officials and creating a navy to patrol the Niger River. The empire reached its zenith under Askia Muhammad Touré, known as Muhammad the Great (reigned 1493–1528). Like his predecessors, however, Muhammad failed to solve the problem of succession. Threatened by military attacks from Morocco in the late sixteenth century and weakened by internal rivalries, the Songhai kingdom collapsed. With the arrival of western explorers, slave traders, and merchants, the great savanna empires were supplanted by African peoples from the coast and forest regions or by Europeans.

As in European feudal kingdoms, the society in these savanna kingdoms was strictly regulated according to class. As in most preindustrial societies, the ruling monarchs controlled much of the wealth and the majority of the people remained pastoralists or small farmers. Vassal states were forced to pay tribute and to provide "volunteers" for the army upon demand. The rich elites and rulers held slaves, but in contrast to slavery elsewhere, the numbers were small and slaves were considered as humans, not merely property. Especially in Muslim areas, they often worked as household servants, not as field laborers.

As in China and the Muslim world, the ruling aristocracy patronized the arts. As previously noted, African artists excelled in sculpture, and many brilliant examples of their craft in stone, wood, and bronze survive. The Nok in northern Nigeria and the Ife and Benin, forest peoples, were expert artisans. The Nok were known for their finely wrought terra cotta sculptures and beadwork. Nok terra cotta humans tend to be highly stylized, while sculptures of animals are highly realistic; Nok sculptures, some of which are almost life size, are finely detailed and often show elaborate hairstyles and beaded jewelry. Many Benin bronzes utilizing the lost-wax method still exist; it is not known whether this technique was indigenous, the product of independent invention, or a cultural exchange from the Nile where the technique was also employed.

Both Mansa Musa and Muhammad the Great brought scholars from Mecca to encourage science and education. Their actions demonstrate how the annual pilgrimages to Mecca facilitated the assimilation and spread of arts and sciences throughout the Islamic world; the annual pilgrimage was undoubtedly a major contributing factor to the strength of Muslim societies. In addition, Muslim pilgrims brought back goods and ideas that were fused with indigenous cultures when the pilgrims returned to their homes, and both ideas and cultures were assimilated and transmuted. Hence, Arabic language words or expressions and Islamic practices are still common among many contemporary West African societies.

Prosperous West African Kingdoms

In common with the kingdoms of gold and salt, other West African states had highly centralized political systems and economies based on trade and agriculture. The Oyo and Benin Empires were ruled by "divine kings," whose welfare was often thought to determine that of their kingdoms. The status of these kings was so high that their subjects sometimes feared that an ailing, sick king meant that the state would weaken and probably die. The Oyo Empire prospered under a series of dynamic kings until the eighteenth century. In conquered areas, village chieftains reported to palace chiefs appointed by the king, who, together with other notables, assisted in his administration.

Benin, perhaps the most powerful kingdom of the centralized states, was already a powerful kingdom by 1300. Under Ewuare the Great (reigned c. 1440–1473), the prosperous kingdom extended from the port at Lagos to the Niger. Although the economies of the western and central African kingdoms had long been indirectly connected with Europe through trade with North Africa and the Muslim world, Benin, a center for overland and sea trade, was

African Gold Mask Pendant. In addition to trading in gold, Africans also created intricate golden jewelry and objects for their own pleasure. This golden mask reveals a high level of expertise and creativity.

Benin Bronze. The oba, flanked by two attendants, wears the dress, collar, and anklets signifying his high rank.

British Museum, London, UK/Bridgeman Art Library

one of the first West African kingdoms to come into direct contact with European traders and explorers.

Portuguese traders described Benin city as a large fortified stronghold at least twenty-five miles in circumference. While the *oba* (king) of Benin and his court resided in a lavish palace decorated with bronze plaques, most of the populace lived in mud houses covered with palm leaves. The city was divided by broad streets and connected to the coast by a good road. Portuguese travelers reported that there were no beggars in Benin, as the king and government officials cared and provided for the poor.

Both the Oyo and Benin societies assimilated and extended the artistic traditions of the earlier Ife kingdoms of western Africa. Benin artists were particularly renowned for their highly realistic bronze sculptures made with the lost-wax process. They also excelled in wood, ivory, and terra cotta sculpture. The oba and notables adorned their dress with finely crafted gold and ivory ornaments. At ceremonial functions, the oba wore robes decorated with red coral beads and carved ivory masks attached to his belt; ivory had religious symbolism and indicated the ruler's divine aspects. Ivory carvings were often handed down to royal successors as a symbol of kingship. As in the Ottoman,

Safavid, and Chinese Empires, the rulers subsidized a lively court art. By controlling the craft guilds, Benin kings guaranteed their acquisition of the finest art works in bronze, gold, and ivory.

Strong kings, assisted by councils of notables, also led the Akan states, in present-day Ghana. Some of these kings were advised by priests in a type of theocratic government. These states were all dependent upon agriculture for revenues, but they also engaged in trade; the most profitable items were gold and kola nuts. The Ashanti, who moved from the interior into the coastal area of present-day Ghana, were the most powerful of the Akan people. Leading strong military forces, the Ashanti kings soon subjugated the peoples living along the coastal regions; by gaining control over the trade routes for gold from the savanna regions they became both rich and powerful.

The Ashanti excelled in making finely wrought and lavish gold objects. The kings held a monopoly over gold nuggets and crafted pieces; the people could own only gold dust. Ashanti kings appeared at state functions dressed in golden hats, bracelets, necklaces, and even gold-decorated sandals. Europeans were so impressed by these displays of wealth that they called the region the Gold Coast. The Ashanti were also known for handwoven cloth known as *kente*. Kente cloth is woven into long strips, which are then sewn together; originally only chiefs and notables wore the kente. Much as clans in Scotland have their own tartans, Ashanti royal families had their own designs, usually in bright greens, reds, blues, and gold.

A Strong Muslim Kingdom in Africa

Our Sultan Haj Idris . . . sought to follow the example of our Lord and Master Muhammad.

So also his exploits when he fought the Barbara, till the earth in its fulness became too narrow for them and the desert too small for them.

So he made the pilgrimage and visited Medina. . . . He was enriched by visiting the tomb of the companions of the prophet Muhammad . . . and he bought in the noble city a house and date grove.

Among the most surprising of his acts was the stand he took against obscenity and adultery, so that no such thing took place openly in his time.

He built the big town near Damasak and made four gates in the town and placed a keeper in charge of each gate and quartered there a detachment of his army. He ordered all his chiefs who were powerful and possessed of a defense force, to build houses and leave part of their equipment there as for instance, the horses, and quilted-armor . . . and coats of mail.

Among the gifts with which God had endowed him, was an impressive appearance. All his followers, small or great, never felt contented except in his presence. Even though he sent large armies in one direction and went in some other direction with a small force himself, his captains were not content to go without him.

Such is the account we have given of the character of our Sultan and his wars in the time when he was king. We have written it after there has passed of his reign twelve years.*

Idris ibn Ali, or Idris Alooma, was the powerful African king of the Bornu kingdom from 1570 to 1602. He was a devout Muslim who extended the faith and his realm through negotiation and military conquest. At the peak of its power, the Bornu kingdom centered on Lake Chad and stretched far into present-day Libya. Many of the exploits and extensive experiences of ibn Ali were recorded by Ahmad ibn Fartua in his *History of the First Twelve Years of Mai Idris Alooma.*

*The Horizon History of Africa *(New York: American Heritage, 1971), pp. 236–238.*

The States of Central Africa

Like many states in West Africa, the Kongo kingdom along the Congo River and the Lunda state were well organized politically and economically. The Kongo capital was on high ground more than 100 miles inland from the coast. Following a matrilineal line, the Kongo kings were often succeeded by their sisters' sons. King Nzinga Nkuwu (reigned 1506–1543), baptized Afonso, was one of the first African monarchs converted to Christianity by Portuguese missionaries.

Afonso I learned to read and write Portuguese and sent a number of officials, including his son Dom Henrique, to Portugal for education and religious training. As his numerous letters to the Portuguese king indicate (see Chapter 9 on the slave trade), Afonso considered himself an equal to European monarchs. Although he adopted Christianity and European dress and habits, Afonso was clearly not a puppet or vassal of the Portuguese. Indeed, the Kongo kingdom governed more people and territory than Portugal. Afonso's alliances and agreements with the Portuguese were made on the basis of equality, and he exercised strict administrative controls over both commerce and the slave trade.

As the foregoing description indicates, the societies in western and central Africa had developed their own unique and durable political organizations long before the advent of European exploration. Trade between African states and the Europeans was initially established on an equal footing and for mutually beneficial economic reasons. During this era, most African states, with some exceptions such as the king of the Kongo, retained their own unique traditional religious beliefs and effectively ignored or resisted attempts by European missionaries to gain converts for Christianity.

Commercial Wealth in East Africa

The fusion of cultures was perhaps nowhere more apparent than in East Africa. Along the coastal regions of Ethiopia and Somalia (the Horn of Africa), and southward along the Kenyan and Tanzanian coasts, city-states based on commerce and trade evolved as the dominant political and economic structures. Owing to the close geographical proximity to the Arabian Peninsula, East African coastal towns had ancient trading ties with Yemen, Persia, and other parts of the Middle East; later they developed commercial contacts with the Greeks and the Roman Empire. Animal skins, ivory, gold from Zimbabwe, and slaves were traded for spears, porcelain, and beads.

By the eighth century, Muslim merchants had begun trading with these coastal cities. Although the Christian kingdoms in Nubia and Ethiopia fought tenaciously against the Muslims, the expansion of Islam along the coastal regions was essentially peaceful. Muslim traders from Arabia and Persia began to settle in the port cities of East Africa, known to the Arabs as the Land of Zanj. Not surprisingly, Muslim sources tend to emphasize the dominance of Muslim culture and governors over these city-states. Because the indigenous Bantu peoples lacked a written tradition, sources describing the extent of their economic and political organization are far fewer than Muslim ones. Information comes from either oral traditions or from written accounts by outsiders.

Good Eating in Mogadishu

We sailed fifteen nights and arrived at Mogadishu, which is a very large town. The people have very many camels. The merchants are wealthy . . . the Sultan of Mogadishu is called Shaikh by his subjects . . . by race he is a Berber. He talks in the dialect of Mogadishu, but knows Arabic. When a ship arrives, it is the custom for it to be boarded by the Sultan's sanbuq [little boat] to enquire whence it has come; they also inquire the nature of the cargo . . . The food of these people is rice cooked with butter . . . with it they serve side-dishes, stews of chicken, meat, fish, and vegetables. They cook unripe bananas in fresh milk, and serve them with a sauce. They put curdled milk [yoghurt] in another vessel with peppercorns, vinegar, and saffron, green ginger and mangoes, which look like apples but have a nut inside. Ripe mangoes are very sweet.*

This passage is from a firsthand account of Mogadishu, written in 1331 by Ibn Battuta, the famous fourteenth-century traveler from Morocco. In over thirty years, Ibn Battuta traveled some 75,000 miles—more than three times the distance covered by Marco Polo—visiting China, Ceylon, Turkey, North and East Africa, and Mecca in Arabia. Ibn Battuta had a keen eye for the smallest detail, and his diaries are full of colorful details about the diet, dress, habits, and culture of the peoples he observed.

*The Horizon History of Africa (New York: American Heritage, 1971), pp. 161–162.

It is apparent, though, that the Muslim/Arab migrants assimilated with the Bantu majority. As these traders intermarried with the indigenous African population, a unique culture was created through assimilation and diffusion. Swahili, an African language infused with many Arabic and Persian words, became the language of trade and inter-communication, and Islam became the dominant religion. It is not always clear from available sources whether these city-states were governed by migrants from Arabia or the Persian Gulf or by indigenous Muslim ruling dynasties.

This new culture prevailed along the coast from present-day Somalia to Tanzania in the cities of Mogadishu, Merca, Brava, and many others, which enjoyed the economic wealth brought by trade. Ivory, gold, and slaves were the primary commodities. By the tenth century, merchants from the Persian Gulf and Oman dominated economic life, extending their trading empire to include the large island of Madagascar and the Comoro Islands. From 1095 to 1291, the Christian Crusaders, avid for riches to take back to Europe, increased the demand for gold and ivory, which came from central Africa through eastern Africa to the eastern Mediterranean, where the Crusaders had established independent feudal kingdoms (see Chapter 8). Gold was brought from Zimbabwe through the port of Sofala to Kilwa in present-day Tanzania. Muslim sources refer to Sofala as the capital of Zanj, or "land of the Bantu," which indicates that Bantu peoples from central Africa had already settled along the southern coast by 900.

Numerous mosques and public buildings along the eastern African coast attest to the wealth of these city-states. Dating from the thirteenth century, the great mosque in Kilwa clearly demonstrates the preeminence of Islamic architectural forms and designs. Many of the mosques and public buildings that remain are remarkably similar to those constructed by the Umayyads and Abbasids in earlier centuries. (See Chapters 5 and 8.)

Zimbabwe. This photograph shows a conical tower and the high circular walls around parts of the vast Zimbabwe complex. The fine granite surface of the walls was likely added by Bantu builders after 1000. Much of the surrounding district still awaits excavation.

© Paul Almasy/Corbis

Inland Cities in Southern Africa

The commercial cities of the coastal regions were linked economically and socially with a series of inland cities ruled by various Bantu societies. Iron production and copper and gold mining provided the economic basis of these cities. They had a flourishing trade with the coastal regions, but it is not yet known whether the merchants who conducted this trade came from the inland cities or the coast.

The massive complex at Zimbabwe is one of the most extensive of these Bantu cities and served as the capital of several Bantu rulers. It includes a hill complex with a huge granite hall, a great enclosure with thirty-foot-high walls and a valley complex. The great enclosure may have housed the rulers' wives, but the purpose of the conical stone tower in its center is unknown. These enormous ruins attest to the architectural skills of the Bantu people. Carbon dating of materials from Zimbabwe reveals that construction probably began around 200 C.E., but most of the buildings left today date from after 1000. Although Europeans originally thought the stone walls were fortresses, these massive complexes were actually built as displays of wealth and power, not for military purposes. It is also thought that the complex had religious importance as a sacred place where one could communicate with the ancestors.

Although the Zimbabwe complex is the most impressive of these Bantu constructions, more than 150 similar ones are scattered along the Zimbabwe-Mozambique border, but only about a dozen have been excavated. The gold jewelry and carved objects found in the Mapungubwe burial mound in northern South Africa indicate the wealth of the society and demonstrate the skill of its artisans. As archaeological research continues in Zimbabwe, more details about the economy, culture, and political and social life of the society will be revealed.

Summary and Comparisons

The cultures in this chapter range from indigenous to derivative in their relationship to Eurasia. In Mesoamerica, the Teotihuacanos, Maya, and Aztecs were the cultural descendants of the Olmec, just as the Babylonians, Assyrians, and Chaldeans had followed the Sumerians. In a larger context, however, Mesoamerican culture as a whole derived little from the Amerindian culture in Peru and the Andes. Contact with Eurasia was nonexistent or insignificant before 1500.

The Mesoamerican cultures that developed after the first century C.E. were essentially clusters of city-states. These states were sometimes aggregated by conquest into larger entities, like the Aztec Empire of the early sixteenth century. The major cities of Mesoamerica usually centered on monumental religious buildings in the shape of flattened pyramids flanked by sacred ball courts. Governments, too, were religion-based, with a single ruler supported by a military elite and a priestly caste that controlled the lower orders. The people of Mesoamerica increasingly turned to human sacrifice to preserve a sense of universal order.

Developmentally, Mesoamerican culture is a paradox: it became quite sophisticated intellectually, employing advanced mathematics and a complex calendar; yet, like the Andean culture, it was technologically backward, lacking metal weapons, the wheel, large draft animals, and heavy transportation. Invading Europeans took full advantage of these deficiencies.

The Inka Empire in the Andean highlands was quite unlike Mesoamerica. A descendant of earlier affluent cultures, the Inka Empire was the most centralized state up to that point in history. A divine emperor presided over a highly structured society, allocating all land, resources, and labor.

Although facing the same problems as the Mesoamericans, the Inka built a remarkable network of roads and supply stations that helped to keep the far-flung empire together. Inka agents collected food into public warehouses and dispensed it, along with clothing and beer, at holidays and state occasions. Sun worshipers, the Inka escaped the bloody religious practices common in Mesoamerica.

The young cultures of sub-Saharan Africa represent various mixes of indigenous and borrowed elements. Before Islam arrived after 700, sub-Saharan Africa was home to indigenous cultures unaffected by Mediterranean influences. Ethiopia saw early development because of its access to the Mediterranean via the Nile River. Here there arose an

CHRONOLOGY

200 B.C.E.	Indians sail to Southeast Asia
1 C.E.	
	Indian influence in Java, Sumatra, Malaya, Burma
	Bantu migrations
	Moche culture rises in Peru
	Teotihuacán begins era of full flowering in Mesoamerica
500	Indian influence in Burma, Thailand, Malaya
	Chinese trade in Southeast Asia
	Maya civilization at its height
	Prince Shotoku's regency in Japan
	Japanese embassy to China
	Kingdom of Axum begins
	Silla unifies Korea
	Spread of Islam in North and East Africa
	Khmer Empire
	Angkor Wat, Borobodur, Pagan built
	Koryo dynasty in Korea
	Feudal Japan, code of Bushido
1000	
	Lady Murasaki, *The Tale of Genji*
	Thais form a state
	Shogunate in Japan
	Maya revival in Yucatán
	Kingdoms of Salt and Gold predominant in West Africa
	Mongols conquer Korea, Southern Sung, Pagan
	East Africa city-states
	Stone complexes in Zimbabwe
	Mansa Kankan Musa leader of Mali
1350	
	Rise of the Aztecs
	Inka Empire expands under Thupa Yupanki
	Moctezuma II becomes ruler of Aztec Empire
1500	

Axum-Kushite trading empire based on Coptic Christianity. However, this empire was cut off from the rest of Christian civilization by the Muslim conquest of North Africa.

In the sub-Saharan savanna of West Africa, a succession of powerful kingdoms—especially Ghana, Mali, and Songhai—arose between the fourth and sixteenth centuries. Based on the salt and gold trade, they built an urban existence on a firm agricultural base. Though illiterate, they were strong politically and militarily. Their ironworking was either a product of independent invention or an import from the Mediterranean. Islam increased its presence in the region after the seventh century.

A third cultural center was the east coast of Africa, where city-states had profited from trade around the Indian Ocean since Greek and Roman times. Here Muslim/Arab culture mixed with indigenous Bantu culture: one major example was the evolution of the Swahili language.

Central and southern Africa saw the Bantu pervade the lower third of the African continent just as Indo-Europeans had peopled Eurasia. By about 1000, the Bantus, metalworking farmers and herders, had developed at least one major urban center in the Zimbabwe area.

Selected Sources

Items indicated with an asterisk (*) are available in paperback.

Bauer, Brian S. *The Development of the Inca State*. 1992. The new standard treatment.

Bovill, Edward W. *The Golden Trade of the Moors: West African Kingdoms in the Fourteenth Century*. 2d ed. 1995. A lively account of Saharan trade routes and the Sudanic kingdoms of West Africa.

Carlson, John B. "Rise and Fall of the City of the Gods." *Archaeology* 16,6 (1993): 58. A look at the Venus warrior cult that provided captives for religious rituals at Teotihuacán.

Carrasco, David. *Moctezuma's Mexico: Visions of the Aztec World*. 1992. A look at Aztec society and culture.

——, ed. *The Oxford Encyclopedia of Mesoamerican Cultures*. 3 vols. 2000. A comprehensive guide to 700 years of history in Mexico and Central America before, during, and after the coming of European invaders.

Coe, Michael D. *Maya*. 3d ed. 1985. The standard work on Mayan historical development.

*——. *Breaking the Maya Code*. 1992. The story of the century-long struggle to decipher the meaning of the Maya glyphs.

*Collins, Robert O., ed. *Problems in African History: The Precolonial Centuries*. Vol. 1. 1992. Includes many subjects for classroom discussion: Bantu origins, slavery, women, and trade, among others.

D'Altroy, Terence N. *Provincial Power in the Inka Empire*. 1992. Reveals the inner political, social, and economic workings of the Inka Empire by studying their operation in a key province.

Davies, Nigel. *The Toltecs*. 1977. A study of the civilization that linked Teotihuacán with the post-classic Maya and the Aztecs.

Fash, William L. *Scribes, Warriors, and Kings: The City of Copán and the Ancient Maya*. 1991. A comprehensive view of one of the great Maya cities and a general survey of current scholarship on the Maya.

"The Glories of Ancient Benin." Films for the Humanities. A short video on the founding of Benin in West Africa, with scenes from the Museum and Palace of Porto-Novo.

Hamdun, Said, and Noel King, eds. *Ibn Battuta in Black Africa.* Rev. ed. 1994. Ibn Battuta's fascinating firsthand narrative of his travels in West and East Africa.

Henderson, John S. *The World of the Ancient Maya.* 1981. Profusely illustrated, focuses on the arts.

The Horizon History of Africa. 1971. A lavishly illustrated account of Africa with many excerpts from primary sources.

Inca. 1995. An informative Time-Life videocassette.

July, Robert W. *A History of the African People.* 4th ed. 1992. A good survey of historical developments throughout Africa.

Kellogg, Susan. *Law and the Transformation of the Aztec Empire.* 1995. Discusses the interface of two legal systems.

"The Lost City of Zimbabwe." Films for the Humanities. Video on the continuing restoration of this great African city.

Malpass, Michael. *Daily Life in the Inca Empire.* 1996. A comprehensive account.

Markman, Roberta H., and Peter T. *The Flayed God: The Mythology of Mesoamerica.* 1992. A combination of original text and contemporary commentary that leads the reader into the mythology of the Mesoamerican cultures.

"Maya Lords of the Jungle" [1980]. British Broadcasting Corporation/Public Broadcasting Associates. This installment of the *Odyssey* program concentrates on agriculture and trade patterns.

Meyer, Karl E. *Teotihuacán.* 1980. An overview of the culture.

Munro-Hay, Stuart. *Aksum: An African Civilization of Late Antiquity.* 1992. A scholarly account of the ancient kingdom in present-day Ethiopia.

Patterson, Thomas Carl. *The Inca Empire: The Formation and Disintegration of a Pre-Capitalist State.* 1991. A special point of view.

Prospouriakoff, Tatiana. *Maya History.* 1993. A well-written alternative to Michael Coe's standard account.

Schele, Linda, and Mary Ellen Miller. *The Blood of Kings: Dynasty and Ritual in Maya Art.* 1986. Text and pictures combine to give the reader insight into Maya religious and dynastic beliefs.

Sharer, Robert J. *Daily Life in Maya Civilization.* 1996. A comprehensive discussion of the topic.

Sweetman, David. *Women Leaders in African History.* 1984. This comprises short biographies of twelve African women, from ancient Egypt to colonial times.

The World Atlas of Architecture. 1984. Lavishly illustrated and fascinating descriptions of building techniques and styles around the world from earliest times to the twentieth century. Includes chapters on African and Mesoamerican civilizations.

 Additional resources, exercises, and Internet links related to this chapter are available at the Book Companion Web site:
http://history.wadsworth.com/upshurcompact4/

COMPARATIVE ESSAY 6
The Development of International Trade

An old merchant said to a person who wanted to find out the truth about commerce: . . . "Buy cheap and sell dear."

The merchant who knows his business will travel only with such goods as are generally needed by rich and poor. . . . Likewise, it is more advantageous and more profitable for the merchant's enterprise, if he brings goods from a country that is far away and where there is danger on the road. . . . They get rich quickly.
Ibn Khaldun, *The Muqaddima: An Introduction to History,* trans. Franz Rosenthal (Princeton: Princeton University Press, 1967), pp. 310–311.

"The business of America is business."
Calvin Coolidge

"What's good for General Motors is good for America; What's good for America is good for General Motors."
Attributed to Charlie "Engine" Wilson, General Motors Corporation, although his actual words were slightly different.

Ibn Khaldun's observations about commerce and trade are as true today as when he wrote in the fourteenth century—a time when international commerce was beginning to flourish. In the twentieth century, industrialists and leaders (like American president Calvin Coolidge or Charlie Wilson of General Motors) have also recognized the important relationship between economic prosperity and national well-being. For centuries, rulers have sought to increase the wealth of their realms; commerce and trade have frequently made major contributions to the growing power of empires and nation states.

By 1500 a well-developed international trade was being carried on among the major civilizations of Africa, Europe, and Asia. From that time to the present, international trade has been a crucial global driving force. Trade among diverse and far-flung parts of the world was made possible by the development of revolutionary advances in the sciences, technology, transportation, and finance that began about five hundred years ago. Since then advances in transportation and communications have shrunk the world to a global village.

It was not always the case. Although international trade had been important for several thousand years before 1500, trade volume grew slowly, and was often subject to interruptions and disruptions caused by wars and politics. Viewing history over the span of several thousand years, we can discern three broad cycles in the rise and fall of trade among civilizations: The first cycle lasted between approximately 500 B.C.E. and 400 C.E., the second cycle spanned between around 600 and 1200, while the third and most recent one began around 1500 and continues to the present.

Cycle 1: International trade in luxury goods or essential raw materials evidently began earlier than 500 B.C.E. In very ancient times, intricate and interlocking trade routes connected civilizations in Eurasia and Africa. For example, a semiprecious stone called lapis lazuli mined in high altitudes in Afghanistan has been found in tombs of ancient Egyptian rulers. During the Bronze Age, tin from Cornwall in Britain may have been traded as far as the eastern Mediterranean. Recent X rays and other tests suggest that Chinese silk fibers were also used in the cloth that wrapped ancient Egyptian mummies over 3,000 years ago. Similarly, when a Chinese general arrived in northwest India in the second century B.C.E., he found that Chinese silks were already available in India. They evidently had reached India via southwestern China and Burma.

These trade routes were regularized and expanded by the Hellenistic kingdoms in Egypt and western Asia, the Roman Empire, the Mauryan Empire in India, and the Han Empire in China. Along these routes people, goods, and ideas intermingled and cosmopolitan towns grew up to provide housing, food, places of worship, and recreation for the merchants.

By 400 C.E. violent invasions disrupted much of this Eurasian trade. The collapse of the Roman and Han Empires had by then reduced the Pax Romana and Pax Sinica to mere memories.

Available technology determined the mode of long-distance trade. Goods were hauled by carts where roads permitted and on pack animals such as oxen, mules, horses, and camels where roads were poor. The animals' carrying capacity severely restricted the quantity of goods that could be carried, so trade was often limited to luxury items. Water transport was always more efficient and much cheaper than land transport. For example, a ten-foot boat could carry as much weight as thirty pack horses. However, the vagaries of wind, storms, piracy, and the lack of navigational charts and compasses hampered shipping. Therefore most ancient sailing ships avoided open seas and hugged coasts, undertaking long-distance sea voyages in stages. Hull, mast, and sail design were primitive compared to those of later sailing vessels and limited the size of waterborne cargoes. As a result boats, too, tended to carry luxury items.

The high cost of transportation ensured that the most costly goods—silk, spices, precious metals, and gems—traveled the longest distances. Most of the cargo carried in ancient trade, both overland and seaborne, went from Asia to Europe. In exchange, Asian producers received silver and gold from Europeans. Large quantities of Roman coins have been discovered in many Indian towns, suggesting that they might have been so common as to be circulated as the local currency. Thus European rulers from the Roman Emperor Augustus on bemoaned the loss of precious metals to Asian lands for ephemeral luxuries such as silk fabrics.

The Western Hemisphere was not involved in the intercontinental trade until the arrival of Europeans at the end of the fifteenth century. Within the region, the lack of any pack animals other than llamas, which would only carry small loads, and the absence of suitable water routes limited commerce. Thus trade between cultures in the Americas was limited to what could be borne on the backs of porters and by canoes along river routes.

Throughout the ages, the wealthy have been major consumers of the goods obtained by long-distance trade. Governments fostered trade by building and maintaining roads and ports and by suppressing piracy; they also derived revenues by taxing commerce. Some governments, most notably Islamic dynasties of West Asia, including the later Ottoman and Safavid Empires, encouraged trade through tax incentives and by inviting outside traders into their realms. In China the Han and T'ang governments encouraged foreign traders to settle in their empire by providing them with residential quarters and places of worship. Successive Chinese dynasties also established markets with the nomads beyond their borders, on the correct assumption that trade was preferable to war.

Cycle 2: The reestablishment of a unified government in China in the sixth century and the gradual restoration of peace and order in Europe following the "dark age" of the barbarian invasions at the fall of the Roman Empire led to a revival of international trade. By the twelfth century, a new cycle of trade peaked. Land and water routes extended from China to western Europe and North Africa, connecting eight overlapping trade zones. The linchpins that linked these zones were Changan in northern China and Canton on the South China coast, Calicut in India, Samarkand in Central Asia, Baghdad in West Asia, Cairo (then called Fustat) in northern Africa, Constantinople at the entrance of the Bosporus in the eastern Mediterranean, and Venice in Italy.

Although governments were more fragmented during the second cycle than the first, international trade flourished perhaps even more than during the previous one. Improved transportation technology was the main reason for this increase. The increased volume of trade satisfied the demands for Asian goods that the Crusaders had stimulated among Europeans since the twelfth century. In East Asia after about 1000, economic advances in Japan and the Sung dynasty's encouragement of exports to raise revenue for defense against the Mongols led to a vibrant international trade in that region.

The second golden age of trade was disrupted in the thirteenth century when nomadic people called the Mongols rudely erupted across Eurasia, causing enormous havoc to lives and material culture. However, Mongol rulers later promoted commerce, especially in luxury goods. Thus the Pax Tartarica, or "Mongol peace," followed the devastation of the Mongol conquests.

In the fourteenth century, a plague or "Black Death" swept Europe and West Asia and also devastated China and India. It wiped out as much as a third of Europe's population and perhaps as much as half the population of India. Recurrent warfare in western Asia, in addition to the high taxes exacted on transit trade by the newly established Ottoman

Empire, contributed to the further disruption of trade between western Europe and India and China. As a result, supplies became irregular and prices rose.

Cycle 3: The third era of intercontinental trade began in the fifteenth century. The impetus came from the newly centralized European states, which adopted policies that led to the development of a new international trading pattern. As a result of advances in the sciences and technology, Europe was propelled to the forefront of world trade. Portugal and Spain developed new trade routes that bypassed the old land and water routes and in the process opened up a new era of world trade.

8

Three Continents: Conflict and Commerce

•

- • The Golden Age of Islam •
- • The Crusades •
- • The Mongol Conquest of Eurasia •
- • The Mongol Legacy •
- • New Dynasties in West Asia •
- • Summary and Comparisons •

The life story of Shagarat al-Durr—slave, wife of one Sultan, stepmother of another, ruler of a dynasty, and murderer—reads like a script for a Hollywood adventure film. Shagarat al-Durr, whose name means "tree of pearls," entered the lavish Mamluk court in Egypt as a slave during the thirteenth century and subsequently married the Sultan. After his death (of natural causes), Shagarat concealed his demise for three months so that her stepson could return from greater Syria and take the throne. However, Shagarat quickly became disenchanted with him, had him murdered, and proclaimed herself ruler. Encouraged to legitimize her position by marrying, Shagarat took a new husband, with whom she shared power for several years, until it was rumored that he planned to take another wife. Shagarat retaliated by having him murdered. But this assassination so enraged Shagarat's many enemies that they conspired to have her assassinated (she was beaten to death with heavy, wooden bath clogs). Her body was thrown from the palace tower to be devoured by dogs. The remains were ultimately buried in a grandiose tomb that Shagarat had built for herself. The memory of this remarkable woman lives on in present-day Cairo, where there is still a street named after her.

Shagarat al-Durr is one of a number of powerful, and sometimes ruthless, women who became politically powerful during an era of empires and absolute rulers. The period 1100–1500 was one of great disruption in the eastern Mediterranean. In West Asia, the Abbasid caliphate ruled over a vast, powerful, and prosperous Islamic state. This golden age of Islam marked a high water point for Islamic sciences, arts, and literature.

The turbulence of the Crusades, coming in the aftermath of the collapse of a unified Islamic empire, lasted several centuries. But those disruptions pale when compared with the havoc wrought by Mongol and Turkish onslaughts across Eurasia in the thirteenth and fourteenth centuries. The Mongol invasions devastated central and West Asian societies, many of which never recovered their former glory or power. The consolidation of Mongol rule in Asia, however, restored trade relations between that continent and Europe.

Another important event of this convulsive period was the creation of the Ottoman state by the Turks of the Anatolian Peninsula. Making effective use of artillery and firearm-bearing infantry, the Ottomans, like the Mongols before them and others after them, created "gunpowder empires." With their technological military superiority, the Ottomans conquered the Balkans and captured Constantinople, thus ending the 1,000-year-old Byzantine Empire.

This period also marked the second cycle of flourishing trade; war and commerce brought the large populations of Europe and Asia into direct contact (as described in the preceding comparative essay). At the beginning of this period, trade between the West and the East flourished amid general prosperity and continued even in times of bitter warfare.

The Golden Age of Islam

The Caliph himself, surrounded by his chief ministers and favorite slaves covered with gold and jewels, resembled a planet amidst a galaxy of stars.

Eunuchs, black and white, with inferior officers of the number of eight thousand, served as a foil to these gems. Silk-and-gold-embroidered tapestries, numbering thirty-eight thousand pieces, ornamented the palace walls, and on a curious tree of gold and silver were perched a variety of birds whose movements and notes were regulated by machinery.

Twenty-two thousand carpets covered the floor, and there floated on the broad stream of the Tigris, before the windows of the palace, thousands of vessels, each splendidly decorated; while a hundred lions, in charge of their keepers, lent a contrast to the glittering scene.*

*Abufelda, "The Caliph of Baghdad Receives an Ambassador from Greece," in Rhoda Hoff, The Arabs: Their Heritage and Their Way of Life (New York: Henry Z. Walck, 1979), pp. 19–20.

This description gives some indication of the richness and splendor of the Abbasid court in Baghdad during what has become known as the golden age of Islam in the eighth and ninth centuries. During the golden age, Islamic society, which was known for its tolerance and intellectual dynamism, achieved a high level of cultural and artistic production. Many Islamic scientific, philosophic, architectural, and artistic creations subsequently formed the basis for scientific and artistic developments in surrounding societies and in the Western world.

Life under the Abbasids

The second Abbasid Caliph, Abu Jafar (reigned 754–775), better known as al-Mansur, established a new fortress capital on the Tigris River, at the site of the village of Baghdad. This circular, walled complex took some 100,000 workers over four years to construct. At its zenith in the ninth century, Baghdad, with a population variously estimated at 800,000 to 2 million, rivaled Constantinople as the largest city of the age. Officially known as Madinat al-Salam (City of Peace), Baghdad became the fabled city of *The Tales of the Arabian Nights*, a collection of highly romanticized and exaggerated stories based on court life under the Abbasids.

Baghdad was dominated by a massive palace that housed the caliph and the administrative complex. With its advantageous location on the Tigris, the capital dominated the trade routes and was a major entrepôt for commerce from the West and East. Thus under the Abbasids the center of Islamic power shifted eastward from Damascus to Baghdad in present-day Iraq.

Under Caliph Harun al-Rashid (reigned 786–809) and his son Mamun (reigned 813–833), the Abbasid Empire reached its zenith of power and wealth. As in the Chinese empires, the government was highly centralized. A grand vizier and an advisory council administered the extensive Abbasid Empire. Taxes were collected for different categories of landowners, and a separate tax was levied on non-Muslims, who did not pay the *zakat,* or Islamic alms, or serve in the army. During the long reign of Harun al-Rashid, the Arabs began to tire of military service, and Turkish forces began to command the military. As the empire declined, they became the masters where once they had been slaves. Similar takeovers by mercenary forces had contributed to the downfall of the Roman Empire.

Abbasid wealth rested primarily upon agriculture and trade efficiently administered by a series of able, dynamic caliphs and advisors. An extensive highway network expedited trade, while a well-organized postal system enhanced communications and also facilitated intelligence gathering; reportedly, old women were particularly able agents. Most of the international trade was with China and India; Muslim traders brought textiles, paper, and porcelains from China and other parts of Asia along overland routes through Samarkand.

Because the Abbasids had the political and social support of the Iranian provinces, Persian influences were particularly strong, and Abbasid rulers often sought to copy the habits and cultural tastes of the old Persian Empire. Under the Abbasids, expert artisans, both from local areas and from other parts of Asia, produced finely decorated porcelains,

Map 8.1 The Abbasid Empire. At the zenith of its power, the Abbasid caliphate based in Baghdad included much of Arabia, present-day Iran, and Afghanistan. Rival Islamic regimes ruled Egypt and North Africa.

carpets, jewelry, metal and inlaid wood products, and innumerable luxury items. Court life under the Abbasids was so lavish that Harun al-Rashid's wife Zubayda reputedly wore shoes studded with jewels and hosted feasts where the food was served on golden plates. Zubayda was typical of upper-class women who lived extravagant lives and sometimes wielded political power. The great majority of the population, however, consisted of peasant farmers and women who not only worked long hours in the fields, but also kept house and raised children.

With enormous power and wealth at their disposal, the Abbasid caliphs became famous patrons of intellectuals and artists. Under Abbasid rule, Baghdad became a center for learning and the arts. Although Muslim sources make little mention of the event, Charlemagne sent a mission in 797 to secure safe passage for Christian pilgrims to Jerusalem. After his delegates returned with stories about the untold wealth of Baghdad, the city became a symbol for the glories of the Muslim dominions.

Abbasid Decline

By the ninth and tenth centuries, the once mighty Abbasid caliphate was showing signs of decay. A major problem was that its rulers were constantly threatened by rival dynasties from within the empire, as governors appointed from Baghdad sought to establish their own dynasties. In general, the more distant a province was from Baghdad, the more likely it was to become independent. In the future, the vast Ottoman Empire would have similar problems controlling its provincial governors.

Weakened by the growing economic strength of rival Muslim rulers in North and West Africa, the rulers in Baghdad turned increasingly to Persian and Turkish leaders for military and political support. The power of Baghdad was also undermined by religious schisms and the weakness of the caliphs, who preferred the pleasures of the court to

The Good Life in Baghdad

When I wandered about the city after a long absence, I found it in an expansion of prosperity. Affluence is abundant among the upper rank.... This may be seen in the case of their purchase of arms inlaid with gold, ornamented vessels, and splendid furniture. They cover their walls with embroidery and silk brocade, and take an interest in planting flowers in their gardens, even to the extent that they have rare flowers brought to them from India.

They indulge in luscious food to the point of buying game and fruit out of season.... When it is hot they place their chairs among water gushing from statues of lions and among forms of birds and apples which they chisel in marble. When their bodies have obtained sufficient water to refresh the soul, they place fans on the ceiling....

They indulge in clothes and ornamentation and in riding horses with silk brocade and heavy finery of silvery, to a degree which no affluent nations before them have reached.*

These excerpts from a letter by an Arab nobleman visiting Baghdad to his father in the latter part of the eighth century give some indication of the vast wealth and luxury of life in the Abbasid capital.

*"Muslim Culture in Baghdad," trans. John Damis, in Ilse Lichtenstadter, Introduction to Classical Arabic Literature (New York: Schocken Books, 1974), pp. 357–362.

administrative or military duties. Empires before and after the Abbasids have been weakened by rulers who have preferred opulent lives to the hard work of administering vast territories or the rigors and perils of the battlefield. The actual collapse of the Abbasid Empire will be described later in the chapter.

The Glories of Muslim Spain

The Muslim Umayyad dynasty in Spain rivaled the glories of the Abbasids. By 710 the Umayyads had crossed the Strait of Gibraltar, and, after being ousted from Damascus by the Abbasids, established a rival caliphate in 756; the new Umayyad Empire included Spain and western North Africa (present-day Morocco and Algeria). Under Caliph Abd al-Rahman I (reigned 756–788), who had escaped the Abbasid takeover in Damascus, the Umayyads ruled until 976 from al-Andalusia in southern Spain. Subsequent Muslim rulers continued to govern parts of Spain until their final defeat by the Christian forces of King Ferdinand and Queen Isabella in 1492.

Córdoba, the capital of the Umayyad Empire in the West, became one of the richest cities in Europe and exported goods to the East and West. Education was highly valued, and Abd al-Rahman III (reigned 912–961) established dozens of free schools and libraries. He also encouraged Jewish scholarship at a time when minorities were vigorously persecuted in the rest of Europe. Thus Muslim Spain became a dynamic center for the arts and sciences.

While Jews were suffering persecution at the hands of Christians in most of Europe, Spanish Jews lived in relative harmony with Muslims; many adopted Arab names and spoke Arabic. A noteworthy Spanish Jew who made valuable cultural contributions was Rabbi Musa bin Maymun, also known as Moses Maimonides (1135–1204), who spent most of his adult life in Egypt. As court physician to the Egyptian sultan Salah ed-Din (reigned 1174–1193), Rabbi bin Maymun wrote treatises based on empirical methods that criticized the still authoritative opinions of classical Greece. Subsequently, he wrote *The Guide for the Perplexed,* a philosophical interpretation of Judaism for those seeking a rational basis for their faith. His openness to Aristotle antagonized more traditional Jews, but Christian thinkers such as Thomas Aquinas soon adopted his analysis of the connection between revelation and reason.

Unfortunately, the Umayyads' political and military power did not match their cultural renown. The Muslim territories under Umayyad authority were continually plagued by civil wars in which local provincial governors or military commanders established rival governments. To save the empire, successive caliphs recruited outside forces, many from Africa; however, these mercenaries founded their own rival kingdoms in Africa, which frequently threatened Umayyad domination in Muslim Spain. To protect the empire from rival Muslim forces and from attacks from hostile Christian armies, fortified towns were built along the coastal areas. These ruins may still be seen along the coasts of Spain and Portugal.

By the end of the eleventh century, the Muslim Empire in Spain was clearly on the retreat in face of the military advances by the famous Spanish Christian hero, al-Cid, who also fought as a mercenary with Muslims. By the fifteenth century, Muslims in Spain held only the small kingdom around Granada, where the highly secular Nasrid rulers built lavish pleasure palaces that remain the epitome of "Moorish" (Moroccan) architecture in the West. After years of fierce fighting, the forces of Queen Isabella and King Ferdinand defeated the Nasrids and entered Granada in January 1492. As Boabdil, the last Muslim monarch in Spain, looked down on his lost capital and wept, his mother allegedly said, "You weep like a woman for what you could not hold as a man." Boabdil escaped into exile, and several centuries of Muslim rule in Spain came to an end. For Christendom, the conquest of Granada with its great al-Hambra palace in some ways compensated for the earlier loss of Constantinople to the Ottomans in 1453.

In face of massive persecutions by the Spanish monarchy and Catholic church, Muslims and Jews either converted or fled to the relative safety of Muslim-dominated territories in Africa or the eastern Mediterranean. Many of those immigrants were merchants or highly skilled artisans whose exodus promoted the cultural and economic development of the Ottoman Empire. Their departure also impoverished Spain, hereafter the home of a small, wealthy elite and a large, poor peasantry. Although the Spanish monarchs swiftly moved to eradicate all traces of Muslim domination, the centuries of Muslim presence had made an indelible mark on the culture of the Iberian Peninsula, and Muslim/Arab artistic styles are still readily recognizable in the music and much of the architecture and language of Spain and Portugal.

Islamic Theology, Philosophy, and Science

Abbasid and Umayyad rulers actively supported philosophers and theologians. Islamic intellectuals were particularly instrumental in preserving and subsequently translating Greek works into Arabic. Had Islamic writers and thinkers not recognized the importance of keeping classical thought alive, many of the books and writings of Greek philosophers that were to form the basis of much subsequent European intellectual development might well have been lost forever. Since Islam had not separated the functions of government and religion, Islamic philosophers were also keenly interested in exploring the relationship between the spiritual and the so-called rational worlds.

Influenced by Plato and Aristotle, Ibn Sina (Avicenna, 980–1037) emphasized that prophecy could be based upon the intellect as well as upon the emotions. Another renowned philosopher, Ibn Rushd (Averroes, 1126–1198) also argued for the necessity of harmonizing revelation and reason. Ibn Rushd, known as "prince of the learned," was an Islamic judge who served in Córdoba and Seville and for a short time also acted as court physician. As a Muslim renaissance man, Ibn Rushd wrote on subjects as diverse as Aristotle, medicine, and astronomy.

By contrast, Muhammad al-Ghazali (1058–1111) argued that the spiritual, even mystical, qualities of revelation were far more important. Orthodox Muslim theologians generally agreed with al-Ghazali's approach, and Ibn Rushd's works were eventually labeled heretical. Indeed, al-Ghazali became one of the most widely read and cited of all philosophers in the Islamic/Arab world.

Islamic rulers were also enthusiastic patrons of scientific endeavors. Under the Abbasids, Baghdad became a major scientific center, much like Hellenistic Alexandria

The Better Half

Women are superior to men in certain respects: it is they that are asked in marriage, desired, loved and courted, and they that inspire self-sacrifice. . . . An indication of the high esteem in which women are held is that if a man be asked to swear by God to distribute his possessions all that comes easily to him, but let him be asked to swear to put away his wife, and he grows pale, is overcome with rage, protests, expostulates, gets angry and refuses—God created a child out of a woman without the intervention of any man, but He has never created a child out of a man without a woman.*

This passage is from an *adab,* or graceful, sophisticated essay, by Abu Uthman 'Amer ibn Bahr al-Faqaimi al-Basri al-Jahiz (d. 869). Al-Jahiz, the grandson of a black slave, lived from the gifts of rich patrons in the Abbasid caliphate; he is reputed to have written more than 200 books.

*Al-Jahiz, "Women's Superiority to Men," trans. D. M. Hawkes, in The Islamic World, ed. William H. McNeill and Marilyn Robinson Waldman (New York: Oxford University Press, 1973; reprint, Chicago: University of Chicago Press, 1983), p. 131.

under Ptolemaic rulers. Translating voluminous materials into Arabic, Islamic scientists preserved both the Greek traditions and Persian and Indian texts. Arab mathematicians studied and enlarged upon Indian traditions of numerical reckoning, including the concept of zero. Arab scholars were particularly interested in geometry and astronomy and were especially advanced in the development of navigational devices such as the astrolabe. They also made substantial progress in the study of optics.

Arabic astronomers were familiar with the works of Indian and Persian scientists as well as treatises from the Greek. They were particularly influenced by the Ptolemaic (earth-centered) system and were keen observers of the heavens and climatic changes. New tables were developed on the basis of observations, particularly of solar and lunar eclipses. By 1259, in the reign of Hulagu, Muslim scientists had established what was perhaps the first professional observatory, with over a dozen full-time astronomers. Many stars are still known by their Arabic names, and remains of the Muslim observatory built at Samarkand by the grandson of Timurlane still exist.

In the field of medicine, Muslim doctors not only translated Greek medical writings, but also wrote treatises on problems as diverse as kidney stones, smallpox, nutrition, and the relationship between the psyche and the body. In the eleventh century, Ibn Sina, a prolific writer in scientific subjects as well as in philosophy, wrote a fourteen-volume work, *The Canon of Medicine,* and a twelve-volume one, *The Book of Healing.* In Seville, the doctor Abu L-Ala Ibn Zuhr or Avenzoar (d. 1130) was known for his clinical diagnoses and was far ahead of his time in advocating medical experimentation. The Ibn Zuhr family carried on the tradition of medicine for five generations. A son, Abu Marwan (d. 1161), a friend of Averroes, wrote a manual of medical technique.

Writing in both Hebrew and Arabic, Rabbi bin Maymun (Maimonides) became so famous that reputedly an Iraqi doctor traveled to Egypt to hear him lecture. The scientific achievements of Rabbi bin Maymun show the relatively open nature of Muslim society during this golden age. Likewise, the ease with which many Muslim intellectuals and scientists moved from place to place attests to the overall unity in culture, language, and society even in the far reaches of the Muslim world.

Hospitals also flourished under Islamic rule; Arabic speaking doctors became renowned for their work in ophthalmology, surgery, pharmacology, and human anatomy. Islamic inventors were also fascinated with mechanical devices. In the book *Automata,* or *The Book of Knowledge of Ingenious Mechanical Devices,* written about 1206, the inventor Ibn al-Razzaz al-Jaziri drew designs for dozens of whimsical contraptions. His inventions, reminiscent of Archimedes' creations in Hellenistic times, range from devices for pumping water to automatic washbasins. As none of these devices is extant, it is not known whether the designs were ever actually constructed or were merely the fantasies of a creative mind.

Islamic scientists also devoted considerable efforts to trying to turn base metals into valuable gold or silver (alchemy), just as did many in medieval Europe. Alchemy proved to be a scientific dead end, but in the process of experimenting, Islamic scientists gained some valuable skills.

Major Architectural Achievements

Early Islamic architects quite literally built on the foundations of Byzantine or Persian edifices, and they rapidly altered these earlier forms into a unique style. Mosques were initially constructed around a large open courtyard with a fountain where the faithful could wash before prayers. Simple, unadorned loggias and halls, used for community gatherings that helped bond the society together, surrounded the courtyard. In the central hall, a *mihrab* (prayer niche) pointed east toward Mecca, the direction for the faithful to pray. Minarets, or towers, for calling the faithful to prayer were constructed above the roof of the main halls.

As the Islamic communities grew richer, they ornamented their mosques and public buildings with elaborate designs, often based on various calligraphic renditions of verses from the Qur'an. The Great Mosque at Damascus and the Dome of the Rock and the al-Aqsa Mosque in Jerusalem are among the most important of the surviving early Islamic monuments. Built over an earlier Christian basilica, the Great Mosque in Damascus had a huge great hall and splendid mosaics depicting trees and village scenes. The Dome of the Rock in Jerusalem, completed in 691, is octagonal in plan and is decorated in sumptuous blue-glazed tiles and topped with a dome that was later covered in gold. Owing to decay caused by climatic extremes and destruction by conquest, few of the great architectural monuments built by the Abbasids in Baghdad remain.

The Ibn Tulun mosque in Cairo is an outstanding example of Mesopotamian work. Ibn Tulun was appointed governor of Egypt in the mid-ninth century by the Abbasid caliph, but he soon established an independent regime. A great patron of the arts, Ibn Tulun financed numerous buildings and developments in Cairo. The Mosque bearing his name was built between 876 and 879 and is noted for the huge central courtyard—for centuries second in size only to the courtyard surrounding the Ka'bah in Mecca—and for its simplicity of design. The minaret of Ibn Tulun is unusual because it is square and has an outside staircase, recalling the ancient ziggurats of Mesopotamia.

The caliphs in Muslim Spain were also enthusiastic builders. Begun in 785, the Mosque at Córdoba underwent numerous alterations and additions, including the build-

The Great Mosque, Córdoba. The Great Mosque was begun by the Umayyad prince Abd al-Rahman I. The horseshoe pillars form a forest of marble and decorated stucco. By placing the arches in two layers, one above the other, the architects achieved the illusion of greater height. The Córdoba mosque has been enlarged several times and remains one of the outstanding architectural achievements of the Islamic world.

© Paul Almasy/Corbis

ing of a Christian church in the center of the mosque following the Christian conquests of the fifteenth century. The Holy Roman Emperor Charles V, generally no lover of the Muslim world, is reputed to have said of this addition, "They have taken something extraordinary and made it ordinary." The Córdoba mosque has a huge central dome with a "forest" of horseshoe arches in two tiers in what was an original development in Islamic architecture. The Great Mosque at Qairawan (Kairouan) in Tunisia has a similar "forest" of marble columns within the main hall.

In Spain, the al-Hambra, or Red Castle, and the summer palace, the Generalife, are the most elaborate and best known of the Muslim monuments that still survive. Built during the fourteenth century, these pleasure palaces have highly sophisticated systems of water fountains, gardens, and ornately decorated and ornamented salons. They are indicative of the secular nature of the Nasrid regime; mosques were added almost as afterthoughts. Sporting lavish stucco decorations throughout and an outstanding "court of the lions," the al-Hambra, in particular, remains among the most famous and best-preserved examples of secular Islamic architecture.

Islamic Literature and the "Lively Arts"

In addition to their work in philosophy and theology, Muslim writers developed a lively literary tradition as well. Muslims universally regarded the Qur'an as the highest achievement in the Arabic language. Hence, early Arabic writers used the flowing cadences and style of the Qur'an as the model for both prose and poetry.

In pre-Islamic Arabia, poetry had long been regarded as the ultimate literary form, and long narrative poems were passed down through the generations by oral transmission. After the advent of Islam, a strong written tradition developed, and poets enjoyed lavish court patronage under both the Umayyads and the Abbasids. Thus poetry continued as the most highly esteemed creative form in Islamic societies.

Political and historical events were popular subjects for early Muslim writers. Poets were often employed to glorify conquests or to vilify political opponents of particular rulers. For example, the renowned classical Arabic poet known by the irreverent pen-name al-Mutanabbi, or "The Pretender to Be a Prophet" (915–965), wrote in praise of one ruler:

> Whither do you intend, great prince? We are the
> 　herbs of the hills, and you are the clouds:
> We are the ones time has been miserly towards
> 　respecting you, and the days cheated of your presence.
> Whether at war or at peace, you aim at the heights,
> 　whether you tarry or hasten.
> Would that we were your steeds when you ride forth,
> 　and your tents when you alight!

Al-Mutanabbi's motto was, "Live honorably or die heroically."

Often written in the vernacular, love poems were also extremely popular. For example, the twelfth-century Córdoban poet Ibn Quzman, who came from a noble Arab family, was noted for mixing colloquial Andalusian language with classical Arabic. Ibn Quzman was a master storyteller who successfully blended irony, cynicism, and dramatic language in a manner similar to European writers such as Dante and Boccaccio.

In the Arab world, music was closely linked to poetic traditions, and under the court influences of the Umayyads and Abbasids, Arabic music gradually fused with the musical traditions of the Byzantines, the Syrians, and other Eastern empires. Caliphs patronized musicians and the very popular poet-singers. In Baghdad, Caliph Mamun had many Greek classical essays on music translated into Arabic; these formed the foundation for scholarly works on nomenclature and musical modes.

Based largely on quarter tones, Arabic music stressed melodies with complex nuances and ornamentation. A number of Arabic instruments influenced Western instruments. The lute was derived from the 'ud, a pear-shaped stringed instrument, various percussion instruments from the drums, and the medieval rebec from the *rabab*, a single-stringed instrument played with a bow. Arabic musicians also played a wide variety of flutes and the *ganun,* a trapezoid-shaped stringed instrument similar to the zither. Musicians in Spain incorporated both Arabic and Western musical forms into their work; later, returning crusaders also brought Arabic musical instruments and songs back to Europe.

In the Spanish courts of Córdoba and Granada, singers elaborated romantic themes, which were then copied and expanded by the romantic troubadours in Europe. "Moorish" traditions, or musical traditions transferred from Morocco, are still found in the popular flamenco music of Spanish Gypsies. Depictions of musicians and dancing groups were also popular subjects for artists and potters in the Iberian Peninsula and Persia (present-day Iran).

During the Islamic golden age, potters were well-known for their sophisticated glazes, particularly the lusterware technique. Because Muslim tenets disparaged the depiction of the human form as encouraging idolatry, Muslim artists became experts in the application of geometric patterns and "arabesques," ornate designs of plant forms in interlaced patterns, and in the use of Qur'anic inscriptions or other written forms to decorate their creations. The beautiful and elaborate penned writing called calligraphy was a highly prized skill that was amply rewarded by court patrons. Persian influences during the Abbasid caliphate prompted depictions of human forms in manuscripts and in painted miniatures portraying court life or favorite legends and stories. Poetry and architecture, however, remained the most esteemed artistic endeavors.

The Crusades

> O race of Franks . . . race chosen and beloved by God! From the confines of Jerusalem and from Constantinople a grievous report has gone forth . . . that a race from the kingdom of Persians, an accursed race, a race utterly alienated from God . . . has invaded the lands of [Eastern] Christians and has depopulated them by the sword, pillage, and fire. . . . The labor of avenging these wrongs [is placed] . . . upon you. . . . Enter upon the road to the Holy Sepulchre; wrest that land from the wicked race, and subject it to yourselves. . . .*

> *Robert the Monk, "The Speech of Pope Urban II at Clermont," trans. D. C. Munro, *Translations and Reprints from the Original Sources of European History*, rev. ed. Series I, vol. 1, no. 2 (Philadelphia: University of Pennsylvania Press, 1902), pp. 5–8.

As Pope Urban II gave his rousing speech in the city of Clermont, France, in 1095, the crowd shouted, "It is the will of God! It is the will of God!" Much to Urban's surprise, his call for the Christian world to unite and attack the Muslim "infidel" in the Holy Lands received a tremendous response. Many devoted believers were deeply committed to securing the holy sites for the Christian world. Urban's speech, given in response to an appeal from the Byzantine emperor for troops to assist him against the Muslims, helped initiate the Crusades, a series of Christian military expeditions against the Muslims in the eastern Mediterranean. The Crusades worsened European-Muslim relations by intensifying religious fanaticism and fostering long-lasting, deep-seated cultural prejudices. They also had a profound effect on East-West commerce. They initially disrupted trade patterns, but eventually boosted Western desire for Eastern commodities, a desire that would strongly affect the history of the world in the centuries to come.

Crusading Zeal

There were four main reasons for the Crusades. First, the pope hoped to unite the entire eastern Mediterranean and the divided Christian faith under the banner of the Latin church. Second, the Italian city-states, with their large navies, hoped for commercial gains and were therefore keen supporters of the Crusades. Third, the Byzantine Empire was in a severe decline and could no longer act as a buffer between the Muslim East and the Catholic West. Finally, the Seljuk Turks, declining in military power, were no longer able to ensure the safety of the Christian pilgrims visiting the holy sites.

By 1097 some 30,000 knights, primarily Frankish and German, were ready to conquer the "infidel" and secure the Holy Land for Christendom while reaping their share of booty and glory. They were preceded by a Peasants' Crusade, a band of land-hungry peasants who journeyed east, only to have their hopes deflated in an alien land; the survivors quickly returned home.

The Divided Muslim World

Initially, the crusaders met with military success largely because of the political weakness of the Muslim/Arab world at the end of the eleventh century. The pressures of the religio-political schisms that had arisen within the Abbasid Empire in the tenth and eleventh centuries had undermined the strength of the Muslims to resist outside attacks. Local rulers in North Africa and central Asia all at one time or another pulled free of Abbasid control while rival Turkish and Iranian forces usurped the power of the Abbasid caliphs. Under the *atabeg* system, slaves (atabegs) acted as tutors to the royal princes and subsequently rose to key positions; often, however, the one-time slaves overthrew their former masters. The atabegs then hired new slaves as tutors for their sons, and the entire system repeated itself. The atabegs and Turkish mercenaries often joined forces to take control from the Abbasid rulers. In 861, Caliph Mutawakkil (reigned 847–861) was assassinated by Turkish mercenaries, who continued to put puppet caliphs in power. At one time, three blind former Abbasid caliphs were reduced to begging on the streets of Baghdad.

By 945, following the takeover of Baghdad by the Iranian-based Buyids in 932, the Abbasid caliphate had effectively ceased to exist. Although Baghdad technically remained the center of the caliphate, the empire was increasingly ruled by various Persian and Turkish forces. Just as strong rulers in European nations competed for control or dominance over the papacy, so, too, did regional rivals within West Asia and Africa compete for control over the caliphate.

Ultimately, the rival Fatimid caliphate in Cairo challenged the preeminence of the caliphate in Baghdad. The Fatimids, adherents of the Shi'i branch of Islam, claimed descent from the seventh Imam and Fatima, the Prophet's daughter and wife of Ali. After becoming the dominant military force in North Africa, the Fatimids conquered Egypt in the second half of the tenth century. They moved their capital to the newly built city of Cairo and from there proceeded to take southern Syria by 969, thereby gaining control over two of the key trading routes in the Muslim world. They then established bases in northern Syria and Damascus and subsequently posed a serious economic and military danger to Baghdad. Thus two rival caliphates existed, one in Cairo and one in Baghdad, each dedicated to the eradication of the other.

Fatimid economic strength was based primarily on the sale of agricultural products and gold, purchased by European merchants. Under the Fatimids, Cairo became an economic and cultural center. Great builders, the Fatimids used the money from agricultural

© Bettmann/Corbis

Pope Urban II Blesses Crusaders. Using the occasion of a church council, the pope appealed for a military expedition to take Jerusalem. Nobles and the clergy—and many pious poor people—responded enthusiastically.

productivity and commerce to construct numerous mosques, public buildings, and, in particular, al-Azhar University. Established in 972, al-Azhar is the oldest active university in the world and has been a major theological center for the training of Islamic theologians until the present.

With the expansion of the Seljuk Turks out of Anatolia (present-day Turkey) in 1037, the fragmented political situation in West Asia became even more complex. The Seljuks replaced the old order in Baghdad with their own form of loosely associated kingdoms, each allied to a specific family. This governmental structure contributed to further political disarray. After conquering most of Persia and Mesopotamia, from 1084 to 1117, the Seljuks moved into Syria, where they clashed with the Fatimids.

Acting out of self-preservation, the local rulers aligned with whatever side appeared the stronger at the time. To add to their problems the Fatimids were plagued by the same difficulties the Abbasid Empire had faced; namely, numerous mercenary elements, particularly Berbers, within the army and a firmly entrenched atabeg system. The Fatimids' war against Byzantium in 1055 further weakened the Fatimids.

In 1060 the Mamluks, former Turkish slaves from central Asia, rebelled in Cairo, hastening the collapse of the Fatimid dynasty. That rebellion provided the signal for separatist movements throughout the empire. Syria became the battleground of local rival forces. Leaders in Damascus played off Berber forces within the army who, in turn, threatened the Fatimid rulers. Religious minorities, including the Druze, Maronites, and

LIVES AND TIMES ACROSS CULTURES

Schools and Universities

In early societies, education of the youth was the responsibility of parents, who generally trained their children from very early ages in the skills and crafts that they themselves followed. But as societies evolved, the education of youth became more systematized and formalized. Ruling families and wealthy elites often hired private tutors to teach their children, particularly sons, reading, writing, mathematics, martial arts, and other skills needed by future leaders. In the Roman empire, Pliny the Younger put up "matching funds" for a school in his hometown so that students would not have to travel far from home.

In ancient Egypt, as well as in the Christian and Islamic worlds, temples, churches, or mosques were centers for formalized education. The curriculum stressed theology, religious law, and spiritual matters. In Islamic societies this involved the memorization of the entire Qur'an, often at a very early age. One of the first universities in the world, al-Azhar, was estab-lished by Islamic rulers of Egypt in the 900s. Its original goal was to train young men in theology and legal studies. Over the centuries al-Azhar has remained one of the preeminent universities in the Islamic world and its curriculum has been expanded to educate present-day students, including women, in a broad range of skills, including engineering and medicine.

Formal education was generally reserved for boys. Some societies, as in ancient Greece, actively discouraged teaching girls to read and write. In most societies only girls from privileged families were educated at home, and the curriculum often focused on the so-called feminine skills of weaving, music, and household management. Corporal punishment was common; flogging was the traditional means of punishment in Europe, and the bastino, a whip cracked over the bare feet of students, was used in much of Africa and western Asia.

Alawites, proceeded to create their own governments in Syria. In present-day Lebanon and Syria, these minorities continue to be political forces and sometimes rivals for power. Local emirs, whose feudal domains resembled those in Europe, also sought to expand at each other's expense.

The Seljuks sometimes persecuted and extracted heavy taxes from Christian Arab minorities—a reason why some Arab Christians initially were eager to assist the crusaders. European Christian pilgrims to the holy places in Palestine were also poorly treated by the Seljuks, who charged high tariffs and made it difficult for the pilgrims to enter. Under the Seljuks, merchants also found it increasingly difficult to conduct business. Torn by civil strife, the area became unsafe for travelers and merchants. Those who were brave enough to attempt the journey inland were often heavily taxed in every village; each emir wanted to obtain his share of the wealth that passed through his area. Lacking any central control, each local ruler was free to do as he pleased.

By the late eleventh century, on the eve of the Crusades, Syria was in the throes of political collapse and economic stagnation. The Byzantine Empire and the ambitious mercantile Italian city-states had already taken advantage of this political weakness to attack along the frontiers of the Islamic Empire. Thus, when the call for the Crusades went out and it became obvious that the crusaders had a good chance of acquiring footholds along the eastern Mediterranean, the Italian city-states were prepared—for a price—to offer their services to the crusaders. Italian merchants, ready to deal with Christians or Muslims, soon followed the knights.

The Crusader States

Moving into Asia, the heavily armed crusaders met little unified opposition. Wearing red crosses on their chests, they assembled in Constantinople, crossed Anatolia, and reached Antioch in the fall of 1097. In June 1098, with the aid of the large Christian Armenian population, they captured the city. After a brief respite they moved quickly down the coast and took Jerusalem in 1099. The crusaders massacred the civilian population of Jerusalem—mostly eastern Christians and Jews. It was reported that human blood ran knee-deep. Many Jews were herded into the central synagogue, which was then burned to the ground. Following this massacre, the knights gathered at the Church of the Holy Sepulchre where, after some debate, they proclaimed Godfrey of Bouillon, a French nobleman, as king. Godfrey continued the war against the Muslims and extended Christian-held territory. About 3,000 knights remained around Jerusalem, more settled in Antioch, and a small group settled in Edessa. Successive European rulers continued to enlarge their territory. By 1123, the crusader states reached their zenith, controlling the Syrian coastal regions and Palestine. However, people in the nearby predominantly Muslim and Arab provinces in Arabia and Iraq were not greatly affected by the Crusades and viewed the wars as frontier skirmishes along the fringes of the Islamic world.

In the areas controlled by the crusaders, the ruling barons organized their states into feudal domains based on familiar European patterns. Each fief, granted to favorites and to those knights who had rendered particular service for the crown, became more or less an independent entity. The controlling barons were only loosely tied to each other by the common threat of attack by the Muslims. Each lord was responsible for the defense of his own land, but on the occasion of a severe attack, the lords united forces. To protect their territories, the crusaders built imposing fortresses or castles, which were imitations of those in Europe. Scattered on hilltops in West Asia, many of these still survive as the main physical remains of the Crusades.

The European feudal system was superimposed upon the existing Arab village system. As the two structures closely resembled each other, the native population was little affected. Under both methods, the people rendered tribute to a lord or emir; they also had specific military obligations to fulfill in time of war.

Under the crusaders, agriculture remained the backbone of the state economy; cereals and fruits were the main crops. The crusaders attempted to enlarge the already existing industries such as sugar refining, soap making, and glassblowing. Jewelry making continued to flourish in Jerusalem.

Despite their apparently sound economy, the crusader states were in a precarious position. Both the church and the military orders, such as the Templars, were exempt from taxation. In addition, the various Italian city-states, which often provided both the

Map 8.2 The Crusader States and Empire of Salah ed-Din. Although the first two Crusades relied on overland routes, later crusaders traveled east primarily by sea. At their greatest extent, the crusaders' holdings formed only a small coastal strip amid extensive Islamic territories, and by 1190 they were rather easily retaken by Salah ed-Din.

financial backing and sea transport for the crusaders, enjoyed special extraterritorial rights. The small crusader states were dependent upon these Italian city-states for protection and for banking and finance. Indeed, the Italians were the major financial beneficiaries of the Crusades. Finally, the crusaders expended considerable energy and money on fighting one another and in repelling attacks from Muslim/Arab forces. The pressures of internal divisions, coupled with external threats from the surrounding Muslim territories, made it impossible for the Frankish crusader states, hemmed in by their geographic position, to have either security or a sound economy.

Muslim Counterattacks

The Muslim community did not sit back and let the crusaders have free political and commercial movement. Each petty emir fought tenaciously to keep his sovereignty. Strong warriors, often of Turkish origins, emerged to counterattack against the crusader kingdom. Zengi (reigned 1127–1146), the Turkish emir of Mosul (in present-day Iraq), and his son Nur-ed-Din (reigned 1146–1174) were the first great challengers to the crusaders. Faced by a Muslim opposition from the north, the crusaders, recognizing the internal divisions within the Muslim world, appealed to the Fatimid kingdom in Egypt for assistance. However, Nur ed-Din managed to outmaneuver both the Fatimids and the crusaders and succeeded in placing one of his own supporters, Salah ed-Din (Saladin, reigned 1174–1193) in charge of Egypt. Salah ed-Din, of Kurdish origins, moved swiftly to unite the Muslims and to lead the attack against the crusaders. His actions ended the Fatimid Shi'i domination and returned Egypt and the surrounding territory to Sunni rule. The battle of Hittin on July 4, 1187, ended any chance of crusader expansion into the heartland of the Arab world. On the offensive, Salah ed-Din continued to attack the crusaders' strongholds and eventually took Jerusalem in 1187.

The loss of Jerusalem provoked the Third Crusade, which attracted the flower of European knighthood, including King Richard the Lion-Hearted of England, Holy Roman Emperor Frederick I (Barbarossa), and Philip II of France. After Frederick drowned in Asia Minor in 1190, the other two kings quarreled, and Philip returned to France. Although Richard secured a truce that allowed Christians access to Jerusalem, the Third Crusade failed to defeat Salah ed-Din militarily. Salah ed-Din often pardoned his enemies, let captured prisoners go free, and provided lavish hospitality for Christian leaders. His honesty and chivalry earned him the respect of both Muslims and Christian crusaders.

Coping with Rude Franks

Everyone who is a fresh emigrant from the Frankish lands is ruder in character than those who have become acclimatized and have held long association with the Moslems. Whenever I visited Jerusalem I always entered the Aqsa Mosque, beside which stood a small mosque which the Franks had converted into a church. When I used to enter the Aqsa Mosque, which was occupied by the Templars, who were my friends, the Templars would evacuate the little adjoining mosque so that I might pray in it. One day I entered this mosque, repeated the first formula, "Allah is great," and stood up in the act of praying, upon which one of the Franks rushed on me, got hold of me and turned my face eastward saying, "This is the way thou shouldst pray!" A group of Templars hastened to him, seized him and repelled him from me. I resumed my prayer. The same man, while the others were otherwise busy, rushed once more on me. The Templars again came in to him and expelled him. They apologized to me, saying, "This is a stranger who has only recently arrived from the land of the Franks and he has never before seen anyone praying except eastward." Thereupon I said to myself, "I have had enough prayer." So I went out and have ever been surprised at the conduct of this devil of a man, at the change in the color of his face, his trembling and his sentiment at the sight of one praying toward the qibla [toward Mecca].**

Muslims called the crusaders "Franks," or those from the west or foreigners. To the average Muslim the Franks seemed remote and even barbarous. The Templars were a Christian religious and military order created to protect visiting pilgrims. In his autobiography (published as *Memoirs of an Arab-Syrian Gentleman*) Usamah Ibn-Munquidh wrote a highly personal account of his relations with the crusader knights; his memoirs are an insightful look at the clash of two cultures. In the above excerpt, Usamah Ibn-Munquidh describes his encounter with some knights when he attempted to pray at the al-Aqsa mosque in Jerusalem.

*William H. McNeill and Marilyn Robinson Waldman, eds., The Islamic World *(New York: Oxford University Press, 1973; reprint, Chicago: University of Chicago Press, 1983), p. 188.*

At Grips with the Infidel

I was at my father's side during the battle of Hittin, the first I had ever seen. When the king of the Franj found himself on the hill, he and his men launched a fierce attack that drove our own troops back to the place where my father was standing. I looked at him. He was saddened; he frowned and pulled nervously at his beard. Then he advanced, shouting "Satan must not win!" The Muslims again assaulted the hill. When I saw the Franj retreat under the pressure of our troops, I screamed with joy, "We have won!" But the Franj attacked again with all their might, and once again our troops found themselves grouped around my father.

Now he urged them into the attack once more, and they forced the enemy to retreat up the hill. Again I screamed, "We have beaten them!" But my father turned to me and said, "Silence! We will have crushed them only when that tent on the hill has fallen." Before he had time to finish his sentence, the king's tent collapsed. The sultan then dismounted, bowed down and thanked God, weeping for joy.*

In this firsthand account, Salah ed-Din's son describes the fierce battle of Hittin, where his father defeated the crusaders.

*Amin Maalouf, The Crusades through Arab Eyes (New York: Schocken Books, 1987), pp. 192–193.

The failure of the Third Crusade foreshadowed the demise of the crusader states. As Christian control over the Holy Land lessened, Pope Innocent III called for new attacks on Egypt, the Muslim power base since Salah ed-Din. The pope hoped to regain the holy places and to reunite Eastern Orthodox and Roman Catholic Christians. When the Venetians demanded exorbitant fares for transporting the Christian armies, however, the crusader knights agreed to conquer Zara, a city on the Adriatic coast, for the Venetians. In spite of the pope's arguments that Christians should not attack other Christians, the crusaders took Zara in 1202. In 1204, when a deposed and disgruntled Byzantine emperor promised them enormous payments if they would restore him to his throne in Constantinople, the crusaders seized the Byzantine capital. When the emperor failed to deliver on his promises, the crusaders looted the city and established the short-lived Latin Empire of Constantinople (1204–1261).

Although the crusaders ostensibly reunified the Christian world, in fact they embittered the Eastern Orthodox Christians. The schism, or division, between Eastern Orthodox churches and the Roman Catholic church widened, and persists today, despite twentieth-century attempts by the Roman Catholic popes and Eastern patriarchs to heal the wounds.

The attack on Constantinople discredited both the papacy and the crusading enterprise. It also crippled the Byzantine Empire so badly that the Byzantines proved unable to withstand later Ottoman Turkish expansion into southeastern Europe.

Renewed political divisions in the Muslim world after Salah ed-Din's death in 1193 enabled the crusaders to reestablish control over much of the territory they had lost. By the mid-thirteenth century, however, continued attacks by the Mamluk rulers from Egypt placed the crusader states once again on the defensive. After a protracted defense, the last crusader territory, Acre, fell in 1291.

Cultural and Commercial Exchanges

Although the Crusades were aggressive militaristic ventures, they produced a number of long-lasting cultural exchanges. The Muslim world introduced the crusaders to a wide range of new foods and luxury items, including silks and brocades, perfumes, and soaps. Some crusaders became so attracted to the different way of life that they joined it, intermarrying and becoming assimilated with the indigenous populations. Those who returned to Europe introduced the new commodities, particularly textiles, to their homelands. In a comparable fashion, republican Roman soldiers who had served in the Hellenistic East brought aspects of that life home.

Seeing the demand for these items, the Italian traders were not content to confine their activities simply to supplying the crusader states; instead, they sought to establish direct trade with the whole Muslim world. Such contacts with the Muslims gave the Italians a chance to tap into the land and sea trade routes to India, central Asia, and East Asia.

Eyewitnesses related with some surprise that trade continued across the frontiers even in times of open warfare. Salah ed-Din encouraged this trade, and various treaties between the Muslim state and the crusaders ensured free passage of goods. Even after the crusaders were ousted from the region, the Italian merchants continued their lucrative trade, which profited the Italian city-states and provided the economic basis for the artistic achievements of the Italian Renaissance.

The most important item of trade between the East and West were spices, especially cinnamon from India, cardamom from Aden, and ginger and pepper from Indonesia. Although the crusader states raised cotton for export, Egyptian cotton was also in high demand, as were Egyptian linen and dates. Precious stones, particularly coral from Ceylon and pearls from the Persian Gulf, were desirable luxury items. Porcelain from China was shipped to Egypt via Aden. Silks and brocades manufactured in Syria were major trading items, as were metal goods from Mosul and Cairo. Damascus was a key center for industry and commerce and profited as a stopping point for pilgrims on their way to Mecca. Jerusalem remained important solely for its religious monuments and as a seat of government.

On the negative side, the era of the Crusades intensified religious animosities between the Christian and Muslim worlds; to some extent these have persisted until the present. The Crusades also fostered further religious disputes between Roman Catholic and Eastern Orthodox Christians. As previously noted, many indigenous eastern Christians suffered persecutions at the hands of both Latin Christians and the previously usually tolerant Muslims, who came to view them as collaborators with the crusaders. In actuality, in spite of having been under Muslim control for over 400 years, nearly half the Arab population along the eastern Mediterranean was Christian when the crusaders arrived. Outraged by the excesses and massacres committed by the crusaders, many eastern Christians subsequently converted to Islam; still others converted to avoid persecution by zealous Muslim leaders. As a consequence, the Crusades ironically proved instrumental in making the eastern Mediterranean predominantly Muslim.

The Mongol Conquest of Eurasia

Then in 1206, the Year of the Tiger, after Chinggis had unified the people of the felt-walled tents, they assembled at the source of the Onon river. There they hoisted the white banner with nine pennants and gave Chinggis the title "Khan". . . . And having finally imposed order on the Mongolian tribes, Chinggis Khan issued a decree:

"I wish to bestow favours on all those who have served me in establishing this nation. I shall make you all commanders of units of a thousand men."

So he decreed, naming ninety-five trusted companions to command ninety-five thousand men. Then he issued a further decree:

"I have appointed ninety-five men—including my sons-in-law—to be commanders over ninety-five thousand.". . .

And he added: "At the time when I, protected by Eternal Heaven, was setting the entire nation in order, you were my eyes and ears. The entire nation shall be divided between my mother, my brothers, my sons and myself. The people of the felt-walled tents shall be divided and the people of the wooden-doored dwellings shall be separated according to their tribes. And let no one presume to countermand my orders!"*

*Urgunge Onon, trans., Chinggis Khan: The Golden History of The Mongols, rev. by Sue Bradbury (London: Folio Society, 1993), pp. 102–103.

This passage recounts how Genghis Khan became ruler of all Mongols in 1206, organized his men into thousand-man units, and rewarded his faithful lieutenants and relatives with commands and the promise of a share of his conquests. Genghis Khan was one of history's most feared conquerors—his name conjured up terror through much of Europe and Asia. The path of the Mongol army in the thirteenth century was strewn

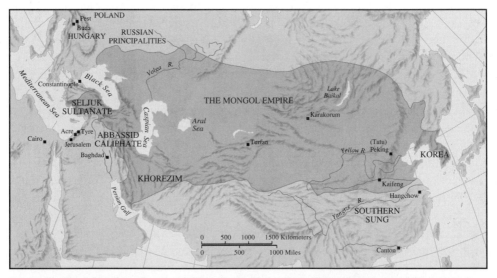

Map 8.3 The Mongol Empire under Genghis Khan. Genghis Khan and his immediate successors conquered a huge empire that stretched from Korea to the shores of the Black Sea. The conquests brought the Mongols unprecedented wealth, but at the expense of terrible destruction and millions of slaughtered victims.

with unprecedented death, devastation, and suffering. Erupting out of the North Asian steppes, the Mongols conquered China, central Asia, Persia, and Russia, creating the largest land empire in Eurasian history. As a result, to this day, Mongols hold him in the deepest reverence. Mongol legend says that he will return and once again lead them to greatness.

Genghis Khan, the World Conqueror, 1155–1227

The Mongols originally roamed the steppes south of Lake Baikal in present-day Russia. They hunted and herded and, when possible, raided the settled peoples nearby for loot. Mongol custom dictated that men obtain wives from outside their own tribe. A man could have as many wives as he could afford but accorded preeminence to

Genghis Khan. Genghis Khan was a powerfully built man with alert eyes and a luxuriant beard, as seen in this idealized portrait by a Chinese artist.

IRC www.historypictures.com

the first wife. Custom prescribed that the heir marry all his late father's wives except his own mother, and that brothers marry their widowed sisters-in-law. Tribal wars to gain territory, seize cattle and horses, and capture slaves and wives were endemic. Mongols worshiped a great god and spirits; shamans or priests interpreted the spirit world for them. Until the thirteenth century, the Mongols had no written language.

Genghis's given name was Temuchin; he was the oldest son of a minor Mongol chief. At age nine, his father took him to the camp of his mother's tribe to arrange a marriage with the chief's daughter, named Borte, then ten years old. En route home, his father was poisoned by an enemy and died. The next few years were full of hardships for Temuchin, his mother, and brothers, because they were cast out by the dead chief's clan. He was hardened by the struggle of these years, claimed his bride, and, with his father-in-law's support, began to rebuild his tribe.

Soon after his marriage, an enemy raided Temuchin's camp and captured his wife and animals. By the time he rescued her from her abductor, she was the mother of an infant boy. Temuchin named him Juji which means "guest" in Mongol, an indication of his doubtful paternity. Borte bore him three more sons. They and Juji would be their father's principal heirs. Temuchin so distinguished himself as a leader in war and in organization that he was acclaimed Genghis Khan (Universal Ruler) by the Mongol tribes in 1203.

It was Genghis's good fortune that the traditionally powerful states that surrounded Mongol territory were suffering from internal divisions at the time of his rise. The Chin Empire, to which Genghis was initially vassal, was situated to the south of the Mongols. Since its victory against the Sung in the mid-twelfth century, the Chin had ruled all North China. Chin prosperity peaked in the late twelfth century, the result of a succession of good harvests and the heavy tribute in silks and silver that it received from the Southern Sung government annually. Its decline began in 1194 when the Yellow River burst its dikes, flooded large areas, and then changed its channel to the sea. Years of famine followed. Government currency manipulations added to the economic chaos. By the thirteenth century, the Chin dynasty was in irreversible decline. Because the Chin were conquering nomads themselves, they had no deep roots in China, and despite partial Sinicization did not enjoy the full support of their Chinese subjects. Even in decline, however, the Chin remained a major power. According to the census of 1195, the Chin Empire had a taxpaying population of 48.5 million and an army of over 500,000, including 120,000 cavalry troops. In addition, the Chin possessed impressive defenses in the Great Wall and numerous heavily fortified cities.

Two other states bordered Mongol lands, the Kara-Khitai to the west and the Hsi Hsia to the southwest. The Persian Empire and the caliphate of the Abbasids were located further west. Both had been weakened by domestic dissent and by the schism and struggles between the Sunni and the Shi'i branches of Islam.

Fired by ambition to rule the world, and backed by his warriors, Genghis began his conquests. Even though the Mongol population was minuscule compared with that of the opposing states, the Mongols' control of the interior line of communications prevented their enemies from coordinating their defenses or forming alliances with one another. Nevertheless, Genghis Khan's victories over all his enemies were spectacular feats of generalship.

Genghis began by attacking the Hsi Hsia, a Buddhist nation situated in northwestern China next to the borders of Tibet, and the weakest of his three neighbors. Its people were proto-Tibetans called Tanguts. He had little difficulty ravaging the Hsi Hsia countryside, but suffered considerable losses at first because his soldiers had no experience in storming walled towns. Accounts say that Genghis took his first walled town by cunning and ruse. He sent a message to the defending commander that he would raise the siege and retire in return for a ransom of 1,000 cats and 10,000 swallows. The astonished defendants complied. Then Genghis ordered his men to tie tufts of cotton wool to the tails of the animals, set them afire, and release them. The frightened birds flew to their nests and the cats ran back to their lairs, and in so doing setting innumerable blazes in the town. Amidst the resulting confusion, the Mongols stormed the walls and captured the town. Later, Genghis used more traditional methods to take walled towns by employing siege engineers whom he had captured. In 1209 the Hsi Hsia surrendered, acknowledged Genghis as overlord, and agreed to pay him tribute.

In 1211 Genghis Khan declared war on his next enemy, the Chin. His army of 150,000 ravaged the northern Chinese countryside, leaving famine and pestilence in its wake. Only the few towns that surrendered without resistance were spared. Captured civilians were driven in front of Mongol troops as cannon fodder or as filling for moats. Any town that resisted was razed and its people put to the sword. In six months, ninety towns lay in ruins. The Chin capital, located near present-day Beijing (Peking), fell in 1215 and was systematically looted and then torched. It burnt for a month and then lay in complete ruin. The booty was sent to Mongolia by caravan. "Useful" men such as

Mongol Terror

"The Tangqut are a powerful, good and courageous people, but they are fickle. Slaughter them and take what you need to give to the army."

That summer Chinggis Khan pitched his camp on the Snowy mountain. He sent soldiers out against those of the Tangqut people who had rebelled against him. . . . The whole tribe was completely wiped out. Then he showed favour to Bo'orchy and Muqali, saying: "Take what you want, until you can carry no more. . . . Make their fine sons follow behind you, holding your falcons. Bring up their daughters to arrange your wives' skirts". . . .

By plundering the Tangqut people, by making their leader [who had surrendered to the Mongols] change his name [to humiliate him] before he suffocated him, Chinggis Khan destroyed the mothers and fathers of the Tangqut even to the seed of their seed, until they were no more.

Then he issued a decree saying:

"While we eat, we will talk of our victory, how we finished them off and saw them die. And we will say to ourselves: 'That is the end. They are no more.'"

Because the Tangqut people made promises they did not keep, Chinggis Khan had hunted them down a second time. On his return, on the 12th day of the 7th lunar month in the Year of the Pig, 1227, he died and was taken up to Heaven, and many of the Tangqut slaves were given to the Lady Yisui [one of his wives who accompanied him on his last expedition].*

This is the chilling account of how Genghis Khan dealt with the Tanguts who had dared rise up against the Mongols after surrendering to them. Genghis Khan used terror and extreme brutality as a means of psychological warfare, killing millions in the process.

*Urgunge Onon, trans., Chinggis Khan: The Golden History of The Mongols, rev. by Sue Bradbury (London: Folio Society, 1993), pp. 152–154.

artists, craftsmen, engineers, astrologers, and philosophers were spared but taken captive. Some women became slaves or concubines; all others were massacred.

One of the captives from the Chin court who was spared was the scholarly Yeliu Chu-ts'ai. He was a nomad by descent but was a fervent admirer of Chinese culture. A professional astrologer, he became a powerful advisor in the Mongol court. He had the unique distinction of successfully dissuading Genghis from committing some of his worst atrocities. A typical nomad, Genghis hated and despised sedentary people and decided to order the extermination of all people in conquered northern China so that their farmland could be turned into pasture for Mongol horses. Chu-ts'ai made a calculation of the annual taxes the victims paid and noted that the sum was greater than could be produced by the same land used for grazing. The appeal to Genghis's greed succeeded, and the people were spared.

The remnant Chin government entrenched itself in the well-defended city of Kaifeng and the war dragged on. After conquering Manchuria in 1216 and Korea in 1218, Genghis put deputies in charge of the Chin campaign and turned west. In 1218, he destroyed the Buddhist kingdom called Kara-Khitai to unblock his route west. After annexing the territory of the Kara-Khitai, Genghis's empire touched that of the Khorezim Empire, which included modern Persia and part of Afghanistan and central Asia and was populated by Christians and Muslims. Between 1219 and 1221, he attacked the larger army of the Khorezim with his force of 200,000 soldiers. As in China, the Mongols committed wholesale butcheries, sparing no civilians except those useful to them, whom they deported to Mongolia. Much of central Asia and northern Persia were systematically laid waste and depopulated. For example, Genghis reputedly massacred 700,000 people at Merv, sparing only 80 craftsmen. A small group of Turkic tribesmen nearby, the ancestors of the Ottoman Turks, were among the few who escaped. They fled westward to Asia Minor, where they were given asylum by the Seljuk Turks. Mongol armies advanced as far west as the Christian kingdom of Georgia in the Caucasus and to the Crimean Peninsula on the Black Sea, but did not consolidate these far-flung conquests until a later time.

In 1223 Genghis began his homeward trip. He was infuriated that the Chin still resisted and that the Hsi Hsia were in revolt. In 1226 he once again took the field against the Hsi Hsia, repeating atrocities against them. Their capital city, Ninghsia, did not fall until 1227, after Genghis's death. According to his wish, the entire population of the city and most of the people of the kingdom were put to the sword. According to Chinese records, only 1 percent of the people survived. The Hsi Hsia written language was lost, and their irrigation works were wrecked or abandoned because not enough people were left to work them. The fields were choked by sand and the land became desert. The region never regained its population or prosperity.

Genghis Khan's Heritage

Genghis died in 1227 at seventy-two, the result of falling from a horse while hunting. The guards who escorted his cortege back to Mongolia left nothing but death behind, for any living thing unlucky enough to have encountered the procession was slaughtered. Finally, at home in Mongolia, he was buried on top of Mount Burkan-Kaldun, a site he had loved since his youth. He is still revered by his people as Genghis the Heaven-Sent, and many Mongols hold the messianic hope that one day he will rise again and lead them to new glory.

To his immediate successors Genghis left two main legacies, as conqueror and as a law-giving administrator. As a conqueror he had no peer and laid the groundwork for the largest land empire in the world. Like Alexander the Great, he was a military genius. However, unlike Alexander, who neglected to consolidate his conquests, Genghis and his successors were superb adapters and improvers of selected existing government and military practices. For example, centuries earlier the Chinese had packed gunpowder in bamboo tubes and propelled them as missiles. In resisting the Mongols, the Southern Sung replaced the bamboo tubes with cast-iron barrels, thereby inventing the first cannon in warfare. Mongols quickly adopted cannons in besieging walled cities, with devastating effect. Cannons quickly spread to Europe and were in use there by the early fourteenth century.

Genghis was also a master of other aspects of warfare. He inspired fanatical devotion and loyal service from a group of outstanding generals. His cavalry were the most skilled horsemen in the world. He was meticulous in doing all the necessary groundwork before embarking on a campaign. Well served by spies, he gathered information about his enemies. He also accumulated needed supplies and provisions and protected his lines of communications. Genghis was also a master of psychological warfare. To inspire terror and demoralize his enemies into surrender without resistance, he deliberately committed

LIVES AND TIMES ACROSS CULTURES

Treasures from Royal Tombs

Across the ancient world from Egypt to China, many cultures held that people needed in the next life the material goods they had enjoyed while alive. Thus surviving relatives buried treasured items with their loved ones. Royal tombs were therefore packed with artifacts, and, because this was common knowledge, they have been the targets of tomb robbers and treasure hunters from antiquity up to the present. Archaeologists, too, search for ancient royal graves, but with the goal of learning about ancient times. They have made spectacular finds since the late nineteenth century, and their quest continues.

In 1829 a seven-year-old German boy, Heinrich Schliemann, was given a copy of the *Iliad*. He became convinced that the events described by Homer were real and not mythology and devoted his later life to finding Mycenae, home of the Greek king Agamemnon, and Troy, the city Agamemnon's victorious men destroyed. Schliemann's boyhood dream came true in the 1870s when he made the spectacular discoveries of both Mycenae with its royal tombs, and the Troy of the *Iliad* with its hoard of treasures. His finds also transformed the Trojan War, about 1200 B.C.E., from myth to history.

In 1922 an English Egyptologist, Howard Carter, found the tomb of King Tutankhamon ("King Tut") of Egypt, who died around 1350 B.C.E. Although it had been looted in antiquity, thousands of treasures, including a solid gold sarcophagus and the mummified body of the king, remained intact, making this discovery one of the most spectacular from ancient Egypt.

In 221 B.C.E. Ch'in unified China, inaugurating the imperial era. Giving himself the title of First Emperor, this megalomaniacal ruler began to construct a huge mausoleum for himself, which he reputedly furnished with fabulous treasures. It was looted after his dynasty fell in 206 B.C.E., but till now the huge mound that surmounts the tomb had not been excavated. However, farmers drilling a well in the 1970s discovered huge underground pits surrounding the mound that yielded over 7,000 life-sized pottery horses and men intended to guard the ruler in death.

In 1227 Genghis Khan, the ruthless and fearsome Mongol conqueror, died while campaigning. His remains were returned to Mongolia for elaborate burial with vast treasures, reputedly including the crowns of seventy-eight subjugated rulers. The site's exact location remains unknown, and several recent expeditions have failed to locate it.

Numerous known tombs as well as those still awaiting discovery will furnish work for generations of future archaeologists and scholars.

acts of cruelty of the greatest magnitude and spread tales of the bloody orgies his men had reveled in during previous campaigns. He made terror a system of government and a method of diplomacy. Any foe that dared resist him found no mercy; any city that loosed one arrow against his forces could expect all its inhabitants (except those whose skills he could use) to be massacred. Thus he ensured success. His career brought glory to Mongols but slavery and ruin to millions of others. As a Muslim poet lamented, no survivors were left to weep for the dead in his path. The devastation caused by his campaigns disrupted the economies and the trade routes across Asia for a generation.

Genghis looked on the empire he conquered as clan property, so clan members and his supporters formed the ruling class. To improve communications and administration, he supervised the invention of an alphabet for the Mongol language, based on the Turkic Uighur script. He set up an efficient postal system that sped information and government business across the far-flung empire. He promulgated the first written law code for Mongols called the Yasa. It decreed religious toleration, exempted the clergy from taxation, forbade washing and urinating in running water (which shows how precious water was to nomads), and prescribed the death penalty for spying, desertion, theft, adultery, and butchering animals in the Muslim manner. He further ordered that no future decrees of Mongols could conflict with the Yasa.

Genghis also created an administrative structure to rule his empire, and since few Mongols had the requisite skills or inclination for the undertaking, he employed conquered peoples, such as Yeliu Chu-ts'ai. After an area was fully subdued, he would even permit the remaining population to return and rebuild their cities so that they could begin paying taxes to him. To his subjugated populace, Genghis was surely the most frightful and monstrous curse imaginable. The Chinese had never suffered such barbarities; few of the Buddhist Hsi Hsia people survived, and the Muslim and Christian peoples were cruelly battered. It is no wonder that the Christian Europeans called him the Scourge of God.

Genghis Khan's measures succeeded in the short term, and his heirs continued to expand the empire he created for half a century. In the long term his plans failed because his people could not combine their pastoral way of life with the needs of governing sedentary populations. Most opted to change, became sedentary, were corrupted by the luxuries they enjoyed, and adopted the religions of their conquered subjects.

Mongol Domains under Genghis Khan's Heirs

Near death, Genghis Khan assembled his sons and grandsons. His eldest son, Juji, had predeceased him. The sons of Juji and the surviving three sons of Genghis and Borte were his heirs. Juji's sons received Russia, the westernmost of the conquered lands, located farthest from home, according to Mongol custom. This area was the least well defined; its western limit was described as the point "as far as the soil has been trodden by the hooves of Mongol horses." Juji's sons became known as khans of the Golden Horde. The second son, Chagatai, received central Asia; Ogotai, the third son, received Chinese Turkestan, while Tului, the youngest son, received the homeland, as well as North China. Genghis designated Ogotai to succeed him as grand khan, subject to confirmation by an assembly of Mongol leaders.

Two years after Genghis's death, the assembly met in Karakorum in Mongolia and formally elected Ogotai the second grand khan. After forming an alliance with the Southern Sung, Ogotai and Tului then resumed the war against the Chin. When Kaifeng was captured in 1233, its last ruler committed suicide and all North China fell under Mongol rule. The Mongols and the Southern Sung soon disputed over the division of spoils. In 1235 Ogotai declared war against the Southern Sung, which was not totally subdued until 1279.

Earlier the Mongols had conquered Manchuria and forced the submission of Korea. Koreans were assessed an annual tribute of 10,000 pounds of cotton, 3,000 bolts of silk,

Map 8.4 The Mongol Empire in 1255. Genghis Khan's successors added to his extensive conquests to create the largest land empire the world had ever seen, stretching from Korea in the east to the heart of Europe. Mongol military force held the empire together under a great khan from the house of Genghis.

2,000 pieces of gauze, and 100,000 large sheets of paper. Otter skins were later added. Between 1217 and 1258, the Mongols repeatedly invaded and ravaged Korea, carrying off prisoners and looting the land. For a time the Korean kings of the Koryo dynasty sought safety on an offshore island, but eventually they had to submit. Many Koreans were later impressed to serve in Kubilai Khan's forces that invaded Japan.

In 1237 a major force set out to conquer Europe to secure the patrimony of Juji's sons. Led by another of Genghis's grandsons, Batu, it swept across Russia and captured Moscow, Kiev, and other principal cities. The fall of Kiev ended the Kievan (or Ukrainian) phase of Russian history. The Mongol juggernaut then advanced through Poland, East Prussia, and Bohemia and swept into Hungary, seizing the cities of Buda and Pest on the Danube River. By the end of 1241, Mongol forces had advanced to the border of the Holy Roman Empire and were at the northern coast of the Adriatic Sea.

Unable to unite against the mighty foe, the rest of Europe was saved in 1241 by Ogotai's death. This event forced the Mongol princes and generals to rush back to their homeland to elect a new grand khan, and the threat to Europe ended. Batu withdrew his forces to the lower Volga Valley, where they remained and created the khanate called the Golden Horde. Europeans had ruefully learned that Mongols were not the people of Prester John, the legendary Christian king of the east, in whom they had hoped to find an ally against the Muslims.

Ogotai's early death and the lack of an obvious leader and heir almost caused a civil war among the Mongols. His widow temporarily assumed the regency while different factions of Genghis's family vied for power. Not until 1246 did the assembly elect Ogotai's son the third grand khan, but he was immediately challenged by rival claimants. Civil war was averted only because the new grand khan died within two years of his election.

To ensure a peaceful succession, the assembly now turned to the house of Tului, Genghis's youngest son. It elected Mongke, Tului's eldest son, the fourth grand khan. Mongke was an able general and made the conquest of the Southern Sung his first priority. He personally directed the campaign and took his younger brother Kubilai with him. He appointed another younger brother, Hulagu, to conquer West Asia, while leaving the youngest, Arik-Boke, in charge of Mongolia.

Mongke's sudden death while campaigning in China brought about civil war. He had intended Arik-Boke to succeed him as grand khan, but Kubilai disagreed. In 1260 he convened an assembly in China that elected him fifth grand khan. Contending that an assembly convened outside the Mongol homeland was invalid, Arik-Boke called a rival assembly at Karakorum, the capital of the whole empire, which elected him grand khan. In the civil war that followed, the descendants of Ogotai and Chagatai supported Arik-Boke, while Hulagu declared for Kubilai. Fighting lasted for four years, with Kubilai the victor. He pardoned his brother, but hostile feelings between various branches of the family survived the protagonists, and some Mongols never recognized Kubilai as the legitimate grand khan. With Kubilai's election, the unity of the Mongol Empire ended forever.

Kubilai Khan's Empire

In 1260 Kubilai Khan established his capital at Peking, the former Chin capital that his grandfather had destroyed. He chose Peking because Karakorum in Mongolia was too far from major population centers and therefore no longer feasible as capital of the entire empire. He called the city Tatu, or Great Capital in Chinese; in Mongolian it was called Khanbalik, city of the khan.

Kubilai Khan resumed the conquest of the Southern Sung for several reasons. In Mongol eyes the success of a ruler was measured by how much new territory and wealth he could bring to his people, and southern China was a rich prize. For decades the Southern Sung government had assiduously developed trade with Southeast Asia, another source of wealth that Mongols would be happy to tap. Conquest of the south would also bring valuable political benefits, for although Kubilai ruled northern China, the traditional heartland of Chinese civilization, control of all Chinese territories would confer legitimacy and remove a possible source of danger.

Conquest of the south proved to be slow and arduous. The terrain was unsuited to Mongol cavalry operations, which forced Kubilai to develop an infantry force, employ new weapons and tactics, and create a navy to counter the Sung navy. Hulagu helped by sending Arab engineers, who devised powerful catapults capable of throwing huge rocks over long distances, flame throwers, fragmentation bombs, and other war machines that could breach the formidable defenses of Sung fortress cities.

The Southern Sung resisted with determination. One strategic city in central China withstood a Mongol siege for five years before it finally fell. Fear and hatred of the Mongols also served to rally the people around the Sung government, which enjoyed wide support as the legitimate dynasty.

Despite its resistance, the end of the Southern Sung was only a matter of time. In 1259 the Mongols destroyed the southwestern kingdom of Tali, in present-day Yunnan province. Mongol conquest of Tali had sent many of its inhabitants fleeing southward, where they found a home in modern Thailand, calling themselves the Thai, or free people. Control of Tali allowed the Mongols to attack the Southern Sung with two pincers. The capital city, Hangchow, surrendered in 1276 without the slaughter that had characterized the fate of many other cities that had resisted the Mongols.

Sung loyalists continued to resist while retreating ever southward. During its last decades, the Sung throne was occupied by young boys, hardly the dynamic leaders that the desperate times needed if the fortunes of the dynasty were to be revived. The last Sung emperor drowned in 1279, as his last ships were overwhelmed. A few loyalists fled to Annam, Champa, and Thailand. In 1271 Kubilai Khan had already adopted a Chinese dynastic name, Yuan, meaning the first. This dynasty ruled China until 1368.

Kubilai also consolidated Mongol dominion in Korea. The heir to the Korean throne became hostage in his court; later this Korean prince was married to one of Kubilai's daughters. Marriages between Korean kings and Mongol princesses was continued by Kubilai's successors. In time the Korean royal family became a mere branch of the Mongol ruling house. At least once a year a Korean tribute mission would travel to Tatu, and a Mongol garrison was stationed in Korea, controlling it with an iron hand.

In his last years, Kubilai attempted to establish control over the many states of Southeast Asia. He first sent envoys to the states to demand submission and tribute. If a state refused, he would declare war to force it to submit. Annam (present-day northern Vietnam) submitted voluntarily in 1265, sending tribute and receiving in return a calendar from Kubilai (from early times a symbol of political submission to Chinese overlordship). Later, when the king of Champa (present-day central and southern Vietnam) refused to become the great khan's vassal, Kubilai decided to punish him. To do so, he demanded that Annam cooperate with him and allow Mongol troops passage on the route south. When the King of Annam refused that demand, he too found himself the target of Mongol attack. When the Mongol expedition arrived at Hanoi, they found that the Annamese king had fled. Mongol troops soon bogged down in Annam and Champa. The terrain was unsuitable for cavalry action, and Mongol warriors fell prey to tropical heat and diseases, while their morale plummeted in the face of guerrilla attacks.

Despite the difficulties the Mongols experienced in securing and holding Annam and Champa, the government of these states also realized the high cost of resistance. In compromise they submitted to Mongol overlordship and agreed to send tribute regularly; in return, Mongol forces would withdraw from their territories. After the Mongols ravaged Pagan in present-day Burma (Myanmar), the Burmese also accepted Mongol overlordship. Next Mongol envoys were dispatched to Ceylon and the Malabar Coast to demand tribute. In the case of Ceylon, they were also in search of Buddha's relics, for by now

Kubilai and many of his followers had converted to Buddhism. Kubilai's last tribute-enrolling expedition was dispatched to Java in 1292. It consisted of 1,000 ships, a 20,000-man army, one year's provisions, and 40,000 ounces of silver for expenses. It was a costly failure.

Kubilai's inconclusive and stalemated campaigns against his cousin Khaidu Khan in central Asia ultimately brought a mutual recognition of the legitimacy of each other's dominion. Kubilai conceded he could not control central Asia, while Kaidu agreed not to make incursions into China. Kubilai's house had now become primarily a Chinese dynasty, identifying with some aspects of China's distinctive history and traditions. Other branches of Genghis's family went their separate ways.

The Last Mongol Conquests in West Asia and Russia

In 1255 Mongke had sent his brother Hulagu with a large army to West Asia, to destroy the fortress of the Assassins and to bring about the submission of the caliph. Entrenched in their almost impregnable fortress of Alamut and other strongholds south of the Caspian Sea for over a century, the Assassins, members of a heretical Muslim sect, had been a great menace to both Muslim rulers and the crusaders. (They were called the Hashishans, because of the use of hashish in their rituals; the word *assassin* is a corruption of *hashishan*.) It took the Mongol army three years to wipe out the Assassin forts and to kill their leader, called the "Old Man of the Mountain."

Hugalu next demanded that the caliph submit to Mongol overlordship, and when he refused, the Mongols besieged Baghdad. The fall of Baghdad in 1258 was followed by six days of pillage and massacre. The Caliph Musta'sim was captured, forced to reveal where his treasures were hidden, and then killed. Then the Mongols overran Mesopotamia and Syria up to the Mediterranean coast, completing the conquest of West Asia begun by Genghis Khan.

Hulagu was poised to attack Egypt in 1259 when he received news of Mongke's death. He left the command of his front forces to a general and returned to participate in the succession struggle. The battle at the Spring of Goliath (A'in Jalut) in present-day Israel in 1260 was a turning point in the history of Mongol conquests. Here, in Hulagu's absence, the Mamluk rulers of Egypt decisively defeated the Mongol forces and shattered the spell of their invincibility. When Hulagu was ready for another test, he found out too late that Mongol instructors sent by the khans of the Golden Horde (who had turned Muslim) had taught the Mamluks Mongol cavalry tactics. Thus ended Mongol dreams of further westward conquest.

Egypt and North Africa were thus saved from Mongol invasion. Egypt would continue to be a powerful bastion against the Mongols, and because Baghdad was under Mongol control, Egypt also became the political center of Islam. Hulagu supported Kubilai, acknowledged the latter as Great Khan, and was in turn recognized as the il-khan, or regional ruler, of western Asia from Persia westward.

India was the only major area in Asia not conquered by the Mongols. It was saved for two reasons. First, the Delhi Sultanate that controlled northern India possessed a powerful army and was acquainted with Mongol fighting methods. Second, Genghis Khan's descendants became preoccupied with wars among themselves, sapping them of the manpower necessary to invade India.

From the middle of the thirteenth century to its end, the rulers of the Golden Horde, already masters of a realm that extended from the steppes of southern Russia to central Asia, launched great drives to conquer Poland and Lithuania. Although they failed, the region was widely devastated and depopulated. Afterwards the Polish government called in German settlers to the area; their descendants accounted for the ethnic German minority in the region that persisted to the twentieth century.

By the late thirteenth century the conquests of the Mongol people were over and Genghis Khan's realm had lost its unity in the civil wars between his descendants. The next phase of Mongol rule would be consolidation, followed by rapid decline. These topics will be discussed in the next section.

The Mongol Legacy

Within the bounds of this royal Park there are rich and beautiful meadows, watered by many rivulets, where a variety of animals of the deer and goat kind are pastured, to serve as food for the hawks and other birds employed in the chase, whose pens are also in the grounds. . . . Frequently, when he [Kubilai Khan] rides about this enclosed forest, he has one or more small leopards carried on horseback, behind their keepers; and when he pleases to give direction for their being slipped, they instantly seize a stag, goat, or fallow deer, which he gives to his hawks, and in this manner he amuses himself.

In the centre of these grounds, where there is a beautiful grove of trees, he has built a Royal Pavilion, supported upon a colonnade of handsome pillars, gilt and varnished. . . . The roof, like the rest, is of bamboo cane, and so well varnished that no wet can injure it. . . . The building is supported on every side like a tent by more than two hundred very strong silken cords. . . . The whole is constructed with so much ingenuity of contrivance that all the parts may be taken apart, removed, and again set up, at his Majesty's pleasure.*

*Marco Polo, The Travels of Marco Polo, ed. Manuel Komroff (New York: Boni and Liveright, 1928), pp. 106–107.

Marco Polo's description of Kubilai Khan's pavilion and hunting park at his summer capital Shangtu (the Xanadu of Samuel Coleridge's poem) is quite revealing about the grandson of Genghis Khan. On the one hand, he continued his nomadic heritage, living in a pavilion that is a glorified tent and enjoying his hunting. On the other hand, his lifestyle was already modified by his contact with the settled civilization of his Chinese subjects. Genghis Khan had moved from one encampment to another; Kubilai Khan traveled among several capital cities. While his grandfather hunted in the wild, Kubilai sometimes hunted in an enclosed artificial game park. And whereas his forefathers lived in tents made of felt and animal hide, his tent was made of fine fabric, and its opening was fastened by silken cords. The rapid assimilation by some Mongols to the life modes of their sedentary subjects became a source of tension between them and their compatriots who abided by the nomadic way of life, and ultimately contributed to the speedy collapse of their empires.

After the heroic phase of conquest was over, Genghis Khan's grandsons were faced with ruling large agricultural and urban populations of many different cultural backgrounds. Since the Mongol rulers were warriors inexperienced in the complex tasks of government, they needed to enlist the aid of their non-Mongol subjects in order to govern. In time, each ruler inevitably identified with the interests and needs of the people he ruled. Additionally, the center of the empire, present-day Mongolia, was insignificant economically and culturally compared with several of the conquered parts. Thus, when Mongol rulers were pulled several ways by the competing interests of their different subjects, the Mongol way often lost. Nonetheless, the heirs of Genghis who ruled large parts of Europe and Asia left a lasting impact. The four Mongol states were:

1. The Yuan dynasty (1279–1368), ruled by Kubilai Khan and his descendents, controlled China, Mongolia, and peripheral lands.
2. The Il-Khanate of Persia (1256–1349) was built by Hulagu Khan and his descendants.
3. The Khanate of the Golden Horde on the lower Volga River was created by the house of Juji; it broke up in the fifteenth century and remnants were completely subjugated by the Russian state in the sixteenth century.
4. The Khanate of Chagatai in central Asia was controlled by the family of Chagatai; its western part was incorporated into Timurlane's empire after 1370.

The Yuan Dynasty

Kubilai Khan (reigned 1260–1294) was the first Yuan emperor of China and Mongolia and overlord of Korea and much of Southeast Asia. He was also the first great khan not acknowledged by all Mongols. As the fifth great khan, he claimed to be ruler of the whole Mongol world and overlord of the other khanates. He was in reality the emperor of China, the largest and wealthiest part of Genghis Khan's empire, but nevertheless not the khan of the entire Mongol world. In crowning himself emperor of China, Kubilai can be compared with Charlemagne, who had been crowned in 800 by the pope as Emperor of the Romans of the West. As emperor of the Yuan dynasty, Kubilai ruled from his capital Tatu (Peking), shifting the axis of the Mongol Empire. As a result Mongolia became a mere province of his expanded Chinese empire.

When conquering the Southern Sung, Kubilai's legions did not pillage and massacre to the same extent that the warriors of Genghis had done earlier. Nevertheless, it was as conquerors that the Mongols ruled reunified China. The people of the Yuan Empire were divided into four hierarchic classes. On top were Mongols, followed by Persians, Arabs, Turks, and other non-Chinese minorities (called light-color-eyed people). Then came the northern Chinese, which included the assimilated nomads who had earlier settled in the region. The southern Chinese, the most recently conquered, came last.

Since most Mongols had neither the inclination nor training to staff and maintain an administration, Kubilai relied heavily on non-Mongols to run the imperial bureaucracy. He and his heirs never trusted the Chinese, however, so they turned to Persians, Arabs, and other central Asians of the Muslim faith. Ahmad, Kubilai's long-time minister of finance,

Kubilai Khan Hunting. This detail of a large painting shows Kubilai Khan, clad in a dragon robe and ermine coat and mounted on horseback, with a female companion. It was painted in 1280 before he became too obese to ride.

was a central Asian Muslim. Muslims usually served as "tax farmers" (people who collected taxes and kept a percentage of the total amount collected) and finance administrators for the Yuan rulers, and they enriched themselves in the process. Ahmad, for example, was notoriously corrupt and was hated for the merciless way he collected taxes for his master. Kubilai also hired a few Europeans, of whom Marco Polo is the best known.

Kubilai favored Muslims and other non-Chinese for several reasons. As a small minority of foreigners, they were easy to control and utterly dependent on their Mongol masters. Muslims were active in the international trade, both overland with West Asia and by sea with Southeast Asia and India. Since Mongols benefited from international trade, they rewarded the Muslims who were active in it. Finally, whether consciously or not, the Mongols used the Muslims as scapegoats to divert Chinese anger from themselves—an endeavor that was partially successful. Chinese writings of this period were bitter about the excesses and financial manipulations of the Muslim officials and merchants.

The non-Chinese staff of the Mongol rulers was still inadequate to administer China, so Chinese were recruited to fill numerous subordinate positions, where they were carefully watched by their Mongol supervisors. All state documents had to be written in Mongol, a language the Chinese were not allowed to learn. When finally the Confucian

The Bitter Pill of Foreign Rule

According to our Great Yuan system, people are reckoned in ten classes. First, officials; second, clerks . . . seventh, craftsmen; eighth, "entertainers" [actors, prostitutes]; ninth, Confucian scholars; tenth, paupers. . . . Ah! how low! Those who are sandwiched under the "entertainers" and above the "paupers" are the Confucian scholars of today! The Emperor, feeling sorry for these people, ordered that two school professors be installed for each circuit and district in the Chiangnan provinces. . . . These school officials look noble but are actually debased. Their salaries are not even sufficient to save them from cold and hunger. The worst among them have sunken faces, needle-sharp Adam's apples, and firewood-like bones.*

This passage, written by a scholar who lived through the fall of the Southern Sung into the Yuan dynasty, describes the suffering of the scholars during Mongol rule and their pitiful, poverty-stricken state. Although the Yuan codes did not in fact classify people into these ten classes, the bitter statement indicates how the once respected Confucian scholars had fallen from the pinnacle of society to among the poorest and most despised.

*Sherman E. Lee and Wai-Kam Ho, Chinese Art under the Mongols: The Yuan Dynasty (1279–1368) (Cleveland: Cleveland Museum of Art, 1968), p. 77.

civil service examinations were reinstituted, half the top degrees had to be awarded to Mongols, regardless of qualification.

Yuan economic policy was designed to produce revenue for the Mongol ruling class and not to promote general well-being. It favored trade, since trade brought revenue and rare luxuries for the rulers and their allies. The Yuan government made sure that the roads were kept open and safe for travelers so that international trade flourished, and luxury goods were traded among the Mongol realms. To the extent that agricultural prosperity underpinned international commerce and increased tax revenue, the Mongol government fostered agricultural recovery, but it did not allow the peasants to benefit. Thus the prosperity observed by Marco Polo was superficial and enjoyed only by the ruling groups, merchants, and privileged foreigners. To most Chinese the Yuan era was a period of unparalleled degradation. Millions were pauperized and an unprecedented number of people became slaves. Northern China was especially devastated and depopulated; even in southern China, which had escaped the worst Mongol depredations, vast acreages were turned into pasturage and parkland for the Mongol lords.

Kubilai, like his forebears, was tolerant of any religion that helped promote obedience and stability. He protected Christians, befriended Muslims and Taoists, and above all paid honor to Buddha. He particularly favored Tibetan Buddhism, partly because the Tibetan Buddhist clergy identified him with the Boddhisatva of Wisdom and portrayed him as a universal Buddhist emperor that all must obey. The magic and rites of Tibetan Buddhism, which somewhat resembled the Mongols' traditional shamanism (animism and belief in magic), were easy for Mongols to relate to. Thus the Mongols of the homeland became Buddhists of the Tibetan church.

Kubilai Khan died in his eightieth year. In death as in life, he was pulled between the two worlds he dominated. He was not buried in a sumptuous mausoleum in the manner of Chinese rulers. Rather, his remains were returned to Mongolia and laid to rest near those of his grandfather and father. A Mongol assembly in Tatu ratified his appointment of a grandson (since his favorite son and heir had predeceased him) as next emperor and great khan.

Kubilai ruled long and accomplished much. He maintained the Mongolian Peace (Pax Mongolica), under which his realm began to recover. His cosmopolitan court opened up East and West to each other, and his lavish patronage of the arts led to wide interchanges of ideas. These positive achievements must be weighed against the misery of the great mass of his subjects. His successors were lesser men who did not share his vision. Thus the Pax Mongolica did not measure up to the sustained and genuine accomplishments of either the Pax Romana or Pax Sinica that more than a thousand years earlier had given the world so much.

The Yuan dynasty did not long survive Kubilai's death. Power struggles quickly divided the royal family. In the twenty-six years between 1307 and 1333, seven rulers occupied the throne, none surviving beyond age thirty-five. Many of the early deaths were due to palace coups and murderous intrigues, but some can be attributed to diseases caused by excessive indulgence. Mongols loved a strong drink called *koumiss* made of fermented mare's milk. Kubilai's father and other kinsmen had died early from alcohol-related causes. Kubilai himself drank heavily and excessively in his old age, and suffered from diseases associated with alcoholism; he was also extremely fat. In their love of strong alcoholic drinks Mongols are akin to the ancient Macedonians; Philip II and Alexander the Great both loved strong drink and feasting, and were likely alcoholics.

Other factors also contributed to the downfall of the Mongols. The government became increasingly extortionate and inefficient, and natural disasters contributed to a worsening economic situation. As famines spread, so did peasant revolts. South China led in uprisings against Mongol rule. In 1368 troops of a southern-led rebel movement captured Tatu. The remaining Mongols fled northward back to the steppes.

The Il-Khanate of Persia

Hulagu was invested by his elder brother Kubilai Khan as il-khan, or regional ruler, and settled down to rule Persia and part of Mesopotamia. In the continuing power struggle between Genghis's descendants, Hulagu and Kubilai, brothers who ruled empires with sedentary populations, were allied against the Golden Horde of southern Russia and the Chagatai khans of Turkestan, who upheld the traditional nomadic Mongol way of life. The Golden Horde, now Muslim, was also allied with the Egyptian Mamluks. Thus the il-khans' lands were ringed by hostile neighbors.

Persian Muslims were most numerous among Hulagu's subjects. Just as Kubilai favored foreigners and minorities to staff his administration, Hulagu employed Jews, Christians, and Buddhists to run his government and had many Chinese soldiers in his army. Hulagu died in 1265 at age forty-eight. He had held to his Mongol faith, although his principal wife was a Christian and his son and successor was also married to a Christian, the daughter of the Byzantine emperor.

Hulagu's son was confirmed by Kubilai as il-Khan of Persia, but Kubilai could not provide effective military support for the il-khans because their territories were separated by the hostile Chagatai khanate. Faced with the Mamluks, the il-khan turned to the non-Muslim West for assistance. He sent ambassadors to the pope and to European monarchs to offer alliances against the Mamluks and even promised to support the return of Jerusalem to Christian rule should they succeed in ousting the Mamluks from Palestine. But by now crusading zeal had gone out of the Europeans, who moreover remembered earlier Mongol savageries against them. The proffered alliance was declined.

Around 1300 the il-khan announced his conversion to Islam and changed his title to sultan, in the Muslim fashion. In so doing he also renounced his vassalage to the great khan (ruler of Yuan China), because he was not a Muslim. The conversion showed a growing identification with the subject Persians and was also a political tactic aimed at weakening the alliance between the Golden Horde and the Mamluks by depriving them of a religious reason to oppose the il-khanate in Persia. The conversion also ended the favored status of the minority religious groups. The Buddhists in the il-khanate fared worse as a result of their ruler's conversion: they were persecuted as polytheists; some were forcibly converted to Islam. Civil wars between members of the ruling house ended the dynasty in 1349.

Like Yuan China, Persia under the il-khans was superficially prosperous. Merchants benefited from the international trade that passed through their land. A luxury-loving court and aristocracy encouraged crafts and certain cultural activities, especially painting and architecture. Meanwhile the peasants and ordinary people were burdened with crushing taxation and financial mismanagement. Many peasants, in addition, had their fields and crops regularly destroyed by the Mongol nomad lords who made their annual migration north and south through the countryside. Finally the il-khans resorted to printing paper money with no backing (as the Yuan government had also done with similar results) and brought on financial ruin.

The Golden Horde

The westernmost part of Genghis's empire, ruled by the descendents of Juji and called the Khanate of the Golden Horde, stretched from the Carpathian Mountains and the northern shores of the Black Sea across the Caspian Sea to the Aral Sea. Unlike the Mongol rulers of China and Persia who adopted some of the sedentary ways of their subjects, the Mongols on the Eurasian steppes maintained their ancestral nomadic habits, assimilating the indigenous nomads.

The Khans of the Golden Horde ruled southern Russia from Sarai, their capital city on the lower Volga River. Because they were furthest from the Mongol homeland, they were the first to go their own way. After successful campaigns to the north and west from 1240 to 1242, they received the submission of all Russian princes, who were required to go to Sarai to tender personal homage and to offer tribute in gold, silver, fur, cattle, and young men and women slaves.

The khans found indirect rule lucrative and effective. They appointed one Russian ruler grand prince and authorized him to keep the other rulers in line. The position of grand prince was not hereditary, however, and since the khan could invest any Russian prince with the position, he was able to sow dissension among the Russian princes and

Mongol Rule through Victims' Eyes

The Mongols rank high among the most ruthless conquerors and exploitative rulers the world has seen. They used armies of occupation to rule and mercilessly exploit conquered lands. The following quotation is from the *Chronicles of Novgorod, 1016–1471*, written by monks of that Russian city, which was spared because it paid human and material tribute to the Mongol rulers. It recounts the terror tactics the Mongols used to conquer their enemies, putting to death the inhabitants of whole towns that dared resist.

[In 1238] foreigners called Tartars came in countless numbers, like locusts, into the land of Ryazan . . . and

thence they sent their emissaries to the Knyazes [leaders] of Ryazan . . . demanding from them one-tenth of everything: of men and Knyazes and horses—of everything one tenth. And the Knyazes of Ryazan . . . without letting them into their towns, went out to meet them. And the Knyazes said to them: "Only when none of us remain then all will be yours." . . . The Tartars took the town on December 21 . . . and they killed the Knyaz and Knyaginya, and men, women, and children, monks, nuns and priests, some by fire, some by the sword, and violated the nuns, priests' wives, good women and girls in the presence of their mothers and sisters.*

*Robert Michell and Nevil Forbes, trans., The Chronicle of Novgorod, 1016–1471, vol. 5 (London, 1914), pp. 81–84.

promote loyalty and subservience to himself. The princes of Moscow gradually proved their loyalty to the Golden Horde, and therefore won continued confirmation as grand princes. In this way Moscow became second only to Sarai in importance during the Mongol period. Mongol expeditions periodically burned towns and ravaged crops to punish disobedience and to instill fear.

Mongol power lasted in Russia without effective challenge until 1380, when the prince of Moscow defeated the Mongols in the major battle of Kulikovo. Although weakened, Mongol authority continued for another hundred years. Finally in 1480, Ivan III, Prince of Moscow, renounced his and Russia's allegiance to the khan. The Golden Horde split up, and after the sixteenth century, in a reversal of events, the rulers of Russia would absorb the Horde's successor states one after another into the Russian Empire. Russians called the descendants of the Mongols Tartars.

Two major factors account for the longevity of Mongol power over Russia. One was the disunity among the Russian princes, who succumbed to the Mongol policy of divide and rule. Since Russia was simultaneously threatened by Lithuanians and Germans to the west, Mongol overlordship even afforded some Russians a measure of protection against their western enemies. Another reason was Russia's relative cultural backwardness compared with China and Persia, so that the Russian way of life was less a model for Mongol emulation than Chinese and Persian ways. Thus Mongols in Russia remained distinct and did not assimilate.

In the fourteenth century, the Golden Horde converted to Islam. This act placed an insurmountable barrier between the Mongols and their Christian subjects. It raised the Russian struggle for independence into a crusade for Orthodox Christianity, and allowed Russians to turn to their religion for identification and consolation. This religious difference continued to accentuate the division between Russian and Mongol and later prevented the full integration of Mongols into Russian life.

The Khanate of Chagatai

The region including present-day Chinese Turkestan and the central Asian republics of the former Soviet Union was assigned to Chagatai, Genghis's second son. It consisted of landlocked steppe grasslands and was home of mostly Turkish-speaking nomads. There were few cities that could provide wealth, but the khans were able to draw substantial revenues from international luxury trade along the famed Silk Road that passed through their territory.

The Chagatai Khanate was surrounded by the three empires ruled by other branches of the Genghis clan: Yuan China, the Il-Khanate of Persia, and the Golden Horde of Russia. Since it could not expand outward, its leaders turned their energies inward, concentrating on destructive and complicated dynastic struggles and civil wars. Because the civil wars concerned the descendants of Genghis Khan, they often drew in other branches of the clan, and because its geographic position was central to the whole Mongol imperial structure, politics in the Chagatai Khanate came to have consequences for the Mongol Empire as a whole. The bitter wars, especially those against Kubilai Khan, helped destroy the already shaky structure of the Mongol Empire.

The Chagatai Khanate broke up in the fourteenth century. The peoples in the western portion embraced Islam. Mongols from the eastern part allied with the remnant Yuan Mongols who had been expelled from China. They reverted to the ways of their ancestors, staging plundering raids against the Chinese. This was a fatal mistake, because whereas China was weak and divided at the time of the first Mongol incursions, it was now united and strong under the new Ming dynasty. In revenge, a Chinese army hammered into Karakorum in 1388 and burned to the ground what remained of the once grand capital. The Chinese then chased the Mongols further northward and smashed their last pretense of power. By the fifteenth century, only memories and legends remained.

The Empire of Timurlane

In 1369, as the Chagatai Khanate was breaking up, a Turkish leader established himself in Samarkand and began a career of conquest as remarkable and terrible as that of his ancestor Genghis Khan. Known in the west as Timurlane or Tamerlane (Timur the Lame), he first consolidated his power over central Asia and conquered Persia and Mesopotamia. He next defeated and captured the Ottoman sultan (descended from the Turks who fled Genghis Khan and finally settled in Anatolia), invaded the realm of the Golden Horde, and turned north, briefly occupying Moscow. He next proceeded southward and eastward, marched through Afghanistan and descended on India, sacking Delhi in 1399. After a massacre that lasted for three days, he left India, taking with him large numbers of captives. Complete anarchy desolated northern India in the wake of his depredation. He was planning to attack China when he died in 1405 at the age of seventy.

Although a devout Muslim, Timurlane was regarded as another scourge of God by Christians and Muslims alike, because he plundered and slaughtered his way across Eurasia, massacring Muslims, Christians, and Hindus indiscriminately. His men relished cru-

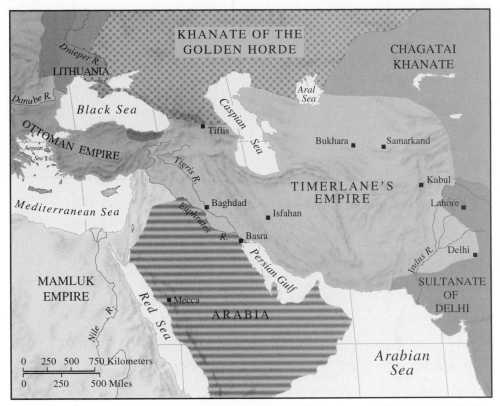

Map 8.5 Timurlane's Empire. Timurlane subjugated twenty-seven states, and his empire stretched from India to Anatolia. His dream of creating a lasting empire was not realized, however, because he left no capable heir.

elty and reenacted some of the worst atrocities committed by Genghis Khan, such as building pyramids from the severed heads of captives. He left depopulated lands in his wake. Some, such as Mesopotamia, would never recover fully, because his men irrevocably wrecked the irrigation system that had sustained the population. On the other hand, he was the lavish benefactor of Samarkand, capital of his short-lived empire, where he brought the loot of continents and the captives of many lands, to build and decorate a city he never found time to live in.

Unlike Genghis, who consolidated his conquests and left an empire to his heirs, Timurlane moved too quickly to forge an enduring empire. His empire split up and collapsed after his death. His was the last assault of the Mongol era.

The Legacy of Mongol Imperialism

The Mongol invasions had both negative and positive long-term results. In the short term there was destruction and devastation wherever Mongol armies had swept through. The population of China was reduced by half as a result of the massacres and other horrors

Timurlane's Tomb. Timurlane was buried in his capital, Samarkand. Although he spent little time there, the city benefited enormously from the loot he sent back from all the lands he conquered and ravaged.

that the invaders inflicted. Similar drastic population declines took place in Persia and other lands they conquered and ravaged.

Everywhere Mongol rule contributed to the brutalizing of society; some of the barbarous practices they introduced persisted after their collapse. For example, when the first Chinese emperor of the succeeding Ming dynasty died, a large retinue of his concubines was killed to serve him in the next world. Since such inhuman practices had died out in China over 2,000 years earlier, their revival can be attributed to precedents recently introduced by the Mongols.

Mongol rule was blatantly racial and helped define Chinese national consciousness. Mongol discrimination against Chinese was especially humiliating to the scholar-gentry. The fact that foreigners had collaborated in the Mongol rule of China brought about the isolationist and antiforeign policies of the succeeding dynasty. Such policies were in marked contrast to the confident cosmopolitanism of the earlier Han and T'ang eras. In Persia the rule of the il-khans helped solidify modern Persian boundaries and sense of identity.

In Russia, where overthrow of the Mongol yoke resurrected an independent nation, the centuries of humiliation served to forge a national, religious, and racial consciousness among the Russian people. Mongol domination cut Russia off from Europe, turned it inward, and isolated it from the advances brought about by the Renaissance. Subsequent Russian fear of the "yellow peril" can be traced to Mongol rule. Mongol destruction of the Grand Duchy of Kiev and occupation of southern Russia turned Russia's power center northward to Moscow, whose rulers rose to power as servants to the khans and then led the liberation of Russia from the Mongol yoke.

The Mongol conquest brought about the spread of the Turkish ethnic/linguistic group throughout West Asia. Turks had played a role in West Asia since the ninth century, but Mongol rule gave them an unprecedented opportunity to expand. The first people conquered by Genghis, the Turks far outnumbered and were more advanced than the Mongols; as a result they were co-opted into Mongol armies and administration. The Turkish Uighur script was adopted to make Mongol a written language. Later, most Mongols began to speak Turkish, which became the dominant language across the Eurasian steppes. By the fourteenth century the peoples of the Chagatai Khanate and the Golden Horde thought of themselves as Turks rather than Mongols. Only the small remnants who were chased back to Mongolia by the Chinese retained their Mongol identity, although that was also altered by conversion to Tibetan Buddhism. In Mongolia a modified Tibetan script was adopted for the alphabet, replacing the Uighur one.

The Mongol conquests reshaped religious patterns in Asia. Though they initially put Islam on the defensive, Mongols in western Asia soon embraced the religion of their subjects, with several important consequences. One was the end of Arab dominance of the Muslim world. Arab leadership was replaced by that of the Turks. Another was the collapse of Asian Christianity, both Nestorian and Catholic. The Nestorian Christian church, found across Asia from Syria to China, had roots that went back for centuries. Both Kubilai's and Hulagu's chief wives were Nestorian Christians, as were many other Mongols and Turks. Their faith did not survive the tumult of events, except in small pockets. The Catholic West's rejection of an alliance proffered by the il-khans resulted in the collapse of a Western Christian bridgehead in the Holy Land, which was conquered by Muslim Mamluks. Buddhism was wiped out in central Asia, but the Tibetan branch of Buddhism was accepted by Mongols of the homeland when Kubilai patronized that church. Mahayana Buddhism remained dominant in China.

The postconquest Pax Mongolica revived commercial and cultural exchange across Eurasia; travelers and their goods moved in safety as never before. Europeans, who had become addicted to the luxury products of Asia long before the Mongol invasions, were again able to acquire such products.

The demand for luxury goods stimulated the creativity of craftsmen. For example, the best cobalt was mined in Persia, and the best porcelain was made in China. During the Yuan, Persian cobalt was brought to China and was used by Chinese potters to decorate ceramics. The result was the blue and white china of that era that is still considered unsurpassed in the world. Chinese called the cobalt-decorated porcelains "Mohammedan blue wares." Turks, Egyptians, and Europeans marveled at the thin, translucent Chinese porcelains. They snapped up these Chinese exports and later learned to make porcelains themselves. Early Turkish porcelains made in Isnik and European porcelains such as Delft ware showed distinct Chinese influence. Persians adapted Chinese portrait painting techniques to produce miniature paintings.

New Dynasties in West Asia

History makes us acquainted with the conditions of past nations as they are reflected in their national character. The writing of history requires numerous sources and much varied knowledge. Historians . . . have committed frequent errors in the stories and events they reported. This is especially the case with figures, either of sums of money or of soldiers. . . . They offer good opportunity for false information. A hidden pitfall in historiography is disregard for the fact that conditions within nations and races change with the change of periods and the passage of time. When politically ambitious men overcome the ruling dynasty and seize power, they inevitably have recourse to the customs of their predecessors and adopt most of them. At the same time, they do not neglect the customs of their own race. This leads to some discrepancies between the customs of the new ruling dynasty and the customs of the old race.*

*Ibn Khaldun, *The Muqaddimah [Introduction to History]*, trans. Franz Rosenthal (Princeton: Princeton University Press, 1969), pp. 11, 24–25.

Born in Tunisia in 1332, Ibn Khaldun, who studied the patterns of change in civilizations over long spans of time, was a pioneer in the study of the philosophy of history. His analytical yet encyclopedic studies are early examples of rational attempts to trace patterns of change while centering on human beings as the main instruments of change. In the passage quoted here, Ibn Khaldun could well have been describing the world in which he lived. During Ibn Khaldun's lifetime, sweeping changes and military upheavals transformed the old Islamic/Arabic empires and brought about the emergence of several new competing centers of power.

After the disruptions caused by the Crusades and the Mongol invasions, West Asia split into three rival political entities: the Persians in present-day Iran; the Mamluks in Egypt, who had repelled the invading Mongols and thereby fell heir to a major portion of the old Islamic Empire; and the Ottomans in present-day Turkey. With some variations, these divisions have persisted until the present.

The Flowering of Islamic Culture in Persia

In Persia and Iraq, the Mongol ruler Hulagu had established the il-Khanate dynasty, which had practiced religious toleration. Although the early il-Khanate rulers had favored Buddhism, the majority of their subjects remained Muslim. In hopes of converting the il-Khanate to Christianity, several popes sent missions to the capital of Tabriz, but these attempts failed. Over successive decades, il-Khanate rulers intermarried with Persian or Turkish Muslims, converted to Islam, and adopted the Persian language, known as Farsi (the Persian word for "Persian").

During the Arab conquests, Persian culture and language had been preserved and, as noted in the discussion of the early Islamic empires, had influenced many Islamic/Arab cultural forms, including art, architecture, and literature. Persian writers, particularly Firdawsi (c. 920–1020) in the *Shahnama* (Book of Shahs), helped to glorify and popularize Persian history. Just as Homer's *Iliad* and the Chinese Book of History relate tales from the mythological and ancient past, so too does the exceedingly long, 120,000-line *Shahnama* chronicle Persian history. The hero, Rustam, with his trusty horse Rakhsh, slays enemies, falls in love, mistakenly kills his own son, and lives over 500 years. This massive epic remains one of the greatest Persian cultural achievements.

As a result of the Mongol conquest, Persia had been freed from Arab domination, and it subsequently continued to develop along separate linguistic, political, and cultural lines. Persian became the language of the court and later heavily influenced literary Turkish. The il-Khanate introduced Chinese and Indian cultural influences and thereby freed Persian artists and scholars from some of the more puritanical constraints of Islamic/Arab culture. For example, the depiction of the human form, discouraged by strict adherents to Islam, became fairly commonplace among Persian artists. The vibrant Persian literary tradition, which developed separately from the Arabic tradition, furthered the division between the two societies, as did the continued predominance of Shi'i practices and interpretations of Islam among most Persians.

Persian poetry exemplifies these new influences. Persian poetry had already been heavily influenced by Sufism, or Islamic mysticism, which was generally frowned upon by Sunni Muslim communities. Sufis advocated using a variety of modes, including dance, music, poetry, and song, to attain unity with God.

Under the il-Khanate rulers, Persian poetry developed in several innovative ways. New meters and subject matter were introduced, as were rhyming couplets. As a result, Persian poetry—and, for that matter, other cultural fields—became more varied than the Arabic forms, which tended to remain static and traditional. Persian poets composed long epic and lyrical poems celebrating love, wine, women, and song. Rhyming quatrains such as these from *The Rubaiyat* by Omar Khayyam, who was also a noted astronomer, remain among the most widely read and quoted poetical works in the world.

> Here with a little Bread beneath the Bough,
> A Flask of Wine, a Book of Verse—and Thou,
> Beside me singing in the Wilderness—
> Oh, Wilderness were Paradise enow!
>
> . . .
>
> The moving finger writes; and, having writ,
> Moves on: nor all your piety nor wit
> Shall lure it back to cancel half a line,
> Nor all your tears wash out a word of it.

Following the collapse of the il-Khanate and the chaos of Timurlane's invasions, a powerful new dynasty, the Safavids, emerged in Persia. The Safavids perpetuated and augmented the Persian cultural identity. The dichotomy between Persian and Arab societies—although both remained Islamic—has persisted until the present.

The Mamluk Dynasties

With the destruction of the Islamic state in Baghdad, Egypt became another center for Muslim cultural expression under the patronage of the new Mamluk dynasties. The first Mamluks, mostly of Turkish and Mongol origins, were former slaves and professional soldiers. These slaves were brought from outside Muslim territory to huge slave markets in Syria and Egypt where rulers who had themselves been slaves purchased them. The new owners educated the Mamluks (literally, those possessed or owned) and then freed them in a formal ceremony. The newly freed slaves were given a state subsidy and entered the service of ruling households. The slaves became the masters following the collapse of the descendants of Salah ed-Din's dynasty.

The Mamluks did not follow the principle of hereditary succession. A son did not inherit his father's position; instead, power was passed on to new slaves who had been raised to become generals or administrators. Although this process ensured a degree of upward mobility and a constant infusion of new, ambitious leaders, it also frequently led to bloody struggles for power. Indeed, the average reign of a Mamluk sultan was only six years. Throughout history, dynasties and governments have struggled with the problems posed by rules of succession and the passing on of leadership (see Comparative Essays 4 and 5).

The first twenty-four Mamluk rulers were known as the Bahri (river rulers); they were followed by a succession of so-called Burji (tower Mamluks), who took their name from having been quartered in the towers of the Citadel fortress, overlooking the city of Cairo. The Burji Mamluks were predominantly Circassian (a region in the Caucasus) in origin. The Mamluks successfully maintained Egyptian control over the Syrian provinces and, under Baybars (reigned 1260–1277), succeeded in driving the crusaders out of the region. Crucially, they also succeeded in repelling four major invasions by the Mongols. Unable to extend his authority over North Africa, and with a keen sense of power politics, Baybars established alliances with potential enemies, including Sicily, Seville, and the Turks.

Mamluk government was based on a strictly hierarchical, feudal system of allegiance of vassals to higher-ranking officials. In addition to their obvious military prowess, the Mamluks were also known for their cruelty and corruption, and as zealous converts to Islam were not as tolerant of minorities as their predecessors. Essentially foreign rulers, the Mamluks excluded most Egyptians from positions of authority, and many never learned Arabic.

The Mamluks sought to legitimize their rule by fervent support of Islamic institutions. Although many of them were not personally religious, the Mamluks gave sanctuary to

A Fable

*Fairuz [the intelligent hare] watches the king of the elephants entering the lake and seeing the reflection of the moon. . . . He notices the movement of the moon's image. . . . Hanging like a canopy over the scene is a deep blue sky with a golden moon.** *

The book of fables, *Kalila wa Dimna,* is a fascinating example of the transfer of culture from one society to another over hundreds of years. Originally written in Sanskrit, the book is a collection of fables much like those of Aesop or the French tales of Reynard, the wily fox. These fables all teach basic lessons of ethics and behavior. *Kalila wa Dimna,* named after the two jackals who are the heroes of the stories, was brought to Persia in the sixth century. Ibn al-Muqaffa translated it into Arabic in the 700s. The stories were still popular during the reign of the Mamluks; a lavishly illustrated copy from 1354 has survived, and it reveals the timeless quality of these tales. The manuscript also demonstrates the skill and sophistication of the artists who worked under Mamluk patronage.

*Kalila wa Dimna, from a fourteenth-century manuscript, ed. Esin Atil (Washington, D.C.: Smithsonian Press, 1981), p. 42.

the exiled Abbasid caliph (Islam's spiritual leader) from Baghdad. Successive caliphs had no real power, but the presence of the caliphate in Cairo gave the Mamluks legal authority throughout much of the Islamic world. The acceptance of Mamluk authority by the holy cities of Mecca and Medina provided a further stamp of legitimacy.

By protecting the trade routes and encouraging commercial activities, the Mamluks made Egypt the most prosperous Islamic state during much of the fourteenth and fifteenth centuries. Because the Mamluks were keen patrons of the arts, they encouraged artisans, particularly metalworkers and textile manufacturers, to settle in their territories, often providing them with substantial financial rewards. However, Mamluk attempts to monopolize the trade in luxury goods and heavy taxation ultimately caused many merchants to shift their activities away from Egypt.

The Mamluks supported building trades and social welfare projects. Many of the medieval monuments remaining in the modern city of Cairo date from the period of Mamluk rule. In addition to huge complexes of hospitals, schools, and mosques, they erected massive mausoleums for themselves and their wives and children. The great Islamic university, al-Azhar, and other Islamic schools prospered under Mamluk patronage. Scholars from throughout the Islamic world flocked to Egypt, which became a center of intellectual activity.

The life of Ibn Khaldun, the best-known of these scholars, demonstrates the overriding cultural unity of the Islamic world, a unity that overcame continual political upheavals and divisions. At various times in his life, Ibn Khaldun worked in his native Tunisia and in Morocco, Granada (the last Arab stronghold in Spain), and Egypt. He was sent as an emissary to negotiate with the King of Castile in Spain, and he even met with Timurlane after the fall of Damascus. Not surprisingly, Ibn Khaldun's historical studies deal extensively with the problems of establishing good governments and the negative effects created by political rivalries.

Despite the insights of Ibn Khaldun, the Mamluks continued their perpetual infighting, which seriously undermined their power and made them increasingly vulnerable to outside threats. Failing to forge a united front, the Mamluks fell in 1517 to the superior political and military organization of the Ottoman Turks.

The House of Osman

As the nomadic Turkish tribes converted to Islam, they devoted their traditional warrior way of life to protecting Islam from internal and external threats. Turkish warriors, adherents of Sunni Islam, viewed themselves as the "guardians" of Islam and fought tenaciously along the religious frontier between Islam and Christianity, particularly against the Byzantine Empire. Known as *ghazis,* these warriors amassed booty and slaves in their fights against the enemies of Islam, and many of their leaders established separate emirates (principalities). One of the Turkish emirs, Osman (reigned 1299–1326), was the founder of one of the greatest world empires, the Ottoman Empire (*Ottoman* is an Italian corruption of Osman). Between 1300 and 1320, Osman, leading his ghazi warriors personally into battle, began to extend his authority from his capital at Bursa out into the Anatolian Peninsula.

Map 8.6 Ottoman Empire in 1461.
From its small territory in central Anatolia, the Ottoman Empire had defeated the old Byzantine Empire, making Istanbul its new capital. From there the Ottomans conquered much of the rest of the Anatolian Peninsula and the Balkans, known as Rumeli.

Clearly, the army was a key institution in the creation of the Ottoman Empire. Originally, the army was composed mostly of volunteers from the nomadic Turkish tribes, but as it grew, recruitment and organization of the army were formalized. As Osman's power increased, other ghazis, attracted by the promise of wealth, joined him. These Islamic warriors were guided by a strict code of behavior, similar to the European knights' code of chivalry.

The creation of the *janissary* corps (from the Turkish term *yeni cheri*, or new soldiers) was a uniquely Ottoman military innovation. Male child slaves taken from predominantly Christian communities under Ottoman control became janissaries, trained from childhood to become professional soldiers. The janissaries learned Turkish, became Muslims, and owed loyalty only to their immediate superiors and to the Ottoman rulers. Like the professional warriors in ancient Sparta and the samurai warriors in Japan, the janissaries became known for their fighting zeal and professionalism. They lived, ate, and fought together and became a highly cohesive force. Janissaries did not marry until they retired from active military service, and even after marriage often continued to take their meals with their colleagues.

When the empire was at its zenith, the janissaries were a key force in the extension and power of the state. As the sultans became weaker and less dynamic, however, the janissaries often revolted against them. Not infrequently, the sultans, like Roman emperors under the control of their personal bodyguards, ruled only at the pleasure of the janissaries, who had the power to oust or even to assassinate them. But the potential threat of the janissary forces was not evident during the early centuries of Ottoman rule. Wisely, Osman and his son Orhan (reigned 1326–1360) willingly accepted outside recruits and formed alliances with Greeks in the captured territories. Such alliances, often reinforced through marriage (for example, Orhan married the daughter of a Greek noble), helped the Ottomans to consolidate their conquered territories.

Ottoman rulers gave land to soldiers as a reward for bravery and success on the battlefield; as a result, some soldiers held huge fiefs and retired as wealthy landowners who frequently hired overseers to manage their holdings. Similarly, the collection of taxes was often "farmed out" to professional tax collectors, a system that resulted in pervasive abuses and corruption. Booty from war and tax revenues on land remained the two major sources of income for the Ottoman Turks, who generally looked down on business and trade. Although the Ottoman government encouraged trade and kept the trade routes in good repair, the commercial life of the empire was in the hands of non-Muslim and non-Turkish merchants and artisans, who often amassed large fortunes from lucrative trade with Europeans.

The whole Ottoman economy was strengthened by the booty gained in warfare. Merchants and craftspeople joined together in *akhis,* which were similar to the European guild. Often members of the guilds were also members of the same *sufi* or mystical Islamic order. Hence, the religious and economic institutions were highly cohesive. The Ottomans followed the Islamic precept of allowing freedom of worship for all "people of the Book." Through the "millet" system (the Islamic system for governing religious minorities), they granted considerable autonomy to the many heterogeneous religious and ethnic groups under their control. For example, the large Jewish community in Ottoman-controlled lands enjoyed considerable prosperity under Ottoman rulers.

The Ottoman sultans rapidly expanded their empire at the expense of Byzantium. Taking the title of sultan, by 1362 Murad I (reigned 1360–1389), Orhan's young warrior son, had successfully led his forces into Thrace (in present-day Greece and Turkey) and took Adrianople, which became the new Ottoman capital of Edirne. Pushing his army further into the Balkans, at Kosovo in 1389 Murad decisively defeated the Serbian rulers but lost his life in the process. The military defeat at Kosovo is still remembered by the people of contemporary Balkan nations. Through the marriage of his son Bayezid to the daughter of a leading emir in Anatolia, Murad nearly doubled Ottoman holdings in Asia.

Bayezid (reigned 1389–1402) immediately sought to consolidate his own position. He had his only brother—a possible rival—killed, thereby establishing a tradition: for the next several hundred years, new Ottoman sultans had their siblings assassinated or imprisoned within the imperial palaces. Having secured sole possession of the leadership, Bayezid then moved to avenge his father's death with further victories in Europe. He surrounded Constantinople and closed the Bosporus and the Dardanelles.

In face of this renewed threat to Christian authority over Constantinople, rulers in Europe, particularly Sigismund, the king of Hungary and later Holy Roman Emperor, were roused to action. Bayezid forsook the siege of Constantinople to meet the crusading Christian forces at Nicopolis in 1396. Attacking directly into the center of the Ottoman forces, the Europeans were routed, and many were taken as slaves or held for ransom.

Enjoying the fruits of victory, Bayezid was the first Ottoman sultan to establish the trappings of a royal court.

Had Bayezid concentrated on the Balkan territories, he might have continued to enjoy unparalleled military success; however, he aimed to extend Ottoman control over all of Asia Minor, and this led to disaster. As his forces began attacking rival Turkish emirates in Asia, he aroused the anger of Timurlane. At the battle of Ankara in 1402 Bayezid's army was defeated, and he was taken prisoner. Placed in a cage as a prize of war, Bayezid probably died en route to Timurlane's capital of Samarkand. The Balkans were lost, but Timurlane turned over the Anatolian territories to Bayezid's sons. After swearing allegiance to Timurlane as his vassals, the sons promptly began fighting among themselves. When Timurlane died in 1405, his loosely fashioned empire dissolved into competing, rival local emirates.

The Conquest of Constantinople

The restoration of the Ottoman Empire was a long and complicated process. After a decade of internecine fighting, Mehmed I (reigned 1413–1421) became sultan. He created a fleet to challenge Venetian dominance over the Aegean Islands, the Anatolia coast, and other coastal regions of the eastern Mediterranean. After several confrontations, Mehmed and the Venetians negotiated an uneasy peace. He and his successor, his son Murad II (reigned 1421–1451), fought tenaciously to restore Ottoman control over most of the Balkans and even raided into Hungary. Known for his piety and adherence to the ghazi warrior traditions, Murad attracted a loyal following of old Ottoman families. He resumed the siege of Constantinople but was forced to lift it in face of renewed revolts in Asia Minor.

Under Murad's patronage, Turkish arts flourished. A new literary tradition glorifying the warrior ethos of the early Ottomans developed and gained popularity. Like the Roman Emperor Diocletian and the later Holy Roman Emperor Charles V, Murad twice announced his retirement for a life of study and contemplation, but attacks by Hungarian and Balkan leaders, who apparently thought the empire would collapse with Murad's departure, impelled his return to the battlefield.

Under Murad's leadership, Ottoman forces easily conquered Serbia, Bosnia, and parts of Greece. Many Eastern Orthodox Christians willingly aligned with the Ottomans who, unlike the Roman Catholic Hungarian leaders, were relatively tolerant of adherents to the Eastern Christian rites; some even sent their sons as hostages to the sultan, and others willingly converted to Islam.

When Murad II died in 1451, his son, Mehmed II (reigned 1451–1481), became the new sultan. Competent and well educated, Mehmed knew several languages and was a student of philosophy. All Ottoman rulers were skilled in a trade, and Mehmed was an accomplished gardener who worked in the royal gardens for relaxation between battles. He was also an efficient administrator who established highly centralized systems of taxation and bureaucracy.

Upon accession to the throne, Mehmed II immediately launched his plans for a total assault on Constantinople. He assembled a fleet at Gallipoli and amassed a huge supply of armaments, including cannon, gunpowder, timbers, and bows and arrows. Although the Mongols, as previously mentioned, had primitive cannon, the Ottomans effectively utilized forged metal cannon to gain strategic advantages over their enemies and thereby became one of the first "gunpowder empires."

To assist in taking Constantinople, Mehmed II constructed Rumeli Hisar, a massive fortress on the European shore of the Bosporus opposite the fortifications built by his great-grandfather. He then had siege cannon moved into position, and when all the preparations were in order, the actual siege began, in April 1453. It lasted fifty-four days. Mehmed even had ships hauled up a wooden ramp to the Golden Horn in order to bombard the city from all directions. With the city completely surrounded, Emperor Constantine called for help from Rome, but by this time most of the Byzantine citizens preferred the toleration of the Ottoman Muslims to the noted intolerance of the Roman papacy.

Mehmed II. In this portrait by the Turkish artist Sinan Bey, Mehmed II is depicted not as an able military commander but as a cultured gentleman. An expert gardener, Mehmed was known for his love of flowers; here he enjoys the scent of a favorite rose blossom.

Finally, on May 29, 1453, the city walls were breached and the Ottoman forces entered the fabled city. After three days of pillage, Mehmed entered the city and proclaimed Istanbul (the Turkish name for the city) the new Ottoman capital. Eyewitness accounts relate that Mehmed was much taken with the glory of the city and was determined to create an even more glorious capital for himself.

Mehmed II, now "the Conqueror," encouraged artisans and merchants from around the world to settle and work in Istanbul and embarked on an ambitious program to make the city a capital worthy of the new Ottoman Empire. For the Christian world, the fall of Constantinople marked the end of the old Roman Empire and the beginning of an era of Ottoman Muslim control over the eastern Mediterranean.

Summary and Comparisons

The spectacular military and political success of the Muslims from the seventh century onward produced an era of affluence and cultural achievement known as the golden age of Islam. It reached its zenith under the Abbasid caliphs in Baghdad at the time of the early medieval period in western Europe. Assimilating many diverse peoples, a new

CHRONOLOGY

950	
	Fatimid caliphate established in Cairo
1000	al-Azhar University established
	Arab scholars and scientists: trigonometry, geometry
	Ibn Sina (Avicenna)
	Rise of the Seljuk Turks
1100	
	Crusaders conquer Jerusalem
	Trade between Europe and Asia increases
	Salah ed-Din reconquers Jerusalem
	Genghis khan leads the Mongols
	Ibn Rushd (Averroës)
	Rabbi Musa bin Maymun
1200	
	Mongols conquer northern China, Russia, eastern Europe
	Kubilai Khan ascends Mongol throne
	Marco Polo visits China
	Mamluks rule in Egypt and Syria
	Mongols convert to Buddhism and Islam
1300	
	Ottomans conquer Anatolia
	Omar Khayyam, *The Rubaiyat*
	Timurlane conquests
	Mongol Yuan dynasty ends in China
1400	Ottomans capture Constantinople
	al-Hambra (Red Castle)
	Ivan III renounces allegiance to the Golden Horde

Islamic/Arabic amalgam developed in culture and the arts. Muslims acted as a conduit for the transmission of Greek and Roman learning to later generations. The T'ang dynasty in China, the Guptas in India, and the Ghanaian kingdoms in West Africa fostered similar cultural contributions.

Schisms fragmented the Abbasid Empire into rival components. Earlier empires in the region had been weakened and torn apart by similar problems. The coastal areas along the eastern Mediterranean fell to a small army of Christian crusaders from Europe.

The Crusades were launched by European Christians of the Roman Catholic church to end Muslim control of the Holy Land and establish European–style feudal kingdoms in the eastern Mediterranean region. Ultimately, the Crusades failed, but they contributed to the rising prosperity of the Italian city-states by spurring European demand for Asian goods and thus promoting international trade. On the negative side, the Crusades caused tension and mutual intolerance between Christians and Muslims.

In the early thirteenth century, Genghis Khan led the Mongol nomads out of the grasslands north of China to create the largest land empire in history. For millions of people in Korea, China, Persia, the Arab world, Russia, and eastern Europe, the Mongol conquest was a cataclysmic event that brought death and destruction; it also cut off Russia from the rest of Europe.

The empire of Genghis Khan remained essentially united until his grandson's generation, when, as in so many earlier empires, civil wars led to its collapse. With little culture and no tradition of settled government, the Mongol rulers recruited foreigners to control their empires. As in the Roman and other earlier empires, when the Mongol rulers became corrupt and decadent, their subject peoples rose up and overthrew them. The Mongols of the heartland and those who ruled China became Buddhists; the others converted to Islam.

Mongol rule did have some beneficial effects, including international trade in luxury items and security for merchants under the Pax Mongolica. But slavery and oppression remained the lot of the Mongol subjects; unlike the Romans and Muslims, the Mongols did not grant citizenship to conquered peoples or generally assimilate them. In marked contrast to earlier empires in Egypt, Mesopotamia, India, and the Western Hemisphere, the Mongol Empire did not bequeath many monuments or enduring cultural achievements to future generations.

Mongol invasions did not destroy the culture or religious zeal of the Muslims. Under Mongol and later Safavid rule, the Persians established their own linguistic and cultural traditions, with strong influences from Chinese, Indian, and Sufi (Islamic mystical) traditions.

The Mamluks, former slaves, established their own dynasties in Egypt and greater Syria. They helped to preserve Islamic traditions and encouraged architecture and the arts, but, as with so many dynasties around the world, political disunity led to their defeat.

Beginning in the thirteenth century, the Turkish leader Osman and his successors extended Ottoman control into Europe and across Anatolia, forming a frontier society based on a strict adherence to Islam. Despite a temporary setback at the hands of Timurlane in Asia, by the mid-fifteenth century the Ottomans controlled most of the Balkans and Anatolia. In 1453, Mehmed II conquered Constantinople, destroying the last vestiges of the Byzantine Empire. Like the Chinese in the Sui and T'ang Dynasties, the Ottomans established a highly centralized government with rule emanating from the top down and following a dynastic line through the ruling family. Many empires in the ancient world had been organized along similar principles.

Selected Sources

Items indicated with an asterisk (*) are available in paperback.

Allen, T. T. *Mongol Imperialism.* 1987. A study of the overall effects of Mongol rule.

*Babinger, Franz. *Mehmed the Conqueror and His Time.* 1978. A colorful account of the outstanding Ottoman leader.

Chambers, James. *The Devil's Horsemen: The Mongol Invasion of Europe.* 1979. A good, short account of the origins and results of the Mongol incursion into Europe in 1241.

De Hartog, Leo. *Russia and the Mongol Yoke: The History of the Russian Principalities and the Golden Horde.* 1996. A good, recent book on how the Mongols dominated Russia.

Esposito, John L., ed. *The Oxford History of Islam.* 2000. An excellent, up-to-date reference work, with chapters on culture, art and architecture, the sciences, and philosophy during the golden age.

*Fletcher, Richard. *Moorish Spain.* 1993. Short introductory text with emphasis on cultural and social life.

*Grousset, René. *The Empire of the Steppes: A History of Central Asia.* 1970. Trans. Naomi Walford. A classic study of nomadic peoples and empires from the ancient Huns on.

*Hart, Henry. *Venetian Adventurer.* 1956. Good biography of Marco Polo.

*Hillenbrand, Carole. *The Crusades: Islamic Perspectives.* 1999. A lavishly illustrated reader, with discussions of the socioeconomic and military effects of the Crusades on Christian-Muslim relations.

Kwanten, Luc. *Imperial Nomads: A History of Central Asia, 500–1500.* 1979. A study of the influence of nomads, especially Turks and Mongols, on the civilization of China, Persia, and Russia.

Langlois, John D., Jr., ed. *China under Mongol Rule.* 1981. A collection of articles on many topics.

Lister, R. P. *Genghis Khan.* 2000. A vivid, short biography.

*Maalouf, Amin. *The Crusades through Arab Eyes.* 1987. A highly readable account of Arab/Islamic reaction to the crusaders, with descriptions of how the Arabs overcame political divisions to oppose the European invaders.

Mernissi, Fatima. *The Forgotten Queens of Islam.* 1993; reprinted 1997. An insightful look at numerous powerful women in the early Muslim empires.

Nicolle, David. *The Mongol Warlords.* 1990. On the rise and rule of the Mongols.

Ratchnevsky, Paul. *Genghis Khan: His Life and Legacy.* 1991. Well-written, based on the latest scholarship.

*Riley-Smith, Jonathan, ed. *The Oxford Illustrated History of the Crusades.* 1995. An excellent, recent account, with superb photographs, maps, and chronologies.

*Rossabi, Morris. *Khubilai Khan: His Life and Times.* 1988. The only English-language biography of the first Mongol ruler of China, and a good one. It brings to life the man and his times.

——. *Voyage From Xanadu: Rabban Souma and the First Journey from China to the West.* 1992. This is a tale of a trip that was the reverse of Marco Polo's journey.

Twitchett, Denis, and John K. Fairbanks, eds. *The Cambridge History of China.* Vol. 6: *Alien Regimes and Border States, 907–1368.* 1994. This comprehensive and authoritative book is written by many experts.

 Additional resources, exercises, and Internet links related to this chapter are available at the Book Companion Web site: http://history.wadsworth.com/upshurcompact4/

COMPARATIVE ESSAY 7
European Imperialism through the End of the Seventeenth Century

I came to get gold, not to till the soil, like a peasant.
Hernán Cortés (William Prescott, *The History of the Conquest of Mexico* [Chicago: University of Chicago Press, 1966], p. 47)

Tell me, by what right or justice do you hold these Indians in such a cruel and horrible servitude? On what authority have you waged such detestable wars against these peoples, who dwelt quietly and peacefully on their own land? Wars in which you have destroyed such infinite numbers of them by homicide and slaughter never before heard of? Why do you keep them so oppressed and exhausted, without giving them enough to eat or curbing them of their sicknesses from the excessive labor you give them, and they die, or rather, you kill them, in order to extract and acquire gold every day?
Fray Antonio de Montesinos (George Sanderlin, ed., *Bartolomé de Las Casas: A Selection of His Writings* [New York: Knopf, 1971], p. 81)

Not only have [the Indians] shown themselves to be very wise people and possessed of lively and marked understanding, prudently governing and providing for their nations . . . and making them prosper in justice; but they have equalled many diverse nations of the world, past and present, that have been praised for their governance, politics and customs, and exceed by no small measure the wisest of all of these, such as the Greeks and the Romans, in adherence to the rules of natural reason.
Bartolomé de Las Casas (Lewis Hankey, *All Mankind Is One* [De Kalb: Northern Illinois Press, 1959], p. 77)

Cortés's statement, made to the secretary of the governor of Hispaniola, aptly describes the motive that drove him and other Spanish adventurers beyond the coast into uncharted territory, risking their lives and doing battle with Indian forces many times larger than their own. The conquistadors not only seized the treasures they found, but enslaved the Amerindians and compelled them to work in the mines for their further enrichment and that of their masters. Fray Antonio de Montesinos's sermon, part of which is quoted above, initiated the Dominican campaign against slavery. Influenced by what he heard, Las Casas joined the order in 1511 and took the lead in the effort to arouse the conscience of Spain. In his many writings he attempted to refute the argument that the

Amerindians were inferior and should be considered as the natural slaves of the Spaniards. Las Casas's plea before the King was so eloquent that new laws were passed in 1542, resulting in the amelioration of the lot of the Amerindians.

The urge of strong and dynamic states to subjugate weaker ones dates back to the earliest civilizations. The word "imperialism," which is used to designate this drive, suggests the use of force to establish and maintain domination. The forms of imperialism varied from region to region, depending on the nature of the governments involved and the level of civilization of the conquered population. In some instances foreign rule was exercised through local tribal chiefs. In others it was administered directly through colonial administrators. The motives for expansion were mixed, but political, economic, religious, and strategic interests were the most important.

During the early modern period, imperialism was largely, but not exclusively, a European phenomenon. Prior to the eighteenth century, several major Asiatic states also dominated weaker neighbors. In 1453 the Ottoman Turks breached the walls of Constantinople, completing their conquest of the thousand-year-old Byzantine Empire. Early in the sixteenth century they conquered Syria, Palestine, and Egypt, creating a state that stretched from the Danube to beyond the Nile and posing a major threat to western Europe. In China the Ming emperors' expansion to the northwest was primarily defensive in nature, designed to forestall renewed Mongol invasion. More impressive were their great maritime expeditions that ventured thousands of miles south and west into the Indian Ocean, the Persian Gulf, and the Red Sea. These voyages, however, were intended essentially to proclaim the resurgence of China, to promote commerce, and to gain geographic knowledge. As the Chinese established no overseas naval bases and planted no colonies, the early expeditions had no lasting effect. Issuing from central Asia, the Moghuls embraced the Islamic religion and invaded India, uniting the country's many petty principalities. Babur, the founder of the Moghul dynasty, and his descendants established an empire that, at its peak, embraced almost the entire subcontinent.

In the late fifteenth century, Europeans embarked on an exploratory burst that changed the course of history. By then improvements in navigational techniques and ship design had made possible long ocean voyages. Then, too, the centralized monarchies could look outward, having attained relative internal peace and stability and possessing the material resources to carry through large-scale enterprises. Portugal, a seafaring nation with a long Atlantic coastline, began the process of opening new worlds to Western peoples. A series of Portuguese expeditions slowly inched along the west coast of Africa and rounded the Cape of Good Hope before a fleet, captained by the intrepid Vasco da Gama, reached India in 1498. The fear that Portugal would dominate the sea lanes spurred Spain to underwrite Columbus's famous journey to find a new route to the Far East. By the seventeenth century other nations, notably England, France, and the Netherlands, had entered the scramble for overseas empires, establishing footholds in Africa and parts of Asia and annexing large territories in the Western Hemisphere.

The desire for profit was the dominant motive for overseas exploration. Monarchs funded exploratory voyages, hoping to find new sources of gold and silver. Merchants and traders also had reason to look abroad. For centuries Asia had supplied Europe with luxury goods and spices, essential for the preservation of food and in pharmaceutical products. The cost of Asian goods was exorbitant because each intermediary who handled them took huge profits. Thus western European commercial interests were anxious to bypass the middlemen and go directly to the source.

Competing European powers tried, usually unsuccessfully, to gain effective control over high-priced commodities. For example, the Dutch jealously guarded their monopoly over nutmeg from the Dutch Indies, even going so far as to treat the seeds with lime to prevent their propagation elsewhere. Ultimately the English were able to break the monopoly and established nutmeg plantations in the Caribbean.

Although the importance of religious zeal has probably been exaggerated by historians, it certainly ranks high among the reasons that drove Europeans across the seas. The crusading impulse against non-Christians was still very much alive in the fifteenth century, particularly among the Spanish and Portuguese whose commitment to Catholicism had been reinforced during the reconquest of the Iberian Peninsula. The Iberian nations spearheaded the movement to convert heathens and to identify supposedly lost Christians in the east who might serve as allies against Islam. Christian missionaries had little success in Asia because the adherents of Hinduism, Buddhism, Islam, and Confucianism resisted conversion. On the other hand, Spanish and Portuguese missionaries were much more successful in the Western Hemisphere, where they compelled the surviving indigenous Amerindians to abandon their traditional faiths. France, regarding itself as the "eldest daughter of the Catholic church," sent missionaries to Indochina and other areas of the world. Although not as zealous to win over converts, Protestant Netherlands and England used their colonies to rid themselves of religious dissenters.

The lure of adventure was another factor prompting Europeans to probe the unknown. They yearned to see for themselves the distant lands and cultures that so differed from their own. Stories abounded about the existence of exotic lands in Asia, popularized by early travelers like Marco Polo, and about the mythical Christian kingdom of Prester John in Africa.

Finally, national rivalry also stimulated imperialism. In the seventeenth century, the English, Dutch, and French governments joined in the search for trade and empire partly because of nationalistic hostility toward Spain and Portugal. Not only did they compete against one another for new lands, but they frequently intruded into the overseas colonial possessions of Spain and Portugal.

Several different patterns of European colonization emerged during this period. The first and oldest form was the fortified trading post, initially established by the Portuguese and later emulated by other European powers in Africa and East Asia. As European states expanded, they often conquered territories possessing the desired commodities. For example, Spain seized control of the gold and silver supply of Mexico and Peru, the Dutch took over much of the spice trade by conquering most of the East Indian islands, and many of the imperial European nations annexed sugar-producing regions in the Caribbean and Brazil. When there were not enough indigenous laborers to work the sugar plantations, black slaves were imported in large numbers from Africa, thereby altering the racial composition of many parts of the Western Hemisphere.

Beginning in the seventeenth century, the English and the French, in particular, created "new Europes," or areas in which a flood of European immigrants replaced the small local populations. Colonies of settlements were established for various economic, political, and religious reasons. The English, Dutch, and French created such colonies on the eastern coast of North America. Spanish and Portuguese settlers had come a century earlier, and in spite of their scant numbers had succeeded in transplanting key aspects of European culture to Latin America. Western Europeans did not attempt to form settlements in Asia, where the dense population provided sufficient labor for their economic exploitation.

Emerging Global Interrelations

•

• The Rival Ottoman and Safavid Empires •

• The Culture of the Renaissance in Europe •

• European Nation-States and the Reformation •

• African Kingdoms, European Contacts, and the Slave Trade •

• European Colonial Empires in the Western Hemisphere •

• Summary and Comparisons •

Wednesday, November 28, 1520, we debouched from [the Strait of Magellan, at the tip of South America], engulfing ourselves in the Pacific Sea. We were three months and twenty days without getting any kind of fresh food. We ate bisquit, which was no longer bisquit, but powder of bisquit swarming with worms. . . . It stank strongly of the urine of rats. We drank yellow water that had been putrid for many days. We also ate oxhides . . . and sawdust from boards. Rats were sold for one-half ducados apiece, and even [then] we could not get them. [But the worst was that] the gums . . . of some of our men swelled [from scurvy], so that they could not eat under any circumstances and therefore died. . . . Had not God and His blessed mother given us . . . good weather we would have all died of hunger in that exceeding vast sea. Of a verity I believe no such voyage will ever be made again. . . .

On Monday, September eight [1522] we cast anchor near the quay of [Seville, Spain] . . . with only [twenty-one] men and the majority of them sick. . . . Some died of hunger; some deserted . . . and some were put to death for crimes. . . . We had sailed fourteen thousand, four hundred and sixty leguas [about 40,000 miles] and furthermore completed the circumnavigation of the world from east to west. . . . Tuesday we all went in shirts and barefoot, each holding a candle, to visit [shrines]. . . .*

*Antonio Pigafetta, in Charles E. Nowell, ed., Magellan's Voyage around the World (Evanston, IL: Northwestern University Press, 1962), pp. 122–124, 259.

The (appropriately named) Portuguese ship *Victoria*, which limped into the harbor near Seville on September 6, 1522, with its sick and ragged surviving crew, had made history by circumnavigating the globe. Although the expedition's commander, Ferdinand Magellan, did not live to savor the triumph, his crew had done what no humans had done before.

Magellan's expedition was the culmination of a century of European voyages of discovery that had begun with Prince Henry the Navigator of Portugal. The European appetite for adventure and taste for the luxuries of Asia dated back to the First Crusade (1096–1099); Marco Polo's accounts of his travels in the thirteenth century had also created great interest in Asian lands far removed from Europe. But not until the fifteenth century did advances in shipbuilding and navigational knowledge permit oceangoing vessels to sail around the Cape of Good Hope and across the Indian Ocean to Asia. At the end of the century, Christopher Columbus sailed across the Atlantic and stumbled onto a "New World" in the Western Hemisphere while seeking an alternative route to Asia. Magellan proved the existence of such a route by sailing around South America, past Cape Horn, and across the Pacific to Asia.

Whereas major civilizations had developed in relative isolation from each other in the preceding 5,000 years, the voyages of discovery of the fifteenth and sixteenth centuries began to meld the world into an interrelated whole. The earth today is truly an interdependent "global village."

This chapter begins with a discussion of the highly centralized and powerful Ottoman and Safavid Empires, based in western Asia, and their interactions and confrontations with one another and with Europe. Commercial interactions between Asian empires and Europe had fueled Europeans' appetites for Asian luxury goods and also helped to foster the new intellectual and artistic climate of the Renaissance, which began in Italy and spread through the rest of Europe. Following a description of the Renaissance, this chapter will trace the development of centralized monarchies in Europe and the religious and political changes brought about by the Reformation.

The chapter will then examine how European horizons in the fifteenth century expanded to include—for Europeans—the newly discovered continents of Africa south of the Sahara and North and South America. The impacts of the slave trade on African societies and the Western Hemisphere will be described. The chapter closes with a discussion of the creation of colonial empires by Europeans in the Western Hemisphere.

The Rival Ottoman and Safavid Empires

The Sultan was seated on a rather low sofa, not more than a foot from the ground and spread with many costly coverlets and cushions embroidered with exquisite work. Near him were his bow and arrows. His expression . . . is anything but smiling, and has a sternness which, though sad, is full of majesty.

The Sultan's head-quarters were crowded by numerous attendants, including many high officials. All the cavalry of the guard were there . . . and a large number of Janissaries. . . . The Sultan himself assigns to all their duties and offices, and in doing so pays no attention to wealth or the empty claims of rank. . . . He only considers merit and scrutinizes the character, natural ability, and disposition of each.

The Turks were quite as much astonished at our manner of dress as we at theirs. They wear long robes which reach almost to their ankles, and are not only more imposing but seem to add to the stature; our dress, on the other hand, is so short and tight that it disclosed the forms of the body, which would be better hidden.

What struck me as particularly praiseworthy in that great multitude was the silence and good discipline. . . . Each man kept his appointed place. . . . The officers . . . were seated; the common soldiers stood up. The most remarkable body of men were several thousand Janissaries, who stood in a long line apart and so motionless that . . . I was for a while doubtful whether they were living men or statues. *

**The Turkish Letters of Ogier Ghiselin De Busbecq*, trans. Edward S. Forster (Oxford: Clarendon Press, 1927), pp. 58–62. Another brief excerpt of the letters can be found in Peter N. Stearns, ed., *Documents in World History*, vol. 2 (Oxford: Clarendon Press, 1988), pp. 73–77.

In these words, the imperial ambassador for the Holy Roman Empire described the court of Suleiman the Magnificent, the ruler of the Ottoman Empire. While Christian Europe was entering a period of religious turmoil (discussed later in the chapter), Suleiman's empire and its powerful rival, the Safavid state in Persia, were both in the ascendant. Indeed, the Ottoman Empire profited from Christian turmoil and dynastic rivalries, extending its rule into central Europe and advancing to the gates of Vienna. Religious differences also existed in the Islamic world, however; the Ottoman and Safavid states were sectarian as well as political rivals. Although Ottoman taxation of international trade helped to stimulate European interest in developing new trade routes to Asia, the two Muslim empires were far too strong in this period to feel adverse effects from European expansion.

Ottoman Territorial Expansion and Government

Immediately following the conquest of Constantinople in 1453, the Ottoman Sultans moved to extend their control over the Balkans. Aided by the rugged terrain in the region, the predominantly Christian but politically divided Balkan peoples repelled Ottoman advances until late in the sixteenth century. Papal calls for crusades against the Ottomans were ignored as Europeans, more interested in economic gains than religious confrontations with the Muslim Ottoman government, sought to establish commercial and political relations.

Sultan Selim I (reigned 1512–1520) sought territorial gains in the east and south. After successfully thwarting the threat of expansion by the Safavid emperors in Persia, in 1517 Selim routed the Mamluks in Egypt and gained control of Palestine and Syria. The defeat of the Mamluks gave the Ottomans control over most of the Arab world, including the key Muslim cities of Mecca, Medina, and Jerusalem. The Ottoman rulers moved the caliphate to Istanbul and assumed leadership over the Sunni Islamic world. They now viewed themselves as the guardians of Islam and the military might of their empire as the Sword of Islam. Later, the sultans also took the title of caliph.

Ottoman expansion continued during the reign of Suleiman the Magnificent (reigned 1520–1566), when the empire reached the apex of its power. Suleiman brilliantly led his armies against rulers in central Europe and in 1521 seized the Serbian capital of Belgrade. In an age of mighty kings, Suleiman was probably the most powerful and dynamic. He was a successful military commander and a clever diplomat; competing European powers, such as France, sought and secured his protection. By exploiting the rivalry between the Austrian Habsburg emperors and the French kings, Suleiman's forces conquered most of Hungary. His political alliance with the French soon expanded into mutually beneficial economic relations.

Map 9.1 Ottoman Expansion. The Ottomans expanded rapidly throughout the fifteenth and sixteenth centuries, conquering vast territories around the Black Sea, in the Balkans, and in the Arab provinces along the eastern Mediterranean and North Africa.

In 1529 Suleiman laid siege to Vienna, but because of overextended communication lines and heavy rainfall that made transporting heavy cannon difficult, the Ottoman forces failed to take the city before the onset of winter. Because the Janissaries (the elite, professional soldiers of the Ottoman army) and the cavalry refused to campaign during the winter months, Suleiman was forced to retreat without taking the Habsburg capital. Reportedly, the Ottoman army left behind sacks of coffee, a new product that soon gained popularity among the Europeans.

At its height in 1566, Suleiman's empire incorporated Hungary and the Balkan Peninsula; extensive territory around the Black Sea; the entire Anatolian Peninsula; Arab territories bordering the eastern Mediterranean and the Red Sea; Egypt and the northern Sudan; most islands in the eastern Mediterranean, including the strategic islands of Rhodes and Crete; and the coastal areas of North Africa east of Morocco.

Like many emperors in other powerful empires before him, Suleiman failed to leave a worthy successor to his throne. Influenced by his most beloved wife, Hurrem Haseki ("the Joyous One"), to make her son the successor, Suleiman had his favorite and more able son killed, just as rulers in China and the Roman Empire had killed members of their own families in order to ensure their own power or the succession of particular favorites. Following Suleiman's death in 1566, Hurrem Haseki's son succeeded to the throne as Selim II, but this alcoholic, nicknamed The Sot, proved unworthy of his capable and abstemious father. Ottoman military and naval supremacy waned under his rule, and at the Battle of Lepanto in 1571, the navies of the Habsburgs and the Italian city-states crushed the Ottoman fleet. This defeat marked the beginning of a military decline that lasted more than 200 years.

The administration of the Ottoman Empire, like the Safavid in Persia and the earlier T'ang in China, was highly centralized. The Sultan acted as the supreme political, religious, and military ruler, subject only to divine law. Below him, the grand vizier and the divan (imperial council) were responsible for political and economic administration. Ottoman administration was highly complex and required a multitude of bureaucrats, drawn from an elite whose prestige was based on ownership of land and booty acquired in military campaigns. They were responsible for matters as diverse as the translation of documents to the supervision of the vast royal palace complex of Topkapi in Istanbul, where the Sultan maintained his harem, with separate chambers for his mother, wives, children, and servants.

Without a firm tradition of primogeniture (succession of the eldest son), all the half-brothers in the harem were potential candidates for the throne. Consequently, wives, mothers, sisters, and sons often intrigued to gain the sultan's favor. As the example of Hurrem Haseki demonstrates, the mothers and favorite wives of sultans could exercise considerable political power. When the sultans were strong rulers, the harem did not pose a threat to effective government. For example, the first ten sultans, from 1299 to 1566, all led their military forces directly into battle and were personally in charge of military strategy and governmental policy. Indeed, the personal dynamism and strength of the first Ottoman sultans were major factors in Ottoman expansion. However, the less able sultans who succeeded Suleiman frequently became virtual prisoners of the royal court, the harem, and the Janissaries.

Like the Safavids in Persia, Ottoman rulers placed the major provinces under appointed governors who ruled for about two years. As authorities in Istanbul correctly feared, provincial governors often tried to establish their own bases of authority. Generally, the central Ottoman government retained tight controls over its Anatolian territories, which lay close to Istanbul. The more distant European and Arab territories tended to enjoy more autonomy.

Suleiman the Magnificent. Here Suleiman, who wrote poetry under the pen name *muhibbi*, or beloved, wearing a white turban, stands before an archway inscribed with the name of Allah. Through the arch may be seen the mosque of Suleiman.

© Bettmann/Corbis

Elegy for Suleiman the Magnificent

That master-rider of the realm of bliss
For whose careering steed the field of the world was
*   narrow.*

The infidels of Hungary bowed their heads to the
*   temper of his blade,*
The Frank admired the grain of his sword.

He laid his face to the ground, graciously, like a fresh
*   rose petal,*
The treasurer of time put him in the coffer, like a jewel.

May the sun burn and blaze with fire of your parting;
In grief for you, let him dress in black weeds of cloud.

Weeping tears of blood as it recalls your skill,
May your sword plunge into the ground from its
*   scabbard.*

May the pen tear its collar in grief for you,
*The standard rend its shirt in affliction.**

This elegy was written by Muhammad Baki (1527–1600), one of the greatest Ottoman poets. It is a lyrical idealization of the imperial ruler, much in the vein of the celebrations of great rulers as mighty heroes in ancient Greek and Latin poetry.

*Wayne S. Vucinich, The Ottoman Empire: Its Record and Legacy, trans. Bernard Lewis (Princeton: Van Nostrand, 1965), pp. 146–147.

The administration was financed through new wealth acquired from the expansion of the empire and from taxes. The collection of taxes was assigned to "tax farmers," who collected as much as possible from a given territory in return for a percentage of the total amount collected. As in Rome and China, tax farming became a source of abuse and corruption within the empire.

Founded by the military, the Ottoman Empire remained dependent upon the army, which, like the government, was rigidly structured. The Janissaries, along with the cavalry, were the backbone of the military. They quickly adapted to the use of European military technology, especially siege and field artillery, and became a major military force of the age.

In this Islamic empire, the Sheik al-Islam was responsible for religious life, and since there was no separation of civil and religious law, he served as supreme judge, handing down *fatwas*, or legal opinions. In the provinces, *qadis* (judges) appointed by Istanbul joined with local experts in religious law to settle legal disputes. They also served as overseers of such charitable religious endowments as orphanages, soup kitchens, and hospitals.

Social and Economic Life in the Ottoman Empire

During the golden age of the empire under Suleiman, Ottoman society was remarkably open. The Ottomans did not see fit to settle Turkish tribes throughout their empire; most Turks remained peasants scattered in remote and poor agricultural villages throughout the Anatolian Peninsula. Ottoman rulers initially made no attempt to impose the Turkish language or customs on their subjects or to force non-Muslims to convert to Islam. On the contrary, Ottoman society allowed diversity, and considerable "upward mobility" occurred. Under the millet system, religious and ethnic minorities retained their own educational, religious, and judicial institutions, and enjoyed considerable economic autonomy in return for the payment of an additional tax. Arabs, Armenians, Christians, and Jews were able to reach the highest levels of society, and some served as advisors and doctors to the sultan himself. Only the sultanate was denied them, for it was solely reserved for the heirs of the Osman rulers. This open society, remarkable for the age, was one of the sources of Ottoman strength.

The Ottoman Empire was at the center of a lively international trade from East to West and West to East that persisted despite rivalries among Western and Eastern monarchs. Istanbul and Cairo became major centers on the route between India and Europe. Slaves, gold, and ivory were transported from sub-Saharan Africa through Cairo to European markets. New foodstuffs like potatoes, tomatoes, and tobacco came from the Western Hemisphere into the Ottoman Empire and into Asia. Coffee from Ethiopia and Yemen was traded to Europe. Coffeehouses became major gathering spots for the elite in Ottoman, Safavid, and European cities. The use of tobacco quickly spread from Europe to the Ottoman Empire, where pipe smoking became a common practice among both men and women.

Despite the rich trade that passed through the empire, the Ottoman elite, reflecting the values of a still predominantly agrarian society, held commerce, banking, and most manufacturing businesses in low esteem. As a result, they permitted and encouraged subject peoples (such as Armenians) and foreigners to organize and maintain these economic activities. Under the system of capitulations, which had also been used by the Mamluks and the Safavids, foreign Christians living in the empire were given freedom of activity and were exempted from Ottoman taxes and laws. When the empire flourished, these special privileges fostered international trade and increased revenues, but as the empire declined and European nations grew stronger, the capitulations enabled Europeans and minorities to dominate economic life.

Ottoman authorities encouraged international trade across their domains in part, of course, to benefit the imperial treasury. Taxes on trade had often gone uncollected in the Arab provinces in the period of political instability before the Ottomans conquered them. The Ottoman government began to collect these taxes with more efficiency, and in some cases raised them. Traders in turn raised prices, which angered European consumers, especially those at the end of the line. Consequently, the newly centralized and energetic nations became increasingly eager to find new trade routes to Asia.

Cultural and Artistic Achievements

The noteworthy cultural achievements of the Ottoman Empire began at the top. According to custom, Ottoman Sultans were all trained in a craft, and some achieved considerable artistic and literary skill. Suleiman, for example, was an accomplished goldsmith. Ottoman Sultans were great patrons of the arts; and as in most Islamic societies, literary skills, especially the ability to write poetry, were much admired. An accomplished poet in his own right, Suleiman strongly supported the cultural life of Istanbul in an effort to make his court the most splendid of the age. The Turkish language continued to develop, borrowing many words from both Arabic and Persian. Some poets wrote in Turkish and Arabic. Turkish historians chronicled the development of the empire and the exploits of the military, and although most literature was highly derivative of Persian or Arab forms, a lively folk literature continued to flourish.

Like many imperial rulers, Suleiman was also a great builder. He financed the construction of monumental buildings, many designed by Sinan, one of the most prolific architects of all time. Originally a slave from the conquered Greek provinces, Sinan was recruited as a Janissary and became a military engineer. His skills attracted the attention of the sultan, who enlisted him as the royal architect. Living to the (at the time) incredible advanced age of ninety-nine, Sinan designed buildings to commemorate Ottoman imperial power. His massive, interconnecting buildings surmounted by domes became the hallmark of Ottoman architecture throughout the empire. Although the Suleimaniye complex of mosque, schools, hospital, bath, shops, and cemetery in Istanbul is the largest of Sinan's creations, the Selimiye Mosque in Edirne, outside Istanbul, finished in 1575, is generally considered his masterpiece.

In the fine arts, Ottoman artisans synthesized earlier Islamic/Arab designs and techniques with Chinese and European motifs and crafts. They decorated Sinan's structures with Isnik (named after a Turkish city) tiles whose glazed surfaces contained painted floral designs. Clearly an imitation of Chinese porcelains, these tiles still retain their crystal-clear coloring. Such glazing techniques and designs were copied in much of Europe. Ottoman artisans also produced textiles, silver work, bookbindings, and calligraphy of remarkable beauty and luxury. The Ottomans were known for their woven textiles and carpets. "Oriental" carpets from Turkey and Persia became popular decorative items among wealthy classes around the world. Although Ottoman culture, like Roman culture, has been criticized for its lack of originality, the synthesis of disparate cultural ideas and motifs from West and East enabled Ottoman artisans to fashion unique objects of remarkable beauty.

The Imperial Safavids

During the sixteenth and seventeenth centuries the Ottoman Empire's chief rival in the Muslim world was the neighboring Safavid Empire centered in Persia (present-day Iran). The Safavid realm differed from that of the Ottomans in two major respects. First, it was based upon Shi'i Islam rather than on Orthodox Sunni Islam. Second, the Safavids maintained and reinforced the separate identity of Persian society and language. In contrast, the Ottoman Empire sought to assimilate many new cultural styles while retaining cultural pluralism. The Ottomans made no attempt to impose their language or values over the diverse peoples they ruled. In particular, the Arabs, the single largest linguistic and ethnic group within the empire, were allowed to retain their linguistic and cultural identity.

Founded by Shah Isma'il, who ruled from 1500 to 1524, the Safavid Empire reached its zenith under Shah Abbas the Great (reigned 1587–1629), an autocrat who ruled with an iron hand. He killed or blinded three of his five sons and, like Suleiman the Magnificent, left no able successor. In the Safavid Empire, as in most other empires, whenever the central authority was strong, the local chieftains remained submissive, paid taxes, and rendered homage to the shah. Whenever the shah or central authority was weak, the local rulers assumed more power. One of Shah Abbas's first moves in consolidating his power was to curb the influence of the local chieftains.

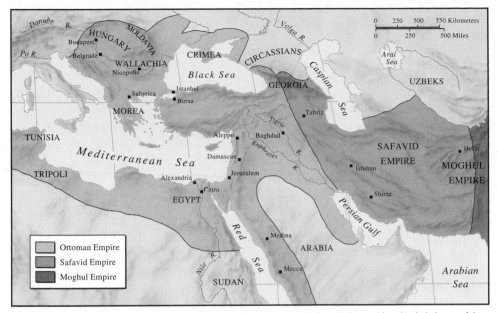

Map 9.2 The Ottoman and Safavid Empires. By 1689 the Ottoman Empire had reached its zenith and included most of the Arab provinces of the eastern Mediterranean, the holy cities of Mecca and Medina, and most of North Africa. However, the Safavid Empire, with its glorious capital at Isfahan in Persia, competed for control in the region; despite many wars, neither empire could conquer its rival.

The populace of Safavid Iran consisted largely of peasants who lived in small rural villages. There were a few nomadic pastoralists as well as a small urban middle class that engaged in cottage industries and trade. In this predominantly rural setting, the Safavid government was organized along feudal lines, and officials acquired fiefs from the shah in return for services to the central government. The Safavids divided their territories into provinces, placed under the administration of appointed governors. The shahs also depended upon the *ghulams,* or slave elite. Obtained mainly from central Asia, these slaves were converts to Islam and gradually achieved prominent positions in the royal court, thereby following a tradition in other Muslim empires.

The mullahs, or Shi'i clergy, also exercised considerable power within the empire; like the feudal landowners, the mullahs tended to be more powerful whenever the shah was ineffective. Their authority was particularly strong in rural areas, where the peasants looked to them for both religious and political guidance.

Taxes, land, and commerce were the major sources of wealth in the Persian economy. Crown lands were owned directly by the royal court to use as it wished; as in the Ottoman Empire, state lands were given as payment or rewards to officials or army officers, generally for a specific time, after which they reverted to the crown to be parceled out again at the pleasure of the court. Some land was owned directly by religious authorities; the revenues from these lands provided the mullahs with an independent source of income and also helped to finance mosques, religious schools, and welfare projects for the poor.

The Safavid Shah Writes to His Ottoman Rival

Shah Isma'il of Persia to the Ottoman Sultan Selim [c. 1514]:

Now to begin: Your honored letters have arrived one after another. . . . Their contents, although indicative of hostility, are stated with boldness and vigor. The latter gives us much enjoyment and pleasure, but we are ignorant of the reason for the former. . . . In the time of your late blessed father . . . when our royal troops passed through the lands of [eastern Anatolia] . . . complete concord and friendship was shown on both sides. . . . Thus now, the cause of your resentment and displeasure yet remains unknown. If political necessity has compelled you on this course, then may your problems soon be solved.

Dispute may fire words to such a heat

That ancient houses be consumed in flames. The intention of our inaction in this regard is twofold:

(1.) Most of the inhabitants of the land of Rum are followers of our forefathers. . . .

(2.) We have always loved the . . . Ottoman house. . . . Nevertheless, there is no cause for improper words: . . . At this writing we were engaged upon the hunt near Isfahan, we now prepare provisions and our troops for the coming campaign. In all friendship we say do what you will.

Bitter experience has taught that in this world of trial

He who falls upon the house of Ali always falls. Kindly give our ambassador leave to travel unmolested. . . . When war becomes inevitable, hesitation and delay must be set aside, and one must think on that which is to come. Farewell.*

In this letter Shah Isma'il of Persia very diplomatically, but firmly, expressed his views on the conflict between the Safavid (Persian) and the Ottoman Empires. Between them, these two great Muslim empires dominated much of the eastern Mediterranean and West Asia from the fifteenth to the nineteenth centuries and were almost continually in a state of war with one another. Although neither succeeded in destroying the other, the perpetual conflicts drained the economic and military strength of both, thereby contributing to their downfalls.

*William H. McNeill and Marilyn Robinson Waldman, eds., The Islamic World (New York: Oxford University Press, 1973; reprint, Chicago: University of Chicago Press, 1983), pp. 342–344.

The manufacture and sale of textiles, particularly silk fabrics and carpets, was a major source of Safavid income. Soon after coming to power, Shah Abbas added the silk-producing areas in the north to his empire. Although Abbas did not directly confiscate the land, the sale of silk became a royal monopoly. Anxious to expand the silk industry, Abbas encouraged foreign traders and Christian communities, particularly the Armenians, who formerly had been silk producers, to settle in his domain. Although earlier Safavid rulers had persecuted religious minorities and forced religious conversion to Shi'i Islam by sword, Abbas was known for his relative tolerance. To some extent, his more liberal policies regarding the Armenians and other Christian minorities, who dominated the silk manufacturing and commercial trade with the West, were motivated by economic considerations.

To strengthen the Persian economy, Shah Abbas established a new Safavid capital in Isfahan, situated at an intersection of key trade routes. He moved a number of Armenians into a new community on the outskirts of the city and provided interest-free loans for them to rebuild their houses and businesses. As a result of Shah Abbas's tolerance and patronage, Isfahan quickly became a world center for trade in luxury textiles.

In search of new markets, Shah Abbas sent emissaries with samples of luxurious silks to Venice, Spain, Portugal, Holland, Russia, and Poland. Foreign traders were encouraged to establish businesses in Persia by special financial inducements, including tax breaks. These privileges contributed to an economic boom from which the royal court benefited. As early as 1617, agents from the English East Indian Company arrived along the Persian Gulf and petitioned the shah for permission to trade. By the middle of the seventeenth century, Bandar Abbas on the Persian Gulf had become a major seaport for trade with Europe. The Safavids also enjoyed a lively trade through northern routes with Russia. Trade through the northern provinces often continued even during periods of open warfare with the Ottoman Empire.

Control of the silk trade provided the Safavid rulers with the economic means to extend their control over all of Persia. As was true for the sultans in the Ottoman Empire, when the central authority of the Shahs was strong, the special privileges for foreign communities were not a threat. However, as subsequent Safavid leaders became weaker, and the European nations strengthened and augmented their global power, these privileges enabled foreign governments, acting in support of their subjects, to undermine the central government and to dominate Persia.

Architecture, the Fine Arts, and Literature in Persia

Literature, painting, music, and architecture flourished under the Safavids. Like imperial rulers in China, Egypt, Rome, and elsewhere, the Safavids encouraged and patronized the arts. The new capital of Isfahan became a glittering cultural center; as the Persians said, "Isfahan is half the world." Shah Abbas ordered numerous mosques, inns, schools, and baths built in Isfahan and along the important trading routes. His Shah Mosque in Isfahan with its ornate tile work, large entrance facades, and bulbous dome epitomizes Safavid architecture at its best. Safavid artists also continued to excel in painting complex miniatures on paper and ivory. Many such miniatures adorned and illustrated Persian manuscripts.

The Safavids and the aristocrats were conspicuous in their love of luxury items. They lived lavishly and wore ornate silk and gold-brocaded attire. Persian artisans were noted for their skills in weaving gold brocade and large, extremely fine carpets. Many weavers of carpets were women and children. European traders often

Persian Silk Robe. This elaborate brocaded taffeta robe in rich blues, oranges, and gold shows the floral designs favored by high-ranking Safavid courtiers.

The Textile Museum, Washington, D.C., 1985.5.1, Ruth Lincoln Fisher Fund commented on the conspicuous consumption of Safavid lifestyles. Nonetheless, the Safavids were early believers in recycling. Every seven years the used clothes from the royal court were burned and the gold and silver threads collected for use in new garments. For relaxation, the upper class enjoyed games such as chess (a Persian invention) and polo. The entire population participated in religious festivals marking the Shi'i calendar, particularly services commemorating the death of Ali (the Shi'i believe that the ruling authority of the Muslim community should have passed through Ali's descendants) and the martyrdom of his son, Husayn. Husayn's death was reenacted in protracted and moving passion plays.

Indeed, much Safavid literature was devoted to religious themes, and the Safavids financed numerous religious schools that reinterpreted and reinforced Shi'i theological tenets. Religious differences between the Shi'i Safavids and Sunni Ottomans were one of the sources of conflict between the two empires. In contrast to the religious written works, romantic love poetry continued to be highly popular, and Persian poets and poetry dominated and influenced literary life in both the Ottoman and Moghul Empires. Like the Ottoman sultans, Safavid rulers also encouraged writers to immortalize their military and political achievements in long histories and biographies.

Wars between the Rival Empires

Throughout their long histories, the Ottomans and Safavids were rivals for control over the territories around the Tigris-Euphrates Valley (present-day Iraq). As Sunni Muslims, the Ottomans also clashed with the Shi'i Safavids over domination of Islamic territories and interpretations of basic Islamic doctrines. The long struggle drained both of needed military power and resources. Neither delivered a fatal military blow to the other, but debilitating intermittent warfare made both increasingly vulnerable to other outside enemies.

The conflicts began when Suleiman's father, Selim I, initiated a "holy war" against the Shi'i and the Safavid dynasty. In 1514 Ottoman forces equipped with cannon decisively defeated the Safavids in the northern provinces of present-day Iran, but Selim failed to follow through on his victory. Suleiman continued the struggle by launching several campaigns against the Safavid ruler, Shah Tahmasp, who employed a policy of "scorched earth" as a defensive measure, thereby forcing the Ottomans to bring all their supplies with them. Suleiman successfully conquered the major northern city of Tabriz, but found it costly to maintain its control. In 1555 his difficulties holding the northern territories forced him to arrange a treaty with the Safavids. Suleiman retained Iraq, with the major trading center of Baghdad and a port on the Persian Gulf, but had to withdraw from the northern Persian provinces.

The Safavids countered Ottoman power by allying with the Habsburgs, the major Ottoman enemy in eastern Europe. Taking advantage of the power vacuum following Suleiman's death, Shah Abbas occupied present-day Iraq and parts of the Anatolia Peninsula. By 1623 the Ottomans, now strengthened by internal reforms, took advantage of Safavid weakness after Shah Abbas's death to oust the Safavids from these territories. A peace treaty between these two mighty empires in 1639 established boundaries that approximate those of present-day western Iran.

In spite of several attempts to implement internal reforms, the Safavid Empire never regained the power wielded by Shah Abbas. As a consequence, it was ill prepared to meet the challenges of expansionist neighbors. By the eighteenth century, tribes from Afghanistan began to expand into Safavid territories and by 1722, Afghan forces took Isfahan. Safavid weakness allowed Ottoman forces then to move into northern Persian provinces. Under Shah Tahmasp II, the Safavids unsuccessfully counterattacked the Afghan forces. The assassination of Nader Shah in 1747 ended the Safavid dynasty. With the collapse of effective centralized government, numerous rival local rulers vied for political and military control until the Qajar dynasty emerged as the dominant power in 1794.

The Culture of the Renaissance in Europe

If then we are to call any age golden, it is beyond doubt that age which brings forth golden talents in different places. That such is true of our age, he who wishes to consider the illustrious discoveries of this century will hardly doubt. For this century, like a golden age, has restored to light the liberal arts, which were almost extinct: grammar, poetry, rhetoric, painting, sculpture, architecture, music . . . and all this in Florence. Achieving what had been honored among the ancients, but almost forgotten since, the age has joined wisdom with eloquence, and produce with the military art . . . and in Florence it has recalled the Platonic teaching from darkness into light.*

*Letter of Marsilio Ficino to Paul of Middleburg, trans. M. M. McLaughlin, in *The Portable Renaissance Reader* (New York: Viking, 1953), p. 79.

In this excerpt, the Florentine philosopher Marsilio Ficino (1433–1499) expresses his joy at living in a time of intellectual revolution, sparked by a reawakened interest in the values and culture of ancient Greece and Rome. Ficino and his contemporaries scorned what they perceived as the ignorance and barbarism of the "dark ages," the thousand years between the collapse of the Roman Empire and their own era, to which they applied the term *Renaissance,* meaning "rebirth" in French. They believed that they were living in a "golden age" that had broken abruptly with the immediate past.

Although Renaissance thinkers were aware of the contrast between their own and the medieval period, they failed to appreciate the full dimensions of their age. To them, the revival of cultural antiquity was the outstanding characteristic of their progressive era. Yet artistic creativity was only one aspect of the Renaissance. In fact, changes affected every element of European society—political, social, and religious as well as cultural. Nor did the Renaissance develop in complete isolation from the era that preceded it. Indeed, the Renaissance continued many trends of medieval civilization. The difference lay in the faster pace of change, not in the creation of something entirely new.

This is not to say that there were no differences in attitude between the Middle Ages and the Renaissance. The medieval cultural perspective had centered on theology, with emphasis on God's will, human sinfulness, and heavenly existence after earthly life. That outlook permeated all intellectual life: education, philosophy, theology, art, and architecture. Medieval religion had firmly rejected life in this world as evil, useless, and perilous to the salvation of the soul. Abandoning secular culture in favor of a monastic life seemed to many the surest way to gain salvation and please God. During the Renaissance, however, thinkers, writers, and artists made man, not God, the chief center of interest. They glorified the human body as beautiful and the human intellect as capable of unlocking the deepest mysteries of nature by rational processes. Renaissance thinkers known as humanists argued that God in fact wanted men to engage in political and civic life, to create and discover, and to marry and have families. In short, fulfillment within the secular sphere was in accord with God's will. Thus a major innovation of the humanists was to reconcile the new urban culture and life with Christianity and the possibility of salvation.

The Origins of the Renaissance: Italian Literature and Humanism

The Renaissance was an age of rapid transition, linking medieval to early modern ways of life. The chronology of the Renaissance raises some problems for historians in deciding when it began and how long it continued. Most accept early fourteenth century as the start and mid-sixteenth century as the end. The Renaissance began and took shape in Italy before spreading across the Alps.

There are many reasons why Italy was the birthplace of the Renaissance. For one thing, the survival of Roman artistic and architectural heritage and the continued use of Latin had kept memories of classical civilization alive. Italy also had profited from both Islamic and Byzantine cultural influences. Trade remained important in Italy, which gave rise to early modern capitalism, and furnished the material resources for cultural development. Less feudal than northern Europe, Italy enjoyed renewed vigor in its urban centers in the wake of the Crusades. Political developments fostered the growth of independent city-states, and prominent commercial cities like Genoa, Venice, and Milan competed with one another in cultural as well as commercial affairs. These cities gave rise to an affluent, middle/upper class with the leisure for education and a sense of political responsibility. Such individuals sought models of civic duty, social responsibility, and governmental values. The urbanized, sophisticated world of ancient Greece and Rome provided just such models in an extensive body of literature and art. Thus, the humanists returned to classical literature and found inspiration there for an active life of political involvement and reasoned analysis of morals and beliefs.

The early Renaissance in Italy during the fourteenth century centered on a few eloquent writers from Tuscany (the area around Florence) who stimulated interest and delight in the physical world. Francesco Petrarca, or Petrarch (1304–1374), sometimes called the father of humanism, idolized the ancient Roman authors and emulated their literary compositions and writing styles; he also adopted the ancient writers' secular outlook on life in his own works. Petrarch as a man of letters gained enduring fame from his poetry, written in the Tuscan vernacular. A keen observer of nature, he wrote tender sonnets and exquisite odes in celebration of his burning love for Laura, a married woman whom he adored at a distance. Although Petrarch expresses real love for a living woman and rhapsodizes over her physical features, his devotion to her is essentially spiritual, so that a conflict between body and mind underlies his poems. Being ambitious and desiring fame and fortune, he struggled against the medieval notion that God

LIVES AND TIMES ACROSS CULTURES

Racy Tales

Renaissance writers, with their interest in describing society as they observed it, tended to be tolerant of human behavior. The following racy passages illustrate how far Renaissance society had departed from Christian moral restraint.

The first excerpt centers on an adulterous relationship. A young wife, Petronella, tells her lover, Gianello, to get into a tub when her husband returns home unexpectedly. Petronella explains that she has sold the old tub to a man who is inspecting it from the inside. Gianello leaps out of the tub and expresses satisfaction with it, except for an area that is coated with a hard substance. The wife tells her husband to climb into the tub to scrape it off.

While she was busy instructing and directing her husband in this fashion, Gianello, who had not fully gratified his desires that morning before the husband arrived, seeing that he couldn't do it in the way he wished, contributed to bring it off as best he could. So he went up to Petronella, who was completely blocking up the mouth of the tub, and in the manner of a wild and hot-blooded stallion mounting a Parthian mare in the open fields, he satisfied his young man's passion, which no sooner reached fulfillment than the scraping of the tub was completed, whereupon he stood back,

Petronella withdrew her head from the tub and the husband clambered out.*

The second excerpt contains a wife's justification for taking on a lover.

As you can see, Lusca [her maid], I am young and vigorous, and I am well supplied with all the things a woman could desire. In short, with one exception I have nothing to complain about, and the exception is this: that my husband is much older than myself, and consequently I am ill provided with the one thing that gives young women their great pleasure.**

The third excerpt describes a young man's clumsy and crude efforts to seduce a noble Parisian lady.

"Would you like a bolt of bright crimson velvet, striped with green, or some embroidered satin, or maybe crimson? What would you like—necklaces, gold things, things for your hair, rings? All you have to do is say yes. Even fifty thousand gold pieces doesn't bother me. . . . "

"No. Thank you, but I want nothing from you."

"By God," said he, "I damned well want something from you, and it's something that won't cost you a cent, and once you've given it you'll still have it, every bit of it. Here"—and he showed her his long codpiece—"here is my John Thomas, who wants a place to jump into."***

* *Giovanni Boccaccio,* The Decameron, *trans. G. H. McWilliam (London: Penguin, 1995), p. 494.*
** *Ibid., p. 534.*
*** *François Rabelais,* Gargantua and Pantagruel, *trans. Burton Raffel (New York: Norton, 1990), p. 201.*

wished men to renounce the material things of this world. Petrarch's work thus exemplifies the typical Renaissance propensity to elevate the secular.

The new interest in worldly life that marks Petrarch's thought is evident also in the work of his friend, Giovanni Boccaccio (1313–1375), the first great Italian prose writer. His *Decameron* is concerned with everyday life, portraying people from all social classes, often with a strong satirical flavor. With Boccaccio, the lustfulness and earthy wit of the lower classes enter serious literature during the Renaissance. In contrast to Dante's *Divine Comedy*, the *Decameron* is sometimes termed the "Human Comedy."

Although many humanist literary works were written in Italian, most writers maintained that the Latin of Cicero was the supreme literary language. Shunning "corrupt" medieval Latin, they found in classical literature a purity of style, form, and eloquence absent from most medieval literature, and they argued that to speak and write correctly one should imitate the ancients. Petrarch, for example, developed the finest Latin style of his age. Succeeding Renaissance writers and scholars, stimulated by the migration of Byzantine scholars who had begun to flee Constantinople before its fall in 1453, promoted the study of Greek.

An important aspect of humanist activity was the recovery of manuscripts of classical literary, scientific, and historical works. Searchers discovered many Latin manuscripts in European monasteries and churches. Increasingly, during the fifteenth century, Greek history and literature became available in the West as humanists obtained copies of Greek manuscripts through contacts with Byzantine scholars. Manuel Chrysoloras, a Byzantine diplomat, began a regular course of lectures on Greek in Florence in 1397; his grammar textbook gained wide circulation (it was used by Erasmus, discussed later in this section) and in 1471 became the first Greek grammar to be printed.

The recovery of so many texts gave rise to modern textual criticism, including the disciplines of paleography (the analysis of manuscripts and the handwriting in which they are transcribed) and philology (the critical study of language and literature). Dictionaries, grammars, indices, and commentaries were produced, and the texts of ancient authors were put on a sound footing by scholars who collected and compared manuscripts. From their careful textual studies, the humanists learned how to assess authenticity, showing, for example, that "The Donation of Constantine," used by popes to support their territorial sovereignty over Rome and its environs, was in fact a forgery written 400 years after the Roman emperor's death.

The Genius of Petrarch

[Petrarch] dwarfs his precursors in every respect: he was an immeasurably greater poet and greater man than any of them; his horizons were wider and his influence, never cramped within the limits of town or province, extended over most of Western Europe; he had the vision and the ability to unite the two existing strands of humanism, the literary and the scholarly, and to combine aims which reached for the moon with the capacity for painstaking research; he went further than anyone else in trying to revive within the framework of a Christian society the ideals of ancient Rome, and his attempts to get close to the great figures of the past, and indeed to rival their achievement, though flirting with the vainglorious, unleashed passions and ambitions which were to reanimate the whole cultural legacy of the ancient world and bring it to bear upon contemporary modes of thought and literature.*

Petrarch is the archetypal figure of the humanist as scholar poet. While he assembled a personal library of thousands of manuscripts, with special emphasis on his beloved Cicero, he was no mere antiquarian book collector. He read with intensity and absorbed the thought of the classical authors to his very marrow.

*L. D. Reynolds and N. G. Wilson, Scribes and Scholars: A Guide to the Transmission of Greek and Latin Literature, 2nd ed. (Oxford: Clarendon Press, 1974), pp. 113–114.

Map 9.3 Renaissance Italy. The commercial vitality and political disunity of northern Italy stimulated cultural creativity. Prosperous towns patronized and promoted artists and scholars. A remarkable number of Italian cities contributed significantly to Renaissance thought, literature, and art.

The spread of classical learning was accelerated by print. The use of movable type to print books, a momentous innovation for Europe, though known earlier in China and Korea, is attributed to Johannes Gutenberg of Mainz about 1450. The mass production of texts that printing facilitated soon made the cultural heritage of the classical world and, with it, the Renaissance widely available in Europe.

Classical texts were the basis of humanistic elementary and secondary education; the curricula included literature, mathematics, music, science, and athletics. In contrast to medieval scholars, teachers and students achieved a direct familiarity with classical Greek authorities in most subject areas. Students who received such classical training excelled in law and theology, or became secretaries for princes, prelates, and town councils.

Renaissance historians modeled their work on the classical authors, producing histories of their city or state, rather than the universal histories or annalistic accounts favored by medieval scholars. They departed from medieval precedents in emphasizing politics and stressing the role of human motives over divine intervention. Renaissance historians were also more critical in their evaluation of source materials.

The philosophers of the Renaissance were proponents of the new humanist outlook. Unlike the Scholastics of the late Middle Ages, they tended to prefer Plato to Aristotle because of the former's superior literary style and the more mystical nature of his thought. Marsilio Ficino translated into Latin all the works of Plato as well as many commentaries on his philosophy. Renaissance Platonists drew on Plato's fascination with numbers and harmonies to promote interest in geometry and mathematics. Ficino and the brilliant young scholar Giovanni Pico della Mirandola (1463–1494) also held that humans were free, perfectible individuals, with social responsibilities and a dignity derived from their position midway between the material world and the spiritual God. Pico's "Oration on the Dignity of Man," delivered in Rome in 1486, was a manifesto of humanism:

> O unsurpassed generosity of God the Father, O wondrous and unsurpassed felicity of man, to whom it is granted to have what he chooses, to be what he wills to be! The brutes, from the moment of their birth, bring with them . . . from their mother's womb all that they will ever possess. The highest spiritual beings [angels] were, from the very moment of creation, or soon thereafter, fixed in the mode of being which would be theirs through measureless eternities. But upon man, at the moment of his creation, God bestowed seeds pregnant with all possibilities, the germs of every form of life. Whichever of these a man shall cultivate, the same will mature and bear fruit in him. If vegetative, he will become a plant; if sensual, he will become brutish; if rational, he will reveal himself a heavenly being; if intellectual, he will be an angel and the son of God. . . . Who then will not look with awe upon this our chameleon, or who, at least, will look with greater admiration on any other being? (A. R. Caponigri, trans., Giovanni Pico della Mirandola: Oration on the Dignity of Man [Chicago: Regnery, 1956], pp. 8–9).

Renaissance Art in Italy

During the fourteenth century, Renaissance painters and sculptors, like Italian writers, drew inspiration from classical models. They could do so partly because Roman antiquities (monuments and ruins) were unusually numerous and near at hand and partly because Gothic art, popular elsewhere in Europe, had penetrated only slightly into Italy.

Art in the Middle Ages tended to be subservient to the church and its purposes. The object was to emphasize spiritual aspiration at the expense of physical beauty. Italian painting, usually religious figures against solid backgrounds, had been stiff and flat, with the human form covered almost entirely with clothing. In short, the art of the Middle Ages had tended to ignore nature and the physical features of the human figure, because these were thought to be sources of evil and corruption that distracted from the contemplation of God. Renaissance artists, by contrast, following the lead of the humanists, depicted a world in which nature, human beauty, the family, and even fame were pleasing to God. Because human beings were to fulfill themselves as Christians in this world, the things of this world were now, in wonderful detail, suitable subjects for artists.

A serious difficulty in the imitation of nature in painting was the simulation of movement and depth on a flat surface. A late medieval painter, the Florentine Giotto di Bondone (1266–1337), overcame this obstacle by discarding the flat forms, aloof figures, and formal compositions of the Byzantine style that had dominated Italian painting. Allegedly able to draw a fly so realistically that viewers attempted to brush it away, he skillfully contrasted light and shadow to create an illusion of depth that made his human figures look solid and round. Among the artists influenced by Giotto was Tomasso Guidi (1401–1428), better known as Masaccio. He employed the laws of atmospheric perspective to show objects receding into a background and to make figures appear round and truly three-dimensional. Although only twenty-seven when he died, Masaccio's innova-

The School of Athens. In this painting, Renaissance master Raphael presented his version of the humanist ideal of classical antiquity. Many Greek and Roman cultural heroes are depicted in the dress of sixteenth-century Italians in a setting of Renaissance architecture and sculpture. At the center of the composition, framed by the arch, Plato and Aristotle are deep in discussion.

tions inspired succeeding generations of painters, including Michelangelo and the other giants of the High Renaissance.

The first of these was Leonardo da Vinci (1452–1519), who more than any other person of his age personified the Renaissance ideal of versatility. As an artist, he was keenly interested in the natural world and was a masterly portrayer of human psychology and personality. *The Last Supper* is a careful study of the emotions that each of Jesus' disciples was likely to have expressed on that occasion. In the *Mona Lisa,* he skillfully employed light and shadow and perspective to make the figure fully human, enigmatic and mysterious, and forever fascinating.

The most popular of the Renaissance painters, Raphael Sanzio (1483–1520), excelled in composition and use of soft colors. His *School of Athens* is a symbolic and allegorical portrayal of the classical philosophers Plato and Aristotle with their students. Raphael was best known for his many Madonnas, which are warm, pious, and graceful.

Michelangelo Buonarroti (1475–1564) considered himself a sculptor first of all, but as painter he was unsurpassed in technical excellence and grandeur of conception. He painted with a sculptor's eye and made the muscular male figure his ideal of beauty. His most ambitious project, perhaps the greatest single achievement in Renaissance art, was the painting of the frescoes covering the ceiling of the Sistine Chapel in the Vatican. This masterpiece, which required four years to complete, often with the artist lying flat on his back on a scaffold, depicts nine scenes from the Old Testament, from the creation to the flood.

Sculpture followed a parallel course to painting in its development. The first major artist in this medium was Donato di Niccolì di Betto Bardi, known as Donatello (c. 1386–1466). He drew on models of classical antiquity for inspiration, traveling to Rome to study ancient art remains. His studies included anatomy and the human body, and he employed models. Donatello's *David*, the first nude statue of the Renaissance, is graceful, well proportioned, and superbly balanced.

Michelangelo brought to sculpture the same scientific accuracy, endowment of life, and deep emotion that distinguished his paintings. His statues, whether standing like *David* or seated like *Moses*, show dramatic and emotional postures and expressions. His absolute mastery of sculptural technique powerfully served the Renaissance glorification of man. Especially moving is his exquisite *Pietà*, which depicts a grief-stricken Mary looking at the dead body of Jesus lying across her lap.

Michelangelo's later works exemplify an important change that took place in the art of the sixteenth century. His later sculptures show an exaggeration, elongation, and distortion that heightens their emotional and religious qualities. For example, his crowded *Last Judgment* painting on the Sistine Chapel's end wall is full of violence, tragedy, and horror, in contrast to the classical harmony and restraint of the ceiling figures.

Architects, though slower in exploring new directions, were still more strongly influenced by classical models. In his church designs, Filippo Brunelleschi (1377–1446) combined the Romanesque cruciform floor plan with such classical features as columns, rounded windows, and arches. His greatest triumph was the cupola (dome) atop the Florence cathedral, which echoes both Rome's Pantheon and Constantinople's Hagia Sophia.

The Renaissance Outside Italy

A great watershed in western European literature and thought was the spread of the Renaissance outside of Italy between 1490 and 1530. Italian humanists accepted positions as secretaries and diplomats with northern kings and princes. Scholars from the north studied in Italy and returned home to write and teach humanism. Northern universities incorporated humanist studies into their curricula, and humanist historians used their critical skills in writing the histories of northern lands.

Italian humanism, fostered in the republics and communes of Italy, had a strong civic strain that was believed to be acceptable to God and quite consistent with Christian life. In northern Europe, humanists wrote less about civic and political duty and more about personal morality, though they still drew heavily upon both Christian and pagan (that is, non-Christian Greek and Roman) authors. Although they stressed the Bible and the words of the church fathers over classical writings, northern humanists believed that by absorbing the wisdom of both, they could improve individual morality and revitalize and purify contemporary social and religious life. Nevertheless, like their Italian predecessors, northern humanists also believed, as Thomas More (1478–1535) said, that education in Latin and Greek "doth train the soul in virtue." More, who was a lawyer and diplomat (even becoming lord chancellor of England) as well as a humanist, is best known for his *Utopia*. The *Utopia* contrasted the evil conditions of sixteenth-century Europe with an idealized, peaceful, and prosperous society living communally in accord with reason and Christian values.

The foremost northern humanist was Desiderius Erasmus (c.1466–1536), a native of Rotterdam. His wit, marvelous writing style, and extensive travels earned him international renown and ensured that his works would be "best sellers." Erasmus formulated a humanist religion of simple piety and noble conduct based on a belief in human dignity and free will. He embraced the naturalism, tolerance, and humanitarianism he found in classical writings and used his formidable satiric power to oppose war, violence, ignorance, and irrationality. His *Adages* collected apt sayings from classical Latin writers and the *Praise of Folly* attacked the pedantic dogmatism of scholars and the ignorance of the masses. Erasmus's fresh edition of the Greek New Testament became the basis of various translations into the vernacular languages.

In areas of Europe outside Italy, vernacular literatures, already developing in the thirteenth century, now registered remarkable achievements. In England, Geoffrey Chaucer (1340–1400) made the East Midland dialect the ancestor of modern English. His highly entertaining *Canterbury Tales* are filled with realistic and humorous portrayals of men and women from various social classes and occupations.

By the fifteenth century, humanist stimulation had fostered a quickening of literary achievement in western Europe. In France, François Rabelais (1490–1553) produced a prose masterpiece, *Gargantua and Pantagruel*, that glorified the human and the natural, rejected Christian doctrine and morality, and satirized scholasticism, bigotry, and church practices with bawdy humor. At the abbey where many of the book's episodes occur, the only rule is "do what you will." A little later Michel de Montaigne (1533–1592) introduced the essay as an important literary form. His great collection of *Essays* is a kind of extended intellectual autobiography, ranging over a wide variety of topics in an engaging conversational tone. Characteristic of Montaigne's essays is a healthy skepticism regarding human opinions, doctrines, institutions, and customs, as in the following passage from "On Cannibals":

> I am not so anxious that we should note the horrible savagery of these [cannibalistic] acts as concerned that, whilst judging their faults so correctly, we should be so blind to our own. I consider it more barbarous to eat a man alive than to eat him dead; to tear by rack and torture a body still full of feeling, to roast it by degrees, and then to give it to be trampled and eaten by dogs and swine—a practice which we have not only read about but seen within recent memory, not between ancient enemies, but between neighbors and fellow-citizens and, what is worse, under the cloak of piety and religion—than to roast and eat a man after he is dead. (J. M. Cohen, trans., Michel de Montaigne: Essays [Harmondsworth: Penguin, 1958], p. 113.)

For the most part, the golden age of Spanish literature came somewhat later than that of France. Miguel de Cervantes's (1547–1616) *Don Quixote*, sometimes regarded as the greatest novel ever written, is a rich depiction of human nobility and folly. Cervantes ridicules the nobles' pretensions to be champions of honor by recounting the adventures of a Spanish gentleman who, after reading too many chivalric romances, becomes a wandering knight. Imagining windmills to be giants and inns to be castles, the hero (mis)behaves in accord with those (mis)perceptions. His squire, Sancho Panza, is, by contrast, a practical man untroubled by romantic dreams and content with the simple creature comforts of eating, drinking, and sleeping.

England's literary developments were contemporary with those of Spain and were most impressive in drama. William Shakespeare (1564–1616) drew themes and story lines from Greek and Roman literature and from English history. Extremely adept in the use of language and the analysis of character, he showed a deep understanding of human potential, both for good and for evil. The following is an example:

> What a piece of work is a man! How noble in reason! How infinite in faculty! In form and moving how express and admirable! In action how like an angel! In apprehension how like a god! The beauty of the world! The paragon of animals! (Hamlet 2.2.315–319.)

In an ironic vein reminiscent of Greek tragedy, Shakespeare's heroes are responsible for their own dilemmas and suffer by their own sins and mistakes. His strongest plays express bitterness and overwhelming pathos, as the characters conduct a troubled search into life's mysteries. Of these plays, the later ones present an overall view of the universe as benevolent and just, despite individual tragedy and grief.

Northern Renaissance art represented physical and emotional reality by use of detail, careful observation of nature, and skill in the technique of foreshortening. Jan van Eyck (1370–1440) capitalized on the advantages of oil paints, excelling in the painting of portraits in which the subjects seem to live and breathe; each detail, from a blade of grass to the hair of a dog, is meticulously rendered. Albrecht Dürer (1471–1528) studied the human form carefully and gave attention to both detail and harmonious composition in woodcuts, engravings, and paintings. He admired Martin Luther (see the next section) and often chose biblical themes for his work. Many of his pieces have a pervasive somber and often gloomy quality. The great Spanish painter, Doménikos Theotokópoulos (1541–1614), known as El Greco from his birth on the island of Crete, was an avid admirer of Michelangelo. He used severe colors and elongated features to express Spanish religious zeal in his powerful and emotional paintings. His greatest work, *The Burial of Count Orgaz,* conveys the Catholic spirit of communion among God, saints, and humans.

Architects outside Italy continued to use Gothic techniques in building both churches and secular structures, but as they reached the structural and decorative limits of the Gothic, they began to employ the classical Greco-Roman style revived by fifteenth-century Italians. Those Italian influences are especially evident in central France's Loire Valley chateaux, country houses for French kings, nobles, and wealthy townspeople.

Women and the Renaissance

In the Renaissance, as in earlier periods of European history, education and intellectual professions were accessible almost exclusively to males. Laws were designed to keep women in a subservient role. As a rule they could not hold public office, testify in a court of law, make their own wills, or buy and sell property. Most women from the nobility and wealthy merchant class had few career options: they either entered into arranged marriages or became nuns. A few women, however, did receive schooling based on the revival of classical learning during the Renaissance; they were typically daughters of aristocrats or royalty instructed by fathers or husbands or by private tutors.

Despite the restrictions imposed by male-oriented societies, some females achieved personal and intellectual fulfillment. Christine de Pizan (1365–c. 1430), for example, was the first woman known to have made her living as a professional writer. In 1390, the death of her husband, a secretary at the court of the French king (Charles V), left her with three children, her mother, and two brothers to support. To do so, she developed her skills in a variety of genres: love poetry, literary criticism, histories of eminent women, political theory, religious meditations, a biography of King Charles V, and poetry written for aristocratic patrons; her last work was a poem celebrating the victory of Joan of Arc at the siege of Orléans during the Hundred Years' War (see the next section). She also penned a fascinating autobiography entitled *Christine's Vision*.

Even for learned women, a life of scholarship did not combine easily with wifely duties and maternal obligations of child bearing and rearing. Ginerva Nogarola (c. 1417–1468) and Cataruzza Caldiera (d. 1463), both of whom showed exceptional promise as young women, abandoned their studies and writings altogether after they

Melancholia I. The melancholy figure by Albrecht Dürer sits amid symbols of the new learning of the sixteenth century, suggesting that greater knowledge does not necessarily produce happiness. If meant as a self-portrait, it is a very early example of the "tormented artist" theme so familiar in modern times. The work shows the exquisite detail that a master engraver could achieve.

married and bore children. Described by some humanists as a prodigy, Cassandra Fedele (1465–1558) married reluctantly at age thirty-three and continued her scholarly work only haphazardly, failing to complete any of the three major works she had planned.

There were a few exceptions, however, when privileged women were able to study, write, marry, and have children. Marguerite of Navarre (1492–1549) was one of the greatest women literary writers of the sixteenth century. Although a poet of unusual sensitivity, her fame rests on her principal prose work, the *Heptameron,* a collection of short stories modeled on Boccaccio's *Decameron.*

Some women found themselves in conflict with their family and society as they followed a literary career outside of marriage. Constanza Barbaro (born c. 1419), daughter of a Venetian humanist, became a nun so that she could devote all her time to study. Isotta Nogarola (1418–1466) was probably the best known among women writers who created their own cloistered world. She was trained by a private tutor and at age eighteen started a correspondence with male humanists in Verona. Though her letters show great promise and were praised by some, others advised her that she would have to "become a man" if she wished to continue her career as a writer. Isotta decided against both the alternatives of married life and the nunnery and lived as a recluse in her mother's home, producing some fine Latin verse and an important theological tract.

Women who aspired to paint had to overcome the same disadvantages as those drawn to the intellectual movement. Still, many succeeded in earning a living by selling their works to, or accepting commissions for portraits from, wealthy patrons. Levina Bening Teerline (c. 1520–1576) was invited by Henry VIII to come from Flanders to paint miniature portraits. The English monarch was so delighted with her paintings that he paid her a life annuity of £40, then a generous sum. The portraitist Sofonisba Anguissola (c. 1535–1625), the daughter of an Italian noble family, drew a similar commission from Philip II of Spain, who rewarded her lavishly with a pension, a dowry on her marriage, and appointment as lady-in-waiting to the court.

During the Baroque phase of the Italian Renaissance, Artemisia Gentileschi (1593–c. 1652), trained by her father and other artists, achieved a reputation on a par with that of Leonardo Da Vinci and Michelangelo. She often chose women for her subjects: for example, the biblical heroines Susannah and Judith beheading Holofernes. In another medium Properzia de' Rossi (c.1500–1530) was singled out by the biographer Vasari for the excellence of her relief sculptures in the Church of St. Peter in Bologna and for her great versatility: "[she was] skilled not only in household matters . . . but in infinite fields of knowledge. . . . She was beautiful and played and sang better than any woman in the city." Few women of the Renaissance were able (or allowed) to be so multitalented.

European Nation-States and the Reformation

[At the Diet of Worms in 1521, the spokesman said:] "Martin, how can you assume that you are the only one to understand the sense of Scripture? Would you put your judgment above that of so many famous men and claim that you know more than they all? You have no right to call into question the most holy orthodox faith, instituted by Christ the perfect lawgiver, proclaimed throughout the world by

the apostles, sealed by the red blood of the martyrs, confirmed by the sacred councils, defined by the Church in which all our fathers believed until death and gave to us as an inheritance, and which now we are forbidden by the pope and the emperor to discuss lest there be no end of debate. I ask you, Martin—answer candidly and without horns—do you or do you not repudiate your books and the errors which they contain?"

Luther replied, "Since then Your Majesty and your lordships desire a simple reply, I will answer without horns and without teeth. Unless I am convicted by Scripture and plain reason—I do not accept the authority of popes and councils, for they have contradicted each other—my conscience is captive to the Word of God. I cannot and I will not recant anything, for to go against conscience is neither right nor safe. God help me. Amen." [In the earliest printed version the words "Here I stand. I cannot do otherwise," were added.]*

**Roland H. Bainton, Here I Stand: A Life of Martin Luther (New York: Mentor, 1958), p. 144.*

This exchange was the culmination of a sequence of events that produced the Protestant Reformation, a broad revolt against the medieval church. Although religious dissent was the root of the problem, the Reformation was also intimately bound up with political, social, economic, and intellectual matters. Within a generation of Luther's defiant act, many Europeans had set up separate religious organizations outside the Catholic church, ending the centuries-long religious unity of western Europe. Although the various Protestant denominations disagreed among themselves on minor theological points, they were firmly united in their opposition to Catholicism. The confrontation inspired a long period of bloody strife that would profoundly affect Western civilization.

The Reformation was closely associated with the formation of powerful national states in western Europe, a process that had begun some two centuries earlier. The pride, power, and resources of these states found expression in various forms of political and commercial rivalry, including developing trade overseas (see the following sections). The emergence of these nation-states of western Europe will open this section.

The Centralization of Western European Monarchies

The High Middle Ages had witnessed the resurgent power of the monarchy in Europe as the prelude to the development of the modern state. However, the troubles of four-teenth- and fifteenth-century Europe—civil and foreign wars, economic depression, and the plague—undid much of the earlier work of consolidation. The powers of government came to be divided between the king and his semiautonomous vassals, the great nobles of the realm. Royal vassals maintained private armies, dispensed justice in the courts, and served as advisors and royal officials. The nobles were monarchs in minia-ture, often having the power of life and death over the people in their territories. As a result, a country like France was not a single nation under one king; rather, it was a mosaic of principalities, each with its own ruler. At times of a major threat, vassals would sometimes temporarily join forces under their king.

For the peasants or serfs, it made little difference whether they were exploited by king or duke, because life close to the soil was harsh in either case. For dwellers in manufacturing and trading towns, the situation was less clear. The city fathers longed to win self-rule and, to that end, liked to play one great lord off against another or against the king. At the same time, however, those who aspired to trade over larger areas found the political fragmentation of their country a hindrance.

The trend towards decentralization was dramatically reversed during the second half of the fifteenth century with the emergence of strong, ambitious kings in France, England, and Spain. They ended internal disorders in their lands, reduced the power of the nobility, and extended greater control over their subjects. The achievements of these "New Monarchs" served as examples for lesser kings to follow.

Several factors led to the recovery of the monarchy in western Europe. As already noted, in the centralized states around the world, the European kings needed to generate an assured source of income sufficient to create an army and a bureaucracy under their control. The new towns provided a potential source of new money. In a mutually beneficial arrangement, the kings granted the towns privileges and rights in return for money payments to the royal treasury. In this way, towns and monarchs became allies against the great lords, who often sought to encroach on the independence of both. These arrangements not only reduced the kings' dependence on the great nobles but resulted in the growth of semi-independent towns in early modern Europe.

With the new revenue, the kings moved to abandon feudal levies and create a powerful army. In the traditional feudal levy, vassals supplied forces for temporary service, but so long as the great nobles controlled the military, the king's power was limited. Accordingly, the monarchs began to build up armies of paid soldiers commanded by loyal officers who were willing to follow orders and even make war on the nobles, if necessary.

The kings further strengthened their position through marriages calculated either to neutralize powerful antagonists or to add territory to their own realm. No less important was the development of bureaucracies. Civil servants attached to districts collected taxes and administered in the king's name. Kings selected their officials from outside the nobility and paid them in money and in small, scattered estates instead of huge blocks of territory. In this way, the kings ensured that the officials would be dependent on them and thus loyal to the crown.

In France, the first of the New Monarchs, Louis XI (reigned 1461–1483), inherited a realm devastated by the Black Death and the Hundred Years' War (1337–1453). The latter was a debilitating struggle fought between the English and the French, and among the French, over a maze of feudal claims and commercial competition. At a dark moment for France, a young woman, later known as Joan of Arc (1412–1431) changed the course of the war. Believing herself to be acting at God's urging, she persuaded Charles VII (reigned 1422–1461) to appoint her to a military command. Her prestige reached its height in 1429 when she succeeded in relieving the besieged city of Orléans and cutting a path for Charles to Rheims, where he was properly crowned in the place and manner of his ancestors. Joan, who was later captured and executed, came to symbolize the French national spirit.

Louis XI was nicknamed the "Spider," in part because his misshapen body appeared spiderlike, but more because he devised political traps and plots reminiscent of a spider-web. He attracted the loyalty of the lesser nobility and employed many of them as royal officials. Louis used the army to expand royal power within France, and in a series of adroit, if underhanded, moves, he suppressed the great nobles, already weakened by losses during the Hundred Years' War. At the same time, he curbed town autonomy and asserted administrative control over the provinces. He seldom convened the Estates General, France's rudimentary representative assembly. By his death in 1483 Louis had united France, strengthened its economy, and laid the foundations for royal absolutism.

Like France, fifteenth-century England was wracked by factionalism, which culminated in a civil war (the War of the Roses, 1455–1485) between the great feudal families of Lancaster and York. The civil war ended in 1485 when Henry Tudor, the foremost surviving Lancastrian, seized the crown as Henry VII (reigned 1485–1509) and married Elizabeth of York, the leading Yorkist claimant, thereby uniting the two feuding groups. With peace temporarily assured, Henry set out to centralize his power. He drew his officials from the ranks of the lesser gentry and townsmen and seated many of his councilors in Parliament, where they could manipulate matters to the king's liking. Henry received such ample revenues from customs duties on increased international trade and from fines derived from active law enforcement that he needed to summon Parliament only once in the last twelve years of his reign. He supplemented traditional English law with Roman law for many purposes. Roman law, formulated to govern a far-flung empire, favored central authority over the rights of aristocrats and common people alike and helped Henry legally justify seizing the lands and revenues of "overmighty subjects." At his death in 1509, Henry left a powerful monarchy to his son, Henry VIII.

Events in the Iberian Peninsula paralleled those in France and England. Beginning in the eleventh century, the salient feature of Iberian history was the Christian *Reconquista* (Reconquest) against the Muslims, who controlled most of the peninsula. By the mid-fifteenth century, the three kingdoms of Aragon, Castile, and Portugal dominated the peninsula. Portugal was the first national state to emerge in Europe. There the House of Avis centralized royal administration by suppressing revolts of nobles and executing many of their leaders. Partly as a result of this centralization, Portugal was the first European nation to use its resources to expand overseas (discussed later in this chapter).

The marriage of Ferdinand, King of Aragon (reigned 1479–1516), to Isabella, Queen of Castile (reigned 1474–1504), in 1469 united their two realms into the Kingdom of Spain. Ferdinand and Isabella moved against the nobles, who objected to any increase in the crown's power and opposed the introduction of Roman law, which the royal couple supported. They forged alliances with the towns, ostensibly to combat bandits but actually to counter the power of feudal levies. The Cortes, the representative assembly dominated by the nobility, steadily lost power.

The desire to consolidate their strength led the Spanish rulers to establish the Inquisition, a tribunal for the detection and punishment of heresy. It operated as an agency of the state, free from papal or church control. Ferdinand, who was not religious, did not hesitate to use it as well as an instrument to enforce civil despotism; in particular, to suppress rebellious churchmen and nobles. Most of the inquisition's fury, however, was aimed at achieving religious uniformity. Its officials energetically and carefully examined the religious purity of all, searching for blasphemers and heretics. The officials conducted trials and passed sentence, often gathering information and confessions through torture. The state then executed those found guilty. When Ferdinand and Isabella conquered Granada (1492), the last Muslim outpost on the peninsula, they ordered all unconverted Muslims and Jews to leave the country with only what they could carry. The confiscated property of the religious exiles, coupled with the profits from discoveries overseas, greatly enriched the crown.

The Background of the Protestant Reformation

The Reformation, the religious upheaval that splintered the Roman Catholic church, took place during the sixteenth and seventeenth centuries, at the same time that central-ized monarchy was on the rise in western Europe. Earlier, in 1054, Christianity had split into two main branches, the Eastern or Orthodox church, which prevailed in the Byzan-tine Empire, and the Western or Roman Catholic church, which was dominant in central and western Europe. In the High Middle Ages, the popes had succeeded in centralizing the administration of the church under their control, permitting them to impose religious uniformity and to exercise a potent influence on European political life. The Catholic church reached the height of its power under Pope Innocent III (reigned 1198–1216). Laxity and worldliness characterized Innocent III's successors, weakening the papacy's moral authority and opening the way for increasing defiance and contempt. Papal power eroded at the same time that the prestige of the new national states was on the rise.

The turning point in papal history occurred when the strong and consolidated monarchy of France challenged the secular pretensions of the papacy. The result was the humiliation of the pope, Boniface VIII (reigned 1294–1303), in 1303 and the removal of the papacy to Avignon, in southern France, two years later. From 1305 to 1378 the popes resided at Avignon, where, to all appearances, they became tools of French inter-ests and, consequently, objects of suspicion and hostility to France's enemies. The long period of papal exile at Avignon, known as the Babylonian Captivity, was a minor scan-dal compared to what followed during the next half century.

Pope Gregory XI (reigned 1370–1378) ended the Babylonian Captivity when he moved back to Rome, where he died in 1378. The cardinals met and, amid scenes of mob violence, first elected an Italian pope, Urban VI (reigned 1378–1389), who publicly scolded them for their worldliness and attempted to reduce their revenues. Most of the cardinals thereupon withdrew from Rome, declared Urban's election invalid because it had been held under threat of violence, chose a Frenchman as Pope Clement VII (reigned 1378–1394), and settled with him at Avignon. To the bewilderment of consci-entious Christians, there were now two popes, one at Rome and the other at Avignon, each with competing systems of church administrations, courts, and taxation. Corrup-tion and financial abuses worsened as each pope, seeking to oust the other, became more involved than ever in politics. At the urging of bishops and powerful laymen, a church council was summoned with the object of ending the schism.

The second church council, held at Constance (1414–1417), reunited the Catholic church. The delegates deposed the rival popes and elected a new pope, Martin V (reigned 1417–1431). Radical elements wanted to go further and strip away papal powers and have councils govern the church, but the efforts of these conciliarists were thwarted by papal intransigence and by their own inability to agree. In the meantime Martin and his successors tried to win over the temporal rulers in western and central Europe who had initially supported the conciliarists. The popes achieved their objective, but only after permitting the monarchs to assume more control over the church in their respective countries. Before the end of the fifteenth century, the papacy had once again asserted its dominance over the church, although it was unable to recapture the spiritual and moral leadership it had formerly enjoyed. The price for the papacy's triumph was high. Preoccupied for many years in combating the conciliarist movement and practicing power politics, the popes showed little interest in undertaking the reforms that sincere Christians were demanding.

A number of abuses had arisen in the church in the fourteenth and fifteenth centuries. Simony, the sale of church offices, was one such problem. Some 2,000 church offices were for sale, and the resulting revenues formed a significant part of papal income. A case in point was the Archbishop of Mainz, who paid the astronomical sum of 30,000 ducats for his office—equivalent to fifteen years' salary for a mid-level functionary in the papal bureaucracy. Another serious problem was pluralism, where one individual held several church offices at the same time. Priests and bishops often hired stand-ins to fulfill their duties. In Germany in 1500, more than 90 percent of the parishes were served by part-time priests. The practice of nepotism, giving lucrative church offices to relatives of the higher clergy, was widespread. Churchmen, from the highest rank to the lowest, were frequently affected by the secular spirit of the Renaissance and showed more interest in worldly pleasures and pursuits than in attending to their spiritual responsibilities. Popes led a life of luxury rivaling that of the secular rulers of their time. The church's ever-growing fiscal demands, together with the immorality and secular interests of the clergy, aggravated the resentment and sense of alienation felt by many Christians.

When church leaders did not initiate reform, some priests and laity on the local level tried to make changes, while in other areas, secular princes led popular reform movements. Appealing to scriptural precedents, the life of Jesus, and the activities of the early church described in the Book of Acts, most reformers demanded back-to-basics change. Such was the general situation on All Saints' Eve, 1517, when Martin Luther made his famous demand for reform of church practices and doctrines.

Martin Luther Breaks with the Church

Martin Luther was born in 1483 at Eisleben in Saxony (central Germany), the second son of a moderately prosperous miner. To please his father he went to the University of Erfurt in 1505 to study law. That same year, according to his account, he was caught in a fearsome thunderstorm and thrown to the ground by a flash of lightning. Following his miraculous survival, which affected him emotionally, he entered an Augustinian monastery at Erfurt, where he was ordained a priest in 1507. He returned to the university and became a doctor of theology. From 1511 until his death thirty-five years later, he served as professor of theology at the newly founded University of Wittenberg.

Library of Congress

Luther before the Diet of Worms, 1521. Luther was resolute in his defense, partly because of the support he received from Germans of all classes. His journey to Worms was made triumphant by the acclamation of cheering crowds who lined the road.

Luther's growing reputation as a biblical scholar masked his torment about gaining God's grace and his own salvation. Beyond scrupulous monastic observance, he had been diligent in confessing his sins, praying, and fasting. Yet performing good works, as commanded by the church, did not give him the comfort and spiritual peace he was seeking. Through the study of the Bible he found the answer to his dilemma in one of St. Paul's letters to the Romans, especially in the phrase "the just shall live by faith." It dawned on him that people could be saved only by repenting their sins and throwing themselves on God's mercy and accepting His grace. Salvation was a gift from God as a reward for faith in His mercy and could not be earned by doing good works. This doctrine struck at the heart of orthodox Catholic belief, which held that only through the sacraments of the church could sinners be redeemed and made worthy of salvation. Luther was at first unaware of the conflict. He thought he was simply giving more emphasis to the Bible in Christian education. Only after he was drawn into the indulgence controversy did he realize the revolutionary implications of his religious views.

According to Catholic teaching, an indulgence was supposed to remit punishment in purgatory for sins for which insufficient penance had been done while on earth. It was granted on condition that the sinner was repentant and was willing to perform some pious deed such as going on a crusade or a pilgrimage. By the sixteenth century, however, the practice had become perverted. Church agents made extravagant claims, implying that indulgences secured total remission of sins, on earth and in purgatory, without bothering to mention the acts of contrition and confession demanded of every sinner as

Ottoman Expansion

The Ottoman's expanded rapidly throughout the fifteenth and sixteenth centuries, conquering vast territories around the Black Sea, in the Balkans, and in the Arab provinces along the eastern Mediterranean and North Africa.

Catholics and Protestants in Europe by 1560

Reformation religious upheavals affected most of Europe, with Protestant faiths predominant in the north. Protestantism also made substantial headway in France, the Habsburg dominions, southern Germany, and Poland, but these areas eventually reverted to Roman Catholicism.

The regions shown were the principal sources of slaves.

The figures are for 1526–1810.

From 1526 to 1870 about 10 million slaves were shipped from Africa to:

Europe	175,000
Spanish America	1,552,000
Brazil	3,647,000
British Caribbean	1,665,000
British North America and United States	399,000
French America	1,600,000
Dutch America	500,000
Danish West Indies	28,000

ETHIOPIA

Bunce Island
Freetown
OYO
GOLD COAST Whydah BENIN
Elmina Brass

ATLANTIC

OCEAN

CONGO

Malindi
Mombasa
Da Gama to India

Luanda LUNDA

ANGOLA

Mozambique

Sofala

African states

Dutch colony

Islamicized areas

- - -> Early Portuguese voyages, 1430–1475

- - -> Voyages of Dias and Da Gama

◄— Major slave trade to Western Hemisphere

—> Secondary slave trade to Europe, North Africa, and Asia

⚓ Dutch slave-trading posts

⚓ Portuguese slave-trading posts

▪ Other European slave-trading posts

Da Gama 1497–1499

Dias 1487–1488

Cape Town

Da Gama 1497–149

Dias

INDIAN

OCEAN

0	500	1000	1500 Kilometers
0	500	1000 Miles	

Africa, 1500–c. 1750, and the Slave Trade

By the sixteenth century, Islam had spread throughout much of North and East Africa, while many independent kingdoms and city-states continued to prosper. Along the African coasts, European explorers also founded small trading posts, where the slave trade flourished as growing numbers of Africans were transported as slave labor for plantations in the Western Hemisphere.

Areas of settlements

- French
- English
- Dutch and Swedish (English after 1664)

Areas of forts and trading posts

- French
- English
- Spanish

European Holdings in North America, c. 1685

After nearly a century of activity in North America, the French and the English had secured very disparate colonial holdings. The French presence centered on fur and deerskin trading posts radiating from a small settlement in Quebec. The English controlled an area smaller in extent, but greater in population, dominated by family farms.

a prerequisite for forgiveness. An indulgence, so it was advertised, guaranteed swift entry in heaven for the purchaser himself or for a loved one in purgatory. As one hawker put it: "As soon as the coin in the coffer rings, the soul from purgatory springs." Many flocked to buy indulgences; the huge sums collected went either into the pockets of leading political and church officials or to Rome to pay for such papal projects as Saint Peter's basilica.

Luther was outraged to see poor people being deprived of their hard-earned money under false pretenses. He objected to the sale of indulgences on the grounds that the pope had no control over purgatory and, most important of all, that it did not mandate repentance as a condition for forgiveness of sins. On October 31, 1517, Luther posted a list of ninety-five theses (statements of error) on the church door at Wittenberg. His purpose in doing so was to challenge the defenders of indulgences to a debate. Luther had expected reaction to be confined to the university community, but to his surprise printed copies of his theses circulated throughout Germany, arousing widespread public interest. To the consternation of church authorities, the sale of indulgences fell off sharply.

As Luther was forced by critics to define his theological position, it became increasingly apparent that his beliefs were sharply at odds with those of the Catholic church. In 1520 Pope Leo X (reigned 1513–1521) condemned Luther's teachings and ordered him to recant within two months or face excommunication. Luther responded by publicly burning the document. The pope then formally excommunicated Luther and called upon the Holy Roman Emperor, Charles V, to punish him as a heretic. But Luther had become a national figure, and the German princes did not feel he could be condemned without a hearing.

In the spring of 1521 Luther, under the protection of an imperial safe conduct, appeared before Charles V at a diet (meeting) at Worms. There he refused to recant unless it could be proved that his writings were contrary to Scripture. Branded an outlaw with a price on his head, he traveled home with the assistance of agents of Frederick, elector of Saxony, under whose protection he would remain for the rest of his life. In 1522 Luther returned to Wittenberg where he gathered his supporters and established the first Protestant church.

The rapid spread of Lutheranism was in marked contrast to other reform movements, which had failed to divide the church. Luther was a brilliant theologian and possessed nearly every quality essential to a revolutionary leader. He also enjoyed advantages that had been denied to his predecessors. First, his revolt against Rome occurred when the church was in a state of decline and was being strongly criticized from within. The abuses resulting from the Great Schism and a series of worldly Renaissance popes had lowered public support for the church. Meanwhile, the writings of Erasmus and other humanists generated a critical spirit that challenged many accepted beliefs. Erasmus's scholarly edition of the New Testament (1516) and the publication of the writings of the church fathers, including all of Jerome's letters, in the vernacular, coupled with other humanist texts, revealed that some church doctrines had shaky foundations. Second, the invention of the printing press allowed for the mass production of books, including the Bible, at relatively low cost. Published materials thereafter became available to larger numbers of people, permitting the rapid spread of new ideas. Third, an unusual political situation existed in Germany. Charles V, the Holy Roman Emperor, was committed to maintaining an alliance with the papacy and also wanted to extend his authority over Germany. About half of the 300-odd German rulers supported Lutheranism as a way to resist Charles V. Some among them may have been moved as much by material considerations as by religious concerns. By adopting Lutheranism, the princes could confiscate the rich and extensive Catholic holdings in their domains. Finally, the rising capitalistic classes, finding Catholicism incompatible with the practices of trade and banking, were willing to push for a system that suited them better.

Many of Luther's early followers broke away from his guidance. The largest group to do so was the Anabaptists, a radical religious sect whose social ideas included a refusal to bear arms and the abolition of private property. Luther disavowed them because, apart from sharp religious differences, his views on the social order were extremely conservative. The humanists, who had scorned and ridiculed church practices, hailed Luther for his efforts to restore the purity of Christianity. But the humanists, placing unity ahead of doctrine, wanted to reform the church from within, not start a new religion. When Luther refused to patch up his differences with Rome, most of them, including Erasmus, decided to remain within the Catholic fold. In 1524–1525 the Peasants' Revolt had far more serious consequences. Thousands of downtrodden peasants in southwest Germany, seeking relief from economic and manorial burdens, revolted against their landlords. At first, Luther had shown considerable sympathy for the commoners' cause but, when they resorted to violence, endangering the fabric of society and the structure of the state, he called for their suppression. The princes did so with unspeakable cruelty, causing Lutheranism to lose much of its appeal among the poor of southern Germany.

Luther saw himself not as a social and economic reformer but as a restorer of true doctrine and practices of the early Christian church. In final form, Luther's religion differed from the Catholic church in a number of important ways. Luther believed that salvation came through faith in God rather than through good works, sacraments, and rituals. The true church, he contended, consisted of all believers and not just an organization of ecclesiastics; thus he eliminated the hierarchy of pope, cardinals, and bishops and reduced the importance of the clergy. For Luther, ultimate authority rested with the Scriptures, not with church traditions and papal pronouncements. Of the seven Catholic sacraments, he retained only baptism and communion, the two found in the Bible. He abolished monasteries and the celibacy of the clergy. Luther himself married a former nun, by whom he had six children. He replaced the Latin liturgy with a German service that included Bible reading and the singing of hymns. So that the Bible would be available in German, Luther translated both the New and Old Testaments. Finally, unlike Catholicism, Luther gave the state supreme authority over his church except in matters of doctrine.

The spectacular progress of Lutheranism troubled Charles V, who sought to find an accommodation that would prevent Germany from being divided by religion. His political skirmishing with the Lutheran princes only intensified matters, however, and led to open war in 1546, the same year that Luther died. Although Charles was determined to crush the Lutheran states, he was unable to intervene forcefully because of his preoccupation with wars against the French and the Turks. With neither side able to gain a clear advantage, the Peace of Augsburg in 1555 ended the nine-year conflict. By this compromise sovereign princes and cities were given the right to decide between Catholicism and Lutheranism; subjects who objected to their ruler's choice would be permitted to emigrate. The peace of Augsburg left Lutheranism firmly entrenched in the northern half of Germany. From there it spread to Scandinavia and to the Baltic lands under the control of Sweden. Lutheranism would also have a great influence on all subsequent Protestant movements.

Protestant Reformers after Luther

Luther may have been the first to revolt against the established church, but others soon followed. Ulrich Zwingli (1484–1531) led a reform movement in Zurich, Switzerland, that incorporated many of Luther's teachings. Zwingli believed in the supreme authority of Scripture and simplified church services, taught justification by faith instead of good works, and opposed clerical celibacy. But he went beyond Luther in considering baptism and communion to be merely symbolic ceremonies. These doctrinal differences proved irreconcilable and marked the first in a long series of Protestant schisms. Zwingli also maintained that the church needed to take the lead in imposing Christian discipline on civil life. The Swiss confederation of cantons could not agree on which church to follow, so it allowed each canton to make its own decision.

The reform tradition that Zwingli started in Zurich was carried on by John Calvin (1509–1564) in Geneva a generation later. Calvin, who next to Martin Luther was the most celebrated Protestant leader of the sixteenth century, was born in the French town of Noyon, the son of a prosperous lawyer. His heart was set on becoming a priest, but at his father's insistence, he abandoned theology for law. Early in life he associated with followers of Luther and about 1534 converted to Protestantism. Forced into hiding to avoid persecution, Calvin fled to Switzerland and settled in Geneva where, as a dynamic agent of change, he rose to become virtual dictator of the city.

Calvin outlined his religious views in *The Institutes of the Christian Religion,* published in 1536 when he was only twenty-six. The book was a clear, logical, and superb synthesis of Protestant theology. On the surface Calvin's beliefs resembled those of Luther. He accepted the sinfulness of humans and their impotence to save themselves, denied the value of good works as a means of salvation, regarded the Bible as the sole authority in matters of faith, and rejected all the Catholic sacraments except baptism and communion. But Calvin's differences with Luther were significant enough to rule out collaboration between the two. Calvin favored suppressing anything that was not clearly sanctioned in the Bible, which he regarded as the supreme authority in every aspect of life. Luther, regarding the Bible as a vehicle for Christ's teachings, permitted anything that it did not specifically forbid. Far more than Luther, Calvin stressed the omnipotence of God. Calvin accepted Luther's concept of salvation through God's grace, but believed more strongly than the latter that this priceless gift was granted only to some men. According to Calvin, people were condemned to live in perpetual sin as punishment for

Adam and Eve's fall from grace. But God through his infinite mercy had chosen some human beings to be saved and had damned all the rest to suffer in hell. Men and women could do nothing to change their fate, which was predestined before they were born. The doctrine of predestination was at the core of Calvin's theology. The doctrine itself was not new, but Calvin's emphasis on it was. Luther's belief in justification by faith implied divine predetermination, but he was too consumed with other matters to follow through. Calvin, with his rigorous logic, was driven to carry the doctrine to its ultimate conclusion.

Logically, one might think that if individuals could have no effect on their destiny, they would be indifferent about their personal conduct. Calvin took another position on that point, however: although people had no sure way of knowing who would be saved and who would be damned, those living in accordance with God's will could take it as a hopeful sign. Even if a pious life did not ensure salvation, an immoral life proved that one was not among the chosen. Calvin's doctrine had an enormous appeal. It gave believers a powerful motive to do God's work in order to convince themselves that they would be saved.

Calvinism was not confined to Switzerland. Geneva became a training center for Calvinist preachers who came from many parts of Europe. Impelled by a sense of militancy and dedication, they returned to promote Calvin's teachings in their homeland. Calvinism triumphed in Scotland under the leadership of John Knox (c. 1510–1572), in the German Palatinate, and in the Dutch Netherlands, where it played a major role in overthrowing Spanish tyranny. It gained many converts in England (Puritans) and a vigorous following in France (Huguenots), Bohemia, and Hungary. From Europe Calvinism made its way to America, where it contributed significantly to the growth of constitutional government.

The act that sparked the English Reformation had little to do with Calvinism or church doctrine, however. The king, Henry VIII, wanted to annul his marriage to his wife, Catherine of Aragon, by whom he had only a daughter, Mary. Although England had no law that barred a woman from the throne, Henry and his advisors felt that the country should be ruled by a male. While divorce was contrary to church law, ecclesiastical authorities sometimes allowed marriages to be annulled, especially when monarchs were involved. The problem in this case was that Catherine was the aunt of the powerful Holy Roman Emperor, Charles V, whose troops not only controlled Rome but held the pope captive. Henry was not a patient man; when the pope delayed acting on his request he turned to the compliant Archbishop of Canterbury, Thomas Cramner, who granted the annulment in 1533. The following year Parliament passed the Act of Supremacy, which repudiated papal primacy and declared the king head of an independent Anglican church. In this capacity, Henry subsequently dissolved the monasteries and enriched his treasury with their great wealth.

Despite his break with Rome, Henry continued to think of himself as a devout Catholic. The official theology of the Church of England made few departures from Catholicism. When Henry died in 1547, his nine-year-old son, Edward VI, ascended the throne. During the regency government of the youth, Protestants gradually moved Anglican doctrine closer to mainstream Protestant tenets through the Book of Common

LIVES AND TIMES ACROSS CULTURES

Life in Geneva and Venice in the Sixteenth Century

Under a constitution Calvin helped write, Geneva became a theocratic republic in which the administration of church and state were closely interwoven. Calvin's objective was to transform the city into his version of the ideal Christian community. Ruling with the assistance of a council known as the Consistory, he considered it his duty to supervise every aspect of the city's life and to enforce God's will. Guided by the Bible, laws were passed forbidding such things as idleness, dancing, frivolous pastimes, card playing, profanity, adultery, and marriage to Catholics. There were instructions for the way people dressed, on how women were to arrange their hair, even for the selection of names for infants. Calvin demanded sobriety, regular church attendance, hard work, frugality, and pursuit of a trade. Secret agents were on the lookout for wrongdoing.

Calvin had no tolerance for human weaknesses, and even common sins were punished with unprecedented rigor. The most notorious example of Calvin's harshness was the execution of Michael Servetus, a Spanish refugee, for publicly denying the doctrine of the Trinity. Gradually, as the more liberal-minded people left the city and were replaced by zealots from all over Europe, the character of the city changed. In 1546 John Knox reported that Geneva was the most perfect community of Christ seen anywhere on earth since the days of the apostles.

In many ways unique among Italian cities, Venice stood in sharp contrast to Geneva. Built almost exclusively on trade and shipping, Venice was a rich, highly cultural and cosmopolitan city. It was governed by a hereditary oligarchy of wealthy merchants comprising only about 2 percent of the population. Although members of this aristocracy, as they styled themselves, tolerated no opposition, they ruled wisely and did much to improve the economic welfare of the disenfranchised masses.

Venice was untroubled by internal disorder, social tensions, or party factionalism. Travelers were struck by the paradoxical nature of the city. On the one hand, they saw a city that projected a sober image of republican restraint and judicious modesty, founded on the principles of equality, magnanimity, domestic harmony, and justice for all of its citizens. On the other hand, they reported that Venice was a pleasure-seeking community—full of festive people, indulgent of gambling, of roisterous parties, of the theatre, and of lax sexual mores. As early as the fourteenth century Petrarch noted with disapproval his impression of the city: "Much freedom reigns there in every respect, and what I should call the only evil prevailing—but also the worst—far too much freedom." Freedom was possible because there was no opposition to the government; and there were few grounds for criticism because the government had adopted progressive social policies and secured boundless wealth.

Laws in Venice were enacted without reference to God's will. In fact the government was anticlerical and as a rule ignored interdicts issued by the papacy. During the Counter-Reformation the papacy rejuvenated the Inquisition as a means to maintain orthodoxy and effectively extend the church's power in the Catholic world. Most Catholic countries rallied behind this institution without reservation. However, Venice, long impervious to papal influence, adopted a middle position, designed to contain heresy without compromising the authority of its secular government or severely restricting rights traditionally enjoyed by its citizens.

Prayer. When Edward died without an heir in 1553, the crown passed to Mary, a devout Catholic, who dedicated herself to restoring the Roman Catholic church in England. Persecution of Protestants during Mary's rule earned her the nickname "Bloody Mary." In 1558 the childless Mary died unexpectedly, and the crown went to her Protestant half-sister,

Elizabeth, who quickly restored the Anglican church and declared herself its governor. During her long reign (1558–1603), Elizabeth successfully steered a middle course between Roman Catholicism and Calvinism. The Anglican church's beliefs were spelled out in a modified Book of Common Prayer and in the Thirty-nine Articles, published in 1563.

A great upheaval, such as the Protestant revolt, was bound to produce extremist groups. The most radical among the reformers were the Anabaptists, the ancestors of the modern Mennonites and Amish. They generally came from the lower classes and stressed a literal interpretation of the Scripture, seeking a return to the simplicity of primitive Christianity. The name *Anabaptist* meant "baptize again," and came from their rejection of infant baptism and their belief that only adults capable of free choice should be baptized. Adults who had been baptized as children had to be rebaptized. Generally the Anabaptists rejected any association between church and state, refused to recognize civil authority when it conflicted with their religious ideals, and favored the creation of egalitarian communities like those of the early Christians. Because they posed a religious and political threat to established society, they were intensively and cruelly persecuted by both Catholics and Protestants.

The aim of early Protestant movements was to modify rather than reject the medieval church. All, to varying degrees, retained features of the old Roman church, but their sharp differences could not be harmonized. By the middle of the sixteenth century, Protestantism had triumphed in nearly half of Europe and the existence of the Catholic church itself seemed threatened.

Women and the Reformation

Women showed as much interest in the Reformation as did men. For most women, exposure to Protestant doctrines came through their husbands or fathers. Some, inspired by what they heard and anxious to promote their new faith, did so in ways open to them. Anabaptist women were allowed to preach and administer baptism, and, occasionally, zealous wives of evangelizers were active alongside their husbands from the pulpits. However, larger Protestant groups, as with Catholics, closed the ministry to women. As John Calvin put it: "The custom of the church . . . may be elicited first of all from Tertullian [church father, c. 160–230], who held that no woman in church is allowed to speak, teach, baptize or make offerings; this in order that she may not usurp the functions of men." Apart from the lack of theological training, women serving conspicuously in nontraditional roles would have been objectionable to most men.

The most common venue in which women conveyed their views and feelings was the home. Here they discussed doctrinal matters and instructed occasional visitors and friends on the virtues of their new faith. Some educated women composed hymns or wrote devotional works. Married women taught their children the catechism, pronounced prayers, and sang hymns. There were even instances of noblewomen pressuring their husbands into converting to their faith.

The Reformation affected women not only through new religious ideas but also through institutional and political changes. Protestant reformers stressed the value and sanctity of marriage, challenging the medieval tendency to denigrate women and encourage celibacy. Luther considered marriage a divinely ordained union and a natural vocation for women. Although he and other Protestant reformers exalted the state of marriage and urged that husbands treat their wives in a kindly manner and share authority with them within the household, they nevertheless insisted that women remain subject to men in that union. Convinced that women's primary duty was to obey their husbands and bear children, the reformers did not want them to serve as ministers or hold too many public responsibilities. A strong patriarchal family seemed indispensable to the social stability of the state.

Laws regulating marriage were quite equitable: if a marriage failed, women had the same right as men to divorce and remarry. Unlike Catholics, who permitted only separation from bed and board, Protestant reformers allowed divorce under circumstances such as abuse, abandonment, or adultery. Still, the various Protestant denominations discouraged the breakup of families, permitting divorce only after all efforts to reconcile had failed. Even "liberated" women rarely sought divorce, which was apt to leave them without financial support.

The closing of convents in Protestant territories imposed a cruel hardship on many nuns. Some married or returned to their paternal homes, but most were left alone to face the hazards of life. They took whatever employment was available; some found no work, while others, in desperation, even turned to prostitution.

Protestant leaders, eager to increase biblical literacy and make individuals better Christians, encouraged education for women and men alike. They established schools for both sexes at the primary and secondary levels, as well as academies and colleges to train pastors and male lay church workers. Education gave women an opportunity to find employment as teachers or become authors. Although illiteracy remained pervasive in Europe, a base for expanding educational opportunity had been laid: it proved to be one of the most enduring legacies of the Reformation.

The Roman Catholic or Counter-Reformation

Rome responded hesitantly and slowly to the Protestant challenge and to calls for changes from within. But as hopes for reconciliation dimmed and Protestantism continued to make gains, the Catholic church launched a vigorous counterattack on a number of fronts, a response termed variously the Catholic Reformation or Counter-Reformation. First and foremost, success in halting the spread of Protestantism and reclaiming lost lands depended heavily on reform within the Roman Catholic church. Long before Luther acted at Wittenberg, many sincere and devout Catholics, disturbed at the deterioration of the church, had urged that a general council be held to carry through needed reforms. The popes had resisted summoning a church council, in part because they were mindful of the efforts of the conciliar movement in the fifteenth century to strip them of their authority. Ultimately, however, the pressure for reform became too great, and Pope Paul III (reigned 1534–1549) called for a church council.

The most important work of the council, which met at Trent, in northern Italy, between 1545 and 1563, dealt with doctrinal matters. All doctrines, especially those under Protestant attack, were reaffirmed. They were set out in clear and precise terms and their differences with Protestantism were specified. The council also outlined a comprehensive

Map 9.4 Catholics and Protestants in Europe by 1560. Reformation religious upheavals affected most of Europe, with Protestant faiths predominant in the north. Protestantism also made substantial headway in France, the Habsburg dominions, southern Germany, and Poland, but these areas eventually reverted to Roman Catholicism.

program of reform. It condemned such corrupt practices as simony, pluralism, and nepotism and made provisions for better discipline and higher educational standards among the clergy.

Besides reforming itself, the Catholic church took measures to halt the spread of Protestant beliefs. The council instituted the Index of Forbidden Books—a list of books, periodically revised, that Catholics were forbidden to read. The council also revived and extended the Inquisition to combat heresy and the practice of witchcraft. The work of the Council of Trent created a foundation on which a new, more vibrant Catholic church could be built.

The most effective single weapon of the Catholic church in battling the Protestants was the Society of Jesus, popularly called the Jesuit order. Founded by Ignatius Loyola (1491–1556), a Basque noble and former soldier, the order was modeled on military lines, highly disciplined, and devoted to actively promoting and defending the teachings of the church. Applicants for membership were carefully screened, and those selected had to pass rigorous training and a long apprenticeship. When found ready, they were sent to whatever field seemed most in need of their services.

The Jesuits were effective missionaries, carrying the gospel to nations as far away as China, Japan, and South America. Some became priests and from the pulpits preached simple sermons that stressed morality. As confessors and advisers to kings and princes, they were able to influence state policy to the benefit of Catholicism. They won their greatest fame, however, in the field of education. In Europe the Jesuits built schools or took over existing ones and in many areas were the dominant force in education. Their results were impressive. Through their dedication and zeal, they played a key role in holding southern Germany and France and in bringing Poland and much of Hungary back to Catholicism.

The zealous efforts of the Catholic church to stamp out Protestantism led to bitter religious wars in the late sixteenth century and first half of the seventeenth. England experienced an attempted invasion by Catholic Spain in 1588, and heavy sectarian fighting occurred in the Netherlands, France, and elsewhere in Europe (see Chapter 11). In Germany the Peace of Augsburg proved to be only an uneasy truce. The growing tensions finally erupted into a destructive conflict, known as the Thirty Years' War, which began in 1618 and continued until 1648. Over time, every major power became involved in the struggle, and the character of the war changed from religious to political. Protestant and Catholic armies, mostly composed of mercenaries, crisscrossed the German landscape, wreaking havoc.

The stalemated Thirty Years' War ended in 1648 with the Treaty of Westphalia. Most of the contending major powers demanded and received grants of territory as compensation for their efforts. Politically the settlement practically dissolved the Holy Roman Empire, though it continued to exist as a formal entity. Each German prince was recognized as a sovereign ruler, free to govern his state without interference by the emperor. The key religious clause accorded Calvinist rulers the same right to determine the religion practiced in their territories that Catholic and Lutheran princes had enjoyed since 1555. All in all, Germany was the big loser. Perhaps 300,000 soldiers and civilians were killed during campaigns, and several times that number died from malnutrition and disease. The damage wrecked the economy of the German states and caused many Germans to migrate to North America.

The Treaty of Westphalia, like the Peace of Augsburg, did not quell religious enmities. Religious strife continued to plague Europe, but on a far smaller scale than in the previous century. By regenerating itself and taking the offensive, the Catholic church had staged a strong comeback, stemming the Protestant tide and even winning back some lands that seemed irretrievably lost. But it could not regain domination over all of Western Christendom. After 1648 the religious map of Europe would not change appreciably.

European Expansion

Beginning in the fifteenth century the new European monarchies, which, as discussed earlier in this chapter, had achieved a high degree of national unification, embarked on five centuries of expansion that brought European power to every continent on the globe. Most of the indigenous societies around the world felt the impact of this movement in one way or another. Some were relatively untouched; many were profoundly altered; a number were destroyed. In the process Western society would itself feel the impact of other cultures.

European overseas expansion occurred for numerous reasons. The new national states of western Europe were now sufficiently centralized to support and finance exploration and expansion. Technological advances in navigational systems and ship design enabled sailors to undertake longer voyages. Moreover, Europeans had visions of wealth; gold, pepper, ivory, and slaves from Africa were all valued commodities on world markets. European governments and merchants were also eager to find alternative ocean routes so they could avoid the high import taxes imposed by the Ottoman Empire on goods coming overland from Asia by caravans. For Spain and Portugal, religion also played a role. After the long struggle (*Reconquista*) that ended Muslim supremacy of the Iberian Peninsula, the devoutly Christian rulers of Spain and Portugal were eager to dominate the Islamic states in North Africa and to convert non-Christians. Some Europeans even dreamed of forging links with the legendary African kingdom of the Christian leader Prester John.

Portugal was the first to move. With a long maritime tradition and an advantageous geographic position on the Atlantic, Portugal was the first European nation to look for a seaborne route to tap the wealth of the Atlantic Islands, Africa, and (hopefully) Asia. Beginning in the 1430s, Prince Henry (later called the "Navigator" by the English), the brother of the king of Portugal, used the royal treasury to finance voyages of discovery down the African coast; by 1498 the Portuguese were in Asia. In 1492, with the voyage of Columbus, Spain moved westward to the Americas. A century later, England, France, and the Netherlands joined in. The text will take up European expansion in the context of the cultures of each geographic area the Europeans entered; this chapter will discuss Africa and the Western Hemisphere, and Chapter 10 will deal with Asia.

African Kingdoms, European Contacts, and the Slave Trade

Your people . . . seize many of our people, freed and exempt men; and very often it happens that they kidnap even noblemen and the sons of noblemen, and our relatives, and take them to be sold to the white men. . . .

And as soon as they are taken by the white men they are immediately ironed and branded with fire, and when they are carried to be embarked, if they are caught by our guards' men the whites allege that they have bought them but they cannot say from whom. . . .

And so to avoid such a great evil we passed a law so that any white man living in our Kingdoms and wanting to purchase goods in any way should first inform three of our noblemen and officials of our court . . . who should investigate if the mentioned goods are captives or free men. . . . But if the white men do not comply with it they will lose the aforementioned goods. *

*A letter by King Afonso of the Kongo to the King of Portugal, October 18, 1526, in *Horizon History of Africa* (New York: American Heritage, 1971), p. 334.

In this letter in 1526, King Afonso, a convert to Christianity, complains of the excesses of European slave traders in his Kongo Kingdom. The slave trade became an important aspect of a dynamic and complex situation in Africa during the period from the fifteenth to the seventeenth century. The Portuguese moved down the West African coast and eventually to southern and eastern Africa, beginning the trade for the riches of those regions. In the fourteenth century, when Europeans first began to make extensive contact, many societies in West Africa had been, in economic terms, nearly as prosperous as those in most of Europe. The slave trade substantially altered that balance. As it turned out, the greatest wealth for European traders was to be found in the labor of human beings. The slave trade devastated many regions of Africa; it also profoundly changed the Western Hemisphere (see the following section). The ensuing discussion will focus on a number of African societies beginning about the fifteenth century, when European explorers and traders began to have extensive contact with local African rulers and peoples.

European Entry into Africa

In the early fifteenth century, the Portuguese began to move into Africa. Portugal's first target was Morocco, where it conquered small coastal areas. During the next half-century the Portuguese worked down the West African coast to Angola. The voyages of Bartholomeu Dias in 1487–1488 and Vasco da Gama in 1497–1499 opened up the Cape of Good Hope and East Africa to Portuguese traders and explorers; in 1498 da Gama arrived in India (see Chapter 10). At the East African city-state of Malindi, a king seated on a bronze chair and wearing an ornate robe trimmed in green satin greeted da Gama. The leaders of Malindi welcomed an alliance with the Portuguese as an aid in their commercial rivalry against traders in Mombasa.

Traders and adventurers, the Portuguese were not initially interested in founding colonies in Africa. However, they did establish fortified trading posts at strategic ports along the western and eastern coasts. Fort Sao Jorge was established at Elmina on the west coast in 1482. In 1576 it was followed by Luanda, which became a major center for the transport of slaves from Angola. Along the East African coast the Portuguese extracted tribute from the local rulers of Kilwa and later extended their domination over the older commercial city-states of Malindi and Mombasa.

African forces from the interior frequently attacked the Portuguese enclaves, limiting Portuguese domination to the coastal regions. Mombasa resisted for so many decades that the Portuguese nicknamed it the Island of War. In 1592 the Portuguese finally seized Mombasa and largely destroyed local opposition. Afterward they built a new outpost, called Fort Jesus, which still stands as evidence of Portuguese presence in Africa.

Although the Portuguese struggled to monopolize the African trade routes and the access they provided for the Asian trade, they were quickly challenged by the Spanish, Dutch, English, and other European powers. By 1630 English traders were operating along West Africa; the French and Dutch soon followed them. The Swedes and Danes also competed for territorial footholds in Ghana, or the Gold Coast. The Dutch proved a particularly formidable rival, and by 1610 they had effectively ended Portuguese dominance in the Indian Ocean. These rival European powers build many forts and military installations along the West African coast; these installations were intended primarily to defend the nation's trading interests against competing Europeans, not as protection against the African states.

As Portuguese naval power waned in the seventeenth century, first Mombasa and then other East African city-states revolted. Mombasa requested aid from fellow Muslims, most notably from the *imam* (leader) of Oman, on the Arabian coast. The Omanis, who had a long naval tradition, quickly responded and after several failures succeeded in ousting the Portuguese from Mombasa in 1698 and subsequently from neighboring East African city-states. The Omanis then established a Muslim empire in coastal East Africa that lasted into the nineteenth century.

Dutch Settlements in South Africa

In 1652, at Table Bay in South Africa, the Dutch founded Africa's first European settlement. Originally, the settlement was intended as a reprovisioning station for ships of the Dutch East India Company undertaking the long voyage between Europe and Asia; it was not meant to be an outpost for further Dutch settlement or colonial expansion. However, the persistent need for fresh food supplies led the Dutch East India Company to bring in colonists to establish farms in South Africa in 1657. Slaves were then brought in as forced laborers.

As the colony expanded, the Dutch attacked the indigenous Khoi, who were forcibly dispersed. The colonists recruited single Dutch women so that the predominantly male population of the colony could marry Europeans. French Huguenots who fled the persecution of Louis XIV reinforced the Dutch settlers. These frontier farmers, who called themselves both Boers (farmers) and Afrikaners, were strict Calvinists. Their descendants continued to dominate South Africa well into the twentieth century.

The Boers viewed black Africans as inferior human beings and used their strict Calvinist tenets to justify their attitude of racial superiority. They established a system of strict social and racial stratification in which the Dutch Boers were placed at the top, followed by later Asian immigrants and coloreds (people of mixed race), with blacks at the bottom. This racial hierarchy based on white European domination continued into the 1990s. Racism, the belief in the superiority and inferiority of differing peoples based on race, was not, however, confined to the Dutch in South Africa. It was common in European and American societies and was frequently used to justify the enslavement of African peoples.

The Slave Trade in Africa

The slave trade was a key factor of European expansion and had disastrous results for African peoples. As in many other societies and cultures, slavery had very deep roots in Africa and was known in antiquity. Africans had enslaved other Africans, and, although there were Qur'anic injunctions against such practices, Islamic societies in Africa had perpetuated the system. It persisted throughout Africa and especially in the Sudan in the ninth century, and it was practiced in other parts of the continent as well. African slaves could be found throughout the Islamic world, in India, and perhaps also in China prior to European expansion into these areas. Slavery in Africa and the Islamic world was not based on race or religion, however. Animists, Christians, and Muslims in Africa and elsewhere had historically enslaved members of their own and other religions. As in most civilizations up to this time, Africans acquired slaves from raids or victories in wars. In African and Islamic cultures, slaves were generally treated as part of the family and were integrated into the larger society. Most such slaves in the Islamic world served as domestic servants, concubines, or slave-soldiers.

The extensive trade in African slaves by the Western nations between the late fifteenth and the nineteenth centuries severely affected the social, cultural, economic, and even political life of the African societies. Although experts disagree on how adversely this

The regions shown were the principal sources of slaves.
The figures are for 1526–1810.
From 1526 to 1870 about 10 million slaves were shipped from Africa to:

Europe	175,000
Spanish America	1,552,000
Brazil	3,647,000
British Caribbean	1,665,000
British North America and United States	399,000
French America	1,600,000
Dutch America	500,000
Danish West Indies	28,000

Map 9.5 Africa, 1500–c. 1750, and the Slave Trade. By the sixteenth century, Islam had spread throughout much of North and East Africa, while many independent kingdoms and city-states continued to prosper. Along the African coasts, European explorers also founded small trading posts, where the slave trade flourished as growing numbers of Africans were transported as slave labor for plantations in the Western Hemisphere.

Memoirs of a Slave

The first object which saluted my eyes when I arrived on the coast was the sea, and a slave ship which was then riding at anchor and waiting for its cargo. These filled me with astonishment, which was soon converted into terror when I was carried on board. I was immediately handled and tossed up to see if I were sound . . . and I was now persuaded that I had gotten into a world of bad spirits and that they were going to kill me. Their complexions too differing so much from ours, their long hair and the language they spoke (which was very different from any I had ever heard) united to confirm me in this belief. . . .

I now saw myself deprived of all chance of returning to my native country. . . . I became so sick and low that I was not able to eat. . . . In a little time after, amongst the poor chained men I found some of my own nation. . . . I inquired of these what was to be done with us; they gave me to understand we were to be carried to these white people's country to work for them.*

The slave trade persisted for centuries. In the above excerpt, Olaudah Equiano, from present-day Nigeria, described his reactions to being captured and taken into slavery. Equiano was taken to the West Indies, Canada, England, and the United States; he was freed in 1766 and became a spokesperson for the antislavery movement (see Chapter 11). His memoirs offer a moving testimony to the human cost of slavery and its disruption of African society.*

*Olaudah Equiano, in Modern Asia and Africa, ed. William H. McNeill and Mitsuko Iriye (New York: Oxford University Press, 1971), pp. 82–84.

trade affected African development, none deny its social and economic consequences. Although Muslims and Europeans took some African slaves for sale in Europe, the Canary and Madeira Islands, Muslim North Africa, the Ottoman Empire, and Asia, the vast majority of those taken by the Europeans and their African allies were sent to the Western Hemisphere for sale.

In contrast to the work of slaves in other societies, the overwhelming majority of slaves in the Western Hemisphere were used as agricultural workers on vast cotton, tobacco, or sugar plantations or as laborers in copper and silver mines. As only able-bodied men and women were suitable for such hard labor, most slaves taken from Africa were young males from fifteen to thirty years of age. Although experts disagree on the exact numbers, it appears that between 10 and 15 million Africans were forcibly removed from their homelands to become slaves in the Americas; in addition, possibly several million more were killed or died during armed raids to secure the slaves, and the forced marches and brutal conditions to which the captives were subjected.

The first African slaves were shipped from Spain to Latin America in 1501. By 1518 Spanish slave traders had established direct trade routes between Africa and the Americas. Recognizing the enormous profits to be made in this human traffic, the Portuguese, English, French, and Dutch also engaged in the slave trade. For the most part, European slave traffickers did not capture the slaves, but paid professional African slave traders, or local political leaders, to secure slaves from the interior and to bring them to ports or marshaling yards on the coast. They were then herded into ships for the long voyage to the Western Hemisphere.

Although their African owners or rulers sold some slaves as punishment, most were captured through wars and raids. Slave hunting was a violent activity. Able-bodied men and women were torn from their villages, shackled in chains, and fastened together in long lines by strips of rawhide. These long human chains were then forcibly marched to either the East or West African coast, where European traders purchased them. Many slaves died of abuse or committed suicide before they ever reached the coasts. Others (at least 15 percent) died of inadequate food or diseases in the overcrowded, vermin-infested ships that transported the slaves to the Americas. Slave revolts were not uncommon, particularly among Muslim Africans, especially after they reached the Western Hemisphere.

African leaders who cooperated with European slave traders became rich from the slave trade. They coveted European armaments with which to extend their authority. The Songhai leaders in northwest Africa, for example, sold slaves for horses and guns. On Goree Island off the coast of present-day Senegal, one of the major trading depots for the traffic in human beings, West African women, who often engaged in commerce, controlled the sale of slaves brought from the interior regions. Likewise, some Muslim African traders became wealthy from the slave trade in East Africa and the Sudan. On the other hand, some African leaders sought to stop or to contain the trade. The obas in Benin banned the export of males from their territories until the end of the seventeenth century. King Afonso I in the Kongo also protested the trade and made numerous attempts to control and to curtail it.

In Angola, where the Portuguese were particularly active, Africans fiercely opposed the slave trade and foreign intervention. The Portuguese had made considerable inroads into Angola during the reign of weak monarchs, but in 1623–1624 Nzinga Mbandi ascended to the throne. As strong a ruler as Cleopatra of Egypt or Catherine the Great of Russia, Nzinga was an astute diplomat and politician. Forbidding her subjects to call her queen, Nzinga took the title king and promptly launched a lifelong struggle against the Portuguese. She joined forces with the Dutch against the Portuguese and lured Portuguese slave-soldiers to desert by promising them freedom and land. In spite of several uneasy treaties with the Portuguese, she continued fighting them until her death in

Slave Ship. This diagram shows how slaves were "packed" into ships for the long and often fatal journey to the Americas. Crowded on and below decks, slaves frequently died of asphyxiation, thirst, and disease during the long Atlantic crossing.

1663. No strong ruler followed Nzinga. As a result, the Portuguese were able to prevail, and slave raids increasingly decimated Angolan villages.

While coastal areas of Africa frequently prospered because of the slave trade, many villages, farms, and political institutions in the interior were weakened or destroyed. Damage to the cultural and economic life of African societies varied greatly from region to region. The forced removal of vital segments of their populations had lasting impact on some African societies. Many major states, however, particularly West African states like Benin, survived the attacks. Most African states remained independent of outside rule until the nineteenth century (see Chapter 13).

One of the most abusive and inhumane enterprises shared between Africa and the West, slavery spread throughout much of the Western Hemisphere in the following century. Slavery profoundly altered traditional social, economic, and political patterns in both Africa and the Western Hemisphere.

European Colonial Empires in the Western Hemisphere

Strange people have come to the shores of the great sea [the Caribbean]. . . . Their trappings and arms are all made of iron; they dress in iron and wear iron casques on their heads. Their swords are made of iron; their shields are iron; their spears are iron. Their deer carry them on their backs wherever they wish to go. Those deer, our lord, are as tall as the roof of a house. . . . The strangers' bodies are completely covered, so that only their faces can be seen. Their skin is white, as if it were made of lime. They have yellow hair, though some of them are black[-haired]. Their dogs are enormous, with flat ears and long dangling tongues. . . . Their eyes flash fire. [Referring to a gun:] a thing like a ball of stone comes out of its entrails; it comes out shooting sparks and raining fire. The smoke that comes out has a pestilent odor, like rotten mud. . . . If the cannon is aimed against a mountain, the mountain splits and cracks open.*

**Miguel Leon-Portilla, ed., *The Broken Spears: The Aztec Account of the Conquest of Mexico*, trans. A. M. Garibay and L. Kemp (Boston: Beacon Press, 1969), pp. 30–31.

This vivid description of the Spanish arrival in Mexico was in a report given to Moctezuma, the Aztec ruler, by his spies who observed the landing and advance of the Spaniards in 1519. The presence of the Spanish in the heartland of Mesoamerican civilization was but one aspect of a remarkable phenomenon, the expansion of European power around the globe during the sixteenth century. As has been seen in the previous section, Europeans were already constructing fortified trading posts along the African coast and building up the slave trade. Europeans were also appearing on the shores of Asia (see Chapter 10).

Early European Exploration of the Western Hemisphere

Spanish and Portuguese explorers and settlers were the first Europeans to make a lasting impact on the Western Hemisphere. Christopher Columbus, an Italian financed by Queen Isabella of Castile, led the way. By sailing west, Columbus hoped to find a shorter route to Asia than the one the Portuguese were pursuing around the African coast. He calculated Japan to be about 2,400 miles west of the Canary Islands (off the northwestern coast of Africa), putting Asia within range of the sailing ships of that day. On

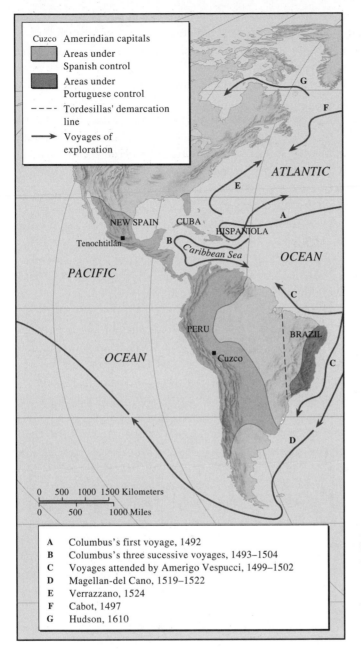

Map 9.6 The Western Hemisphere, c. 1600. After a century of exploration and conquest, Spain had created a huge colonial holding, based in large part on the ruins of the Aztec and Inka Empires. The Portuguese were beginning to create a major colony in Brazil.

A	Columbus's first voyage, 1492
B	Columbus's three sucessive voyages, 1493–1504
C	Voyages attended by Amerigo Vespucci, 1499–1502
D	Magellan-del Cano, 1519–1522
E	Verrazzano, 1524
F	Cabot, 1497
G	Hudson, 1610

October 12, 1492, Columbus made landfall in the Bahamas, approximately where he had calculated Asia to be. Assuming that he was off the coast of Asia, he called the islands the "Indies" and their inhabitants "Indians" (in this text, Amerindians). In 1493 Columbus triumphantly returned to Spain.

In January 1492, just a few months before Columbus's first voyage, the Spanish had conquered Granada, the last Muslim enclave on the Iberian Peninsula. The victory marked the completion of seven centuries of the *Reconquista* (Reconquest) of the Iberian Peninsula from the Muslims, a crusade that left a profound impact on Spanish institutions and practices. The struggle against the Muslims had forged a powerful partnership between church and state in Spanish society. The end of the *Reconquista* left a large number of men who were looking for new and profitable adventures and for new areas for Christianity to conquer.

During the quarter-century after Columbus's landing in the Bahamas, the Spanish occupied the major Caribbean islands. They found that European crops and domestic animals could thrive in the Western Hemisphere. Eventually it became clear that the islands could produce valuable crops of sugar and tobacco. These products, however, required constant attention and thus a large labor force.

To get this labor, the Spanish instituted the *encomienda* system, in which the Spanish king gave individuals control over Amerindian lands and villages. The *encomiendero* had the right to force the Amerindians under his control to work in his mines and fields. This brutal labor system and the ravages of new diseases from Europe, plus secondary factors, killed nearly all of the Amerindians in the Caribbean. Deprived of a native work force, the Spanish imported large numbers of black slaves from Africa.

To avoid confrontation, the Spanish and Portuguese negotiated a treaty to divide the Western Hemisphere between them. Under the Treaty of Tordesillas in 1494, the pope selected a line of longitude in which Spain received everything west of the line and Portugal everything east of it. The treaty technically gave Asia, the East Indies, and Brazil to Portugal, while everything else in the Western Hemisphere went to Spain. In 1500 Pedro Cabral landed in Brazil and formally claimed the area for Portugal. Brazil eventually became a major sugar-producing area.

Meanwhile, Europeans were readjusting their thinking about the nature of the lands that Columbus had found. After two voyages to the Western Hemisphere in which he visited much of the eastern coast of South America, Amerigo Vespucci claimed in 1501 that he had seen a "new land . . . a continent." In 1507 cartographers putting out a new map labeled the area representing present-day Brazil "America" in his honor.

By the early sixteenth century it was becoming clear that Asia was far away from Europe, with the new "America" in between. In 1513 Vasco Núñez de Balboa crossed the Panamanian isthmus and saw what he called the South Sea (the present-day Pacific Ocean), a sea that ships might sail on to Asia if a way could be found to get through or around America to enter it. Various European expeditions searched for a "Passage to India," a water route around or through America that led to Asia. They all failed, confirming the dismaying proposition that America was an unbroken barrier that extended northward and southward from the Caribbean to the stormy and icy waters of the Arctic and Antarctic seas.

In 1519 the Spanish government dispatched an expedition under Ferdinand Magellan to find a passage to Asia that would justify a Spanish claim to some of the southeast Asian Spice Islands held by the Portuguese. Magellan fought his way for thirty-eight days through a stormy water passage (later called the Straits of Magellan) at the tip of South America. Afterwards, Magellan pushed across the enormous stretches of Balboa's South Sea, which Magellan termed the Pacific (from Latin for "calm") Ocean. His men died from lack of water and ate rats to survive. In 1521 he reached the Philippines, where he was killed in a skirmish. His navigator, Juan Sebastián del Cano, and one surviving ship pushed on across the Indian Ocean, reaching Spain in September 1522, three years after their departure. This first circumnavigation of the globe was one of the great epics of human bravery and was the high mark of the age of European exploration. The discoveries of Magellan and del Cano demonstrated that Asia was too far away, and the trip too dangerous, for a successful trade route westward to Asia. Although holding on to the Philippine Islands, Spain would have to derive its main colonial wealth from the Western Hemisphere, not the Eastern.

Spanish Conquests in Mexico and South America

Great wealth was not long in coming to the Spanish. For years Spaniards had heard tales of Amerindian empires of gold and silver on the mainland of present-day Mexico. In 1519 Hernán Cortés organized an expedition of 11 vessels, 550 men, 16 horses, and 10 cannon, and sailed from Cuba to the Mexican coast. Marching inland, Cortés swiftly reached the outer fringes of the Aztec Empire.

Aided by large forces of Amerindian allies disaffected by the parasitic rule of the Aztecs, Cortés and his tiny band of Spaniards defeated the Aztecs and conquered Mexico. The key reasons were clear. Cortés himself gave much credit to his Amerindian allies, both as warriors and porters. The Tlaxcalans, armed with razor-sharp obsidian weapons, were especially effective. The Spanish firearms and cannon, as well as metal armor and weapons, totally outclassed the Aztec's stone-age weapons and cotton armor. In battle the Spanish horses and huge mastiffs, which were unknown to the Amerindians, often unnerved them. Cortés also capitalized on prophecies in Mexican folklore that seemed to foretell his coming.

Disease was perhaps the greatest ally of Cortés. An epidemic of smallpox saved Cortés from an Amerindian revolt in 1520. Since Amerindians did not have natural immunities to the many diseases the Europeans carried, including smallpox, measles, and influenza, the ravages of these diseases continued unabated. When Cortés landed, there were about 28 million persons in the Mexican heartland. Fifty years later the population had plummeted to 3 million. By 1620 only 1 million Amerindians lived in the area. As a result of the massive depopulation, Amerindian culture in the Western Hemisphere was substantially demolished.

In 1532 the Mexican story was repeated in Peru when Francisco Pizarro led a force of 170 men into the Andes, looking for the gold and silver of the Inka Empire. Inka rule centered in the mountains of present-day Peru, Ecuador, Bolivia, and northern Chile. Like the Aztecs, the Inkas had only lately come to power (see Chapter 7). By the time the Spanish arrived, the Inkas ruled about 8 million persons living in an area about half the size of the Roman Empire at its height. The Inka state was a rigid autocracy in which all power focused in the person of the ruler, the Inka; this proved to be a fatal weakness.

Finding this highly structured civilization divided by civil war and racked by an epidemic, Pizarro captured, imprisoned, and murdered the Inka ruler Atahualpa and destroyed every element of the Inka leadership; by 1533 he had gained control over the empire.

The *conquistadores* in Mexico and Peru were well rewarded for their ruthless daring. They robbed the Amerindians of their gold and silver objects and then searched for deposits to mine. In both Mexico and the Andes they found substantial supplies of gold and huge amounts of silver. Their search for precious metals and other opportunities for wealth took them into the southern third of the present-day United States, throughout Central America and across much of South America outside Brazil. A very rich lode was discovered at Cerro Potosí in Bolivia in 1545, which supplied enormous quantities of silver to the Spaniards. Potosí had a population of 160,000 persons in 1650, when the silver mine was at its most productive. It shrank to a minor town of 8,000 persons by 1825, when the mine had been largely depleted.

To exploit the wealth of the Inka Empire, the Spanish instituted a forced labor regime that was, if anything, more brutal than those in Mexico or the Caribbean. Inka rulers had demanded *mit'a* (forced labor) from their subjects. The Spanish claimed that their own demand for forced labor was an extension of the mit'a; under the Inkas, however, mit'a demands were harsh, but could be met without starvation and other ills that became prevalent under the Spanish. The dangerous and arduous labor in the mines killed many Amerindians. Coupled with recurrent epidemics, the Andean population declined in the same proportion as in Mexico, with the same devastating cultural results.

It is likely that the Amerindians gave their conquerors syphilis in exchange for the terrible plagues that had been let loose among them. Syphilis raged for decades as an epidemic, mortal disease in Europe. Eventually it became a slow-acting but still immensely dangerous disease.

In the middle of the sixteenth century, the Amerindians were proclaimed subjects under the protection of the crown. As such they could no longer be legally enslaved, but many were still worked to death in the mines, businesses, and fields of their Spanish overlords. Over time, racial interrelationships created many individuals of mixed ancestry called *mestizos,* who eventually formed a major element in the Latin American population.

Based on the toil of this Amerindian and *mestizo* work force, fleets carried enormous wealth in silver, hides, gold, dyes, cacao, and quinine from the mainland of the Western Hemisphere to Spain. The Spanish monarchy, from its share of the precious metals and from taxes, received 40 percent of the value of these shipments. Two fleets from Spain carrying food, clothing, wine, tools, household items, and a few settlers sailed to the Western Hemisphere annually, but the goods sent over were inadequate for the colonial population.

The Spanish and Portuguese, in name at least, made their colonies Roman Catholic. In many areas church teachings mixed with indigenous Amerindian and African religious practices. Some of the Spanish religious leaders went to great lengths to destroy all remnants of the Amerindian heritage on the grounds that their pre-Conquest culture was based on devil worship, sodomy, and cannibalism. A Spanish bishop destroyed all the pre-Conquest Maya books that he could locate because they contained aspects of the old religion. Of the hundreds of Maya books that once existed, only four survived to modern times. In many areas Catholic churchmen were responsible for exploration and settlement. Some priests also led the fight for more humane treatment for the Amerindians.

Several aspects of the Western Hemisphere were transmitted to Europe. Foods such as potatoes, maize, several varieties of peppers, tomatoes, chocolate, and many others became a part of the European diet; maize became a staple in China.

Rival Empires in the Western Hemisphere

By the middle of the sixteenth century, the Spanish and Portuguese had used the Western Hemisphere as an arena to create enormous colonial empires. Unlike the collection of fortified coastal towns and trading depots set up by the Portuguese in Africa and Asia, the Spanish colonies constituted a territory many times larger than Spain itself. Portugal created an equivalently huge colony in Brazil.

During most of the sixteenth century, while the Spanish and Portuguese exploited the riches of Latin America, the English, French, and Dutch, preoccupied with religious wars and other domestic problems, stayed home. Late in the century, however, these nations were ready to compete with the Spanish and Portuguese; in particular, they had devised effective economic incentives to foster their own colonialism. The Spanish and Portuguese had allowed a small percentage of their business community to monopolize opportunities abroad, thus limiting available investment resources. In contrast, the English, French, and Dutch governments encouraged merchants and bankers to invest in overseas commerce by granting charters to new "joint stock" companies specializing in trading and colonization. Participants in joint stock companies had their risks limited to the proportion of their investment; this restricted liability encouraged smaller investors to put their money in new overseas companies. Investment was further encouraged by

Forced Labor in Peru, 1652

According to His Majesty's warrant, the mine owners on this massive range have a right ... to 13,300 Indians in working and exploitation of the mines. It is the duty of the Corregidor of Potosi [governor] to have them rounded up and to see that they come in from all the provinces. . . . These Indians are sent out every year under a captain. . . . This works very badly, with great losses and gaps in the quotas of Indians, the villages being depopulated. . . . After each has eaten his ration, they climb up the hill, each to his mine, and go in, staying there from that hour until Saturday evening without coming out of the mine; their wives bring them food, but they stay constantly underground, excavating and carrying out the ore from which they get the silver. They all have tallow candles, lighted day and night; that is

the light they work with, for as they are underground, they have need of it all the time. The mere cost of these candles used in the mines ... will amount every year to more than 300,000 pesos, even though tallow is cheap in that country, being abundant; but this is a very great expense, and it is almost incredible, how much is spent for candles in the operation of breaking down and getting out the ore.*

The above description of forced Amerindian labor in silver mines provided insight both into the working conditions for the miners and attitudes of Spanish observers. This report revealed rather more concern over the cost of candles than for the health or well-being of the Amerindian workers.

*"The Potosi Mine and Indian Forced Labor in Peru," in Antonio Vasques de Espinosa, Compendium and Description of the West Indies, trans. C. U. Clark (Washington: Smithsonian Institution, 1942), pp. 623–625, in Peter N. Stearns, ed., Documents in World History, vol. 2 (New York: Harper & Row, 1988), pp. 83–84.

LIVES AND TIMES ACROSS CULTURES

New Stuff on Your Plate

We have already seen two important results of European conquests in the Western Hemisphere: one was the migration of millions of Europeans and Africans to the Americas, and the second was the spread of diseases, especially smallpox, which decimated the Amerindian populations. A third effect was the reciprocal introduction of new foods. Europeans brought with them both field crops and livestock. Wheat now supplemented the indigenous maize, and citrus fruits and grapes also enjoyed local success in the Americas. On the other hand, cash crops like sugar, rice, bananas, and tobacco (indigenous) enriched the landowning elite in the Americas.

Before Columbus, the Amerindians had domesticated only dogs, turkeys, ducks, alpacas, and llamas—none of which provided much food or hauling power. Worst of all, the Amerindians had few animals that could turn grass into meat. The European introduction of sheep, goats, swine, cattle, and horses varied the diet of many and furnished powerful draft animals. Later, horses, cattle, and sheep became the basis of full-scale Amerindian herding and riding cultures among, for example, the Navaho and the Apache.

At the same time, Amerindian field and tuber crops had a tremendous impact in Europe after 1500.

Maize and potatoes spread through the Eastern Hemisphere, superseding indigenous staples because they supplied more nutrients per hectare.

The potato, native to the cool valleys of the Andes, adapted very readily to temperate northern Europe, providing the dietary mainstay from Ireland to Russia. The Dutch peasant family portrayed in Van Gogh's *The Potato Eaters* could just as well have been Peruvian. Maize, native to warm Mesoamerica, was adopted in much of southern Europe; its cultivation in Africa increased steadily till, by the 1990s, it had become the leading consumer crop on that continent. Maize and sweet potatoes became major crops in Asia, surpassed only by rice and wheat. Other Amerindian foods that proliferated around the world were tomatoes, squash, certain beans, and peanuts. Manioc (cassava) was an important food crop, first in Brazil and later in Africa.

Enormous economic consequences flowed from the improvement of diet ensured by maize and potato farming. In the British Isles, for example, the new crops spurred population growth, thereby furnishing both the labor and the consumer basis for the Industrial Revolution.

---

easier access to marine insurance. The wealth brought into Europe from the Western Hemisphere later helped to fuel further European expansion into Asia (see Chapter 10).

At first the northern nations concentrated on finding a share of the Asia trade. During the sixteenth century, despite the discouraging news of earlier explorers, many northern Europeans hoped that a water route to Asia might yet be found somewhere in the northern latitudes. Beginning in 1497 English, French, and Dutch expeditions hunted for a "Northwest Passage" around North America, but to their dismay found the northern seas clogged with impenetrable ice. However, the explorers did learn that the northern parts of North America contained valuable timber and furs and that the North Atlantic teemed with fish.

As hopes of finding a northern route to Asia faded, the northern European nations turned their attention to the Western Hemisphere. Since Spain and Portugal monopolized the wealth of the most valuable parts of the Americas, England, France, and the Netherlands had to fight their way in. In the beginning this meant smuggling goods and slaves into the Spanish colonies; the Dutch were particularly active in this. Soon the interlopers were attacking Spanish and Portuguese ships laden with wealth bound for Europe. Pirates, both freelance "buccaneers" and marauders secretly outfitted by European governments, pillaged the "Spanish Main," raiding Spanish silver fleets and attacking Caribbean ports.

By the mid-seventeenth century, the English, French, and Dutch were strong enough to attempt the conquest of the Spanish and Portuguese colonies in the Western Hemisphere, as well as in Africa and Asia. The Spanish and Portuguese held on to their main possessions in the Americas, but the newcomers did capture a number of small islands in the West Indies, turning them into agricultural plantations for growing sugar and tobacco. To work the crops, the English, French, and Dutch shipped in slaves from their trading posts in West Africa. The constant importation of slaves into the European plantation colonies quickly transformed the racial composition of the eastern fringe of the Western Hemisphere, replacing the original Amerindian population with a few Europeans and masses of black slaves.

Map 9.7 European Holdings in North America, c. 1685. After nearly a century of activity in North America, the French and the English had secured very disparate colonial holdings. The French presence centered on fur and deerskin trading posts radiating from a small settlement in Quebec. The English controlled an area smaller in extent but greater in population, dominated by family farms.

Slavery in Virginia. In 1619, at Jamestown, England's Virginia colony, a Dutch ship has landed with the first blacks offered for sale. The Virginians stare at the strangers, trying to gauge the economic and social consequences of purchasing them. Their decision to buy slaves radically transformed the racial composition of the Western Hemisphere.

© Bethmann/Corbis

During the seventeenth century the northern European states established new colonies on the east coast of North America. The Dutch, Swedes, and French were primarily interested in developing a lucrative fur trade with the Amerindians, but their colonies proved to be only modestly profitable, considering the cost of maintenance and defense. To cut down on costs, they brought over a few farmers to provide food.

In 1607 the English established a new kind of colony on the east coast of North America. In such colonies, often termed "New Europes," large numbers of European settlers landed, killing off or driving out the Amerindian inhabitants and setting up replicas of European society. The English authorities had originally hoped to trade with the Amerindians for skins and furs, as the French and Dutch were doing. Failing that, they wanted to find or grow the products that had made the Spanish and Portuguese rich: gold, silver, silk, spices, and tea. They had other motives as well: outflanking the Spanish; converting Amerindians to Christianity; and removing from England some of its criminals, paupers, unemployed, religious dissenters, and political unreliables. English leaders believed that the work of these people would be profitable to the merchant trading companies. Encouraged by such "boosters" as Richard Hakluyt and with varying degrees of pressure by the government and the trading companies, more than 100,000 settlers came to English North America by the middle of the seventeenth century.

To the disappointment of the English investors, many of the colonies produced little in the way of Asian and Latin American wealth. North of Chesapeake Bay, the natural products were timber, fish, grain, and meat; only the first was wanted in England. The foodstuffs, however, could be sent to the Caribbean, allowing the planters there to keep their slaves at work exclusively growing sugar and tobacco. From the Chesapeake southward, the English had more luck: Here settlers could grow tobacco and (later) rice, indigo, and cotton—all valuable products. Slave traders brought in slaves from the Caribbean and from Africa to raise these products; as a result some areas from the Chesapeake southward rapidly took on the brutal economic and social characteristics of the plantation culture of the Caribbean and Brazil.

By the mid-seventeenth century, the center of economic power in Europe had shifted from the Iberian to the North European nations. Having sufficient power and economic stability, these nations created, enlarged, and protected their colonial empires. Increasingly efficient in mercantile and banking affairs, they augmented the profits obtained from their colonies and avoided dissipating their wealth in European wars. Many English and Dutch families became wealthy from overseas trade, and company investors plowed profits from their colonial enterprises into new manufacturing and trading projects in Europe (see Chapter 11).

Summary and Comparisons

The fifteenth, sixteenth, and seventeenth centuries were marked by the rise and fall of absolutist states. The Ottoman and Safavid Empires were flourishing; several of the Atlantic-facing nations of Europe were building up centralized monarchies; and the papacy was beleaguered. The Renaissance reissue of classical histories and biographies gave some new perspective to this process. Largely as a result of European exploration and expansion, the Aztec and Inka Empires in the Western Hemisphere were overthrown.

Authoritarian government was well established in the Ottoman and Safavid Empires. Although old enemies, these empires were remarkably similar. Each was highly centralized politically and economically, and their cultural and social life shared a common Islamic heritage. Differences did exist, however, because the Ottoman Empire adhered to Sunni Islam while the Safavids were ardent believers in Shi'i Islam.

As a leading military power in the eastern Mediterranean, the Ottomans successfully absorbed the Balkans, Hungary, and the Arab lands of the eastern Mediterranean and North Africa. Ottoman attempts to take Vienna and to destroy Safavid power failed. The Ottoman Empire reached its zenith under Suleiman the Magnificent, a great patron of the arts, but steadily declined in world status afterwards.

The Safavid Empire entered its golden age under Shah Abbas, who created a new, glorious capital at Isfahan and made Persia a cultural center. Control of the silk industry provided the Safavids with economic wealth and enabled them to become patrons of the arts. Like the Ottoman Empire, the Safavids encouraged trade with European nations

CHRONOLOGY

1300	
	Petrarch and the Italian Renaissance
	The Black Death
	Renaissance in northern Europe
1450	
	Johannes Gutenberg's printing press
	Benin kingdom in West Africa
	End of Muslim rule in Spain
	Voyage of Christopher Columbus
1500	Centralization of western European monarchies
	Leonardo da Vinci
	Michelangelo Buonarroti
	Desiderius Erasmus
	Beginnings of the Safavid Empire
	Voyages of Balboa and Magellan
	Martin Luther's ninety-five theses
	Spain conquers Aztecs and Inkas
	Ottoman Turks conquer Arab territories
	Suleiman the Magnificent
	Suleimaniye complex in Istanbul
	John Calvin
	Afonso I, king of the Kongo
	Henry VIII
	Roman Catholic Reformation
	Slave trade in Africa
	Queen Elizabeth I
	Shah Abbas the Great
1600	William Shakespeare
	British and French establish colonies in North America
	Miguel de Cervantes, *Don Quixote*
	The Thirty Years' War
	"King" Nzinga in Angola
	Ashanti kingdom
	Louis XIV, the Sun King
	Dutch make settlement in South Africa
1700	

and granted special privileges to European traders. Both the Safavids and the Ottomans also maintained economic links with Asia, where other centralized empires flourished during the sixteenth and seventeenth centuries.

During these centuries European societies also underwent profound changes. In Europe, the otherworldly orientation of the Catholic church gave way to a secular outlook in thought and in art. Spurred on by refugee scholars who fled Ottoman advances in the eastern Mediterranean, Italy became the center of a remarkable intellectual, literary, and artistic reawakening called the Renaissance. Deriving inspiration from recently recovered manuscripts by classical authors of Greece and Rome, and from contacts with Islamic scholars, humanists produced superb works in history, philosophy, and philology. Drawing from nature, painters and sculptors now concentrated on capturing and interpreting the world about them. By the sixteenth and seventeenth centuries, the practices and perspectives of the Italian Renaissance also spread into western Europe. Vernacular literature flourished, and humanism became a strong force. France, England, and Spain enjoyed golden ages of literary productivity, particularly in drama.

During the fifteenth and sixteenth centuries national monarchies also developed in western Europe. These national monarchies established territorial unity and centralized governmental functions, and their monarchs overcame the opposition of the nobles by allying with towns and relying on advisers and bureaucrats from outside the aristocracy. Expanding centralized monarchies also had impacts on the relationships of European governments with the Catholic church.

The Protestant Reformation of the sixteenth century had several causes. A weakened papacy lowered popular support and abuses of simony, indulgences, and pluralism stirred reformers to action. Luther and Calvin led the movement to break with the Catholic church and to establish Protestant Christianity. Within the Roman Catholic church, humanists and clergy led reforming activities, and Pope Paul III made reform a churchwide activity. The Council of Trent reaffirmed traditional Roman Catholic doctrines and sought to eliminate abuses. Religious wars disrupted European societies until 1648, when the Treaty of Westphalia recognized both Protestant and Catholic states in Europe.

The newly unified European states along the Atlantic Ocean had also amassed the economic resources and technology necessary to explore new trade routes. Spurred on by Ottoman taxes on goods from Asia, and to some degree by a desire to make converts to Christianity, they began to search for routes to Asia that they could control. In the process they explored much of the globe and brought European power not only to Asia but to Africa and the Western Hemisphere as well.

The Portuguese, Dutch, French, and English all established trading routes along the coasts of Africa. The Portuguese were initially strongly entrenched in both West and East Africa, but they gradually lost their favored positions to the Dutch and English.

In East Africa, indigenous African and Arab opposition drove out the Portuguese, who had been weakened by Dutch naval victories in the Indian Ocean. In South Africa, the Dutch established a permanent colony based on the racial supremacy of the white

Boers. This initially small colony would have many long-term ramifications for the history of South Africa.

Finally, the slave trade, which lasted some 400 years, affected all of Africa. Millions of Africans were shipped by force to the Americas. Although some Africans cooperated and benefited from this trade, many, like "King" Nzinga of Angola, fought against it. The slave trade had many disastrous results on individual African societies, particularly in the interior of the continent. In spite of the negative impacts of the slave trade, most of Africa remained independent and continued to develop under its own political and cultural institutions until the nineteenth century.

During this era, Spain led the European expansion across the Atlantic and established a vast empire, exceedingly rich in silver, in Mexico and South America. In the course of this conquest, the great majority of Amerindians died from European diseases. Europeans also transformed the Caribbean into sugar and tobacco plantations worked by black slaves who lived and died under brutal conditions. Portugal established a similar plantation-based economy in Brazil. Three key characteristics of Iberia—paternalistic government, aristocratic privilege, and mercantilist economics—were essentially replicated in Latin America, but in this case imposed on populations who were predominantly Amerindian and black. Amerindian and black culture—especially food, clothing, textiles, music, and speech—modified the lifestyles of Europeans, both in Latin America and elsewhere.

In the seventeenth century, the French, Dutch, and English also became active overseas. Although they failed to find passages to Asia through the Arctic ice, the northern European states did establish colonies on the Atlantic seaboard of North America and used the wealth from these colonies for financial and industrial developments in Europe. Thousands of Europeans settled in North America, displacing and often massacring the Amerindians. These colonies began to exhibit more liberal social, political, and religious values and practices than Europe.

These major upheavals mark the beginning of a remarkable five-century period in which some European nations extended their power into four other continents. In the process they destroyed or profoundly altered many indigenous cultures in the Western Hemisphere and also in Africa and Asia. As a result of these developments, the center of political and economic power shifted from Mediterranean to Atlantic societies.

Selected Sources

Items indicated with an asterisk (*) are available in paperback.

Adas, Michael, ed. *Technology and European Overseas Enterprise: Diffusion, Adaptation, and Adoption.* 1996.

*Atil, Esin. *The Age of Sultan Suleyman the Magnificent.* 1987. Lavishly illustrated discussion of art, crafts, and culture during the zenith of Ottoman power.

Augustijn, Cornelius. *Erasmus: His Life, Works and Influence.* Trans. J. C. Grayson. 1991. Presents a balanced account of Erasmus's life and works.

*Bailyn, Bernard. *Origins of American Politics.* 1970. Examines colonial roots of American political theory and practice.

*Balewa, Abubakar Tafawa. *Shathu Umar.* 1967. A novel about the life of a slave by a former prime minister of Nigeria.

Barber, Noel. *The Sultans.* 1973. Readable account of the Ottoman Empire, based on the lives of the Sultans.

Benesch, Otto. *The Art of the Renaissance in Northern Europe.* 1965. Well-illustrated presentation relating northern European art to contemporary trends in thought and religion.

Bethell, Leslie, ed. *Colonial Spanish America.* 1987. *Colonial Brazil.* 1988. Both books contain essays concerning Latin America from the conquest to independence. Noted authorities write about rural society and the hacienda, urbanization, and Amerindian cultures matters.

*Bouwsma, William J. *John Calvin: A Sixteenth-Century Portrait.* 1988. An essential biography of Calvin.

Boxers, Charles R. *Four Centuries of Portuguese Expansion, 1415–1825.* 1969. Overview of Brazil within the context of the Portuguese Empire.

Braudel, Fernand. *The Mediterranean and the Mediterranean World in the Age of Philip II.* Abridged 1992. Excellent background for understanding Spain and Spanish transplantations in the Americas.

Brown, Judith C., and Davis, Robert C., eds. *Gender and Society in Renaissance Italy.* 1998. A useful collection of essays on the interplay between gender and society.

*Costain, Thomas B. *The Moneyman.* 1947. Historical novel on the life of a French merchant.

Cutter, Donald C. *Quest for Empire: Spanish Settlement in the Southwest.* 1996. An overview of Spanish policies.

Ferro, Marc. *Colonization: A Global History.* 1997. A good general account.

Fuentes, Carlos. *The Buried Mirror: Reflections on Spain and the New World.* 1992. Excellent introduction to Spain and the Americas; beautifully crafted with prints, maps, and artwork.

*Goodwin, Godfrey. *A History of Ottoman Architecture.* 1971; reprinted 1992. Includes hundreds of illustrations and dozens of floor plans for mosques, government complexes, and homes; also a particularly informative chapter on Sinan, the noted Ottoman architect.

"Gorée: Door of No Return." Films for the Humanities. A moving historical description of Gorée, a slave-trading center in West Africa.

Green, Guy, dir. *Luther.* 1974. Stirring film interpretation of Luther's reforming activities.

Grimm, Harold J. *The Reformation Era: 1500–1650.* 2d ed. 1973. Focuses on the religious issues and personalities of the Reformation era.

*Haring, Clarence H. *The Spanish Empire in America.* 1975. An authoritative study that is sympathetic to the Spanish.

*Hodgson, Marshall G. S. *The Venture of Islam: The Gunpowder Empires and Modern Times.* Vol. 3. 1974. Scholarly analysis and truly global approach to the confrontation of Islamic states, including the Ottoman and Persian Empires and Muslim India, with the West.

*Innes, Hammond. *The Conquistadors.* 1969. A lively, beautifully illustrated account.

The Isfahan of Shah Abbas. 1987. This 28-minute film is a stunning visual presentation of Safavid culture with narration by art expert Oleg Grabar.

Jensen, De Lamar. *Reformation Europe.* 1992. The best one-volume account.

Joffe, Roland, dir. *The Mission.* 1986. A visually spectacular film about a Jesuit mission in the jungles of Brazil and its destruction by the greed of merchants and factionalism within the church.

*Kinross, Patrick Balfour. *The Ottoman Centuries: the Rise and Fall of the Turkish Empire.* 1977. Well-written account of Ottoman history, with good analysis of strengths and weaknesses of the empire.

Labalm, Patricia, ed. *Beyond Their Sex: Learned Women of the European Past.* 1980. Contains a number of useful articles analyzing educational and scholarly roles open to females in Renaissance society.

*Leonard, Irving A. *Baroque Times in Old Mexico: Seventeenth-Century Persons, Places, and Practices.* 1959. A colorful insight into the society and culture of Latin America.

Leon-Portilla, Miguel. *The Broken Spears: Aztec Accounts of the Conquest.* 1962. An enduring classic, employing Amerindian accounts of the fall of the Aztecs.

——. *Pre-Colombian Literatures of Mexico.* 1992. An anthology of poetry and prose, including indigenous accounts of the Conquest.

*Maalouf, Amin. *Leo Africanus.* 1986; reprinted 1992. A novel based on the celebrated traveler's life, with vivid, historically accurate descriptions of Moorish Spain, Timbuktu, and Italy during the Renaissance.

Marks, Richard L. *Cortés: The Great Adventurer and the Fate of Aztec Mexico.* 1993. A biography of the Spanish conqueror against the backdrop of a clash between the Aztec and European civilizations.

Marshall, Sherrin, ed. *Women in Reformation and Counter-Reformation Europe.* 1989. Explores the role and status of women in the Reformation era, and their contribution to spiritual renewal and reform.

*Morison, Samuel E. *Christopher Columbus, Mariner.* 1983. A lively, if traditional, introduction to Columbus.

Oberman, Heiko O. *Luther: Man between God and Devil.* Trans. E. Walliser-Schwarzbart. 1989. Examines Luther and his theology against the intellectual currents of the later medieval world.

*Pernoud, Regine. *Joan of Arc, by Herself and Her Witnesses.* Trans. Edward Hyams. 1969. Powerful biography; also the film *Joan of Arc,* dir. Victor Fleming, 1948, starring Ingrid Bergman.

*Perroy, Edouard. *The Hundred Years' War.* 1965. Combines social and political history with military events.

*Perry, Glenn E. *The Middle East: Fourteen Islamic Centuries.* 3d ed. 1997. Concise overview of the region from early times to the present day.

Ptak, Roderich, ed. *Portuguese Asia: Aspects in History and Economic History, Sixteenth and Seventeenth Centuries.* 1987.

Rubin, Nancy. *Isabella of Castile: The First Renaissance Queen.* 1991. A lively biography of the strong-willed queen.

Sale, Kirkpatrick. *The Conquest of Paradise: Christopher Columbus and the Columbian Legacy.* 1990. A fervent exposition of the concept that a sickly, dispirited post–Black Death Europe essentially destroyed the environment, native population, and indigenous culture of the Americas.

Shaffer, Peter. *The Royal Hunt of the Sun.* 1981. A moving play depicting the story of the capture, imprisonment, and execution of the Inka emperor by Pizarro.

Sobel, Dava. *Galileo's Daughter.* 1999. Based on the surviving letters of his illegitimate daughter, a cloistered nun in Florence, this study reveals much about Galileo the man, accenting his struggle to reconcile his scientific discoveries with his beliefs as a good Catholic.

*Stone, Irving. *The Agony and the Ecstasy.* 1961. An historical novel based on Michelangelo's life; also the basis for a movie of the same title.

Suleiman the Magnificent. 1987. This one-hour film, produced by the National Gallery of Art, is a colorful, historically accurate account of the Ottoman empire at its zenith.

*Thompson, Vincent Bakpetu. *The Making of the African Diaspora in the Americas 1441–1900.* 1988. Full account of the slave trade and its cultural impacts.

Williams, Selma. *Demeter's Daughters.* 1976. A survey of the various roles of women in British North America, stressing the stories of individuals.

Wölfflin, Heinrich. *Classic Art: An Introduction to the Italian Renaissance.* 3d ed. 1968. Brief, comprehensive, well-illustrated introduction to this large topic.

Wood, Betty. *The Origins of American Slavery: Freedom and Bondage in the English Colonies.* 1997.

Zili, Madeline C. *Women in the Ottoman Empire.* 1997. A scholarly study of the lives of women over the many centuries of Ottoman rule.

Zophy, Jonathan W. *A Short History of Reformation Europe.* 1997. A concise, readable overview of the period. Tailored for students who have not had much exposure to the subject.

——. *A Short History of Renaissance Europe.* 1997. Like its above companion, a useful introduction for the beginning student.

 Additional resources, exercises, and Internet links related to this chapter are available at the Book Companion Web site: http://history.wadsworth.com/upshurcompact4/

Romanizing Chinese Words

Two systems are in current use for romanizing Chinese words. The Wade-Giles system has been in use longer than the Pinying system. Scholars of China use both equally. Newspapers tend to use the Pinying system for the People's Republic and the Wade-Giles system for the Republic of China. This book follows the Wade-Giles system for pre-1949 China and the Pinying system for the post-1949 era. The following table equates some of the Wade-Giles and other conventional spellings with the Pinying spelling used in this text. Since not all words differ in the two systems, only those words that do are included.

Wade-Giles	Pinying	Wade-Giles	Pinying
Canton	Guangzhou	Kwangsi	Guangxi
Ch'an	Chan	Kwangtung	Guangdong
Chao	Zhao	Lao Tzu	Laozi
Chekiang	Zhejiang	Li Po	Li Bo
Chengchow	Zhengzhou	Loyang	Luoyang
Ch'ien-lung	Qianlong	Mao Tse-tung	Mao Zedong
Ch'in	Qin	Nanking	Nanjing
Ching-te Cheng	Jingdezhen	Peking	Beijing
Ch'ing	Qing	Shang-ti	Shangdi
Chou	Zhou	Shantung	Shandong
Chu Hsi	Zhu Xi	Shansi	Shaanxi
Chu Yuan-chang	Zhu Yuanzhang	Shensi	Shanxi
Chungking	Chongqing	Sian	Xi'an
Fukien	Fujian	Sinkiang	Xinjiang
Hangchow	Hangzhou	Sung	Song
Honan	Henan	Szechuan	Sichuan
Hopei	Hebei	T'ang	Tang
Hsiung-nu	Xiongnu	T'ang T'ai-tsung	Tang Taizong
Hung-wu	Hongwu	Taoism	Daoism
K'ang-hsi	Kangxi	Tatung	Dadong
Kansu	Gansu	Tien	Tian
Kiangsi	Jiangxi	Tz'u-hsi	Cixi
Kiangsu	Jiangsu	Wu-ti	Wudi
K'ung Fu-tzu	Kong Fuzi	Yang-tze	Yangzi
Kuomintang	Guomindang	Yung-cheng	Yongzheng

Glossary

●

Abbasid dynasty   The caliphs resident in Baghdad from the 700s C.E. until 1252.

Abbot/abbess   The male/female head of a monastery/nunnery.

Absolutism   A form of government in which the sovereign power or ultimate authority rested in the hands of a monarch who claimed to rule by divine right and was therefore responsible only to God.

Abstractionism   A twentieth-century school of painting that rejected traditional representation of external nature and objects.

Academy   The school founded by Plato; Aristotle is its most famous student.

Actium, Battle of   The decisive 31 B.C.E. battle in the struggle between Octavian Caesar and Marc Antony, in which Octavian's victory paved the way for the Principate.

Agincourt   The great victory of the English over the French in 1415, during the Hundred Years' War.

Agricultural revolution   The substitution of farming for hunting and gathering as the primary source of food by a people.

Ahimsa   The Buddhist doctrine of not harming other living creatures.

A'in Jalut   A decisive thirteenth-century battle in which the Egyptians turned back the Mongols and prevented them from invading North Africa.

Ajanta Caves   Caves in central India that are the site of marvelous early frescoes inspired by Buddhism.

Allah   Arabic title of the one God.

Alliance of 1778   A diplomatic treaty under which France aided the American revolutionaries in their war against Britain.

Anabaptists   Radical Protestant reformers who were condemned by both Lutherans and Catholics.

Analects   The body of writing containing conversations between Confucius and his disciples that preserves his worldly wisdom and pragmatic philosophies.

Anarchism   A political theory that sees all large-scale government as inherently evil and embraces small self-governing communities.

ANC   The African National Congress. Founded in 1912, it was the beginning of political activity by South African blacks. Banned by politically dominant European whites in 1960, it was not officially "unbanned" until 1990. It is now the official majority party of the South African government.

Ancien régime   The "old government"; the pre-Revolutionary style of government and society in eighteenth-century France.

Angkor Wat   A great Buddhist temple in central Cambodia, dating to the twelfth-century C.E. Khmer Empire.

Anglo-French entente   The diplomatic agreement of 1904 that ended British-French enmity and was meant as a warning to Germany.

Anglo-Russian agreement   The equivalent to the Anglo-French entente between Britain and Russia; signed in 1907.

Animism   A religious belief imputing spirits to natural forces and objects.

Anschluss   The German term for the 1938 takeover of Austria by Nazi Germany.

Anthropology   The study of humankind as a particular species.

Antigonid kingdom   One of the Hellenistic successor kingdoms to Alexander the Great's empire.

Anti-Semitism   Hostility toward or discrimination against Jews.

Apartheid   The Afrikaans term for segregation of the races in South Africa.

Appeasement   The policy of trying to avoid war by giving Hitler what he demanded in the 1930s; supported by many in France and Britain.

Archaeology   The study of cultures through the examination of artifacts.

Arianism   A Christian heresy that taught that Jesus was inferior to God. Though condemned by the Council of Nicaea in 325, Arianism was adopted by many of the Germanic peoples who entered the Roman Empire over the next centuries.

Aristocracy   A social governing class based on preeminence of birth.

Arthasastra   An early Indian political treatise that sets forth many fundamental aspects of the relationship of rulers and their subjects. It has been compared to Machiavelli's well-known book The Prince and has provided principles upon which many aspects of social organization have developed in the region.

Aryans   A nomadic pastoral people from Eurasia who invaded the Indus Valley and other regions in about 1500 B.C.E.

Ashikaga clan   A noble Japanese family that controlled political power as shoguns from the 1330s to the late 1500s.

Atatürk, Mustafa Kemal   The "father of the Turks"; a World War I officer who led Turkey into the modern age and replaced the Ottoman Empire in the 1920s.

Audiencia   The colonial council that supervised military and civil government in Latin America.

August 1991 coup   The attempt by hard-line Communists to oust Gorbachev and reinstate the Communist party's monopoly on power in the Soviet Union.

Ausgleich **of 1867**   The compromise between the Austro-Germans and Magyars that created the "Dual Monarchy" of Austria-Hungary.

Austro-Prussian War   The conflict for mastery of Germany won by the Bismarck-led Prussian kingdom in 1866.

Authoritarian state   A state that has a dictatorial government and some other trappings of a totalitarian state but does not have the same degree of control of the populace and the economy.

Avesta   The holy book of the Zoroastrian religion.

Axis Pact   The treaty establishing a military alliance between the governments of Germany, Italy, and Japan; signed in 1936.

Axum   The center of the ancient Ethiopian kingdom.

Aztec   Last of a series of Amerindian masters of central Mexico prior to the arrival of the Spanish; developers of the great city of Tenochtitlán (Mexico City).

Babylon   Most important of the later Mesopotamian urban centers.

Babylonian Captivity   The transportation of many Jews to exile in Babylon as hostages for the good behavior of the remainder; occurred in the sixth century B.C.E.

Bakufu   The military-style government of the Japanese shogun.

Balance of power   A distribution of power among several states such that no single nation can dominate the others.

Balfour Declaration   The 1917 public statement that Britain was committed to the foundation of a "Jewish homeland" in Palestine after World War I.

Bantu   A language spoken by many peoples of central and eastern Africa; by extension, the name of the speakers.

Barbarian   Greek for " incomprehensible speaker"; uncivilized.

Baruch Plan   An idea put forth early in the Cold War in which all countries would pledge not to make atomic bombs and to allow international inspections; it was rejected by the Soviet Union.

Battle of the Nations   Decisive defeat of the army of Napoleon by combined forces of Prussia, Austria, and Russia in October 1813 at Leipzig in eastern Germany.

Bay of Pigs invasion   A failed U.S.-backed invasion of Cuba by anti-Castro exiles in 1961.

Bedouin   The nomadic inhabitants of interior Arabia; they were the original converts to Islam.

Benedictine Rule   The rules of conduct given to his monastic followers by the sixth-century Christian saint Benedict.

Berbers   Pre-Arab settlers of northern Africa and the Sahara.

Berlin blockade   The 1948–1949 attempt to squeeze the Western allies out of occupied Berlin by the USSR; it failed because of the successful Berlin Airlift of food and supplies.

Berlin Wall The ten-foot-high concrete wall and "death zone" erected by the communist East Germans in 1961 to prevent further illegal emigration to the West.

Bhagavad-Gita The best-known part of the *Mahabharata,* it details the proper relations between the castes and the triumph of the spirit over material creation.

Big bang theory The theory that the cosmos was created by an enormous explosion billions of years ago.

Bill of Rights of 1689 A law enacted by Parliament that established specific rights of English citizens and placed certain limits on royal powers.

Black Death An epidemic of bubonic plague that ravaged most of Europe in the mid-fourteenth century.

Blitzkrieg ("lightning war") A war conducted with great speed and force, as in Germany's advance into Poland at the beginning of World War II.

Bodhisattva In Buddhism, an enlightened being that helps others to reach *nirvana.*

Boer War/Boers The armed conflict, 1899–1902, between the Boers (the Dutch colonists who had been the earliest European settlers of South Africa) and their British overlords; won by the British after a hard fight.

Bohemia Traditional name of the Czech Republic, dating from the tenth century C.E.

Bolsheviks The minority of Russian Marxists led by Lenin who seized dictatorial power in the October Revolution of 1917.

Boule The 500-member council that served as a legislature in ancient Athens.

Bourgeoisie The urban middle class; usually commercial or professional.

Boxer Rebellion A desperate revolt by peasants against the European "foreign devils" who were carving up China in the new imperialism of the 1890s; it was quickly suppressed by Western powers.

Brahman In Hindu theology, the title of the impersonal spirit responsible for all creation.

Brahmin The caste of priests, originally found among the Aryans and later spread to the Indians generally.

Bread and circuses The social policy initiated by Augustus Caesar aimed at gaining the support of the Roman proletariat by supplying them with essential food and entertainment.

Brest-Litovsk Treaty of 1918 The separate peace between the Central Powers and Lenin's government that took Russia out of World War I.

Brezhnev Doctrine The doctrine, enunciated by Leonid Brezhnev, that the Soviet Union had a right to intervene if socialism was threatened in another socialist state; used to justify the use of Soviet troops in Czechoslovakia in 1968.

Bronze Age The period when bronze tools and weapons replaced stone among a given people; generally about 3000–1000 B.C.E.

Burning of the books China's Legalist first emperor attempted to eliminate Confucian ethics by destroying Confucian writings and prohibiting its teaching.

Bushido The samurai code of honor.

Byzantine empire The continuation of the Roman imperium in its eastern provinces until its fall to the Muslim Turks in 1453.

Caliph Arabic for successor (to Muhammad); leader of Islam.

Carthage Rival in the Mediterranean basin to Rome in the last centuries B.C.E.; it was destroyed by Rome.

Caste A socioeconomic group that is entered by birth and can only rarely be exited from.

Caudillo A chieftain (that is, a local or regional strongman) in Latin America.

Central Intelligence Agency A Cold War creation of the United States, this organization, among other activities, sought to overthrow or destabilize countries deemed too receptive to communism.

Chaeronea The battle in 338 B.C.E. in which Philip of Macedon decisively defeated the Greeks and brought them under Macedonian rule.

Ch'an Buddhism Founded by the semilegendary Indian monk Bodhidharma, this Chinese branch of Buddhism (Zen in Japan) focused on meditation and an intuitive understanding of reality.

Chartism A British working-class movement of the 1840s that attempted to obtain labor and political reform.

Chavin   Early Peruvian Amerindian culture.

Cheka   An abbreviation for the first Soviet secret police.

Chichén Itzá   Site in the Yucatan of Mayan urban development in the tenth to thirteenth centuries.

Ch'ing dynasty   The Manchu dynasty that ruled China from 1644 to 1911.

City of God, The   Written by Augustine in the fifth century C.E., it calls for ultimate allegiance to God, not to earthly rulers.

Civil Code of 1804   Napoleonic law code reforming and centralizing French legal theory and procedures.

Civil constitution of the clergy   1791 law in revolutionary France attempting to force French Catholics to support the new government and bring clergy into conformity with it.

Civil rights   The basic rights of citizens, including equality before the law, freedom of speech and press, and freedom from arbitrary arrest.

Civilization   A complex, developed culture.

Code Napoleon   A system of laws promulgated by Napoleon that upheld many of the ideals of the French Revolution while continuing the subjugation of women and the suppression of unions.

Cold War   The ideological conflict between the Soviet Union and the United States after World War II.

Collective farms   Large farms created in the Soviet Union by Stalin by combining many small holdings into one large farm worked by the peasants under government supervision.

Command economy   The name given to communist economic planning in the Soviet Union after 1929.

Committee of Public Safety   The executive body of the Reign of Terror during the French Revolution.

Commonwealth of Independent States (CIS)   The loose confederation of eleven of the fifteen former Soviet republics formed after the breakup of the Soviet Union in 1991.

Congress of Vienna   A meeting of the major and minor powers of Europe in 1815, called to decide the fate of France and the future of Europe after the defeat of Napoleon. It developed informal structures that kept war in Europe at low levels throughout much of the nineteenth century.

Conquistadores   Title given to sixteenth-century Spanish explorers/colonizers in the New World.

Conservatism   An ideology based on tradition and social stability that favored the maintenance of established institutions, organized religion, and obedience to authority and resisted change, especially abrupt change.

Consuls   Chief executives of the Roman republic; chosen annually.

Contras   One side of the 1980s civil war in Nicaragua, it was composed in large part of people loyal to the former dictator Somoza; they fought against the Sandinistas.

Coral Sea, Battle of   The naval engagement in the southwest Pacific during World War II that ended the Japanese invasion threat to Australia.

Corpus Juris   "Body of the law"; the final Roman law code, produced under the emperor Justinian in the mid-500s C.E.

Cottage industry   A system of textile manufacturing in which spinners and weavers worked at home in their cottages using raw materials supplied to them by capitalist entrepreneurs.

Creationism   A cosmology based on Christian tradition that holds that the universe was created by an intelligent Supreme Being.

Creole   Term used to refer to whites born in Latin America.

Crimean War   Conflict fought in the Crimea between Russia on one side and Britain, France, and Turkey on the other, from 1853 to 1856; ended by the Peace of Paris with a severe loss in Russian prestige.

Cultural relativism   The belief that no culture is superior to another because culture is a matter of custom, not reason, and derives its meaning from the group holding it.

Culture   The human-created environment of a group.

Cuneiform   Mesopotamian wedge-shaped writing begun by the Sumerians.

Cynicism   A Hellenistic philosophy stressing poverty and simplicity.

Daimyo   Japanese nobles who controlled feudal domains under the shogun.

Dasa Sanskrit term for "slave" used by Aryans; refers to the dark skin color of Indus Valley peoples.

D Day June 6, 1944; the invasion of France from the English Channel by combined British and American forces.

Declaration of Independence The 1776 document approved by the Continental Congress in Britain's American colonies; it asserts the colonies' independence from Britain and provides a logical explanation for doing so.

Declaration of the Rights of Man and Citizen The epoch-making manifesto issued by the French Third Estate delegates at Versailles in 1789.

Decolonization The process of becoming free of colonial status and achieving statehood; occurred in most of the world's colonies between 1947 and 1962.

Deductive reasoning Arriving at truth by applying a general law or proposition to a specific case.

Delian League An empire of satellite Greek states under Athens in the fifth century B.C.E.

Democracy A system of government in which the majority of voters decides issues and policy.

Demographic transition The passage of a large group of people from traditional high birthrates to lower ones, induced by better survival rates among children.

Depression A severe, protracted economic downturn with high levels of unemployment.

Descent of Man The 1871 publication by Charles Darwin that applied selective evolution theory to mankind.

Destalinization The policy of denouncing and undoing the most repressive aspects of Stalin's regime; it was begun by Nikita Khrushchev in 1956.

Détente Relaxation of tensions; the term used for the toning down of diplomatic tensions between nations, specifically between the United States and the Soviet Union during the Cold War.

Dharma A code of morals and conduct prescribed for one's caste in Hinduism.

Diaspora The scattering of the Jews from ancient Palestine.

Diffusion theory Description of the spread of ideas and technology through human contacts.

Directory The five-member executive organ that governed France from 1795 to 1799 after the overthrow of the Jacobins and before Napoleon gained control.

Divine right theory The idea that the legitimate holder of the Crown was designated by divine will to govern; personified by King Louis XIV in the seventeenth century.

Domino theory The belief that if the communists succeeded in Vietnam, other countries in Southeast and East Asia would also fall (like dominoes) to communism; a justification for the U.S. intervention in Vietnam.

Dorians Legendary barbaric invaders of Mycenaean Greece in about 1200 B.C.E.

Dream of the Red Chamber The best-known of the eighteenth-century Chinese novels.

Duce, il "The Leader"; title of Mussolini, the Italian dictator.

Duma The Russian legislature created by Tsar Nicolas II.

Dynastic state A state in which the maintenance and expansion of the interests of the ruling family is the primary consideration.

East India Company A commercial company founded with government backing to trade with the East and Southeast Asians. The Dutch, English, and French governments sponsored such companies starting in the early seventeenth century.

Economic nationalism A movement to assert national sovereignty in economic affairs, particularly by establishing freedom from the importation of foreign goods and technology on unfavorable terms.

Edo Name of Tokyo prior to the eighteenth century.

Eightfold Path The Buddha's teachings on attaining perfection.

Emir A provincial official with military duties in Muslim government.

Empirical data Facts derived from observation of the external world.

Empirical method Using empirical data to establish scientific truth.

Enclosure movement An eighteenth-century innovation in British agriculture by which formerly communal lands were enclosed by private landlords.

Encomienda   The right to organize unpaid native labor by the earliest Spanish colonists in Latin America; revoked in 1565.

Encyclopédie, The   The first encyclopedia; produced in mid-eighteenth-century France by the philosopher Diderot.

Enlightened absolutism   An absolute monarchy where the ruler follows the principles of the Enlightenment by introducing reforms for the improvement of society, allowing freedom of speech and the press, permitting religious toleration, expanding education, and ruling in accordance with the laws.

Enlightenment   The intellectual reform movement in eighteenth-century Europe that challenged traditional ideas and policies in many areas of theory and practice.

Epicureanism   A Hellenistic philosophy advocating the pursuit of pleasure (mental) and avoidance of pain as the supreme good.

Equal field system   Agricultural reform favoring the peasants under the T'ang dynasty in China.

Era of Stagnation   The period of Brezhnev's government in the Soviet Union (1964–1982), when the Soviet society and economy faced increasing troubles.

Era of Warring States   The period of Chinese history between about 500 and 220 B.C.E.; characterized by the breakdown of the central government and near-constant feudal war.

Essenes   A Jewish religious group that lived near the Dead Sea at Qumran from around the middle of the second century B.C.E.; some of their ideas were similar to those found in early Christianity.

Estates-General   The parliament of France; it was composed of delegates from three social orders: clergy, nobility, and commoners.

Ethnic, Ethnicity   The racial, cultural, or linguistic affiliation of an individual or group of human beings.

Ethnic cleansing   The policy of killing or forcibly removing people of another ethnic group; used by the Serbs against Bosnian and Kosovar Muslims in the 1990s.

Etruscans   The pre-Roman rulers of most of northern and central Italy and cultural models for early Roman civilization.

European Economic Community   An organization that blossomed after World War II, it fostered economic cooperation among member states, eventually becoming today's European Union.

Excommunication   The act of being barred from the Roman Catholic community by decree of a bishop or the pope.

Existentialism   Twentieth-century philosophy that was popular after World War II in Europe; it insists on the necessity to inject life with meaning by individual decisions.

Exodus   The Hebrews' flight from the wrath of the Egyptian pharaoh in about 1250 B.C.E.

Extended family   Parents and children plus several other kin group members.

Factory Acts   Laws passed by Parliament in 1819 and 1833 that began the regulation of hours and working conditions in Britain.

Fallow land   Land left uncultivated for a period to recover fertility.

Fascism   A political movement in the twentieth century that embraced totalitarian government policies to achieve a unity of people and leader; first experienced in Mussolini's Italy.

Fashoda crisis   In 1898 British forces and French forces, both bent on increasing the imperial holdings of their respective countries, came head-to-head in Fashoda in the Sudan. Diplomacy averted a war between the two countries.

Feminism   The belief in the social, political, and economic equality of the sexes; also, organized activity to advance women's rights.

Fertile Crescent   A belt of civilized settlements reaching from lower Mesopotamia across Syria, Lebanon, and Israel and into Egypt.

Feudal system   A mode of government based originally on mutual military obligations between lord and vassal; later often extended to civil affairs of all types; generally supported by landowning privileges.

Final Solution   Name given by the Nazis to the wartime massacres of European Jews.

First Consul Title adopted by Napoleon after his coup d'état in 1799.

First Emperor (Shi Huangdi) The founder of the short-lived Qin dynasty (221–205 B.C.E.) and creator of China as an imperial state.

First Industrial Revolution The initial introduction of machine-powered production; began in late-eighteenth-century Britain.

Five Pillars of Islam Popular term for the basic tenets of Muslim faith.

Five-Year Plan First introduced in 1929 at Stalin's command to collectivize agriculture and industrialize the economy of the Soviet Union.

Floating world A term for ordinary human affairs popularized by the novels and stories of eighteenth-century Japan.

Forbidden City The center of Ming and Ching government in Beijing; entry was forbidden to ordinary citizens.

Four Noble Truths The Buddha's doctrine on human fate.

Fourteen Points The outline for a just peace proposed by Woodrow Wilson in 1918.

Franco-Prussian War The 1870–1871 conflict between these two powers, resulting in humiliating defeat for France and German unification.

Frankfurt Assembly A German parliament held in 1848 that was unsuccessful in working out a liberal constitution for a united German state.

Führer, der "The Leader" in Nazi Germany—specifically, Hitler.

Fujiwara clan Daimyo noble clan controlling the shogunate in ninth- to twelfth-century Japan.

Geisha Women in feudal Japan who entertained men with good conversation, dance, singing, and occasional sexual favors; similar to the *hetairai* of ancient Athens.

Gentiles All non-Jews.

Gentry Well-to-do English landowners below the level of the nobility; played an important role in the English Civil War of the seventeenth century.

Geocentric "Earth centered"; theory of the cosmos that erroneously held the Earth to be its center.

Gestapo Hitler's secret police, responsible for intimidating the population and helping to rid

Germany of "undesirables" such as Jews and leftists.

Ghana The earliest of the extensive empires in the western Sudan; also a modern African state.

Ghetto Italian name for the quarter restricted to Jews.

Gilgamesh One of the earliest epics in world literature, originating in prehistoric Mesopotamia.

Glasnost The Russian term for "openness"; along with *perestroika,* it was employed to describe the reforms instituted by Gorbachev in the late 1980s in the Soviet Union.

Glorious Revolution of 1688 The English revolt against the unpopular Catholic king James II and the subsequent introduction of certain civil rights restricting monarchic powers.

Golden Horde The Russia-based segment of the Mongol world empire.

Gothic style An artistic style, found mainly in architecture, that came into general European usage during the thirteenth century.

Gracchi brothers Roman noble brothers who as consuls unsuccessfully attempted reform in the late republican era.

Great Depression Originating in 1929 in the United States, this global decline in economic output spread throughout the world, causing high unemployment and political unrest; it was a major reason Hitler came to power in Germany.

Great Elector Frederick William of Prussia (1640–1688); one of the princes who elected the Holy Roman Emperor.

Great Leap Forward Mao Zedong's misguided attempt in 1958–1960 to provide China with an instantaneous industrial base rivaling that of more advanced nations.

Great Proletarian Cultural Revolution The period from 1966 to 1969 when Mao inspired Chinese youth to rebel against all authority except his own; caused great damage to the Chinese economy and culture.

Great Purge The arrest and banishment of millions of Soviet Communist party members and ordinary citizens at Stalin's orders in the mid-1930s for fictitious "crimes against the State and Party."

Great Schism A division in the Roman Catholic church between 1378 and 1417 when two (and for a brief period, three) popes competed for the allegiance of European

Christians; a consequence of the Babylonian Captivity of the papacy in Avignon, southern France.

Great Trek The march of the Boers into the interior of South Africa, where they founded the Orange Free State in 1836.

Great Zimbabwe The leading civilization of early southern Africa.

Greens A pro-environment, moderately leftist political movement that began in West Germany in the 1970s and has since spread throughout Europe and to other parts of the world.

Grossdeutsch versus Kleindeutsch The controversy over the scope and type of the unified German state in the nineteenth century; *Kleindeutsch* would exclude multinational Austria, and *Grossdeutsch* would include it.

Guild A medieval urban organization that controlled the production and sale prices of many goods and services.

Habsburg dynasty The family that controlled the Holy Roman Empire after the thirteenth century; based in Vienna, they ruled Austria until 1918.

Hacienda A Spanish-owned plantation in Latin America that used native or slave labor to produce export crops.

Hagia Sophia Greek name ("Holy Wisdom") of the cathedral in Constantinople, later made into a mosque by Ottoman Turkish conquerors.

Hajj The pilgrimage to the sacred places of Islam.

Han dynasty The dynasty that ruled China from about 200 B.C.E. to 221 C.E.

Hanoverians The dynasty of British monarchs after 1714 that came from the German duchy of Hanover.

Harappa An early Indus Valley civilization.

Hegira "Flight"; Muhammad's forced flight from Mecca in 622 C.E.; marks the first year of the Muslim calendar.

Heliocentrism Opposite of geocentrism; recognizes the sun as center of the solar system.

Hellenistic A blend of Greek and Asiatic cultures, extant in the Mediterranean basin and Middle East between 300 B.C.E. and about 200 C.E.

Helots Messenian semislaves of Spartan overlords.

Heresy "Wrong" belief in religious doctrines; often severely persecuted by Christian authorities, including the punishment of execution.

Hetairai High-class female entertainer-prostitutes in ancient Greece.

Hieroglyphics Early Egyptian writing consisting of pictographs and symbols for letters and syllables.

Hinayana Buddhism A strict, monastic form of Buddhism claiming a closer link with the Buddha's teaching than Mahayana Buddhism; often called Theravada.

Historiography The writing of history so as to interpret it.

History Human actions in past time, as recorded and remembered.

Hitler-Stalin Pact of 1939 The treaty of nonaggression between Hitler and Stalin in which each agreed to maintain neutrality in any forthcoming war involving the other party.

Hittites An Indo-European people who were prominent in the Middle East around 1200 B.C.E.

Hohenzollerns The dynasty that ruled Prussia-Germany until 1918.

Holocaust The mass executions perpetrated by the Nazi regime of Germany during World War II; its chief victims were 6 million Jews, but hundreds of thousands of gypsies, homosexuals, and others also perished.

Holy Roman Empire First constituted by Charlemagne, the Holy Roman Empire was a concept that served both political and religious purposes; it was eventually controlled by the Habsburgs centered in Austria, but it essentially had lost all its meaning by the early nineteenth century.

Hominid A humanlike creature.

Homo sapiens "Thinking man"; modern human beings.

Hoplites Heavily armed infantry soldiers in ancient Greece in a phalanx formation.

Huguenots French Calvinists, many of whom were forced to emigrate in the seventeenth century.

Humanism The intellectual movement that sees humans as the sole arbiter of their values and purpose.

Hungarian Revolution The Hungarians' attempt to free themselves from Soviet control in October 1956; crushed by the Soviets.

Hyksos A people who invaded the Nile delta in Egypt and ruled it during the Second Intermediate Period around 1600 B.C.E.

Ideographs Written signs conveying entire ideas and not related to the spoken language; used by the Chinese from earliest times.

Iliad The first of the two epics supposedly written by Homer in eighth-century B.C.E. Greece.

Impressionists Members of a Paris-centered school of nineteenth-century painting focusing on light and color.

Indian National Congress Organized in 1885, this secular organization promoted Indian nationalism and lobbied for increased rights of Indians; it became a major force in the struggle for Indian independence.

Individualism Emphasis on and interest in the unique traits of each person.

Inductive reasoning Arriving at truth by reasoning from specific cases to a general law or proposition.

Indulgence The remission of part or all of the temporal punishment in purgatory due to sin; granted for charitable contributions and other good deeds. Indulgences became a regular practice of the Christian church in the High Middle Ages, and their abuse was instrumental in sparking Luther's reform movement in the sixteenth century.

INF (Intermediate Nuclear Forces) Treaty Negotiated by Mikhail Gorbachev and the Reagan administration in the mid-1980s, it removed all medium-range nuclear missiles from Europe.

Inflation A sustained rise in the price level.

Inka Title of the emperor of the Quechuan peoples of Peru prior to arrival of the Spanish.

Inquisition A systematic attempt by the Roman Catholic church to enforce its religious orthodoxy; the Inquisition tortured and executed hundreds of thousands of people suspected of heresy.

Institutes of the Christian Religion John Calvin's major work that established the theology and doctrine of the Calvinist churches; first published in 1536.

Intelligentsia Russian term for a social group that actively influences the beliefs and actions of others, seeking reforms; generally connected with the professions and media.

Iranian Revolution The fundamentalist and anti-Western movement led by the Ayatollah Khomeini that seized power from the shah of Iran through massive demonstrations in 1979.

Iron curtain A metaphor employed by Winston Churchill early in the Cold War, it refers to the divide between western and eastern Europe caused by Soviet domination in the latter region.

Isis A chief Egyptian goddess, represented by the Nile River.

Isolationism A foreign policy in which a nation refrains from making alliances or engaging actively in international affairs.

Jacobins Radical revolutionaries during the French Revolution; organized in clubs headquartered in Paris.

Janissaries An elite troop in the Ottoman army, created originally from Christian boys from the Balkans.

Jesuits Members of the Society of Jesus, a Catholic religious order founded in 1547 to combat Protestantism.

Jewish War A rebellion of Jewish Zealots against Rome in 66–70 C.E.

Jihad Holy war on behalf of the Muslim faith.

Judea One of the two Jewish kingdoms emerging after the death of Solomon when his kingdom was split in two; the other kingdom was Samaria.

Justification by faith Doctrine held by Martin Luther whereby Christian faith alone was the path to heavenly bliss.

Ka'bah The original shrine of pagan Arabic religion in Mecca containing the Black Stone; now one of the holiest places of Islam.

Kali Wife of the Hindu god Shiva, she was both the cosmic mother and the goddess of destruction.

Kamakura shogunate The rule by members of a noble Japanese family from the late twelfth to the mid-fourteenth century in the name of the emperor, who was their puppet.

Kami   Shinto spirits in nature.

Kampuchea   Native name of Cambodia, a state of Southeast Asia bordered by Thailand and Vietnam.

Karma   In Hindu belief, the amounts of good and evil done in a given incarnation.

Karnak   The site of a great temple complex along the Nile River in Egypt.

Kashmir   A province in northwestern India that Pakistan also claims.

Kellogg-Briand Pact   A formal disavowal of war by sixty nations in 1928.

KGB   An abbreviation for the Soviet secret police; used after *Cheka* and *NKVD* had been discarded.

Khmers   The inhabitants of Cambodia; founders of a large empire in ancient Southeast Asia.

Kiev, Principality of   The first Russian state; flourished from about 800 to 1240 C.E., when it fell to Mongols.

Kleindeutsch   "Small German"; adjective describing a form of German unification that excluded the multinational Austria; opposite of *Grossdeutsch*.

Knight   Type of feudal noble who held title and landed domain only for his lifetime; generally based originally on military service to his overlord.

Korean War   1950–1953 war between the United Nations, led by the United States, and North Korea; precipitated by the invasion of South Korea by North Korea.

Krishna   An important Hindu god who gives core religious teachings in the *Bhagavad-Gita*.

Kshatriyas   The warrior class of Aryan society.

Kuomintang (KMT)   The political movement headed by Chiang Kai-shek during the 1930s and 1940s in China.

Kurds   A group of people located in an area comprising eastern Turkey, northern Iraq, northern Syria, and northwest Iran; the Kurds have unsuccessfully sought an independent state and have fought with the governments of Turkey and Iraq.

Kush   Kingdom in northeast Africa that had close relations with Egypt for several centuries in the pre-Christian epoch.

Kyoto   Ancient capital of the Japanese Empire and seat of the emperor.

Labour party   Political party founded in 1906 by British labor unions and others for representation of the working classes.

Laissez-faire   "To let alone." An economic doctrine that holds that an economy is best served when the government does not interfere but allows the economy to self-regulate according the forces of supply and demand.

Lascaux   Site of Paleolithic cave paintings in France.

Late Manchu Restoration   An attempt by Chinese reformers in the 1870s to restore the power of the central government after the suppression of the Taiping rebellion.

Lateran Treaty   A 1929 agreement between the pope and Mussolini in which the pope gained substantial sums of money and control over education, while Mussolini gained greater political and economic control of Italy.

League of Nations   An international organization founded after World War I to maintain peace and promote amity among nations; the United States did not join.

Lebensraum   "Living space." The doctrine, adopted by Hitler, that a nation's power depends on the amount of land it occupies; thus, a nation must expand to be strong.

Left   The reforming or revolutionary wing of the political spectrum; associated originally with the ideals of the radical French Revolution.

Legalism   A Chinese philosophy of government emphasizing strong authority.

Legislative Assembly   The second law-making body created during the French Revolution; it was dominated by the Jacobins and gave way to the radical Convention.

Legitimacy   A term adopted by the victors at the Congress of Vienna in 1815 to explain the reimposition of former monarchs and regimes after the Napoleonic wars.

Legitimacy, principle of   The idea that, after the Napoleonic wars, peace could best be reestablished in Europe by restoring legitimate monarchs who would preserve traditional institutions; it guided Metternich at the Congress of Vienna.

Lepanto, Battle of   Decisive 1571 naval defeat of the Ottomans at the hands of the Habsburgs and Italian city-states; it marked the beginning of the long decline of the Ottomans.

Liberalism   An ideology based on the belief that people should be as free from restraint as possible. Economic liberalism is the idea that the government should not interfere in the workings of the economy. Political liberalism is the idea that there should be restraints on the exercise of power so that people can enjoy basic civil rights in a constitutional state with a representative assembly.

Locarno Pact   An agreement between France and Germany in 1925.

Long March, the   6,000-mile fighting retreat of the Chinese Communists under Mao Zedong to Shensi province in 1934–1935.

Lyric poetry   Poetry that celebrates the poet's emotions.

Maastricht Treaty   Signed in 1991 by members of the European Community; committed them to closer political and economic ties.

Macao   Portuguese island colony just off China's coast; founded in 1513.

Maghrib or **Maghreb**   Muslim northwest Africa.

Magna Carta   A "great charter" issued in 1215 by King John of England that gave the aristocracy substantially increased powers, especially over taxation, and created a more uniform justice system.

Mahabharata   A Hindu epic poem; a favorite in India.

Mahavira   "Great hero." The term refers to Vardhamana, the founder of Jainism in the sixth century B.C.E.

Mahayana Buddhism   A more liberal, looser form of Buddhism; originating soon after the Buddha's death, it de-emphasized the monastic life and abstruse philosophy in favor of prayer to the Buddha and the bodhisattvas who succeeded him.

Mahdi rebellion   A serious rebellion against European rule in the Sudan in the 1890s, led by a charismatic holy man ("mahdi") and ended by his death and British attack.

Mali   The African Sudanese empire that was the successor to Ghana in the 1300s and 1400s.

Manchu   Originally nomadic tribes living in Manchuria who eventually overcame Ming resistance and established the Ching dynasty in seventeenth-century China.

Manchuria   Large province of northeastern China, seized in the nineteenth century by Russia and Japan before being retaken by the Maoist government.

Mandarins   Chinese scholar-officials who had been trained in Confucian principles and possessed great class solidarity.

Mandate   Britain and France governed several Asian and African peoples after World War I, supposedly as agents of the League of Nations.

Mandate of heaven   A theory of rule originated by the Chou dynasty in China, emphasizing the connection between an imperial government's rectitude and its right to govern.

Manor   An agricultural estate of varying size normally owned by a noble or the clergy and worked by free and unfree peasants/serfs.

Marathon   The battle in 490 B.C.E. in which the Greeks defeated the Persians, ending the first Persian War.

March on Rome   A fascist demonstration in 1922 orchestrated by Mussolini as a preliminary step to dictatorship in Italy.

Maritime expeditions (China's)   Early fifteenth-century explorations of the Indian and South Pacific Oceans ordered by the Chinese emperor.

Marshall Plan   A program proposed by the U.S. secretary of state George Marshall and implemented from 1947 to 1951 to aid western Europe's recovery from World War II.

Marxism   The political, economic, and social theories of Karl Marx, which included the idea that history is the story of class struggle and that ultimately the proletariat will overthrow the bourgeoisie and establish a dictatorship en route to a classless society.

Mass education   A state-run educational system, usually free and compulsory, that aims to ensure that all children in society have at least a basic education.

Matriarchy   A society in which females are dominant socially and politically.

Matrilineal descent   Attribution of name and inheritance to children via the maternal line.

Maya   The most advanced of the Amerindian peoples who lived in southern Mexico and Guatemala and created a high urban civilization in the pre-Columbian era.

Medes   An early Indo-European people who, with the Persians, settled in Iran.

Meiji Restoration   The overthrow of the Tokugawa shogunate and restoration of the emperor to nominal power in Japan in 1867.

Mein Kampf   *My Struggle;* Hitler's credo, written while serving a prison term in 1924.

Mercantilism   A theory of national economics popular in the seventeenth and eighteenth centuries, it aimed at establishing a favorable trade balance through government control of exports and imports as well as domestic industry.

Meritocracy   The rule of the meritorious (usually determined by examinations).

Messenian Wars   Conflicts between the neighbors Sparta and Messenia that resulted in Sparta's conquest of Messenia around 600 B.C.E.

Messiah   A savior-king who would someday lead the Jews to glory.

Mestizo   A person of mixed Amerindian and European blood.

Metics   Resident foreigners in ancient Athens; not permitted full rights of citizenship, but did receive the protection of the laws.

Mexican Revolution   The armed struggle that occurred in Mexico between 1910 and 1920 to install a more socially progressive and populist government.

Middle Kingdom   The period in Egyptian history from 2100 to 1600 B.C.E.; followed the First Intermediate Period.

Milan, Edict of   A decree issued by the emperor Constantine in 313 C.E. that legalized Christianity and made it the favored religion in the Roman Empire.

Militarism   A policy of aggressive military preparedness; in particular, the large armies based on mass conscription and complex, inflexible plans for mobilization that most European nations had before World War I.

Ming dynasty   Chinese empire lasting from 1368 to 1644; it overthrew the Mongols and was replaced by the Ch'ing dynasty of the Manchu.

Minoan civilization   An ancient civilization that was centered on Crete between about 2000 and about 1400 B.C.E.

Missi dominici   Agents of Charlemagne in the provinces of his empire.

Modernism   A philosophy of art of the late nineteenth and early twentieth centuries that rejected classical models and values and sought new expressions and aesthetics.

Mohenjo-Daro   Site of one of the two chief towns of the ancient Indus Valley civilization.

Moksha   In Hinduism, the final liberation from bodily existence and reincarnation.

Monarchy   Rule by a single individual, who often claims divine inspiration and protection.

Mongol yoke   A Russian term for the Mongol occupation of Russia, 1240–1480.

Mongols   Name for collection of savage nomadic warriors of Central Asia who conquered most of Eurasia in the thirteenth century.

Monotheism   A religion having only one god.

Monroe Doctrine   The announcement in 1823 by U.S. president James Monroe that no European interference in Latin America would be tolerated.

Mughal   A corruption of "Mongol"; refers to the period of Muslim rule in India.

Mulatto   A person of mixed African and European blood.

Munich Agreement   The agreement coming from 1938 meetings between Hitler and the British and French prime ministers that allowed Germany to take much of Czechoslovakia; the agreement confirmed Hitler's belief that the democratic governments would not fight German aggression.

Munich beer-hall putsch   The failed attempt by Hitler to seize power by armed force in 1923.

Mutual deterrence   The belief that nuclear war could best be prevented if both the United States and the Soviet Union had sufficient nuclear weapons such that even if one nation launched a preemptive first strike, the other could respond and devastate the attacker.

Mycenaeans   An early and rich Greek culture centered on Mycenae that was destroyed by the

"Sea Peoples" and the influx of Dorians from the north.

Mystery religion   One of various Hellenistic cults promising immortal salvation of the individual.

Nantes, Edict of   A law granting toleration to French Calvinists that was issued in 1598 by King Henry IV to end the religious civil war.

Napoleonic settlement   A collective name for the decrees and actions by Napoleon between 1800 and 1808 that legalized and systematized many elements of the French Revolution.

National Assembly   The first law-making body during the French Revolution; created a moderate constitutional monarchy.

Nationalism   A sense of national consciousness based on awareness of being part of a community—a "nation"—that has common institutions, traditions, language, and customs and that becomes the focus of the individual's primary political loyalty.

Nationalities problem   The dilemma faced by the Austro-Hungarian Empire in trying to unite a wide variety of ethnic groups, including, among others, Austrians, Hungarians, Poles, Croats, Czechs, Serbs, Slovaks, and Slovenes in an era when nationalism and calls for self-determination were coming to the fore.

Nationalization   The process of converting a business or industry from private ownership to government control and ownership.

Nation-state   A form of political organization in which a relatively homogeneous people inhabits a sovereign state, as opposed to a state containing people of several nationalities.

Natural rights   Certain inalienable rights to which all people are entitled; include the right to life, liberty, and property, freedom of speech and religion, and equality before the law.

Natural selection   The Darwinian doctrine in biology that changes in species derive from genetic changes that confer an enhanced ability to survive and reproduce.

Navigation Acts   Laws regulating commerce with the British colonies in North America in favor of Britain.

Nazism   The German variant of fascism created by Hitler.

Neanderthal man   A species of *Homo sapiens* flourishing between 100,000 and 30,000 years ago and that mysteriously died out; the name comes from the German valley where the first remains were found.

Négritude   A literary term referring to the self-conscious awareness of African cultural values; popular in areas of Africa formerly under French control.

Neo-Confucianism   An eleventh- and twelfth-century C.E. revival of Confucian thought with special emphasis on love and responsibility toward others.

Neolithic Age   The period from about 7000 B.C.E. to the development of metals by a given people.

Nerchinsk, Treaty of   A 1714 treaty between China and Russia that settled border issues between the two great powers in eastern Asia.

New China movement   An intellectual reform movement in the 1890s that attempted to change and modernize China by modernizing the government.

New Deal   The economic policies of U.S. president Franklin Roosevelt; designed to combat the effects of the Great Depression, they included aspects of Keynesian economics and the first significant social welfare programs in the United States.

New Economic Policy (NEP)   A policy introduced at the conclusion of the civil war that allowed for partial capitalism and private enterprise in the Soviet Union.

New Kingdom or **Empire**   The period from about 1550 to 700 B.C.E. in Egyptian history; followed the Second Intermediate Period. The period from 1550 to about 1200 B.C.E. was the Empire.

Nicaea, Council of   A fourth-century conclave that defined essential doctrines of Christianity under the supervision of the emperor Constantine.

Nicheren sect   A Japanese sect of Buddhism founded by the monk Nicheren; it stressed its supremacy over other religions and glorified Japan.

Niger River   The great river draining most of the African bulge.

Ninety-five Theses   The challenge to church authority put forth by Martin Luther in 1517.

Nineveh The main city and later capital of the Assyrian Empire.

Nirvana The Buddhist equivalent of the Hindu *moksha;* the final liberation from suffering and reincarnation.

Nonaligned nations A large group of countries, most of which became independent after World War II, that desired Cold War alliances with neither the United States nor the Soviet Union.

North American Free Trade Agreement (NAFTA) An agreement signed by the United States, Canada, and Mexico in 1993 that liberalized trade among these nations.

North Atlantic Treaty Organization (NATO) An organization founded in 1949 under U.S. aegis as a defense against threatened communist aggression in Europe.

Nuclear family Composed of parents and children only.

Nuclear test ban The voluntary cessation of above-ground testing of nuclear weapons by the United States and the Soviet Union; in existence from 1963 to the present.

Nuremberg Trials Trials conducted in Germany after World War II to determine and punish war guilt among high German officials, resulting in several executions.

October Revolution of 1917 The Bolshevik coup d'etat in St. Petersburg that ousted the Provisional Government and established a communist state in Russia.

Odyssey The second of the two Homeric epic poems, it details the adventures of the homeward-bound Ulysses coming from the siege of Troy; see also *Iliad.*

Oil boycott of 1973 The temporary withholding of oil exports by OPEC members to Western nations with governments friendly to Israel; led to a massive rise in the price of oil and economic dislocation in many countries.

Old Kingdom The period of Egyptian history from 3100 to 2200 B.C.E.

Old regime/old order The political and social system of France in the eighteenth century before the Revolution.

Old Testament The first portion of the Judeo-Christian Bible; the holy books of the Jews.

Oligarchy Rule by a few.

Olmec The earliest Amerindian civilization in Mexico.

Open Door Policy An early-twentieth-century agreement among the major Western powers that all should have access to trade with weakened China.

Opium Wars Conflicts that occurred in 1840–1842 on the Chinese coast between the British and the Chinese over the importation of opium into China. The Chinese defeat began eighty years of subordination to foreigners.

Oracle bones Animal bones used as a primitive writing medium by early Chinese.

Orange Free State One of the two political entities founded after the Boers' Great Trek in South Africa.

Orders/estates The traditional tripartite division of European society based on heredity and quality rather than wealth or economic standing, first established in the Middle Ages and continuing into the eighteenth century; traditionally consisted of those who pray (the clergy), those who fight (the nobility), and those who work (all the rest).

Organization for Pan African Unity (OAU) The present name of the association of African nations founded in 1963 for mutual aid.

Organization of American States (OAS) An organization founded in 1948 under U.S. auspices to provide mutual defense and aid.

Organization of Petroleum Exporting Countries (OPEC) Founded in the 1960s by Arab governments and later expanded to include several Latin American and African members.

Origin of Species, On the Charles Darwin's book that first enunciated the evolutionary theory in biology; published in 1859.

Osiris A chief Egyptian god, ruler of the underworld.

Ostpolitik German term for Chancellor Brandt's 1960s policy of pursuing normalized relations with West Germany's neighbors to the east.

Ostracism In ancient Greece, the expulsion of a citizen for a given period.

Paleolithic Age The period from the earliest appearance of *Homo sapiens* to about 7000 B.C.E., though exact dates vary by area; the Old Stone Age.

Paleontology   The study of prehistoric things.

Palestine Liberation Organization (PLO)
An organization founded in the 1960s by Palestinians expelled from Israel; until 1994 it aimed at destruction of the state of Israel by any means. Superseded by the autonomous Palestinian Authority created in 1997.

Pan-Africanism   The concept of African continental unity and solidarity in which the common interests of African countries transcend regional boundaries.

Panama Canal   A canal built across the isthmus of Panama. Completed in 1914 by the United States, it linked the Atlantic and Pacific Oceans, helping international commerce and extending American naval power.

Pan-Arabism   A movement after World War I to assert supranational Arab unity, aimed eventually at securing a unified Arab state.

Pantheism   A belief that God exists in all things, living and inanimate.

Paris Commune   A leftist revolt against the national government after France was defeated by Prussia in 1871; crushed by the conservatives with much bloodshed.

Parthenon   The classic Greek temple to Athena on the Acropolis in Athens's center.

Patriarchy   A society in which males have social and political dominance.

Patricians (*patres*)   The upper class in ancient Rome.

Patronage   The practice of awarding titles and making appointments to government and other positions to gain political support.

Pax Mongolica   The Mongol peace; between about 1250 and about 1350 in most of Eurasia.

Pax Romana   The "Roman peace"; the era of Roman control over the Mediterranean basin and much of Europe between about 31 B.C.E. and 180 C.E. or later.

Peace of Augsburg   Pact ending the German religious wars in 1555, dividing the region between Lutheran and Catholic hegemony.

Peaceful coexistence   The declared policy of Soviet leader Khrushchev in dealing with the capitalist West after 1956.

Pearl Harbor, bombing of   A surprise attack on December 7, 1941, by Japanese planes on the American navy at Pearl Harbor, Hawaii; it brought war between the United States and Japan.

Peasants' Revolt   An uprising in southern German states in 1524–1525; it was ruthlessly suppressed after the peasants were denounced by Martin Luther.

Peloponnesian War   The great civil war between Athens and Sparta and their respective allies in ancient Greece; fought between 429 and 404 B.C.E. and eventually won by Sparta.

Peon   A peasant in semislave status on a hacienda.

Perestroika   The Russian term for "restructuring," which, with *glasnost*, was used to describe the reforms instituted by Gorbachev in the late 1980s.

Persepolis   With Ecbatana, one of the twin capitals of the Persian Empire in the 500s B.C.E.

Persian Wars   The conflict between the Greeks and the Persian Empire in the fifth century B.C.E., fought in two installments and ending with Greek victory.

Persians   An early Indo-European tribe that, along with the Medes, settled in Iran.

Petrine succession   The doctrine of the Roman Catholic church by which the pope (the bishop of Rome) is the direct successor of St. Peter.

Pharaoh   The title of the god-king of ancient Egypt.

Philosophes   A French term referring to the writers and activist intellectuals during the Enlightenment.

Phoenicians   An ancient seafaring people living along the coast north of Palestine; they dominated trade in the Mediterranean.

Phonetic alphabet   A system of writing that matches signs with the sounds of the oral language.

Pictographic script   Uses symbols and graphs only, with no alphabet; used in Chinese writing.

Piedmont   "Foot of the mountains"; the Italian kingdom that led to the unification of Italy in the mid-nineteenth century.

Platea   The land battle that, along with the naval battle of Salamis, ended the Second Persian War with a Greek victory over the Persians.

Plebeians   The common people of ancient Rome.

Pogrom   Mob violence against local Jews.

Polis   The political and social community of citizens in ancient Greece.

Politburo   The ruling council of the Soviet Union; it came under the firm control of Joseph Stalin, but reasserted substantial power upon the dictator's death.

Polytheism   Belief in many gods.

Popular sovereignty   The doctrine that government is created by and subject to the will of the people, who are the source of all political power.

Post-Impressionist   A term for late nineteenth-century painting that emphasized color and line in revolutionary fashion.

Praetorian Guard   The imperial bodyguard in the Roman Empire and the only armed force in Italy.

Precedent   What has previously been accepted in the application of law.

Predestination   The belief, associated with Calvinism, that God, as a consequence of his foreknowledge of all events, has predetermined those who will be saved (the elect) and those who will be damned.

Prehistory   The long period of human activity prior to the writing of history.

Primogeniture   A system of inheritance in which the estate passes to the eldest legitimate son.

Princeps   "The First" or "the Leader" in Latin; title taken by Augustus Caesar.

Principate   The reign of Augustus Caesar from 27 B.C.E. to 14 C.E.

Proconsuls   Provincial governors and military commanders in ancient Rome.

Proletariat   Poverty-stricken people without skills; also, a Marxist term for the propertyless working classes.

Provisional Government   A self-appointed parliamentary group exercising power in republican Russia from March to October 1917.

Psychoanalysis   A psychological technique that employs free associations in the attempt to determine the cause of mental illness.

Ptolemaic Kingdom of Egypt   The state created by Ptolemy, one of Alexander the Great's generals, in the Hellenistic era.

Punic Wars   The three conflicts between Rome and Carthage that ended with the complete destruction of the Carthaginian Empire and the extension of Roman control throughout the western Mediterranean.

Puranas   A collection of mythical stories about Hindu gods and goddesses.

Purdah   The segregation of females in Hindu society.

Purgatory   In Catholic belief, the place where the soul is purged after death for past sins and thus becomes fit for heaven.

Puritans   The English Calvinists who were dissatisfied by the theology of the Church of England and wished to "purify" it.

Pyramid of Khufu (Cheops)   The largest pyramid; stands outside Cairo.

Quadruple Alliance   The diplomatic pact to maintain the peace established by the Big Four victors of the Napoleonic wars (Austria, Britain, Prussia, and Russia); lasted for a decade.

Quantum theory   A theory in physics describing the discontinuous nature of energy. Energy can come only in certain amounts, or quanta.

Quechua   The spoken language of the Inca of Peru.

Qur'an   The holy scripture of Islam.

Raison d'état   The idea that the welfare of the state should be supreme in government policy.

Ramayana   A Hindu text that illustrates important aspects of the religion; its heroes, Rama and his wife Sita, are worshiped as the embodiment of the ideal man and woman, especially Sita.

Realpolitik   "Politics of reality." Politics based on practical concerns rather than theory or ethics.

Reconquista   The recapture of Muslim Spain by Christians; it was completed during the reign of Ferdinand and Isabella.

Red Guard   The youthful militants who carried out the Cultural Revolution in China during the 1960s.

Reform Bill of 1832   Brought about a reform of British parliamentary voting and representation that strengthened the middle class and the urbanites.

Reign of Terror   The period (1793–1794) of extreme Jacobin radicalism during the French Revolution.

Relativity theory Einstein's theory that holds, among other things, that (1) space and time are not absolute but are relative to the observer and interwoven into a four-dimensional space-time continuum and (2) matter is a form of energy.

Reparations Money and goods that Germany paid to the victorious Allies after World War I under the Versailles Treaty.

Republican government A form of governing that imitates the Roman *res publica* in its rejection of monarchy.

Restoration (English) The period of the 1660s–1680s when Charles II was called by Parliament to take his throne and was thus restored to power.

Revolution A fundamental change in the political and social organization of a state.

Revolutions of 1989 The throwing out of the Communist governments in eastern Europe by popular demand and/or armed uprising.

Rig Veda The oldest of the four Vedas, or epics, brought into India by the Aryans.

Romanov dynasty Ruled Russia from 1613 until 1917.

Rome, Treaty of The pact signed by six western European nations in 1957 that is the founding document of the European Union.

Rubaiyat The verses attributed to the twelfth-century Persian poet Omar Khayyam.

Russo-Japanese War The 1904–1905 conflict that resulted in defeat for Russia, which weakened the position of the Tsar; simultaneously, the international power and prestige of Japan increased substantially.

Safavid The dynasty of Shiite Muslims that ruled Persia from the 1500s to the 1700s.

Sahel The arid belt extending across Africa south of the Sahara; also called the Sudan.

Salamis The naval battle that, with the battle of Platea, ended the Second Persian War with a Greek victory.

SALT (Strategic Arms Limitation Treaty) Two agreements between the United States and the Soviet Union that placed caps on certain types of nuclear weapons.

Samaria One of the two kingdoms into which the Hebrew kingdom was split after Solomon's death; the other was Judea.

Samsara The reincarnation of the soul; a concept shared by Hinduism and Buddhism.

Samurai Japanese warrior-aristocrats of medieval and early modern times.

Sandinistas A left-wing revolutionary group that overthrew the Somoza dictatorship in Nicaragua and found itself the target of the Reagan administration during the 1980s.

Sangha Groupings of Buddhist monks or nuns; one of the "Three Jewels," along with the *dharma* (teachings) and the Buddha.

Sanhedrin The Jewish governing council under the overlordship of Rome.

Sanskrit The sacred language of India; came originally from the Aryans.

Sardinia-Piedmont See Piedmont.

Sati The practice in which a widow committed suicide at the death of her husband in India; also called *suttee*.

Satrapy A province under a governor or *satrap* in the ancient Persian Empire.

Savanna The semiarid grasslands where most African civilizations developed.

Schlieffen Plan The strategic doctrine employed by Germany at the beginning of World War I; it was designed for a two-front war with France and Russia. The bulk of German military forces quickly swept through Belgium into France while fewer forces stayed in the east to hold off the slow-mobilizing Russians.

Schutzstaffel (SS) Hitler's bodyguard; later enlarged to be a subsidiary army and to provide the concentration camp guards.

Scientific method The method of observation and experiment by which the physical sciences proceed.

SDI Strategic Defense Initiative, also known as "star wars." A plan put forth by the Reagan administration to build a space-based missile defense system.

Second Front The reopening of a war front in western Europe against the Axis powers in World War II; eventually accomplished by the invasion of Normandy in June 1944.

Second Industrial Revolution The second phase of industrialization that occurred in the late 1800s after the introduction of electricity and the internal combustion engine.

Second International   Association of socialist parties founded in 1889; after the Russian Revolution in 1917, the Second International split into democratic and communist segments.

Secret speech   Premier Nikita Khrushchev of the USSR gave an account in February 1956 of the crimes of Josef Stalin against his own people that was supposed to remain secret but was soon known internationally.

Secularism   The rejection of supernatural religion as the arbiter of earthly action; emphasis on worldly affairs.

Seleucid kingdom of Persia   The successor state to the empire of Alexander the Great in most of the Middle East.

Self-determination   The doctrine that the people of a given territory or a particular nationality should have the right to determine their own government and political future.

Self-strengthening   The late nineteenth-century attempt by Chinese officials to bring China into the modern world by instituting reforms; it failed to achieve its goal.

Seljuks   Turkish converts to Islam who seized the Baghdad government from the Abbasids in the eleventh century.

Semitic   Adjective describing a person or language belonging to one of the most widespread of the western Asian groups; among many others, it embraces Hebrew and Arabic.

Seppuku   An honorable method of ritual suicide performed by Japanese samurai; it involved disembowelment with a short sword.

Serfdom   Restriction of personal and economic freedoms associated with medieval European agricultural society.

Seven Years' War   Fought between France and England, with their allies, around the world, 1756–1763; won by England with major accessions of territory to the British Empire.

Shang dynasty   The first historical rulers of China; ruled from about 1500 to about 1100 B.C.E.

Shari'a   The sacred law of Islam; based on the Qur'an.

Shiite   A minority sect of Islam; adherents believe that kinship with Muhammad is necessary to qualify for the caliphate.

Shintoism   The earliest religion in Japan, it was polytheistic and stressed the importance of nature; it placed little or no emphasis on theology or ethical conduct.

Shiva   An important member of the Hindu pantheon; he, along with his wife Kali (Durga), is both the creator and the destroyer.

Shogunate   The government of medieval Japan in which the *shogun*, a military and civil regent, served as the actual leader while the emperor was the symbolic head of the state and religion.

Sikhs   Members of a religious group founded in the sixteenth century C.E. by a holy man who sought a middle way between Islam and Hindu belief; centered on the Punjab region in northern India.

Silk Road   A route linking China with the Mediterranean region; it opened during the Han dynasty and was an important conduit for ideas and goods.

Sino-Soviet conflict   Differences in the nature of socialism were accentuated by conflict over proper policy vis-à-vis the United States in the 1950s and 1960s in the twin capitals of Marxist socialism, Moscow and Beijing.

Six Days' War   The 1967 conflict between Israel and its neighbors in which Israel gained much territory.

Social Darwinism   The misadaptation of Darwinian biology to human societies; it stressed competition and struggle between humans and justified the rule of the powerful over the weak.

Social Democrats   Noncommunist socialists who refused to join the Third International and founded independent parties.

Socialism   An ideology that calls for collective or government ownership of the means of production and the distribution of goods.

Socratic method   A form of teaching that uses a question-and-answer format to enable students to reach conclusions by using their own reasoning.

Solidarity   The umbrella organization founded by Lech Walesa and other anticommunist Poles in 1981 to recover Polish freedom; banned for eight years, but continued underground until it was acknowledged as the government in 1989.

Songhai   A West African state, centered on the bend of the Niger River, that reached its fullest extent in the sixteenth century before collapsing.

Sophists   Wandering scholars and professional teachers in ancient Greece who stressed the importance of rhetoric and tended toward skepticism and relativism.

Soviets   Councils of workers' and soldiers' deputies formed throughout Russia in 1917; played an important role in the Bolshevik Revolution.

Spanish Civil War   Conflict in Spain lasting from 1936 to 1939 in which authoritarian forces led by Generalissimo Francisco Franco, with the help of Adolf Hitler, triumphed over Republican forces.

Sparta   A militaristic Greek city-state that vied with Athens for power in the Peloponnesian War.

Springtime of the Peoples   The spring and summer of 1848 when popular revolutions in Europe temporarily succeeded.

Stalingrad, Battle of   The 1942 battle that marked the turning point of World War II in Europe.

Stalinist economy   Involved the transformation of a retarded agrarian economy to an industrialized one through massive reallocation of human and material resources directed by a central plan; imposed on the Soviet Union and then, in the first years after World War II, on eastern Europe.

Stamp Act   A law enacted by the British Parliament in 1765 that imposed a fee on legal documents of all types and on all books and newspapers sold in the American colonies.

State   The term for a territorial, sovereign entity of government.

Stoicism   A Hellenistic philosophy that emphasized human brotherhood and natural law as guiding principles.

Stonehenge   A Neolithic stone arrangement in southern England with a layout based on astronomical principles.

Successor states   Usual term for the several eastern European states that emerged from the Paris Treaty of 1919 as successors to the Russian, German, and Austro-Hungarian Empires.

Sudan   The arid belt extending across Africa south of the Sahara; also called the Sahel.

Sudras   One of the four classes of Aryan society; included serfs and servants.

Suffrage   The right to vote.

Suffragists   Those who advocate the extension of the right to vote (suffrage), especially to women.

Sufi   Arabic name for a branch of Islamic worship that emphasizes emotional union with God.

Sui dynasty   Ruled China from about 580 to about 620 C.E.; ended the disintegration of central government that had existed for the previous 130 years.

Sultanate of Delhi   The government and state erected by the conquering Afghani Muslims after 1500 in northern India; immediate predecessor to the Mughal Empire.

Sumerians   The creators of Mesopotamian urban civilization.

Sung dynasty   The dynasty that ruled China from about 1127 until 1219, when the last ruler was overthrown by the Mongol invaders.

Sunni   The majority group in Islam; adherents believe that the caliphate should go to the most qualified individual and should not necessarily pass to the kin of Muhammad.

Supremacy, Act of   A law enacted in 1534 by the English Parliament that made the monarch the head of the Church of England.

Swahili   A hybrid language based on Bantu and Arabic; used extensively in East Africa.

Sykes-Picot Agreement   A secret 1916 pact between the British and French to divide up Ottoman holdings in the Middle East after World War I; at the same time the British were promising Arabs independence after the war.

Taipings   Anti-Manchu rebels in China in the 1860s.

Taj Mahal   The beautiful tomb built by the seventeenth-century Mughal emperor Jahan for his wife.

Tale of Genji   First known novel in Asian, if not world, history; authored by a female courtier about life in the Japanese medieval court.

T'ang dynasty   Ruled China from about 620 to about 900 C.E. and began the great age of Chinese artistic and technical advances.

Tao Te Ching   "The Way and its Power," a text attributed to Lao Tzu; it discusses the

"Tao," the universal source of everything, and also presents ways for attaining the Tao and the best methods of government.

Taoism (Daoism) A nature-oriented philosophy/religion.

Tariffs Duties (taxes) imposed on imported goods; usually imposed both to raise revenue and to discourage imports and protect domestic industries.

Tel el Amarna The site of great temple complexes along the Nile River in Egypt.

Theravada Buddhism A strict monastic form of Buddhism entrenched in Southeast Asia; same as Hinayana Buddhism.

Thermidorean reaction The conservative reaction to the Reign of Terror during the French Revolution.

Third Estate The great majority of Frenchmen: those neither clerical nor noble.

Third International An association of Marxist parties in many nations; inspired by Russian Communists and headquartered in Moscow until its dissolution in 1943.

Third Reich The third German empire, self-proclaimed by Hitler. The first was the empire of Charlemagne, the second that of 1871–1918.

Third Republic of France The government of France after the exile of Emperor Napoleon III; lasted from 1871 until 1940.

Third World A term in use after World War II to denote countries and peoples in underdeveloped, formerly colonial areas of Asia, Africa, and Latin America; the First World was the West under U.S. leadership, and the Second World was the communist states under Soviet leadership.

Thirty Years' War A devastating conflict lasting from 1618–1648, it ravaged central Europe. It involved questions of power and religion, and it ended with an agreement that each ruler would determine the religion in his territory.

Tiananmen Square, massacre on The shooting down of thousands of Chinese who were peacefully demonstrating for relaxation of political censorship by the Communist leaders; occurred in 1989 in Beijing.

Tien The supreme but impersonal deity of Chou dynasty China.

Time of Troubles A fifteen-year period at the beginning of the seventeenth century in Russia when the state was nearly destroyed by revolts and wars.

Titoism The policy of neutrality in foreign policy combined with continued dedication to socialism in domestic policy that was followed by the Yugoslav Marxist leader Tito after his expulsion from the Soviet camp in 1948.

Toltec An Amerindian civilization centered in the Valley of Mexico; succeeded by the Aztecs.

Torah The first five books of the Old Testament; the Jews' fundamental law code.

Tordesillas, Treaty of A 1494 treaty brokered by the pope, it divided the New World between Portugal and Spain, awarding Brazil to Portugal and all the lands west to Spain.

Tories A nickname for nineteenth-century British conservatives; opposite of Whigs.

Totalitarianism The attempt by a dictatorial government to achieve total control over a society's life and ideas.

Trench warfare Warfare in which the opposing forces attack and counterattack from a relatively permanent system of trenches protected by barbed wire; characteristic of World War I.

Trent, Council of The council of Catholic clergy that directed the Counter-Reformation against Protestantism; met from 1545 until 1563.

Triple Alliance A pact concluded in 1882 that united Germany, Austria-Hungary, and Italy against possible attackers; the members were called the Central Powers.

Truman Doctrine The commitment of the U.S. government in 1947 to defend any noncommunist state against attempted communist takeover; proposed by President Harry Truman.

Twelve Tables The first written Roman law code; established about 450 B.C.E.

Tyrant In an ancient Greek *polis* (or an Italian city-state during the Renaissance), a ruler who came to power in an unconstitutional way and ruled without being subject to the law.

Ulema   A council of learned men who applied the *shari'a* in Islam; also, a council of religious advisers to the caliph or sultan.

Umayyad dynasty   The caliphs resident in Damascus from 661 to 750 C.E.

Uncertainty principle   The theory in physics that denies absolute causal relationships of matter and, hence, predictability.

Unequal treaties   Chinese name for the diplomatic and territorial arrangements foisted on the weak Ching dynasty by European powers in the nineteenth century; also, the commercial treaties forced on just-opened Japan by the same powers and the United States.

United Nations   Created in 1945, it is the world's most extensive international organization.

Upanishads   The Hindu holy epics dealing with morals and philosophy.

Utopian socialism   The dismissive label given by Marx to previous theories that aimed at establishing a more just and benevolent society.

Vaisyas   The landholder and artisan class of Aryan society.

Vassal   In medieval Europe, a person, usually a noble, who owed feudal duties to a superior, called a suzerain.

Vedas   The four oral epics of the Aryans.

Vernacular   The native oral language of a given people.

Versailles, Treaty of   Negotiated in 1919, it established the League of Nations, created several new states in Europe, set procedures for imperial control of the Middle East, and imposed harsh punishments upon Germany.

Vichy regime   A puppet state in the south of France during World War II, its leaders generally did the bidding of Nazi Germany.

Viet Cong   Pro-independence supporters of Ho Chi Minh active in South Vietnam during the Vietnam War.

Viet Minh   Ho Chi Minh's North Vietnamese troops.

Vishnu   A Hindu god who, through his nine incarnations, saves the world from destruction; in one incarnation he was Krishna, in another Gautama Buddha.

Vizier   An official of Muslim government, especially a high Turkish official equivalent to prime minister.

Wandering of peoples   A term referring to the migrations of various Germanic and Asiatic tribes in the third and fourth centuries C.E. that brought them into conflict with Rome.

War of the Roses   An English civil war between noble factions over the succession to the throne in the fifteenth century.

Wars of the Austrian Succession   Two 1740s wars between Prussia and Austria that gave important advantages to Prussia and its king, Frederick the Great.

Warsaw Pact   An organization of the Soviet satellite states in Europe; founded under Russian aegis in 1954 to serve as a counterweight to NATO.

Watergate   A scandal involving criminal acts by President Nixon; it led to his resignation in 1974.

Waterloo   The final defeat of Napoleon in 1815 after his return from Elban exile.

Wealth of Nations, The   The short title of the path-breaking work on national economy by Adam Smith; published in 1776.

Weimar Republic   The popular name for Germany's democratic government between 1919 and 1933.

Westphalia, Treaty of   The treaty that ended the Thirty Years' War in 1648; the first modern peace treaty in that it established strategic and territorial gains as more important than religious or dynastic ones.

Whigs   A nickname for British nineteenth-century liberals; opposite of Tories.

"White Man's Burden"   A phrase coined by Rudyard Kipling to refer to what he considered the necessity of bringing European civilization to non-Europeans.

World Bank   A monetary institution founded after World War II by Western nations to assist in the recovery effort and to aid the Third World's economic development.

Yalta Conference   Conference in 1945 in which Franklin D. Roosevelt, Josef Stalin, and Winston Churchill (the "Big Three") met to attempt to settle postwar questions, particularly those affecting the future of Europe.

Yamato state   The earliest known government of Japan; divided into feudal subdivisions ruled by clans and headed by the Yamato family.

Yin/yang   Taoist distinction between the male and female characteristics of the universe.

Yom Kippur War   A name for the 1973 conflict between Israel and its Arab neighbors.

Yuan dynasty   Official term for the Mongol rule in China, 1279–1368.

Zama, Battle of   Decisive battle of the Second Punic War; Roman victory in 202 B.C.E. was followed by absorption of most of the Carthaginian Empire in the Mediterranean.

Zen Buddhism   The Japanese form of Ch'an Buddhism.

Zionism   A movement founded by Theodor Herzl in 1896 to establish a Jewish national homeland in Palestine.

Zoroastrianism   A religion founded by the Persian Zoroaster in the seventh century B.C.E.; characterized by worship of a supreme god, Ahuramazda, who represents the good against the evil spirit, identified as Ahriman.

Zulu wars   A series of conflicts between the British and the native Africans in South Africa in the late nineteenth century.

Index

•

NOTE: **Boldface** numbers indicate illustrations.